1/16 R

THE CRESCENT
AND
THE ROSE

Sir Robert Sherley

THE CRESCENT
AND THE ROSE
Islam and England during
the Renaissance

BY SAMUEL C. CHEW

1965

OCTAGON BOOKS, INC.

New York

Reprinted 1965
by special arrangement with Oxford University Press

OCTAGON BOOKS, INC.
175 FIFTH AVENUE
NEW YORK, N. Y. 10010

LIBRARY OF CONGRESS CATALOG CARD NUMBER: 65-25888

Printed in U.S.A. by
NOBLE OFFSET PRINTERS, INC.
NEW YORK 3, N. Y.

96073

TO

L.E.C.

WHO SHARES MY MEMORIES

OF LANDS AND LIBRARIES

Voi credete

Forse che siamo esperti d'esto loco;

Ma noi siam peregrin, come voi siete.

Dianzi venimmo, innanzi a voi un poco,

Per altra via che fu sì aspra e forte

Che lo salire omai ne parrà gioco.

PURG. II.

PREFACE

THE subject of this book suggested itself long ago when the writer was engaged upon a study of the only English poet of renown who has ever had first-hand experiences of the life of the Levant or come into intimate relations with its peoples. We have here to do, however, not with the Age of Byron but with the English Renaissance. As approximate temporal limits (occasionally transcended) have been chosen the year 1453 and the year 1642, that is, the period from the downfall of the Byzantine Empire to the downfall of the older English drama. In geographical range the inquiry embraces the Ottoman Empire and Persia, with an occasional venture into the further East and at one point into Moslem Spain. The plan adopted is neither strictly historical nor strictly topographical but a combination of both. At times we may seem to wander far from Islam; but the Moslems were never, in the Near and Middle East, wholly absent from the anxious thoughts of Elizabethan travellers, even when their interests were fixed, to the exclusion of the immediate present, upon classical or biblical associations or upon the marvels of the Orient. The point of view is that of a student of English literature, and the focus of the inquiry is upon London, not Stamboul or Baghdad or Isfahan. By way of preliminary apology and as a shelter behind an illustrious precedent may be cited the words which Gibbon appended in a note to the opening sentence of his fiftieth chapter: 'As I shall display much Arabic learning, I must confess my total ignorance of the Oriental tongues, and my gratitude to the learned interpreters, who have transfused their science into the Latin, French, and English languages.'

The Elizabethan form of the Prophet's name, Mahomet (with the accent on the antepenult) is, though incorrect, everywhere employed rather than the usual modern English form, Mohammed, or the more correct Muhammad, because

vii

the retention of the old form obviates a discordance between
the present narrative and the numerous quotations from old
writers. But the spelling Mohammedan, though inconsistent,
is used, because Mahometan and its variants seldom occur
in the quotations and are disconcertingly archaic. In general
the Elizabethan names of the Ottoman sultans are used, as
is *Koran* instead of *Quran*. The old spelling of English words
is retained save in a few cases where modernized texts have
been employed; but long *s* has been discarded, *u* and *v* and
i and *j* are given their modern values, and contractions are
expanded. Line-references to Shakespeare are to the one-
volume Oxford edition. Entries in the Index serve the purpose
of a bibliography by sending the reader to titles in the text
or notes; such titles are generally abbreviated; and London
is the place of publication unless there is an indication to the
contrary. For bibliographical details of printers and book-
sellers reference may be made to the *Short Title Catalogue*.
Where necessary, dates are altered to the New Style, but
the ten days' lag in the Julian Calendar is ignored as im-
material. The word 'Christendom' is generally used to embrace the Catholic and Protestant states of western Europe
but is occasionally used in a wider sense. The loose but
convenient term 'Elizabethan' covers the whole period unless
a more specific indication is necessary.

Since the book was conceived other scholars have published,
or have assembled, the results of somewhat similar investigations. The inquiry was barely begun when a brief article by Professor Louis Wann (*Modern Philology*, xii,423f.) provided a convenient classification of Elizabethan dramas on oriental themes.
Had Professor E. H. Sugden's *Topographical Dictionary of the
Works of William Shakespeare and His Fellow-Dramatists* (Manchester, 1926) appeared at an earlier date it would have
afforded welcome short-cuts; as it is, it has lightened the
task of checking references to a large body of dramatic literature read long ago. The work of revising the first draft of
this book was in hand when the writer learnt of the existence
of a dissertation, deposited in typescript in the Widener
Library of Harvard University, on Turks, Moors, and Persians

in Elizabethan and Stuart Literature, by Dr. W.G.Rice. When an opportunity to examine this thesis occurred, it turned out that though Dr. Rice's work covers a considerable portion of the ground here surveyed and part of his general plan is similar, the emphasis, tone, and point of view are unlike those of the present book.

Every student who has worked in the British Museum retains grateful memories of the erudition, efficiency, courtesy, and patience of the members of its staff. To Professor Rhys Carpenter, sometime Director of the American School of Classical Studies at Athens, the writer is under obligations for permission to have direct access to the fine collection of English and foreign books of travel which is in the Gennadeion. At Bryn Mawr College Professor Carpenter has given counsel on several special points; and other colleagues who have been of assistance in one way or another are Professor T.R.S. Broughton, Professor S.J.Herben, Professor M.K.Woodworth, and Dr. Richard Bernheimer. Miss Marie Louise Terrien, Reference Librarian at Bryn Mawr, elucidated several matters that were obscure. Mrs. Kenneth Robbins transcribed a number of texts in the British Museum at a time when that library was inaccessible to the writer. Miss Sarah T. Ramage's expert typing eliminated many slips of the pen. Lord Leconfield has kindly given permission to reproduce the Sherley portraits at Petworth. A pleasant memory is of several visits to Santa Maria della Scala in Trastevere to discuss Sir Robert and Lady Sherley with the Reverend Father Marcellino Dorelli. Another pleasant encounter was with Dr. Walter Livingston Wright at Constantinople; a specialist in Turkish history, he furnished some valuable bibliographical notes. The deepest obligation is to her who has shared the happiness and the weariness—increasing the pleasures, mitigating the pains—of adventures in the Levant and among books.

S.C.C.

Bryn Mawr College,
June 1937

NOTE ON ABBREVIATIONS

Few abbreviations are employed; but *C.S.P.* stands for *The Calendar of State Papers* (*Dom.* = *Domestic*); *D.N.B.*, for *The Dictionary of National Biography*; E.E.T.S., the Early English Text Society; *O.E.D.*, *A New English Dictionary* (Oxford); *P.M.L.A.*, *Publications of the Modern Language Association of America*; and Hazlitt's Dodsley, W. Carew Hazlitt's edition of Robert Dodsley's *Collection of Old English Plays.*

CONTENTS

ILLUSTRATIONS

THE CRESCENT
AND
THE ROSE

THE CRESCENT AND THE ROSE

CHAPTER ONE

TALES AND TALE-BEARERS

I

CHAUCER says that merchants are the fathers of tidings and tales and that the wallets of shipmen and pilgrims are full of lies.[1] The propensity of returned travellers to pull the long bow in stories of their adventures is pleasantly satirized in William Bullein's *Dialogue against the Fever Pestilence* (1564), an attractive curiosity of literature inspired by the belief that since the melancholy man is the special prey to the plague the best preventive of the disease is an antidote to melancholy. One of the most amusing figures in this dialogue is Mendax, the lying traveller. In Ethiopia he had seen Solomon's tomb, made of crystal and as large as Westminster Abbey. The eating of a certain herb gives you, he says, the power during four hours of the night to see through this crystal; and within the tomb are Solomon and four hundred ladies, 'daunsing with noble graces in riche attyre.' In the isle called Ruc in the Great Khan's land Mendax had seen, among many other wonders, the 'sciopodes having but one foote, which is so broad that thei cover all their bodies for the raine and the Sonne.' Elsewhere the anthropophagers ate a hundred friars sent out by the Spanish Inquisition to convert them. Mendax himself escaped only through the friendly offices of a witch who turned him into a dog; and in this disguise he fed upon the friars' bones. 'My boy was so stronglie bewitched that he is a dogge still. This same is he; he was a gentleman of a good house; he understandeth us well, and sometyme was a proper man.'[2] In similar vein Joseph Hall ridicules the 'sweet-sauc'd lies of some false traveller' who tells of his adventures in India, his sight of

1 *Canterbury Tales*, 'Man of Law's Prologue,' ll.128f.; *The House of Fame*, ll.2121f.
2 *A Dialogue bothe pleasaunt and pietifull against the Fever Pestilence*, ed. M.W. and A.H.Bullen, E.E.T.S., Extra Series 52 (1888), pp.99 and 103f.

'the antique tombes of Palestine,' the magic wall of glass at Damascus, the great bird ruc, the mermaids that haunt the southern seas, the race of headless men, and other such marvels.[1] There is similar but more good-natured fooling in Samuel Rowlands's description of the experiences of a boastful traveller:

> His wondrous travels challenge such renowne,
> That Sir John Maundivell is quite put down.
> Men without heades, and Pigmies hand-bredth hie,
> Those with one legge that on their backes do lie,
> And doe the weathers injurie disdaine,
> Making their legges a penthouse for the raine.[2]

Another writer, one Baptiste Goodall, attempts to differentiate between actual wonders that are to be seen in foreign lands and the incredible marvels about which lying tales are told. The ruins of Rome or the pyramids of Egypt twelve miles round are more astonishing, because they are real, than 'foothigh pigmeyes, dogg-eard men,' and other such fabulous creatures.[3]

You cannot trust travellers, for they all lie 'cheaper than a beggar.'[4] 'Thou art no traveller,' says Dekker, 'the habit of lying therefore will not become thee; cast it off.'[5] When Dorothy Osborne had read 'The Story of China' by the Portuguese traveller Fernando Mendez Pinto, her comment was: 'You must allow him the privilege of a travellour and hee dos not abuse it, his lyes are as pleasant harmlesse ones as lyes can bee, and in noe great number considering the scope hee has for them.'[6] 'Travellers ne'er did lie, though fools at home condemn 'em,' says Antonio;[7] but since he was shipwrecked on an enchanted island when he said this, his words are not to be construed as evidence that Shakespeare gave credence to tales of the marvellous; in fact the usual scepticism of the stay-at-

---

1 *Satires*, IV,vi.
2 *The Letting of Humours Blood in the Head-Vaine*, 1600, Satire i; *Works*, Hunterian Club, i,48. Compare the attack on lying travellers, too long to quote, in Thomas Lodge, *Wits Miserie, Works*, Hunterian Club, iv,41f.
3 *The Tryall of Travell or, 1 The Wonders of Travell, 2 The Worthes of Travell, 3 The Way to Travell*, 1630, Sig. C₁ᵛ.
4 Ben Jonson, *Cynthia's Revels*, II,iii,99.
5 *The Seven Deadly Sinnes of London*, 1606; ed. H.F.B.Brett-Smith, p.26.
6 *Letters*, ed. G.C.Moore Smith, Oxford, 1928, p.48.
7 *The Tempest*, III,iii,26f.

home is implied in his remark. George Wither rebukes this scepticism:

> There's a number too, that doe suppose,
> All that beyond their little reason growes
> Is surely false; and vainely doe uphold
> That all reports which travellers unfold
> Of forraine lands are lies: because they see
> No such strange things in their owne parish be.[1]

But this protest against parochialism is very unusual. It was the part of the returned wanderer to tell of the wonders he had seen; and equally it was the part of the stay-at-home to doubt his word.

Such reports and rumours of marvels have from time immemorial come into western Europe from the Levant and from the further parts of the Orient. Today the progress of science has pushed back and back the frontiers of the Lands of Wonder; but during the period of the Renaissance—in this respect, as in so many other respects, an epoch which exhibits no complete solution of continuity from the Middle Ages—these lands were of vast extent, embracing not only the further East (upon which our subject barely impinges) and the new-found western hemisphere (with which we have nought to do) but especially those countries that during the past centuries had fallen under the dominion of aggressive and expanding Mohammedanism.

The history of the Chosen People and the events centring in the life of Christ made it natural, indeed inevitable, that this should be the case. There was biblical authority for the belief that Moses learned how to practise magic from

> those Ægyptian wisards old
> Which in star-rede were wont have best insight.[2]

Samuel Daniel apostrophizes 'mysterious Egypt' as the breeder of wonders; [3] and an English traveller who calls Egypt 'the fountaine of all science' visited that country in the hope

---

1 *Abuses Stript and Whipt*, 1622; *Poems*, Spenser Society, p.230.
2 Spenser, *The Faerie Queene*, V, Prologue, viii. See Exodus vii,11; Acts, vii,22.
3 *Cleopatra*, IV,iii, Chorus.

'to finde some sparke of those cinders not yet put out.'[1] The undeciphered hieroglyphic inscriptions confirmed the general belief that the ancient Egyptians had been astrologers, magicians, wizards, and soothsayers. 'Your hieroglyphick was the Egyptian wisdom,' says a character in a play;[2] Massinger says that one may be instructed 'by a true Egyptian hieroglyphic,'[3] and Jonson's Subtle asks: 'Was not all the knowledge of the Ægyptians writ in mystic symbols?'[4]

Biblical themes lent themselves easily to the process of oriental decoration: the stories, for example, of those famous women, the Queen of Sheba and godly Queen Esther and Judith and Salome; the adventures of Daniel at the court of the great monarchs of Mesopotamia. From the parts of the East came the mysterious pagan prophet who foresaw the rising of a star over Israel, and thence came the Three Kings, following the guidance of that star. When the Holy Family fled from Herod's wrath into Egypt, their journey thither and their sojourn in the land were marked by miraculous happenings. Out of Syria came Saint Peter and Saint Paul to suffer martyrdom in Rome; and Saint James followed his way to Compostella; and the Maries and their gipsy servant, escaping from persecution, landed on the coast of the Midi. Conscious-stricken Pilate passed from place to place in Europe, and even after death his accursed body could not find repose.[5] Saint Mark's body, after strange vicissitudes, rested in Venice,

1 Sir Henry Blount, *A Voyage into the Levant*, 1636, p.3.
2 William Cavendish, Duke of Newcastle, *The Country Captain*, 1649, II,ii. Compare the amusing song by Mercurius in Thomas Randolph's *Hey for Honesty*, 1651 (*Poetical and Dramatic Works*, ed. W.C.Hazlitt, 1875, p.479):

From Egypt have I come,   A Chaldee me begot,
  With Solomon for my guide: Old Talmud was his name;
By chiromancy I can tell,   In hieroglyphics he excell'd,
  What fortunes thee betide.   Through Nilus ran his fame.

3 *The Guardian*, II,iii.
4 *The Alchemist*, II,iii,202f. In Sir William Berkeley's play *The Lost Lady* (Hazlitt's Dodsley, xii,609f.) a female character assumes a disguise as 'an Egyptian lady' and pretends to be a soothsayer. By Egyptian a gipsy is of course often intended.
5 Legend had it that Pilate found refuge in the gloomy recesses of Mount Pilatus near Lucerne. After his death his body was thrown into a lake but the water cast it forth. Some said that he dwelt within the lake, and in stormy weather the foam upon the water tossed itself in the manner of one washing his hands. In hell Sir Guyon saw Pilate deep drenched within a river but extending his arms high above the flood and washing his hands perpetually (*The Faerie Queene*, II,vii,61).

and the bodies of the Three Kings in Cologne. During the early Christian centuries Europe was strewn with relics from the Holy Land. Portions of the Manger from Bethlehem were exhibited in Santa Maria Maggiore in Rome; and Saint Veronica's handkerchief was in Saint Peter's, where was also the lance of the Roman soldier; [1] and the Title of the Cross was in Santa Croce. The Shroud of Christ was to be seen at Turin and His seamless Coat at Treves; and fragments of the True Cross and spines from the Crown of Thorns were scattered through a thousand churches. Angels, it was said, had carved the Most Holy Bambino in Santa Maria Ara Coeli from an olive tree in Gethsemane. To Lucca in the ninth century, borne across the Mediterranean in a ship manned by no human sailors, had come the Santo Volto, the true Likeness of the Lord, fashioned by angels out of cedar-wood of Lebanon. Centuries later other angels carried through the air the Virgin's House, the Santa Casa, from Nazareth to Loretto. Innumerable were, and still are, the bones and snippets of clothing, the trinkets and utensils and instruments of torture, relics of the apostles and martyrs and saints and confessors and virgins, which, brought out of the Levant, rested, and still rest, beneath Christian altars and in Christian reliquaries. They directed the minds of the devout to holy meditations and had their part in filling the popular imagination with dreams and fantasies of the East.

Nor were these associations limited to memorials of primitive Christianity. From the time of Herodotus travellers wrote of the wonders of the East. Having assumed divinity in Egypt and having passed beyond the boundaries of the Hellenic world, Alexander the Great took on, in popular tradition, the aspect of a supernatural being. He was the first of western kings whose fame underwent such a transformation. The medieval story-tellers of Charlemagne, not content with his actual historical contacts with the Arabs in Spain, imagined for him strange adventures in the Levant. Similar tales were told of Frederick Barbarossa, at whose court eastern necromancers practised soothsaying and who received an embassy from the

---

1 The lance had been in Hagia Sophia. After the fall of Constantinople the Sultan Bajazet II sent it to the pope.

Tartar potentate who in the distorting and magnifying popular memory became Prester John.[1] The folk in general and the story-tellers in particular did not forget the intimate relation of Frederick II with the Arab world; and memories long survived of the exotic oriental menagerie, the tigers and leopards and camels, belonging to him.[2] Folklorists and students of the origins of romance have traced to India innumerable tales of the marvellous and fantastic which through the medium of Persian and Arabic literature came along the trade routes into the Latin world.[3]

No episode of far travel was better calculated to quicken the pulses of imaginative readers than that of Marco Polo's journey through the Desert of Lop, 'the abode of many evil spirits which amuse travellers to their destruction,' where, says Marco, if separated by some accident from their companions these travellers

1 The domain of Prester John, whether in Asia or Africa, was beyond the frontiers of Islam and therefore does not directly concern us. But since Europeans for long cherished the hope that this Christian monarch would give them aid against the Moslems a few words may be devoted to him here. Medieval writers (Marco Polo, *Mandeville*, etc.) place his kingdom in India; and this tradition survives in the statement in John Rastell's interlude of *The Four Elements*, *c*.1518, that 'India Major [is] the land of Prester John' (Hazlitt's Dodsley, i,32) and in Rabelais's unfulfilled promise that he will tell how Panurge married the daughter of the king of India, Presthan (*Pantagruel*, i, chapter 34). After much discussion and uncertainty it came to be agreed during the Renaissance that he ruled over Abyssinia. The conflict of testimony is seen in a legend upon Sebastian Cabot's Map, 1544, where we read of a king in central Africa 'whom some call Prester John' but 'this is not Prester John, because Prester John had his empire in eastern and southern India.' Stephen Batman says that Presbiter John Emperor of the Abissines 'is without doubte to bee reckoned among the greatest monarchies of our age' (*Batman uppon Bartholome*, book xvii, chapter 45). Benedick offers to bring Don Pedro 'the length of Prester John's foot'— a daring feat but not so dangerous as to stay and confront Beatrice (*Much Ado About Nothing*, II,i,278). Nashe (*Lenten Stuffe*, *Works*, ed. McKerrow, iii,172) and Dekker (*Old Fortunatus*, II) refer to this potentate. There is a long account of him in Robert Johnson's English epitome of Giovanni Botero's *Relationi Universali* (*The Travellers Breviat*, 1601, pp.169f.). William Lithgow says that 'the Great Turke is inforced to pay yearely the tribute of forty thousand Sultans of gold to Prester Jehan, least he impede and withdraw the course of Nylus . . . and so bring Ægypt to desolation' (*Rare Adventures*, p.281). This report, which is traceable long before Lithgow repeated it, is suggestive of Great Britain's present anxiety about the control of the head-waters of the Nile. On the Portuguese search for Prester John see Edgar Presage, *The Portuguese Pioneers*, 1933, pp.214f. See in general Sir Henry Yule's article on Prester John in the *Encyclopædia Britannica*, eleventh edition; Sir E.Denison Ross's chapter (ix) in *Travel and Travellers in the Middle Ages*, ed. A.P.Newton, 1926; C.R.Beazley, *John and Sebastian Cabot*, 1898, p.233; and Arthur Tilley, 'Rabelais and Geographical Discovery,' *The Modern Language Review*, ii (1907), 323.
2 Ernst Kantorowicz, *Frederick the Second*, translated by E.O.Lorimer, New York, 1931, p.311; P.K.Hitti, *History of the Arabs*, 1937, p.610.
3 Gaston Paris, 'Les Contes orientaux dans la littérature française au moyen age,' *La Poésie du Moyen Age*, second series, third edition, Paris, 1906.

hear themselves called to by their names, and in a tone of voice to which they are accustomed. Supposing the call to proceed from their companions, they are led away by it from the direct road, and not knowing in what direction to advance, are left to perish. . . Sometimes . . . these spirits assume the appearance of their travelling companions, who address them by name and endeavour to conduct them out of the proper road. . . These spirits of the desert . . . are said at times to fill the air with the sounds of all kinds of musical instruments.[1]

Very similar was the experience of the fourteenth-century wanderer Friar Odoric when he passed through a certain valley and saw therein things strange and terrible. In the pages of Hakluyt the Elizabethans could read his story:

> I saw many dead bodies, and in the sayd valley also I heard divers sweet sounds and harmonies of musike . . . whereat I was greatly amazed. This valley . . . into the which whosoever entreth dieth presently, and can by no meanes passe alive thorow the middest thereof . . . I was tempted to go in, and to see what it was. At length, making my prayers, and recommending my selfe to God in the name of Jesu, I entred, and saw such swarmes of dead bodies there, as no man would beleeve unlesse he were an eye witnesse thereof. At one side of the foresayd valley upon a certaine stone I saw the visage of a man, which beheld me with such a terrible aspect, that I thought I should have died in the same place. But always this sentence, the Word became Flesh and dwelt amongst us, I ceased not to pronounce, signing my selfe with the signe of the crosse, and neerer then seven or eight pases I durst not approch unto the said head: but I departed and fled. . . When the men of that country knew that I was returned out of the valley alive, they reverenced me much, saying that I was baptized and holy, and that the foresayd bodies were men subject unto the devils infernall, who used to play upon citherns, to the end they might allure people to enter, and so murther them.[2]

Jean de Bourgogne, the author of *The Travels of Sir John Mandeville*, among his many unacknowledged borrowings from

---

1 *The Book of Ser Marco Polo, the Venetian, concerning the Kingdoms and Marvels of the East*, translated and edited by Sir Henry Yule, third edition, revised by Henri Cordier, 1929, chapter 39. On the Desert of Lop as it affected the English imagination see J.L.Lowes, *The Road to Xanadu*, Boston, 1927, pp.489f.
2 *Itinerarium fratris Odorici . . . de Mirabilium Orientalium* (1330); Hakluyt, iv,440 (all references to Hakluyt are to the MacLehose edition, Glasgow, 1903f.).

Friar Odoric's narrative, took thence portions of the above passage and worked them into his description of the Vale Perilous.[1] Such mysterious and awful tales came to the Elizabethans not only from Marco Polo and Odoric and Mandeville directly but as paraphrased by the cosmographers. Thus, in the tiny English abridgment of Sebastian Munster's huge work there is an account of 'certaine illusions of devils about Tangut' which, save for a shift in geographical position, is identical in substance with Marco Polo's description of the seducing devils of Lop:

> There be heard the voyces of spirits and devils, which goinge solitarily will call other by their names, fayning and counterfayting the voyces of their companions, the which, if they can by anye meanes, do leade men oute of the waye to destruction. There be heard sometimes in the ayre the consentes and harmonye of musicke instrumentes.[2]

The 'noyses, sounds and sweet aires' and the 'thousand twangling instruments' which filled Prospero's island were, though harmless and delightful, occurrences of a like order; and in *Comus* the Lady's memory was thronged with a thousand fantasies

> Of calling shapes, and beckoning shadows dire,
> And airy tongues that syllable men's names
> On sands and shores and desert wildernesses [3]

drawn from her reading of these travellers' tales.

Even the Near East, centuries after these medieval wanderings were over, was not quite free from such supernatural horrors. When Milton's exquisite lines were recited at Ludlow Castle, only six years had passed since an Englishman, voyag-

---

1 The earliest English edition is that of Richard Pynson, 1496, with the colophon: 'Here endeth the boke of John Maunduyle, knight, of wayes to Jerusalem and of marveylys of ynde.' Three other editions followed before that which was doubtless best known to the Elizabethans: *The voiage and travayle of syr John Maundevile*, 1568. The description of the Vale Perilous is in chapter 31.

2 *A Briefe Collection and compendious extract of straunge and memorable thinges gathered out of the Cosmography of Sebastian Munster*, 1574, folio 88ᵛ.

3 *The Tempest*, III,ii,147f.; *Comus*, l.205f. Robert Burton cites the passage quoted from Marco Polo as an example of the mischiefs wrought by terrestrial devils (*The Anatomy of Melancholy*, I,2,i,2).

ing through the Ægean, came upon an island close to Milos which was called on his map Anania.

> But the Greekes I had in my shippe named it l'Isola de Diavoli, because they say no men inhabite there, but is infested with divels; and that when they moore their cables upon the shore. . . they all loose of themselves, unless they make them fast, making a crosse with the endes of everie two cables. One of them said that not long before he was there with the Florentine gallyes, and they were moored without a crosse, and in the night they heard a loud voice out of the sea that bad them quickly rowe away, and cry'd 'Hala! Hala! ' for their cables were loose, which they found to be true.[1]

Such was a supernatural horror to be met with, in the full seventeenth century, on a principal route of trade between Christendom and the Ottoman Empire.

Besides the cries and wailings of demons and the music of their instruments other dreadful sounds might be heard in the East. In the thirteenth-century narrative of Friar John of Pian de Carpini, which in Hakluyt's version supplied the Elizabethans with an abundance of information, in the main astonishingly accurate, on the customs, manners, laws, religion, government, literature, history, warfare, wealth, cattle, victuals, and superstitions of oriental peoples, we read of Tartars travelling through the desert:

> This people were not able to endure the terrible noise, which in that place the sunne made at his uprising: for at that time of the sunne rising, they were inforced to lay one eare upon the ground, and to stoppe the other close, least they should heare that dreadfull sound.[2]

In Cathay there was a lake of which no less reliable a traveller than Anthony Jenkinson brought home a report (but he de-

1 Sir Kenelm Digby, *Journal of a Voyage into the Mediterranean* (1628), ed. John Bruce, Camden Society, 1868, p. 53. Like beliefs linger in the Greek islands to this day; see W.W.Hyde, *Greek Religion and its Survivals*, Boston, 1923, chapter v. For a modern parallel to these seducing spirits of the East see E.G.Browne, *A Year among the Persians*, Cambridge, 1926, p.180.
2 *Libellus historicus Joannis de Plano Carpini, qui missus est Legatus ad Tartaros* (1246); Hakluyt, i,149.

pended upon what was told him) that from its depths rose a 'most sweet harmony of bells' while beneath its waters might be seen 'stately and large buildings.' [1]

Strange and fearful monsters, grotesque parodies of humanity, were to be met with—or more often heard of—in eastern lands. The sciapods were there which 'have but one foote, and that so great that when they lye downe on theyr backes and woulde keepe them from the sunne, the shadow of that onely legge doth comfort them'; [2] and the dog-headed folk; [3] and a people 'of foul stature and of cursed kynde, that han non hedes but here eyen ben in here scholdres' [4] of whom Othello told Desdemona and in whose existence Gonzalo was ready to believe when he had seen the wondrous shapes of the enchanted island. [5] Five specimens of such monstrosities are the subject of one of Sebastian Munster's illustrations, and similar outlandish folk appear in other cosmographies. Upon the map of Asia in the Basle edition, 1540, of Ptolemy's *Geography* we see a sciapod and a cynocephalus and two 'men whose heads do grow beneath their shoulders' and a couple of anthropophagi (cheerful little people) busily carving up a human body for their dinner. [6] Some of these creatures are either depicted or

---

1 Hakluyt, iii,457.
2 *Straunge and memorable thinges*, folio 82ʳf. Interesting material on the sciapods and other creatures touched on in the text is scattered through C.R.Beazley, *The Dawn of Modern Geography*, 1897–1906. See also A.P.Newton's chapter (viii) on 'Travellers's Tales of Wonder and Imagination' in *Travel and Travellers in the Middle Ages*. Professor Lowes treats of this lore with his inimitable charm and excited enthusiasm in *The Road to Xanadu*, pp.119f. On the sciapods see, among many writers, Vincent of Beauvais, *Speculum historiale*, I,xciii; *Mandeville*, chapter 18; Caxton, *The Mirrour of the World* (ed. E.E.T.S., p.72, and sources there cited); and Emile Mâle, *L'Art religieux du xiiiᵉ siècle*, fig.23, p.55. On the related cyclopods see John of Carpini in Hakluyt, i,154.
3 On February 2, 1577, the Earl of Sussex's Men acted at Hampton Court a play, now lost, entitled *The History of Cenocephali* (or *Cenocephals* or *Cynocephali*—the title has been variously read). See A.Feuillerat, *Documents relating to the Office of the Revels in the Time of Queen Elizabeth*, pp.256 and 265; G.M.Sibley, *The Lost Plays and Masques*, Cornell University Press, 1933, p.25. This piece, if the title warrants the guess, must have introduced dog-headed men. Compare the outlandish *dramatis personae* in the lost *Tamar Cam* on which see p.518, note 1, below.
4 *Mandeville*, chapter 23. Reports of these people go back of Vincent of Beauvais (*Speculum historiale*, XXXI,cxxvii) to Pliny, *Historia naturalis*, V,vii. The authority of Mandeville is cited by Ralegh for the existence of such creatures (*The Discoverie of Guiana*, 1596; ed. Hakluyt Society, p.85; also in Hakluyt, x,406).
5 *The Tempest*, III,iii,46; *Othello*, I,iii,144f. See J.M.French, 'Othello among the Anthropophagi,' *P.M.L.A.*, xlix (1934), 807f.
6 Reproduced in French's article cited in the previous note. These and other monstrosities—pygmies; men with huge ears; others with enormous lips—are traceable

'*Monstrous Forms 'twixt Africa and Ind*'

described on the famous mappemond of Hereford cathedral.[1]
They were well known to the Elizabethans. Better from books
than from table-talk with foreigners, says Joseph Hall, arguing
against the necessity to travel, can we learn of the world's
wonders.

> Out of our bookes can we tell the stories of the monocelli, who lying
> upon their backes, shelter themselves from the sunne with the
> shadow of their one only foot. . . We can tell of those cheape-
> dieted men, that live . . . without meat, without mouthes, feeding
> onely upon aire at their nostrils. Or of those headlesse easterne
> people that have eyes in their breasts. . . Or of those . . . that
> cover their whole body with their eares.[2]

'All the monstrous forms 'twixt Africa and Inde'[3] are to be
met with in the cosmographies and geographies, the travel-
books and compilations of zoological knowledge:[4] the basilisk
and his close relative the cockatrice;[5] the mantichora, a

back through the medieval bestiaries to Isidore of Seville, Honorius of Autun,
Gervais of Tilbury, Solinus, and yet further into the past, to Lucian's *True History*,
1 to Pliny, to Herodotus. They are, indeed, fantasies of the folklore of many countries.
2 See Lowes, op.cit., p.110 and references in his notes.
3 *Quo Vadis? A Just Censure of Travell*, 1617, pp.38f.
4 *Comus*, ll.606f.
One of the most important Elizabethan books on natural lore and kindred subjects
is *Batman uppon Bartholome, his booke de Proprietatibus Rerum, Newly corrected and
amended with such Additions as are requisite*, 1582. This is one of the most direct
links between Elizabethan culture and the Arabian science of the Middle Ages. The
English Franciscan Bartholomew compiled his treatise 'On the properties of things'
(*c.*1240) from translations of the Arabian literature. The English translation of
Bartholomew was made by John of Trevisa in 1398. This was first printed by Wyn-
kyn de Worde, with illustrations, in 1495. This was reprinted as *Bartholomeus de
Proprietatibus Rerum*, 1535, an edition occasionally cited in the present volume.
Stephen Batman adds his own quaint commentary. See further *The Legacy of Islam*,
Oxford, 1928, p.238. The popular Jacobean work on fauna is Edward Topsell's
Historie of Foure-Footed Beastes, 1607, a version of Conrad Gesner's *Historiae
Animalium*, the first edition of which, in five splendidly illustrated folio volumes,
appeared at Zurich in 1553, followed in 1563 by the German version: *Thierbuch: das
ist ein kurtze beschreybung aller vier fussigen Thieren*. Gesner and his English disciple
continue the tradition of the bestiaries, of Bartholomeus Anglicus, and other nat-
uralists.
5 See P.A.Robin, *Animal Lore in English Literature*, 1932, pp.83f., 181f. When Richard
compliments Anne upon the beauty of her eyes (*Richard III*, I,ii,150f.), she exclaims: 'Would they were Basiliskes to strike thee dead!' A modernized text should
have an apostrophe to indicate the possessive case; that is, her wish is not that
her eyes were basilisks but that they were the eyes of a basilisk; but this small
emendation has not been made in any edition. The name 'basilisk' was given to
a kind of cannon (see *1 Henry IV*, II,iii,58; Marlowe, *The Jew of Malta*, III,v,31).
As a figure of speech it occurs constantly in Elizabethan literature; see, for example,
3 Henry VI, III,ii,187; Spenser, *The Faerie Queene*, IV,viii,39.

'dreadful hiddeous Ægiptian beast';[1] the splendid, solitary phoenix of Arabia;[2] the ferocious unicorn.[3] Among the flora of

[1] Pliny's description of this monster (*Historia naturalis*, viii,21), drawn from Ctesias and Aristotle, is translated almost word for word in the anonymous Jacobean tragedy *Tiberius* (ed. W.W.Greg, Malone Society, 2070f.), with the added detail that it is an 'Egyptian beast.' The mantichora is an intrusion into Egypt; report generally assigned it to India. The association with Egypt is probably due to confusion with the crocodile because of the attribute of a seducing voice given the mantichora by Solinus (Golding's translation, 1587, p.198). Skelton places it vaguely in 'the mountains' (*Philip Sparrow*, Chalmers' *English Poets*, ii,292). Pictures of it are sometimes found in the bestiaries, whence through a succession of intermediaries one of them came into Topsell, *Foure-Footed Beastes*, pp.441f. See also *The Elizabethan Zoo*, ed. M.St.C.Byrne, p.76. On the etymology and curious fortunes of the name see *O.E.D.* and for further details, Robin, op.cit., p.80.

[2] On the variants of the legend see Robin, op.cit., pp.36f. which, however, is not complete. To survey the accounts of the fabulous bird would carry us far beyond our limits to Herodotus, Tacitus, Ovid, Pliny, the *Physiologus*, Solinus, Tertullian, Saint Ambrose, Isidore of Seville, Jacobus de Vitriaco, Roger of Neckam, Alan de l'Isle, *Mandeville*, Caxton, and many other encyclopaedists and cosmographers. The phoenix is an oft-recurring figure in Elizabethan imagery. Consult the concordances to Shakespeare and Spenser and compare also: John Lyly, *Euphues and His England, Works*, ed. R.W.Bond, ii,86, and *Endymion*, III,iv; Thomas Nashe, *Christ's Tears over Jerusalem, Works*, ii,50, and *Preface to Astrophel and Stella*, ibid. iii,331; George Peele, *The Arraignment of Paris*, V,i,151; the following anonymous plays, *Selimus*, 2010, *Tiberius*, 100, *Revenge for Honour*, V,ii,35f. (and T.M.Parrott's note in George Chapman, *Tragedies*, p.726); Dekker, *Old Fortunatus*, II,ii; Ford, *The Lady's Trial*, II,i; William Rowley, *All's Lost by Lust*, II,ii,43 and IV,ii,4f.; Robert Greene and Thomas Lodge, *A Looking-Glass for London and England*, II,i; Michael Drayton, *Idea*, xvi; Herrick, *Ode to Endymion Porter*, ll.17f.; and *A Nuptiall Song*, ll.25f.; Davenant, *Albovine*, III,i and *The Platonic Lovers*, II,i (*Works*, 1872, i,48 and ii,35); Marston, *Histriomastix*, III,i; Milton, *Paradise Lost*, v,270f. and *Samson Agonistes*, ll.1700f.; and the numerous parallels assembled in Massinger, *The Maid of Honour*, ed. E.A.W.Bryne, Bryn Mawr, 1927, IV,iii,68, and in *The Great Duke of Florence*, ed. Johanne Stochholm, Bryn Mawr, 1933, III,i,184. The variations played upon the theme of the phoenix are numerous. Sir William Alexander, Earl of Stirling, for example, pondering upon the Day of Judgment, imagines that that dread event will interrupt the last phoenix in the very process of renewing its youth (*Doomes-Day*, Third Hour, 28; *Poetical Works*, ed. L.E.Kastner and H.B.Charlton, Manchester, ii [1929]). An exception to the almost universal localization of the phoenix in Arabia is the statement of Miguel de Castanhoso that it lives in Abyssinia; see *The Portuguese Expedition to Abyssinia in 1541–1543*, ed. R.S.Whiteway, Hakluyt Society, 1902, p.236. Sebastian's scepticism as to the bird's existence (before his arrival on Prospero's island) may have been encouraged by the French traveller Nicolas de Nicolay who closes his account of the phoenix with the remark: 'Il croira cecy qui voudra: quant a moi, il me semble, que parler du Phoenix n'est autre chose, que fabolizer' (*Navigations*, Antwerp, 1575, p. 229). This was accessible to Elizabethan readers in Washington's translation of Nicolas de Nicolay, *Navigations*, 1585, folio 123ᵛ. A like opinion is expressed later by Sir Thomas Browne, *Vulgar Errors*, III,xii.

[3] See Odell Shepard, *The Lore of the Unicorn*, Boston, 1930; Robin, op.cit., pp.74f.; C.G.E.Bunt, 'The Lion and the Unicorn,' *Antiquity*, iv (1930), 425f. The notion that the creature pays homage to a pure virgin derives from the *Physiologus* and occurs frequently in medieval literature but is rare in Elizabethan literature. On the curious method of capturing a unicorn by 'betraying' it with trees see Topsell, op.cit., p.711; Byrne, *The Elizabethan Zoo*, p.91; and compare *Julius Caesar*, II,i,204; *Timon of Athens*, IV,iii,339f.; *The Faerie Queene*, II,v,10; and especially Chapman, *Bussy d'Amboise*, II,i,119f. References to the therapeutic use of the unicorn's horn, whether fashioned into a drinking-cup or in powdered form, are numerous; see, for example, Thomas Lodge, *A Treatise of the Plague*, 1603, Sig. H₃ᵛ; Jonson, *Every*

eastern lands were marvels rivalling those of the animal kingdom: the palm-trees, for example, which 'flourish most when
bow'd down fastest'; [1] or the apples of Sodom, fair to look upon
but within bitter dust and ashes. [2]

The actual experiences and adventures of travellers, exaggerated in the retelling and, by a process familiar to us all,
more richly coloured in memory than they were in the reality,
did little or nothing to lessen the credulity with which these old
traditions of the East were accepted at home. It is true that
travellers' tales were proverbially untrustworthy; true, too,
that among travellers were some of sceptical mind. But both
the critical instinct and the necessary accumulation of testimony were lacking to differentiate the fabulous from the real;
and the analogies between the two classes were sometimes disconcertingly close.

What distinction must perforce be made between the roc
and the carrier-pigeon? Both were wonderful and both beyond
the reach of occidental experience. Levantine merchants and
officials of the Ottoman government made use of carrier-
pigeons long before they were known in Europe. In the thirteenth century the Crusaders learned from the Syrians how to
train carrier-pigeons to convey military information; but this

---

Man out of His Humour, V,v,82; Dekker, *The Wonderful Yeare*, 1603 (*Plague-
Pamphlets*, ed. A.P.Wilson, p.23); Webster, *The White Devil*, II,i,14f.; Burton,
The Anatomy of Melancholy, II,4,i,1; Sir Thomas Browne, *Vulgar Errors*, III,xxiii;
Topsell, op.cit., p.720. On unicorns at Mecca see p.427, below.

1 *Revenge for Honour*, II,ii,29. Lyly says: 'It is proper for the Palm tree to mounte;
the heavyer you loade it the higher it sprowteth' (*Euphues: The Anatomy of Wit*;
Works, i,191); and again, with the analogy of the palm in mind: 'So fast a roote
hath true love taken in my hart, that . . . the more it is loaden the better it beareth' (*Euphues and His England*; *Works*, ii,76). Massinger uses the image impressively:

> I will, like a palm tree,
> Grow under my huge weight

(*Believe As You List*, I,i). An English traveller in the Levant reports unquestioningly that the palm cannot be suppressed 'but shooteth up against all opposition'
(George Sandys, *Relation of a Journey*, 1615, p.102). One of the emblems surrounding
the portrait of King Charles I at his prayers in the 'ΕΙΚΩΝ ΒΑΣΙΛΙΚΗ' (1649)
is a palm-tree from whose fronds dangle two weights; a scroll round the trunk bears
the inscription 'Crescit sub pondere Virtus' and a couplet in 'The Explanation of the
Emblem' runs:

> Though clogg'd with weights of miseries
> Palm-like depress'd I higher rise.

No source of this curious belief has been discovered in classical authors.
2 See p.81, note 1, below.

knowledge seems to have been forgotten by the West, and Renaissance Europe received with incredulity reports of these birds. At the very close of the sixteenth century an Englishman at Aleppo was disquieted lest his account of them be disbelieved. The Turks, he says,

> have one thing most usual among them, which though it be right wel knowne to all of our Nation that knowe Turkie, yet it exceadeth the credite of our homebred countriemen, for relating whereof (perhappes) I may be held a liar, having authoritie so to doe (as they say and thinke) because I am a traveller.

After which characteristic remonstrance he gives a description of the birds merchants employ to communicate with each other from town to town, sending information as to what goods are on hand and what commodities are in demand.[1] Another Englishman conveys to us the sense of astonishment with which he first heard of these pigeons at Tripoli in Syria:

> My Host told me a strange thing, namely that in Alexandria of Ægypt . . . there was a dove-cote, and that also at Cairo (or Babylon), farre within the Land of Ægypt, there was another dove-cote; and because it much concernes the merchants, to have speedy newes of any commodity arriving, he assured mee that they used to tie letters about the neckes of the doves at Alexandria, and so to let them loose, which doves having formerly bred in the dove-cote at Cayro, did flie thither most swiftly. . . This I beleeved not, till I came to Haleppo, and telling it for a fable to the English merchants there, they seriously affirmed the same to be true.[2]

The near alliance of the fabulous and the real is again exemplified in the analogy between the ashes of the phoenix and the eggs of chickens incubated in the sand. New birds came forth from each. European incredulity about the process of artificial incubation was perhaps in part due to the fact that one of the

---

1 William Parry, *A New and Large Discourse of the Travels of Sir Anthony Sherley*, 1601, p.11f.
2 Fynes Moryson, *Itinerary*, ii,52 (MacLehose edition). Linschoten, Sanderson, Biddulph, Sandys, and Della Valle are among the travellers of the period who report on the use of carrier-pigeons in one or another place in the Levant. Sandys's description is cited by Isaac Walton, *The Compleat Angler*, chapter 1. Davenant refers to messages being brought 'about the neck of a Barbary pigeon' (*The Platonic Lovers*, I,i; *Works*, ii,8).

' Crescit sub pondere Virtus '

earliest reports of it was in *The Travels of Sir John Mandeville*.[1] But succeeding centuries had produced an ample number of witnesses to verify this report; [2] and it is consequently somewhat surprising to catch a suggestion of doubt in Bacon's note that 'eggs, as is reported by some, have been hatched by the warmth of an oven.' [3] The contemporaneous waning belief in the phoenix and waxing belief in incubation are characteristic of a period when credulity was yielding place to scientific knowledge.

Once more, what logical necessity was there to compel one to reject reports of the existence of the unicorn and accept reports of the existence of the rhinoceros? Until a live specimen of the latter creature could be produced, was not his single horn as remarkable as that of the fabulous monster with which he was sometimes confused? Without entering into the much-debated question of the origin of the belief in the existence of the unicorn—whether it is to be found in the rhinoceros or in the tusk of the narwhal or in the horns of an antelope seen fleetingly in silhouette, it is to be noted that Conrad Gesner and Edward Topsell (who follows him) clearly differentiate in texts and illustrations between the two beasts. Gesner's picture of the rhinoceros is taken, as he admits, from Dürer's well-known engraving; but Topsell, reproducing it from Gesner, makes the misstatement that Gesner had seen a live specimen of the animal in Portugal. There is no evidence that any rhinoceros was exhibited in England during our period; and a designer of a Lord Mayor's Show prided himself upon the ingenious artificial model of one which he introduced into the procession as a rare

1 Chapter vii.
2 Breydenbach saw the incubators in Egypt (*Peregrinations*, 1486); Sebastian Munster describes the process (*Straunge and Memorable Thinges*, folio 91); Sandys and Sanderson and an anonymous writer in Hakluyt (v,333) are among those who saw and wondered. Lithgow visited the incubating furnaces in Tunis (*Rare Adventures*, p.334). James Howell, though he never saw the phenomenon, was fascinated by accounts of it (*Familiar Letters*, i,66). Incubation is referred to twice in the drama of the period. Surley says to Subtle: 'You should hatch gold in a furnace, Sir, as they do eggs in Egypt' (*The Alchemist*, II,iii,127f.); and in *Revenge for Honour*, I,i,66, it is said of one whose mind is filled with schemes that he 'hath hatched more projects than the ovens in Egypt chickens.' Whence did William Rudyerd, who addressed some lines to Richard Lovelace, derive the notion that 'chickens hatcht in furnaces produce or one limbe more, or one limbe lesse than nature bids'? (Lovelace, *Poems*, ed. C.H.Wilkinson, Oxford, 1925, ii,6).
3 *Natural History*, #856; *Works*, ii,25.

curiosity.[1] In fact, so rare was this animal that more than a century later, when one was exhibited at Stuttgart in 1748, a medal was cast in its honour, showing on one side the beast under a blazing sun and giving on the other its weight and certain facts about its enormous appetite. This same rhinoceros occasioned great excitement in Venice when it was shown there during the carnival of 1751. It is the subject of Pietro Longhi's well-known picture, now in the National Gallery.[2]

Small wonder that the Elizabethans believed in the existence of the unicorn when there was evidence of the existence of such creatures as the rhinoceros, the camel, the elephant, and the crocodile. The camel and the dromedary were both known to them from various picture-books; Topsell reproduces both with reasonable accuracy. Polonius could recognize the resemblance between a 'humped' cloud and a camel. Thomas Coryat's last pamphlet is adorned with a picture showing the adventurous traveller riding upon a camel led by naked negroes.[3] In Spenser's pageant of the Seven Deadly Sins Avarice rides camel-back, the symbol suggesting not only the general connection of the beast with the Orient and the Orient with all manner of wealth but the particular association of the camel which finds it hard to pass through the needle's eye with the rich man who finds it hard to enter into the Kingdom of Heaven; and there had probably descended to Spenser the tenuous medieval tradition interpreting the camel's hump as the emblem of the rich man's burden of superfluities.[4] There is no record that there were camels in the menagerie at the Tower of London during Elizabeth's reign; but a generation later Londoners had a good opportunity to acquaint themselves with the actual appearance of the beasts when, about 1623, a small herd owned by King James could be seen daily grazing in Saint James's Park.[5]

1 See p.467, below.
2 Pompeo Molmenti, *La Storia di Venezia nella Vita Privata*, Bergamo, 1926, iii, 252 and 254.
3 *Mr. Thomas Coriat to his friends in England sendeth greeting*, 1618, title-page and recurring twice among the preliminary poems. Compare Topsell, op.cit., pp.92f., 97f. Camels are delineated frequently in paintings and tapestries of the period.
4 *The Faerie Queene*, I,iv,27. See J.L.Lowes's interpretation in *P.M.L.A.*, xxix (1914), 425. Corflambo, the pagan giant, rides on a dromedary (*The Faerie Queene*, IV,viii,38).
5 *C.S.P.,Dom.*, *1623-5*, p.13.

What is more remarkable, considering the immensity of the creatures and the smallness of the ships in which they were transported, is the fact that at one time or another within our period there were two or three elephants in England. 'The fellow with the elephant' was a well-known character in London.[1] By one poet he is classed with two other showmen, Banks who owned the famous performing horse and a man who played with an ape; another poet ranked this elephant with the Lord Chancellor's tomb and the new water-works among the most notable sights of the city.[2] A quarter of a century later another elephant was owned by King James.[3] Sir Thomas Browne, refuting the ancient notion that elephants have no joints in their legs, remarks that some years earlier Englishmen had an opportunity to see for themselves that they could bend their joints;[4] he is referring either to yet a third specimen or else one or the other of these. A living model was, then, at hand for the artist who adorned another pamphlet by Coryat with a cut showing him riding upon an elephant. 'I have rid upon an elephant,' he had written from India, 'determining one day (by Gods leave) to have my picture expressed in my next Booke, sitting upon an Elephant.'[5]

Strange creatures such as these served to confirm the truth of travellers' tales of eastern lands. Englishmen were notoriously inquisitive about far-fetched curiosities. 'Any strange beast there makes a man,' said Trinculo. 'When they will not give a

1 Jonson, *Every Man out of His Humour*, IV,vi,60.
2 John Donne, *Satires*, i,80; *Poetical Works*, ed. Grierson, i,148, and ii,101f.; Sir John Davies, *Epigrams*, xxx and vi; *Works*, ed. A.B.Grosart, i,334 and 318.
3 See p.18, note 5, above. After the Restoration specimens were not uncommon in London.
4 *Vulgar Errors*, III,i. The Shakespearean commentators have abundantly illustrated the words of Ulysses: 'The elephant hath joints, but none for courtesy: his legs are legs for necessity, not for flexure' (*Troilus and Cressida*, II,iii,114); but they have not noted that this statement contradicts two ancient beliefs: that the elephant has no joints and that it is the most courteous of animals. Chapman, Middleton, William Rowley, and other writers of the period refer to its lack of joints, drawing from this an image of stubbornness. A corollary of this belief is that it sleeps standing. Other notions are that it will not drink of clear water for fear of beholding its own deformities; that its breath draws forth serpents from their holes; that it shows an appreciation of beautiful women; that it goes in quest of the mandrake root; and that its seasons of amorousness are very infrequent but of the wildest fury. See further Golding's translation (1587) of Solinus, p.116, and Topsell, op.cit., pp.190f.; also G.C.Druce, 'The Elephant in Mediaeval Legend and Art,' *The Archaeological Journal*, Second Series, xxvi (1919), 1f.
5 *Thomas Coriate Traveller for the English Wits*, 1616, p.24.

doit to relieve a lame beggar, they will lay out ten to see a dead Indian.' [1] Trinculo was meditating on the possibility of making his fortune by taming, transporting to England, and exhibiting there the monster which he had stumbled upon on the sea-shore. His design was rational and his hopes plausible, for he doubtless knew that Englishmen had been willing to pay to see dead crocodiles. 'Of late years,' says Stephen Batman, 'there hath bene brought into England, the cases or skinnes of such Crocodiles to be seene, and much money given for the sight thereof; the policy of strangers laugh[s] at our folly, either that we are too wealthy, or else that we know not how to bestow our money.' [2] One can imagine the chatter and the gasps of wonder as a crowd of Londoners gazed at the stuffed carcasses. Before their eyes lay specimens of the creatures which beguiled unwary travellers with hypocritical tears and as they devoured their victims wept over them; [3] the noisome reptiles which were so dangerous that the dogs of Nile dared not pause to drink of the river but lapped water as they ran; [4] the 'foure-footed mischiefs,'

---

1 *The Tempest*, II,ii,32f.
2 *Batman Uppon Bartholome*, xviii, chapter 33. The apothecary in *Romeo and Juliet* (V,i,43) has a stuffed alligator hanging in his shop.
3 *Lachrimae crocodili* provoked two explanations. When it wept, did the creature merely anticipate the gesture of the Walrus who amid sobs and tears gulped down the largest oysters? Or did it weep aloud to attract its human victims, somewhat in the manner of the devils of Lop? Topsell remarks that authorities differ on this point (*The Historie of Serpents*, 1608, p.135). Vincent of Beauvais, upon whom rests the responsibility of popularizing the notion of the crocodile's tears among the medieval compilers of bestiaries, implies (*Speculum naturale*, xviii,106) that there was no conscious deception on the creature's part; and this view is as old as the *Physiologus* (compare *Bartholomeus de Proprietatibus Rerum*, 1585, xviii, chapter 33). But the general Elizabethan view was that there was treachery as well as hypocrisy in its tears. Compare *Selimus*, ll.441f.:

> Even as the great Ægyptian crocodile
> Wanting his prey, with artificial tears
> And fained plaints his subtil tongue doth file
> To entrap the silly wandering traveller.

Spenser's notion is that the crocodile weeps to deceive his victim (*The Faerie Queene*, I,v,18), and when (ibid. V,vii,7) the goddess Isis rests her foot upon a crocodile the symbol is of guile. Compare the analogous symbolism in the figure of Saint Theodore standing upon a crocodile in the Piazetta of San Marco at Venice. The image occurs times beyond number in Elizabethan literature. A few striking examples are: Lyly, *Euphues: The Anatomy of Wit*; *Works*, i,220; Nashe, *Pierce Penilesse*; *Works*, i,184; Nicholas Breton, *Wits Private Wealth*, 1639; *Works*, ed. Grosart, ii, *p.*, p.11; Lewis Machin and Gervais Markham, *The Dumbe Knight*, IV,i; Hazlitt's Dodsley, x,194. Sir John Hawkins tells the same thing of the alligator (Hakluyt, x,40). George Wither somewhat curiously associates treachery not with the crocodile's tears but with its smiles (*Abuses Stript and Whipt*, p.8; *Poems*, Spenser Society, p.36).
4 Pliny, viii,61; Ælian, *Varia Historia*, i,4; Golding's Solinus, Sig. N₁ᵛ. 'The Dogs of Egypt drinke water by snatches,' says Lyly (*Euphues and His England*; *Works*,

THOMAS CORIATE
Traueller for the English
VVits : Greeting.

From the Court of the Great MOGVL, *Resi-*
dent at the Towne of ASMERE, in
Easterne INDIA.

Printed by W. Iaggard, and Henry Fetherston.
1616.

'*I have rid upon an Elephant*'

as Golding calls them, which have 'few friends in the world, except the bird Trochilus';[1] beasts the more terrible because so difficult to destroy, their scales being proof against iron.[2] The carcasses brought into England have long since disappeared; but the chances of time have permitted the survival of a similar specimen elsewhere. Under the colonnade of the Patio de los Naranjos at Cordova there hangs, dusty and desiccated, a dead crocodile. It has hung there for centuries.

Monsters of the Nile were not the only gruesome curiosities that one could bring home from Egypt. John Sanderson, an English merchant who was in Egypt in 1586, has this to record of his visit to the tombs at Sakkara:

> The Momia . . . ar thowsands of imbalmed bodies, which weare buried thousands of years past in a sandie cave, at which ther seemeth to have bine some cities in tims past. We were lett doune by ropes as into a well, with wax candles burninge in our hands, and so waulked uppon the bodies of all sorts and size, great and smaule, and some imbalmed in little earthen potts, which never had forme; these ar sett at the feet of the great bodies. They gave no noysome smell at all, but ar like pitch, beinge broken; for I broke of all parts of the bodies to see howe the flesh was turned to drugge, and brought home divers heads, hands, arms, and feete for a shewe.

ii,56). Compare Gabriel Harvey: 'The wittier sort tasteth, and flieth: as the Dog from Nilus' (*Foure Letters, and certaine Sonnets*, 1592; ed. G.B.Harrison, *Bodley Head Quartos*, p.41). Also Marston, *Sophonisba*, III,i,201f.; Dekker, *The Wonderful Year, Plague-Pamphlets*, ed. Wilson, p.41; Purchas, xi,364.

1 Golding's Solinus, p.148; Topsell, *The Historie of Serpents*, pp.126f.,131,135; Herodotus, ii, chapter 68; Pliny, viii,25; Bartholomeus Anglicus, op.cit., xviii, chapter 33 (a charming description of the bird 'cuschillus' cleaning the crocodile's mouth). George Sandys (*Relation of a Journey*, p.100) vouches for the truth of the phenomenon, saying that he has seen the bird making a meal by picking the crocodile's teeth. Lyly twice uses the image of the trochilus, adding some details not discoverable in his classical sources (*Euphues: The Anatomy of Wit; Works*, i,193; *Euphues and His England; Works*, ii,144). In Spenser's description of 'a little Bird cal'd Tedula' (*Visions of the World's Vanity*, iii) the name, which occurs nowhere else, is probably a printer's error. Francis Rous likens the poet's subservience to his patron to the bird's action in picking 'a Serpents jawes' (*Thule, or Virtues Historie*, 1598, II,vi,4; ed. Spenser Society, p.123). John Webster alone touches the subject with imagination (*The White Devil*, IV,ii,224f.).

2 Marlowe, *1 Tamburlaine*, IV,i,10f.; Nashe, *Have with You to Saffron-Walden; Works*, iii,96; Topsell, op.cit., p.126f.; Hakluyt, x,40. The Earl of Stirling says: 'His scaly armour is no proofe for fire' (*Doomes-Day*, Third Hour, stanza 65). This will be at the Day of Judgment; but elsewhere (*Tiberius*, ed. cit., ll.2070f.) we read of one weapon to which the hard-pressed traveller may have recourse:

> Fling wilde fire at the Crokadile,
> For nothing else can pierce his brazen skales.

We bought allso 600 lb. for the Turkie Company in peces, and brought into Ingland in the Hercules, together with a whole bodie. They are lapped in 100 doble of cloth, which rotton and pillinge of, you may see the skinne, flesh, fingers, and nayles firme, onelie altered blacke. One little hand I brought into Ingland to shewe, and presented it to my brother, who gave the same to a doctor in Oxford.[1]

In Samuel Purchas's text of Sanderson's narrative a marginal gloss adds the information that the 'momia' that was entire was carried to the residence of Sir Edward Osborne (the wealthy merchant-adventurer) in Filpot Lane and remained there until it was sold to the apothecaries.[2]

II

OCULAR proof was, then, not wanting in the shape of out-landish monsters to substantiate the stories told by returned wanderers to Englishmen who stayed at home. There was doubtless an eager audience for such stories in every tavern and by many a fireside. That there was a larger audience for those who put their tales into print is evident not only from the number of travel-books but from the number of editions through which the more popular of them passed. Of such 'arm-chair travellers' who never ventured far from home Robert Burton is typical. In the comfort and security of his library he inveighed against the monotony of his existence

1 *Travels in the Levant*, pp.44f. The objects in the little earthen pots may have been mummied embryos, or Sanderson may have been referring to the canopic jars in which were placed the entrails of the dead. 'Pillinge of' is apparently 'pealing off.' For another description of the purchase of a mummy and its transportation to Europe see Pietro della Valle, *Viaggi*, Rome, 1658–62, i,204f. Thevenot, Bruin, and Monconys, among other travellers of the seventeenth century, describe the mummy-pits of Memphis and tell of their purchases. There was an established trade in pow-dered mummy which, because of the presence in it of bitumen and also for magical reasons, was a recognized article in the Levantine and European pharmacopoeia. See the article on Mummy in the *Encyclopædia Britannica*, and the commentators on *Othello*, III,iv,75 and on Jonson's *Volpone*, IV,iv,14. Descriptions of mummies and their tombs furnished writers of a meditative turn of mind with matter for melancholy reflections. The Earl of Stirling broods upon the 'ridiculous care' with which the Egyptians preserved their dead, 'to scorn corruption and to mock the dust' (the most eloquent line in all his enormous poem on *Doomes-Day*, Fourth Hour, stanza 95). Compare the magnificent passage in Sir Thomas Browne's *Urn-Burial*, chapter 5. The 'Fragment on Mummies' attributed to Browne is a nineteenth-century fabrication, an extraordinary bit of pastiche.
2 *Pilgrimes*, ix,419 (MacLehose edition).

('still, still the same'), while enjoying vicariously the adventures of voyagers of greater hardihood and restlessness. With unwearying diligence he transferred their anecdotes and observations to the pages of his great book. In the 'Digression of Ayre,' that magnificent expatiation and exercise for his recreation in which he considers the virtue of a change of climate as a cure for melancholy, he visits in imagination many parts of the East.[1] He would test the truth or falsity of 'Marcus Polus the Venetians narration'; would censure the 'lies' of all Plinies, Solinuses, Strabos, and Sir John Mandevilles; passing Madagascar he would see 'that great bird Rucke'; and in Arabia he would search out the phoenix. He knows as well as though he had been there that 'about Damascus . . . is a paradise, by reason of the plenty of waters,' while 'the desarts of Arabia [are] barren, because of rockes, rolling seas of sand, and dry mountaines; . . . uninhabitable therefore of men, birds, beasts, void of all greene trees, plants and fruits, a vast rocky horrid wilderness, which by no art can be manured.' All this and much more he saw in his mind's eye as he voyaged through strange seas of thought.

Thomas Dekker who, so far as we know, was never out of England and probably seldom away from London, needed only the 'universal Map' made by those 'two honest Card-makers Peter Plancius and Gerard Mercator' to acquaint himself with 'the old raine-beaten world' and all 'the spicke and span new-found worlds.' With such enthusiasm did he con his cards that, as he says, 'Prester John and the Sophy were never out of [his] eye.' He came to know his way about Constantinople 'and could have gone to the great Turkes Serraglio (where he keepes all his wenches) as tollerably and farre more welcome, then if I had beene one of his Eunuches.'[2] On the low plane of his laborious fancy, as he studies the

---

1 *The Anatomy of Melancholy*, II,ii,3.
2 *Newes from Graves-end*, 1604; *Plague Pamphlets*, ed. Wilson, p.66. *Ortelius his Epitome of the Theatre of the World* was freshly available in an augmented English edition, 1603, when Dekker wrote. The complete *Theatrum* was reissued in England in 1606; and in 1610 there was an amplified edition *with new mappes wanting in the Latin editions*. Plancius's *Orbis terrarum typus* was not reissued in England. *Mercators Atlas* was not englished till 1635, and in the following year it had to compete with another English version printed in and imported from Holland.

Orbis terrarum typus of Plancius and the projection of the world by Mercator, he reflects something of the enthusiasm of a greater poet whose imagination was fired by the contemplation of Abraham Ortelius's map of Asia to picture the far-flung conquests of Tamburlaine.[1] In *Old Fortunatus* Dekker indulges in another flight of fancy. A Chorus 'wafts us overseas' in the fashion Ben Jonson satirized, reciting a swift summary of the travels of Fortunatus.[2] From Famagusta in Cyprus, traditionally his native place,[3] Fortunatus journeys to Asian shores; he visits the Tartar's palace, the courts of barbarian kings, and the Turkish court, where he 'revels with the Emperor of the East.' At length he arrives in Babylon of Egypt, that is, Cairo,[4] where he tells the Soldan of his various adventures: his ride in a chariot drawn by unicorns and his visits to the great Tartarian Cham, to Prester John, and to the Turkish Solyman.[5]

Another glimpse into the mind of a student who did his travelling in his library is afforded us by Henry King in a poem complimenting Sir Henry Blount upon his *Voyage into the Levant* (1636). 'From my Countreys smoke I never mov'd,'

1 Ethel Seaton, 'Marlowe's Map,' *Essays and Studies by Members of the English Association*, x (1924).
2 The Chorus before Act II. Compare the account of his travels which Fortunatus gives his sons, *Dramatic Works*, ed. Pearson, i,117.
3 Dekker's topography is vague; he seems to think that Cyprus is a town. 'This path leads thee to Cyprus,' he writes; and he refers to 'the streets of Cyprus.' See *Old Fortunatus*, I,i and ii.
4 On the origin of the name Babylon for Cairo (or for the Roman citadel whose ruined walls are still visible in Old Cairo) see Baedeker's *Egypt*, ed. 1929, pp.46 and 114. The identity of name with the Mesopotamian city sometimes caused Cairo to be called Babylon the Less or Babylon of the Egyptians; sometimes a distinction was made between Cairo and Babylon, somewhat farther south (see, for example, Robert Greene, *Orlando Furioso*, I,i, where the Soldan of Egypt holds his state 'in Cairye and in Babylon'). The name Grand Cairo was needed to embrace Cairo proper, Babylon, and Bûlâq. Sometimes the two Babylons caused confusion; see for example the Table of Names attached to Abraham Hartwell's translation of G.T.Minadoi's *Historia della Guerra fra Turchi et Persiani* (*History of the Warres betweene the Turkes and the Persians*, 1595, *sub* 'Cairo'). Not understanding the matter, no commentator has explained Spenser's reference (*The Faerie Queene*, II,ix,21) to the 'Egyptian slime' with which King Ninus built the walls of Babylon. Why 'Egyptian slime' for the walls of a city on the Euphrates? The geographical epithet is due to a confused association of the two cities in the poet's mind. The author of *Mandeville* had been careful to distinguish between the two: 'That Babylone that I have spoken offe where that the Soudan duelleth is not that gret Babylone where the dyversitee of languages was first made' (chapter vi).
5 Dekker's chronology is hazy, for, having had an audience with Sultan Solyman, Fortunatus is presently at the court of King Athelstane in England.

says King wistfully; but he has always had a curiosity to see foreign lands, and, for want of a better way, has had to stray through the world with Ortelius and Mercator as his guides. In this fashion he has visited Egypt and Arabia and degenerate Greece. 'Wrapt in pity and amaze' he has often contemplated the vast territory of the Sultan of Turkey, musing on the daring steps whereby this potentate has become 'the Asian fear and scourge of Christendome.' A higher Ordinance willed that this growth of power should come to pass, since the days when

> 'mongst a lawless straggling crew
> Made up of Arab, Saracen, and Jew,
> The world's disturber, faithless Mahomet,
> Did by Imposture an opinion get.

Centuries later, Ottoman—that is, Othman or Osman I, the founder of the Empire—based his rule upon the ruins of the eastern kingdoms. Amurath (Murad II) displayed 'his horned Crescents' on the plains of Servia, until his defeat at Croya (a battle in which the Albanian hero Scanderbeg was victorious) set a limit to his conquests. All this, says King, he has often read; and he has also perused many books about Turkish manners and their way of life:

> Their frequent washings, and the several Bath
> Each Meschit to it self annexed hath;
> . . . how just and free
> To inoffensive Travellers they be;

and so forth. But not until he read Blount's narrative did he cease to doubt these curious truths.

> The solid depths of your rare history
> . . . looks above our gadders trivial reach,
> The Common Place of travellers, who teach
> But Table-talk; and seldomly aspire
> Beyond the Countres Dyet or Attire.

In contrast to such trivialities Blount's book reveals 'the Policy and Manage of each State' and deserves to be the 'Rule' of all who travel in the Levant.[1]

1 'To his Noble and Judicious Friend Sir Henry Blount upon his Voyage,' *Poems*, ed. John Sparrow, 1925, pp.76f.

In the fashion of the time friends contributed such commendatory poems to volumes of *Travels* and *Voyages* as they
did to books in all departments of literature. William Lithgow's
first short narrative, *A Most Delectable and True Discourse*
(1614), has five such pieces. One admirer hails him as 'William
of the Wilderness'; another marvels at his temerity:

> Thou durst go like no man else that lives;
> By Sea and Land alone in cold and raine,
> Through Bandits, Pirats, and Arabian Theeves.

Many other similar poems introduce the later complete account of the same traveller's experiences in strange lands.
Between the lines of the poems in facetious vein which Thomas
Coryat's friends contributed to his various publications one
can detect an admiration for that fantastic wanderer's courage
and endurance. Innumerable other such tributes are extant,
inspired in part by a literary convention but also by the admiration and something like envy with which the stay-at-home
regarded the man who had passed from land to land, seen
strange cities, and consorted with people well-nigh fabulous.

The growth of the fashion of visiting foreign lands occasioned
at the close of the sixteenth century and during the first decades
of the seventeenth a good deal of comment which, though
generally prompted by the journeys of young aristocrats to
France and Italy, applies also to travel in the Levant. Francis
Bacon would allow a young man to travel provided he is
accompanied by a wise tutor. His special concern is that the
competent traveller should observe the conduct of public affairs and make the acquaintance of men occupying offices of
responsibility. It is needful, he says, to have some knowledge
of a country's language before setting forth to visit it. The
traveller should carry some map or book describing the country. He should keep a diary, noting therein all important
buildings; not neglecting 'comedies, such whereunto the better sort of people do resort' but not paying disproportionate
attention to other public spectacles. He should not remain too
long in one place. 'Let him sequester himself from the company
of his countrymen' and consort as much as possible with

citizens of the country. When he returns home, 'let his travels appear rather in his discourse, than in his apparel or gesture; and in his discourse let him rather be advised in his answers, than forward to tell stories; and let it appear that he doth not change his country manners for those of foreign parts, but only prick in some flowers of that he hath learned abroad into the customs of his own country.'[1]

A treatise more elaborate than Bacon's and closely packed with matter is Thomas Palmer's upon the means to make foreign travel more profitable. Here are considered the various objects sought by official and unofficial travellers; the necessary preparations for a journey; the proprieties of deportment while abroad; the acquisition of strange tongues; the need to exercise the power of observation; the duty to report significant intelligence to the authorities at home; and much else of like nature. Palmer provides warnings against the particular perils which the unwary traveller is likely to meet with in different lands. For example, when he is in Turkey he should 'lie along the ground' while partaking of a meal, and when he meets a native of his acquaintance he should salute him 'with the hatte on, without bending of the knee, without bowing of the bodie, without embracing, without profering of the hand, without conjoyning, without kissing.' By so observing the manners of a country and adapting himself to them a stranger will avoid giving offence.[2]

With the reasonableness and moderation of Bacon's counsel and Palmer's one may contrast Joseph Hall's violent indictment of the moral dangers of travel. The perils that environ young Englishmen in Roman Catholic countries are his particular concern; but his treatise is not without applicability to travel in Moslem countries also. Hall begins his censure with the admission that travel is necessary and lawful for matters of traffic and of state. Only let merchants take heed lest they go so far that they leave God behind them and lest 'whiles they buy all other things good cheape, they make not an ill

---

1 *Essays*, xviii: 'Of Travel.'
2 *An Essay of the Meanes how to make our Travailes into forraine Countries the more profitable and honourable*, 1606.

match for their souls.' He utterly disapproves of travel at a
tender age to gratify curiosity. If youths run moral dangers
even in English universities, how much worse it is to send them
into 'those places which are professedly infectious.' If early
rising 'makes a man healthfull, holy and rich, . . . all falls
out contrary in an early travell': differences in food and climate
are bad for the body; travel is a great enemy to holiness; and
as for riches—'all the wealth of a young Traveller is only in his
tongue.' Englishmen do not need to go abroad for their education, because the reputation of Italy for arms and of Greece
for learning is now 'happily met in one Iland.' There is also
the danger lest one lose the desire to perfect the intellect, for
in some lands (Hall is thinking of Mohammedan countries)
learning is held in disgrace. Moreover, though 'necessity drove
our forefathers out of doores,' there is no such compulsion
today when we can stay at home and read about the wonders of
the world. Hall assumes complacently that opportunities to discover fresh marvels are now exhausted; and he is equally complacent in his willingness to experience in the safety of his home
a vicarious thrill as he reads of the adventures of other men.[1]

Nashe's hero, Jack Wilton, encountered at Rome a banished
English nobleman who poured out to him a flood of invective
against the folly of travelling. That which was the curse of
the Israelites, that they should dwell in a strange land, 'we
Englishmen count our chiefe blessednes: hee is no bodie that
hath not traveld: we had rather live as slaves in another
land . . . than live as freemen and Lords in our owne Countrey.' 'He that is a traveller must have the backe of an asse
to beare all, a tung like the taile of a dog to flatter all, the
mouth of a hogge to eate what is set before him, the eare of
a merchant to heare all and say nothing.' [2] William Biddulph
probably had this passage in mind when he advised would-be
travellers in Turkey to give tribute-money promptly, never to
answer back, to fawn upon the Turks and kiss the hem of their
garments, never to return blow for blow but to receive the

---

1 *Quo Vadis? A Just Censure of Travell as it is commonly undertaken by Gentlemen of
our Nation*, 1617, pp.4,12,20,27,38f.
2 *The Unfortunate Traveller; Works*, ii,297.

buffets of officials with a smile; to be, in other words, like the painted picture of a servant, with a swine's snout (for you must not be dainty), an ass's ears (for you must patiently bear sharp words), and the feet of a hart (for you must be swift to perform what is commanded of you).[1]

It is difficult to discover in the literature of the period any whole-hearted and unqualified commendation of travel. Shakespeare, indeed, says in an oft-quoted passage that 'homekeeping youth hath ever homely wit';[2] but the context does not imply the advice to venture further abroad than the distance from Verona to Milan. Even those who visited foreign lands were almost invariably candid about the risks and inconveniences and humiliations they have had to put up with. Baptist Goodall does celebrate the achievements of the great travellers of Holy Writ, from Adam to Saint Paul; and with a gusto which often gets the better of his syntax he gives a catalogue of the wonders to be seen in different countries. Nevertheless he declares that the greatest happiness of a travelled Englishman is the sight of his native country:

> But see at sea their frothiness is scourged,
> And by a timely pyll there braines are purged,
> Turne taile to travaile now retired to shore,
> Love England now so well theyl out no more.[3]

A character in one of Fletcher's plays says that 'till we are travell'd and live abroad, we are coxcombs';[4] but a prevalent charge against travel was that it turned decent Englishmen into just such conceited showy persons. Human nature being what it is, the stay-at-home resented the affectations of the traveller. It is such a sophisticated fop who, echoing Nashe, says in Jonson's first comedy that 'a man is nobody till he has travelled.'[5] Many are the satiric protests against the fantastic fashions introduced by returned travellers and encouraged by merchants trading into foreign countries. 'Monsieur Traveller,' says Rosalind; 'look you lisp and wear strange suits';[6] and Fletcher characterizes outlandish stockings and

1 *The Travels of Foure English Men and a Preacher*, 1612, pp.84f.
2 *The Two Gentlemen of Verona*, I,i,2.
3 *The Tryall of Travell*, 1630, Sig. H₂ʳ.   5 *The Case Is Altered*, II,vii,34.
4 *The Wild Goose Chase*, I,ii,14.   6 *As You Like It*, IV,i,35.

breeches as 'those types of travel.'[1] William Harrison declares that the notorious mutability of the English is seen in their changing fashions: Spanish one day, French or German another, and 'by and by the Turkish maner is generallie best liked of.' Even the cut of the beard depends upon the foreign style of the moment; 'some are shaven from the chin like those of Turks.'[2] There are fops, Wither remarks scornfully, who disdain the styles of France or Italy because those countries are near at hand and who fetch their fashions from more distant lands.

> We have Morisco gownes, Barbarian sleeves,
> . . . with divers far-fetcht trifles,
> Such as the wandring English gallant rifles
> Strange Countries for.

And he goes on to protest with vigorous irony:

> Our home-made Cloth is now too course a ware,
> For Chyna, or for Indian stuffs we are.
> For Turkey Grow-graines, Chamblets, silken Rash,
> And such like new devised Forraine trash. . .
> (Oh Vanity) our Country yeelds enough,
> What need we Graecian or Arabian stuffe? . . .
> That Opium which a Turk in saftie will
> Devour at once, two Englishmen would kill.[3]

The ground of complaint was not only the foreign fashion of the travelled man's costume but the melancholy sophistication of his demeanour. 'As solemn as a traveller' is a simile of Marston's;[4] and the same satirist exclaims:

> With what a discontented grace
> Bruto the traveller does sadly pace![5]

In an elaborate diatribe against such affected cosmopolitans Barnabie Rich works himself into a very ecstasy of indignation:

1 *Henry VIII*, I,iii,31 (the scene is by Fletcher).
2 *Description of England*, 1577; ed. F.J.Furnivall, New Shakespeare Society, 1877, pp.168f.
3 *Abuses Stript and Whipt*, II,i; *Poems*, ed. cit., pp.216,221f. Castiglione, commenting upon the infinite variety of courtiers' clothes, imitating the fashions of foreign peoples, had remarked: 'Neither want we of them also that will clothe themselves like Turkes' (*The Book of the Courtier*, translated by Sir Thomas Hoby, 1561, Book ii).
4 *Antonio and Mellida*, Induction, 134; *Works*, ed. Bullen, i,12.
5 *Satires*, ii,127f. So also Spenser says that a deportment 'alla Turchesca,' dignified, disdainful and with lofty looks, is characteristic of 'newfangledness' (*Mother Hubberds Tale*, ll.675f.).

Here comes a spruce fellow now, and if hee be not alied to the Fantasticke, yet I am sure the foole and he are so neare a kinne, that they can not marrie, without a Licence from the Pope. Would ye knowe who it is? Mary Sir, it is a Traveller, not of the sort that endevor their travels but of purpose to growe into the hieway of Experience for the better service of their Prince or Country: but of those whipsters, that having spent the greatest part of their patrimony in prodigality, wil give out the rest of their stocke, to be paid two or three for one, upon their returne from Rome, from Venice, from Constantinople, or some other appoynted place. These fellowes in their journeying doe so empty themselves of the little witte they carryed out, that they can make no better return then their mindes full fraught with farre fetcht follies, and their heades over birthened with too many outlandish vanities.[1]

It is noteworthy that this writer associates with Constantinople the practice of putting out a sum of money to be repaid several times over on the traveller's return home. Gonzalo's phrase 'Each putter out of five for one'[2] has called forth a flood of commentary; and what has to be said here will be limited to the bearing of the custom upon travel in the Levant. Ben Jonson's fantastic traveller Puntarvolo announces:

I do intend . . . to travel, and . . . I am determined to put forth some five thousand pound to be paid me five for one upon the return of myself, my wife, and my dog from the Turk's court in Constantinople. If all or either of us miscarry in the journey, 'tis gone; if we be successful, why, there will be five and twenty thousand pound to entertain time withal.[3]

The practice was often nothing more than a wager, as when Will Kemp 'put out' money upon his morris-dance to Norwich or when John Taylor the Water-Poet put it out upon his journey on foot from London to Scotland.[4] But it could also

---

1 *Faultes, Faults, and Nothing Else but Faultes*, 1606, folio 8.
2 *The Tempest*, III,iii,48.
3 *Every Man out of His Humour*, II,iii,245f.
4 *Kemps Nine Daies Wonder*, ed. Dyce, Camden Society, 1840, p.19; John Taylor, *A Kicksey Winsey, or A Lerry Come-Twang; Works*, Spenser Society, pp.196f. Taylor follows this satiric poem with a prose statement 'In Defense of Adventures upon Returnes.' Kemp was paid by some of his debtors; Taylor by none. For other references to the practice of 'putting out' see Beaumont and Fletcher, *The Noble Gentleman*, I,i; Nathaniel Field, *Amends for Ladies*, III,iv; Sir John Davies, *Epigrams*, *Works*, ed. Grosart, i,343; James Shirley, *The Ball*, II,i. See also the discussion in Clare Howard, *English Travellers of the Renaissance*, New York, 1913, p.95.

be a serious form of business speculation. A traveller before
starting upon his voyage 'put out' a sum of money; if he
never returned home the person or group who had assumed
the risk retained the premium; but if he returned he received
anywhere from two to five times the amount according to the
estimate of the dangers of the voyage which had been agreed
upon before his departure. That there were travellers who
considered it wise to make the initial outlay and responsible
moneyed people willing to take the risk is eloquent testimony
to the perils of travel three hundred years ago; and indeed the
travel-literature of the period is strewn with references to
wanderers who never returned home. Fynes Moryson is an
example of the traveller who made a provision of this sort.
Before starting for the Levant he put out some money at the
rate of three for one, placing it among his brethren and some
few kinsmen and dearest friends. To our way of thinking it
argues a strange insensitivity that kinsmen and friends were
willing to gamble upon the chance of his death in foreign
parts; but the Elizabethans felt differently. 'Neither did I
exact this money,' Moryson goes on, 'of any man by sute of
law after my returne, which they willingly and presently paid
me, onely some few excepted, who retaining the very money
I gave them, deale not therein so gentlemanlike with me, as
I did with them.' Moryson denounces those 'base adventurers
for gain' who lay out money where the risk is small; and he
contrasts his brother Henry whose purpose it was to recover
'at least the charges of his journey' when, on setting out for
Constantinople with the intention to proceed thence overland
to Jerusalem (a journey never hitherto undertaken by an
Englishman), he 'put out some four hundred pounds, to be
repaid twelve hundred pounds upon his return from those
two cities, and to lose it if he died in the journey.' As it turned
out, Henry Moryson did die and was buried near Scanderoon,
and the original investment was consequently kept by those
who had assumed the risk. Among the anecdotes with which
Moryson enlivens his narrative is that of an Englishman who
narrowly escaped being captured by Turks and sold into
slavery, and who was so much terrified by this experience that

he returned forthwith to England without visiting Jerusalem, and carried back with him 'a counterfeit testimonie and seale that he had been there, because he had put out much money upon his return.'[1]

III

So far we have been occupied in the main with the prejudices and opinions regarding travel expressed by those who stayed at home. It is time to heed the views of some of those who spoke from personal experience; and of these one of the most important, for the length of his journeys, the scope of his narrative, and the dignity of his character, is this same Fynes Moryson. He was a man of independent means who went abroad not as a political or commercial agent nor because he was banished for public or private reasons, but purely from a desire to see the world. His first journey, accomplished in the years 1591–1595, took him through parts of Europe only; but on his second journey (November 1595 to July 1597) he visited Constantinople, Asia Minor, Syria, Palestine, and other parts of the Ottoman Empire. His *Itinerary*, composed long after his return to England but obviously from careful notes, was originally written in Latin; but this version was not published. An English translation, made by himself, appeared in 1617.[2]

Looking back from the safe harbour of home upon his adventures in distant countries, he has much advice to offer those who would travel.[3] Some of his remarks apply only to travel in Christendom, others to travel in Mohammedan countries, the majority to travel almost anywhere. If he sometimes labours the obvious, he is always judicious and often illuminates the discomforts and dangers of the way and shows how best to adapt one's self to unfamiliar circumstances. To visit foreign countries is, he says, good and profitable; but not all persons are fit to travel: not women, nor feeble

1 *Itinerary*, i,425f.,461.
2 The portions of the work dealing with the Levant were complete; but parts of the chapters on Europe remained in manuscript till the present century. See *Shakespeare's Europe: Unpublished Chapters of Fynes Moryson's Itinerary*, ed. Charles Hughes, 1903.
3 *An Itinerary* . . . *Containing His Ten Yeeres Travell*, Part III, Book i, chapters 1–3; Book ii, chapters 1 and 2. Page references to the selected specimens of Moryson's advice it seems unnecessary to give; all passages are in volume ii of the MacLehose reprint, Glasgow, 1907.

persons, nor the aged, nor those too young; but men of middle
years who have a good foundation of the arts and sciences
and are of 'so ripe discretion as they can distinguish between
good and evil.' The theatre of the world is full of the wonders
of God, and 'the admirable variety thereof represents to us
the incomparable Majestie of God.' A wary mind can apprehend
these good things while avoiding the evil. It is true that vices
and heresies are spread through the world by travellers, but
how should we come by new knowledge if all men stayed at
home? The Holy Gospel would not have been given to the
gentiles if the apostles had not excelled in travelling; and
'Christ himself lived in the flesh as a pilgrim.' Inasmuch as
variety is the most pleasing thing in life, Moryson recommends
both contemplation and action, life at home and life abroad.

> They seeme to me most unhappy, and no better than Prisoners,
> who from the cradle to old age, still behold the same walls, faces,
> orchards, pastures, and objects of the eye, and still heare the same
> voices and sounds beate in their eares. . . Running water is sweet,
> but standing pooles stinke. . . Men were created to move, as
> birds to flie. . . We are Citizens of the Whole World; . . . all our
> life is a Pilgrimage.[1]

Of Moryson's practical precepts for the inexperienced we
shall note only those that apply to travel in the Levant,
omitting those that bear only upon western Christendom. He
has a long list of the matters and objects to be observed in a
strange country: the policy of each state, the reputation of
its prince, the disposition and religion of the people, the
traffic of the merchants, its produce and its prices, the situation
of its cities and their salubrity; and all such special things as
sepulchres, ruins, inscriptions, arches, churches, and the like.
Because memory is weak let the traveller carefully note down
all rare observations, 'for he lesse offends that writes many
toyes than he that omits one serious thing.'

[1] Compare Samuel Purchas's second introductory chapter (*Pilgrimes*, i,135f.) on life
a pilgrimage and Christ and the apostles pilgrims. Compare also the 'Preface a la
Louange des Peregrinations et Observations estranges, declarant l'intention de
l'Auteur' which opens Nicolas de Nicolay's *Navigations, Peregrinations et Voyages,*
Antwerp, 1576. This Moryson had doubtless read either in the original or in Washington's translation.

Let him write these notes each day, at morne and even, at his Inne, within writing Tables carried about him, and after at leasure into a paper booke, that many yeers after he may look over them at his pleasure.[1]

For better protection from the casual stranger these notes may be written in cipher. Money had best be carried in a letter of credit, not in specie; and no store of ready money is to be displayed to the view of strangers. For the modest traveller fifty or sixty pounds sterling per annum will suffice; but this estimate implies long sojourns in a few places, not much moving from place to place; and it does not include luxuries.

Nashe had said that it is impossible 'for anie man to attain anie great wit by travell, except he have the grounds of it rooted in him before';[2] and Moryson counsels the man who would travel to begin beforehand the study of cosmography and of foreign languages. As soon as he is settled in a country he should hire a teacher, frequent native society, shun his own countrymen, and avail himself of every opportunity to practise the tongue without fear of being laughed at. An Englishman must also accustom himself to doing without various amenities easily procurable at home. 'We use too much the helpe of our servants, so as we scarcely make ourselves ready' (that is, dress ourselves) without assistance. Moreover Englishmen 'despise the company of meane people at bed and board.' Such insular prejudices can be corrected, Moryson suggests amusingly, if before journeying further an Englishman lives for a while in Germany, where he will have to shift for himself and 'learne to feed on homely meat and to lie in a poore bed.'

Avoid the company of one's own countrymen, for if such

---

1 Other travellers allude occasionally to their habit of 'writing up' by night at an inn the hasty jottings of their table-books. Surviving specimens of such note-books must be of the utmost rarity. One is in the Folger Shakespeare Library; another is described in Quaritch's Catalogue, No. 500: *Writing Tables with a Kalendar for xxiiii yeeres, with sundry necessarye rules,* 1601. This contains, besides the calendar, an almanac, a series of short prayers, calculating tables, weights and measures, a list of English highways, illustrations of English and foreign coins, and other practical information valuable to a traveller. These items supplement the actual tablets which are blank pages specially prepared so that notes can be spunged off and the surface used again and again. Compare *Hamlet,* I,v,98f.; *2 Henry IV,*iv,i,201.

2 *The Unfortunate Traveller; Works,* ii,299.

companions are apprehended or in difficulties one is likely to be held accountable and drawn into danger along with them. Best content one's self with 'such consorts as the way yeelds'; and when chance companions fail have always some good book in the pocket, which will make 'innes and many irksome things' more tolerable. At inns the traveller should lock his chamber-door, sleep with his sword by his side and his purse under his pillow ('but always foulded with his garters or something hee first useth in the morning, lest he forget to put it up before hee goe out of his chamber').

Some say the traveller should discipline himself beforehand so as the better to endure privation when it comes; but on the contrary, says Moryson, cherish the body so long as you can, the better to fortify it against future hardship. He is doubtful of the value of knowing how to swim. It is of little avail in a shipwreck and the swimmer is often pulled under by those who clutch at him. A good chicken-coop thrown overboard will serve him better than his own skill. If he can swim, Moryson recommends that the traveller conceal the fact. He does not approve of travelling on foot. 'Let them stay at home and behold the World in a Mappe, who have not the meanes for honest expenses.' Much good advice follows on the best ways to preserve the health, with remarks on air, diet, purging, exercise, sleep, and accidents. The traveller should conform so far as possible to the apparel of the people among whom he sojourns. 'In the hot clymes of Turkey, they ware thicke garments, but loose, and a thick Tulbant upon their heads, but hollow, and borne up from their heads, and they shave their heads, all to make the Sunnebeames to have lesse power upon their bodies.' The traveller must suppress any desire to criticize or to speak out boldly. He will naturally desire to see the sights and observe the customs of a place; wherefore 'let him be, so he seem not to be curious.' He must be very patient and slow to pick a quarrel. In Turkey not only must a Christian not risk an altercation; he may not so much as carry a weapon or look a Turk in the face without courting a bastinado. Of thieves there is no great danger in the Ottoman Empire, because travellers usually band together in great caravans. Solitary journeying is out of the question for foreigners there. They had best join a company of merchants; but sometimes one may obtain permission to travel in the retinue of some basha or provincial governor or with a troop of the Sultan's horsemen.

Moryson offers various observations upon the effect of climate upon races of men. The covetousness and prodigality of the Turks are characteristics due, he thinks, not to their geographical situation but to the corruption and tyranny of their government and to their ignorance of the liberal and manual arts. He notes the rapidity with which people age in southern climes: the Turks think a woman of five-and-twenty is too old to love or be loved, and there are few men with gray heads. Southern people are, he says, most neat and cleanly of body, much addicted to the use of the bath, and unable to endure the least spot of dirt upon their apparel. This is notably true of the 'tulbant' of white linen which the Turks wear upon their heads. Their houses are kept free of all filth; and above all they are 'curious in keeping their Churches, in which it were no small trespasse so much as to spet (which in common conversation they take for an offence, as if he that spets were wearie of their company).' Observations such as these shed as much light upon the manners of England as upon those of the Turks.

When Moryson penned his caution against travelling on foot he probably had in mind those two sturdy pedestrians, Thomas Coryat and William Lithgow, whose narratives of adventures in many lands had appeared respectively in 1611 and 1614.

Thomas Coryat lives in the memory of students of English literature as a picturesque and mirth-provoking figure of Jacobean England where he seems to have been a kind of privileged buffoon at court. The contemporary testimony to his absurd demeanour and to his irresistibly comic appearance has obscured the remarkable feats of courage and endurance which he achieved in his wide wanderings. Inheriting a small competence, he set out upon his travels in 1608; and having visited many European countries returned to England in 1610, and in the following year published *Coryats Crudities, Hastily*

gobled up in Five Moneths Travels. The reputation of this book
was coloured by the mock-heroic tributes, more than sixty in
number, contributed by poets and poetasters among Coryat's
friends and acquaintances; and two pamphlets published in the
same year—*Coryats Cramb* and *The Odcombian Banquet*—enhanced this facetious notoriety. In 1612 he set out again; and
this time, sailing from Venice, he came to Constantinople;
thence journeyed through Greece and parts of Asia Minor; and
from Smyrna he crossed the Mediterranean to Egypt. A
sojourn at Cairo was followed by a visit to the Holy Land.
Joining a caravan in Syria, he went on to Mesopotamia; passed
through southern Persia; and came by way of Kandahar and
Lahore to Agra. There Sir Thomas Roe, the agent of the
East India Company, procured for him an audience with
Jahangir, the Great Mogul. This was in the autumn of 1616.
During his travels Coryat, who from his youth had possessed
a remarkable gift of languages, had pursued the study of
Persian, and to such good purpose that he was now able to
deliver an oration in that tongue before the Mogul. A copy of
the Persian original and an English translation of this address
he sent home to his mother; and for her information he out-
lined his proposed further itinerary which was to include
Babylon (that is, Baghdad), Nineveh (near the modern Mosul),
Persia, and a more extended exploration of Egypt than he had
had time for on his way eastward. This communication ends:
'Expect no more letters from me after this till my arrivall in
Christendom.' [1] It was his last message home. He had accomplished but the first stage of his westward journey when in
December 1617 he died near Surat in northern Bombay. In
subsequent years an occasional Englishman passing that way
saw his tomb. 'On the left hand of the road [near Surat],' says
John Fryer, 'lies Tom Coriat, our English Fakier. . . He was
killed with kindness by the English Merchants, which laid his
rambling Brains to Rest.' [2] The Reverend Edward Terry also
visited the tomb, and on his return to England devoted some
twenty pages of the narrative of his own travels to 'Some

1 *Mr. Thomas Coriat to his friends in England sendeth greeting,* Sig. Eᵛ.
2 *A New Account of East India and Persia,* Hakluyt Society, i,253.

particulars to revive the memorie of that (now almost forgotten) English Pilgrim Tom Coriat.' [1] Terry's estimate of Coryat: 'His knowledge and high attainments in several languages made him not a little ignorant of himself' is superficial and betrays a misunderstanding of his subject, for Coryat was no simpleton, and if he was willing to be made the butt of ridicule it was not without a shrewd sense of what we might call its 'publicity-value.' That he was a keen observer is as apparent to any reader of the *Crudities* as that he was a tireless traveller; and it is greatly to be regretted that save for the two little pamphlets compiled from letters to his mother and to certain friends and for a few additional fragments published by Purchas [2] we have no narrative of his experiences in the Levant and the further East. Such a narrative, planned on the scale of the *Crudities*, would have been one of the most vivid and valuable accounts of early travel in the Orient.

William Lithgow is sometimes described as a disciple of Thomas Coryat, but the label is inaccurate, for the two men had little in common beyond their astonishing feats of pedestrian travel and were, moreover, very different in temperament and reputation. Nor was it the fame of the *Crudities* that prompted Lithgow to go upon his journeys, for he had made several comparatively unambitious peregrinations in Europe long before that book appeared and the wider wanderings were begun in 1610. An unattractive but unforgettable figure, as strongly marked an individual as any we shall meet with in this book, Lithgow was a hard, dour, truculent, and pugnacious Scot. During the second decade of the seventeenth century he covered in the course of three journeys some thirty-six thousand miles (according to his own calculation) of highways and by-ways of Europe, nearer Asia, and North Africa. His first long journey, lasting for three years, took him to Constantinople, the principal islands of the eastern Mediterranean, Syria and

1 *A Voyage to East-India*, 1655, pp.58f.
2 *Pilgrimes*, 1625; ed. MacLehose, x,389f. The pamphlets of 1616 and 1618 were reprinted in the edition of 1776 of the *Crudities* but are not in the MacLehose edition. They may be found in *Early Travels in India, 1583–1619*, ed. William Foster, pp.234f. On the problem of the site of Coryat's now vanished tomb see ibid., p.239. In Henry Hutton's *Follie's Anatomy*, 1619 (Percy Society, 1842, p.15) Tom Tospot, who has 'travell'd all Earths globe a-foote,' is obviously a caricature of Coryat.

Palestine, and thence through the desert of Sinai to Egypt, whence in a roundabout fashion he made his way home. The result for literature was *A Delectable and True Discourse of an admired and painefull peregrination* (1614).[1] His second journey took him in 1613–16 to Algiers, Fez, and Tunis, and was notable for his penetration far south into the Libyan desert. On a third journey, undertaken with the intent to visit the court of Prester John, he fell into the hands of the Spanish authorities at Malaga, was suspected of being a spy, and before his release suffered grievous torments which seem permanently to have warped his already sardonic and querulous disposition. On his return to London he exhibited his 'martyred anatomy' to King James; but despite repeated pleas he obtained no satisfactory redress, and in 1622, in a fit of rage, he assaulted Gondomar, the Spanish ambassador, for which offence he was imprisoned for about a year. In 1632 he published *The Totall Discourse of the Rare Adventures and Painefull Peregrinations of long Nineteene Yeares Travayles.*[2] Of this the first 'book' and some other sections are an expansion of his little volume of 1614; the remainder deals with adventures of subsequent date. His style is a curious amalgam of tortuous euphuism and extravagant redundancy on the one hand and of racy realism and downrightness on the other. His strongest passion is a bitter hostility to the Roman Catholic Church, expressed with a vehemence that is extraordinary even for that age of religious fanaticism. By comparison, his comments upon Mohammedanism seem tolerant. His abundant erudition when he deals with antiquities was probably at second-hand, drawn after his return home from works of scholarship and antiquarianism; but here he is merely typical of the writers of early travel-books who seldom posssed a strict literary conscience and while making a parade of their learning with ostentatious notes and glosses, in reality

1 The long title continues with a list of countries, cities, rivers, lakes, seas, and so forth visited by the author. The book was reprinted in 1616 and was used by Purchas (x,447f.).
2 The complete title is thirty lines long; see the facsimile facing p.xxvii of the Mac-Lehose reprint to which henceforth reference is made unless the edition of 1632 is indicated.

frequently pillaged from their predecessors with no acknowledgment whatsoever. But of modern men and manners Lithgow is an acute, albeit often a scornful, observer, recording what he has seen for himself and distinguishing these observations from what he has picked up from hearsay. He gives a hundred lively pictures of Levantine life. Courageous yet cautious, wearied often and not seldom disgusted with his wandering way of life, he nevertheless persevered in a strange desultory way that is rather pathetic; and he has left us an invaluable record of travel through the countries of Islam.

In the same year in which Lithgow set out for the Levant (1610) another Englishman made a similar but shorter and less arduous journey through the same part of the world. This was George Sandys, the son of the Archbishop of York. His rank and easy circumstances enabled him to command comforts beyond the reach of the wayworn Lithgow. His journey, an ambitious extension of the European tour which, though not yet so common as it became at a later date, was then often the finishing touch to the education of a gentleman, took him to the Ionian Islands and the Ægean; to Smyrna and what were thought to be the ruins of Troy; and to Constantinople, where he was the guest of Sir Thomas Glover, the English ambassador. Thence he went to Egypt and from there, after an extended stay, to Palestine. He was home again before the close of 1611. In leisurely fashion and with a plentiful supply of authorities from which to enrich his narrative with classical allusions he composed *A Relation of a Journey . . . Containing a description of the Turkish Empire, of Ægypt, of the Holy Land, of the Remote Parts of Italy, and Ilands adjoyning* (1615).[1] Nothing so beautiful and delightful as the copperplate illustrations in this handsome volume had been provided in any earlier English travel-book. They include views of Constantinople from the Bosphorus, views of Jerusalem, a view of the pyramids and

---

1 The pretty engraved title-page illustrates a curious assortment of divinities, abstractions, and historical personages: 'Veritas,' 'Constantia,' 'Achmet' (the reigning Sultan), 'Isis,' etc. There were new editions of the *Relation* in 1621, 1627, 1632, and 1637. It was largely used by Purchas. A modern edition of this pleasant book is a desideratum.

the sphinx with European travellers and native dragomans in the foreground, and admirably accurate plans of the Church of the Holy Sepulchre in Jerusalem and the Church of the Nativity at Bethlehem. The narrative, though a little long-winded and somewhat heavily weighted with classical learning, is not only informative but generally entertaining. Occasionally, as when he says of Smyrna that 'now violated by the Mohametans, her beautie is turned to deformitie,' Sandys mourns the decay of countries once glorious; and occasionally, as when he refutes Pierre Belon's identification of the site of Troy, he shows an archaeological turn of mind; [1] but generally he is interested in the present rather than in the past and for the most part his attention is concentrated upon matters of commerce and agriculture. But one's attention is held by the expectation, frequently gratified, of picturesque and out-of-the-way bits of information not merely drawn (as is his detailed account of the Turkish government and religion) from earlier writers but based upon his own observations. Thus, he describes the Turkish watchtowers on the islands of the Ægean which smoke by day and blaze by night to give warning of the approach of enemies; he laments the condition of the Christian slaves who hew marbles on one of the islands of the Sea of Marmora for the new mosque being erected in Constantinople; [2] he describes not unsympathetically the holiday dancing of the 'merry Greeks' though he condemns them as a cowardly and cruel people; he reports upon the excellence of the manuscripts at Mount Athos; he has a pleasing taste for oddities of folklore and folk-custom, as when he notes the prohibition of burial on the island of Delos [3] or records the curative value of a certain kind of earth or describes the ceremonies and organization of the pilgrim caravan from Cairo to Mecca. Sandys's interest in antiquities became more pronounced after his arrival in Egypt; [4] and his description of Jerusalem is so accurate and so

---

1 *Relation*, pp.15 and 22f.
2 Ibid., p.27. This was the mosque of Sultan Achmet (Ahmed I) whom Sandys characterizes at length, pp.73f.
3 Ibid., p.11. Compare Baedeker's *Greece*, ed. 1909, p.245.
4 See his curious discussion of the religion of the ancient Egyptians, p.103, and the plate, p.133, illustrating half a dozen Egyptian gods.

nearly exhaustive that it might almost serve as a guide-book today.[1]

With Sandys we may associate an aristocratic traveller of somewhat later date, Sir Henry Blount, whose *Voyage into the Levant* (1636) inspired Henry King's poetic tribute. Little allowance has to be made for the partiality of friendship, for Blount deserved King's praise. He was already experienced in European travel when in 1634 he sailed from Venice to Spalato and made his way thence through the Balkan peninsula to Constantinople. His account of the great city has a freshness that is often wanting in descriptions of a place about which so much had already been written. He was there shortly after the devastating fire of 1633 whose ravages he observed. He went on to Rhodes and Egypt, where he made an expedition quite out of the ordinary into the Fayûm. From Egypt he returned to England. Blount was a serious-minded traveller and a conscientious and competent observer of Turkish life, interested in the problems of commerce and administration and determined to test for himself the truth or falsity of occidental opinion of the Turks. His unprejudiced outlook upon the world of Islam and his dispassionate desire to observe independently and report fairly upon the admirable features as well as upon the shortcomings of that alien civilization appear often in his narrative. His candour is illustrated by the shrewd remark about Cairo, that the presence of such a multitude of men, of such divers races, would quickly breed confusion, famine, and desolation 'if the Turkish domination there were nothing but sottish sensualitie, as most Christians conceive.' Noteworthy, too, is his commendation of the 'incredible civilitie' of Turks to foreign visitors.[2]

Moryson, Sandys, and Blount were well-to-do gentlemen of

---

1 Compare Henry King, 'To my honoured Friend Mr. George Sandys,' *Poems*, ed. Sparrow, p. 82:

> When in delightful raptures we descry
> As in a Map, Sions Chorography
> Laid out in so direct and smooth a line,
> Men need not go about through Palestine:
> Who seek Christ here will the streight Rode prefer,
> As neerer much then by the Sepulchre.

2 *A Voyage into the Levant*, pp.75 and 2f.

education and refinement; Coryat was an eccentric not easily classifiable nor in fact typical in any way; Lithgow was an adventurer kept by loyalty to his religion and country from degenerating into the type known at a later date as the 'rogue Englishman.' These five men are representatives of those who travelled if not precisely for pastime at any rate with no practical political or commercial object in view but to see the world and to broaden their comprehension of their fellow-men. We must now consider other sorts of travellers. In later chapters we shall meet with representatives of the large class of agents and factors who penetrated into Islamic countries in search of outlets for trade, courageous men in the employ of one or another of the great mercantile companies. In their upper ranks this type merged into that of the diplomatic agent or consul who resided at Constantinople, Smyrna, Aleppo, Joppa, or some other trading-centre in the Levant. Several such men will make their appearance in subsequent pages. There were also merchants of wealth and some social position whose affairs took them from time to time into the East.

One such merchant has lately been rescued from oblivion— John Sanderson, who until recently led a dim posthumous life in the pages of Samuel Purchas.[1] Sir William Foster discovered in the British Museum a manuscript folio containing copies of Sanderson's business and private letters together with miscellaneous memoranda and, what is very curious, an autobiography. All this interesting material he published in 1931.[2] Sanderson visited the Holy Land three times. He was a member of John Davis's expedition which set out for India by the Cape route. His varied adventures included shipwreck, attacks by Spaniards, and a visitation of the plague at Aleppo. He passed much time at Constantinople, serving there for a while as English agent while the ambassador was accompanying the Sultan on a military campaign. From his letters we can discern the difficulties encountered by English merchants and negotiators at the Porte during the early years of the Levant Com-

1 *Pilgrimes*, ix,412f.
2 *The Travels of John Sanderson in the Levant, 1584–1602*, ed. Sir William Foster, Hakluyt Society, 1931.

pany's activities. Besides troubles against which it was impossible to guard one's self, such as piracy and losses by storms at sea, there was the constant need to bribe customs officials and courtiers; there was the need to counterplot against the untiring conspiracies of French and Italian agents anxious to thwart the English; there was the difficulty of acting in concert with fellow-Englishmen whose morale had been weakened through long sojourn in the Levant and who passed their time in riot and loose living; and there were more technical troubles relative to credits and bills of exchange and falling markets. It took shrewd and intrepid men to carry on in such circumstances; and Sanderson's papers reveal him as such a man. If his temper appears to have been ungovernable, that is not surprising. He possessed grit and determination in abundance; and if not an amiable person he had one very attractive characteristic which it is strange to find in combination with his other traits: so great a love of music that even when he lay dying, as was thought, of the plague at Aleppo, with an open coffin made ready by his bed, his chief grief was for the beloved lute which by accident he had fallen on in his sickness and had broken to pieces. He survived, to pass his later years in London where he died in 1627. We shall encounter him more than once in the course of this book; and many of his fellow-merchants will also cross our path. We know of them generally from letters, trade-reports, charters, and other documents that came into the hands of Hakluyt or Purchas. These men of large affairs had neither the time nor inclination to compose books about their travels.

The chaplains or 'preachers' attached to the English consulates and factories in the East had the leisure and training to express themselves on paper, and several important volumes of travel are from their pens. In 1600 William Biddulph set out from England to assume his duties as preacher to the Company of English Merchants at Aleppo. With him journeyed two merchants, a jeweller, and a gentleman. By sea this party came to Constantinople where they met Henry Lello, the English ambassador. Thence Biddulph dispatched a long letter 'to a learned Gentleman in England, wherein the author discourseth of his voyage hither.' This was the first of many such communications, sent from ports of call on the voyage to Tripoli and from Syria and Jerusalem. In Jerusalem the party broke up, some members returning home.[1] From Biddulph's letters and from a few other documents someone who concealed his identity under the pseudonym 'Theophilus Lavender' compiled *The Travels of Certaine Englishmen. . . Begunne in the year of Jubile 1600, and by some of them finished this year 1608. The others not yet returned* (1609).[2] This is commended on the title-page as 'very profitable for the help of Travellers and no lesse delightful to all persons who take pleasure to hear of the Manners, Government, Religion, and Customes of Forraine and Heathen Countries.' The editor's Address to the Reader is of interest as evidence of the value for edification set upon such narratives and also for the light it casts upon contemporary literary ethics. He says that he first became interested in the travels of William Biddulph and his brother Peter when he saw 'a Copie of a Voyage to Jerusalem by Land.' The natural inference from this statement is that one of the letters was already in print; but the allusion is probably to a manuscript copy in circulation in London. Into the editor's hands came letters which Bezaliell Biddulph, now dead, had received from his kinsman. These were supplemented by other letters from Peter. The editor admits that he has not asked the consent of the brothers, one of whom is still beyond seas while the other is too modest to publish them himself. But public good is above private; and therefore he has taken this liberty with personal communications to private friends. He believes that the letters may teach Englishmen to love and obey their

1 It is difficult to distinguish between William Biddulph and his obscure brother Peter. One would expect the former to remain at his post as preacher at Aleppo and the latter to return to England; but it seems to have been William whom Sanderson, as we shall see, met in Saint Paul's and about whom Kitely gossiped maliciously to Sanderson. In later years a William Biddulph was a factor in India associated with Sir Thomas Roe (see *The Embassy of Sir Thomas Roe*, ed. William Foster, Hakluyt Society, index); but whether he was the same person as our travelling preacher is not apparent.

2 In 1612 the letters were reissued with a slightly altered title, beginning: *The Travels of Foure English Men and a Preacher* and continuing as in the first edition except that the date when some of the company completed their journey is changed from 1608 to 1611. Biddulph's letter dealing with the region of Lebanon reappeared in Purchas, viii,248f. The entire narrative was reprinted in *A Collection of Voyages and Travels*, 1745, volume i, and in Osborne's *Voyages*, 1747, volume vii.

gracious sovereign when they read of foreign tyrants; and English wives may see how blessed is their lot compared with that of foreign slaves; the poor how much better off they are than they who live elsewhere on grass and water like brute beasts; and all men how excellent are our inns compared with the sleeping quarters provided in those far countries. He confesses to having taken liberties with his texts. He has reduced many short letters into four long ones; rearranged their dated order into a chronological or topographical scheme; and added some matter drawn from conversations with the returned travellers or from other travellers of credit. (This last admission accounts for the suspicious resemblances of some passages in the book to earlier narratives; the description of Constantinople, for example, owes much to Nicolas de Nicolay.) The reason for the abrupt conclusion of the narrative after the description of Jerusalem is, the editor explains, that he had no letters about the return voyage nor would the authors furnish him with any particulars about what was merely tedious, troublesome, and dangerous.

Parts of the book are commonplaces of Renaissance travel-literature; but since it was subjected to editorial tampering it is unfair to accuse the authors of plagiarism. In other parts it is evident that the observations are at first-hand. Thus, in his third letter Biddulph writes:

> About 8 miles from Scanderone we came to a towne called Bylan, where there lieth buried an English Gentleman, named Henry Morison, who died there coming downe from Aleppo, in company with his brother Master Phines Morison, who left his Armes in that Countrie, with these verses underwritten:
>
> > To thee deare Henry Morison,
> > Thy brother Phines here left alone
> > Hath left this fading memorie,
> > For monuments and all must die.

As Moryson's *Itinerary*, in which this same epitaph is given, was not published till years later, this is a fair test of Biddulph's trustworthiness. Again, in Jerusalem Biddulph and his party met Henry Timberlake (or Timberley) and his companion

John Burrell. Timberlake mentions this encounter in his *True and Strange Discourse of the Travailes of two English Pilgrims* (1603). The excited enthusiasm with which Biddulph writes when he has to do, not with mere antiquities, but with the present state of affairs in the Levant is in itself a warrant of his reliability. The appalling picture of the lot of oriental Jews and Christians in countries under Ottoman domination is evidently drawn by an eye-witness of these miseries. Occidentals fare better, he remarks, because they can appeal to their consuls who in turn can rely upon the good offices of their ambassadors. Such remarks as these sound authentic. On the other hand, the sketch of Mohammedanism is just such as travellers were often wont to provide for their readers and may well be one of the interpolations of Biddulph's editor.

In Sanderson's correspondence we catch a momentary view of the rivalries and jealousies of Englishmen whose paths crossed in the Levant. In January 1609, when Biddulph's book was hot from the press, Sanderson wrote from London to his friend John Kitely in Constantinople, warning him to preserve letters and other documents carefully lest they fall into the hands of the unscrupulous; and he continues:

> Many most malitious and in thier foolishe humours triomphes uppon papers and letters of others and spares not to put in printt matters of wournot newes and ould date, with malitiouse additions and faulse flatteries, as by the inclosed you may perceave; which I tore out of a booke sett out to the wourld, nominated the Travails of Divers Inglishmen into Africa, etc., by one Theophilus Lavender; a sweet and virtiouse name, and yet the booke stinkes of lies and foolerye. . . Most of it conteynes Master William Biddles letters written to divers his worshipful frends in Ingland, in treating of his travails, etc.

Sanderson, after these incoherencies, goes on to say that report has it that the volume was published without Biddulph's consent. There had been an unfriendly encounter between the two men in Constantinople; and now in London Sanderson refused to speak to Biddulph when they chanced to meet. 'Upon Sunday last,' he tells Kitely, 'in Poules Bidle passed by me and gave me a conjoye; but my hart rosse at his gotes beard, that I had no power to speake to him.' Kitely's comment on this is that Biddulph 'hath shewed more beard then witt or religion in all his ten yeares travils.' Kitely passes on to Sanderson some gossip he has picked up about the gross drunkenness and debauchery Biddulph practised at Aleppo. As for the editor of the *Travels*, 'I would take some paines with my penne,' he says, 'to perfume Theophilus Lavender. . . I smell his kinsman, Theologus Spickenard.' [1] The point of this exchange of innuendoes is lost after three centuries, but it is a safe inference from these angry sneers that Sanderson and Kitely suspected the name 'Theophilus Lavender' to be a pseudonym for someone, possibly a kinsman of Biddulph.

The altered title of the reissue of Biddulph's book, with his quality as 'preacher' displayed, was probably prompted by emulation of a volume that appeared in 1611. This volume touches upon so many subjects that concern us in the present book that its title may be given in full: *The Preachers Travels. Wherein is set downe a true Journall, to the confines of the East Indies, through the great Countreyes of Syria, Mesopotamia, Armenia, Media, Hircania and Parthia. With the Authors returne by the way of Persia, Susiane, Assiria, Chaldaea, and Arabia. Containing a full survew of the Knigdom [sic] of Persia: and in what termes the Persian stands with the Great Turke at this day: Also a true relation of Sir Anthonie Sherleys entertainment there: and the estate that his Brother, M. Robert Sherley lived in after his departure for Christendome. With the description of a Port in the Persian Gulf, commodius for our East Indian Merchants: and a briefe rehearsall of some grosse absudities [sic] in the Turkish Alcoran. Penned by J. C. sometimes student in Magdalen Colledge in Oxford.* The initials stand for John Cartwright. The narrative is of an expedition begun in February 1599, when in an unofficial capacity he set out for the East with John Midnall. Cartwright starts his story at Scanderoon whence he and his companion travelled to Antioch and Aleppo. After lingering in Syria for two months, they went overland to the Euphrates. There they parted company,

1 *The Travels of John Sanderson*, pp.259f.,264f.

Midnall proceeding down the river to the Persian Gulf [1] and
Cartwright crossing Mesopotamia to the Tigris. Having penetrated Kurdistan, Armenia, and the Taurus region, he entered
Persia and arrived at Kasvin. At that time, as we shall see in
a later chapter, Sir Anthony Sherley had departed for Europe
but his brother Robert was a hostage there and by him the
clergyman was entertained. Cartwright conceived a great admiration for the Sherley brothers, and the publication of his
book long afterwards was timed to spread knowledge of their
adventures and of their political and commercial designs. But
The Preachers Travels is of interest in itself as well as for its
connection with the Sherleys. Cartwright has an attractive
talent for bringing home the appearance of strange places by
likening them to places familiar to Englishmen, as when he
describes the Euphrates 'as broad as the Thames at Lambeth'
and 'almost as fast as the River of Trent.' He has an eye for
detail, as when he describes the crowded 'bassars' of the
Shah's capital and the buildings of sun-dried brick; for beauty,
as when he describes the Persian gardens; for splendour, as
when he characterizes Shah Abbas as a man of martial disposition and exorable nature, and courteous and affable; and
for curious lore, as when he repeats the old report that the
Caspian Sea is part salt, part fresh, or when he tells the story
of the King of the Assassins and his mountain paradise. He
has much to say about Mohammedanism, especially in its
Persian form, the Shi'a heresy. He notes with sympathy the
miseries of Christian populations subject to 'that monster of
Turkish tyranny.'[2] Cartwright returned home by way of the
desert route through Arabia roughly parallel with the course of
the Euphrates. His narrative closes on his arrival at Aleppo.

Once more in England, he was appointed in 1602 chaplain

1 Midnall's original intention seems to have been to go only so far as Aleppo. The expansion of his plans probably accounts for his separation from Cartwright. His subsequent activities at Agra (where he seems to have attempted to forestall the East
India Company) lie beyond our purview. He obtained concessions which he offered
to the Company but which were declined. On a second journey to the East (1611)
he fell ill and died at Agra. His tombstone, the oldest English monument in India,
is still standing. A summary of some of his papers is in Purchas. See further on
Midnall, Sir William Foster's article in *The Gentleman's Magazine*, August, 1906;
Foster, *England's Quest of Eastern Trade*, chapter xvii; and *Early Travels in India*,
ed. Foster, pp.49f.

2 *The Preachers Travels*, pp.12,49f.,61f.,54,16f.,52f.,71f.

to the expedition sent out by the East India Company to discover a north-west passage to the Indies. Before long this expedition put back to England, having accomplished nothing; and its failure was attributed to the faint-hearted counsel of the chaplain, who was accused of having been the 'perswader and mover' of the captain and crew to give over the voyage and return home. The directors of the Company accordingly required Cartwright to surrender 'the gowne and apparell' in which, had all gone well, he was to have figured at the court of the Emperor of China.[1] Recalling the hardihood he had displayed so recently in the East, one suspects that his cautious advice was inspired not by cowardice but by sound judgment.

A third far-travelled 'preacher' was the Reverend Edward Terry who was chaplain to a fleet sent out by the East India Company in 1616 and at Agra was appointed chaplain to Sir Thomas Roe. After his return to England in 1619 Terry wrote an account of his experiences. His manuscript came into the hands of Samuel Purchas who published it in slightly abridged form.[2] Terry settled down to the life of an English clergyman, and keeping his narrative by him expanded it to seven or eight times its original size by introducing abundant expatiations upon divinity and morals, many of them but loosely connected with his subject. Thus swollen almost beyond recognition, it reappeared in 1655 as *A Voyage to East-India. Mix't with some Parallel Observations and inferences upon the storie, to profit as well as delight the Reader*.[3] Beneath the frontispiece-portrait of the author is the following solemn couplet:

> In Europe, Africk, Asia have I gonn;
> One journey more, and then my travel's don.

By the time he came to compose the enlarged version of his narrative the worthy Mr. Terry's thoughts were so fixed upon

1 *The Dawn of British Trade to the East Indies as recorded in the Court Minutes of the East India Company, 1599–1603*, ed. Henry Stevens, 1886, p.232; Sir W.Wilson Hunter, *A History of British India*, 1899, i,268.
2 *Pilgrimes*, ix,1f.
3 Slightly condensed and without the author's name it reappeared in 1665 in a volume containing also a translation of the *Viaggi* of Pietro della Valle. This condensed text was reprinted in 1777. Much use of Terry's narrative is made in *The Embassy of Sir Thomas Roe to the Court of the Great Mogul, 1615–1619*, ed. Foster, Hakluyt Society, 1899.

that coming journey to the heavenly country that the memories
of his travels to the court of the Grand Mogul nearly forty
years before must have been dim indeed.

One more 'preacher' and we shall have done with this
preliminary survey of some characteristic travellers who have
left records of their experiences in the Levant. The Reverend
Charles Robson was chaplain to the English factors at Aleppo.
In a letter intended, it is claimed (it would seem sincerely),
solely for private perusal and addressed to a clerical friend in
England, Robson told of his voyage through the Mediterranean
and of his life as 'preacher' at Aleppo. His brief narrative is
lively and straightforward, almost modern in manner, with a
minimum of the elaborate stylistic artifices of most travel-
books of the period. In some of his comments and observations
we catch the first suggestions of the diary of an intelligent
tourist of today. In the islands of the Ægean he tried to converse
in classical Greek with the inhabitants but they understood
not a word. At Smyrna he was disappointed to find that 'the
famous primitive Church' was now 'all buried under the
beastly new Turkish Shrine'; and though he saw the mitre
of Saint Policarp he was sceptical as to its authenticity,
believing it to have been 'the cappe of some Turkish Santone,
for it is overwrought with Turkish letters.' Scanderoon he
found 'full of the carcases of houses, not one house in it, it
having beene a little before sackt by the Turkish Pyrats.' Of
the country around Aleppo he writes that it 'aboundeth as
of old with superfluities of all necessaries; unhappy in nothing
but the cursed Lords of it'; 'the unhusbanded plaines' blame
the slothfulness and stupidity of their owners; and he breathes
a prayer that 'the Lord when it pleaseth him will cast out
these usurpers and . . . restore it to the true owners, the
Christians.' Robson's pious prejudices are amusingly and
forcefully revealed in his description of the ancient aqueduct
whose waters now 'wash the stinking feet of the profane Turkes
before they enter into their bawling devotion'; but even deeper
prejudices are apparent in the remark that in a certain cave
the Shi'a Moslems reverence the print of a man's hand which
is said to be 'Ali's as much as our Lady's pictures are reverenced

in Spain or Italy 'but with farre lesse pompe, farre less superstition, farre lesse Idolatry.' In a later chapter we shall see
that Protestants either coupled Mohammedans with Roman
Catholics in their abhorrence or else conceded certain virtues
to the Moslems in order to emphasize the iniquities of Rome.
After offering some brief remarks upon recent public events
in the East, Robson brings his friendly and intelligent letter
to a close with a request for news from England. The title-
page of his book bears this recommendation:

> The witnesse of the eye doth farre excell
> The witnesse of the eare in high degree:
> What others doe by hearesay onely tell,
> This man most plainely with his eye did see.[1]

IV

TRAVEL in the Levant was not, comparatively speaking, so
arduous and strenuous an undertaking in the Elizabethan
period as it became in the nineteenth century. So long as the
roads at home were unimproved, swamps not drained, and
the amenities to which modern western peoples are accustomed
were unknown, the inconveniences of travel in the Near East,
though they differed in degree, did not differ in kind from the
inconveniences of travel in England. The dangers in Mohammedan countries were scarcely more serious than they were
in England; in Turkey there were religious fanatics but on
the very outskirts of London there were highwaymen. In
some respects travel in the Levant may have been more agreeable than a journey undertaken at home. Take, for example,
the testimony to the cleanliness of the Turks; the implication
is that in this matter conditions in Islam contrasted favourably
with those in England. Or note the reports of the civility of
the Turks towards strangers; the implication is that one did
not always meet with such courteous treatment in Christendom. And—what is very important—the means of locomotion
were much the same in Europe and the East. A man who had
journeyed from London to Edinburgh at the beginning of the

1 *Newes from Aleppo*, 1628, pp.9f.,13f.

seventeenth century was in large measure initiated into the dangers and discomforts of a journey from Constantinople to Antioch. He was accustomed at any rate to leisurely movement, long delays, dirty lodgings, execrable roads, constant danger, and probably bad food. The great Victorian explorers of the Near East who left behind them the modern comforts and conveniences of England had more hardships to bear, because the contrast was greater, than their Elizabethan predecessors bore. Palgrave and Burton and Doughty certainly are proof that there was no decline in determination and fortitude during the intervening centuries, though one need not go so far as to say that they were more intrepid adventurers than the men we have met or are to meet in this book.

Those to whom the reader has now been introduced do not include any official ambassadors or agents at the Porte or any of the many Englishmen who, on regaining their freedom, published narratives of their captivity among the Turks or Moors. Several of the most remarkable travellers of the age will make their appearance later. The intention so far has been to suggest the personalities of about a dozen representative Englishmen who brought home typical reports and impressions of Islam. The further intention has been to suggest some of the many and varied preconceptions of far-off, dangerous, and romantic countries that were in the mind of 'the well-wishing adventurer in setting forth.'

CHAPTER TWO

THE CLASSICAL AND BIBLICAL PAST

I

VENICE was the vestibule to Islam. In the later decades of
Elizabeth's reign, after commercial treaties had been arranged
with the Porte, many Englishmen travelled to Constantinople
by sea in vessels of their own nationality. Some journeyed
overland through the Balkans and yet others, having sailed
so far as Patras, continued on their way through Greece. But
Venice remained one of the most convenient ports of departure.
The day of the pilgrim was departing and that of the tourist
was dawning in Shakespeare's England; but the general
manner of procedure in preparation for a voyage remained
much as it had been and it is therefore permissible to draw
our evidence from the counsel given in earlier generations
to those intending to make a pilgrimage to the Holy Land.
From the time when the Turks began to dominate the eastern
end of the Mediterranean it was necessary to take special
precautions and to come to such terms as could be effected
with 'infidels' who were more fanatical than the Saracens
had been. In Roman Catholic countries the need to assure
safe conduct for pilgrims was an important motive for keeping
on good terms with the Turks, and emissaries were occasionally sent to the Levant to carry on the necessary negotiations.[1]
After the Reformation no special provision was made for
Protestants, who, being grouped with Christians of the Latin
communion, often suffered mortifications and perils from their
fellow-travellers in addition to those imposed upon them by
the Turks.

Fynes Moryson remarks that in former times a pilgrim-ship,

1 The Baron des Hayes de Courmenin was sent by France on such a mission. In his
Voiage du Levant fait par le Commandement du Roy, Paris, 1624, p.271, he argues
for peaceful relations with the Porte as advantageous to commerce, as a protection
to Christians of the East, and as enabling Christians to visit the Holy Places.

a galley especially engaged for passengers to Palestine, sailed annually from Venice on Ascension Day; but 'this custom is growne out of use, since few are found in these daies who undertake this journey, in regard of the Turkes imposing great exactions, and doing foule injuries to them.'[1] After the use of a pilgrim-ship was abandoned, the usual procedure was to engage quarters in a merchantman. William Wey, who made the pilgrimage to Jerusalem twice, in 1458 and 1462, had the advantage over later travellers of sailing in a hired galley. To those who might make the same journey he gave advice based upon his own experiences. Before leaving Venice, 'chese yow,' he says, 'a place in the seyd galey in the overest stage; for in the lawyst under hyt ys ryght smolderyng hote and stynkyng.' He offers suggestions as to the supplies of food, the cooking utensils, and the bedding to be taken along, each pilgrim having to provide for himself; and he discusses also the problem of exchange between England and Syria and the most convenient way of carrying funds. The practical end which he had in view is shown also by the brief glossary and list of phrases in modern Greek which he supplies.[2] Drawn partly from Wey's treatise is the *Informacon for pylgrymes unto the holy londe* which Wynken de Worde printed in 1498.[3] The author's name and the precise date when he made his pilgrimage are unknown. The practical advice and homely details regarding proper provisions and precautions here given make very vivid to us the discomforts and hardships with which not pilgrims only but all travellers were afflicted. The pilgrim should secure accommodations on an upper deck for the sake of the cool fresh air. Choose a chamber amidship to escape the pitch and roll and so keep your 'brayne and stomache in tempre.' Padlock your door whenever the vessel calls at a port. Be sure to make a covenant with the ship's master for everything: the time of departure, time of arrival, fresh bread, fresh water, and 'hot meete twyes at two meeles.'

1 *Itinerary*, i,447.
2 *The Itineraries of William Wey*, Roxburghe Club, 1857. The first Itinerary contains more information about the Holy Places; the second, more about the way thither.
3 Wynken de Worde reprinted the book in 1515 and again in 1524. The Roxburghe Club's reprint is of 1824; and in 1893 a facsimile of the edition of 1498, with an introduction by E.Gordon Duff, appeared.

But take with you two barrels of wine and one of water, and biscuits, bread, cheese, and so forth, so that if the master gives you 'feble brede, feble wine and stynking water' you may fall back upon your own supplies. Take also a cage of 'half a dosen of hennes or chekyns to have wyth you in the shippe.' Many other provisions are suggested, including a variety of the spices indispensable to the Englishman. Procure also a small cauldron and a frying-pan, dishes, platters, cups, and saucers. From a shop near Saint Mark's can be purchased a bed, mattress, feather-bed, pillow, sheets, and quilt. On your return the dealer will buy all this back even if this bedding be badly worn. Take with you also a barrel 'for a sege for your chambre in the shyppe. It is full necessary yf ye were syke that ye come not in the ayre.' Counsel of the same sort is found in two other sixteenth-century narratives of pilgrimages. One is by the chaplain who accompanied Sir Richard Guylford (or Guildford) and the Prior of Giseburn to the Holy Land.[1] The other, which borrows heavily from the *Informacon for pylgrymes* and from the account of Guylford's journey, is the so-called 'Diary' of Sir Richard Torkyngton (1517).[2] It has little independent value.

The sheer discomfort of the voyage must have been great. The *Informacon* describes with painful realism the seasickness, the close quarters, the stench of the bilge, the constant need to be on guard against pilfering galley-slaves. Turkish vessels might lie in the way and have to be circumvented.[3] When the remnant of Guylford's party were on their way back to Europe (for both the knight and the prior died in the Holy Land), they were warned that 'a grete army of Turkes gayleys and fustes' which 'had lately taken many sayles of cristen men' were lying in wait for them; and these poor pilgrims were indeed miserable, for in the midst of a great storm when they

1 *The Begynnynge and contynuance of the Pylgrymage of Sir Richard Guylforde*; ed. Sir Henry Ellis, Camden Society, 1851. The chaplain's name is unknown.
2 *Ye Oldest Diarie of Englysshe Travell: being the hitherto unpublished narrative of the Pilgrimage of Sir Richard Torkington to Jerusalem in 1517*, ed. W.J.Loftie, [1884], pp.7f. Excerpts had been published in *The Gentleman's Magazine*, lxxxii (October, 1812) and in T.D.Fosbrooke, *British Monachism . . . New edition to which [is] added Peregrinatorium religiosum, or Manners and Customs of ancient Pilgrims*, 1817.
3 *Pylgrymage of Sir Richard Guylforde*, ed. Ellis, p.11.

'fearfully sange *Salve Regina* and other Antymes' and their
ship was almost dashed upon the rocks (the covetous captain
not having provided sailors enough to govern the ship properly
in such an emergency), they had no haven into which to flee
'but into Turkey or Barbary, into the handes of the Infidels
and extreme enemys of our Cristen fayth.'[1] Great was their
relief when after many anxieties they reached Venice. At a
later date not the Turks only were to be feared. Roman Catholic pilgrims had to beware of the renegade English corsairs
who infested the Mediterranean.[2] On the other hand, an
English Protestant might find himself in peril from fanatical
Roman Catholics. Laurence Aldersey, for example, a merchant
of London, was in a critical situation when in the midst of a
storm his religious principles made him stubbornly refuse to
join in the singing of *Salve Regina*. 'They sayd I was no good
Christian, and wished that I were in the middest of the sea.'
Two friars who bore him better will than did the rest of the
company intervened on his behalf and protected him from
being treated like a Jonah.[3] On a like occasion Captain John
Smith was actually tossed into the sea and had to swim for
his life.[4] There were other perils besides the dissensions of
rival sects. The vessel in which John Locke voyaged to Palestine in 1553 might have been engulfed by a waterspout had
not a conjuration, uttered in the nick of time, driven it off.
On the same voyage a drunken Dutchman raised such a riotous
disturbance that he had to be put under hatches.[5] William
Biddulph and his party had alarming adventures at sea.
Among the Cyclades a fearful storm and the incompetence
of the sailors combined to put them in extreme danger. Each
man called upon his God to save him. The captain requested
one Newport, an English merchant, to ask an English doctor
who was on board to cast upon the waves some relics which

1 Ibid., p.61.
2 Father Castela, *Le Sainct Voyage de Jierusalem*, Paris, 1612, p.97, tells of the
   captain's fear when two English vessels were sighted; 'les Anglois,' he declares,
   'sont estimez en ces cartiers la, les plus grands escumeurs et voleurs qui soient en
   la mer du levant.'
3 Hakluyt, v,202f.
4 *The True Travels, Adventures and Observations of Captaine John Smith*, 1630, chapter ii; *Travels and Works*, ed. Edward Arber and A.G.Bradley, 1910, ii,826.
5 Hakluyt, v,76f.

he had with him from Jerusalem; these relics would calm the tempest. Master Newport was sure the doctor had no such relics. Nothing was then left for the superstitious papists, says Biddulph, save weeping and wringing of hands, 'calling upon Hee Saints and Shee Saints.' The captain accused the doctor, whom he had seen continually reading in a book, of having raised the tempest by his wicked arts; and the sailors were about to cast him into the sea when, as luck had it, the storm subsided. Biddulph tells of another captain who in a storm prayed to the Virgin, promising a votive candle as tall as his ship's mast if she would come to their rescue. The mate protested that it was impossible to keep this promise; but the captain replied that in the emergency he would promise anything and that if they came out of the peril alive the Virgin would be content with some candles of ordinary size. In yet another desperate storm a mariner reminded the Lord that he was not a common beggar and did not trouble Him every day and promised that if the Lord delivered him this once he would never pray to Him again.[1]

The usual course taken by the pilgrim-ship or, in later times, by the merchantman carrying pilgrims was by way of Patras, Zante, Candia, Rhodes, and Cyprus to Joppa. The pious traveller seldom turned aside from his intention to make what speed he might to his holy destination; but those who travelled for curiosity and to see the world were not so single-minded and some of them included Greece in their itinerary. Let us, then, leave the pilgrims for a while and inquire into the impressions made by Greece upon wandering Englishmen.

II

ENGLISHMEN who visited Greece were generally en route to some other country, seldom sojourned long in the land, and rarely took particular note of their surroundings except to remark upon the degenerate condition of the inhabitants. Pilgrims of the older generations had small opportunity to record details and less inclination, for they touched at but a

1 Condensed and paraphrased from the first Letter in *The Travels of certaine Englishmen*, 1609.

few ports and their thoughts were upon higher things. Merchants of Elizabeth's time were desirous to arrive as soon as might be at their destination and were anxious for their personal safety in a perilous part of the world. Accordingly their scanty comments are generally about Turkish rule and the signs of Greek subserviency; and they have little to say about the ruins of classical antiquity. It is true that their narratives are ornamented with quotations from classical authors and with allusions to mythical or historical events associated with one site or another; but one suspects that such erudite allusions were often assembled after the traveller's return home. Occasionally there is some intelligent scepticism as to the authenticity of sites and monuments and occasionally there is manifest a genuine, if uncritical, antiquarian enthusiasm. But it remains a fact that English travellers of the Renaissance did not compose any such serious topographical works about Greece and the region of the Ægean as did the French travellers Pierre Gilles, Pierre Belon, and Nicolas de Nicolay.[1] To account for this strange contrast between the intellectual interests of France and England it is not sufficient to say that England was farther off than France from the Hellenic area, for she was also farther off from Italy, a country about which Englishmen wrote in copious detail; and English travellers who are singularly reticent about Greece often write abundantly about Constantinople, Jerusalem, or Cairo. The closer relations which existed between France and the Ottoman Porte probably had something to do with the scholarly activity

1 Belon, who was Gilles's companion, inherited much of the material which he had assembled. Nicolas de Nicolay in turn made use of Belon and commends him as a diligent observer. The work of Petrus Gillius (Pierre Gilles) is *De Topographia Constantinopoleos et de illius antiquitatibus Libri quatuor*, Lyons, 1561, supplemented by his *De Bosphoro Thracio*, Lyons, 1561. Renaissance travellers could obtain an abundance of well-digested classical lore from these treatises. Thomas Coryat carried with him copies of both and to his 'great greife' lost them one day and never recovered them (*Thomas Coriate Traveller for the English Wits*, pp.45f.). Belon's book is *Les Observations de plusieurs Singularitez et choses memorables, trouvees en Grece* [etc.], Paris, 1553. This famous and charming book contains, more methodically arranged than is usual in travel-books of the time, a vast quantity of information on the topography, antiquities, languages, fauna, flora, curiosities, and so forth of the Near East. It is illustrated with woodcuts.—On the beginnings of archaeological research in Greece, Ionia, the islands of the Ægean, and Constantinople, with an account of Englishmen in Greece, see W.G.Rice, 'Early English Travellers to Greece and the Levant,' *Essays and Studies in English and Comparative Literature*, University of Michigan, 1933.

of French travellers, for diplomacy and archaeology have often gone hand in hand into foreign countries. But it is perhaps not fanciful to discern the real explanation in the fact that English travellers, oppressed with a sense of the vast solution of continuity between the glorious classic past and the shameful desolation of their own day, were disillusioned and spiritually depressed as they journeyed through Greece.

Fynes Moryson is a case in point. Save for some perfunctory remarks upon Greek geography he is absolutely silent about this country in that portion of his *Itinerary* which he published. In the part of his manuscript which he suppressed and which remained unpublished till the present century he speaks of the baseness of the inhabitants, 'trodden underfeete' by the Turks, 'used like borne slaves,' and unable to enjoy the fruits of their toil, nay bereft of their very children who are taken for tribute, obliged to turn Mohammedan, and trained for service in the Ottoman army. 'The Greekes,' he says, 'are more despised by the Turkes then any other Christians, because they lost their liberty and Kingdome basely and cowardly, making small or no resistance against the Turkes conquest.'[1] That the most thoughtful of our early travellers did not consider this indictment worth publishing renders it the more severe. *Guarda e passa!* he seems to exclaim.

'Poor despised Grecians' is a phrase of Dekker's.[2] The same estimate of the decadent heirs of a once mighty civilization is implicit in the expression 'Merry Greek.' It occurs in our old drama in the sense of a lively or frivolous fellow, sometimes with the connotation of rascal and, when applied to a woman, of harlot.[3] It derives ultimately from the Roman contempt for the Greek adventurers who resorted to the capital of the Empire, and some vestige of this origin remains occasionally in English usage, as when the parasite in *Ralph Roister Doister* is named Merrygreek. But it received a heightened significance from the reports of travellers who observed the shamelessness

1 *Shakespeare's Europe*, ed. Charles Hughes, p.495.
2 *The Seven Deadly Sinnes of London*, 1606; ed. Brett-Smith, p.8.
3 Shakespeare's Cressida refers to Helen as 'a merry Greek' (*Troilus and Cressida*, I,ii,116); Massinger associates together 'the merry Greek' and the Venetian courtesan (*The Guardian*, II,v).

and light-hearted indifference with which the modern Greeks accepted the overlordship of the Turks. Thus, William Parry remarks that in Candia the manners of the inhabitants

> do verify our English proverb, which termeth any man pleasantly disposed (by reason of wine or otherwise) a merry Greek; alluding to these Greeks that always sit drinking and playing the good fellows before their doors: some dancing arm in arm up and down the town: some others making some other sports to procure laughter; and thus gamesomely do they pass their time, as if they were created but for the matter of pleasure: So that to me it seemed no little wonder that that nation which heretofore made all the world admire their wisdom and learning, who (in regard to themselves) held all the world besides but barbarians and barbarous, should now become such cup-shop companions, tripping their nimble wits with quick and subtle wine, thereby turning all their deep policy into deep carousing and shallow jocundity.[1]

Parry's companion, George Manwaring, says: 'They may well be called merry Greeks, for in the evenings, commonly after they leave work, they will dance up and down the streets, both men and women.'[2] George Sandys bears like testimony:

> They are in a manner releast from their thraldome, in that unsensible of it: well meriting the name of Merrie Greekes, when their leasure will tolerate. Never Sunday or holiday passes over without some publike meeting or other: where intermixed with women, they dance out the day, and with full crownd Cups enlengthen their jollitie.[3]

A people of this temperament practised instinctively the virtue of hospitality; and to this virtue even the dour Lithgow bears witness. It is true that a merchant with whom he travelled from Patras to Athens cheated him unconscionably, but he expresses his gratitude to the Athenians who 'exceeding kindly banqueted' him for four days and with 'great regard and estimation . . . honoured travellers.' Nevertheless Lithgow's final estimate of the Greeks was unqualifiedly condemnatory. 'They are,' he says, 'wholly degenerate from their Aunces-

---

1 *A New and large Discourse* (Sir E.Denison Ross, *Sir Anthony Sherley*, p.104).
2 *A True Discourse* (ibid., p.179).   3 Purchas, viii, 100.

tors, . . . being the greatest dissembling lyers, inconstant, and uncivill people of all other Christians in the World.' [1] The reputation of the Candiotes [2] was the worst. For this there was scriptural authority [3] which was substantiated by the experience of modern travellers. In Crete 'there be ryght evil people,' says a voyager to the Holy Land.[4] Lithgow pictures the lawlessness of the island's inhabitants, from whom he barely escaped with his life. 'A barbarous and uncivill people, . . . tyranicall, blood-thirsty, and deceitfull' is his verdict.[5] This reputation explains what may have been a proverbial expression analogous to our 'Go to Jericho,' for it was on the way down to Jericho that a certain man fell among thieves. So Webster has: 'Send him to Candy,' meaning to perdition; [6] and Fletcher has:

1 *Rare Adventures*, pp.62,67f.,105.
2 The classical name Crete was usually employed by the Elizabethans in their allusions to any of the myths associated with the island; but the name Candia, used with precision of a town on the island, was extended on some sixteenth-century Italian maps and occasionally in the drama (e.g., *Twelfth Night*, V,i,65) to embrace the whole island. In seventeenth-century usage the name Crete was obsolescent and later fell wholly into disuse, to replace Candia again only in recent times.—The usual Elizabethan form of Candia was Candy. The word 'candy,' a sweetmeat, comes from the Persian *qand* meaning crystallized sugar; but the Elizabethans, knowing nothing of the etymology, doubtless associated the sweetmeat with the island, which, as it happened, did, like neighbouring Cyprus, raise sugar-cane. When Greene writes (*Friar Bacon and Friar Bungay*, III,ii): 'Candy shall yeeld the richest of her canes' he is thinking not of Persia but of the island. So Dekker (*The Shoemaker's Holiday*, III,i) describes a ship from Cyprus 'laden with sugar-candy.' Compare Fletcher and Massinger, *Beggars' Bush*, I,iii,64. Candia was famous for its wines. Lithgow (*Rare Adventures*, p.71) says that 'this Ile produceth the best Malvasy,' a wine which takes its name from the eparchy of Malevyzi and is not to be confused with Maumsey, named from Monemvasia in the Peloponnesus. Henry Glapthorne (*The Ladies Priviledge*, III,i; *Works*, ii,127) describes the wives of London citizens as 'wholsome as pretious Candy wives.' Here the emendation 'wines' is obviously needed. For other commendations of the wines of Candia see Fletcher, *A Very Woman*, III,v; Jonson, *Volpone*, I,i,58; and *A Paradox of a Painted Face* (a poem ascribed to Donne and included in Grierson's edition of Donne's *Poems*, i,457).
3 Epistle to Titus, i,12: 'One of themselves, even a prophet of their own, said The Cretans are always liars.' Saint Paul is quoting Epimenides of Cnossos who called them liars because they said Zeus was buried in Crete. Ovid has the phrase 'Mendax Creta' (*Ars Amoris*, i,298). The liar Mendacio in Brewer's *Lingua* (II,i; Hazlitt's Dodsley, ix,365) is said to have been 'nursed in Crete.' The play on words 'Cretiza cum Cretensi' in the *Adages* of Erasmus reappears in Arthur Edwards's *Damon and Pithias* (Hazlitt's Dodsley, iv,62). See also Lyly, *Euphues: The Anatomy of Wit*; *Works*, i,186; *Euphues and His England*, ibid., ii,24; Gabriel Harvey, *Foure Letters and certaine Sonnets*, 1592; ed. G.B.Harrison, p.50.
4 *The Pylgrymage of Sir Richard Guylforde*, p.13.
5 *Rare Adventures*, p.73.
6 *The White Devil*, II,i,289. The analogy to Jericho (suggested by Professor Sugden) explains Webster's metaphor better than does Mr. F.L.Lucas's theory that Webster had in mind Nashe's statement that the Cretans 'live on serpents' (*The Unfortunate Traveller*; *Works*, ii,299). Nashe had Pliny's authority (*Historia naturalis*, vi,29) for the belief that the Cretans ate serpents. But a transference of the episode of

'Her men are gone to Candy; they are peppered,' [1] that is, they have had rough treatment in a fight.

About the ruins of classical antiquity in Greece Moryson, as we have seen, provided no information whatsoever. Blount also was silent. Sandys occasionally noted the location of a famous monument, but only once or twice did he go out of his way to visit one. Lithgow was at once more enterprising and a little more communicative. Interspersed among his comments upon the modern Greeks we find a few—tantalizingly few—notes on the ruins which he passed by. Thus, as he plodded wearily through the 'desart way' of Arcadia, he 'beheld many singular Monuments and ruined Castles,' whose names he could not learn because he had 'an ignorant guide.' At Sparta he found only 'the lumpes of ruines and memory.' His route led him through the plain of Argolis, but he gives no indication that he so much as remarked the mighty ruins of Mycenæan civilization; and at Corinth, though he gives an inaccurate account of the location of the ancient city, he has nothing to say of Acrocorinth. Athens he found 'now altogether decayed' with but a scant two hundred houses within the still recognizable circuit of its walls and with 'a Castle which formerly was the Temple of Minerva.' That is all he has to say about the Parthenon; but it is more than is said by any other English traveller of the period. Crete apparently interested him more than the mainland of Greece and he is correspondingly more generous of descriptions. His greatest enthusiasm was for a 'Temple of Saturn' beside Mount Ida; this he describes as 'a worke to be admired, of such Antiquity, and as yet undecayed.' This temple cannot be identified with any certainty; he may have visited the Temple of Apollo Pythios near ancient Gortyn; if so and if his description is accurate, it was in a better state of

Saint Paul and the viper (Acts, xxviii,3f.) from Malta to Crete led to the precisely opposite belief that there were no snakes in Crete. 'There is no kind of serpent there,' says Solinus (Golding's translation, 1587, p.72). Compare Moryson, *Itinerary*, ii,83; Peter Heylyn's discussion of Crete in the *Microcosmos*; and Sir Thomas Browne, *Vulgar Errors*, VI,viii. Lithgow's own experiences were to the contrary: 'It is sayd by some Historians, that no venomous animall can live in this Ile; but I saw the contrary: For I kild on a Sunday morning, hard by the Sea-side . . . two Serpents and a Viper . . . Many build upon false reports, but experience teacheth men the trueth' (*Rare Adventures*, p.79).
1 *The Double Marriage*, II,iii.

preservation than it is today.[1] Not far from this site he came
to the great quarry west of Hagii Deka which was then, and
still is, pointed out by the islanders as the Labyrinth of Minos.
This he would gladly have viewed better, but for fear of stum-
bling into hollow places he dared not enter it, having no candlelight. He had no means to test the validity of the identification
in this case; but sometimes his scepticism hindered him from
accepting unquestioningly what was told him. On Chios, in the
dark subterranean chamber called Homer's Sepulchre, he was
of two minds, obviously wishing to believe. 'I saw an auncient
Tombe,' he says, 'whereon were ingraven Greeke letters, which
we could not understand for their antiquity; but whether it was
this Tombe or not, I doe not know, but this they related, and
yet very likely to have been his Sepulcher.' He was in a more
doubting mood when, having landed on the coast of Asia Minor
opposite Tenedos, he hired a Janissary to guide him to the so-
called ruins of Troy. There the tombs of the 'valiant Champions' of the Greeks and Trojans were pointed out. 'Well I
wot,' says Lithgow, 'I saw infinite old Sepulchres, but for their
particular names, and nominations of them, I suspend, neither
could I beleeve my Interpreter, sith it is more than three thousand and odde yeares agoe, that Troy was destroyed.' Nevertheless his pride in the accomplished pilgrimage to Troy is shown
by the fact that at this point in his narrative he affixed the
'Effigie' representing him in Turkish habit and turban and
standing among the ruins.[2]

These same tombs stirred the sensibilities of the more emo-
tional Tom Coryat. 'It grieved me to the heart,' he says, 'that
I coulde not learne either by inscriptions, or any other meanes,
whose Monuments these were: for it is vaine to be induced by
conjectures, to say they were these or these mens; onely I hope
no man will taxe me of a rash opinion, if I beleeve'—and he
goes on to offer his own guesses.[3] Coryat had a quicker eye for
antiquities, a more intelligent interest in them, and a greater
willingness to take notes of them than most of his fellow-

[1] Baedeker's *Greece*, ed. 1909, p.427.
[2] *Rare Adventures*, pp.63,67,78,91,109.
[3] 'Master Coryates travels to, and Observations in Constantinople and other places
in the way thither,' Purchas, x,397.

travellers. The only antiques Lithgow seems to have troubled to take away with him were 'three peeces of rusted money' which he found at Troy; but Coryat owned something much more precious. He picked up in Bythinia 'a very curious white marble head of an ancient Hero or Gyant-like Champion'; and writing home, he asked that a message be conveyed to 'that famous Antiquarie' Sir Robert Cotton that 'to this head will his best antiquities whatsoever veyle bonnet' [1]—that is, take off their hats, as we say.

Not until the beginning of the seventeenth century, when Sir Thomas Roe and William Petty, acting as agents for the Earl of Arundel, began to collect antiquities on an ambitious scale, was the rapacity of the Turks stirred to an appreciation of their pecuniary value. Hitherto no official protection had been afforded the monuments; and then and for long after-wards the Turkish government was the worst offender. Their vandalism was on a par with that perpetrated by the popes against the ruins of ancient Rome. George Sandys noted that the ruins of Troy were 'lessened daily by the Turkes, who carried the Pillars and stones unto Constantinople, to adorne the buildings of the great Bassas.' Of Delos the same writer remarks complacently that 'the ruines of Apollos Temple are here yet to be seen, affoording faire Pillars of marble to such as will fetch them.' [2] How unrestricted were the exertions of antiquarians in a remote locality not guarded by the Turks is shown by Sir Kenelm Digby's narrative of his visit to Delos (which by a slip he calls Delphos) in 1628. The passage is worth quoting at length:

> I went with most of my shippes to Delphos, a desert iland, where staying till the rest were readie, because idlenesse should not fixe theer mindes upon any untoward fansies (as is usuall among seamen), and together to avayle myselfe of the conveniencie of carrying away some antiquities there, I busied them in rolling of stones downe to the sea side, which they did with such eagernesse as though it had bin the earnestest businesse that they came out for, and they mastered prodigious massie weightes; but one stone,

---

1 *Thomas Coriate Traveller for the English Wits*, p.44.　　2 Purchas, viii,94.

Loe here's mine Effigie, and Turkish suite;
My Staffe, my Shasse, as I did Asia foote:
Plac'd in old Ilium; Priams Scepter thralles:
The Grecian Campe design'd; lost Dardan falles
Gird'd with small Simois: Idaes tops, a Gate;
Two fatall Tombes, an Eagle, sackt Troyes State.

William Lithgow among the Ruins of Troy

the greatest and fairest of all, containing 4 statues, they gave over after they had bin, 300 men, a whole day about it, whiles the dispatching some businesse with some Venetians come from Tino detained me abord. But the next day I contrived a way with mastes of shippes and another shippe to ride over against it, that brought it downe with much ease and speede. In the little Delphos [i.e., Little Delos] there are brave marble stones heaped up in the great ruines of Apollos temple, and within the circuit of it is a huge statue, but broken in two peeces about the wast, which the Greekes told me was Apollo. It weigheth att least 30 tonnes, and time hath worn out much the softnesses and gentilenesses of the worke, yet all the proportions remaine perfect and in grosse: the yieldinges of the flesh and the musculous partes are visible, so that it is still a brave noble piece, and hath by divers bin attempted to be carried away, but they have all failed in it.[1]

With the genuine, if rudimentary, connoisseurship evinced by Digby one may contrast Sir Thomas Roe's distaste for 'old idolls' that are battered and defaced. He confesses to the Earl of Arundel that he does not see much beauty 'in ruines, that only showe there was once bewtye'; and reporting that he has had a piece of sculpture brought on mule-back from Angora, he describes it as wanting 'a hand, a nose, a lip' and as 'so deformed, that she makes me remember a hospital.' Again, he writes to the Duke of Buckingham that he is not 'so fond of antiquitye . . . [as] to court it in a deformed or misshapen stone.'[2]

Roe was interested in ancient coins (his collection went ultimately to the Bodleian) but, as these passages show, he disclaimed any connoisseurship in the matter of sculpture. It was no part of his official duties as an ambassador to the Porte to search out, secure, and ship to England statues, fragments of statues, inscriptions, and other antiquities. But he could not risk the displeasure of influential friends in England who requested him to undertake such tasks for them. One of these friends was Archbishop Laud, and for him Roe ferreted out Greek manuscripts. He told the Patriarch of Constantinople

1 *Journal of a Voyage into the Mediterranean, A.D. 1628*, ed. John Bruce, Camden Society, 1868, p.57.
2 *The Negotiations of Sir Thomas Roe*, 1740, pp.495,534.

roundly that 'his old books rott and rust by him, among ignorant Greeks, that never will understand, nor make use of them' and that 'in right they belong to the church of God, that will publish them. I find hee scarse knowes the names of many, I am sure, nor their contents.' Roe offered to furnish in exchange a complete library of classical authors.[1] More difficult to satisfy than Laud's tastes, if not more exacting, were those of the Earl of Arundel, especially when the activities of the ambassador and other agents made the Turks conscious of the value of antique sculpture. In the task of discovering and acquiring—by persuasion, purchase, bribery, or downright theft—such objects of art Roe was assisted by Arundel's two personal agents, John Markham (who died while engaged in the work) and William Petty, who in the prosecution of his quests endured great hardships, including a shipwreck which involved the (fortunately temporary) loss of his collections. Roe's difficulties were enhanced when the Duke of Buckingham presently appeared as a rival of Arundel. The Duke's more fastidious but less well trained taste required that the marbles sent him be entire, and consequently he was harder to please than the Earl who was content with fragments as well as entire statues.

On the Porta Aurea, the gate close by the Seven Towers at Constantinople, there were certain works of sculpture which Roe describes as 'twelve tables of fine marble, cutt into historyes, some of a very great relevo, sett into the wall, with small pillars, as supporters.' His efforts to procure these for Buckingham are amusingly related in a letter:

> Promise to obteyne them I cannot, because they stand upon the ancient gate, the most conspicuous of the cyttye, though now mured up, beeing the entrance by the castell called the Seaven Towers, and never opened since the Greeke emperors lost yt; to offer to steale them, no man dares to deface the cheefe seate of the grand signor: to procure them by favour, is more impossible, such envy they beare unto us. There is only then one way left; by corruption of some churchman, to dislike them, as agaynst their law; and under that pretence, to take them downe to bee brought into

1 Ibid., p.414.

some privat place; from whence, after the matter is cold and un-
suspected, they may be conveyed.

Nothing came of this ingenious plan to bribe a 'churchman' to
declare these reliefs intolerable as contrary to the Islamic law
against images; and when Roe attempted to proceed openly
he was met by the guardian of the 'castle' with the objection
that 'those statues were enchanted' and that harm would be-
fall the city if they were removed. Arguments were of no avail;
and in the end Roe had to write Buckingham that 'though I
could not gett the stones, yet I allmost raised an insurrection in
that part of the citty.' [1]

Roe's search for Greek manuscripts brought him into contact with the clergy of the Orthodox Church; but though on
more than one occasion he used his influence to protect these
divines from the Turks his correspondence shows no curiosity
about the liturgical ceremonies of the Eastern communion.
Such books as Edward Brerewood's *Enquiries touching the
Diversity of Languages and Religions* (1614) supplied English
readers with an abundance of information on this subject. Of
Brerewood's work Samuel Purchas made use in his account of
'the condition of life in which the Greekes now live,' where
there is a long description of orthodox doctrine and ceremonial.
The information here provided on the plan of their 'temples'
(especially the enclosed 'quire'); their holy days and four
annual seasons of fasting; their orders of monks (which include
'no Abbylubbers nor begging Friers'); their system of auricular
confession; and their liturgy (notably the ceremony of cutting
the consecrated bread with 'a little speare in forme of the
speare wherewith the Souldiers pierced Christ') and much else

1 Ibid., pp.386f.,512.—The earliest critical account of the collections assembled for
the Earl of Arundel by Roe and Petty is John Selden's *Marmora Arundelliana: sive
saxa Graece incisa*, 1628. The many passages referring to his archaeological activities in Roe's correspondence have been extracted from the *Negotiations* and reprinted together in Adolf Michaelis, *Ancient Marbles in Great Britain*, translated by
C.A.M.Fennell, Cambridge, 1882, pp.184f. Compare his chapter i: 'The Arundel
Marbles and other Early Collections.' See also Mary F.S.Hervey, *The Life, Correspondence, and Collections of Thomas Howard Earl of Arundel*, Cambridge, 1921,
chapter xx; and W.G.Rice's study referred to, p. 60, note 1, above.—Evelyn (*Diary*,
September 19, 1667) describes the marbles as 'miserably neglected and scatter'd
up and downe about the garden and other parts of Arundel House.' It was through
his good offices that the son of the collector was persuaded to present a good many
of the pieces to Oxford.

is in the main accurate.[1] Travel-books both English and continental often contain information of this kind and impressions of the relations existing between the Greek Christian authorities and the Turkish administration. These, however, have generally been gathered not in Greece but in the Holy Land.

III

WE now rejoin the company of pilgrims voyaging from Venice to the Holy Land. Among them there may be a few English Protestants, led on as much by curiosity as by piety, men who have not undertaken the long journey as a discipline for their souls. On another, less arduous, pilgrimage centuries earlier Chaucer's Parson prayed to Jesus to grant him wit enough to show his companions

> the way, in this viage,
> Of thilke parfit glorious pilgrimage,
> That highte Jerusalem celestial.[2]

But the conception of the actual physical pilgrimage to the Holy Land as the counterpart, for the body's discipline, of the soul's wayfaring to the Celestial City is foreign to Protestant thought. The theme of the Pilgrimage of Human Life, of life as a journey from the City of Destruction to the Celestial City, is found times beyond number in medieval literature, whether expressed in a homely *exemplum* for use in a parochial sermon or in the sublime poem in which Dante narrates the pilgrimage of the soul from sin, through contrition and absolution, to salvation. Hymns of longing for the Heavenly City were sung in the churches of Elizabethan England; [3] and we have, on the one hand, pure allegory, as in *The Pilgrim's Progress*, and, on the other, descriptions of the sights and wonders of the Holy Land, as in Thomas Fuller's *Pisgah-Sight of Palestine*. But our literature is the poorer for the lack of any such combination of

1 Purchas, i,422f.
2 *Canterbury Tales*, 'Parson's Prologue,' ll.48f.
3 The hymn 'Jerusalem my happy home,' first published in the anonymous *Song of Mary the Mother of Christ*, 1601, Sig. F₁, has various less familiar counterparts. See, for example, the anonymous *Pilgrim's Song* in *Select Poetry Chiefly Sacred of the Reign of King James the First*, ed. Edward Farr, Cambridge, 1847, pp.109f. Compare John Welles, *The Soules Progresse to the celestiall Canaan*, 1639.

allegory and guide-book as *Le Pelerin Veritable de la Terre Saincte auquel soubs le Discours figuré de la Jerusalem antique et moderne est enseigné le chemin de la Celeste* (Paris, 1615). On the title-page of this pleasant treatise is represented a pilgrim wearing a gown upon which is embroidered the Jerusalem Cross. Female figures, personifications of Health, Prudence, Charity, Abundance, Hope, Faith, and Patience, are his companions upon the way. The text begins with an elaborately wrought analogy between the way to Jerusalem and the way of Salvation; and what follows is at once a guide-book for visitors to the Holy Land and a devotional manual. The Protestant Englishman was out of sympathy with this state of mind. Samuel Purchas twice thought it necessary to utter caveats against pilgrimages. He writes:

> Although I denie not that a place dignified with holy actions or passions, may be a Place to the memorie or affection exciting holinesse, yet for Religion of place to leave or neglect our place and calling in Religion, is superstitious; and to ascribe sanctity to the place, is Jewish.

Again, he urges his countrymen who 'adventure this Jerosolymitan Pilgrimage' not to endanger 'the best Pilgrimage, which is the peaceable way of a good Conscience to that Jerusalem which is above.' [1] If he was no mere sceptical scoffer like William Lithgow but serious, sober, and inclined naturally to contemplation, the point of view of the Englishman who travelled to Jerusalem was probably generally like that of Fynes Moryson who assured his readers that he went there without thought to expatiate any sin or to merit any grace but simply out of emulation and curiosity; yet when he found himself there, though he offered worship to God alone, yet 'the very places strucke me with a religious horrour, and filled my mind, prepared to devotion, with holy motives.' [2]

This is not to say that Protestant travellers were not as curious as Catholic pilgrims to note all places along their way which possessed a holy relic or were associated with any of the saints. For example, John Aldersey saw at Patras the tomb of

---

1 Purchas, viii,19; ix,478.   2 *Itinerary*, ii,1.

Saint Andrew 'and the boord upon which he was beheaded, which boord is now so rotten, that if any man offer to cut it, it falleth to powder, yet I brought some of it away with me.' [1] And at Famagusta in Cyprus John Locke was shown one of the water-pots which Jesus used in working his first miracle at Cana.[2] At Ephesus could be seen the Cave of the Seven Sleepers and the fountain which Saint John used in baptizing.[3] Beyond Rhodes [4] was Saint Helen's Gulf where the mother of Constantine cast into the sea one of the nails of the Cross to still a tempest.[5] In Cyprus, where there were distracting associations with the classical past,[6] was preserved the cross of the Penitent Thief.[7] At Beirut there was shown the place where Saint George slew the dragon in order to deliver the daughter of the king of that country.[8] These are a few examples of the sacred sites and

1 Hakluyt, v,40.—The *Itinerarii Terre Sancte* by Bartholomeus Salignac, Lyons, 1525, gives a list of all the relics and holy places the pilgrim will pass en route.

2 Hakluyt, v,76f.

3 The tradition that Saint John, 'the Eternal Witness,' was not dead but sleeping in his tomb at Ephesus occurs in *Mandeville*, whose author claims to have seen the earth stirring 'as there weren quykke thinges under' (*Travels*, chapter iv). Compare *The Golden Legend*, chapter ix. The tradition is at least as old as St. Augustine.

4 The thoughts of Elizabethans who visited Rhodes were not upon classical antiquities but upon the siege of 1522 when Solyman the Magnificent won this outpost of Christendom. Of the siege the finest English narrative is that in Hakluyt (v,1f.). Marlowe strangely perverts history when he says (*The Jew of Malta*, II,ii) that when the 'hideous force' of Turks 'environed Rhodes,'

> Small though the number was that kept the town,
> They fought it out and not a man survived
> To bring the hapless news to Christendom.

On the contrary, Solyman granted liberal terms to the Knights, who were permitted to depart, and after some years of indecision (spent in Crete and elsewhere) were granted by Charles V an asylum in Malta. For dramatizations of the siege see p.496, note 1, below.

5 *The Pylgrymage of Sir Richard Guylforde*, p.14. For a characteristic scoffing Protestant comment see Anthony Munday, *The Englishe Romayne Life*, 1582; ed. G.B.Harrison, pp.76f. The story is told by Gregory of Tours. It has been seriously argued by a modern Roman Catholic scholar that Saint Helena did not cast overboard so holy a relic but lowered it by a rope into the sea and hauled it on board again (Balduino Bedini, *The Sessorian Relics of the Lord's Passion*, Rome, 1928, p.71).

6 From the temple of Aphrodite at Paphos in Cyprus come the epithets Paphian and Cyprian. Moryson (*Itinerary*, i,460) reports that the earth, herbs, and water of Cyprus have a taste of salt 'which Venus loved well.'—To a fine gauze exported from the island was given the name cypress; Shakespeare, Ben Jonson, Milton, and other poets allude to it. Dekker (*Old Fortunatus*, I,i) mentions the 'great bell' of Saint Michael's church in Cyprus; and Professor Sugden suggests that this is the 'dreadful bell' in *Othello*, II,iii,177; but that was more probably in the citadel.

7 *Mandeville* reproves those who make men believe that this is the Cross of Christ (chapter v). The largest fragment of the cross of the Penitent Thief has for centuries been exhibited in Santa Croce in Rome.

8 Henry de Beauvau, *Relation journalière du Voyage du Levant*, Toul, 1608, p.130.

relics to be seen at or near the ports where vessels touched on the voyage to Palestine.

Save for those travellers who entered the Holy Land from Syria or those who crossed the Sinai desert from Egypt, the usual port of entry was Joppa. 'As soone as we hadde syght of the Holy Land,' wrote a pilgrim of early Tudor times, 'we sange *Te Deum*, and thanked joyously Almyghty God, that had yeven us suche grace to have ones the syght of that most holy land.' [1] Before landing, the mariners were wont to sing a litany; [2] and as soon as they were ashore pilgrims flung themselves down and kissed the earth. [3] The Moryson brothers were Protestants, not Catholics, but Henry, when they landed, flung himself impetuously upon the ground and in doing so hit his nose and, as Fynes tells us, 'voided much blood at the nose; and howsoever this be a superstitious signe of ill, yet the event was to us tragicall, by his death shortly after happening.' [4]

Once ashore, new troubles assaulted the travellers and they were made painfully aware of the fact that they were in a hostile as well as in a holy land. The rapacity of the Arabs is on record from the eleventh century when Ingulphus and his companions found themselves *eviscerati de infinitis pecuniis*.[5] Though the 'Sarsenes wyl go talkyng wyth yow and mak goyd chere . . . they wyl stele fro you that ye have and they may.' [6] Guard well your 'knyves and other smale Japes ye beare uppon you' lest the Saracens steal them, is the warning given by the author of the *Informacon*. Mamelukes and Saracens registered each pilgrim's name; and then they were crowded together to await the departure of the caravan. Guylford and his companions were put in a cave where they lay 'upon the bare, stynkynge stable ground, as well nyght as daye, right evyll intreated by the Maures.' At this time Guylford (who later

1 *The Pylgrymage of Sir Richard Guylforde*, p.15.
2 Torkyngton's *Diary, Gentleman's Magazine*, lxxxii, 317.
3 On the verso of the title-page of *Le Pelerin Veritable* there is a panoramic view of the Holy Land, and in the foreground a pilgrim is kneeling upon the seashore, kissing the ground.
4 *Itinerary*, i,463.
5 Quoted by Ellis in his introduction to *The Pylgrymage of Sir Richard Guylforde*.
6 William Wey, *Itineraries*, p.7.

died) and one of his friends were 'sore seke'; and 'with greet dyffyculte and outragyous coste,' writes their chaplain, 'we purveyed camellys for them and certayne Mamelukes to conducte theym in safty to Jherusalem, which intreated us very evyll, and toke moche more for theyr payne thenne theyr covenaunt was.' [1] The *Informacon* counsels celerity in the choice of an ass or mule for the journey up into the mountains; otherwise you will get an inferior beast.

Whether they ascended into Judea from the coast or entered Palestine from the North or South, travellers were surrounded by perils on the march; and these dangers became more critical after Selim the Grim had wrested the land from the Mameluke sultans of Egypt and added it to the Ottoman Empire (1517). The caravan of which William Lithgow was a member from Damascus to Jerusalem was guarded by soldiers, and by night each traveller carried a light. The leader 'most dexteriously discharged . . . the function of his calling, not with insolencie, but with prudent and magnanimous virilitie'; and Lithgow was grateful to him for his 'diligent care of that benigne caravan.' [2] Christians were not always so efficiently protected. Father Castela, for example, was in constant danger from robbers within and without his caravan when he crossed the Sinai desert; and Henry Timberlake in the same journey had to bribe heavily his Arab guides who persistently threatened him as a 'Guaire' (Giaour) or unbeliever. The pilgrim-garb which Timberlake wore did not avail him when, singing and praising God, he and his company came to the walls of Jerusalem; for though his friend Master Burrell, who spoke some Greek, was admitted, Timberlake was thrown into prison. In reply to his remonstrances 'the Turks flatly denied that they had ever heard either of my Queen or country.' At length he was released through the mediation of a Moor whom he had befriended on an earlier stage of his journey and who was on his way to Mecca. [3] It was of course to a Christian's advantage to win the goodwill of a Mohammedan fellow-traveller.

1 *Pylgrymage*, pp.16f.
2 *Rare Adventures*, pp.188f.
3 *A True and Strange Discourse of the Travailes of two English Pilgrimes*, 1603. The author's name appeared first on the title-page of the edition of 1616. The exception-

In Jerusalem visitors from western Europe were taken in charge by the Padre Guardiano, the warden of the Franciscan monastery. Meals and lodgings were provided at a small fixed price and guidance was nominally free not only to the Holy Places of the city but to the near-by sacred sites. The friars furnished this service in return for the contributions made by Catholic princes towards the maintenance of the Holy Places. Timberlake was taxed by the friars with the question why Queen Elizabeth contributed nothing to these funds; and a few years later Lithgow promised to use his good offices with King James in their behalf. No special provision was made for Protestants; they were herded with the Roman Catholics— an arrangement which frequently gave rise to disorder.

The scandalous quarrels among Christians of different sects were the occasion of scornful amusement and scoffing to the Mohammedans. Biddulph describes the unseemly bickering that went on.[1] John Sanderson did not enter the Church of the Holy Sepulchre 'by reason I had a great controversie with the Popish friars,' so that the Greek Patriarch had to entreat him to avoid an uproar.[2] On Palm Sunday the Father Guardian had to beg Lithgow 'to abstaine from scandalizing and mocking our Rites and ordinary Customes, which at this great Feast wee must performe.' 'To the which,' says Lithgow, 'we condiscended and promised to give no occasion of offence.'[3] Even when there was no violence there was apt to be subdued illfeeling, as Fynes Moryson discovered when he attempted to dispute with some Greek priests about the old belief that Jerusalem was the centre of the world. When the texts they quoted were interpreted by Moryson in a non-literal sense, 'they grew angry and said that the Scriptures must be beleeved, in spite of all Cosmographers and Philosophers. It had been vaine to dispute further with them, there being not one learned man among these Greekes at Jerusalem.'[4]

The number of places in and about Jerusalem visited and venerated by pilgrims increased astonishingly during the

ally entertaining quality of this small book accounts for the several reprints. It is in the *Harleian Miscellany*, ed. 1744, i,327f.; ed. 1809, iii,323f.
1 *Travels of certaine Englishmen*, p.98.   3 *Rare Adventures*, p.219.
2 *Travels into the Levant*, p.108.   4 *Itinerary*, ii,31.

Middle Ages; and this growth may be traced in the narratives of successive pilgrims from the tenth century to the Renaissance. Anywhere from twenty to forty localities are mentioned even in succinct descriptions, and generally many more.[1] Fynes Moryson itemizes no less than ninety-six Holy Places, all indicated on his plan of the city; and this does not include thirty-three places within the Church of the Holy Sepulchre which are separately designated.[2] In English accounts of the sites there is a marked change in attitude as we pass from Catholic pilgrims to Protestant visitors, from the credulous acceptance of everything related by the guide (as seen in Guylford's *Pylgrymage* or Torkyngton's so-called *Diary*) to the courteously suppressed doubts of Moryson and the derisive scepticism of Lithgow.

The visits to the Holy Places were performed solemnly and with minds attuned to serious meditations. The pilgrims met together at the Franciscan monastery and listened to an appropriate discourse by the Father Guardian, 'a ryght holy sermon,' says Torkyngton, on the 'holynesse of all the blyssed choseyn places in the holy londe.'[3] Hymns, anthems, prayers, and antiphones were sung or recited at each station of the *Via Dolorosa* and at each sacred site.[4] Lithgow 'laughed in his sleeve' while these ceremonies were in progress. Timberlake, with better breeding, contented himself with saying silently the Lord's Prayer when he and his companions were directed to repeat Pater Nosters and Ave Marys. Signs of dissension

1 The increase in the number of the Holy Places may be observed by reading in chronological order the fourteen volumes of *The Library of the Palestine Pilgrims' Text Society*. See also C.R.Beazley, *The Dawn of Modern Geography*, ii, chapter 3. In *Le Sainct Voyage* Father Castela notes an amazing number of sites, literally scores upon scores. Even more elaborate is the information in Sigmund Feyerabend's *Reyszbuch dess Heyligen Lands*, Frankfort am Mayn, 1584. This is the most detailed and exhaustive of all Renaissance books on Palestine; not counting preliminary matter and index this folio contains 466 leaves, not pages.

2 *Itinerary*, ii,6f.

3 *Diary, Gentleman's Magazine*, ut cit.

4 Some Roman Catholic treatises combine practical directions with devotional material. Father Castella's book contains many hymns and prayers, including (p.361) a beautiful hymn to be sung at the Tomb of Christ. The *Itinerarii Terre Sancte*, though it gives no hymns, has a series of prayers to be recited at the various sites (folio ixf.). Antoine Regnault, *Discours du Voyage d'Outre Mer au Sainct Sepulcre de Jerusalem*, Lyons, 1573 (an attractive little book with maps and vignettes) contains devotional exercises. There are no analogous English books of the period.

among the Christians were not lost upon the Mohammedans around them.

Within the Church of the Holy Sepulchre were living quarters of a sort, and there were ascetics who passed their entire lives there. The Moslem custodians locked visitors in, sometimes overnight, sometimes, especially during Holy Week, for as much as three days and three nights together. The most elaborate ceremonies took place, then as now, at Easter-tide. In the Middle Ages pilgrims who had carried wooden crosses to Jerusalem cast them down on Mount Calvary in token of the fulfilment of their vows; and annually on Easter-Eve these crosses were burnt by the Father Guardian.[1] This picturesque ceremony is not mentioned by writers of our period; it may have fallen into desuetude or because of the conspicuousness of the crosses may have been forbidden by the Turks. But the ceremonial entrance into Jerusalem on Palm Sunday was still enacted. Lithgow was a spectator of it, and he tells how the Padre Guardiano rode into the city mounted upon an ass amid the shouts of the people; and the clamour so incensed the Turks that they laid about them with their sticks, pulling the Guardian from his steed and beating him cruelly; 'whereat I and other Protestants,' says Lithgow, 'did laugh in our sleeves to behold their foolish Procession, so substantially rewarded.'[2] He witnessed also the ceremony of the *Depositio Crucis* on the evening of Good Friday, when the friars brought forth 'the wooden Portrait of a dead Corpse, representing our Saviour, having the resemblance of five bloody Wounds.' The friars kissed the wounds, 'the Turkes meanewhile laughing them to scorne in their faces, with miserable derision.' This ceremony Lithgow denominates 'a singular dottage of the Romish folly.'[3]

1 See the so-called 'Anonymous' narrative, §§5–6, *Palestine Pilgrims' Text Society*, vi; and Theodorick's *Description* (*c.*1172), ibid., V,iv,20.
2 *Rare Adventures*, pp.218f.
3 Ibid., p. 246.—From an eighteenth-century traveller we learn that at that period the artificial body representing the Dead Christ was fashioned with flexible joints (*Travels through Egypt . . . and the Holy Land . . . By an English Merchant*, 1758). It does not follow from the silence of Renaissance travellers on such repellently realistic details that these features did not then exist; indeed the excessive naturalism of the figures and scenic 'properties' in some of the oldest chapels of the Sacro Monte at Varallo suggests that a similar naturalism was in vogue at Jerusalem. To Moslems it must have seemed offensive and profane.

The same scoffing Englishman describes vividly the annual miracle of the Holy Fire:[1]

> The day before the Resurrection, about the houre of midnight, the whole Sects and sorts of Christians Orientall . . . convened togither, which were about the number of 6000 men, women, and children: for being separated by the Patriarks, in two companies, they compassed the Chapell of the holy Grave nine times; holding in their hands burning Candles, made in the beginning pittifull, and lamentable regreetings, but in the ending, there were touking of kettledrummes, sounding of horne-trumpets, and other instruments, dauncing, leaping, and running about the Sepulchre, with an intollerable tumult, as if they were all mad, or distracted of their wits. Thus is the prograce of their procession performed in meere simplicitie, wanting civilitie, and governement. But the Turkes have a care of that; for in the middest of all this hurly burly, they runne amongst them with long rods, correcting their misbehavior with cruell stroakes; thus are these slavish people, even at the height of their ceremonious devotion strangely abused.[2]

There is no hint here of any awareness that the devout claimed that a miracle had occurred. Probably Lithgow did not clearly comprehend just what was in progress nor why the drums beat and the trumpets sounded. Had he understood what it was supposed was going on, he would not have foregone the opportunity to deride such folly. Doubtless he and all European visitors assumed that the scornful laughter of the Turks and their barbarous beatings of the poor Christians were prompted by mere heartlessness and hostility and the desire to exhibit their power over men who were at their mercy. There seems to have been no understanding of the fact that the ceremonies memorializing the death and resurrection of Jesus Christ were peculiarly profane to the Mohammedan mind. It is significant that no such scenes of ribald laughter and cruelty are recorded as occurring at the Manger in Bethlehem.[3]

---

1 Records of the Holy Fire go back to the historians of the Crusades; the miracle is mentioned by various medieval pilgrims. See Beazley, op.cit., ii,173 and Warner's note in the Roxburghe Club edition of *Mandeville*, chapter xi.

2 *Rare Adventures*, p.240. Compare *A Most Delectable and True Discourse*, Sig. Q₂f.

3 Guylford's chaplain (*Pylgrymage*, p.36) tells us that the Sultan of Egypt intended to tear down the Church of the Nativity at Bethlehem and use its stones to build

From the Garden of the Agony and from the Mount of Olives Christians saw afar off the magnificent mosque in the Temple Area, the Dome of the Rock. The claim made by the author of *Mandeville*, that personal letters presented by him from the Sultan of Egypt won for him permission to visit the 'temple,' [1] may indubitably be numbered among his many lies; for until comparatively recent years no Christian was permitted to come into any part of the *Haram al-Sharif*, the August Sanctuary. Guylford's chaplain is emphatic on this point: 'The Sarrasyns woll suffre no cristen man to come within the sayd Temple, and if he do he shall be compelled incontynently to renye his fayth and crystendome, or ellys he shalbe put to execution of deth by and by.' [2] A century later, Moryson, writing of the whole Area, says: 'In the middest thereof the Turkes had a Mosche for their wicked worship of Mahomet, neither may any Christian come within this circuit, much lesse into the Mosche, either being a capitall offence.' [3] A quaint explanation of this prohibition was that Allah promised that all prayers said in the Temple Area would be granted, and were the Christians allowed to enter they would pray for the downfall of Mohammedanism—'ce qu'ils obtiendroient infalliblement,' adds ironically the French writer who reports this.[4] A good deal of discussion among modern scholars as to the contradictions between the actual structure of the Dome of the Rock and early European pictures of it [5] would have been avoided had the rule

a palace at Cairo but was so frightened by a 'houge, grete serpent' that he abandoned his plan. The story betrays an unawareness of the fact that Moslems pay homage to the place of the birth of Jesus. Lithgow knew better; he notes that Mohammedans 'doe so reverence this monument of Christs birth, as they creepe groveling upon hands and knees to kisse the said stone,' that is, 'a marked stone in the pavement, in which verie place they say the Redeemer of the world was borne' (*Rare Adventures*, p.246).
1 *Mandeville*, chapter xii.
2 *Pylgrymage*, pp.43f.
3 *Itinerary*, ii,8. Compare Lithgow, *Rare Adventures*, p.224.
4 Des Hayes de Courmenin, *Voiage du Levant*, 1624, pp.341f.
5 Erhard Reuwich's famous drawing of the Dome of the Rock in Bernard von Breydenbach's *Peregrinationes in Terram Sanctam* (Mainz, 1486) shows a dome swollen at the base and culminating in a point, a form which it had at no stage in its history. The best explanation of this distortion is that the drawing was made from memory. Adapting the drawing of some unidentified artist (certainly not Reuwich), Carpaccio put the mosque into the background of two of his pictures, the Saint George with the dead dragon in the Schiavoni at Venice and the Preaching of Saint Stephen in the Louvre. (See F.Gilles de la Tourette, *L'Orient et les Peintres de Venise*, pp.137f.). It is recognizable also in the Maries at the Sepulchre attributed to Hubert Van Eyck

against the near approach of Christians been kept in mind. The mosque seen by fifteenth and early sixteenth century travellers such as Breydenbach and Guylford differed considerably, in colour rather than in general form, from the appearance which it presented to later visitors such as Lithgow and Moryson; for Solyman the Magnificent caused most of the exterior decoration in glazed tiles to be added and many of the windows to be pierced through the walls. What we see today, allowance being made for restorations not always skilful, is what travellers saw at the beginning of the seventeenth century.

Pilgrims generally made the long descent from Jerusalem through the Wilderness of Judea to Jericho, the Jordan Valley, and the Dead Sea. Not everyone was so bold as to undertake this journey, for in this lawless region to the danger of Mohammedan fanaticism was added the rapacity of the bedouin tribes. 'We had a great desire to see these places,' says Moryson, 'but were discouraged from that attempt, by the fear of the Arabians and Moores.' [1] Lithgow, loyal to his resolve to rely solely on his own stout legs, made the entire journey on foot, trudging beside his companions who rode donkeys. In the badlands on the hither side of Jordan, while this company floundered through sandy morass, Arabs secreted in the hillocks showered them with arrows. Fortunately no one was wounded. [2] Pilgrims bathed in the Jordan and regularly carried some of its water with them on their return to Europe. It was believed to be virtuous and to have the property of remaining sweet an indefinite time. [3] More out of curiosity than from piety some

---

and in Raphael's Sposalizio. The adaptations of the design of the mosque seen in these paintings and in various Christian churches must have been based, at best, upon drawings made from a distance and probably in haste.

1 *Itinerary*, ii,17.

2 *Rare Adventures*, pp.225f.

3 'Jordan' in the sense of a chamber-pot has been thought to derive from 'Jordan bottle' in which pilgrims carried home the water of the river, through the intermediate sense of a vessel used by alchemists and physicians; but the etymology is doubtful. Jordan almonds are from *jardyne* almonds, i.e., 'de jardin,' and have nothing to do with the river. Compare the well-known false etymology by which the *girasole* (sun-flower) artichoke has become the Jerusalem artichoke.—The notion that the Jordan rose from two springs, the Jor and the Dan, on the slopes of Mount Hermon arose from the location of the tribe of Dan there. The appropriate name Dan for a source required a companion source, Jor. Saint Gerome (Commentary on Matthew, xvi,13) mentions the etymology without approving it. Through Isidore of Seville and later encyclopaedists and through accounts of several pilgrims it came

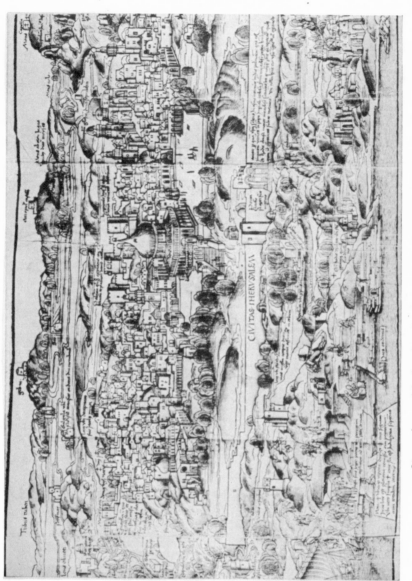

Jerusalem, with the Temple Area and the Dome of the Rock

pilgrims went down to the shore of the Dead Sea,[1] and the intrepid Lithgow seems even to have ventured some distance along its eastern bank among the foot-hills of Moab.

IV

THE grand Levantine tour of some Englishmen embraced Syria and Egypt as well as Palestine. What was their impression of Damascus? Whether one enters Damascus from the defiles of Lebanon or from the rock-strewn Hauran, the impression which the city makes upon the stranger is the same today, despite the ravages wrought by the invasion of European tawdriness, as it made upon travellers three centuries ago. It is still 'the great and splendid Arab city set in a girdle of fruit trees and filled with the murmur of running water.' [2] Englishmen brought home the names which Mohammedans attach to it: a Garden of God, an Earthly Paradise; [3] and told

to the Elizabethans. See, e.g., *Batman uppon Bartholome*, xviii, chapter 9. Lithgow, for once willing to depend upon hearsay, writes: 'This River Jordan beginneth in Mount Libanus, of two Fountaines, Jore and Dan' (*Rare Adventures*, p.229). On the map of the 'Pars Tribus Dan' in Fuller's *Pisgah-Sight of Palestine* (ii,p.106, §7) we see 'Jor Fons' and 'Dan Fons.' Compare Milton's 'double-founted stream' (*Paradise Lost*, xii,145). See further Beazley, op.cit., i,109.

1 Many notions were attached to the Dead Sea: that beneath it was hell; that the ruins of Sodom and Gomorrah were on its shore or to be seen beneath its surface; that the pillar of salt still stood on the shore though difficult of access; that fish washed down from the Jordan floated dead upon its mephitic waters; that birds attempting to fly across it fell into it, killed by the exhalations; that though a living person could not sink in it a corpse sank to the bottom; and so forth. The Idle Lake in *The Faerie Queene* (II,vi,46) probably owes to the Dead Sea the property of bearing up a man in its sluggish waters 'engrost with mud.' On the shore of the Dead Sea grew the Apples of Sodom or Dead Sea Fruit, fair to outward view but filled with ashes and bitter to the taste (Tacitus, v,7; Josephus, IV,viii,4; Golding's Solinus, p.159; Vincent of Beauvais, *Speculum historiale*, i, chapter 67; *Mandeville*, chapter xiii; *Cleanness*, 1042f.; Caxton, *The Mirrour of the World*, ed. Prior, E.E.T.S., p.90 and notes; and so forth). Renaissance travellers differ about this natural curiosity. Father Castela (*Le Sainct Voyage*, p.459) writes as though he had seen and handled the fruit but doubtless he was relying upon ancient tradition or the even more dubious authority of a dragoman. Lithgow cites Josephus but 'affirms the contrary' for 'there is not such a thing . . . as either Trees or Bushes grow neere to Sodom by many miles' (Purchas, x,489; this is altered in *Rare Adventures*, p.228, to 'by three miles,' an instance of Lithgow's revision for greater accuracy). The nineteenth-century traveller Robert Curzon identified the fruit with a species of gall-nut (*Monasteries of the Levant*, ed. D.G.Hogarth, 1916, pp.228f.). Modern scholars hold that the description of the 'vine of Sodom' in Deuteronomy, xxxii,32, is purely figurative, no actual fruit being intended. The most impressive imaginative uses of this piece of nature-lore are in Webster, *The White Devil*, III,i, and Milton, *Paradise Lost*, x,562f.

2 Gertrude L.Bell, *Syria: The Desert and the Sown*, 1907, p.133.

3 Lithgow, *Rare Adventures*, p.184.

the story that when Mahomet approached Damascus he refused to enter in lest the pleasantness thereof move him to
abide therein and ravish his thoughts and desires from heaven.[1]
The associations of the words damask and damascene with
ideas of beauty and luxury and exquisite craftsmanship and
with a sense of refreshment are due in part to the city's reputation for wealth and ease and voluptuousness as well as to the
quality of the commodities that came thence.[2] Biblical associations centred in memories of Saint Paul's sojourn in the city;
and there was also the ancient legend that Adam was created
in a field near by and that Cain slew Abel at Damascus.[3]

Englishmen say little about the Mohammedans of Damascus.
The most interesting portion of Biddulph's letters is that which
has to do with the region of the Lebanon. He gives an intelligent
account of the Maronites and repeats the popularly accepted
notion of the Druses: that they were descendants of the Crusaders who, remaining in Syria and driven to the mountains by
the Saracens, forgot Christianity while retaining certain
Christian forms of worship. Biddulph penetrated far into the
recesses of Mount Lebanon and was disappointed to find that
the famous cedar-trees were now very scarce. This was the
report brought home by all Englishmen. Lithgow thought that
their paucity was more than atoned for by their immensity;
their tops, he says, 'do kisse or enhance the lower cloudes, making their grandure over-looke the highest bodies of all other
aspiring trees.'[4] Sanderson, on the other hand, says that they
are 'of indifferent bignes but not very hudge.'[5]

---

1 Biddulph, *Travels of Foure English Men and a Preacher*, p.79.
2 Damask, a stuff, damson, a fruit, and damascene metal-work reveal their origin in
their names. Damask-roses, first imported into England in the reign of Henry VIII
(Hakluyt, v,229f.), were mixed in colour, red and white (*As You Like It*, III,v,123).
Viola's cheek was 'damask' and among the wares of Autolycus were 'gloves as sweet
as damask roses.' Damask-water was a perfume distilled from this rose and damask-
powder a toilet preparation (see John Rastell, *The Nature of the Four Elements*,
Hazlitt's Dodsley, i,44; Thomas Heywood, *The Royal King and the Loyal Subject*,
IV, *Works*, vi,70). Dekker's costermongers sell 'fine apples of Damascus' (*Old
Fortunatus*, IV,ii).
3 Chaucer, *Canterbury Tales*, *Monk's Tale*, 'Adam'; and Skeat's note on the passage.
Compare *Mandeville*, chapter xiv. Compare also *1 Henry VI*, I,iii,39f.:

> This be Damascus, be thou cursed Cain,
> To slay thy brother Abel, if thou wilt.

4 *Rare Adventures*, pp.170f.
5 *Travels in the Levant*, p.118.

It is surprising that the magnificent ruins of Baalbec, set so conspicuously in the long broad valley between Lebanon and Anti-Lebanon, did not attract the special attention of Englishmen. At that time the temple of Bacchus was practically intact and worship was conducted in the mosque which now lies crushed in ruins beneath pillars which were thrown down by an earthquake in the eighteenth century. Of the gigantic columns of the temple of Jupiter at least nine were then standing whereas only six are erect today. French travellers of the Renaissance described the ruins intelligently,[1] but not till the close of the seventeenth century were they described and illustrated by an Englishman.[2]

Of northern Syria and especially of the city of Aleppo we shall hear more in later chapters. English factors were established there and at Tripoli. The impression we receive from their descriptions and reports is that their minds were upon their business and that Syria, unlike Palestine, did not deeply move the English imagination.

Not so Egypt. There was a ready demand for accounts of the ancient marvels of the Land of Nile. To the Elizabethans as to ourselves the mention of Egypt evoked associations with the mighty river. The mysterious problem of its annual rise and fall[3] was connected with the yet

1 Bertrandon de la Brocquière, *Travels*, translated by Thomas Johnes, p.149; Pierre Belon, *Observations*, folio 152ᵛ.
2 Henry Maundrell, *A Journey from Aleppo to Jerusalem*, Oxford, 1703, pp.133f. Maundrell illustrates his remarks with two engravings, one an attempted reconstruction, the other a general view which shows considerably more of the ruins standing than are erect today.
3 'We seeke to know the strange cause of th'ebs and flouds of Nile,' says John Davies of Hereford (*Nosce Teipsum, Works*, ed. Grosart, i,49). The Earl of Stirling considers all explanations doubtful (*Doomes-Day*, Third Hour, stanza 75). Sir Thomas Browne attempts no explanation but refutes the belief that the phenomenon is unique (*Vulgar Errors*, vi,7). George Sandys (*Relation of a Journey*, p.95) has a copperplate illustration of the figure of Nilus in the Vatican and explains that each cupidlike child playing about the river-god represents one cubit of the annual rise of the river. Shackerly Marmion (*The Antiquary*, I,i; Hazlitt's Dodsley, xiii,429) has the simile: 'A face rugged as Father Nilus is pictured on the hangings,' that is, on a piece of tapestry. The use of the Nilometer or Nilescope, reported by Pliny, Strabo and Plutarch, was observed and reported by travellers of our period (e.g., Sir Henry Blount, *A Voyage into the Levant*, p.39). Strabo described the one on the island of Elephantine at Aswân but that on the island of Rôda near Cairo (still in use), which dates from the eighth century A.D., is the one generally described by English travellers. Its comparative proximity to the pyramids of Gîza probably accounts for Shakespeare's error in placing the instrument in the pyramid (*Anthony and Cleopatra*, II,vii,20f.).

more mysterious problem of its source [1] and with the fe-
cundity of the river-valley. [2] Since classical times its fertility

1 See Fletcher's beautiful masque in *The False One* (III,iv,22f.) in which Isis and
the Seven 'conceal'd Heads' of Nilus take part. Medieval geographers sometimes
use the Latin *caput* not for the source but for the mouth of a river, and this ambiguous
terminology survives in Elizabethan English. In Dekker's 'seven-headed Nilus' (*The
Seven Deadly Sinnes of London*, p.57) we cannot be sure whether the sources or the
mouths are intended (compare Marlowe's 'fifty-headed' Volga, *1 Tamburlaine*,
I,ii,103). Seven was the traditional number of the branches of the Nile in the delta
(Herodotus, Strabo; Pliny says eleven). Hence the phrases 'seven-fold Nile' and
'seven-mouthed Nile' in the literature of the period (*The Faerie Queene*, I,v,18;
Greene, *Orlando Furioso*, I,i; Barnes, *The Devil's Charter*, IV,v; the anonymous
Caesar's Revenge, I,ii; *Paradise Lost*, xii,157). But there was discussion about the
conflicting testimony (Blount, *A Voyage into the Levant*, p.57; Sir Thomas Browne,
Vulgar Errors, vi,8; Fuller, *A Pisgah-Sight of Palestine*, iv,pp.80f.). Sebastian Munster's map of Africa shows three mouths and his map of Lower Egypt nine (*Cosmographiae Universalis Libri VI*, ed. 1550, pp.1113 and 1127). Belon writes of two
navigable branches but his full-page 'portrait' of Alexandria shows seven branches
flowing through the city (*Observations*, folios 92ᵛ and 94ᵛ). Lithgow notes the disagreement of ancient authorities and cites some modern writers who allege there
are four of which the chiefest are Damiota and Roseta but continues with the round
assertion: 'This is false . . . for it hath now eight several mouthes' (*Rare Adventures*, p.281). In Fletcher's masque and in Caesar's threat to the Egyptians that the
Nile may 'raise his seven heads and devour ye' (*The False One*, II,i,216f.) and in
Daniel's

> Draw back thy waters flow
> To thy concealed head

(*Cleopatra*, V,ii) there is no ambiguity; the sources are intended. The mystery of
the river's source or sources supplied writers with a picturesque figure of speech.
'Sans naissance non plus que la riviere du Nil,' says Montaigne (*Essais*, iii,5).
'Which like to Nilus yet doth hide his head' is a simile of Nashe's (*Summers Last
Will and Testament*; *Works*, iii,250). Compare Anthony Brewer, *Lingua*, III,vi;
Hazlitt's Dodsley, ix,401; Jasper Fisher, *Fuimus Troes*, V,i; ibid., xii,523; the anonymous *Tragedy of Tiberius*, l.2931; John Wilson, *The Cheats*, III,iii,141. The old
idea that the Nile was to be identified with the Pison or the Gihon, rivers flowing
from the Garden of Eden, had not completely disappeared (see, e.g., *Batman uppon
Bartholome*, xiii,5; Cartwright, *The Preachers Travels*, p.93; Henry de Beauvau,
Relation Journalière du Voyage du Levant, p.215). Sometimes, as in John Pory's
translation (1600) of Leo Africanus, the idea of the subterranean course of the Nile
is divorced from the notion of its rise in Eden. John Donne commits the common
error in old cosmographies of confusing the Nile and the Niger and tells how the
latter river 'enwombs it self into the earth' (*A Funerall Elegie*, ll.41f.). Father Peter
Paez's claim to have discovered the 'two fountains' whence the Nile gushes forth
dates from 1618 (see J.L.Lowes, *The Road to Xanadu*, p.370 and p.589, note 34).
In general it was pretty well understood, or rather shrewdly guessed, that the annual
rise was occasioned by the melting of snows so far away that months passed before
flood-water reached Egypt. When Lithgow says (*Rare Adventures*, p.281) that the
Sultan of Turkey is forced to pay a yearly tribute to Prester John lest 'he impede
or withdraw the course of Nylus' he is repeating a report which had been current
for long before his time. To the belief that there is a king in the South who dams up

2 The magnificent pageant of the Nile in *The False One* displays the abundant riches
of Ptolemaic Egypt:

> We owe for all this wealth to the old Nilus;
> We need no dropping rain to cheer the husbandman,
> Nor merchant that ploughs up the sea to seek us;
> Within the wealthy womb of reverend Nilus
> All this is nourish'd (III,iv,22f.).

had given rise to the notion of spontaneous generation from the slime left by the receding waters; [1] and from the volume of its waters came the belief that the noise of the cataracts deafened the dwellers upon its banks. [2] The pyramids inspired awe and wonder, speculation as to the purposes for which they were constructed, [3] meditations upon the vanity of regal

the Nile water and releases it at his pleasure George Sandys (*A Relation of a Journey*, p.98) offers the objection: 'What damme can contain such a confluence of waters?' To conclude with this matter, it may be noted that at the end of the seventeenth century the Flemish traveller Cornelis Bruin (*Voyage au Levant*, 1700, chapter xli) passes in review all theories regarding the source and annual rise of the Nile and recommends the problem to the Jesuits who are 'les plus abiles et les plus rusez faiseurs de recherches qu'il y ait au monde'—interesting testimony to the part played by the Jesuits in building the foundations for a scientific orientalism (see Pierre Martino, *L'Orient dans la littérature française*, 1906, pp.115f.).

1 Referred to by Lucretius, Diodorus Siculus, and especially Ovid (*Metamorphoses*, i,416f.; xv,362f. and 375f.). For no very apparent reason this idea of the monstrous spawn of Nile appealed to Spenser; he refers to it three times in *The Faerie Queene* (IV,xi,20; I,i,21; III,vi,8). The first reference is a simple statement; the second with elaborate detail; the third with special attention to the fertilizing power of the sun. Shakespeare describes the sun as 'the fire that quickens Nilus slime' (*Anthony and Cleopatra*, I,iii,69; compare II,vii,31f.). Elizabethan poetry contains many allusions to monsters, serpents, toads, crocodiles, rats, and so forth hatched or bred upon the banks of Nile. See, e.g., Fletcher, *The Maid's Tragedy*, IV,i,232f. (the passage is not by Beaumont); Marston, *The Scourge of Villainy*, vi,66f. and vii,15; Shirley, *The Traitor*, III,i and IV,ii, and *Love Tricks*, II,i; Jasper Fisher, *Fuimus Troes*, III,v; and (of later date) Dryden, *Aureng-Zebe*, II; *All For Love*, V; *Cleomenes*, II,ii (*Dramatic Works*, ed. Summers, iv,104 and 251,vi,348); Pope, *Essay on Criticism*, 40f.

2 The idea had been a commonplace of geographers since Pliny. Lithgow (*Rare Adventures*, p.280) and Sandys (*Relation of a Journey*, p.93) tell of the phenomenon, but neither journeyed so far south as the First Cataract. Petrarch's simile derived from the deafening 'romore' of the Nile (Sonnet lxviii) probably influenced English poets. Compare Massinger, *The Roman Actor*, V,i, and *Valentinian*, V,iv,42f. (the passage is not by Fletcher); J. Gough, *The Strange Discovery*, 1640, I,i; Dekker, *Newes from Graves-ende*, *Plague Pamphlets*, p.94; Shirley, *The Witty Fair One*, III,iv; Sir Aston Cockayne, *The Obstinate Lady*, IV,ii; John Wilson, *The Cheats*, I,iii,110; and Drayton, *Poly-Olbion*, xiii,23f., *Works*, ed. J.W.Hebel, iv,571, where the notion is transferred from Egypt to Westmorland. Montaigne gave a new turn to the idea, suggesting that the inhabitants of the river banks were not deafened by the sound but merely so accustomed to it as to disregard it; and he draws an analogy to the music of the spheres (*Essais*, i,23; the commentators on Montaigne refer to Cicero's *Dream of Scipio*). Anthony Brewer, echoing Montaigne, says of the harmony of the spheres: 'Our ears are so well acquainted with the sound that we never mark it. As I remember, the Egyptians Catadupes never heard the roaring of the fall of Nilus, because the noise was so familiar to them' (*Lingua*, III,vii; Hazlitt's Dodsley, ix,409). Here κατάδουποι, 'down-thud,' properly used of the cataracts themselves, is used in the transferred meaning of dwellers by the cataracts. Thomas Lodge uses the term figuratively: 'In the Catadupe of my knowledge, I nourish the Crocodile of my conceit' (*Wits Miserie and the Worlds Madnesse*, 1596; *Works*, Hunterian Club, iv,29).

3 Writers of the Renaissance are practically unanimous in holding that the pyramids are tombs. The old opinion had been that they were granaries. The author of *Mandeville*, here more than usually perverse (since his source, Boldensele, whom he wilfully defies, is correct), holds that they are the garners built by Joseph for King Pharaoh. 'Summen seyn that thei ben sepultures of grete lords . . . but that is not trewe.' Else, he argues feebly, why the gates to them? And why are they hollow

pride,[1] and strangely inexact descriptions of their shape and size.[2] Christian visitors to Egypt thought of the biblical associations of the land; and innumerable in Elizabethan literature are the allusions to the captivity of the Israelites and to the plagues inflicted upon the Egyptians. More picturesque, because unwarranted by Scripture, were the sites connected with the Holy Family during their Egyptian exile from Herod's wrath. Visitors were conducted to the chapel built on the site where Mary took refuge with the infant Jesus; to the very house where Joseph and Mary lived; to the fig-tree under which the Mother and Child reposed; to the well which was opened for the Blessed Virgin's refreshment by the stroke of an angel's wings.[3]

inside? Besides, 'yee may wel knowe that tombes and sepultures ne ben not made of such gretness ne of such highness'—a beautiful example of question-begging (chapter vii).

1 The thought inspires Richard Knolles to one of his finest passages, in which he describes these 'monuments of the barbarous Egyptian Kings vanity; whose proud Names and Titles time hath worn out of those huge and wonderful Buildings, of purpose made for the vain eternizing of their fame and endless wealth . . . Yet are those places of a loathsome smell, and for darkness thereof, dreadful to behold' (Generall History of the Turkes, ed. 1687, i,369f.). In Fletcher the pyramids inspire the most eloquent passage in all his plays, when Julius Caesar, standing by the body of Pompey, addresses the Egyptians (The False One, II,i,149f.).

2 For descriptions of the interior of the Great Pyramid by travellers who had explored it see Belon, Observations, folio 113[r]f.; John Evesham, 'Voyage into Egypt' (1586), Hakluyt, vi,37; Blount, Voyage into the Levant, pp.45f.; Lithgow, Rare Adventures, pp.275f. One of the plates in Sandys's Relation (p.130) is a cross-section of the interior. Evesham estimated its height as 'twise the heigth of Paules steeple.' Lithgow greatly exaggerated the height of all the pyramids, giving 1126 feet as the altitude of the largest. From the top he made the usual experiment with an arrow, which fell well within the building's base. Richard Knolles (op.cit., i,370) says that some travellers, having climbed to the top of the pyramids, report that 'for the great height of them a man cannot shoot an Arrow so high as the Midst of the lower Tower whereon the Spire standeth.' This is very odd indeed. What was his mental picture of the pyramids? What was the spire? the lower tower? If he, who was steeped in Levantine travel-lore, could betray such confusion, what concept did other men have of the pyramids? Marlowe refers to the pyramids 'which Julius Caesar brought from Africa' (Doctor Faustus, III,i,46f.; compare Dido, III,i,121f.; Massacre at Paris, Sc.ii,ll.43f.). Here he probably means 'obelisk'; the two words were used interchangeably; compare Lithgow, p.276f. and Heywood, The English Traveller, I,i: 'The great pyramid reared in the forum, on four lions mounted' (where all editions read: 'reared in the front'—the necessary emendation is obvious). The confusion between the two words may have caused the confused concept of the shape of the pyramids: on almost all maps and views of the period they are drawn too taperingly; sometimes as spires; once like little match-boxes set on end. See, e.g., Munster, Cosmography, ed. cit., pp.1127 and 1134; H.W.Davies, Bernard von Breydenbach and his Journey to the Holy Land, plate 28; Sandys, Relation of a Journey, pp.50 and 128 (the latter view fairly accurate); J.H.Van Linschoten, Discourse of Voyages, 1598 (the map is reproduced in the MacLehose Hakluyt, vi,176). Even in Thomas Fuller's bird's-eye map of Egypt in A Pisgah-Sight the pyramids, of which but two are depicted, are drawn as slender spires.

3 Hakluyt, v,338 and vi,35f.; Blount, A Voyage into the Levant, p.44; Bruin, Voyage

The Pyramids

Far more closely in Cairo than in Jerusalem were Englishmen brought into contact with the Moslems, for whereas in the Holy City Christian visitors were under the care of Franciscans, in Cairo they had to shift for themselves more or less and depended upon the guidance of their dragomans ('trunchmen'). To attempt a review of the descriptions of Cairo written by travellers of our period would be, as in the like cases of Jerusalem and Constantinople, to enact the functions of a guide-book. Little building of historic or artistic importance has been done there since the Turkish conquest of 1517.[1] To most of the mosques additions and alterations have been made; but of late there has been a good deal of intelligent restoration that has brought some of them back to the appearance they presented in the sixteenth century. Old dwellings have for the most part disappeared; even the famous House of Gamal ed-Din ez-Zahabi, the best preserved example of a home of the wealthy mercantile class to which such a traveller as Sir Henry Blount had letters of introduction, dates only from 1637. New quarters have grown up or been incorporated in the city here and there, and in the nineteenth century a whole European section developed, while thoroughfares were driven through mazes of old streets. In the main, however, the great sights of the city—the mosques and bazaars and citadel and necropolis and the Coptic churches—which the visitor sees today are what the traveller saw three or four hundred years ago.

Of the abundant bustling life of Cairo we have a vivid picture in Lithgow's narrative. He calls it 'this incorporate World, . . . the most admirable and greatest City seene upon the earth,' in which a score of races of men, 'all sorts of Christians' and 'the infinite number of Infidels,' meet and chaffer and are 'diabolically given to all sorts of abhominations.' It was characteristic of this stout pedestrian to put to the test of his 'bruised feete' the dimensions of the place, and round its periphery he walked in what he describes as 'one of

au Levant, chapter 35; and Father Castela, *Le Sainct Voyage*, in the course of his long description of Cairo.

[1] The chief exception is the so-called Alabaster Mosque which was built during the nineteenth century.

the sorest dayes journey that ever I had in my life.'[1] In the older quarters of Cairo the life of the streets was then much the same as it is today. Porters bore their heavy burdens to and fro. Donkey-boys ran behind their mounted clients, thwacking their lazy beasts. Here or there a snake-charmer crouched, playing upon his cithern. Blind people and people with sore eyes and multitudes of beggars; the water-vendors with their bulging goatskins; the sellers of dried cow-dung for fuel because of the scarcity of wood—these and a score of other picturesque details show that Cairene life has changed but little since Lithgow and Blount and Sandys were there. The slave-market was a curiosity to be visited by those of not too tender susceptibilities. A great spectacle was that of the assembling and departure of the Meccan *Haj*. Europeans provided with introductions had opportunities to meet representatives of the higher classes of native society and were impressed with their hospitality and culture. But the effect produced by contact with the masses of the people was less agreeable. 'Extremely addicted to Cozening and Cheating' is Joseph Pitts's verdict on the Cairenes at a somewhat later date; and the mild comment of a French traveller who found it necessary to anchor his boat in mid-Nile as a precaution against brigandage by night is: 'L'une des plus grandes incommoditez qu'il y ait en Egypt est celles des Arabes.' Much the same may be said in the twentieth century![2]

To avoid the rigours of the Sinai desert travellers more often then than now went by sea from Alexandria to Joppa. In a later chapter we shall hear of the adventures of certain Englishmen who were held captive in Alexandria and made their escape. The wealth and commerce of the great seaport touched Marlowe's imagination; his Barabas had 'merchandise untold' in storage there and looked for the coming thence of an argosy.[3] From Aristotle, Strabo, or Pliny

1 *Rare Adventures*, pp.267f.
2 Blount, *A Voyage into the Levant*, especially p.45; Bruin, *Voyage au Levant*, chapter 35; Joseph Pitts, *A True and Faithful Account*, Exeter, 1704; Jouvin, *Le Voyageur d'Europe*, Part vii,p.21; Monconys, *Journal des Voyages*, Lyons, 1665.
3 *The Jew of Malta*, I,i; IV,i. Robert Greene, *Frair Bacon and Friar Bungay*, Scene ix, writes of 'rich Alexandria drugs fetched by carvels.' In *A Knack to Know a Knave* (Hazlitt's Dodsley, vi,570) 'arras hanging' is brought into England from Alexandria.

Marlowe may have learned of the ancient canal connecting the Nile and the Red Sea; he makes his Tamburlaine announce his grandiose design to cut a channel to the Red Sea 'that men might quickly sail to India.' [1]

V

LET us now imagine a company of pilgrims and travellers assembled together at Jerusalem shortly before their departure on the homeward voyage. Some will have been northward into Syria; others will have included Egypt in their itinerary; the majority will have been satisfied with the sight of Jerusalem and the neighbouring places of blessed memories. Into the state of mind of the Roman Catholic pilgrim we need not inquire. But what was the attitude of English Protestant visitors towards the Holy Places and the wonders connected therewith as related to them by their guides, the Franciscans? Thomas Nashe warns those pilgrims who spend half their days in visiting Jerusalem that 'ungainfully you consume good houres,' because 'that Sepulcher which you peregrinate to adore . . . is but a thing built up by Saracens to get mony with, and beguile votive Christians.' [2] This is an egregious libel upon Islam. In the face of the express statement in the *Koran* that Jesus did not die, it is inconceivable that Mohammedans would have manufactured a monument in memory of His death. No Christian visitor—not even a rabid Protestant like Lithgow—either questioned the authenticity of the Tomb

---

1 2 *Tamburlaine*, V,iii,133f. In Ariosto's *Orlando Furioso*, xv, stanza 40, Astolfo on his magical horse flies over 'Trajan's channel,' that is, the canal by which Trajan joined the Nile and the Red Sea. Sir Thomas Browne, *Vulgar Errors*, vi,8, refutes the belief that the old canal was a direct connection from the Mediterranean to the Red Sea. After the discovery of the route to India by the Cape of Good Hope, the Venetians, threatened by the Portuguese with the loss of their trade to the Far East, began negotiations with the Mameluke sultans for the building of a new canal; but the Turkish conquest of Egypt (1517) put an end to this scheme. Later in the century the Turkish governor of Egypt made a beginning with a new attempt; but that, too, came to nothing. On Linschoten's map of Egypt (*Discourse of Voyages unto the Easte and Weste Indies*, 1598; the map is reproduced in the MacLehose Hakluyt, vi,176) the route of the canal is shown, with this annotation: 'A diche begonne in auncient tyme and somewhat attempted of late by Sinan the Bassa to joyne both the Seas together.' Jasper Fisher, *Fuimus Troes*, V,i (Hazlitt's Dodsley, xii,523), uses the project as a figure for something difficult, if not impossible, to accomplish; rather than do such-and-such, 'dig that isthmus down which ties great Afric.' On the ancient canal see further P.K.Hitti, *History of the Arabs*, 1937, pp.32 and 58.

2 *Pierce Penilesse; Works*, i,183.

or suspected the Moslems of palming off an imposture. Their doubts were directed against the extravagances of superstition and the fantastic legends associated with other Holy Places. At Bethlehem even Moryson could not forbear to laugh at the notion of a star coming down through the roof of a church.[1] Moryson is always careful to caution his readers that he sets down precisely what has been shown and told him without guaranteeing the authenticity of any place or the truth of what has been said about it. Lithgow is often more outspoken in criticism. Thus, having been shown the house of Dives he remarks that everyone holds the story of Dives to be a parable 'and although it were a History, who can demonstrate the particular place, Jerusalem having beene so often transformed by alterations?' Again, when shown the fissure in the rock on Mount Calvary, his comment is that 'the slit lookes as if it had been cleft with wedges and beetles' and he derides 'these soule-sunke Friers' who forget that it was the Temple, not the rock, which was rent in twain.[2] (Needless to say, it is Lithgow's memory of the Gospel narrative that is at fault.) William Biddulph discusses at length the distinctions among 'Apparent Truths,' 'Manifest Untruths,' and 'Things Doubt-ful' at Jerusalem. An example of matters in the first category is the site of the city, which, with insignificant shiftings of its boundaries, is undoubtedly the same as in antiquity; of the second, the hole in the roof of the Church of the Nativity through which the star of the Magi descended; of the third, the story of Saint Veronica.[3]

Without note-books and journals (supplemented by one or another of the numerous guide-books and manuals of devotion)

---

1 *Itinerary*, ii,22. William Wey, who wrote part of his first *Itinerary* in execrable verse ('The way to Jerusalem and the Holy Placys in that Same Contre,' *Itineraries*, p.18), has this to say of the star:

> In a depe chapel, tel yow I wyl,
> Where seynt Jerome translatyd the bybyl . . .
> By thys ther ys a place ryght nere
> Of Innocentys scleyne the sepucure . . .
> The ster also the kyngys dyd lede
> Fyl downe yn an hole on that stede [place].

See also, on the 'Cisterne de l'etoille,' Father Castela, *Le Sainct Voyage*, p.391.
2 *Rare Adventures*, pp.221f.,238.
3 *Travels of Foure English Men and a Preacher*, Letter iv.

visitors to Jerusalem could not have kept in mind all they saw and heard. Moryson, as we saw in the previous chapter, advises the traveller to carry with him 'tables' upon which to jot down notes and impressions which he can copy and expand at leisure at his inn. At several points in his *Travailes of Two English Pilgrimes* Henry Timberlake gives us glimpses of the conscientious diarist. After his first long day making the rounds of the Holy Places he was weary of seeing new things and of praying at each site; but before he could go to bed he had, he says, 'much to do in writing my notes out of my table-book.' Again, when locked up with other pilgrims in the Church of the Holy Sepulchre, he was busy all night observing and 'writing down all things I thought note-worthy.'

Pilgrims, then as now, carried away with them relics and souvenirs. Sir Richard Guylforde's companions (Guylforde himself was now dead) were entertained before their departure at 'a right honest dyner' by the Warden and friars of Mount Sion, and after the repast each pilgrim was given a packet containing relics, 'which we toke as devoutly as we coude, and thanked accordyng.'[1] After his return to England William Wey gave to the chapel at Eton College a quantity of such relics—vestments, hangings, little models of the Holy Places, and, along with much else, 'a borde byhynde the queer the length of our Lorde ys sepulkyr.'[2] That is, this board was to be set up in the retrochoir in approximation to the custom obtaining in Christendom of erecting a structure in imitation of the Lord's Tomb. From certain 'poore Christians' John Sanderson purchased 'Crosses, Pater-Nosters, Beades, Rosaries' (made, he was told, from wood from the Mount of Olives), and two girdles the length of the Sepulchre; and from some poor nuns he bought some 'trifles of needle-worke.'[3] Lithgow purchased, besides many other things, not only a girdle but 'a paire of Garters of the Holy Grave, all richly wrought in silke and gold, having this inscription at every end of them in golden letters, Sancto Sepulchro, and the word Jerusalem.'

1 *Pylgrymage*, p.39.
2 On the fly-leaf of the manuscript of the *Itineraries* is a list of 'goodys' which Wey gave to the chapel; see *Itineraries*, Roxburghe Club edition.
3 *Travels in the Levant*, p.110; Purchas, ix,468f.

But he treasured most the turpentine rod, more than three yards long, which he had cut on the banks of Jordan and which he later presented to King James.[1] Moryson enters into many particulars about the articles he saw for sale: 'Divers toies . . . being of no worth, save onely that they were far fetcht, namely, beades for Papists to number their praiers, and also crosses, both made of the earth whereof they say Adam was formed, or of the Olive trees of Mount Olivet . . . Also girdles of the Virgin Mary, and glistering stones of little price (as all the rest are).' The Father Guardian gave Moryson and his companions 'Agnos Dei, Dust and little stones taken from the fore said monuments, for a great treasure to be carried to our friends at home.'[2] The Agnus Dei was a disk of wax stamped with a figure of the Lamb of God; it was worn by the faithful suspended from the neck and was used as an object of devotion.[3] The reference to dust from the monuments will remind anyone who has visited Egypt of the grooves worn in the walls of temples by generations of men who have rubbed them to the height of a man's reach to obtain small quantities of the powdered stone, supposed to possess magical or medicinal properties; but more probably Moryson was thinking of the dust from the 'Milk Grotto' at Bethlehem where the Blessed Virgin's miraculously abundant milk spilled upon the ground. This ground, as an English pilgrim notes, 'ys good for Norces that lake mylk for ther Children.'[4] Lithgow purchased 'a pound weight' of this 'admirable dust' which he

1 *Rare Adventures*, pp.225f.,247.
2 *Itinerary*, ii,36f.
3 In early days the Master of the Merchant Tailors' Company in London was called 'the Pilgrim,' the Company had special privileges at the Church of Saint John of Jerusalem, and the crest of the Company was a silver lamb (John Webster, *Monuments of Honour*, ll.105,220, and 235; *Works*, ed. F.L.Lucas, iii,323f.). The emblematic ship owned by the Company was named 'the Holy-Lambe.' The figure of Prince Henry described by Webster (ibid., 316f.) held in its left hand 'a Circklet . . . charged with foure Holy Lambes, such as our Company choose Masters with.' Webster's editor, Mr. Lucas, and the Clerk of the Merchant Tailors' Company are unable to explain Webster's allusion; but it evidently refers to one or another of two familiar forms of *Sortes*. Either four Holy Lambs, each marked with a different sign, were drawn by lot, or, more likely, since the Lamb was disk-shaped, it was flipped like a coin. The Agnus Dei was supposed, as students of witchcraft know, to have supernatural powers; consequently what had once been a superstitious rite may have degenerated in post-Reformation England into a purely traditional ceremony.—'Agnus Deis' and 'hallowed Girdles' were distributed at Rome as well as at Jerusalem (Anthony Munday, *The English Romayne Life*, ed. Harrison, p.27).
4 Torkyngton's *Diary*, ut cit.

carried to England and presented to Queen Anne. For once his scepticism failed him and he affirms that it has 'the force of a strange vertue.'¹ Its miraculous properties are mentioned by many other writers;² and to this day the visitor to Bethlehem may purchase small packets of the sandy earth. Moryson's further reference to little stones from the monuments speaks eloquently of the dilapidation from which they have suffered through the centuries to provide relics for pilgrims. Already in Guylforde's day (and doubtless much earlier) the hole in the rock on Mount Calvary in which the Cross had rested was lined with copper 'to thentente that no man shulde kutte nor take awaye any parte of the sayde stone.'³ At a somewhat later date this hole was 'trimmed about with silver'⁴ as it is today.

Departing pilgrims were given a certificate or testimonial of their visit to Jerusalem. This document bore the seal of the Franciscan monastery: a figure of Christ with the twelve apostles below.⁵ The better to avoid fraud any 'markable signs' of the pilgrim's face or body, that is, any distinguishable physical characteristics, were sometimes noted in the document.⁶ If the bearer had accomplished any special feat or peculiarly meritorious action, a statement to that effect might be included. Thus, Lithgow obtained a patent testifying that he had saved a friar from breaking his neck during the descent from the Mount of the Temptation; and Timberlake had a letter 'to shew that I had washed myself in the river Jordan.'⁷

1 *Rare Adventures*, p.247.
2 For example, Father Crespet, *Instructions de la Foy Chrestienne*, Paris, 1589, folio 138ᵛ; Father Castela, *Le Sainct Voyage*, p.428; Henry Maundrell, *A Journey from Aleppo to Jerusalem*, p.90.
3 *The Pylgrymage of Sir Richard Guylforde*, p.26.
4 Laurence Aldersey, Hakluyt, v,211.
5 See Lithgow's reproduction of this seal, *Rare Adventures*, p.254. Lithgow quotes the Latin form of the document. Because he had quarreled with the Franciscans Sanderson obtained a certificate from the Greek Patriarch; of this an English translation is in Purchas, ix,480f. For a Latin certificate given John Verney see *Royal Commission on Historical Manuscripts*, Seventh Report, Part I (1879), Appendix, p.508. A copy of the 'Certificate du Commissaire de Jerusalem' given to Roman Catholics is in Anthoine Regnault, *Discours du Voyage d'outre mer au Sainct Sepulchre*, 1573, p.157.
6 Moryson, *Itinerary*, ii,37.
7 Lithgow's 'patent' is described in Purchas, x,492, but is not mentioned in *Rare Adventures*. On Timberlake's special Jordan certificate see *Travailes of Two English Pilgrimes*, towards end.

For a fee, Roman Catholic pilgrims were often made Knights of the Holy Sepulchre. Such knights assembled annually on Palm Sunday at home and performed a processional representation appropriate to the day. This is derided by the English translator of Erasmus's satiric dialogue on pilgrimages:

> They that have been at Hierusalem [he says] be called knightes of the sepulchre, and call one another bretherne, and upon palme-sondaye they play the foles sadly, drawynge after them an asse in a rope, when they be not moche distante from the woden asse that they drawe.[1]

The Padre Guardiano offered to make Lithgow a 'Knight of the Holy Grave,' but knowing 'the condition of that detestable oath'—to pray for the Pope, the King of France, and the King of Spain; to be the enemy of all Protestants; and to 'pay yearely some stipend' to the Franciscans—he declined the honour.[2] Fynes and Henry Moryson were approached with the like offer, but they, too, declined it, knowing that it was merely an 'art to get money from pilgrims.'[3]

The Jerusalem Cross—a large Cross with four small Crosses, one within each arm—was sometimes embroidered on the left shoulder or sleeve of a pilgrim's garment or was, more frequently, tattooed upon his arm. At Bethlehem Moryson stood by while his companions had 'printed the signe of the Crosse with inke and a pen-knife upon their armes, so as the print was never to bee taken out.' 'We would not follow them in this small matter, but excused ourselves,' he says, on the ground that since he and his brother had to pass through Moslem countries 'we durst not beare any suche marke upon

---

1 *A Dialoge or communication of two persons, devysed and set forthe in the laten tonge, by the noble and famose clarke Desiderius Erasmus intituled the pylgremage of pure devotyon,* no place or date (1540), Sig.iiii.—The ceremony derided by Erasmus's translator is that of the Palmesel. Compare the satiric attack on the same ceremony in Barnabe Googe, *The Popish Kingdome,* a rhymed version of Thomas Kirchmayer's *Regnum Papisticum.* The passages in Kirchmayer and Googe are quoted in Karl Young, *The Drama of the Medieval Church,* ii,526 and 532. Wooden figures of Christ riding upon the ass survive in the cathedral-museum at Strassburg, the museum of Nuremburg, the Victoria and Albert Museum, and elsewhere.
2 *Rare Adventures,* p.242.
3 *Itinerary,* ii,41. Among John Sanderson's papers there is a 'Copie of the oath taken at Jerusalem by those that desier ther to be knighted' (*Travels in the Levant,* p.290). Sandys, *Relation of a Journey,* p.124, gives an account of the Knights of the Sepulchre.

our bodies, whereby we might bee knowne.' [1] Lithgow was not so cautious; he had the Cross and the sacred Initials I.H.S. engraved upon his arm, and under them the crown of England and Scotland with the monogram of King James.[2] This juxtaposition of symbols roused the wrath of the Guardiano who accused Lithgow of polluting 'that Holy place with the name of such an Arch-enemy to the Romane Church'; but the friar's fury fell when Lithgow promised to make known the needs of the monastery to King James so that he might allow some 'support to their afflicted lives' and some 'gratuity for maintayning of those Sacred Monuments.' The Reverend Edward Terry goes into particulars concerning the marking process: 'Impressions were made by sharp Needles . . . that pierced only the skin, and then a black Powder put into the Places so pierced, which became presently indelible.' [3]

VI

'O THERE's a brave travelling scholar, one that hath been all the world over, and some part of Jerusalem!' [4] A special prestige attached to one who, whether urged by the old piety or the new curiosity, had visited the Holy Land. Heywood's Geraldine was such a traveller; he bore upon him the 'mark' of Jerusalem. His friends found pleasure in his 'strange discourse'

> About Jerusalem and the Holy Land:
> How the new city differs from the old,
> What ruins of the Temple yet remain,
> And whether Sion and those hills about,
> With the adjacent towns and villages,
> Keep that proportioned distance, as we read.[5]

1 *Itinerary*, ii,41.
2 *Rare Adventures*, ed. 1632, p.285; reproduced facing p.254 of the MacLehose edition. Contrast *A Most Delectable and True Discourse*, 1614, Sig. R₃ᵛ. It is noteworthy that in his first narrative Lithgow is silent about the Cross and the I.H.S. and mentions only the royal crown; in his final narrative, of much later date, when he was perhaps no longer afraid or ashamed to call attention to a 'papist' symbol, he describes the entire 'engraving' and gives a facsimile of it.
3 *A Voyage to East-India*, 1655, p.64. A more detailed description of the process is in Maundrell, op.cit., pp.73f. For other allusions or descriptions see Sanderson, p.290; Sandys, p.156; Lovell's translation of *The Travels of Monsieur de Thevenot*, 1687, i,201; Bruin, *Voyage au Levant*, p.281. The custom of tattooing the Cross and I.H.S. has not yet entirely died out.
4 Thomas Middleton, *No Wit, No Help Like a Woman's*, III,i,141f.
5 Thomas Heywood, *The English Traveller*, I,i.

Contrasted with Geraldine is the stay-at-home Delavil who has accumulated much information about Jerusalem and can talk about monuments and distances and topographical details, but has gathered all this from books only and realizes regretfully that 'knowledge by travel . . . still makes up a complete gentleman.' The tone of this dialogue is that of intelligent antiquarianism; there is no hint of satiric intent despite Heywood's boisterous Protestantism. This is because Geraldine had been moved to travel not for purposes of piety but to acquire foreign languages and to sample the qualities of the women of foreign countries. From the earlier sixteenth century there had been appreciative readers of satires against the fanatical enthusiasm of pilgrims. The shafts of Erasmus's wit had been directed against pilgrims to European shrines, but by implication the Holy Land was included. The Palmer in John Heywood's interlude had been to well-nigh three dozen shrines, all which he mentions; and among them those in the Holy Land:

> At Hierusalem have I bene
> > Before Chrystes blessed sepulture;
> The Mount of Calvery have I sene,
> > A holy place, ye may be sure;
> To Iosophat and Olyvete
> > On fote, God wote, I went ryght bare,—
> Many a salt tere dyde I swete
> > Before thys carkes coulde come there.[1]

But the palmer was more often a character of romance than an object of satire, for stay-at-home Englishmen regarded pilgrimages to Jerusalem rather as a curious and obsolete custom of the superstitious times of the old religion than as feats occasionally accomplished by their own contemporaries. Masquers at court sometimes wore pilgrim-costume; Romeo disguises himself as a pilgrim when he attends the ball given by the Capulets, but he does not reveal his destination.[2]

1 *The Four PP*, ll.13f.; J.M.Manly, *Specimens*, i,484.
2 Two pilgrims on their way to Jerusalem beg a night's shelter in Dekker's *If This Be Not a Good Play the Devil Is in It*, *Dramatic Works*, ed. Pearson, iii,285.

What books had the scholarly Delavil read about Jerusalem? Apart from the large cosmographies, geographies, and world-histories, there was little available in English until the appearance of Thomas Tymme's translation of Christianus Adrichomius, *A briefe description of Hierusalem* (1595), which is provided with a map; and until the publication of Sandys's *Relation of a Journey* (1615) there were no illustrated English books comparable with those that had appeared on the continent. We must imagine that Delavil read foreign tongues. If so, he had doubtless studied Reissner's *Jerusalem, die Alte Hauptstadt der Juden* (Frankfort a-M., 1563) which contains, besides many small engravings of scenes from the Bible and various views of the Holy Places, a large map of Jerusalem and another of the Holy Land. Or he may have studied Zuallardo's *Il devotissimo viaggio di Gierusaleme* (1595) which contains a wealth of illustrations with large maps and plans.[1] Most likely he knew Bernard von Breydenbach's *Peregrinationes in Terram Sanctam* (first published in 1486) which, though not translated into English, was accessible in numerous editions in the original Latin and in German and French translations. This was one of the major sources whence Europeans drew their knowledge of Palestine. The huge panoramic views are famous; and among other remarkable plates are those of Jerusalem, the Church of the Holy Sepulchre, the pyramids, and other objects; of masculine and feminine costumes; and of the Arabic alphabet. It is conceivable that the immense and magnificent folding panorama of Jerusalem which Erhard Reuwich drew for this book was copied in enlarged form to serve as a back-drop for the scene in Heywood's *Four Prentices of London* in which Godfrey points out to his army, as they stand before Jerusalem, the site of Jehovah's house, the *Via Sacra*, the judgment-seat of Pilate, Golgotha, and the Holy Sepulchre.[2] It is difficult to imagine how Godfrey's speech, so full of topographical details, could have been con-

---

1 Father Bernadino Amico's *Trattato delle Piante ed Immagini de Sacri Edifizi di Terra Santa*, which remains famous because the numerous illustrations are by Jacques Callot, appeared at too late a date to be known to Heywood's Delavil.

2 *The Four Prentices of London, Dramatic Works*, ed. Pearson, ii,213f.

vincingly delivered if while he spoke he pointed to a mere blank curtain at the rear of the stage.[1]

The play just mentioned is the only surviving dramatization of the story of the Crusades;[2] in it the romantic attraction of the theme is quite uncontaminated by any Protestant prejudice. It is an absurd and noisy but not altogether displeasing piece designed to appeal to the lower elements of the theatre-going public. The Crusaders are opposed by the Soldan of Babylon (that is, Egypt) and the Sophy of Persia. The Soldan is inclined to moderation and would not molest the Christians provided they commit no violence and desire to visit peaceably 'the ancient Reliques of their Saviours Tombe.' But the Sophy is a fire-eater and counsels battle. The mild words of the one and the challenge of the other are alike greeted with defiance. 'Pagan lords,' says Godfrey,

> We come not with gray gownes, and Pilgrimes staves,
> Beads at our sides, and sandals on our feete,
> Feare in our hearts, entreaty in our tongues,
> To beg a passage to our Prophets grave.
> But our soft Beaver Felts, we have turn'd to iron,
> Our gownes to armour, and our shels to plumes,
> Our walking-staves we have chang'd to Cemytars,
> And so with Pilgrimes hearts, not Pilgrims habits,
> We come to hew our way through your maine Armies,
> And offer at the Tombe our contrite hearts.[3]

1 The use of such back-drops is still disputed but seems proved by passages in *Doctor Faustus* coupled with an entry in a list of Henslowe's properties. Towards the end of Marlowe's play a view of hell is displayed and presently withdrawn. Earlier there is a description of Rome analogous to the description of Jerusalem in Heywood's drama; and it is a striking fact that among the properties listed by Henslowe for use in *Doctor Faustus* is one called 'the sittie of Rome.' What can that have been save a painted cloth to illustrate the description in the text? (See *Henslowe Papers*, ed. Greg, pp.116f.; *Shakespeare's England*, Oxford, 1916, ii,267).

2 On the date of Heywood's play and the problem of its relation to the lost *Jerusalem* (1591) and the lost *Godfrey of Bulloigne* (1594) see *Henslowe's Diary*, ed. Greg, i,13f.,18f., ii,155,166; Sir Edmund Chambers, *The Elizabethan Stage*, iii,340; E.H.C.Oliphant, *The Plays of Beaumont and Fletcher*, pp.175f.; G.M.Sibley, *The Lost Plays and Masques*, Ithaca, N.Y., 1932, pp.65f.,83. Two lost plays bore the title *The Destruction of Jerusalem*; their theme was probably the destruction by Titus. See Sibley, pp.41f. The subject was a favourite one for Tudor and Stuart 'motions' (puppet-shows).—The false tradition that Edward I went on a crusade survives in Greene's *Friar Bacon and Friar Bungay*, II,i, and III,i; and in Peele's *Edward I*, I,i,1. Compare *Mandeville*, chapter vi.—Heywood's *Four Prentices* is based on Richard Carew's unfinished version of Tasso's *Jerusalem Delivered* (1594).

3 *Dramatic Works*, ed. Pearson, ii,213f.

Heywood, as always, knows how to strike the popular note; this is what the London apprentices liked to hear; this is how they would confront the Turks. In their imagination one did not placate and bribe the infidels and submit to all manner of indignities in Palestine; one bore one's self like Godfrey de Bouillon and the other champions. Thus did the theatre provide some compensation for the dread which moved the Elizabethans when they thought of Islam.

CHAPTER THREE

'THE PRESENT TERROR OF THE WORLD'

I

'HE who would behold these times in their greatest glory could not finde a better Scene then Turky.' So wrote an experienced traveller, Sir Henry Blount, who goes on to say that the Turks 'are the only moderne people, great in action . . . whose Empire hath so suddenly invaded the World, and fixt it selfe such firme foundations as no other ever did.' [1] This testimony to the greatness and stability of the Ottoman Empire, expressed sixty-five years after the Battle of Lepanto, is at variance with the views of modern historians who, having the advantage of the perspective of three centuries, have detected the germs of decay in Turkish military organization and political administration long before 1571 and even during the last years of the reign of Solyman the Magnificent. To contemporaries, however, and to the generation that followed, Lepanto appeared to be but a temporary repulse of the Ottoman onset, a triumph indeed and of value as indicating that the hosts of Islam were vulnerable, but with a swift aftermath of disagreement and disunion in Christendom that served as a warning and hushed the celebrations of the victory. Not many years after Lepanto Montaigne, as an argument in support of his contention that the study of the arts and sciences weakens the courage of men and makes them effeminate, remarked that the Turks were a people trained to arms and scornful of learning and were consequently hardier than the more civilized nations. 'Le plus fort estat qui paroisse pour le present au monde, est celuy des Turcs.' [2]

In the fourteenth century a cloud arose in the East and from

1 *A Voyage into the Levant*, pp.2f.
2 *Essais*, i,25. Compare ii,21: 'La race Hottomane, la premiere race du monde en fortune guerriere.' In ii,24, Montaigne describes Sultan Solyman as 'saoul et chargé de tant de monarchies et de puissance.'

the fifteenth till far into the seventeenth the Ottoman peril
hung over Europe. The governors of Christendom watched
the Turkish aggression, encouraged occasionally when the
Turks met with some temporary check, more often dumbfounded as province after province was added to the Empire;
endeavouring, generally in vain, to use the sense of a common
peril for the purposes of a common effort; thwarted almost
always in their plans for united action by internecine religious
and nationalistic prejudices and rivalries. Successive popes
attempted to rally Christendom to a new crusade, yet more
than once acted in concert with the Porte for the purpose of
crushing Venice. The policy of France was in the main pro-
Turk because a strong power in south-east Europe and on the
Mediterranean was required as a counterpoise to the Emperor
Charles V. In times of extreme crisis, when the Turks penetrated far up the valley of the Danube, overran Hungary and
Serbia, established their overlordship in the Balkans, pushed
into Poland, and threatened the very walls of Vienna, it was
possible to sink these differences; but never for very long. In
Roman Catholic propaganda attacks upon Islam were frequently combined with assaults upon Lutherans and Calvinists
and it was asserted that Satan worked for the Turks by stirring
up the hatred of heretics against the true Church. Conversely,
among Protestant controversialists there was a tendency to
associate Rome and Islam together as partners in iniquity;
and the succession of exhortations from Rome on the necessity
of a new crusade prompted some Protestants to advocate a
contrary opinion.[1] Luther himself at first advocated the

1 Opponents of Wyclif called him 'Mahomet.' In the *Dialogue of Comfort* (a debate
between two Hungarian Catholics as to how they are to behave under Turkish tyranny) Sir Thomas More implies a parallel between Henry VIII and the Turk
(R.W.Chambers, *Sir Thomas More*, 1935, p.314). Father Crespet (*Instructions de la
Foy Chrestienne*, 1589, folio 39^r) couples Luther in infamy with the false prophet
Mahomet. He declares that even the Turks would have been horrified to hear of the
'sanglantes tragedies qu'ont joué les heretiques sur le theatre de France et d'Angle-
terre,' for Turks would not have practised on their lowest slaves the cruelties 'qu'ont
exercée et exercent ces faux Chrestiens contre les vrais Chrestiens et fideles cath-
oliques.' On the other hand, Luther declared that the spirit or soul of Antichrist was
the Pope, his flesh or body was the Turk (*Werke*, lx,176; cited by Alphandéry,
'Mahomet-Antichrist au Moyen Age,' *Melanges Hartwig Derenbourg*, p.275). Englishmen contributed to these accusations and counter-accusations. At Antwerp
was published in 1597 and republished in 1603 a treatise of more than a thousand
pages entitled *Calvino-Turcismus, id est, Calvinisticae perfidiae cum Mahumetana*

principle of non-resistance to the Turks on the ground that God had sent them as a visitation for the sins of Christendom; but later, when in 1529 the army of Sultan Solyman approached Vienna, he acknowledged the need to make war against the infidels.

Alliances were formed and dissolved; policies fluctuated and faded away; the confusion was the more confounded as, following the fortunes of the wars, the Turkish armies alternately advanced and retreated in the South-East. European statesmen made feeble efforts to effect some sort of an under-

Collatio. This was originally composed by Dr. William Reynolds and was completed and edited by William Gifford, Archbishop of Rheims (on whom see *D.N.B.*). It provoked a violent reply from Matthew Sutcliffe: *De Turco-Papismo, hoc est De Turcorum et Papistarum adversus Christi ecclesiam et fidem Conjuratione, eorumque in religione et moribus consensiene et similitudine,* 1599; republished 1604. Compare also Thomas Aylesbury, *Paganisme and Papisme parallel'd and set forth in a Sermon,* 1624. Knowledge of the existence of these dead and dreary polemics is necessary for the understanding of various allusions in the literature of the period. In the course of one of his ferocious diatribes against Roman Catholicism Bishop Bale makes his character 'Veryte' say to the Clergy with venomous candour: 'The Turkes, I dare say, are a thousand tymes better than yow' (*King Johan,* ed. J.H.P.Pafford, Malone Society, 1931, l.2257). John Foxe links Pope and Turk together again and again in the *Acts and Monuments.* The same association is established in John Phillips's pious poem *A Friendly Larum:*

> If Mahomet, that prophet false,
> Eternitie doe gaine,
> Then shall the pope, and you his sainctes,
> In heaven be sure to raigne.

This piece contains the prayer:

> As from the Turke, so shield us, Lord,
> From force of popish power.

(*Select Poetry Chiefly Devotional of the Reign of Queen Elizabeth,* ed. Edward Farr, Parker Society, Cambridge, 1845, Part ii,p.528). Falstaff boasts after the battle of Shrewsbury that 'Turk Gregory never did such deeds in arms as I have done this day' (*I Henry IV,* V,iii,46). The allusion to the martial Pope Gregory VII (Hildebrand) is obvious; but why does Falstaff turn him into a Turk? The only explanation offered by the commentators is that Falstaff is whimsical. Spectators at the Globe doubtless saw the point more clearly. A phrase in Purchas (viii,25) exhibits the same linking of words and associations: 'This Urban the second (the second Turban).' Here there is also the association of an elaborate oriental headdress with the papal tiara. In Berne there is a statue representing a heroic female (typifying Switzerland or Liberty or Protestantism) who stands in triumph over two prostrate forms, one of whom wears a tiara, the other a turban. Lodowick Barry's play *Ram-Alley, or Merry Tricks* (IV,i; Hazlitt's Dodsley, x,350) contains a song:

> What can you do for the Great Turk?
> What can you do for the Pope of Rome?

Less definite but none the less unmistakable is Bunyan's association of the moribund Giant Pope with the dead Giant Pagan, for to an Englishman of the seventeenth century 'pagan' was almost synonymous with Mohammedan or more specifically Turk. The connection between the two ideas endures to this day in the ditty beloved of undergraduates about the 'jolly life' of the Pope with his wine and the Sultan with his wives.

standing with remote peoples—the Turcomans and especially
the Persians—in order to bring military pressure against the
Turkish rear. Selfish commercial interests were often stronger
than national pride and religious convictions, and to gain
advantages for trade humiliating terms of peace were accepted
and enormous tributes paid, disguised as free-will offerings of
friendship.

Of what events in this welter of warfare and intrigue was
an Englishman of the later years of Elizabeth's reign mindful,
not a man in public life whose business it was to inform himself of the progress of Turkish aggression and to make plans
to resist it, but an ordinary man whose private affairs obscured
for him the details of far-off events but who, having some
education, was accustomed to talk with his acquaintances
about happenings on the continent of Europe? A precise
answer is of course impossible; we cannot see far into the minds
of men dead so long ago. But in the literature of Tudor England
—not the political pamphlets and treatises nor the state-papers
but the popular literature and more especially the drama—
we may find some sort of guide or gauge with which to measure
the range of popular knowledge of Islam, for the drama is a
fairly accurate reflection of the popular mind. The representation of Mohammedan history and life upon the London stage
is the subject of a later chapter in this book; for the moment
all we need is a rough anticipation of the results to be arrived
at after an examination of the many plays to be considered.
From this survey it appears that a man of average education
and intelligence had in mind the conquests of Tamburlaine
and his humiliation of Sultan Bajazet; the heroic resistance
of Scanderbeg; the fall of Constantinople and the ruthless
cruelty of Mahomet the Conqueror; the alternately advancing
and retreating tides of Turkish forces in the Balkans and the
Danube country (these aggressions and recessions confusedly
remembered); the overrunning of Greece and the islands of
the Ægean; the fall of Syria and Egypt; the loss of Rhodes
and at a much later date of Cyprus; the fall of Budapest and
other Hungarian cities and the successful resistance of Vienna;
the Turko-Venetian wars alternating with periods of peaceful

commercial intercourse; the repulse of the Turks from Malta; the naval encounters in the Mediterranean and the victory of Lepanto; the growth of piracy in the Barbary States; the hostility of Turks and Persians; England's establishment of diplomatic and commercial relations with the Porte; and the grim fact that largely because of the rivalries of the Christian states no definite and decisive barrier had yet been set up against Islam. Added to these impressions of contemporary or comparatively recent events would be memories of the farther past where history merged into legend and romance; for because no clear-cut distinction was made between Turks and Moors, legends of the Moorish invasion of Spain reinforced the sense of the present Ottoman peril, and because no clear-cut distinction was made between Turks and Saracens, legends of the Crusades stood out in vivid colours when calls were heard summoning Christians to arms against the Turks.[1]

II

INDIVIDUAL Englishmen fought as mercenaries or as volunteer adventurers against the Turks but the policy of England was to stand aloof so far as possible from the struggle with Islam. Commercial rivalry with Venice, political and economic rivalry with Spain, religious differences with all the Catholic countries of Europe, and the general calculations of trade-interests alike dictated a policy of neutrality if not of actual friendship with the Turks. Elizabeth even went so far as to make advances to the Porte on the ground that she and the Great Turk were alike enemies of idolaters.[2] Nevertheless there was always in Tudor England an undercurrent of uneasiness and alarm in the face of the Turkish aggression, natural to a Christian people and to a nation whose trade with the East was expanding. At moments of crisis these anti-Moslem sentiments developed into an anxious sympathy with the Catholic powers which were struggling, alone or in various combinations, with the Turks. In England no such immense

1 See Appendix, Synopsis of Ottoman History.
2 Compare the report of Edward Hogan, Elizabeth's first envoy to Morocco, that the king of that country 'beareth a greater affection to our Nation than to others because of our religion, which forbiddeth worship of idols' (Hakluyt, vi,289).

body of historical and propagandist literature on the subject was published as we find in Germany, for the issues were more remote. But thoughtful men did write about the Turks and especially did they meditate upon the problem of how the rise of the Ottoman power had taken place. Innumerable, indeed, are the explanations put forward during the sixteenth century by terrified or bewildered Europeans to account for this sudden and portentous ascent to the heights of power and glory. Let us pass in review some of the most significant explanations put forward, limiting our survey to works by Englishmen and works translated into English. What then were, or were believed to be, the causes of Turkish greatness? The answer to this question will introduce us to a large number of treatises, some general in character, some dealing particularly with the Ottoman Empire. These we shall survey chronologically, describing those that are not more appropriately described elsewhere in this book.

In that curious manual of geographical and ethnological information, the *Introduction of Knowledge* by the traveller Andrew Borde (*c.*1542), there is a chapter on the Turks which begins:

I am a Turk, and Machamytes law do kepe;
I do proll for my pray whan other be a slepe;
My law wyllith me no swynes flesh to eate;
It shal not greatly forse, for I have other meate—

which is a commendably philosophic attitude to adopt towards the dietary regulations imposed by one's religion. Lapsing into prose, Borde gives a brief list of the domains of the Great Turk: 'Besyd his owne possessyons . . . the Sarsons land, . . . the Sophyes lond, and the ylond of Roodes, with many other prevynces.' These, Borde says, the Great Turk holds 'in pesable possession. . . He doth conquere and subdue, as wel by polyce and gentylnes, as by hys fettes of ware.' [1] This jejune statement is an unconscious tribute to the greatest of the Ottoman Sultans, Solyman the Magnificent, who at the time when Borde wrote was on the throne.

---

[1] Andrew Borde (or Boorde), *The fyrst boke of the Introduction of Knowledge*, 1548; ed. F.J.Furnivall, E.E.T.S., Extra Series x, 1870, pp.214f.

The earliest extended account of the Ottoman government in English—not an original work, however, but a translation from the French—is *The order of the great Turckes courte, of hys menne of warre, and of all hys conquestes, with the summe of Mahumetes doctryne* which Richard Grafton published, and perhaps wrote, in 1544.[1] After a preliminary tirade against the Turks there is some information about the organization of the Turkish court, the status of various officials, and the discipline of the army; and this is followed by a military history down to the conquests of Solyman. Christian Europe, it must be remembered, possessed no standing armies but depended in emergencies upon recruits, ill-trained and often resentful, or upon volunteer adventurers; and consequently regarded with awe and admiration the regular professional army, disciplined, uniformed, and organized, which the Ottoman Turks drew from their subject populations.[2] It is not surprising that this formidable fighting-machine is again and again pointed to by Christian publicists as a principal cause of Turkish success.

The military organization and martial discipline of the Turks are so characterized by Peter Ashton in his *Shorte treatise upon the Turkes Chronicles*,[3] a version of the *Turcicarum Rerum Commentarius* of Paulus Giovius. From the time of its publication in 1546 Ashton's treatise was for many years a chief source of information regarding the Ottoman Empire available to the Elizabethans. In an introductory epistle Ashton commends his book as valuable because by perusing Turkish history we may amend our lives, for God 'sufferethe the wicked and cursed seed of Hismael to be a scourge to whip us for our synnes.' The idea that Islam was the scourge of the wrath of God, justly offended by the sins of Christendom, was one often propounded by moralists of the Renaissance. Fear and hatred of the Turks lead Ashton (following Paulus Giovius) to exalt the heroic

---

1 The French original is Antoine Geuffroy, *Briefve description de la court du Grant Turc et ung sommaire du regne des Othmans. Avec ung abrege de leurs . . . superstitions; ensemble lorigine de cinq empires yssuz de la secte Mehemet*, Paris, 1543.

2 See A.H.Lybyer, *The Government of the Ottoman Empire in the Time of Suleiman the Magnificent* (*Harvard Historical Studies*, xviii, 1913), p.317.

3 Ashton translated, not the original Italian text of Paolo Giovio (*Commentarii delle Cose de Turchi*) but the Latin version which had been made by Franciscus Niger Bassianates. Ashton's account of the Sultan's army is at folio cxix[r]f.

qualities of their enemies. An enthusiastic interest in the character and career of Tamburlaine is inspired by his victories over the Turks; and it is with an almost gloating satisfaction that he tells how Tamburlaine 'used Bayazet in stede of a blocke when he toke his horse, and fed hym under his table, lyke a curre.' [1] A like sympathetic prejudice is behind the strangely distorted picture of the religion and policy of the Persian Sophy. The Sophy, it is said, threw down the Mohammedan temples and restored 'the olde auncient temples'; 'he called Mahomet in despite, a bondeman and a vyle boughte drudge.' [2] Needless to say, Shi'a loyalty to 'Ali seldom if ever went to such lengths as these; but Ashton transmutes the heretical Shi'ite detestation of the orthodox Sunni Turks into a general hostility to Islam. Again, the career of Scanderbeg, another successful opponent of Turkish arms, was, it is implied, an example of valour and resourcefulness to Christians and patriots who were struggling against the Turks.[3] A long digression on 'the order and dissiplyne of the Turkysh warfare' leads to some consideration of the strategy to be adopted against them: prompt action and offensive war are advised; the Christian states should invade the Ottoman domains and no longer stand on the defensive, awaiting supinely another invasion of their own territories.[4]

The hardihood and endurance of the Turks are characteristics often emphasized by those who advance explanations for their success in war. Thus, the English epitomist of Sebastian Munster writes:

> The Turkes have a marveylous celerity in doing, a constancy in daungers and observation of the Empyre. They will swimme over very deepe and daungerous waters, they passe over straung hils, and being commaunded they go throughe thicke and thinne headlonge, havinge no regarde of their lives, but of the Empyre. Most apt and readye to suffer fastinge and watchinge. There is no sedition amongest them, no tumult.[5]

'No man goeth armed' in the Sultan's domains, this writer continues, 'but in the time of warre.'

1 *A Shorte treatise*, folios xiii[r].
2 Ibid., folios lxxiiii[r]f.
3 Ibid., folios xxii[r]f.
4 Ibid., folios cxxxiii[r]f.
5 *Straunge and memorable thinges*, folio xxxiv.

The well attested fact that Turkish soldiers, though they might bicker and squabble among themselves, never came to blows with each other [1] casts light upon a passage in *Othello* where the commentators fail us. Othello, remonstrating with his brawling followers, exclaims:

> Are we turn'd Turk, and to ourselves do that
> Which heaven hath forbid the Ottomites? [2]

This may be paraphrased: 'Are we become worse than barbarians in that we do to ourselves that which heaven has forbidden the Ottoman Turks to do to each other?' Strikingly similar to Othello's thought is an anecdote told by Francis Bacon:

> It is memorable, that is reported by a counsellor or ambassador of the Emperor's, touching the censure of the Turks on these Duels: That was a combat of this kind performed by two persons of quality of the Turks, wherein one of them was slain, the other party was converted before the council of Bassaes; the manner of the reprehension was in these words: How durst you undertake to fight one with the other? Are there not Christians enough to kill? Did you not know that whether of you should be slain, the loss would be the Great Seigneours? [3]

The unity of Islam emphasized by painful contrast the divisions and seditions of Christendom. This unity was correctly judged to be a major cause of Turkish victories. In his treatise upon the ruin wrought to commonwealths by Envy, George Whetstone points to that sin as the occasion of the Turkish triumphs, arguing that the contention which Envy set between the Emperor of Constantinople, the Lord of Bulgarie, and the other

1 William Lithgow writes (*Rare Adventures*, p.136): 'I have often heard Turkes brawl one with another most vily, but I never saw, or heard, that they, either in private or publique quarrels, durst strike one another; neither dare they, for feare of severe punishment, imposed on such quarrellers.' Such testimony is frequently met with. See, e.g., *The Travellers Breviat*, 1601, p.41. (This is an epitomized translation by Robert Johnson of the *Relationi Universali* by the Italian diplomat and traveller Giovanni Botero.)

2 *Othello*, II,iii,175f. Another possible paraphrase is: 'Do we destroy ourselves by civil war when heaven has forbidden the Turks to destroy us?' There is no note on the passage in the Furness *Variorum*. The incomprehensible note in the *Arden* edition is: 'Heaven forbade the Turks to destroy themselves by doing it for them in wrecking them.'

3 *The Charge . . . touching Duells*, 1614; James Spedding, *The Letters and the Life of Francis Bacon*, ed. 1890, iv,404f.

Christian princes was the sure foundation of the Great Turk's power.[1] The biographer of Scanderbeg deduces a like lesson for western Europe from the career of that hero; he argues that the disasters that have overtaken the Greeks came from 'their hateful discords and civil warres'; and his book closes with an appeal to France to put away sects and schisms, partialities and divisions.[2]

The problem of the causes of Turkish greatness exercised the mind of Fulke Greville, a philosophic student of public affairs whose thoughts turned frequently to the Levant. He believed that though the Mohammedan religion 'was meere collusion and deceit,' yet the Turks have prevailed upon the Christians because they have been 'first in unity' whereas Christians have 'divided stood, in schisme and sect, among themselves.' Moreover the warlike discipline of the Ottomans has strengthened them.

> The ground which makes most States thus fond of Warre,
> Is that with armes all empires doe increase. . .
>
> Such the religion is of Mahomet,
> His doctrine, onely Warre and hazard teaching:
> His discipline, not how to use but get;
> His Court, a campe; the law of sword, his preaching:
> Vertues of Peace, he holds effeminate,
> And doth, as vices, banish them his State.[3]

There follows a contrasting picture of the Pope who 'lets not contention cease' in Christendom.

Elsewhere Fulke Greville, establishing grandiose general principles from his reading of history and illustrating those principles with particular examples, instances the fall of Constantinople to the Turks as an example of the law by which 'periods in the growth of all States' are ordained.[4] To this solemn conception of the fated course of human events

---

1 *The English Myrror. A Regard wherein al estates may behold the Conquests of Envy*, 1586, Book i, chapter 7.
2 Jacques de Lavardin, *The Historie of George Castriot, Surnamed Scanderbeg* (translated by Z.I.), 1596, pp.334,496.
3 *A Treatie of Warres*, stanzas 64,15 and 17; *Works*, ii,127 and 109.
4 *A Treatise of Monarchy*, stanzas 627–8; *Works*, i,222f.

George Wither gives a purely personal colouring when he
writes:

> The Easterne Kingdomes had their times to florish;
> The Grecian Empire rising, saw them perish;
> That fell, and then the Roman Pride began;
> Now scourged by the race of Ottoman.
> And if the course of things a round must run;
> Till they have ending, where they first begun,
> What is't to me? who peradventure must,
> Ere that befall, lye, moulthr'd into dust.[1]

Much information about the Turks is presented in condensed
form in that very popular work, *The Travellers Breviat*, the
English abridgment of Giovanni Botero's *Relationi Universali*.
The rise of their empire to its present greatness is ascribed in
part to the discords of Christendom, in part to the excellence
of the Turkish army. The Great Turk possesses three instruments with which to terrify the whole world: multitudes of
men, an incorruptible military discipline, and an infinite store
of corn and other provisions. Added to these are the thrift,
patience, and endurance of a soldiery accustomed to a hard
diet and the severest conditions of life. No women are permitted to accompany these armies. The men are never billeted
in towns but always kept in isolated encampments. They do
not fear death because they believe that their destiny is in-
evitably written on their foreheads.[2] The 'Janizars,' drawn
from subject European populations, and the 'Azamoglani'
(men schooled from boyhood in the use of arms and reared in a
discipline that is quite monastic) form the core and mainstay
of the Great Turk's forces. Military command is in the hands
of renegados 'whom he taketh as tithe from their parents in
their childhood.' The sources and extent of the Turkish revenue
are surveyed. The picture presented in this treatise of the
power, organization, discipline, and resources of the Ottoman
Empire is formidable indeed.[3]

1 *Withers Motto*, 1621; *Poems*, Spenser Society, p.674.
2 Compare the *Koran*, iii,145: 'No soul can ever die except by Allah's leave and at a
  term appointed' (Marmaduke Pickthall's translation). Montaigne writes (*Essais*,
  ii,29): 'La Persuasion estant populerement semee entre les Turcs, de la fatale et
  imployable prescription de leurs jours, ayde apparement a les asseurer aux dangers.'
3 *The Travellers Breviat*, 'The Great Turke,' pp.39f.

A similar picture of the Sultan's resources is that drawn from close personal observation by Lazaro Soranzo whose *Ottomanno* was published in 1598. In Abraham Hartwell's translation of this book (1603) Englishmen found a quantity of information on the Turkish Question in general and on the state of the war then raging in Hungary in particular, together with not only a survey of the organization of the Ottoman Empire but also a series of estimates of the character and ability of many individual officials holding positions of power and responsibility. Other portions of the treatise, having to do with such technical problems as the Turkish sources of supply of food-stuffs and timber, the qualities of the Turk as a fighting man, the treasure and revenue of the Sultan, cast light upon the causes of Turkish success, while on the other hand the Turks' lack of engineering skill and the weakness of their naval forces suggest the proper manner of engaging them. Turkish motives in waging war against Christendom are discussed; the problem of the Sultan's probable designs—against whom will he next 'bend his forces'?—is mooted; the possibility of establishing pacific relations with him is debated; and the suggestion is thrown out that the Turks might be overcome by the use of learning instead of violence, that is, by having 'some easie and wittie bookes' disseminated among them in Arabic to expose the 'mad fooleries' of the *Koran* and so undermine their faith.[1] This plan to enfeeble the authority of the *Koran* is based upon an awareness of the close tie between the military prowess of the Turks and the promise of celestial rewards held out for those who die in battle for their religion.[2]

In this same year (1603) there appeared the greatest of English works of the Renaissance period dealing with Turkey. This is: *The Generall Historie of the Turkes, from the first beginning of that Nation to the rising of the Othoman Familie: with all the notable expeditions of the Christian Princes against them. Together with the Lives and Conquests of the Othoman Kings and Emperours. Faithfully collected out of the best Histories, both*

---

[1] *The Ottoman of Lazaro Soranzo. Wherein is delivered as well a full and perfect report of the might and power of Mahamet the Third, Great Emperour of the Turkes now raigning*, 1603.

[2] Compare, for example, Sir Henry Blount, *A Voyage into the Levant*, p.67.

auncient and moderne, and digested into one continual Historie until this present yeare 1603. The author, Richard Knolles (*c.*1550–1610), was a teacher and student who devoted twelve years to the preparation of his great book.[1] Doctor Johnson's opinion was that no other English historian could 'justly contest the superiority of Knolles' and that he displays 'all the excellencies that narration can admit.' He especially commends his 'artful arrangement' of 'a wonderful multiplicity of events,' the purity and elevation of his style, and the clarity of his descriptions and characterizations. 'There is nothing turgid in his dignity, nor superfluous in his copiousness.'[2] Gibbon, on the other hand, sneering at Doctor Johnson, doubted whether 'a partial and verbose compilation from Latin writers' could 'instruct or amuse an enlightened age.'[3] Henry Hallam, taking issue with Johnson who had held that Knolles was unfortunate in choosing to relate the story of 'a remote and barbarous people' about whom 'none desire to be informed,' took issue also with Gibbon and declared that the subject was 'one of the most splendid he could have selected' and that 'we should not err in placing him among the first of our elder writers.'[4] Southey commended 'old Knolles' to Coleridge; and Byron said that the *History* was one of the first books to give him pleasure as a child, influenced his future wishes to visit the Levant, and 'gave me perhaps the oriental colouring which is observed in my poetry.'[5] Today the great book is neglected. An anthology of its best pages would display a fine narrative gift, considerable power of characterization, an admirable talent for reducing to coherence large masses of refractory material, and on occasion real eloquence.[6] But no anthology could do it

1 Knolles revised the second edition, 1610. Anonymous continuators brought the *History* up to date in 1621 and 1631. Thomas Nabbes, the dramatist, issued a fifth edition, revised, in 1638. The sixth edition, 1679, was revised and enlarged by Sir Paul Rycaut, an agent of the Levant Company and a distinguished authority on Turkey. The seventh edition, further expanded and containing a survey of 'the Present State of the Ottoman Empire' by Rycaut (first published separately in 1668) appeared in three folio volumes between 1687 and 1700. In 1701 an abridgment by John Savage appeared.
2 *The Rambler*, No.122; 18 May 1751.
3 *The Decline and Fall of the Roman Empire*, chapter 64.
4 *Introduction to the Literature of Europe*, Part iii, chapter 7.
5 *The Life and Correspondence of Robert Southey*, p.176 (12 March 1804); Byron, *Works*, ed. 1832, ix,141.
6 Such an anthology would include, among other passages, the prefatory address to the

justice. Properly to appreciate the *History* one must read it entire, letting wave after wave of events break upon one's imagination.

Yet Gibbon is correct in calling it 'partial,' for Knolles could not avoid prejudice and his purpose was in part propagandist; and in calling it 'verbose,' for it is mercilessly long (twelve hundred pages); and in calling it a 'compilation.' On his title-page the author expressly called his book a collection and a digest, and in an Address to the Reader he gave a list of his authorities. It would be unprofitable to enumerate them exhaustively, but some indication of the range of his reading and investigations will introduce us to various writers on Turkish history. Anyone fairly familiar with the sixteenth-century historians will remark Knolles's indebtednesses while turning his pages. He certainly used the *Commentaries* of Paulus Giovius and probably possessed Peter Ashton's racy English version of that work. Another early English book on Turkey that he seems to have used is Hugh Gough's *Ofspring of the House of Ottomanno* (undated; later than 1553), a compilation from Paulus Giovius, Bartolomeo Georgievitz, and other continental sources.[1] Here he found, or could have found, much general information on Turkish warfare and military organization, and here is told at great length and with considerable skill the story of Roxolana of which we shall hear in a later chapter. Knolles also had at hand the most ambitious English narrative of Islam that had yet appeared at its date, Thomas Newton's *Notable*

reader, the story of Tamburlaine and Bajazet, the wars of Scanderbeg, the story of the relations of Bajazet II and his sons, the characterization of Selimus (Selim the Grim), the story of Solyman and Roxolana (though Knolles lifts this practically entire from his source), the narrative of the attack on Malta, and the superb account of the battle of Lepanto. For these passages see the *History*, ed. 1687, i,145f.; 193f.; 248f.; 326f.; 512f.; 536f.; ii,589f.; 600f.

1 *The Ofspring of the house of Ottomanno, and offices pertaining to the greate Turkes Court. Whereunto is added Bartholomeus Georgievitz Epitome, of the customes, Rytes, Ceremonies, and Religion of the Turkes: with the miserable afflictions of those Christians, whiche live under their captivitie and bondage* (n.d.).—Of the *De Turcarum Moribus Epitome* by Georgievitz (or Georgevitz) many editions appeared from *c*.1544 till well into the seventeenth century. Though he made use of earlier authorities, especially the *Petit Traicte de l'Origine des Turcqz* by Teodoro Spandugino (Paris, 1519; ed. Charles Schefer, Paris, 1896), Georgievitz, like Spandugino, had had first-hand experience of what he writes, for he had been captured by the Turks in Hungary in 1528 and was a slave for thirteen years before he made his escape. See A.H.Lybyer, op.cit., p.317. On Georgievitz's account of the subject populations was based an anonymous English account, *The Estate of Christians under the subjection of the Turke*, 1595.

Historie of the Saracens (1575). The third section of this work covers briefly the ground which Knolles was presently to make his own.[1] In the later stages of his researches he may have obtained guidance from R.Carr's *Mahumetan or Turkish Historie* (1600), another English derivative from continental originals. But though these English predecessors have to be taken into account, Knolles's chief reliance was upon such continental historians, memoir-writers, and topographers as Busbecq, Chalcondylas, Lonicerus, Minadoi, Barletius, Sabellicus, Secundinus, and Leunclavius.[2] In the case of the story of Solyman and Roxolana he did not hesitate to transfer semilegendary matter from the pages of the novelists to his *History*.

Knolles begins his narrative with the resounding words: 'The glorious Empire of the Turks, the present Terror of the World'; and though he brings it to a close with the comforting conviction that the Turks are not invincible and that there are signs that their power is waning, nevertheless his stories of disasters to Christendom, of Turkish atrocities, of their barbarous cruelties to captives, their frightful executions (as when a prisoner, buried waist-deep in the earth, is made a target for bowmen), their treatment of the bodies of the slain, the plunder and rapine following the fall of besieged cities, the strangling of sons and brothers of the reigning Sultan—such stories were not calculated to soothe fears and lessen alarms. Even in so quiet an anecdote as that of the Turk who said that the loss of

1 *A Notable Historie of the Saracens. Briefly and faithfully describing the originall beginning, continuance and successe as well of the Saracens, as also of Turkes, Souldans, Mamalukes, Assassines, Tartarians and Sophians . . . Whereunto is annexed a Compendious Chronycle of all their yeerely exploytes*, 1575. This compilation from continental writers (chiefly Italian) is divided into three books: the origin, success, and 'encreasing' of the Saracens; the 'declination' of the Saracens with the beginning of the Turks; and 'a true and perfect discourse of Turkishe Affaires for three hundreth yeeres space before Ottomanne [Othman I], for pleasure and varietie very delectable' (folios 85–119). Then follows (folios 120–144) 'A Summarie or breefe Chronicle of Saracens and Turkes, continued from the birthe of Mahomet, their first peevish Prophet and Founder, till this present yeere.'

2 Augerius G.Busbecq, *Itinera Constantinopolitanum*, Antwerp, 1581; Chalcondylas, *De Origine et rebus gestis Turcorum*, Basle, 1556; Philip Lonicerus, *Chronicorum Turcicorum Tomus Primus* [etc.], 1556 *et seq.*; Minadoi, *Historia della Guerra fra Turchi e Persiani*, Venice, 1588 (English translation by Abraham Hartwell, 1595); Marino Barletto, *De Vitis et gestis Scanderbegi*; Sabellicus (Marcus Antonius Coccius), *De pugna inter Venetos et Turcas* (printed in some editions of Chalcondylas and of Lonicerus); N.Secundinus, *Otthomanorum familia, seu de Turcorum imperio historia*, Vienne, 1551; Johannes Lowenklau (Leunclavius), *Historiae Musulmanae Turcorum . . . libri XVIII*, Frankfort, 1591.

The Ottoman Peril: The Emperor versus The Great Turk

Lepanto was as if a man should shave his beard: it would grow again; but the loss of Cyprus by the Christians was, like the loss of an arm, irreparable—even in so trivial a tale there was an implied warning to the seventeenth century lest the experiences of the fifteenth and sixteenth centuries be repeated.

The prefatory address to the Reader begins: 'The long and still declining state of the Christian Commonwealth, with the utter ruin and subversion of the Empire of the East . . . might . . . move even a stony heart to ruth.' Knolles seeks to account for these disasters. The blame is attached in the first place to Satan [1] and then to those ancient heretics whose doctrines helped to shape Islam; but especially it is fixed upon 'the false prophet Mahomet, born in an unhappy hour' and upon his 'gross and blasphemous Doctrines.' The Will of God has permitted Turkish greatness to expand; and various lesser causes have contributed to the catastrophe: the uncertainty of all worldly affairs, the lack of unity in Christendom, the Turks' ardent desire for sovereignty, and their unity and agreement among themselves, their courage, frugality, and temperance.

One of the most closely reasoned political tracts inspired by the Eastern Question at the close of the sixteenth century is René de Lucinge's treatise on the rise, power, and decline of the Ottoman Empire, which Sir John Finett translated into English.[2] The problem here discussed is that of the strategy to be adopted against the Turks; and this involves some consideration of the causes of Turkish success. The Turks, says Lucinge, have always applied their minds to the art of war. Their captains do not stand upon the defensive but wage offensive war, acting at opportune moments, not fighting out of season or dividing their forces or wasting their energy upon subsidiary enterprises. They have the advantage of unity of command. The

---

1 The thought occurs frequently. Thomas Lodge personifies 'Malitious Hatred' as an incarnate devil and says that 'it was he that flesht the Turke upon the Christians' (*Wits Miserie, Works*, Hunterian Club, iv,65).

2 *The Beginning, Continuance, and decay of Estates: Wherein are handled many notable Questions concerning the establishment of Empires and Monarchies. Written in French by R. de Lusinge . . . and translated into English by I.F.*, 1606. The title promises a broader subject than that actually treated. The original French work appeared in Paris in 1588. For the passages cited see Finett's translation, pp.30,128,138,148,160.

soldiers are encouraged by the constant presence of the Sultan in the field. 'It was never seene that the Turkes ever lost battaile through disorder,' that is, because of dissensions or lack of discipline in their ranks. After Lepanto, on the other hand, the Christians let their alliance lapse through jealousies among themselves. Yet the case is not desperate for Christendom. From the recent Persian victories over the Turks Lucinge extracts an augury of Ottoman decline. The best chance of victory is at sea, for Christendom possesses more and better harbours and more expert mariners than Turkey, and 'fighting by sea, wee shall not need to feare their horse.' It is conceivable that a revolt might be stirred up among the Janissaries and in the subject nations; and bribes might win Turkish officers from their allegiance. Lucinge proposes, as Soranzo had done, that books to expose the fooleries of the *Koran* should be disseminated in the Ottoman Empire. These must be innocuously entitled so as not to arouse suspicion and subtly written so as to entice the Turks to read them, thus gradually leading them to doubt the authenticity of the fables in their holy book. The proposal may seem fantastic but it is not unlike the technique of propaganda in modern wars.

In the original or in Finett's translation Lucinge's treatise may have influenced Fulke Greville's meditations upon the Turkish problem. For Greville believed that the best chance of a Christian victory lay in naval warfare. He argues:

> Lepanto likewise proves the Christian's might
> Able by sea to shake the Turkish pow'r,
> When his land-armies all the World devour.

Therefore he urges that England must possess 'a well-fram'd Navy,'

> For whatsoever odds in man or beast
> Betweene the Christian and the Turk there be,
> By delicacy, hardness, industry or rest,
> Our fatal discord, or their unity,
> Yet we that thus on disadvantage stand,
> Stand fast, because he makes his wars by land.

Had the Turk realized this situation, changed his mode of war, and put all his energies upon the ocean, Christendom, Greville declares, would have 'long since been shaken.' [1]

Francis Bacon's thoughts upon the nation which he calls 'the Ottoman family, now the terror of the world' [2] may have been influenced by Lucinge. In 1617 he sent to Sir John Digby at Madrid certain instructions as to the 'noble effects' which would follow the proposed union of the royal families of England and Spain.

> It may be [he writes] the beginning and seed . . . of a holy war against the Turk, whereunto it seems the events of the time doth invite Christian Kings, in respect of the great corruption and relaxation of discipline of war in that empire; and much more in respect of the utter ruin and enervation of the Grand Seigneur's navy and forces by sea; which openeth a way (without congregating vast armies by land) to suffocate and starve Constantinople, and thereby to put those provinces into mutiny and insurrection. [3]

This project of an attack by sea was still in his mind five years later when he denounced the Turks in these terms:

> A cruel tyranny, bathed in the blood of their emperors upon every succession; a heap of vassals and slaves; no nobles; no gentlemen; no freemen; no inheritance of land; no stirp or ancient families; a people that is without natural affection; and, the Scripture saith, that regardeth not the desires of women; and without piety, or care towards their children; a nation without morality, without letters, arts, or sciences; that can scarce measure an acre of land, or an hour of the day: base and sluttish in buildings, diets and the like; and in a word, a very reproach of human society: and yet this nation hath made the garden of the world a wilderness; for that, as it is truly said concerning the Turks, where Ottoman's horse sets his foot, people will come up very thin. [4]

The victory of October 1571 remained the best augury of success. Lepanto 'arrested the greatness of the Turk,' Bacon wrote, [5] and 'hath put a hook into the nostrils of the Ottomans

1 *A Treatise of Monarchy*, stanzas 410 and 575f.; *Works*, i,148 and 203f.
2 *Of General Naturalization*, *Works*, ed. 1824, iii,308.
3 *Works*, vi,158.
4 *An Advertisement touching an Holy War*, *Works*, iii,477.
5 *Essays Civil and Moral*, xii: 'Of Boldness,' *Works*, ii,279.

to this day.' [1] Christian princes, he argued, did not need to seek a pretext for declaring war upon the Turks; Mohammedans hold that to propagate their 'law' they may without provocation wage war upon Christendom (Bacon is thinking of the *Jihad*); consequently 'there lieth upon the Christians a perpetual fear of a war . . . and therefore they may at all times, as they think good, be upon the preventation.' [2]

An analysis of the causes of Ottoman greatness somewhat similar to Lucinge's is made by Edward Brerewood. In the course of his discussion of Mohammedanism and, by inference, the political power of Islam, occurs the following noteworthy passage:

> Of the great spreading and enlargement of [this] religion if the causes were demanded of mee, I should make answere, that beside the justice of Almighty God, punishing by that violent and wicked sect the sinnes of Christians . . ., one cause, I say, of the large spreading of their Religion, is the large spreading of their victories. For it hath ever beene the condition of the conquered, to follow for the most part the religion of the conquerors. A second, their peremptory restraint (even on the paine of death) of all disputation touching their religion, and calling any point into question. A third, their suppression of the studie of Philosophy, by the light whereof, the grossness and vanity of many parts of their religion might be discovered . . . A fourth cause may well bee assigned, the sensuall liberty allowed by it, namely, to have many wives, and the like promise of sensual pleasures to succeed after this life (to the Religious observers of it) in Paradise wherewith men for the greatest part, as being of things wherewith their sense is affected, and whereof they have had certaine experience, are more allured and perswaded, then with promises of spiritual delights, presented only to their hopes, and for which present and sensible pleasures must in the meane time be forsaken.[3]

Whatever secondary causes are adduced, it is rare that a writer does not put in the first place the Will of God. Thus, as an illustration of the terror of Jehovah's wrath and as a warn-

---

1 *An Advertisement touching an Holy War, Works*, iii,474.
2 *Considerations touching a Warre with Spain*, 1629 (written in 1624), *Works*, vi,506.
3 *Enquiries touching the Diversity of Languages and Religions*, 1614, chapter xi: 'Of the parts of the World possessed by Mahumetans,' pp.85f. Compare Purchas, i,318f.

ing to plague-stricken London, Thomas Dekker bids his readers look upon the 'insolent triumphs' of the Turks.[1] Again, Thomas Beard, in the course of his encyclopaedic catalogue of examples of God's judgment upon sinners, is curiously specific. The Byzantine emperors, he says, committed an offence against God when they readmitted images into their churches, and so God suffered the iconoclastic Turks to be the instruments for the execution of His most just wrath, licensing them to commit 'grievous outrages and to make great wastes and desolations in all Christendome.' [2]

Some writers were sufficiently impartial to combine with hostility to Islam respect for certain admirable qualities of the Moslems. Thus, Alexander Ross considers that a prime cause of Turkish greatness is to be found in the 'continual jars, frivolous debates, and needless digladations among Christians.' The scandalous lives of Christians compare unfavourably with the sobriety of Mohammedans. While the sensual element in Islamic dogma is an appeal to the weak and the Turkish tyranny induces those victims who are not firm in their faith to become renegades, the Turkish zeal in practising and propagating their religion, their devoutness and reverence, their simplicity and abstemiousness of life—all are attractive to the thoughtful. Their respect for Moses appeals to the Jews; their respect for Jesus appeals to the Christians.[3]

Many suggestions as to the causes of Ottoman greatness are thrown out by Francis Osborn in the course of his reflections upon the political system of the Turks.[4] Abstinence from wine is one, for wine tends to enervate a man and make him effeminate and is the 'sworne Enemy to Discipline.' The Spartan frugality of their soldiers accustoms them to the rigours of a campaign. Yet by planning their campaigns for summer, when the sufferings from weather are not added to those from war, unnecessary hardships are avoided. In Turkey there are not so many idlers as in Europe, nor so many lawyers and scholars; neither

1 *A Rod for Run-awaies*, 1625; *Plague Pamphlets*, ed. Wilson, p.141.
2 *The Theatre of Gods Judgements*, ed. 1631, pp.157f.
3 ΠΑΝΣΕΒΕΙΑ: or, *A View of all Religions in the World*, 1653, pp.16of. Compare Peter Heylyn, *Cosmographie*, 1652, Part iii, pp.123f.
4 *Politicall Reflections upon the Government of the Turks*, 1656, pp.25f.,46,48,15,57, 61,72,74,99,102f.,110f.

are there 'the European vanities of Horse-rases, Hunting, Hawking, and amorous Entertainments, their plurality of Women quenching with more security in regard to health and lesse Charge, the thirst of Change ordinarily attending the tedious cohabitation with one.' To encourage their 'Resolution in Warre,' the sisters and daughters of the Emperor are often given in marriage to reward 'bravest soldiers of meanest birth.' But the Janissaries are forbidden to marry because single men make tougher soldiers. (Osborn seems not to know that even so long before his time as the reign of Solyman the Magnificent this discipline of the Janissaries had been relaxed and the permission granted to them to marry had been one of the causes of Turkish decline.) Eunuchs are often given places of command, being naturally cautious and not foolhardy; faithful, moreover, because though a 'perfect man' may profit by a change in government a eunuch is better off if the government remains the same. (This reasoning is not clear.) The moderation of their religious doctrine breeds hope rather than fear, for Mahomet and his successors wisely foresaw that

> nothing makes Subjects recoile more from their Obedience, than when they are loaded with a conceit that their Governors lead them in the way to Hell. This gives me occasion to think, that the Goblings armed by the Catholics with so much terrour, may possibly . . . fall foul upon themselves, and bring their Religion into a low contempt, through an apparent delection, or a panick fear.

The one respect in which the Moslem religion is stern—the belief in the inexorableness of fate—conduces to courage. The Sultan himself aids in maintaining order and discipline in his domains, both by the serenity and splendour of his appearance on public occasions and by his policy of heeding complaints against his grandees, thus 'stopping the mouths of his people with a shew of Piety and Justice.' Finally (to have done with Osborn's parade of explanations), 'the Turk finding Printing and Learning the chief fomentors of Divisions in Christendome, hath hitherto kept them out of his Territories.' Here Osborn, like various other writers, betrays an unawareness of the severity of the handicap to literacy among the Turks caused by the use of the Arabic alphabet.

We have now passed in review the most important English writers (and translators of foreign books) who discovered the causes of Ottoman greatness, first and foremost in the Will of God who has used the Moslems as an instrument to punish the wickedness of Christians; then in the natural law by which one empire succeeds another in power; then in the machinations of Satan who prompted Mahomet to promulgate his new religion and who instigated the unhappy divisions in Christendom; then in the impressive contrasting unity of Islam; then in the religious doctrines of the Moslems who are taught that a war against Christians is invariably holy, that the hour of every man's death is predetermined and hence fear is banished, and that sensual pleasures are the celestial reward of the brave; then in the hardihood, temperance, frugality, patience, and endurance of the Turkish soldiery; in their martial discipline, the entire state being organized for warfare; in the skill of their captains and the wisdom of their strategy in which there is no division of forces or wasting of effort; and in the religious zeal which wins the respect of subject populations.

III

In English lamentations for the ruin wrought by Turkish arms and fears of further aggressions and expressions of triumph in the too rare victories of Christendom, hostility to Islam is sometimes combined with hostility to Rome, while at other times, when the danger is critical or the triumph great, the sense of peril or the joy in victory silences for a moment the Christian discord.

At one point in *The Ship of Fools* Alexander Barclay, following his German original, turns from the follies of various types of Christians to those of infidels such as 'sarsyns, paynems, turkes and suche lyke,' for whom he makes a place in the 'folysshe nomber' in his ship. It were better, he says, to despise these wretches and leave them in their 'blynde darkenes,' for they refuse medicine to heal them of their vain idolatry, and no good counsel can move those who have delight only in 'theyr fals mayster, diceytfull Mahumyte.' So numerous are 'these fals forayns' that they overspread sea and land; indeed, so infinite is their foolishness that 'a small volume can nat well comprehende theyr foly.' 'Afryke and asye' 'and of europe great part and quantyte' are blinded with misbelief; 'the houndes of Tartary ar of this sect,' as are the Scithians, 'the owgly Maurians,' and the peoples of 'the londes and Iles adjacent.' Through false enchantments they have been seduced from God their Creator. With these Moslems Barclay associates Jews and 'nygromancians and fals wytches' and

> those wretched houndes of hell
> Which by dispayre with theyr owne handes ar slayne.

But to write more about these misbelievers or to reprove their errors 'were but foly and payne without avayle'—and with that contemptuous remark Barclay dismisses them. The woodcut illustration accompanying this section of his poem portrays a group of outlandish folk (two of whom wear turbans) engaged in a disputation among themselves, while in the background a desperate fool is in the act of hanging himself.[1] To place Mohammedans and suicides in one fellowship is strangely perverse, for the sin of self-destruction is of extreme rarity among Moslems.

On the title-page of Peter Ashton's translation of Paulus Giovius there is the following quatrain:

> Wake up now, Christiens, out of your slumbre,
>   Of the Turkes to recover your long lost glory,
> Feare not theyr strength, theyr power, ne numbre,
>   Sith ryght, and not myght, atchyveth the victory.

On the *verso* of the title-page is a singular poem, headed simply 'Thomas Litell' (apparently the author's name), in which an analogy is drawn between the struggle of ancient Rome with Carthage and Christendom's struggle with the Turks. The poem then continues with this mingled exhortation and lament:

> So O Christendome, Thottoman hath ben everymore
> Thy cruel and heavy foe, and greved the ryght sore.
>   Bloodshed and slaughter he hath wrought,
>   To destroye the al meanes hath he sought.

1 *The Ship of Fooles*, ed. Jamieson, Edinburgh, 1874, ii,188f.

Thy fresh flowers he hath bereved, thy riche, thy stronge,
Thy noble cities they ben his, thou hast more wronge,
    Constantinople, Rhodes, Belgrade,
    Bude hys herytage he hath made.
Whylom whiche were thyne, and shelbe I hope agayne,
For well I wot, that cursed seede shal not long raygne.
    For some Christien Camillus,
    Or Scipio Africanus
(Be of good chere) shall spryng up, which wyll the restore
To joye, ryches, and wealth, double thou had before.
    This blooddye Turkysh Annibal
    His power shall fade and have a fall.
Nowe all ye gentrye of Englande this boke embrace,
For of Christendome so standeth the plyght and case,
    No hystorye is more requisite,
    And it is nowe set forthe with lyght.[1]

With this recommendation of the treatise which follows, this somewhat uncouth rhapsody concludes abruptly.

During the siege of Malta in 1565 the Pope summoned all Christendom to prayers for victory. Even Protestant England responded, a common sense of imminent peril transcending the prejudices of sectarian divisions. The form of prayer issued by the diocese of Salisbury has survived. The preface declares that forasmuch as Malta is besieged with a great army and navy of the Turks, to the extreme peril of the beleaguered Christians, 'it is our part, which for distance of place cannot succour them with temporal relief, to assist them with spiritual aid.' We must implore God to deliver Christians from the rage and violence of enemies whose purpose it is to root out the very name and memory of Christ. 'If they should prevail against the Isle of Malta, it is uncertain what further peril might follow to the rest of Christendom.' The form provides appropriate lessons and psalms, and a prayer which runs in part as follows:

Thine and our sworn and most deadly enemies the Turks . . . now invade thine inheritance. . . The Turk goeth about to set up, to extol, and to magnify that wicked monster and damned soul

1 *A Shorte treatise upon the Turkes Chronicles*, 1546.

Mahumet above thy dearly beloved Son Jesus Christ. . . Wherefore overthrown thine and our enemies, establish thy kingdom, suffer them not to prevail.[1]

As was the anxiety poignant while Malta was threatened so was the satisfaction great when later in the same year the island was relieved. The news reached London promptly [2] and the Archbishop of Canterbury set forth a *Form of Thanksgiving* to be used thrice weekly for six weeks. The eloquence of this prayer testifies to the sense of alleviation from spiritual distress which swept over England.

O God [it runs] who hast of late most sharply corrected and scourged our Christian brethren thy servants with terrible wars and dreadful invasions of most deadly and cruel enemies, Turks and Infidels, . . . [and now] when all our hope was almost past dispersed and put to confusion all those Infidels,

we give Thee humble and hearty thanks for the relief of the afflicted Christians of Malta. Continue Thy mercies and 'as in this, so in all other invasions of Turks and Infidels, save and defend Thy holy Church.'[3]

The Turks acted swiftly to recover the prestige endangered by their repulse from Malta; and the bewilderment occasioned by the rapidity with which, defeated at sea, they struck again on land, is audible in a form of prayer put forth in the following year for the Christians of Hungary and other invaded nations. Whereas, the Preface reads, the Turks were last year repelled from Malta but now invade Hungary 'far more terribly and dreadfully,' it is our duty to pray for our fellow Christians. The prayer that follows and the form of lessons and psalms resemble

1 *A Form to be used in common prayer every Wednesday and Friday, within the city and Diocese of Sarum: to excite all godly people to pray unto God for the delivery of those Christians that are now invaded by the Turk*, 1565; reprinted in *Liturgies and Occasional Forms of Prayer set forth in the Reign of Queen Elizabeth*, ed. W.K.Clay, Parker Society, Cambridge, 1847, pp.519f. A like form was published for the city and diocese of London.

2 *Copie of the last advertisement that came from Malta of the miraculous deliverie of the isle from the Turke*, 1565. Of this the only recorded example is the fragment in the Cambridge University Library.

3 *A Short Forme of Thankesgiving to God for the Delyverie of the Isle of Malta from the invasion and long siege thereof by the great army of the Turkes both by sea and land, and for sundry other victories lately obtained*, 1565; reprinted in *Liturgies*, ed. Clay, pp.524f.

those previously recommended for the Maltese but are somewhat more elaborate.[1]

Though England did not join the coalition of 1571, there were
English volunteers at the battle of Lepanto, among them, it is
said, Sir Richard Grenville. It is strange that the great out-
burst of triumph which resounded through Europe after the
victory did not find expression in England in any special form
of thanksgiving to Almighty God. England—and Scotland—
did, however, celebrate the victory and do honour to the victors.
It is significant that among the few revels of a distinctly Levantine cast at the court of Queen Elizabeth of which records are
extant are those of the season of 1571–2. The account-books of
the Revels-Office show expenditures for costumes for Turks and
Moors;[2] what part these infidels played we do not know, but
doubtless they were discomfited. Since Tudor entertainments
were often patterned 'after the manner of Italy,' it is a valid
surmise that the theme of these revels was inspired not only
by the renewed interest in Levantine life and costume to be
expected immediately after the victory but more particularly
by reports which had come to England of the celebrations at
Venice.[3]

When news of Lepanto reached the City of the Lagoons
the Signory proceeded in state to offer thanksgiving in Saint
Mark's, while the bells of the campanile were rung. An arch
of triumph was erected at the entrance to the Rialto bridge
and the various market-places were festooned with lights.
Trophies of the despoiled Turks were hung in doorways.
Debtors were released from prison. On shops were displayed
signs reading: *Chiuso per la morte dei turchi*. For three days the
city devoted itself to rejoicing, and the streets and canals resounded with songs and shouts and clamour. The poets did
their part in memorializing the triumph, the most ambitious
effort of the kind being Celio Magno's *Trionfo di Cristo per la*

1 *A Form to be used in common prayer . . . for the preservation of those Christians and
their Countries, that are now invaded by the Turk in Hungary, or elsewhere* [1566];
reprinted in *Liturgies*, ed. Clay, pp.527f.
2 A.Feuillerat, *Documents relating to the Office of the Revels in the Time of Queen Elizabeth*, Louvain, 1908, pp.141,157,158,174,180. See below, p.457.
3 The account of these celebrations is drawn from Pompeo Molmenti, *La Storia di
Venezia nella Vita Privata*, ed. 1929, ii,437f.;446;426.

vittoria contro i Turchi, a semi-dramatic composition in a sequence of scenes and songs, performed before the Doge and published the same year. In it King David and several Saints and a Chorus of Angels take part. David compares his warlike deeds with those of Venice. The Chorus hymns the victory and does honour to Saint Justina on whose feast-day the battle had been fought. Saint Peter sings the praises of Pope Pius V; Saint James, the praises of King Philip II; and Saint Mark, the praises of the Venetian Republic. The Archangel Gabriel brings the performance to a close with a hymn of praise to the Holy Trinity. When the next carnival season came round the proud city, still in festive mood, dedicated the masquerade to further celebrations. Young men, costumed as Albanian soldiers in the service of Venice, as Swiss mercenaries, as Turks, as negroes, as fishermen, as what-not, followed with shouts and songs several triumphal cars upon which were allegorical representations of Faith, Venice, and the Three Corners of the World.[1] All this turbulent rejoicing was soon over; and of the innumerable poems and pageants produced in other parts of Italy not a single one was worthy of the occasion. But there were memorials of more lasting value. One of the reliefs on the tomb of Saint Pius V (who died in 1572, the year following the battle) in the Sixtine chapel of Santa Maria Maggiore is a representation of Lepanto. In the Academy at Venice is a painting by Paolo Veronese depicting with grimly realistic detail the hurly-burly of the conflict, while, in the clouds overhead, Venice, portrayed as a kneeling woman grasping a dagger, is presented by Saint Mark to the Madonna, and angels shower flaming arrows upon the Turkish fleet. In the Doge's Palace is still to be seen the same artist's magnificent allegory of the Triumph of Venice at Lepanto.[2] Paintings of the subject were presently sufficiently common in England to make an allusion to one of them comprehensible upon the stage, as is shown by the remark in one of Ben Jonson's plays: 'He looks like a

1 Molmenti, p.446, is here following: *Ordine et dichiaratione di tutta la mascherata nella citta di Venezia la domenica di carnevale MDLXXI* [i.e., 1572, n.s.] *per la gloriosa vittoria contra Turchi*, Venice, 1572.
2 In the public and private collections of Venice are several other paintings entitled 'The Battle of Lepanto,' generally pretexts for assembling a group of splendidly costumed Venetians with a few Turks.

The Battle of Lepanto

PHOTO. ALINARI

Venetian trumpeter in the battle of Lepanto in the gallery yonder.' [1]

Some months after the battle of Lepanto the double wedding of a son and a daughter of the Viscount Mountacute took place, and as part of the festivities on this occasion a masque was devised by George Gascoigne and presented by some of the guests.[2] The idea of performing in a masque originated in the minds of eight gentlemen who, as Gascoigne tells us, had reached in their preparations only the point of causing their garments 'to bee cut of the Venetian fashion' (were they merely following the mode or had they heard of the late splendid *Trionfi*?) when it occurred to them that they needed some excuse for appearing before the wedding-guests in this garb. As Gascoigne puts it in his prefatory explanation: 'Without some demonstration it would seem somewhat obscure to have Venetians presented rather then other countrey men.' In their predicament these gentlemen entreated the poet to devise verses 'convenient to render a good cause of the Venetians' presence.' The obliging poet forthwith invented the following situation. A Boy of about twelve years of age, English on his father's side, Italian on his mother's, was taken captive by the Turks after his father had been slain, and was a galley-slave till rescued by the Venetians 'in their last victory,' that is, at Lepanto. The Venetian vessel was driven by tempests upon the English coast; and that was why he and his rescuers were present at the marriage festival. Following this long explanatory introduction (written in prose) comes the longer poetical 'devise' which the Boy recited to the guests. He told them that his father fought against 'the Turke that Prince of pride' whose vaunt it was

> the greedy fish to glut
> With gobs of Christian carkasses, in cruell pieces cut.

He had served against the Moslems at Rhodes and Chios, and later, having lost his fortune, he sailed eastward to Cyprus just at the time of the Turkish siege of Famagusta. Thus it

1 *Cynthia's Revels*, IV,i,48f.
2 'A devise of a Masque for . . . Viscount Montacute,' *The Posies*, 1575; *Works*, ed. Cunliffe, Cambridge, 1907, i,75f.

came about that with his single ship he encountered the entire Turkish navy. Despite the overwhelming odds, he exhorted his crew to fight. Many a Turk was sent down to hell but in the end the father and some of the crew were slain and the rest taken prisoner:

> Among the which my selfe was tane by Turkes alas,
> And with the Turkes a turkish life, in Turkie must I pass.

For the few months between the fall of Cyprus and the battle of Lepanto the Boy was a galley-slave; and then 'in October last upon the seventh day' the Turks and the Christian allies met in a conflict which is described in a lively, horrific, and alliterative fashion. Smouldering stench stopped noses; fume offended eyes; pots of lime were hurled; parched peas were strewn on decks so that enemies' feet would slip; wild fire flamed in the air;

> The halbert[s] hew on hed, the browne billes bruse the bones,
> The harquebush doth spit his spight, with pretty persing stones,
> The drummes crie dub a dub, the braying trumpets blow,
> The whistling fifes are seldom herd, these sounds do drowne them so.

The wounded and the dying shriek and the ghosts of the slain make lamentation. The Boy, rescued by the victorious Christians, was identified as belonging to the house of Mountacute by the tokens which members of that family wear in their hats to distinguish them from the Capels (Capulets) because of the 'auncient grutch' between the two houses.[1] The last episode in his long story has to do with the tempest which tossed him and his rescuers ashore in England. At the conclusion of his speech there is a dance; and then a 'Trounchman' (an interpreter) translates to the brides and bridegrooms the congratulations of the visiting shipwrecked Venetians. In this wise did a noble English family celebrate at once a double wedding and the great recent victory over the Turks.

---

1 Gascoigne quaintly identifies his Mountacutes with the Montagues of Verona. He had doubtless read Arthur Brooke's *Romeus and Juliet*, 1561, and the story in Paynter's *Palace of Pleasure*. Shakespeare seems to echo Gascoigne in the opening Chorus of *Romeo and Juliet*, l.3; and the bit of dialogue at the opening of I,iv ('speech,' 'apology,' and 'the date is out of such prolixity') may be an allusion, unnoticed by the commentators, to Gascoigne's 'devise.'

While, obviously, Gascoigne's masque does not reach the higher levels of poetic inspiration, it drives forward in its jog-trot 'poulter's measure' rather bravely. Not even so much commendation can be granted to the long, pompous, and tedious poem, *Lepanto*, by King James VI of Scotland.[1] It has not even the virtue of timeliness, for James was but six years old in 1571 and his poem, though of uncertain date, was written long afterwards. Without reckoning the two choruses at the close, of about fifty and ninety lines respectively, it is 915 lines long. The metre is that of Gascoigne's 'devise'— which can scarcely be a coincidence. The introduction of the Archangel Gabriel and of an Angelic Chorus makès it likely that King James knew Celio Magno's *Trionfi di Cristo*, described above. After an invocation to God to 'inflame' his pen James begins his narrative. God places the responsibility for the wickedness of the Turks upon Satan. He sends Gabriel to Venice to incite the Venetians against the Turks. Disguised as a man, the Archangel moves about the city, saying to everyone he meets that the Turks have treated the Venetians outrageously. Presently he has instilled this opinion into the entire populace. After a brief description of the wretched condition to which the Turks have reduced Venice, James tells of the gathering of the allied armies: Greece, Italy, Spain, and the Almains join against the infidels. God weighs in His balance the faults of Christians against the infidelity of the Turks: 'The ballance stood not eaven, but sweid upon the faithlesse side.' The opposing forces prepare for battle; Don John of Austria encourages his followers; and the Turkish

1 *The Lepanto of James the Sixt, King of Scotland*, included, with a separate title-page, in *His Maiesties Poeticall Exercises at vacant houres*, Edinburgh, [1591]. A prefatory reference to certain 'stoln copies' indicates that there had been an earlier unauthorized edition. In the *Stationers' Register*, 7 August 1589 (Arber's *Transcript*, ii,527), there is an entry for 'A Booke intituled *the furious*, translated by James the Sixte kinge of Scottland, with the *le panto* of the same kinge.' No trace of this edition survives save this entry; it may have been suppressed and have been that to which James refers. An entry in the *Stationers' Register*, 11 April 1603 (Arber, iii,232), shows that a London edition was contemplated (though apparently never published) at that appropriate time. *La Lepanthe*, a French version by Du Bartas, is included in the *Poetical Exercises*. There is no modern edition of King James's poem but extracts are in *Select Poetry Chiefly Sacred of the Reign of King James the First*, ed. Edward Farr, Cambridge, 1847, pp.1f., and a facsimile of the first page of the manuscript is in *Lusus Regius being Poems and other Pieces by King James the First*, ed. R.S.Rait, 1901, opposite p.x.

commander Ali-Basha, surveying his men 'with bolde and manly face,'

> did recount among the rest
> What victorie Turks obtained
> On catif Christians, and how long
> The Ottomans race had raignd.

He bids them fear nothing save the flight of the Christians before his men have a chance to fight them. The battle begins. Jaw-bones and brains are strewn about; 'the clinkes of swards, the rattle of Pikes, the whirre of arrowes light, the howles of hurt, the Captaines cryes,' and other hideous noises resound.

> My pen for pitie cannot write
> My haire for horrour stands,
> To think how many Christians here
> Were kild by Pagane hands.

But the Christians achieve the victory, and the poem concludes with a Chorus of Venetians and a *Chorus Angelorum*.

The finest narrative of Lepanto in the various histories and chronicles is that in *The Generall Historie of the Turkes*. Here Knolles, rising to the occasion, gives a quite superb picture of the terror and glory of the battle when 'the Sea [was] stained with Blood, and covered with dead Bodies, Weapons and the Fragments of the broken Gallies.'[1]

The memory of the victory did not quickly fade and 'Seventy-One' remained traditionally a proud year,[2] not eclipsed

---

1 Ed. 1687, ii,589f.

2 'In Anno seventie one, . . . the Battle of Lepanto was fought in't—a most remarkable time' (Webster, *The Devil's Law-Case*, IV,ii,376). 'The last valour show'd in Christendom was in Lepanto, . . . the place made famous by the so-much mention'd battle betwixt the Turks and Christians' (Thomas Randolph, *The Muses' Looking-Glass*, III,iv; *Poetical and Dramatic Works*, ed. W.C.Hazlitt, 1875, p.232). 'That still memorable battle of Lepanto' (*Swetnam the Woman Hater*, 1618, I,iii; *Tudor Facsimile Texts*). Thomas Nashe (*Lenten-Stuffe*, *Works*, iii,185) describes the Yarmouth herring fair as 'a confused stirring to and fro of a Lepanta-like hoast of unfatigable flud bickerers.' The Earl of Stirling, alluding, as a loyal Scot, in complimentary fashion, to King James's poem, has the not very happy conceit that the Turks were 'baptiz'd' in the waters of Lepanto (*Doomes-Day*, Fourth Hour, stanza 65). In the anonymous play *Lady Alimony* (1635; III,i; Hazlitt's Dodsley, xiv,324) a fleet is compared for brave rigging, military strength, virile spirits, and expert commanders to that assembled at Lepanto. In Thomas Nabbes's *The Unfortunate Mother* (II,i) the oath 'on my maidenhead' is described as 'of great antiquity, the cavaliers used it before Lepanto.'

even by the more glorious renown of 'Eighty-Eight.' Since
the allied Christian powers failed to follow up their success,
the momentary triumph remained the unique symbol of the
practicability of united action and unified command and a
proof that the Ottoman Empire was not invincible. But this
was less apparent to contemporary observers than the speed
with which Turkey recovered from her defeat. Just as after
the repulse at Malta she regained her prestige by striking
swiftly and fiercely at Hungary, so after the defeat at Lepanto
she bent every effort to rebuild her navy. Within a year of
Lepanto, *The Travellers Breviat* tells us, the Turkish navy
was whole and entire again, yea, itching to cope with the
Christian Armada, for the Great Turk possessed infinite resources of timber for his ships and of Christian shipwrights
who flocked to Constantinople to work for him. Fears were
not lulled even by the rumours which reached European
publicists of the declining morale of the Ottoman organization.
There is a striking paragraph in Fulke Greville's biography
of Sir Philip Sidney in which, apropos of Sidney's knowledge
of European affairs, he writes of the decay of the Turkish
Empire. Sidney, he says, saw

> the Grand Signior asleep in his Seraglia; as having turned the
> ambition of that growing monarchy into idle lust; corrupted his
> martiall discipline; prophaned his Alcoran in making war against
> his own Church, and not in person, but by his Bashas; consequently
> by all appearance, declining into his people by such but more pre-
> cipitate degrees, as his active ancestors had climbed above them.[1]

Greville is here writing of the weak voluptuary Murad III,
of the rebellion of the Janissaries during his reign, and of his
inconclusive war with Persia.

But such signs of waning power were estimated as of little
consequence. In the year before Lepanto, John Foxe the Martyr-
ologist had preached a Good Friday Sermon at Paul's Cross
on 'Christ Crucified,' concluding with a prayer for the universal state of Christ's Church. From this impassioned and
moving supplication a few phrases may be quoted:

1 *The Life of the Renowned Sir Philip Sidney*, 1652; *Works*, iv,86.

Thy poor church militant here in this wretched earth; sometime a rich church, a large church, an universal church, spread far and wide, . . . now driven into a narrow corner of the world. . . First, the Turk with his sword, what lands, what nations, and countries, what empires, kingdoms and provinces, with cities innumerable, hath he won, not from us, but from Thee. Where Thy name was wont to be invocated, Thy word preached, Thy sacraments administered, there now remaineth barbarous Mahumet, with his filthy Alcoran. The flourishing churches in Asia, the learned churches in Greece, the manifold churches in Africa, which were wont to serve Thee, now are gone from Thee. . . In all Asia and Africa Thy church hath not one foot of free land, but all is turned to infidelity or to captivity.

Foxe proceeded to recite the names of countries lost to Christ in Asia and Africa, noting the possible exception of 'the far Ethiopians' who, according to report, still remained Christians; and continued: 'Now of Europe a great part also is shrunk from Thy church,' to wit: the Empire of Constantinople, Greece, Illyria, with almost all Hungary and much of Austria.

Only a little angle of the West parts yet remaineth in some profession of Thy name. But here (alack) cometh another mischief, as great, or greater than the other. For the Turk with his sword is not so cruel, but the Bishop of Rome on the other side is more fierce and bitter against us. . . Such dissensions and hostility Sathan hath sent among us, that Turks be not more enemies to Christians than Christians to Christians, papists to protestants: yea, protestants with protestants do not agree, but fall out for trifles.[1]

More than twenty years after the great victory Gabriel Harvey asks rhetorically:

Who honoureth not the glorious memory and the very name of Lepanto: the monument of Don John of Austria, the security of the Venetian state, the Halleluia of Christendome, and the Welaway of Turky? . . . Lord have mercy upon thee, o little-little Turke.

1 *A Sermon of Christ Crucified*, 1570. The prayer is reprinted in *A Booke of Christian Prayers*, 1578; in John Strype, *Annals of the Reformation* (ed. 1824, ii,636f.); and in *Private Prayers put forth by Authority during the Reign of Queen Elizabeth*, ed. W.K. Clay, Cambridge, 1851, pp.462f. Strype, p.214, misdates the sermon 1577–8.

Pride may exalt his hawty presumptions, and Prowesse advance his terrible bravery; but there is a God in heaven; and they cannot laugh long, that make the Devil laugh and Christe weepe.

But his confidence in the final triumph of the righteous does not blind Harvey to the gravity of the actual situation towards the close of the century. 'The Turke,' he says, 'a horrible foe to Christian states, [is] not to be daunted, or dismayed, with two or three petty foiles, . . . whose puissance hath long bene and still is the dishonour of Christendome.'[1] A few years later we find an anonymous writer on the policy of the Turks commenting upon 'the excessive heights of their present greatness. The terrour of their name,' he goes on, 'doth even now make the kings and princes of the West . . . to tremble and quake through fear of their victorious forces.'[2]

IV

LAMENTS for the ruin and desolation of ancient civilizations, biblical and classical, were frequently uttered by Englishmen on their return from travel in the Levant. Thus, John Cartwright, having given an account of the miseries of the populations subject to the Turk, declares that 'that monster of Turkish tyranny . . . hath too long raigned and laid the earth desolate.'[3] Lithgow's impressions of Greece are conveyed to his readers with his characteristic vividness and emphasis:

In all that countrey of Greece I could finde nothing to answer the famous relations . . . of the excellency of that land, but the name onely: the barbarousnesse of Turkes and Time having defaced all the Monuments of Antiquity: No shew of honour, no habitation of men in an honest fashion, nor possessours of the Countrey in a Principality. But rather prisoners shut up in prisons, or addicted slaves to cruell and tyrannicall Maisters: So deformed is the state of that once worthy Realme, and so miserable is the burthen of that afflicted people. . . In a word, they are wholly degenerate from their Auncestors in valour, vertue, and learning: Universities they

---

1 *A New Letter of Notable Contents*, 1593; *Works*, ed. Grosart, i,262,264.
2 *The Policy of the Turkish Empire*, 1597, Sig. A₃ᵛ.
3 *The Preachers Travels*, 1611, p.71.

have none, and civill behaviour is quite lost: formerly in derision they tearmed all other Nations Barbarians: A name now most fit for themselves, being the greatest dissembling lyers, inconstant, and uncivill people of all other Christians in the World.[1]

In the Dedication to his *Relation of a Journey* George Sandys says that he offers a narrative of travels in what were formerly the most renowned of countries, 'once the seats of most glorious and triumphant Empires,' now 'wast and overgrowne with bushes,' 'which countries once so glorious and famous for their happy estate are now through vice and ingratitude, become the most deplored spectacles of extreme miserie.' Sandys's picture of contemporary Greece moved Michael Drayton to mourn that

> Th' unlettered Turk, and rude Barbarian trades
> Where Homer sang his lofty Iliads.[2]

The same narrative inspired Lucius Carey, Viscount Falkland, to mournful meditations upon the decay of Greece and the sad and perilous condition of the Orthodox Eastern Church, caught between Roman Catholicism and Mohammedanism. After praising Sandys's book as 'a work much lastinger' than the pyramids which it describes, one which teaches 'the frailty of humane things,' Falkland continues:

> We know that towne is but with fishers fraught,
> Where Theseus govern'd, and where Plato taught:
> That spring of knowledge, to which Italy
> Owes all her arts and her civility,
> In vice and barbarisme supinely rowles;
> Their fortunes not more slavish than their soules.
> Those churches, which from the first hereticks wan
> All the first fields, or led (at least) the van, . . .
> Lie now distrest between two enemy-powers,
> Whom the West damns, and whom the East devoures.
> What state than theirs can more unhappy be,
> Threatened with hell, and sure of poverty.[3]

1 *Rare Adventures*, pp.65 and 105.
2 'To Master George Sandys,' ll.71f.; *Works*, ed. J.W.Hebel, iii,206f.
3 'To My Noble Friend, Mr. George Sandys,' *Poems*, ed. Grosart, in *Fuller Worthies' Library, Miscellanies*, 1871, pp.79f.

In identical mood Henry King, having perused Blount's
Voyage into the Levant, mourns the changed condition of him
who was

> Once the worlds Lord, now the beslaved Greek,
> Made by a Turkish yoak and fortunes hate
> In language, as in mind, degenerate.[1]

The Earl of Stirling rises above his usual pedantic and pedestrian level when he portrays the condition of Christianity in
the Levant:

> The Eastern Churches first did Christ embrace,
> And drew their faith from fountaines that were pure,
> What famous Doctours, singular for grace,
> Have clear'd those parts, though at this time obscure?
> What glorious Martyrs crowning there their race,
> The fyrie tryall, gold-like did endure?
> To thinke of them my soule for anguish groanes;
> Ah, that base Turkes should tread upon their bones! [2]

The grief of Phineas Fletcher is not for the oppression of the
Orthodox Church but for the decay and disappearance of
classical arts and letters:

> Where once the lovely Muses us'd to sing,
> And chant th' Heroes of that golden age;
> Where since more sacred Graces learn'd to string
> That heavn'ly lyre, and with their canzons sage
> Inspirit flesh, and quicken stinking graves,
> There (ah for pitty!) Muses now are slaves,
> Graces are fled to heav'n, and hellish Mahomet raves.[3]

The reports of returned travellers of the ruin wrought by
the Turks in the countries they had overrun were confirmed
by the presence of refugees from Greece and other invaded
lands in England. So early as 1455-6 gifts of money were made
by the English exchequer to four exiled Greeks.[4] Early in the
sixteenth century the custom began in England of collecting

1 'To My Noble and Judicious Friend Sir Henry Blount upon his Voyage,' *Poems*,
  ed. John Sparrow, pp.76f.
2 *Doomes-Day*, Ninth Hour, Stanza 53; compare Second Hour, Stanza 28.
3 *The Apollyonists*, iii,13.
4 H.L.Gray, 'Greek Visitors to England in 1455–1456,' *Haskins Anniversary Essays*,
  Cambridge, Massachusetts, 1929.

alms for the redemption of prisoners of the Turks.[1] In 1563 there were Greek refugees at Oxford offering books (that is, probably, Greek manuscripts) for sale; one of these exiles hoped to obtain employment from the Queen as a copyist of Greek manuscripts.[2] In the account-books of Winchester College there are about a dozen items of various dates between 1595 and 1626 concerning disbursements of small sums to such deserving objects of charity.[3] One of these gifts was to a Greek archbishop who was travelling about England to collect funds for the redemption of his fellow-countrymen from captivity. Other recipients are described as .poor Greek scholars, travelling Greeks, and in one case two 'Chaldeans.' *The Odcombian Banquet* gives us a glimpse of one poor refugee. Here Thomas Coryat is described as eager to improve his knowledge of modern Greek. He practised that tongue with a Greek beggar who haunted the aisles of Saint Paul's. 'The greatest Politicke'—that is, the most influential statesman— 'that advances into Paules hee will quitte, to go talke with the Grecian that begges there; such is his humilitie; and doth grieve inwardly he was not borne that Countreyman for that purpose.' A marginal gloss elucidates this somewhat obscure statement: 'Not to beg, but to talke Greeke the better with the natural Grecians.'[4] A similar fleeting glimpse of foreign refugees is afforded us by Dekker who describes

> the Hungarians in Paules, who have a Priviledge to holde out their Turkish History for any one to reade. They beg nothing, the Texted Past-bord talkes all; and if nothing be given, nothing is spoken, but God knowes what they thinke.[5]

How dextrous is this sketch of those unfortunates who, knowing no English, proffer a card or sign on which is written their

1 In 1518 Richard Pynson printed on a single folio sheet Pope Leo X's authorization of J. Sargy to collect alms for prisoners of the Turks. The only surviving copy is in the British Museum. It begins: *These be the articles of the popes Bulle.* Another unique document, probably from the same press, *c.* 1515, is in the Bodleian. It has no title but is an Indulgence in English in favour of the redemption of Lady I. Lascarina's children from the Turks. See *Short Title Catalogue,* 15473.
2 See W.G.Rice, 'Early English Travelers to Greece and the Levant,' ut cit., pp.240f.
3 *Annals of Winchester College,* ed. T.F.Kirby, 1892, pp.297 (cited by Rice, op.cit.).
4 *The Odcombian Banquet: Dished foorth by Thomas the Coriat and Served in by a number of Noble Wits,* 1611, Sig.B^{v}f.
5 *Dekker His Dreame, Works,* ed. Grosart, iii,7.

sad history! The 'privileges' mentioned by Dekker were probably issued by local authorities; in the few cases where surviving records show that the central government took a hand we have probably to do with refugees of some importance. Thus, in 1623 one John Albertus, a Greek, was granted a licence to have a general collection for his relief taken throughout England.[1] His must have been a case of notable misfortune, or else he was a person of some influence. Again, in 1626 the Council allowed one Contarini Paleologus to make a collection for the redemption of his relations from the Turks.[2] Not all these Levantines were mere beggars. We find, for example, four Greek monks, or men habited as monks, who landed at Dover, professing the desire to study at the English universities.[3] Three Greek scholars, two of them in clerical orders, were established at Balliol College in the seventeenth century; one of them, named Nathaniel Conopius, is said to have been a composer of music.[4] John Evelyn used to see Conopius when he was an undergraduate at Oxford, and he notes that he was 'the first I ever saw drink coffee.'[5] Where licences to beg were not needed or at any rate not granted, passports or other credentials might be issued to the deserving; thus we have record of a 'safe conduct for a Grecian.'[6] Swindlers sometimes fell foul of the law. In January 1624, a Macedonian and a Syrian, with their interpreter (a Londoner), were arrested on a somewhat unusual charge. They had in their possession a Latin letter addressed by King James to foreign princes, recommending them to their kindness. It was suspected that this letter was a forgery; but the accusation brought against the prisoners was that they had had printed an English translation of this document with alterations so contrived as to make it appear that the King commended them to the charity of his own subjects.[7] This case confirms Lithgow's warning to his countrymen to beware of such dissembling knaves:

1 C.S.P.,Dom., 1623–5, p.111.
2 Ibid., 1625–6, p.557.
3 Ibid., 1603–1610, p.548.
4 H.W.Carless Davis, *Balliol College*, 1899, pp.114f. (cited by Rice, op.cit.).
5 Preliminary autobiographical matter which opens the *Diary*, under date 10 May 1637.
6 C.S.P.,Dom., 1623–5, p.499.
7 Ibid., p.148.

I must give the Kings Kingdomes a caveat here, concerning vaga-
bonding Greekes, and their counterfeit Testimonials: True it is,
there is no such matter, as these lying Rascals report unto you,
concerning their Fathers, their Wives, and Children taken Captives by the Turke: O damnable invention! How can the Turke
prey upon his owne Subjects, under whom, they have as great
Liberty, save onely the use of Bels, as we have under our Princes. . .
And therefore looke to it, that you be no more gulled, golding them
so fast as you have done, least for your paines, you prove greater
Asses, than they do Knaves.[1]

Lithgow's violent rhetoric is also confirmed by the reliable
Sir Thomas Roe's statement that the Greeks who toured
Europe asking alms to redeem their countrymen held in captivity were 'no better than counterfeits.' [2] Whether rogues or
honest men, some of these refugees doubtless picked up a
little English, the better to recount their sad stories to the
charitably inclined; and from them Englishmen in taverns
or on the streets or by church doorways would obtain picturesque and pathetic anecdotes of the miseries of the Near
East.

Among the beggars who infested the streets of London were
many discharged veterans of foreign wars, and though most
of these had served in the Low Countries there were some who
had fought as volunteers against the Turks. 'I have knowne
men,' says a character in one of Webster's plays, 'that have
come from serving against the Turke; for three or four moneths
they have had pension to buy them new wooden legges and
fresh plaisters; but after 'twas not to bee had.' [3] Jonson's
Brainworm nourishes a like grievance. He claims to have
fought in all the late wars 'by land and sea, any time this
fourteene yeeres, and follow'd the fortunes of the best Commanders in Christendome.' Twice he had been shot at the
taking of Aleppo; once at the relief of Vienna. 'I have beene
at Marseilles, Naples and the Adriatique gulfe, a gentleman-
slave in the galleys.' While pulling at the oars he had been
'most dangerously shot in the head, through both the thighs,'

1 *Rare Adventures*, p.106.   3 *The White Devil*, V,i,132f.
2 *Negotiations of Sir Thomas Roe*, 1740, p.103.

yet, 'being thus maym'd, I am void of maintenance, nothing left me but my scarres, the noted markes of my resolution.'[1] In another play one veteran meeting another exclaims: 'You and I have sweat in the Breach together at Malta.'[2] In one of the Beaumont-Fletcher plays there is an elderly man who tells how in his youth he had turned to the profession of arms and for twenty years 'wore the Christian cause upon [his] sword.' At the siege of Buda he suffered cold and heat and 'thrice was . . . made a slave and thrice redeemed.'[3]

Not only from refugees and discharged soldiery but from news-sheets and *corrantos* Londoners obtained information and impressions of events in the Near East and in the parts of Europe threatened by Islam. Here are the titles of some of these ephemeralities. *The triumphant victory of the Imperyall Mageste against the Turks . . . in Steuermarke by a Capytayne named Michael Meschsaer*, 1582. In 1594 there was entered for publication *A Most great and wonderful and miraculous victorie obteyned by the christians against the Turkes in Hungarie*;[4] and four months later: *Newes from the Levant Seas.*[5] *The wonderfull mercy of God shewed towards the Christians against the Turks*, translated from the German, was published in 1593. *Good Newes from Florence: of a famous victorie obtained against the Turkes*, 1614; *Newes from Turkie, or the Death of Achmet.* 1618; *Good newes to Christendome*, 1620; *Newes from Turkie and Poland*, 1623; *A true and faithfull relation of the death of Sultan Osman*, 1622; *The strangling and death of the great Turke*, 1622 (these two on the assassination of Othman II)— these are other specimens of the same sort of publications.

1 *Every Man in His Humour*, II,iv,58f.
2 Webster, *The Devil's Law-Case*, IV,ii,634.
3 *The Captain*, II,i. The allusion may be to the Archduke Matthias's unsuccessful siege of Buda in 1602; but the veteran's triple misfortune seems to suggest the three takings of the city in 1527-9, by Solyman the Magnificent, by Ferdinand, and again by Solyman. If the dramatists expected their audience to respond to such an allusion, they reckoned on a good deal of popular knowledge of a disaster eighty-odd years before. There was, however, a play, now lost, entitled *Vayvode* (*Henslowe's Diary*, ed. Greg, ii,197), which doubtless had to do with the fighting around Budapest and with other stirring events in the life of Zapolya, the Voivode of Transylvania; and this may have kept these long-past events in mind.
4 *Stationers' Register*, 20 April 1594 (Arber, ii,647). Compare the translation by R.C[hurche] of Martin Fumée's *Historie of the Troubles in Hungarie*, 1600.
5 *Stationers' Register*, 19 August 1594 (Arber, ii,657).

Prophecies of the overthrow of the Turks were naturally popular. In the case of one report of a Persian victory over the Turks this augury that the Ottoman Empire is not invincible is coupled with an astrological prediction of the fall of Constantinople.¹ A curious book (a tiny quarto of only four leaves) is: *Strange and Miraculous Newes from Turkie. Sent to our English Ambassadour resident at Constantinople. Of a Woman which was seene in the Firmament with a Book in her hand at Medina Talnabi where Mahomets Tombe is. Also severall Visions of Armed men appearing in the Ayre for one and twenty dayes together. With a Propheticall interpretation made by a Mahumetan Priest, who lost his life in the maintenance thereof*, 1642. The woman who appeared in the heavens was none other than the Blessed Virgin Mary; the book she held in her hand was the Bible. At the sight of her the aerial armies were put to flight. A 'dervice' (dervish) described and expounded this miraculous vision in such heretical and pro-Christian terms that with the consent of the Beglerbeg the Turks tortured and slew him. There was a ready market for other kinds of books which in one way or another fomented prejudices against the Turks. Thus, so late as 1607 there appeared a book entitled *The Turkes Secretarie* which contains a translation of the correspondence of Sultan Mahomet II with various potentates.² This collection, of whose authenticity there is some doubt, had had a considerable circulation in Latin during the sixteenth century.³ Its belated appearance in English dress was perhaps due to emulation of a tiny pamphlet entitled *Letters from the Great Turke* which had been published in 1606.⁴ This claimed to be a translation of letters

1 *A Discourse of the bloody and cruell Bataile, of late lost by the great Turke Sultan Selim. And also of the taking of the strong towne of Sernan, with the number there slaine and taken, and the great store of Artillery and munitions of warre lost in the taking of the saide Towne, 1579. Translated out of the French into English,* [1579].

2 *The Turkes Secretarie, conteining his . . . letters . . . to divers emperours, kings, princes,* [etc.]. *With severall answers to the same. . . Translated out of the Latine copie,* 1607.

3 The Latin text of this correspondence is included, for example, in *Epistole Turchi,* collected by Laudivius, Lyons, 1520.

4 *Letters from the great Turke lately sent unto the holy Father the Pope and to Rodulphus naming himselfe King of Hungarie, and to all the Kinges and Princes of Christendome. Translated out of the Hebrew tongue into Italian, and out of the Italian into French and now into English out of the French coppie. Maximus horror, maxima virtus,* 1606. This is a quarto of twelve pages.

which the reigning Sultan Achmet had sent to the Pope and other rulers of Christendom. In this flamboyant and bombastic communication the Sultan styles himself 'Champion of Babilon, God of the Earth, Barron of Turkie, . . . and future Conqueror of Christendome.' [1] He expresses the expectation 'to be the onely Monarche of the whole earth before the expiration of two yeares,' and in return for the promise of freedom of worship demands the submission of all Christians to him. The document may be a fabrication; if not, its tone was singularly ill-advised at a time when Turkey was signing with Austria the first peace not imposed by her upon the vanquished but negotiated between equal powers. In three later years translations of somewhat similar documents appeared in England. These are: *The Greate Turkes Defiance to Sigismond the Third. With replie. Englished by M.S.*, 1613; *True Copies of the insolent letter lately written by the Great Turke*, 1621; and *A Vaunting letter sent from Sultan Morat*, 1638.

V

PREJUDICES against the Turks reached a climax in the oft-expressed notion that they were incarnate devils or at any rate the chosen followers of Satan, that they all derived from hell or were all going there. How closely the Sultan was associated with Satan in the popular imagination is evident from some quotations earlier in this chapter. Another such quotation, perhaps the more significant for being quite casual and off-hand, may be cited from a play where a character is described as strutting 'as if he were a gentleman-usher to the Great Turk or to the devil of Dowgate.' [2] In an early interlude Satan boasts that many of all nations come to his palace:

---

1 In *1 Henry VI*, IV,vii,73f. apropos of the 'silly stately style' of titles of honour, a character exclaims:

> The Turk, that two-and-fifty kingdoms hath,
> Writes not so tedious a style as this.

Compare the dignities of Bajazet listed in *1 Tamburlaine*, Act III; the titles in Greene's *Alphonsus King of Arragon*, III,ii; the list of the Sultan's 'bombastical titles' in James Howell, *Familiar Letters*, i,178; and the titles attached to many Levantine documents in Hakluyt.

2 *Wily Beguiled* (anonymous), Hazlitt's Dodsley, ix,285.

> All the Jews and all the Turks,
> Yea, and a great part of Christendom,
> When they have done my will and works,
> In the end they fly hither all and some.[1]

Another poet says that 'the Italian Turke' comes from hell.[2] The epithet here attached to the Turk is noteworthy because it exemplifies the instinct to associate the traditional wickedness of the Turks with a strain of Machiavellianism. This is seen in some characterizations of the Turks upon the stage. The most familiar example is Ithamore, the Turkish slave whom Marlowe's Barabas purchases in the slave-market at Malta. In answer to the question how he was accustomed to spend his time when he was a free man, Ithamore replies:

> In setting Christian villages on fire,
> Chaining of eunuchs, binding galley slaves.
> One time I was an hostler in an inn,
> And in the night time secretly would I steal
> To travellers' chambers, and there cut their throats:
> Once at Jerusalem, where the pilgrims kneel'd,
> I strewed powder on the marble stones,
> And therewithal their knees would rankle so
> That I have laugh'd a-good to see the cripples
> Go limping home to Christendom on stilts.[3]

When allowance is made for the element of caricature, such conduct is not very different from that of some Turks at the Holy Sepulchre, as reported by English travellers.

Of even grosser fiendishness is the character of Mulleasses in John Mason's play *The Turk*. The plot of this violent drama centres in the ambition of an Italian named Borgias to become Duke of Florence and afterwards, with the aid of the Great Turk, King of Italy. Mulleasses, a Turk visiting Florence while Borgias's son is in Constantinople, is professedly Borgias's agent in these designs but in secret is conspiring against him. In action and dialogue the play is shot through with dark

---

1 *The Disobedient Child* (anonymous), Hazlitt's Dodsley, ii,310.
2 Thomas Robinson, *The Life and Death of Mary Magdalene* (c.1620), ed. O.H.Sommer, E.E.T.S., 1899, l.873.
3 *The Jew of Malta*, II,iii,203f.

villainy, obscure 'policy,' lust, and murder. No source has been discovered for this sinister amalgam. Both Borgias and the Turk subscribe to the doctrines of *The Prince* and give frequent expression to their Machiavellian philosophy.[1] Mulleasses prays to Mahomet to liberate him from the dictates of conscience and from the fools' philosophy that inculcates honesty.[2] His actions are, it is sufficient to say, thoroughly in accord with this petition. He possesses a slave named—or styled—Eunuchus who in soliloquy acquaints us with the story of his life:

> Howso'ere my fortunes make me now a slave
> I was a free borne Christians soone [son] in Cyprus,
> When Famagusta by the Turke was sackt:
> In the division of which Citty spoyles,
> My fortunes fell to Mulleases lot.

He was castrated and for sixteen years subjected 'unto the vilde command of an imperious Turke'; and at length was bestowed by his master upon the wife of Borgias to be an agent of her lusts.[3] The dramatist probably intended that the repulsive character of Eunuchus should illustrate the horrible degeneracy of Christians so miserable as to fall into the hands of the Turks.

The contrasting situation of a Turkish slave in Christian hands is found in Robert Davenport's play *The City Night-Cap*. Antonio had captured this Turk in a sea-fight off Palermo.[4] For purposes of the intrigue which need not be explained this slave changes garb with his master and immediately thereafter, mistaken for Antonio, is slain by Philippo. The scene is an arresting one. The slave, speaking in soliloquy, complains that Antonio 'twits' him with his capture, and goes on:

1 *The Turke. A Worthie Tragedy*, 1610 (*Stationers' Register*, 1609); ed. J.Q.Adams, Bang's *Materialien*, Louvain, 1913. On the Machiavellianism of the play see Adams's discussion, p.xviii, and the text of the play *passim*.
2 Ibid., ll.688f. Compare ll.880f.
3 Ibid., ll.443f.
4 'Thou art my slave,' says Antonio; 'I took thee (then a Turk) in the fight thou know'st we made before Palermo.' The reference is not to the long-past Saracenic occupation of Palermo but to some sea-fight or (less probably) to one of the raids conducted during the fifteen-seventies.

> I did command
> Men as he did there, Turks and valiant men:
> And though to wind myself up for his ruin,
> That I may fall and crush him, I appear
> To renounce Mahomet, and seem a Christian,
> 'Tis but conveniently to stab this Christian. . .
> I'll wait him with a pistol, O sweet revenge!
> Laugh, our great prophet; he shall understand,
> When we think death far off, he's nearest hand.

At this moment Philippo shoots the slave, who dies commenting upon the irony of his fate: 'Mine own words catch me!'[1] In this fashion the Machiavellian and fiendish Turk is caught in his own trap.

With the popular English notion of the trickery and treachery of the Turks went the notion of their sensuality and lasciviousness. To Shakespeare the word Turk almost invariably suggested images of lustfulness and cruelty. 'In women outparamour'd the Turk,' says Edgar in *King Lear*.[2] Henry V, ascending the throne, reassures the fearful nobles:

> This is the English, not the Turkish court;
> Not Amurath an Amurath succeeds,
> But Harry Harry.[3]

Elsewhere the exclamation 'What? thinke you we are Turkes or infidels?' is equivalent to an assurance that no one will be executed without cause.[4] 'Stubborne Turkes' are 'never train'd to offices of tender courtesy.'[5] When war threatens it is said paradoxically that 'Peace shall go sleep with Turkes and infidels.'[6] Analogous examples might be adduced from many other Elizabethan plays. In general 'Turk' is a term of reproach among the Elizabethans,[7] sometimes in the alliterative and belittling form 'a Turk of tenpence.'[8] The expression

1 *The City Night-Cap*, V,i; Hazlitt's Dodsley, xiii,176f.
2 III,iv,91.
3 *2 Henry IV*, V,ii,47f.
4 *Richard III*, III,v,40.
5 *The Merchant of Venice*, IV,i,32f.
6 *Richard II*, IV,i,139.
7 Iago says: 'It is true or else I am a Turk' (*Othello*, II,i,114). A similar locution occurs in Beaumont and Fletcher, *The Captain*, IV,v.
8 'What gentry can be in a poor Turk of tenpence' (Marlowe, *The Jew of Malta*, II,iv); 'Give me a valiant Turk, though not worth ten pence' (Middleton and Rowley, *A Fair Quarrel*, III,i).

'To turn Turk' is very common, sometimes in the literal sense of embracing Islam, as when a Mohammedan commander asks: 'What say these prisoners? will they turne Turke or no?'[1] The title of Daborne's drama *A Christian Turn'd Turk* has a double meaning, religious and political, for the protagonist Captain Ward is a traitor to England and embraces Mohammedanism. Hamlet uses the term metaphorically: 'If the rest of my fortunes turn Turke with me,' that is, if my fortunes betray me. Sometimes there is no implication of treachery but merely of fantastic or contemptible changes in condition, as in this passage: 'This is to turn Turk; from a most absolute, complete gentleman to a most absurd, ridiculous, and fond lover.'[2] The phrase 'An you be not turn'd Turke' in *Much Ado About Nothing*[3] has been inadequately annotated by the editors. It has the special meaning, or at any rate glances with a *double entendre* at the special meaning, to become a prostitute. When Massinger's Paulina says 'I will turn Turk,' Gazet replies: 'Most of your tribe do when they begin in whore.'[4] Again, Dekker's Hippolito exclaims to Bellafront: ' 'Tis damnation if you turn Turk again!'[5] What may have been another proverbial expression of contempt seems to be echoed in the title of a lost play, *A Turkes Too Good for Him.*[6]

So far as is known, no inn or tavern in Elizabethan London was called the Turk's Head; but it must be remembered that no clear distinction was popularly drawn between Turks and Saracens; and the analogous Saracen's Head was a common

1 Thomas Kyd (?), *Soliman and Persida*, III,v.
2 John Cooke, *Greenes Tu Quoque or the City Gallant*, Hazlitt's Dodsley, xi,226.
3 III,iv,56. The phrase in *Hamlet* (III,ii,292) may contain the same implication, since Hamlet calls Fortune a strumpet.
4 *The Renegado*, V,iii.
5 *1 Honest Whore*, IV,i; *Dramatic Works*, ed. Pearson, ii,59. Compare also Marston, *The Dutch Courtesan*, II,ii,46: 'Vat sall become of mine poor flesh now? mine body must turn Turk for twopence.' This connotation survived into the eighteenth century in the slang name 'Turkish-shore' for the disreputable districts on the Surrey side of the Thames opposite London and Westminster. See W.G.Rice, 'To Turn Turk,' *Modern Language Notes*, xlvi (1931), 154, citing *The Dictionary of the Canting Crew*, c.1700, *sub* 'Turkish Shore.'—For a convincing interpretation of the obscure words of the Third Madman in Webster's *Duchess of Malfi*, IV,ii,94f.: 'Greeke is turn'd Turke, we are onely to be sav'd by the Helvetian translation,' see F.L.Lucas's note in his edition of Webster, ii,183.
6 G.M.Sibley, *The Lost Plays and Masques*, p.166.

sign. Though the tradition among innkeepers was that this sign owed its origin to the fact that the mother of Thomas à Becket was reputed to have been a Saracen, it is more likely that the sign is a late reflection, through the romances, of memories of the Crusades, or else was brought into England by pilgrims returning from the Holy Land. Veterans of later wars in the Levant may have helped to prolong its popularity. 'Do not undervalue an Enemy by whom you have been worsted,' said John Selden. 'When our Countrymen come home from fighting against the Saracens and were beaten by them, they pictur'd them with huge bigg terrible faces (as you still see the Signe of the Saracen's head is) when in truth they were like other men, but this they did to save their owne creditts.' [1] The explanation is far-fetched, for the motive was, obviously, to caricature one's enemy. How the sign happened to become so popular is not clear. It was that of the inn at Ware which contained the famous 'great bed.' The inn at Islington in which is laid the scenes of Thomas Jordan's *Walks of Islington and London* also bore the name. That the head was grotesque in features and of a red or garish colour is an inference from several allusions to the most famous inn of this name, that which stood beyond London Wall outside of Newgate near Smithfield. Richard Tarleton compares a gentleman with a red face to 'the Saracens Head without Newgate.' [2] Thomas Delony likens a man with blood smeared upon his face to 'the Sarazins Head without Newgate.' [3] Dekker's Tucca, railing at Horace, says: 'Dost stare, my Sarsens Head at Newgate, dost gloat?' [4] Staring was certainly a striking trait of these grotesques, for Joseph Hall writes:

> His angry eyes look all so glaring bright
> . . . like a painted staring Saracen.[5]

1 *Table Talk*, ed. Pollock, p.136.
2 *Tarleton's Jests*, ed. J.O.Halliwell, Shakespeare Society, 1844, p.12. This inn was standing so recently as the eighteen-sixties. Dickens describes it.
3 *The Gentle Craft*, ed. A.F.Lange, *Palaestra*, xviii, Part ii, p.60.
4 *Satiromastix*, l.577; *Dramatic Works*, ed. Pearson, i,200. In *The Shoemaker's Holiday*, V,i, Dekker likens a character to a Saracen's Head.
5 *Satires*, VI,i.

The features were distorted and monstrous. Nashe describes a man 'that has a sulpherous big swolne head like a Saracen.' [1] Dekker says that the swollen eyelids of victims of the plague were 'as monstrous as a Sarazens.' [2] Nicholas Breton describes a man as having 'a Sarazins face, his nose too long for his lips, his cheekes like the jawes of a horse, his eyes like a Smithes forge.' [3] In all these cases the writers are certainly thinking of the grotesque inn-sign. It was a familiar sight to Londoners of the day. [4] When the Witch in *Macbeth* threw into the cauldron a 'nose of Turk' the image suggested to the audience must have been of a monstrous, garish, and comically loathsome visage painted upon a board swinging over a tavern door. For though, as we have remarked, there is no record of a Turk's Head inn in Elizabethan London, in the early seventeenth century the printer and bookseller John Barnes had in Fleet Street his shop 'at the sign of the Great Turk'; and at a later date this sign became very prevalent. [5] An image of a Turk or a large Turk's Head was sometimes employed as an archery butt. Among the varieties of archery discussed by William Camden is the sport of 'shooting at the Turke.' [6] Among 'those sports that are lawfull' Henry Chettle names 'Turkes' along with skoyles and nineholes. [7] One of Dekker's characters exclaims: 'If I stay, I pray God I may be turned to a Turk, and set up in Finsbury, for boys to shoot at.' [8]

1 *The Unfortunate Traveller, Works*, ii,247.
2 *The Meeting of Gallants at an Ordinarie*, 1604; *Plague Pamphlets*, ed. Wilson, p.109.
3 *Wonders Worth the Hearing*, 1602; ed. Grosart, p.7.
4 The house occupied by Sir Christopher Wren in Friday Street, which remained almost unaltered till its demolition in 1844, was the Saracen's Head (private residences, like inns, had signs, not numbers). At Daventry John Byng 'housed at the Saracen's Head—pronounc'd the Serjeant's Head; say Saracen and you wou'l not be understood' (*The Torrington Diaries*, ii,118). For other late taverns of this name see H.D.Eberlein and A.E.Richardson, *The English Inn, Past and Present*, 1926, Index. See also Larwood and Hotten, *The History of Sign-Boards*, 1866, pp.429f.
5 Robert Boulter published *Paradise Lost* at the Turk's Head in Bishopgate Street. Doctor Johnson often took supper at the Turk's Head in the Strand; and it was at another Turk's Head in Soho that he organized the Club in 1763. The growing fashion of coffee-drinking popularized this and analogous tavern-signs: the Great Turk, the Three Turks, the Turk and the Slave, The Sultan Morat, the Sultan Soliman, and so forth.
6 Preface to the *History of Elizabeth*, ed. 1569 (cited by Sugden, *Topographical Dictionary*).
7 *Kind-Harts Dreame*, [1592]; ed. G.B.Harrison, p.61.
8 *The Shoemaker's Holiday*, III,i.

Analogous grotesque expressions of racial and nationalistic prejudices are to be seen in popular resorts to this day.

A very different device or ensign was the Ottoman Crescent, which lent itself to a variety of poetic images. To the simple mind it suggested the simple image of the new moon's beauty, as when William Parry writes of 'that most admirable Cresset, who for his glittering and divine glory provokes many nations of the world to performe divine adoration thereunto.' [1] Sir Philip Sidney imagines that 'the Turkish new-moon,' as it waxes, will 'fill his hornes . . . on Christian coast.' [2] The Earl of Stirling uses the same figure when after a survey of the disasters wrought by the Turkish power— Constantinople fallen, the Mamelukes overthrown, Rhodes conquered, Hungary taken—he describes the Turks' 'gaping Moone, not fill'd with kingdomes wonne.' [3] In Dekker's imagination there is a strange association, verbal rather than pictorial, of the crescent moon and the horns of an angry bull:

> The Turkish Halfe-Moone on her silver Hornes
> Tosses the Christian Diadem, and adornes
> The Sphaere of Ottoman with Starry light
> Stolne even from Those under the Crosse who fight.[4]

The pallid moon suggests to George Wither, in his tribute to the dead Prince of Wales, that the Turks were fearful because the Prince had been so promising a leader of Christendom that his very name struck terror into foreign foes and 'the turkie Moone look't pale.' [5] Sir John Denham has in mind the supposed maleficent power of the moon when he writes:

> The Mahomets Crescent by our fewds encreast,
> Blast'd the learn'd Remainders of the East.[6]

Fletcher likens a Turkish defeat to the change of moons into falling meteors:

1 *A new and large discourse of the Travels of Sir Anthony Sherley*, 1601, p.2.
2 *Astrophel and Stella*, xxx.
3 *Doomes-Day*, Fifth Hour, stanzas 78–83.
4 *Dekker His Dreame; Non-Dramatic Works*, ed. Grosart, iii,15.
5 *Prince Henries Obsequies*, 1622, Elegy 37; *Poems*, Spenser Society, p.395.
6 *The Progress of Learning; Poetical Works*, ed. T.H.Banks, New Haven, 1928, p.118.

All their silver crescents then I saw
Like falling meteors spent, and set forever
Under the cross of Malta.[1]

The most memorable use of the image occurs in Milton's
magnificent description of the retreat of the Persians from the
horns of the Turkish crescent. Here the image is extended to
suggest at once the two enveloping flanks of a mighty army
and the points of enormous clutching pincers.[2] The device
sometimes occurs on title-pages of books dealing with the
Near East.[3] Thus, in the edition of 1553 of Georgievitz's
Profetia we see two cuts, one of the Roman Emperor with the
double-headed eagle; the other of the Ottoman Sultan with
the crescent and a star. The star, however, is rare at this
date and is not an essential part of the design. The theme
of two of the engravings on the title-page of Michel Baudier's
Religion des Turcs is the inconstancy of the moon contrasted
with the *Lux Certa Salutis*.

1 *The Knight of Malta*, II,i.
2 *Paradise Lost*, x,432f.
3 The crescent, be it remembered, is an Ottoman symbol, unknown to Islam till the
  Turkish conquests, and to this day is not used by the Shi'ites. But in the popular
  imagination of Renaissance Christendom it often symbolized Islam in general. In
  this loose, broad sense it is employed in the title of this book.

CHAPTER FOUR

'THE GREAT TURK'

I

SPRUNG from nomads of the Asiatic hinterland and for long
dependent upon other nations for transport at sea, the Turks,
when they had captured Constantinople, found it to their
advantage to revive the commercial arrangements that had
existed between Byzantium and the European states. Since the
later years of the fourteenth century there had been treaties
between the Ottoman government and the two Italian repub-
lics of Genoa and Venice to insure the safe passage of vessels
bringing grain from Russia and Anatolia; and it was but an
extension of these treaties when, shortly after 1453, Genoa and
then Venice obtained concessions for direct trade with the
Porte. For a long while the two Italian cities, first in the field
and often in bitter rivalry with each other, controlled what was
almost a monopoly of this trade, though subject to interruptions during periods of war. In 1535, however, formal capitulations were conceded to France, and by this arrangement the
French ambassador was constituted the official protector of
Europeans in Constantinople not otherwise represented diplo-
matically. This state of affairs occasioned acrimonious disputes
between the French and English envoys at the close of the
sixteenth century.

During the first half of that century there were only isolated
cases of English voyages to the Levant in quest of trade. Merchants had to face the hostility of Venice and Genoa and at a
later date of Marseilles, the high duties imposed at various
ports, and the illegal but none the less unavoidable exactions of
unscrupulous Turkish officials. There are records of such
voyages at infrequent intervals from about the year 1511. In
1513 a consulate or commercial agency was set up on a precarious basis on the island of Chios. In 1534 two ships went out

to Crete and returned badly battered. Anthony Jenkinson's journey through Asia Minor and Syria in 1553—a journey which made him a recognized authority on trading conditions in the Levant—was probably undertaken with a view to obtaining information regarding the possibility of initiating local trade in Turkey and the practicability of tapping some of the trade which came from the further East by way of Mesopotamia or the Red Sea. But nothing developed immediately from this exploratory tour. Between 1566 and 1581 the trade through Russia into Persia, which for all its dangers, difficulties, and delays was on the whole profitable, was responsible for a neglect or at any rate a postponement of English efforts to build up a trade with Turkey. Commerce was indeed carried on, but not in English bottoms. A considerable percentage of Venetian shipping plied between the Levant and the English Channel Ports. So late as 1575 a Venetian argosy was wrecked off the Isle of Wight. This disaster may have been in Shakespeare's memory when he pictured his Merchant of Venice as anxious for the fate of two of his argosies, one of which was bound for Syria, the other for England. It is significant that when English diplomatic and commercial relations with Turkey had been put upon a basis that permitted the immensely profitable voyage of the *Hercules* in 1587, this Venetian trade was abruptly discontinued; no more argosies came to England. In sum, then, the early efforts of England to obtain markets in the Levant were sporadic, infrequent, and not well concerted. Besides the rivalry with Marseilles and the two Italian cities there was the danger from pirates, not only Algerine, Moorish, and Turkish but also Maltese and Greek; and—a point not always sufficiently regarded by writers on this subject—there was in England the popular fear and detestation of the Turk. One must not exaggerate the influence of such popular sentiments. The man of business would not permit religious or racial prejudices to stand in his way if he saw an opportunity to develop new markets in the land of the infidel. Nor did such considerations move Queen Elizabeth. The long delay in establishing an embassy at Constantinople was due to the fact that the need for it did not arise until Anglo-Turkish commercial relations had been put upon a reasonably secure basis with the promise of profit; and by the time that that need arose there was an even stronger motive to action, for as Anglo-Spanish relations grew more strained Elizabeth saw in the Sultan a potential ally. We have already remarked that in one communication she did not scruple to describe herself to the image-hating Moslem as one who shared his detestation of the worshippers of idols, that is, the Roman Catholics.[1] Yet the fact remains impressive that the English government did not enter into diplomatic relations with the Porte till a hundred and thirty years after the fall of Constantinople; and at a much later date James I was reluctant to receive an emissary from the Sultan on the ground that to welcome an infidel would be unbecoming to a Christian Prince.

The memory of the profitable though sporadic voyages of the first half of the sixteenth century survived in London and, about 1575, steps were taken to regularize English trade with Ottoman ports. For this purpose two great London merchants, Edward Osborne and Richard Staper, sent agents to Constantinople who secured a safe-conduct for their negotiator William Harborne. Harborne's activities resulted, after vexatious delays, in an interchange of letters between Queen Elizabeth and Sultan Murad III (Amurath). The Sultan was so deeply impressed that Harborne was able in 1580 to secure a grant of capitulations guaranteeing the safety of English merchants, the right to trade, and the permission to establish consulates.[2] When this agreement had been reached, the English government issued Letters Patent to 'The Company of

1 We may pursue a little further this matter of the common ground between Mohammedans and Protestants, to cite an incident of much later date. The Reverend John Corvel, who was the Levant Company's chaplain at Constantinople from 1670 to 1679, tells of a long debate on religious issues between Sir Thomas Baines and one Vani Effendi, a great 'preacher' among the Turks. 'Sir Thomas told what kind of Christian he was, viz., he would rather dye then worship either crosse, Pictures, Images, or the like.' On hearing this the 'preacher' wept, saying he had not thought 'any Christian came so near true Musselman, but that they all had been Idolaters' (Early Voyages and Travels in the Levant, ed. J.T.Bent, Hakluyt Society, 1893, p.271).
2 In The Gentleman's Magazine, lxii (1792), Part ii,p.1071, there is quoted a letter, dated 25 March 1581, from the Sultan to Queen Elizabeth, sending greetings and wishing her 'happy succes in all [her] accions.' Doubts as to the authenticity of this communication were later expressed (ibid., lxiii (1793), Part i,p.31); but the date is in favour of its genuineness. The letter is reprinted in John Nichols, Progresses of Queen Elizabeth, 1823, ii,302.

Merchants of the Levant,' dated 11 September 1581, in which Edward Osborne, as governor, was associated with other merchants, not to exceed twenty in all. These privileges were granted them 'because they had found out and opened a trade in Turkey, not known in the memory of any man now living to be frequented by our progenitors.' A memorandum or 'brief remembrance' which the elder Hakluyt communicated some years later to a friend who was being sent into Turkey is a lively memorial of these searchers after new markets for English woollens and other commodities. Hakluyt bids him observe the industries and products of Constantinople and endeavour to arrange for various 'vents,' 'for the benefit of our poor people: for a large vent found, it setteth many on work.' [1]

II

THE agreement of the English merchants with Turkey was effected in spite of the intense opposition of Venice. The activities of Venetian agents in Constantinople were reported in England; and of the consequent prejudice against Italian merchants there is a curious reflection in the drama. It has not hitherto been noticed that Robert Wilson's *Three Ladies of London* (published in 1584 but written in 1581 [2]) has an intimate bearing upon the history of the founding of the Levant Company. Because of its resemblances in situation and occasionally even in phraseology to *The Merchant of Venice* this play has received a good deal of attention from historians of the drama. It is a late and in all respects save one an uninteresting morality in which Love and Conscience are corrupted by Lady Lucre. But amid the activities of these tedious abstractions there is a series of episodes of which the protagonist is the startlingly

1 Hakluyt, v,229f.
2 On the title-page of the edition of 1584 are the initials 'R.W.' Wilson's authorship is generally accepted. The text is in Hazlitt's Dodsley, vi,245f. The date has been determined from a topical reference to contributions of money received from England by the Pope 'in Queen Mary's time' (ibid., p.272). Sir Edmund Chambers (*The Elizabethan Stage*, ii,380) discusses the date but does not remark upon the connection of the play with the organization of the Levant Company in 1581. This topical allusion disproves Fleay's conjecture (*Chronicle History of the London Stage*, p.40) that the play is identical with *The Jew*, commended two years earlier by Stephen Gosson in *The School of Abuse* (ed. Shakespeare Society, p.30). Gosson's description of *The Jew* does not in the least fit *The Three Ladies of London* and, as is generally agreed, shows that a play similar to *The Merchant of Venice* was in existence in 1579.

concrete figure of an Italian merchant, Mercatore, who associates with Lady Lucre and trades in London and Turkey. Lucre instructs him as to England's exports and imports:

> Thou must carry over wheat, pease, barley, oats, and vetches, and all kinds of grain,
> Which is well sold beyond sea, and bring such merchants great gain.
> Then thou must carry beside leather, tallow, beef, bacon, bell-metal and everything,
> And for these good commodities trifles into England thou must bring.

As examples of such trifles she mentions beads, amber, coral, crystal, 'and every such babble that is slight, pretty and pleasant.' [1] This counsel might be thought to provide interesting confirmation of the opinion of modern historians that the principal English motive in establishing eastern trade was not (as it was formerly thought to be) to obtain oriental goods for the English market but to exploit foreign markets for English products. But Lady Lucre's eye is not really upon a favourable balance of trade; she is a wicked temptress and is counselling that England be deprived of valuable commodities and receive in exchange mere baubles. Presently she sends Mercatore to trade 'amongst Moors, Turks and Pagans.' [2] In Turkey he encounters one Gerontus, a Jew, to whom he is indebted for loans amounting to three thousand ducats. These loans are two years overdue. Gerontus remonstrates gently with his debtor and courteously accepts his renewed promise to pay. But Mercatore is again faithless and Gerontus is forced to threaten him with imprisonment. [3] They appear before a Turkish judge, where the villainous Mercatore, availing himself of the law of the realm that a conversion to Islam cancels any debt contracted hitherto, announces his intention to 'turn Turk.' 'Lay your hands upon this book,' says the judge; and he bids Mercatore repeat after him the formula of renunciation of Christianity. The worthy Jew, scandalized by this desecration, offers to forego the interest on the debt and be content merely with his principal. 'Not a denier,' says Mercatore; 'me will be a Turk,

I say. Me be weary of my Christ's religion.' Loath to bear the responsibility for the wretch's apostasy, Gerontus freely forgives him the entire debt, whereupon Mercatore declares that 'not for all da good in da world me forsake-a my Christ!' The judge's rebuke: 'You did more for the greediness of the money than for any zeal or goodwill you bear Turkey' does not a whit embarrass the shameless Mercatore.[1] The Jew has no redress. The contrast between the moderation, self-control, and generosity of this Jewish money-lender in his dealings with the Italian merchant and the greed and cruelty of Shylock in dealing with the Merchant of Venice has struck every reader of *The Three Ladies of London*; but the topical significance of the episode has been overlooked. Wilson has drawn the character of a rascally and unprincipled Italian merchant who cheats a Jew and is reproved by a Turk; and the portrayal of Mercatore in this contemptible role coincides precisely in date with the newly developed rivalry between English and Italian commercial interests in Turkey.

III

THE first ship belonging to the Levant Company, the *Great Susan*, set sail in January 1583, having on board Harborne—now Sir William Harborne—who proceeded to Constantinople not only as the merchants' agent but as Queen Elizabeth's first duly accredited ambassador to the Great Turk. On his arrival he found that the French ambassador and the Venetian agents had exerted themselves during his absence to persuade the Sultan to withdraw the concessions which he had granted to the English; but he was able to thwart these machinations. Doubtless the various and costly presents which he presented to the Sultan—evidence of the wealth of his royal mistress—were strong arguments in his favour. These gifts included three mastifs, three spaniels, two bloodhounds, 'two little dogs in coats of silk,' various clothes and utensils, a basin and ewer, two silver poppinjays, a clock set with jewels and elaborately decorated (valued at five hundred pounds), and many other

1 Ibid., pp.353f.

articles.[1] We shall hear more of the part played by gifts in the diplomatic negotiations with the Porte.

From Hakluyt may be gleaned a few notes by way of illustration of the impression made by Constantinople upon this first English visitor of high rank. Harborne was entertained at a Turkish feast where the bill of fare included 'mutton boiled and roasted, rice diversely dressed, fritters of the finest fashion, and dishes daintily dight with pretty pap.' He was permitted to visit Hagia Sophia but was required to put off his shoes before entering; and not understanding this Moslem custom he thought he was being subjected to a humiliation because he was a Christian and would profane the mosque. The sight of a whirling dervish who 'turned him continually and cried Hough very hollowly' remained in his memory. There are no interesting records of his observations of other historic buildings in the city. He used his influence to procure the release of Christian slaves, among them Edward Webbe, the master-gunner, of whose hardships and far wanderings we shall hear in Chapter VIII. Harborne, according to Webbe, 'did behave himselfe wonderfully wisely, and was a speciall meanes for the releasement of me and sundrie other English captives.' [2] Thomas Nashe boasts loudly that Harborne 'mollified' 'the adamantinest tyranny of mankind' and so 'noised the name of our Island . . . that not an infant of the curtaild skinclipping pagans but talk of London as frequently as of their Prophet's tomb at Mecca.' [3] Most of these captives were freed not from Constantinople or other eastern parts of the Ottoman Empire but from the Barbary States over which Turkey was at the time exercising a fairly

1 Incidents from Harborne's embassy are from Hakluyt, v,243f.—On the Levant Company see M.Epstein, *The Early History of the Levant Company*, 1908; A.C.Wood, *A History of the Levant Company*, Oxford, 1935; W.R.Scott, *The History of Joint-Stock Companies*, ii,83f.; Sir William Foster, *England's Quest of Eastern Trade*, 1933, chapter vi; J.T.Bent's introduction to *Early Voyages and Travels in the Levant* (see p. 152, note 1); and Sanderson's *Travels in the Levant*, ed. Foster. Foster, in *England's Quest*, assembles information on the sporadic voyages of the earlier sixteenth century, drawn in the main from Hakluyt. On two fifteenth-century voyages to the Levant, combining the carriage of pilgrims and the trade in spices, see E.M.C.Wilson, 'The Oversea Trade of Bristol,' in *Studies in English Trade in the Fifteenth Century*, New York, 1933, pp.226f. Both these voyages were disastrous, the first (1446) through shipwreck, the second (1456) through the hostility of the Genoese.
2 *The Rare and Most Wonderful Thinges which Edward Webbe . . . hath seene and passed in his troublesome Travailes*, 1590; ed. Arber, p.28.
3 *Lenten Stuffe, Works*, iii,173.

strict control. That Harborne did not always intervene successfully is shown by a letter addressed to a eunuch in a Moslem
household in Constantinople, a forlorn creature named Rowley
from Bristol, who had been captured, castrated, and sold. All
the ambassador could do in this case was to counsel patience,
virtuous action, and loyalty to the Christian faith.[1] It was
Harborne's duty on several occasions to advise visiting Englishmen as to the safest quarters for them in the city—that is, in
Galata, not Stamboul. From other testimony we learn that in
any Mohammedan city 'the surest lodging for a Christian . . .
is in a Jew's house, for if he have any hurt, the Jew and his
goods shall make it good, so the Jew taketh great care of the
Christian for fear of punishment.'[2] The regard which the
Turks bestowed upon him enabled Harborne to promote his
employers' interests in various parts of the Sultan's dominions.
During his term of office a consulate was established at Aleppo
(1586) which became a convenient hospice and sometimes a
place of refuge for English travellers. A commercial agency was
also set up at Smyrna. In the political sphere he accomplished
something in line with Queen Elizabeth's hopes when she
sent him out to Turkey, for he persuaded the Sultan to threaten
Spain just at the time when the Great Armada was being prepared for the attack on England.

When the original privileges granted to his employers lapsed
in 1588, Harborne returned to England. Delays followed,
caused in part by disputes with English merchants trading with
Venice and in part by the war with Spain, which rendered voyages in the Mediterranean perilous. At length, in 1592, by a new
charter the Levant Company, still under the governorship
of Sir Edward Osborne, and now enlarged to a group of fifty-
three merchants, was permitted to form a fellowship for twelve
years (dating from 1588, when the first charter lapsed). Harborne's services in travelling or causing agents to travel 'to
find out and set open a trade in merchandise and traffics
into the lands . . . of the Great Turk' were cited in this new
document, and the Company was commended for success in

1 Hakluyt, v,282.
2 Ibid., v,271.

securing 'good and profitable vent and utterance of the commodities of our Realm' and in effecting the release of many captives.[1]

Late in this same year, 1592, there was published at Lyons the *Responsio ad Edictum*, an attack on Queen Elizabeth, English policy, and the Church of England, by the English Jesuit, Father Robert Parsons.[2] To this Francis Bacon replied in his *Observations on a Libel*. One count only in the accusations concerns us: that England was a confederate of the Great Turk. If this means, says Bacon, that English merchants keep an agent in Constantinople, what about the Emperor, the King of France, the King of Spain, the Senate of Venice? All have for a long time had ambassadors there. 'If the Turk hath done some special honour to our ambassador (if he be so termed),' the responsibility for that rests upon the King of Spain, 'for that the honour we have won upon him by opposition hath given us reputation through the world.' 'If he [the author of the *Responsio*] mean it because the Turk seemeth to affect us for the abolishing of images, let him consider then what a scandal the matter of images hath been in the church, as having been one of the principal branches whereby Mahumetism entered.'[3] Bacon, it will be noted, implies that the status of the English agent at Constantinople was not the same as that of the representatives of the continental powers. Harborne's salary and the expenses, it is true, were paid by the Levant Company; but he held his appointment from the Queen and was a genuine ambassador. To make a point against the Roman Catholic controversialist Bacon may have deliberately taken advantage of the fact that after Harborne's return to England the affairs of the Company were left in charge of Edward Barton, his secretary, who was not appointed as his successor till 1593.

The renewal of the charter gives point to the praise of Elizabeth at the close of *The True Tragedie of Richard III*:

---

1 The text of the charter is in Hakluyt, vi,73f., where may be read the elaborate rights and regulations laid down for the Company.
2 *Per D. Andraeam Philopatrum ad idem* [that is, *Elizabethae Reginae Edictum, November 29*] *Responsio*, Lyons, 1592. Parsons's authorship is not absolutely certain.
3 James Spedding, *The Letters and the Life of Francis Bacon*, ed. 1890, i,204.

The Turke admires to heare her government . . .
The Turke hath sworne never to lift his hand,
To wrong the Princesse of this blessed land.[1]

Barton, who had been in England for consultation with the
Company, was now knighted and returned to Constantinople.
An account of his voyage and of his reception at the Porte
(where he offered elaborate gifts to the Sultan) forms the opening portion of a narrative in Hakluyt by Richard Wrag, a
merchant who went on to Tripoli, Aleppo, Ormuz, and India.[2]
The new ambassador's long residence in Turkey, combined
perhaps with personal qualities concerning which we have a few
hints, made him *persona gratissima* with the Sultan. John
Sanderson noted the 'extraordinary esteme' in which he was
held, adding that so great was his influence that he 'made and
displaced both princes and patriarks'[3]—which was probably an
exaggeration. After the accession of Sultan Mahomet III Barton
accompanied him on his campaign against Hungary and the
revolted Danubian provinces. His secretary Thomas Glover
(afterwards ambassador) wrote a narrative of Barton's experiences on this campaign; and this Purchas published many
years later with an apology for the action of a Christian envoy
in accompanying the Great Turk in a war against Christians.[4]
Barton's intimate relations with Turkish officialdom caused
concern to his employers, and after his death they warned
his successor, Henry Lello, to confine himself to his proper
duties.[5]

Barton's career in Turkey affords us an interesting and
rather pathetic early example of the Englishman who, in the
modern phrase, 'goes Balkan,' that is, whose moɹale declines
in exotic surroundings. John Sanderson, who had known him
in England, made his first visit to Constantinople while he was
ambassador and actually performed his functions in the capital
during Barton's absence with the Turkish armies. Sanderson

1 On other grounds the play has been dated *c*.1592; the immediate timeliness of the
   allusion here noted seems to settle the matter.
2 Hakluyt, vi,94f.
3 *Travels in the Levant*, p.61.
4 Purchas, viii,304f.
5 Sir William Foster, *England's Quest of Eastern Trade*, p.74.

is one witness of this deterioration. He found that life in the Levant had effected a sad alteration in the ambassador, who 'from serving God devoutly and drinking puer water' had come to 'badnes stoutly and much wine.' The serious-minded merchant paints a disquieting picture of life at the English embassy at Galata, where poisoners and filthy livers, 'garboylers,' assassins, drunkards, and harlots rioted. Members of the staff of the embassy 'plied their whores so, that at one time was rumord to be in the house seventeen; but the ambassiator caused all to depart except his owne, with whome and alcami he waisted his alowance.' Sanderson remonstrated with him. 'But what availed my counsell? Pride and selfewill was to[o] rife in all.' [1] Like testimony may be read between the lines of William Biddulph's remark that Lello, the next ambassador, 'in many ways exceeded' Barton, 'especially in his religious carriage and unspotted life.' [2] Fynes Moryson, however, records his gratitude for the courteous entertainment 'with lodging and dyet' which 'this worthy Gentleman' afforded him during his stay in Constantinople in 1597.[3] This may mean no more than that like many another wastrel Barton was affable and hospitable; or it may be that Barton reformed his way of life shortly before his end. For in 1597 he died, worn out, according to Lello, by the hardships of the Turkish campaign.[4] He was buried outside the gate of the Greek monastery on the island of Chalcis or Halki in the Sea of Marmora, which when Biddulph visited it a few years later was known as 'Barton's Island.' There his tomb is still to be seen.[5] Some correspondence ensued with his successor on the 'insolent corses of excesse and ryot' of which Barton had been guilty, exceeding all reasonable bounds; and Lello was cautioned that a curb must be kept upon the expenses of the embassy.[6]

The twelve-year monopoly granted by Elizabeth to the

---

1 Sanderson's 'Autobiography,' prefixed to his *Travels in the Levant*, p.13.
2 *The Travels of certaine Englishmen*, 1609, p.40.
3 *Itinerary*, ii,101.
4 Letter from Lello to Sanderson, in the latter's *Travels*, p.174.
5 Sanderson, *Travels*, p.296; Corvel's 'Diary,' in *Early Voyages and Travels in the Levant*, ed. Bent, p.282.
6 *The Dawn of British Trade to the East Indies as recorded in the Court Minutes of the East India Company, 1599–1603*, ed. Henry Stevens, 1886, p.269.

Company expired in 1600. For a variety of reasons the merchants now proceeded with caution. Disputes between Lello and the French at Constantinople involved delays. The war with Spain and the Barbary pirates made trade in the Mediterranean increasingly hazardous. The project of direct trade with the further East by way of the Cape of Good Hope was being discussed, and such commerce would lessen the profits of voyages to Turkey which depended in part upon goods from India that came westward through the Ottoman Empire. There was, furthermore (in May 1600), a dispute with the Privy Council over the payment of certain special import levies, and this occasioned an order closing down the Company's operations till the question was settled. For a while it seemed likely that other merchants, not members of the Company but interlopers, would take over the Turkish trade on whatever terms the government dictated. However, an agreement was reached at the end of 1600 renewing the monopoly for fifteen years, but it was not until the following spring that Lello defeated the French machinations (largely by bribery) and extracted new privileges from the Sultan. Then, on the accession of James I in 1603, came the royal proclamation against monopolies. To the Levant Company this was, so to speak, a blessing in disguise, for on the surrender of their monopoly they were excused from the payment of a large sum due the government. 'This did not mean,' says Sir William Foster, 'that the merchants engaged in the trade intended to abandon it. They knew that the government could not contemplate the loss of the revenue derived therefrom, and they had a shrewd idea that they had only to hold out to get their privileges renewed on a more favourable basis.' [1] Their calculations proved correct. In December 1605, King James renewed their charter with greatly extended privileges and the Company entered on a long period of orderly administration and great prosperity. It is to this time that Peter Mundy looked back when, writing many years later of his long sojourn at Constantinople, he said that the

---

1 Foster, *England's Quest of Eastern Trade*, p.76. For details of these delays and negotiations see ibid., p.73f. and W.R.Scott, *Joint-Stock Companies*, ii,87. The text of the new capitulations of 1601 was first published in Sanderson's *Travels*, pp.282f.

English merchants there spent their time 'verie commodiously with pleasure, love and amitye amonge themselves.' [1]

IV

LELLO's tenure of office coincided with the stay of two Englishmen at Constantinople about whose visits we have an abundance of picturesque information. To introduce the first of these men we must return to an earlier stage in the Company's history. While Barton was ambassador, Sultan Amurath had died (1595) and Mahomet III reigned in his stead. This change of sovereignty caused a temporary lapse of the capitulations of 1581. Custom required that an assortment of gifts, brought by a special envoy, be laid before the Sultan in advance of the granting of fresh privileges. Barton persuaded the Turks to waive the requirement of the special envoy but they declined to forego the usual presents. In 1598, when the new Sultan had already reigned three years, the gifts which were *de rigueur* had not yet been sent to him. Barton's death had rendered the gifts all the more necessary, for Lello was new to office and had not yet won the imperial favour which had been lavished on his predecessor. The problem of such gifts was a delicate one because, as

1 *Travels of Peter Mundy in Europe and Asia, 1606–1667*, ed. Sir Richard C. Temple, Hakluyt Society, 1907f., i,22.—Lello's successor in 1606 was Sir Richard Glover. The circumstances of Lady Glover's death at Constantinople are sufficiently curious to be noted here. Of this event John Sanderson, then residing in London, wrote to John Kitely, his friend in Turkey: 'His Lordship I take to be of to[o] manly and heroyacall spiritt to be amated at the decease of one wife. . . Counsell His Lordship to interr hir ther. My opinion is that in the monastary of Calcose Ile, where that wourthy Bartons body lieth, ether by or therabout, with some marble monument, wilbe more laudable then to bring hir corps for Ingland. You knowe it is Christian buriall; and peradventure yf by sea she should be transported, every storme would hassard hir truncke [coffin] to be buried overbourd; most mariners ar superstitiouse in that respect. And all reson and order would that, wher the tree fauleth, ther it should lie' (*Travels*, p.259). The strange sequel is an illustration of Professor Grierson's remark that 'at this period the most fantastic poetry was never more fantastic than life itself.' John Kitely communicated Sanderson's advice to Glover; but the wise and practical counsel, expressed with so much sympathy, did not prevail, for the ambassador refused to inter the corpse, saying: 'She is buried already in branne, which is a kind of earth, and it is no sinne to keepe her.' (On this process compare: 'I have eaten foure of these egges, the rest I have put in branne to preserve,' *Two Wise Men and All the Rest Fooles*, VII,ii,95). Kitely, reporting Glover's macabre devotion, adds: 'Sight of her herse oftentimes revives his melancholy passions.' How close is this situation to that in Chapman's *Monsieur D'Olive* where the bereaved husband refuses to permit the burial of the body of his beloved wife, and to that in the play of *Charlemagne* (almost certainly by Chapman) where the distracted emperor, victim of a potent charm, dotes on the corpse of his mistress! There are situations analogous though less close in Massinger's *Duke of Milan* and in the anonymous *Second Maiden's Tragedy*.

a contemporary remarks, the Grand Seigneur 'taketh all Presents of the Christian Princes to be as tributes: and for such they are registered in his Records: which being once begun, he looketh for a continuance thereof, as of duty; and the greater value that the Present is made, the greater duty and subjection he taketh hold of thereby.' [1] Again and again during the sixteenth century European states, those of the Danubian region more especially, paid the 'Turkish tribute,' saving their self-respect with the pretence that such payments were free-will offerings of friendship. The exaction of this tribute is an important *motif* in Marlowe's *Jew of Malta;* and Falstaff refers to 'the Turk's tribute' that is paid by certain states.[2] Even so late as 1656 Francis Osborn wrote that 'repute hath swell'd the Sultan's power to such vast Monstrosity, and so farre dazled the eyes of Christian Princes, weakened by divisions in Religion, that they dare not look upon him without a Present.' [3]

To give an idea of the size and costliness of certain New-Year's gifts, Dekker says that they were 'more in number and more worth then those that are given to the Great Turk.' [4] Not only did the Sultan have to be placated but his high officials as well; presents to them were nothing else than bribes. 'The pride of the Turkish Visiers or Bashawes is so great,' says Coryat, 'that when a Christian Ambassador doth either bring them or send them a Present of great worth, they have not the honestie as to thanke him.' [5] *The Travellers Breviat* informs us that the ordinary sources of Turkish revenue are supplemented by confiscations and presents; no ambassador dares appear empty-handed; and no trifles are accepted—presents must be rich and grand.[6] How costly they were is shown by the fact that in 1605 James I made to the Levant Company a grant of no less than £ 5,322 'for a present to the Grand Seigneur.' [7] And costliness was not enough; they must be rare, intricate, odd, and elaborate, to awaken the jaded interest of a cloyed poten-

1 Ellis, *Original Letters*, First Series, iii,83f.
2 *2 Henry IV*, III,ii,334.
3 *Political Reflections on the Government of the Turks*, p.83.
4 *The Wonderful Year*, 1603; *Plague Pamphlets*, p.9.
5 Purchas, x,427.
6 *The Travellers Breviat*, pp.41f.
7 *C.S.P.,Dom., 1603–10*, pp.270 and 311.

tate. Albumazar, the astrologer and inventor, says to his assistant:

> The perpetual motion
> With a true 'larum in't, to run twelve hours
> 'Fore Mahomet's return, deliver it safe
> To a Turkey factor: bid him with care present it
> From me to the house of Ottoman.[1]

In the very year in which the merchants of the Levant Company were planning to make a gift to Mahomet III Ben Jonson makes one of his characters say: 'I have a present for thee; our Turkie company never sent the like to the Grand Signor.' [2]

Towards the close of 1598 an English organ-builder, Thomas Dallam (who in later life constructed several of the finest instruments in England [3]) brought to completion an elaborate and complicated organ which, played by hand or at regulated intervals by clock-work, would give forth melodies while artificial birds chirped and clapped their wings and wooden angels set trumpets to their lips. Master Dallam obtained permission to set up his instrument in the banqueting-hall at Whitehall where he performed upon it before the Queen. She condescended to be pleased; and her Council, doubtless after consultation with the Turkey merchants, were pleased also, for the organ solved for them a difficult problem. On 31 January 1599, it was recorded: 'A great and curious present is going to the Grand Turk.' [4] The gift was the organ, and Dallam was engaged to accompany it, set it up in the Seraglio, and teach the Sultan's servants how to perform upon it. Commanded to make ready to depart within a month, he purchased with excited haste the necessaries for the voyage ('the which I bought upon very short warning, having no friend to advise me in anything'): clothing and spices and a small pair of virginals to beguile the tedium of the voyage.

---

1 Thomas Tomkis, *Albumazar*, 1615, I,v; Hazlitt's Dodsley, xi,318.
2 *Every Man in His Humour*, I,ii,81f.
3 See the article on Dallam in the *D.N.B.*, written, however, before the publication of his 'Diary' and containing no reference to his voyage to Turkey.
4 *C.S.P.,Dom.*, *1598–1601*, p.156.

Some years after his return he wrote a narrative of his adventures which he entitled 'The Account of an Organ Carried to the Grand Seigneur and Other Curious Matter.' [1] This delightful record is unique in interest for us, for it is not consciously 'literary' or stylized but is the candid revelation of a plain man's interest and wonder and at times alarm when he found himself in circumstances altogether beyond his experience or expectations. A quiet, modest, and unsophisticated craftsman, as his narrative shows him to have been, he was of none of the usual types of Englishmen who ventured into the East.

On 5 February 1599, he had himself, his chest, and his virginals rowed down the Thames to Gravesend, where he clambered aboard the ship *Hector*. A fellow-voyager was John Sanderson, returning to Constantinople to assume his duties as consul and treasurer of the embassy. Dallam does not refer to him nor does Sanderson mention Dallam by name, though he knew about the organ. The two men probably did not associate together on ship-board and perhaps did not even meet, for Sanderson was of superior social status and was probably provided with better quarters.

At Zante Dallam had his first impressions of the Levant. He and two companions set off to climb a hill, but, frightened at the approach of a native herdsman, one of the trio lay all day in some bushes while Dallam and Ned Hale were entertained at a monastery and attended mass. 'Nether he nor I had ever sene any parte of a mass before; nether weare we [any]thinge the wyser for that.' At Rhodes a misadventure befell the party. Some Turks and 'Jues' (Dallam's spelling is delightful!) came aboard, and for their delectation the organist performed upon the virginals so sweetly that they embraced and kissed him. Then he and some friends went ashore, and as they were drinking at a tavern, up came a couple of stout Turks who said 'Parlye Franko, sinyore?' Two of the travellers who knew the *lingua franca* fell into converse with these strangers, but another Turk, who had heard Dallam

---

1 It is now known, not quite accurately (for it is not a day-.by-day record), as Dallam's 'Diary.' It remained in manuscript till published by the Hakluyt Society together with Corvel's 'Diary' in *Early Voyages and Travels in the Levant*, ed. Bent, 1893.

play and consequently bore him 'kindness and som love,' made a sign to him to hasten back to the ship; so he quietly departed, but the two linguists were arrested, and later released from prison only after trouble, delay, and expense. At the Cape of the Janissaries on the Asiatic side of the Dardanelles the travellers went ashore to see 'the rewins of the wales and housis in Troye' and with a hammer Dallam broke off a piece of marble from the ruins to carry home as a souvenir.

Constantinople was reached the middle of August. Their arrival was promptly reported by the Venetian ambassador, who was closely watching this English bid for Turkish favour. The English, he wrote, counted upon the effect of their gift. 'Il presente poi sara di un artificiosisimo organo, che serve per horologio et che suona da stesso diversi moteti.' There were also, he adds, other gifts, including a coach for the Sultana and many suits of cloth; but the latter were found on unpacking to be 'fioriti et guasti,' mouldy and spoiled; and the English were anxious.[1]

Worse had happened than the spoiling of some bolts of cloth, for when the great organ, which had been carried in the ship's hold, was unpacked, Dallam found to his distress that 'all glewinge worke was clene decayed' by reason of the heat of the hold and the 'hootnes of the cuntrie.' 'Lyke wise divers of my mettle pipes were brused and broken.' The work of repair occupied a considerable time but at length Dallam reported to Mr. Lello that his skill and patience had made the instrument even better than it was when he had performed upon it before Queen Elizabeth. Lello had the organ set up in his own house for a preliminary inspection by various Turkish officials.[2] The ambassador told Dallam that the Levant Company would be well content if it pleased the Sultan for a single day. 'Yf it doo not please him at the firste sighte, and performe not those thinges which it is toulde him that it can dow, he will cause it to be puled downe that he may trample it under his feete. And than we shall have no sute granted, but all our

1 *C.S.P.*, *Venetian*, iv,375. Sanderson (*Travels*, p.181) mentions the coach and its cost—£600; adding that it was 'very well excepted' (accepted).
2 This we learn not from Dallam but from Sanderson, *Travels*, p.177.

charge will be loste.' One is not surprised to read that the organist had 'smale comforte' in this 'frindly spetche.'

The part of the Seraglio chosen to house the instrument was an apartment not calculated to alleviate his anxieties. He describes it as 'no dwellinge house, but a house of pleasur, and lyke wyse a house of slaughter,' for 'in this litle house, that emperor that rained when I was thare[1] had nynetene brotheres put to deathe in it, and it was bulte for no other use but for the stranglinge of everie emperor's bretherin.' Dallam did not exaggerate, for the room to which he refers was the *Kaweh* or 'cage' where Mahomet III on his accession four years earlier had caused nineteen of his brothers to be put to death. This massacre had shocked Europe, accustomed though men were to stories of Ottoman atrocities.[2] For this murderous despot Dallam had now to make music.

The critical day arrived: 24 September 1599. Lello had told Dallam that there was no chance of his being permitted to see the Sultan, and he was concealed behind curtains in an anteroom. When with his retinue the Great Turk had entered and was seated in his chair of state, 'all being quiett and no noyes at all, the presente began to salute the Grand Sinyor.' No condensed paraphrase can do justice to the craftsman's pride implied in Dallam's account of the performance.

[1] This phrase shows that Dallam was writing after the death of Mahomet III in 1603.
[2] Sanderson, who was in Constantinople at the time of these murders, wrote to a friend that the deceased Sultan's '19 sonnes weare strangoled in their brothers presence. . . The next day at none [noon] we sawe them passe by to buryall; which was to be pittied, beinge inosents, thoughe Turks' (*Travels*, p.141; letter of 25 January 1596). Compare the Venetian *bailo's* account of the massacre in *C.S.P.*, *Venetian*, ix, No.328. In 1597 Fynes Moryson saw and noted the coffins of the late Sultan's 'male children, which (according to their manner) are strangled by his Successour assoone as he was dead' (*Itinerary*, ii,100). Dryden's lines in *Aureng-Zebe*, Act I:

> When Death's cold Hand has clos'd the father's eye,
> You know the younger sons are doom'd to die

were perhaps written with this particular massacre in mind. The most notorious earlier case, at the accession of Selim the Grim, involved the death of two elder, not younger, brothers. Pope is less specific when he likens the jealous Atticus to the Turk who bears 'no brother near the throne.' On the legal origin of the custom of putting to death the Sultan's brothers on his accession see A.J.Toynbee, *A Study of History*, iii,33, note 1.—A nineteenth-century oriental despot eclipsed the atrocities of the Sultans of the Renaissance; King Thebaw of Burma had eighty brothers, uncles, nephews, and other relatives, male and female, slaughtered horribly at Mandalay. See F.Tennyson Jesse's vivid narrative of this horror in *The Lacquer Lady*; and compare the brief account in *The Cambridge History of the British Empire*, v (1932), 435.

First the clocke strouke 22; than the chime of 16 bels went of[f], and played a songe of 4 partes. That beinge done, tow personagis which stood upon the corners of the seconde storie, houldinge tow silver trumpetes in there handes, did lifte them to theire heades, and sounded a tantarra. Than the musicke went of[f], and the orgon played a song of 5 partes twyse over. In the tope of the orgon, being 16 foute hie, did stande a holly bushe full of blacke birds and thrushis, which at the end of the musick did singe and shake theire wynges. Divers other motions there was which the Grand Sinyor wondered at.

When the performance was over, the Sultan asked an attendant whether the organ would ever do the same again, and the official, who really knew nothing about the matter but did not dare disappoint his formidable master, replied that it would perform at the next hour. The awkward thing was that Dallam had set the machinery to go off only four times a day. Behind the curtain there was a hurried consultation with the trembling musician, who instructed the attendant how to push a little pin when the clock next struck; this would release the mechanism for another performance. All went well and 'the Grand Sinyor sayed it was good.' But the Sultan was an observant person and he had remarked that while the instrument was making music automatically the keys went up and down though no fingers touched them. It was so contrived, he was told, that a man could play upon it. Is there anybody about who can play? asked the Sultan. The maker of the organ, he was told. 'Fetche him hether,' said the Sultan. Dallam was fetched from behind the curtain and was so 'dazzled' with the display of the four hundred guards, dwarfs, mutes, eunuchs, and 'padgis' (pages) who formed the Sultan's retinue that for some minutes he was as dumb and impotent as any of them. He was indeed in a predicament, for to play upon the organ he would have to turn his back upon the Great Turk and the penalty for such disrespect, he had been informed, was instant death. Moreover, the enthusiastic potentate was sitting as close as possible to the instrument, and while playing Dallam could not avoid touching him; and to touch even the hem of his garments meant instant death. Poor terrified organist! However, the Sultan graciously made way for him and he began to play; but while playing, says Dallam, 'I thought he had bene drawinge his sorde to cut of[f] my heade.' But he lost his head neither literally nor figuratively, and having performed to Mahomet's satisfaction he was dismissed and retired backwards from the awful presence.

His success was in fact embarrassingly complete. Mahomet was so much pleased that he wished to retain Dallam as an official entertainer. There came messengers to offer the organist, if he would remain at Stamboul, 'tow wyfes, ether tow of his Concubines or els tow virgins of the beste I could chuse my selfe.' Dallam replied that he had a wife and children in England, 'thoughe in deede I had nether wyfe nor childrin, yeat to excuse my selfe I made them that answeare.' Obstacles were then put in the way of his departure, and meanwhile a 'drugaman' from the English embassy ('a Turke but a Cornishman born') showed him the sights of Stamboul. One day, after giving an organ-concert for the Sultan, he lingered in a court of the Seraglio to watch thirty young concubines playing at ball. At first he thought they were boys, but their long hair 'and other plaine tokens' convinced him that they were women 'and verie prettie ones in deede.' He loitered so long that his guide stamped his foot angrily as a signal to give over looking, 'the which I was verie lothe to dow, for that sighte did please me wondrous well.' (Almost we hear the voice of Samuel Pepys!)

Word came at length that Dallam might depart for England. On 18 November Sanderson noted that the vessel which was to take 'the workmen of the instrument' was waiting for a favourable wind.[1] Dallam and his assistants sailed only so far as Volo, across the Ægean. Thence they rode through northern Greece, 'verrie muche trubled wethe shepheardes doggs, the which weare like to pluck us of[f] our horsis.' In the neighbourhood of Parnassos they were pestered by four ruffianly 'Turks' who followed them for several days and tried to persuade their dragoman to cut off their heads. The drago-

[1] *Travels in the Levant*, p.185.

man wisely temporized. He was by birth an Englishman named Finch, 'in religion a perfit Turke, but he was our trustie frende.' Dallam had hoped to be entertained at Patras by Mr. Jonas Aldredge, the English consul, but that official 'was gone 40 myles from home to hange a Jew.' It seems a curious occupation for a consul, but Dallam offers no explanation, as though it were the most natural thing in the world. Sailing westward, they had near Gibraltar a sharp encounter with a Spanish ship, which was driven off. No details of the fight are extant, for at this point some pages of the 'Diary' are missing. Then, 'our vitals [victuals] beinge verrie badd,' Dallam was invited by the English merchants aboard to dine in their cabin (which shows that the organist, an artisan, was not voyaging in such comfort as his betters could command). While they were dining they 'harde the crye of a mearmaide, like as yf one had hailed our shipe: but our bootswane forbid any man to make answeare or to louke oute.' Consequently Dallam did not add the sight of a mermaid to his experiences—but he heard one plainly.[1] With no further adventures he reached Dover at the end of April 1600. His return home gave point to an allusion in a play of the same year: 'Thy brother's like the instrument the Merchants sent over to the great Turke: You need not play upon him, hee'le make musicke of himselfe, and hee bee once set going.'[2]

The *Hector* carried to England presents from the Sultana to Queen Elizabeth and with the gifts a letter written in Italian at the Sultana's command by a Jewess named Esperanza Malchi. The gifts are therein described and catalogued: 'una vesta, et una cintura, et doi faeiolli [kerchiefs] lavorati de horo [gold], et tre lavorati di seta, . . . et un collar di

1 For other instances of the late survival of belief in mermaids see J.L.Lowes, *The Road to Xanadu*, pp.491f. Professor Lowes does not mention Dallam's experience.
2 *Jack Drums Entertainment*, 1601, Act III; reprinted in *The School of Shakespeare*, ed. Richard Simpson, ii,169. Marston's authorship of this anonymous piece is generally admitted. It is dated from various allusions in the text (among which Sir Edmund Chambers does not mention this to the organ) 1600.—What is the 'ingenious instrument' in *Cymbeline* (IV,ii,186f.) which 'sounds' when Cadwel 'gives it motion'? The commentators usually answer, an aeolian harp. It is obvious that Shakespeare was put to it to account for 'solemn music' in a cave in the deep country. Possibly he had in mind some such instrument as Dallam's organ which made music by itself when once set going.

perle et rubini, . . . una corona di diamenti.' In return the Sultana requests the Queen to send her 'aque destillati . . . per la facia et hogli [oils] hodoriffere per le mani'; also silks and woollens if in England there are any of a quality 'convenient per una tanta alta Reggina.'[1]

Not every gift sent to an oriental potentate met with the appreciative reception accorded Dallam's organ. Very different, for example, was the fate of the virginals, the coach, and other presents sent in 1615 by the East India Company to the Grand Mogul Jahangir and delivered to him by Sir Thomas Roe. The Mogul's minister inspected them beforehand; he 'misliked not' the virginals but scorned the coach and 'sayd it was little and poore.' Roe wrote home indignantly to his employers: 'The presents you have this yeare sent are extreamely despised'; the 'perspectives' being of the sort one might buy for sixpence apiece and the pictures 'not all woorth one Penny.' The virginals at first gave Jahangir 'good content' but he tired of the music presently and dismissed the musician. As for the coach, he had the furnishings all ripped out and gorgeous new fittings installed.[2]

To return for a moment to Dallam. When he had married and set about founding that 'dynasty' of organ-builders of whom the *Dictionary of National Biography* tells us, did he ever in idle moments join the company of those who, says Nashe, 'tell a whole legend of lies of their travels unto Constantinople'?[3] Did he use to call to mind the thirty concubines playing at hand-ball in the court of the Seraglio? Did he ever regret his refusal of the offer of two wives on condition that he would accept the appointment as court-organist to the Great Turk?

Today the apartments of the Seraglio have become a museum and the visitor to the treasury of the Sultans wonders at the display of florid taste: the jewelled dressing-table from

1 *Original Letters*, ed. Sir Henry Ellis, First Series, iii,52f. The Spanish flavour of the Italian suggests that the writer was a member of one of the colonies of Jewish refugees from Spain who settled in Constantinople and Salonica.
2 *The Embassy of Sir Thomas Roe*, ed. Foster, Hakluyt Society, 1899, i,67,97,118; ii,323, note 3. At the last reference will be found the Reverend Edward Terry's long account of the episode.
3 *Pierce Penilesse, Works*, i,169.

Russia, the repoussé silver and silver-gilt objects, the garish enamels, the ponderous rock-crystal ornaments, the jewel-studded thrones and pearl-embroidered pillows, and all the vast collection of medals, decorations, bibelots, objets d'art, and gewgaws. Eyes weary of the tawdriness rest with satisfaction upon the truly magnificent collections of Chinese porcelains of all periods. But one looks in vain for Dallam's organ.

V

ANOTHER Englishman who was in Constantinople during the reign of Mahomet III found himself in a situation less unusual though much more perilous than that in which the organist had been placed. Sir Thomas Sherley, Junior, passed most of his long sojourn in prison. He was the elder brother of Sir Anthony Sherley and Sir Robert Sherley who will claim our attention in later chapters in this book. They are associated especially with the story of Anglo-Persian relations, whereas their brother's career impinges upon our subject only in the region of the Ægean and at Constantinople.[1]

Thomas Sherley, the son of Sir Thomas Sherley of Wiston Manor in Sussex, was born in 1564. In his early manhood he saw some fighting in the Low Countries and in Ireland, and won the favour of Queen Elizabeth, only to sacrifice it by contracting a hasty and secret marriage.[2] Debts and extravagances dragged him down and after spending some time in Germany[3] he was presently launched upon the picturesque and disreputable career of a privateering adventurer, a buccaneer. His first victims were some poor Portuguese sailors.[4] In succeeding years he was in difficulties of one kind or another; and meanwhile his two brothers had become characters of international notoriety. Anthony à Wood says of him:

1 For contemporary and later works on the Sherley brothers, most of which have to do with Anthony and Robert, see p.339, note 1, below, and other references in Chapters VI and VII. Certain details in Thomas's career will become clear when we arrive at the story of his brothers' adventures.
2 [E.P.Shirley], *The Sherley Brothers*, pp.5f.
3 Historical Manuscripts Commission, *Hatfield MSS*, vii,130; ix,371.
4 *C.S.P.,Dom., 1598–1601*, p.97.

Ashamed to see the Trophies and Atchievements of his two younger Brothers . . . worn like Flowers in the Breasts and Bosoms of Foreign Princes, whilst he himself wither'd upon the Stalk he grew on, [he] left his aged Father, and . . . undertook several Voyages into Foreign Parts, to the great Honour of his Nation, but small enrichment of himself.[1]

Wood is too kindly; no honour came to Sherley's country and no enrichment to himself.

It was in April 1602 that he put out from Southampton with four ships and two pinnaces, to conduct an outrageous raid upon two villages on the coast of Portugal.[2] The success of this venture encouraged him to undertake something on a larger scale. Sharing the antipathy to the Turks which was the mainspring of his brothers' actions, he formed the design to conduct a 'private war' against Turkish commerce. Report of these intentions reached the Levant Company whose merchants were already alarmed for their trade because of the anti-Ottoman conduct and policies of the second brother, Anthony; and they petitioned Sir Robert Cecil to have Thomas's purposes prevented; otherwise the English factors resident in Turkey would suffer great loss. Cecil acted promptly and endeavoured to have Sherley 'stayed'; but it was too late; Sherley, having forcibly obtained a ship, the *Golden Dragon*, had already sailed with a band of desperadoes.[3]

In the Mediterranean he seized a Venetian galley. The Doge and Senate were at this time protesting frequently to England against the outrages of English corsairs; and for Sherley's act of piracy the English government promised full satisfaction should it be possible to apprehend him. The Venetian envoy at London, reporting this, added that it was thought that Sherley would either dispose of his booty somewhere in the Barbary States or else, rounding the Cape of Good Hope, attempt to join his brother Robert in Persia.[4]

Actually he sailed eastward, harrying the coast of Greece

---

1 *Athenae Oxoniensis*, second edition, 1721, i, column 552.
2 John Chamberlain, *Letters*, ed. Sarah Williams, Camden Society, 1861, pp.132 and 144.
3 *Hatfield MSS*, xii,99,399,576.   4 *C.S.P., Venetian*, ix,537f.

and the islands of the Ægean.[1] It was one of these exploits that led to disaster. According to one account Sherley had captured a Turkish vessel after an eight-hour fight in which he lost a hundred men. The prize disappointed expectations; the crews threatened mutiny; and to conciliate them their commander consented to a raid upon the small island of Zea (Kea, the ancient Keos).[2] Sherley's own justification was that his ship sprang a leak which forced him to put into harbour.[3] Anthony Nixon, who is Sherley's mouthpiece and whose book *The Three English Brothers* (1607) is the only contemporary narrative of this affair, puts the most favourable light possible upon it. He tells of the growing discontent of Sherley's crews; one became mutinous; another quit him altogether; and he was left with but one ship. On 15 January 1603, he landed with a hundred men on Zea. Dividing them into two parties, he surprised the unsuspecting islanders, who fled to the woods and rocks behind their little town. He was then doubtful as to how to proceed, and while he hesitated report came that 'a great rabble of the Islanders had gathered head together.' Sherley's men murmured among themselves and were afraid. He commanded them to make a soldier-like retreat at an easy pace to their ship. But his followers were 'now changed from mutineers to cowards'; their retreat was hasty and disorderly; and Sherley, in the rear, was captured. 'He found himself,' says Nixon, 'forsaken of his own men, and nowe in the handes of a trustlesse, bloody, and barbarous people.'[4] Nixon puts no blame upon Sir Thomas; but Henry Lello told Cecil that Sherley had threateningly demanded food of the inhabitants of Zea and that a riot had followed in which two of the islanders were killed and Sherley and two companions captured.[5]

1 Ibid., ix,543.
2 This is the account in the *Genealogica Historia Domus de Sherley* (MS. Harl. 4023), followed by Briggs in his sketch of the Sherleys, *Journal of the Royal Asiatic Society*, First Series, vi,78f.
3 Letter to Burghley, February 1603, cited by E.P.Shirley.
4 *The Three English Brothers*, 1607, Sig.C₃ʳ. Anthony à Wood says that on his return to England Sherley 'printed or caused to be printed' a narrative of his voyages. Wood adds that he has not seen this book. The reference is evidently to Nixon's work. See further on Nixon Chapters VI and VII, below.
5 Lello to Cecil, 26 February 1603; cited by E.P.Shirley.

For three days the crew of the *Golden Dragon* remained in the harbour, but they made no effort to rescue their leader and presently sailed away. Their ship was last heard of in Levantine waters as a peril to Christian and Turkish commerce. Meanwhile, after a month's detention on Zea, Sherley was taken across the water to Negroponte (Euboea) and handed over to the Turkish authorities. There he was, says Nixon, 'committed into a darke dungeon, and with a great gally chain bound fast with a slave . . . which greeved him worst of all.' He was, however, permitted to communicate with the English consul on Zante; and word was sent by a disinterested third party that ransom had best be forthcoming quickly before the Turks discovered that they held a gentleman of consequence, when they would assuredly demand more.[1] Nothing came of these negotiations; Sherley stubbornly refused to disclose his identity; and in July 1603 he was transferred to Constantinople, travelling overland on mule-back loaded with chains. In Constantinople he was 'put into a filthy common Gaole; where . . . he founde no other bedde to lie upon, but the cold stones.' To force him to reveal his name the Turks placed him in the stocks and even stretched him on the rack, and in the intervals of torture he was 'vexed continually with lyce.' When at length it was discovered that he was a brother of Sir Anthony Sherley, whose anti-Turkish propaganda was notorious, hostility towards him redoubled. From John Kitely (Sanderson's friend at the English embassy) he received assistance or at least sympathy;[2] and he was also befriended, according to Nixon, by a kindly Jew who counselled him to compromise on a smaller ransom with the promise to pay more after he was liberated. Sir Thomas had then, says Nixon, 'a Woolfe by the eare, wherein there was danger, either to hold or let goe; doubting whether he were best follow the counsell of a Jewe, or trust the cruelty of a Turk.' Twice condemned to death, he was twice reprieved, probably because of the conviction that sooner or later a large ransom would be forthcoming. He continued (in Nixon's words) to 'bare out the brunt of many a cold and bitter hour' and was on

1 *C.S.P., Venetian*, ix,544f. 2 Sanderson, *Travels in the Levant*, p.256.

the very verge of execution when a message arrived from King James I.[1]

Queen Elizabeth, as will appear more fully when we come to the story of the other Sherley brothers, had been hostile to them all; but King James, who had reasons to be friendly towards them, appealed to the Sultan for Sir Thomas's release.[2] This royal gesture was remarkable, for James's prejudices revolted at the thought of corresponding with the Great Turk, revolted so violently indeed that shortly after his accession he had refused to sign important commercial letters to the Sultan, 'saying, that for Merchants causes he would not do things unfitting a Christian prince.'[3] His plea for Sir Thomas had no immediate effect. The fact was that the continuity of English foreign policy was being maintained by Cecil, who had reasons to sympathize with Turkish indignation against Sherley and who, it seems, privately instructed Lello to make no representations on behalf of the imprisoned buccaneer. In any case Lello was likely to be less than half-hearted in such a cause, because his principal policy at the Porte had been to further an Anglo-Turkish alliance against Spain and the chances of accomplishing this would not be improved by pleading for an offender against Turkish subjects. Consequently Sherley languished in gaol for more than two years, writing woe-begone letters and accusing Lello of inactivity. One of these letters, addressed to his brother Anthony in June 1605, he entrusted to a certain friar who betrayed him by turning it over to Lello. The ambassador annotated it marginally and forwarded it to Cecil. Letter and glosses are alike querulous.

King James persisted, and Sir Thomas wrote to thank him for his efforts, adding not very tactfully that the King's first letter to the Great Turk had 'turned absolutelye into smoake.'

---

1 *The Three English Brothers*, Sig.E^r.
2 *C.S.P., Venetian*, x,35. On the whole episode see E.P.Shirley, *The Sherley Brothers*, pp.43f. A facsimile of King James's letter of 31 May 1605, renewing his appeal for Sherley's release, is in the *Bulletin of the School of Oriental Studies*, vii,Part 2. For yet another appeal from King James see Maggs's Catalogue, No.452 (*Bibliotheca Asiatica*, 1924), item 105.
3 Thomas Wilson to Sir Thomas Parry, 12 June 1603; *Original Letters*, ed. Ellis, First Series, iii,84.

Bribes were offered and accepted; 'with money,' Lello wrote, 'this State will sell any offence or error whatsoever.' At length the Sultan yielded, saying to Lello, 'Notwithstanding this man's fault I present him to the King of England.' [1] The Venetian envoy judged this to be a noteworthy act of grace, for the depredations of English pirates had aroused anger in Constantinople.[2] After his liberation in December 1605, Sherley remained for about ten weeks in the capital, 'taking a view and survey of . . . the city, observing their laws, customs and ceremonies, beholding their courts, synagogues and temples; with other things not unworthy a stranger's observation.' [3] In the spring he went to Naples where he passed several months [4] and before the end of 1606 he was once more in England and presently in trouble.

His activities had made the merchants of the Levant Company his bitter enemies; and for his part Sir Thomas, in revenge for his imprisonment, did what he could to foster prejudice in England against the Turks.[5] By way of retaliation a Turkish agent in London (of whom something more will be said presently) fomented the suspicions of the Levant merchants against him.[6] There were, moreover, rumours that he was in some way connected with the Tyrone rebellion in Ireland, and he was suspected of being in correspondence with his disloyal brother Anthony who was then in Spain. It is not surprising, therefore, that he was placed under arrest on 16 September 1607. The following day he addressed an humble petition for pardon to Cecil: 'I have done nothinge out of malis,' he declared, 'but have offended through weakness and ignorans.' [7] What is surprising is that, according to the record, he was 'sent to the Tower for turning Turk.' [8] He was, needless to say, violently anti-Turk; and though the phrase means strictly to embrace Islam, there is no other evidence that he had become a Mohammedan and it is extremely unlikely that he had done so. We

1 E.P.Shirley, op.cit., pp.43f.   2 C.S.P., Venetian, x,311.
3 Briggs, op.cit., from the *Genealogica Historia.*
4 Toby Matthew to Dudley Carleton, 8 August 1606; E.P.Shirley, op.cit., p.51.
5 C.S.P., Venetian, xi,39. The Venetian envoy reports that Sherley has 'done the Turks a bad turn here.'
6 Ibid., xi,72.
7 *Stemmata Shirleiana*, p.267.   8 C.S.P.,Dom., 1603–10, p.370.

have noted in an earlier chapter the looser meaning of the
term, equivalent to becoming a traitor; but in an official document we expect precise charges. Perhaps the Turkish agent
or the Levant Company or both had spread a report that
Sherley was a renegade, hoping thereby to strengthen prejudice
against him. In the following year a similar report was circulated, as we shall see, against Sir Francis Verney; and because
of the scandalous lives of Captain John Ward and other rogue
Englishmen the words buccaneer and renegade were at the
time almost synonymous in the popular imagination. The
charge may have been trumped up against Sherley to conceal
something else. It is unlikely that through sheer bravado he
had pretended a conversion to Islam.

At all events the accusation was not pressed against him
and he was soon at liberty. His later life was unadventurous
and forlorn: an improvident second marriage; too numerous
progeny; an undistinguished term in Parliament; two imprisonments for debt [1]—these matters require no attention from
us. In 1617, while in the Fleet prison, he composed a *Discours
of the Turkes*.[2] A bitter prejudice, natural in the circumstances,
informs this treatise. The Turks 'are all pagans and infidells,
Sodomites, liars, and drunkardes,' proud, scornful, and cruel.
Their forces are now 'soe decayed' that the Sultan is but a
'shaddowe of greatnes.' Sherley has much to say of military
affairs; he has a low opinion of Turkish strategy. He discusses
the state of trade and the difficulties of Christian merchants
who suffer from Turkish insolence. There is a brief description
of Constantinople and of some of the islands of the Ægean.
The long remainder of the discourse has to do with states and
cities of Europe. The treatise is almost wholly lacking in biographical interest and is very dull.

After the forced sale of Wiston, his ancestral home, Sherley
retired to the Isle of Wight where he was living so late as 1625.

1 On his children see E.P.Shirley, op.cit., pp.100f. On his debts and imprisonments
see *Stemmata Shirleiana*, p.268; Dalrymple, *Memorials*, second edition, p.65; *Court
and Times of James I*, p.178.
2 The manuscript is in the Library of Lambeth Palace, number 514 in the Catalogue
of 1812. It extends to seventy leaves plus an index. Bound in parchment, it is in
good preservation. It has been recently published by Sir E.Denison Ross, *Camden
Miscellany*, xvi (1936).

The date of his death is unknown. His memory lives, so far as it may be said to live at all, through his association with his romantic brothers. The friends and relatives in England who interested themselves in the fortunes of the family naturally connected the eldest brother with Anthony and Robert. Whoever it was that inspired the publication of a batch of pamphlets and the presentation of a drama to interest the public in the affairs of the Sherleys—and it is almost certain that Sir Thomas himself was one source of inspiration—would not permit that eldest brother to be ignored or neglected. After all, to the Jacobean public he was something of a hero; he had defied the terrible Turk. But to our taste he is not an attractive figure; a dangerous, headstrong, and yet ineffectual buccaneer in his adventurous days; a nonentity thereafter.

VI

THE Turkish agent in London who made representations against Sir Thomas Sherley is worth a moment's attention not only because he was the first Turkish official to visit England but because he gave a new word to the English language. Towards the close of July 1607, this Turk, whose name was Mustapha, arrived in England, announcing himself as an emissary of the Sultan but claiming the rank not of ambassador but merely of *Cha'usch*, that is, an official agent or messenger.[1] Though warnings had been sent by Lello and Glover that Mustapha's claims were counterfeit and that he was a person of no standing,[2] the English government was reluctant to risk offending the Sultan, and the envoy was provided with board and lodging for himself and his followers. Sanderson describes him as 'a stalkie personable fellow.'[3] Another description of him is of 'a man of a goodly presence and a gallant spirit, social, affable, and full of intertainment to all comers'; tactful withal, in that he was willing to dispense with Turkish fashions

---

1 The title *Cha'usch* is defined in the 'Table' or glossarial index to Hartwell's translation of Minadoi's Turco-Persian *History* as 'a Nuntio, or an Embassadour'; but actually it does not imply the latter exalted status. Massinger oddly interprets 'chiaus' as gardener (*The Renegado*, III,iv).
2 Sanderson, *Travels in the Levant*, p.244; from *S.P.,Turkey*, v, folio 38 (cited by Sir William Foster).
3 Sanderson to Glover, 27 August 1607; *Travels*, p.240.

and adapt himself to English customs, as when dining with Sir Thomas Low, the governor of the Levant Company, he not only sat upon a chair instead of cross-legged upon a carpet but even drank a toast to King James. His retinue was not prepossessing. 'He is come,' says the same observer, 'but slenderly attended, with some dozen of Turkes, wherof three only are civilly appareld, the rest looking like the ambassadors that came to Josua with old shoes and threed-bare apparel.' [1]

No emissary, even with quite unimpeachable credentials, coming from the Great Turk would be received cordially at any Christian court, for in addition to the prejudice on religious grounds there was the suspicion that his commission embraced the task of fomenting differences among the nations of Christendom. Says one of Fletcher's characters: 'I will make one of you dissemble, as if the devil should be sent from the Great Turk, in the shape of an ambassador, to set all the Christian princes at variance.' [2] King James, who was in the country at the time of Mustapha's arrival in midsummer and who was none too willing to receive a Moslem envoy, did not grant him an audience till September. Thereafter he had conferences with the Levant merchants and at least one other audience, this time in private, with the King. In November, with his passage furnished by the merchants, he left London for Constantinople where he arrived in May 1608. Glover was forced to admit that Mustapha's account of his reception in England made a good impression upon the Sultan. But Mustapha had left behind him in London a different impression. A report got abroad (traceable perhaps ultimately to Lello's and Glover's protests) that the English had entertained as the Sultan's envoy a man who was little better than an impostor. Hence the point of the following bit of dialogue from *The Alchemist*:

Dapper: What do you thinke of me,
           That I am a Chiause?
   Face: What's that?
Dapper: The Turke was here—
           As one would say, doe you thinke I am a Turke? . . .
   Face: This is a gentleman, and he is no Chiause. [3]

1 An unidentified correspondent to Sir Thomas Hoby, *Original Letters*, ed. Ellis, First Series, iii,85f.   2 *The Fair Maid of the Inn*, IV,ii.   3 *The Alchemist*, I,ii,25f.

Gifford's explanation of this passage is that 'in 1609 Sir Robert
Shirley [*sic*] sent a messenger or Chiaus . . . to this country
as his agent from the Grand Seignior and the Sophy to trans-
act some . . . business' and that this person 'decamped' after
having 'chiaused the Turkish and Persian merchants' in London out of four thousand pounds. The notion that Sir Robert
Sherley ever sent any messenger from the Sultan is of course
ridiculous, and equally so the notion that one and the same
messenger could have represented the Sultan and the Shah
and have transacted business with Persian as well as Turkish
merchants; the date 1609 is incorrect; there is no record that
Mustapha cheated the merchants out of any money; and certainly he did not decamp, for he was sent home honourably
at the expense of the Levant Company. Yet the latest editor
of *The Alchemist* has pronounced Gifford's explanation to be
'very satisfactory.'[1]

The later fortunes of the word are due not to the notoriety
of the original incident but to the fame of Jonson's play. Jonson
used 'chiause' as a synonym for 'Turk'—Dapper says so in
so many words; and with the word 'Turk' were associations
of treachery. Hence the verb 'to chiaus' (in various spellings)
comes to mean 'to cheat' and the substantive to have the
odd variety of meanings: a cheater, or one who is cheated,
or a trick, a sham, a cheat.[2] Thus did Mustapha, the first Turkish
envoy to come to England, personable fellow and gallant
spirit though he was, leave an inappropriate imprint upon
the language.

VII

THERE are very few allusions to the Levantine merchants in
Elizabethan literature. One we have already noted in *Jack*

---

1 Professor Hathaway's note in the Yale edition of the play. The *O.E.D.*, as Hathaway
remarks, regards Gifford's explanation with suspicion.
2 James Shirley (*Honoria and Mammon*, II,iii; *Works*, vi,28) uses the verb with the
meaning 'to cheat'; but John Ford (*The Lady's Trial*, II,i,256) associates 'chouses'
with 'gulls' and Samuel Butler (*Hudibras*, III,iii,531f.) has 'a sottish Chews,'
equivalent to a stupid gull. In Sir George Etherege (*Love in a Tub*, V,ii) and William Congreve (*Love in a Wood*, I,i) the meaning has shifted back to a cheat or cheater.
Yet Doctor Johnson defines the word as 'a bubble, a tool, a man fit to be cheated.'
The rustic clown in *The Variety*, 1649, a comedy by William Cavendish, Duke of
Newcastle, is named 'Chiause.'

Drum's Entertainment. A character in another play is said to have suffered 'some great losses on the sea' through a brother who is a 'Turky merchant.' [1] Thomas Heywood has a traveller who thinks that the new Royal Exchange in London is a finer mart than any at Rome or Frankfort or Venice; and he goes on:

> I have been in Turkies great Constantinople;
> The merchants there meet in a goodly temple,
> But have no common Burse. [2]

He had not observed accurately; for the Bezestan in Constantinople was in function much like the Exchange in London and was, in fact, likened to it by various visitors. Goods imported from Turkey are rarely mentioned. A Turkish weapon is said to be as fine a blade as any from Damascus or Toledo. [3] A swaggering soldier boasts that the Great Turk gave him a rapier in reward for 'mighty monst'rous marshal-like behaviour' [4]—but this gift can scarcely be classified as a Turkish import. Nashe mentions cloaks 'faced with Turkey grogeran' [5] (a sort of mohair), and it is into a cloak of similar material that Dekker describes a gallant as changing after dinner. [6] In the inventory of Volpone's effects there are nine Turkey carpets; [7] there are other allusions to such carpets, which appear to have been a staple import; [8] and when Antipholus of Ephesus describes a desk 'that's cover'd o'er with Turkish tapestry' [9] what he really refers to is a small carpet used as a table-cloth, for no tapestry was made in Turkey. [10] Shakespeare also refers to cushions from Turkey. [11] These are the only direct

---

1 *The Merry Devil of Edmonton* (anonymous), I,i,78f.
2 *If You Know Not Me You Know Nobody*, II; *Works*, i,296.
3 Fletcher and Massinger, *The Elder Brother*, V,i,45.
4 Samuel Rowlands, *Looke To It: For Ile Stabbe Ye*, 1604, p.17; *Works*, Hunterian Club, i.
5 *The Unfortunate Traveller*, *Works*, ii,300.
6 *The Gull's Hornbook*, chapter iv.
7 *Volpone*, V,iii,1.
8 Lyly, *Euphues and His England*, *Works*, ii,189; Marlowe, *2 Tamburlaine*, I,iii,43 (the scene is in the Levant, of course, but the allusion is evidence of acquaintance in England with the article in question); Beaumont and Fletcher, *The Coxcombe*, IV,iii.
9 *The Comedy of Errors*, IV,i,105. In the same scene the Merchant, dunning Antipholus, says: 'I am bound for Persia and want guilders for my voyage.'
10 *Shakespeare's England*, ii,128.
11 *The Taming of the Shrew*, II,i,349.

allusions to the Turkish trade. Their paucity perhaps points to a lack of popular demand for such goods; and we know that at times the warehouses of the Levant merchants were gorged with stocks which they found it difficult to market.

Nowhere in the Tudor-Stuart drama is there any reference to coffee. England became acquainted with it only gradually and it did not become a staple article of import till the second half of the seventeenth century. The earliest mention of the drink by a European writer appears to be that in a report to the Venetian Senate by the *Bailo* at Constantinople, Gian-francesco Morosini in 1585.[1] He wrote that the Turks were accustomed to drink 'un' acqua negra, bollente quanto possono sofferire, che si cava d'una semente che chiaman *kahvé* la quale dicono che ha la virtù di far stare l'uomo svegliato.' To William Lithgow has often been accredited, incorrectly, the earliest description to appear in an English book. But more than a decade before he wrote, two companions of Sir Anthony Sherley on his journey into Persia told of the habit of coffee-drinking which they had observed among the Turks at Aleppo. William Parry describes the Turks as sitting 'as Tailers sit upon their stalle, crosse-legd for the most part, passing the day in banqueting and carowsing, until they surfet, drinking a certain liquor which they do call Coffe, which is made of a seede much like mustard seede, which will soone intoxicate the braine, like our Metheglin.'[2] Manwaring, another member of Sherley's party, observed the Turks passing away the time in 'friendly meeting' in the 'very fair houses where this koffwey is sold.'[3] About ten years later Lithgow was entertained by Turks at Constantinople; and concerning the refreshment provided he wrote:

The usuall courtesie they bestow on their friends, who visite them is a Cup of Coffa, made of a kind of seed called Coava, and of a blackish colour; which they drink so hote as possible they can, and

1 Molmenti, *La Storia di Venezia nella Vita Privata*, iii,280. The date of this quotation is seven years earlier than that given by D.G.Hogarth (*The Penetration of Arabia*, ed. 1905, p.43) and P.K.Hitti (*History of the Arabs*, 1937, p.19) for the first mention of coffee by a European writer. See also *O.E.D.*, *sub.* 'coffee.'
2 *A new and large Discourse of the Travels of Sir Anthony Sherley*, 1601, p.10.
3 George Manwaring, *A True Discourse of Sir Anthony Sherley's Travel into Persia* (written in 1601 or 1602), in *The Three Brothers*, 1825, pp.27f.

is good to expell the crudity of raw meates, and hearbes, so much by them frequented. And those that cannot attaine to this liquor, must be contented with the cooling streames of water.[1]

About the same time George Sandys watched the sociable gatherings of the Turks:

There sit they chatting most of the day, and sippe of a drinke called Coffa . . . in little China dishes, as hot as they can suffer it: black as soote, and tasting not much unlike it, . . . which helpeth, as they say, digestion, and procureth alacritie.[2]

From Sandys Burton seems to have obtained his information about coffee, which he includes among the 'Alteratives and Cordials, corroborating, resolving the reliques, and mending the temperament.' His description contains no indication that he had ever seen or tasted the drink or that it was used in his time in England:

The Turks have a drink called Coffa (for they use no wine) so named of a berry as black as soot, and as bitter . . . which they sip still of, and sup as warm as they can suffer; they spend much time in those Coffa-houses, which are some what like our Ale-houses or Taverns, and there they sit chatting and drinking to drive away the time, and to be merry together, because they find by experience that kinde of drink so used helpeth digestion, and procureth alacrity.[3]

The Levant Company made no effort to introduce coffee into England, and though the early expeditions of the East India Company brought home a certain amount of it, the commodity did not make its appearance in the sale lists at East India House till so late as 1660. There is doubtless a connection between its recognition as a staple import at that time and the publication in the previous year of a tiny two-page tract or pamphlet entitled *The Nature of the drink Kauhi, or Coffe, and the Berry of which it is made. Described by an Arabian Phisitian* (Oxford, 1659). The Arabic original of this treatise is printed on the page opposite the translation. The

1 *Rare Adventures*, p.136.   2 *Relation of a Journey*, p.66; Purchas, viii,146.
3 *The Anatomy of Melancholy*, II,v,i,5.

translator—his name does not appear on the title-page—was Dr. Edward Pocock, the famous Arabist. The brevity of this pamphlet permits, and its curiousness warrants, its quotation entire:

> Bun is a plant in Yaman, which is planted in Adar, and groweth up and is gathered in Ab. It is about a cubit high, on a stalk about the thicknesse of one thumb. It flowres white, leaving a berry like a small nut, but that sometimes it is broad like a bean; and when it is peeled, parteth in two. The best of it is that which is weighty and yellow, the worst, that which is black. It is hot in the first degree, dry in the second: it is usually reported to be cold and dry, but it is not so; for it is bitter, and whatsoever is bitter is hot. It may be that the scorce is hot, and the Bun it selfe either of equall temperature, or cold in the first degree. That which makes for its coldnsse [sic] is its stipticknesse. In summe it is by experience found to conduce to the drying of rheumes, and flegmatick coughes and distillations, and the opening of obstructions, and the provocation of urin. It is now known by the name of Kohwah. When it is dried and throughly boyled, it allayes the ebullition of the blood, is good against the small poxe and measles, and bloudy pimples; yet causeth vertiginous headheach, and maketh lean much, occasioneth waking, and the Emirods, and asswageth lust, and sometimes breeds melancholly. He that would drink it for livelinesse sake, and to discusse slothfulnesse, and the other properties that we have mentioned, let him use much sweet meates with it, and oyle of pistaccioes, and butter. Some drink it with milk, but it is an error, and such as may bring in danger of the leprosy.

The drink was, then, for a long while regarded as a medicine, a specific against certain, or rather uncertain, diseases; but one to be used with caution because in inexpert hands it might cause a variety of disorders ranging from vertigo to leprosy. It is not surprising that the demand for it was of slow growth. It was, moreover, costly stuff, not easily obtainable, the taste for it an acquired one, the art of preparing it delectably not easily learned. The first *café* in Europe was opened in Marseilles in 1676; that a great seaport having close relations with the Orient and thronged with Levantine sailors should have taken the initiative is natural. The story is a familiar one, though not well authenticated, that when the siege of

Vienna was raised in 1683 and the Turks retired, the victorious Viennese discovered in the abandoned camp of their enemies supplies of coffee the use of which they were taught by prisoners and presently popularized throughout Europe. It is also told that the crescent-shaped rolls, still known as croissants and eaten on the continent with morning coffee, were first shaped and baked in celebration of the relief of Vienna. In the same year, 1683, and possibly because of the new Viennese fashion, a *caffe* was opened on the Piazza San Marco in Venice. Others quickly followed; in 1720 Florian's, which still flourishes after an uninterrupted history of more than two centuries. In England the chocolate-houses of the Restoration Period yielded precedence slowly to the coffee-houses which became a characteristic feature of Dr. Johnson's London. At this point, having far outrun our temporal limits, we break off this subject and return to Constantinople.

VIII

In the Baron des Hayes de Courmenin's *Voiage du Levant* (1624) the four routes from western Europe to Constantinople are discussed. That by sea is the cheapest but it is dangerous from storms, rocky coasts, and corsairs. That by way of the Danube is the longest but most comfortable. To go into the heel of Italy and thence cross into Greece has the advantage of covering much of the distance in Christian territory. Or one may cross the Adriatic from Ancona or Bari to Spalato or Ragusa and thence proceed overland: a rugged way but well protected because one can join a merchant caravan which always has an armed guard. This last route was the one followed by Sir Henry Blount; he gives some interesting details of his itinerary. Having agreed with a Janissary at Venice who was to serve as guide and guard, he embarked with a party of Turks and Jews. He was the only Christian in the company, an advantageous situation, he tells us, since it obviated the danger of drawing on himself prejudices and punishments which might have been occasioned by the misdemeanours of other Christians. Landing at Spalato, the party crossed Bosnia; travelled by way of Belgrade, Buda and Sophia; and so to Adrianople and Constantinople. From Spalato this was a journey of fifty-two days.

It is not easy to give a generalized description of Constantinople during the two centuries with which we have specially to deal. Its population at the beginning of the seventeenth century is given in a contemporary manual for travellers as 700,000 souls, an estimate that is probably an exaggeration and certainly guess-work.[1] Of its citizens the great majority were crowded within the walls of Stamboul. Galata, across the Golden Horn, was a commercial and foreign quarter stretching along the shore; and behind it Pera, now a vast residential district, was then a vineclad slope upon which were scattered houses, among them that of the English ambassador. The general appearance of the great city as the voyager approached it from the Sea of Marmora was much the same then as now; nothing has altered the unrivalled majesty of its situation, with Seraglio Point projecting into the Bosphorus and shutting off the view of the Golden Horn till one's vessel rounds the Point, and the dome of Hagia Sophia rising behind the palaces and gardens of the Seraglio, and the circle of walls and towers, with the grim Seven Towers at the farthest landward boundary of the city. Not very obvious save to those searching for analogies between Rome and 'New Rome' were the Seven Hills.[2] Time, war, earthquake, and fire had made by the year 1600 many changes in the old Byzantine city which Bertrandon de la Brocquière had visited and described a few years before it was captured and pillaged by the Turks.[3] There had been much destruction in 1453, and the terrible earthquake of 1509 did irreparable damage to Byzantine antiquities. Constantinople has always been scourged by fires; even today no topographical feature is more conspicuous than the great vacant areas where fire has more or less recently destroyed quantities of the ramshackle wooden houses whose

1 *The Travellers Breviat*, p.39.
2 The analogy is often drawn. See, for example, Petrus Gillius (Pierre Gilles), *De Topographia Constantinopoleos*, 1561, pp.28f.; Des Hayes de Courmenin, *Voiage du Levant*, p.101.
3 *Le Voyage d'Outremer*, ed. Charles Schefer in *Recueil de Voyages*, Paris, 1892, xii. There is an English translation by Thomas Johnes, 1808.

fellows, still standing, seem to attend a like fate.[1] Successive sultans had erected numerous splendid mosques. Those two magnificent monuments of Ottoman greatness, the Mosque of Bajazet II and the Mosque of Solyman the Magnificent, were among the most imposing features of the city in the later sixteenth century. The Yeni Djami Mosque in its superb situation fronting the Golden Horn opposite Galata remains in the memory of the modern visitor perhaps more clearly than any other Mohammedan building in Stamboul; but when Sanderson, Dallam, and Sherley were in Constantinople it was in course of construction and a little later work on it was interrupted, not to be resumed till the sixteen-sixties. The Mosque named for the boy-sultan Achmet I (the so-called Blue Mosque) close by Hagia Sophia was begun just after Dallam's and Sherley's time. Glover must have often watched it a-building; and by the time of Blount's visit it was finished. The slender minarets which rise here and there about the city and are so beautiful when seen from the heights of Pera were, most of them, already characteristic landmarks. Those that completed the Mohammedan alterations of Hagia Sophia were already built.

The days when the awed pilgrim could witness the magnificent liturgical ceremonials of the Orthodox Church [2] were long since past; and though the popular report, which lingered long in Christendom, that Mahomet the Conqueror had turned the Church of the Holy Wisdom into a brothel was a gross exaggeration of the desecration which had accompanied the sacking of the city, Hagia Sophia was profaned in the minds of Christians. Testimony differs as to whether access to it was permitted or forbidden to Christians; it is probable that the regulations varied in strictness at different times. Belon, for

---

1 Nicolas de Nicolay (*Navigations*, p.92) and Thomas Coryat (in Purchas, x,421) comment upon the frequency of fires. Biddulph (*Travels of Foure English Men and a Preacher*, p.21) gives an account of the fearful conflagration of 14 October 1607, when some three thousand houses were destroyed. Sir Henry Blount saw and describes (*Voyage into the Levant*, p.25) 'that horrid gap made by fire, Ann. 1633, when they report seventie thousand houses to have perished.'

2 Of great splendour must have been the Mystery of the Three Children in the Fiery Furnace as acted liturgically in Hagia Sophia in the fifteenth century. Bertrandon de la Brocquière saw it in 1433. See his *Travels*, translated by Thomas Johnes, p.223.

example, says that entrance was prohibited;[1] but various
Christian travellers describe the interior. Fynes Moryson entered Hagia Sophia 'with the Janizare my guide, trusting to
his power to defend me,' for (he explains) 'the Turks cannot endure that unwashed Christians . . . should enter their
Mosches.' He describes the roof as 'beautified with pictures
of that rich painting, which the Italians call alla Mosaica,
shining like enameled work, which now by antiquity were
much decaied, and in some parts defaced.'[2] John Sanderson
reported that 'of the pictures of all sorts (as the painted imagis)
the Turks have scraped out the eyes.'[3] Not till about 1625
did the Turks cover some of the mosaics with whitewash,[4]
and so recently as 1717 Lady Mary Wortley Montagu described
the pictures of the saints as 'still very visible in Mosaic work,
and in no other ways defaced but by the decays of time; for
it is absolutely false,' she continued, 'though so universally
asserted, that the Turks defaced all the images that they
found in the city.' In her time the mosaics of the roof were
fast falling away, and she was presented with a handful of
the debris.[5]

The slave-market where Christian captives and prisoners of
war were sold attracted the attention and roused the sympathy
of European visitors. The French traveller Philip du Fresne-
Canaye has a vivid and shocking picture of conditions in the
Bezestan or Exchange as they existed about the year 1573.
Of the sale of young women he writes:

> Ceux qui veulent acheter leur levent le voile qu'elles ont sur le
> visage; et pour connaître si elles ne sont peintes ou fardees leur

1 *Observations*, p.74.
2 *Itinerary*, ii,94. Compare Sandys's more detailed description: 'The roofe compact
and adorned with Mosaike Painting: an Antique kind of worke, composed of little
square pieces of Marble; gilded and coloured according to the place that they are
to assume in the figure or ground, which set together as if embossed, present an
unexpressable stateliness' (*Relation*, p.31). The reference to the 'figure' is noteworthy, as is the aesthetic appreciation evinced.
3 *Travels in the Levant*, p.71. So also Nicolas de Nicolay had noted that 'aux images
de Mosaique et autres de platte peinture, les Turcs ont crevé les yeux' (*Navigations*,
p.104. In the English translation by T.Washington,Jr., 1585, this passage is at
folio 57ʳ).
4 'La Voûte est toute garnie de Mosaique, que les Turcs ont blanchie en quelques en-
droits' (Des Hayes de Courmenin, *Voiage du Levant*, p.103).
5 *Letters*, ed. Galignani, 1837, i,290.

crachent a la figure, regardant en la bouche, tâtant et comptant les
dents pour voir si elles ne sont pas postiches ou gatées. . . Après
quoy ils viennent aux bras et aux mains, puis aux jambes et cuisses,
et, de là, passent jusque sur la croupe examinent les parties le plus
secrètes. . . Les pauvrettes . . . se laissant malmener tenant les
yeux baissés et eteints.[1]

Lithgow likewise saw girls 'strip'd starke naked' in the open
market.[2] But Moryson says that 'the buyers, if they will, take
them into a house, and there see them naked, and handle them
(as wee handle beasts to know their fatness and strength).'[3]
Biddulph's experience was that 'if Christians be mooved in
compassion' to purchase slaves in order to set them at liberty,
'the Turkes will sell them exceeding deare to them, but cheape
to a Musselman.'[4] In a later chapter, on the corsairs of the
Barbary States, we shall recur to this matter of the slave-
markets in Mohammedan countries.

The monuments of antiquity in Constantinople are described with such monotonous regularity and such close resemblances in phraseology by Renaissance travellers that one
has reason to suspect that later visitors are relying upon the
descriptions of their predecessors. There is a wearisome repeti-
tiousness in these descriptions of the mosques and palaces,
the hippodrome, the conduits, the obelisque, the Column of
Constantine, the Burnt Column, the Serpentine Column, the
so-called Tomb of Constantine, the aqueduct, the Seven Towers, and so forth. The interest of the modern reader is roused
only when a monument is in question which has been altered
or destroyed since the Renaissance. Travellers of the early
sixteenth century saw, and some of them described, the eques-
trian statue of Achilles which was destroyed in 1525.[5] Again,
of the three heads on the famous Serpentine Column but one
is in existence today and that is in the Archaeological Museum;

1 *Le Voyage du Levant*, ed. H.Hauser, p.95; cited by F. Gilles de la Tourette, *L'Orient et les Peintres de Venise*, pp.88f. Compare the description of the slave-market in Richard Grafton's *Chronicle*, ed. 1809, ii,429.
2 *Rare Adventures*, p.122.   3 *Itinerary*, ii,95f.
4 *Travels of Foure English Men and a Preacher*, Letter ii. Compare the description in Des Hayes de Courmenin, *Voiage du Levant*, p.109.
5 Prosper Merimée, *Description de Constantinople en 1503*, cited with Merimée's source by F.Gilles de la Tourette, *L'Orient et les Peintres de Venise*, p.87.

but all three were in place when Sanderson described this monument,[1] and more than a century later Lady Mary Wortley Montagu wrote of the 'three serpents twisted together, with their mouths gaping.' [2]

The imperial menagerie maintained in an ancient building which was popularly believed to have been Constantine's palace was an unfailing object of interest to European visitors; and their detailed accounts of it carry the implication that by contrast similar collections in western Europe (such as that at the Tower of London) were but poor affairs. The animal which inspired the greatest interest was, it would seem, the giraffe. Pierre Belon provides not only a description but a woodcut illustration of a specimen.[3] John Sanderson, a traveller usually austere and matter-of-fact and seldom moved to enthusiasm, wrote:

> I had the wewe [view] of many animalls, as olifants, tame lions, tame spotted catts, as bigge as little masties. . . The admirablest and fairest beast that ever I sawe was a jarroff, as tame as a domesticale deere. . . He was of a very great hieth; his foreleggs longer then the hinder; a very longe necke; and headed like a cambel. . . This fairest anymale was sent out of Ethiopia to this Great Turks father for a present. To Turks the keeper of him would make him kneele, but not before any Christian for any mony.[4]

Fynes Moryson devotes a paragraph to the same beast, 'newly brought out of Affricke.' By reason of his long neck, says Moryson, 'he many times put his nose in my neck, when I thought myselfe furthest distant from him, which familiarity of his I liked not.' [5] Michel Baudier tells of a giraffe which was brought into the hippodrome for the Sultan's delectation; his account may be quoted from Grimestone's quaint translation of which we shall hear more presently:

> It is not only beautiful of it selfe, but it is also gentle and very tractable: it hath a head like a Stagge, armed with two little hornes halfe a foot long, covered with haire; the eares, the feet and the taile are like unto a Cow: It hath a neck like unto a Camell, it

1 *Travels in the Levant*, p.76.
2 *Letters*, i,291.
3 *Observations*, folio 118ᵛ.

4 *Travels in the Levant*, p.57.
5 *Itinerary*, ii,96.

hath hard knobs upon the hams and brest: The skin is speckled like unto a Leopard; and some beleeve that it is that Cameliopardalis of the Ancients.

In the hippodrome with this giraffe was an elephant. 'This beast,' says Baudier, 'being brought before the Grand Seigneurs window, lifted up his head to looke on him, then he bowed it downe very low in signe of reverence.' [1]

The interest of Europeans centered with a natural though often prurient curiosity upon the Seraglio, that forbidding labyrinth of gardens and pools, kiosks and courts and halls which was the more alluring because it was closed save in the most exceptional cases to Europeans and because in it were practised, or were reported to be practised, barbarous cruelties and extravagant sensualities which were none the less frequently described for being characterized as indescribable. The visitor to Constantinople who was neither a diplomat [2] nor, like Thomas Dallam, an indispensable artisan, had generally to be content with what information or misinformation he could pick up without the walls of the imperial residence. Few casual travellers had the good fortune which came to Sir George Courthope during his sojourn in the capital; and because he saw much more of the Seraglio than did most travellers this is an appropriate place to say something about his wanderings. His recollections are surprisingly detailed and picturesque considering that he did not set them down till forty years after his youthful sojourn in the Levant.[3] His

1 *The History of the Imperiall Estate of the Grand Seigneurs*, pp.91f.

2 No English ambassador of the period published an account of his mission to Constantinople and his impressions of the city. Two Frenchmen who went there on diplomatic business may therefore claim a moment's attention. Henri de Beauvau's *Relation Journalière du Voyage du Levant* contains, besides the usual descriptions of the city's sights, a more detailed account of the Seraglio with particular attention to the ceremony (in which he took part) of the reception of the French ambassador (pp.40f.). In Des Hayes de Courmenin's *Voiage du Levant*, pp.134f., there is a similar account of diplomatic ceremonial. The author evokes for us a vivid picture of the crowds of attendants in the imperial apartments: the eunuchs, mutes, dwarfs, pages, and buffoons; and in the women's chambers the Sultana and the odalisques. He was a special agent of the King of France to settle various problems connected with the Holy Places in Jerusalem.

3 *Memoirs of Sir George Courthope*, ed. Mrs. S.C.Lomas, *The Camden Miscellany*, xi (1907), 91f. Courthope's memory is generally very accurate, but he makes occasional slips, as when he writes: 'We passed by water from Pera to Galata,' Pera being on the hill-slope above Galata and on the same side of the Golden Horn. Compare the next note.

first contact with Moslems was at Negroponte where his vessel anchored to take on fresh water. The inhabitants, who had had disagreeable experiences with thievish sailors, would not consent to any traffic unless a Christian was first surrendered as a pledge. Negotiations were conducted by a renegado of Italian birth and led to a bargain by which hostages were exchanged. The Moslem hostage who was taken on board burst into 'a flux of tears' at the sight of a leg of pork at the captain's table; but after he was assured that no one intended to force him to eat it, all went well and 'we parted very good friends.' So they crossed the Ægean and came to Smyrna whence with a 'druggerman' and a bodyguard they made five days' journey on horseback to see the temple of Diana at Ephesus.[1] From Smyrna to Constantinople Courthope travelled overland without misadventure. The distant prospect of the capital from the Asiatic shore, its surrounding waters, its shipping, its cypress trees, and 'golden spires' moved him in memory to liken it to a paradise. A closer impression was less attractive, for 'when we went into the city we had all the dogs of the city following us, some with doublets on, catching at our feet: we asked the meaning of it, they told us the dogs could tell the inhabitants when there were strangers come to town.'[2]

The Sultan's absence from his capital provided Courthope

1 Ibid., p.117. Courthope's description of this site is puzzling. 'We rode,' he says, 'to see the Ephesian Church, and Diana's Temple, which is built in a quagmire but sunk an incredible way in the earth so that we went down into it with a candle, but saw nothing but vast rooms under ground, supported by marble pillars.' It would not surprise us to find Courthope confusing the Ephesian Church with the Temple of Diana, for in old days the Church of Saint John on the hill near the site of the temple was identified with the Artemisium. The ruined church had vast subterranean chambers. The real difficulty is that Courthope describes a descent through the quagmire to pillared rooms sunk deep underground. Evidently, writing many years after his visit, his memory played him false. It is impossible to suppose that he had any knowledge of the ruins that existed under twenty feet of silt. This was not removed till Wood identified and excavated the site sixty-odd years ago. After Wood's time it quickly silted up again. Before Hogarth recleared it, it looked, he says, 'as hopeless as an ancient site can look—an immense water-logged pit choked with a tangled brake of thorns and reed' (*The Wandering Scholar*, ed. 1925, p.232). According to Professor T.R.S.Broughton, who has recently visited Ephesus, the site has again begun to choke up; and today the visitor will be inclined to agree with Courthope that it is not 'worth the pains and expence the Journey cost us' (p.117).
2 *Memoirs*, p.119. The pariah dogs are mentioned by other travellers; when Coryat was in Constantinople they had been 'banished' from the streets as a means of combatting the plague (Purchas, x,429).

with an opportunity to see the Seraglio and he was permitted to see more than was generally accessible even to the most privileged foreigners. He describes the richly adorned rooms, the gaudy nicknacks, and the pleasant gardens; and like other Europeans he carried away scandalous rumours of the sadistic enjoyments of the Great Turk. In one of the gardens he saw a pond made entirely of porphyry. Into it, says Courthope, the Sultan

> putteth . . . his Concubines stark naked and shooteth at them with certain pellets that stick upon them without any damage to their bodies. And sometimes he lets the water in such abundance upon them . . . that being above their heights they all bob up and down for life; and when his pleasure is satisfied with the sport, he lets down the water, and calls the Eunuchs who wait upon his women, to fetch them out if alive.[1]

This sort of story meets the reader of the old travel-books again and again; and these tales helped to establish the conception of the cruelty and lasciviousness of the Turk.

Courthope saw all the sights of the city accessible to the ordinary visitor; for more details than his memory retained or he had room for in his narrative he refers his readers to Robert Withers's *Description*, a book to which we shall come in a moment. On his journey homeward he visited what he thought were the ruins of Troy; and on Mitylene he fell into serious difficulties through a false accusation, was arrested, and was in danger of mistreatment. Arguments, explanations, and bribes won his freedom, however, and he and his companions set sail for Malta with all possible speed, 'for fear of any after-clap, they having power enough over us if they had made any use of it.'[2]

The account of the Seraglio to which Courthope refers had been published in the great collection of Samuel Purchas[3] with a foreword in which the editor stated that the author, Robert Withers, had been educated in Constantinople and had unusual opportunities to see the 'unholy Holies' of the Great Turk. This *Description* was reprinted separately in 1650

1 *Memoirs*, p.123. 2 Ibid., pp.128f. 3 ix,321f.

with a short introduction by John Greaves, who makes the curious statement that the manuscript had been given him in Constantinople and that on later inquiry he learned that it was by Withers.[1] Withers has a genuine feeling for the marvellous situation of the Seraglio with its prospects over the Golden Horn, the river, and the sea; its gardens, lakes, cypress walks, terraces, summer-rooms, and grazing gazelles. In spite of the architectural confusion caused, as he tells us, by reconstructions and additions at different periods, he has a fairly clear grasp of the plan of the palace: courtyards and chambers for the guards; rooms of state, judgment-hall, dining apartments, hospital, storerooms, and kitchens (of which he lists no less than nine, one for each rank of the hundreds of inhabitants of the Seraglio). He reveals a particular interest in food and cooks; but he also delights in ceremonies, describing minutely the public appearances of the despot, the courts of justice, the reception of ambassadors, the elaborate processions, and all the homage paid to the Grand Seigneur. On an occasion when the Sultan was away on a hunting expedition he was permitted to penetrate into some of the private apartments, including the quarters for the eunuchs, those dismal barracks which the tourist visits today. One suspects, however, that for the particulars regarding the women's apartments he relied upon hearsay; certainly he was never in the Harim, those suites of rooms and baths so enticing to the European imagination, now so forlorn, and always so different in their dark and stuffy dreariness from the occidental notion of their voluptuousness. Towards the close of his book Withers wanders away from his proper subject and discusses at some length the religion of the Moslems.

No recollection of the Mohammedan East recurs more often in the narratives of European travellers than that of the lack of bells in the Christian churches. Church-bells were associated with the tenderest and most solemn emotions of every occidental Christian, and there was perhaps no contrast between the customs with which he was familiar in his own country

---

1 *A Description of the Grand Signor's Seraglio, or Turkish Emperours Court,* 1650; reprinted in 1653.

and those of Islam that struck him more forcibly than the substitution for their sweet sound of the shrill falsetto voices of the muezzins' calls to prayer. This is remarked upon by visitors to many cities of the Near East but it must have been especially noticeable in Constantinople where so large a number of mosques were concentrated. Of the prohibition of the use of bells a fifteenth-century pilgrim offers the explanation that 'when Jerusalem was lost the bells were all cast down, for heathens of the rite of Mahomet cannot endure bells, because they have a commandment in their Alcoran not to use bells for the service of God, nor to suffer them to be so used.' [1] There is no such specific commandment in the *Koran* but there is an early *hadith* or tradition that the Caliph Omar once removed some little bells from a slave girl's legs, saying 'I heard the apostle of God say there is a devil with every bell.' [2] Another explanation, evidently manufactured to fit the case, is that 'in the beginning of Mahumetisme, by the sound of a Bell, the Christians had assembled and done the Moslemans great mischiefe' [3]—but what they did, and when, is not stated. Lithgow, whose protest that the Greeks are not molested by the Turks nor their way of life interfered with is qualified by the admission that the use of bells is prohibited, remarks that the Turks 'contrafact and contradict all the formes of Christians.' [4] Whatever the reason—and it is probable that it is based upon dislike of Christian ceremonies reinforced with the authority of the *hadith* mentioned above—the prohibition was almost universal. Two exceptions are noteworthy. In Scio Coryat visited an Orthodox monastery 'famous for the Bels that are therein, in number foure, not for the greatnesse thereof, but that those Coloiri onely of all the other Greekish monkes of the whole Greekish territorie, are suffered to use them.' [5] A visitor to the Maronite settlements on Lebanon noted that this Christian sect uses bells 'which are prohibited

1 *The Wanderings of Brother Felix Fabri*, translated by Aubrey Stewart (*Library of the Palestine Pilgrims' Text Society*, viii), i,426.
2 Alfred Guillaume, *The Traditions of Islam*, p.118.
3 Purchas, ix,105.
4 *Rare Adventures*, p.106. Compare *A Most Delectable and True Discourse*, Sig.H4ʳ.
5 Purchas, x,395.

other Nations.' [1] Some travellers contrast the church-bells of
Christendom with the muezzins' call of Islam. Thus William
Parry writes picturesquely:

> They have no use of Belles, but some priest three times in the day
> mounts the toppe of their church, and there, with an exalted voyce
> cries out, and invocates Mahomet to come in post, for they have
> long expected his second coming. [2]

That Parry did not trouble to inform himself of the meaning
of the muezzins' call is not surprising; these travellers had
little curiosity about such matters. [3] His interpretation of the
summons to prayer as an invocation to Mahomet to return
to earth is a confused recollection of something he has heard
about expectations of the coming of the Mahdi. It would be
profitless to quote other writers who refer to the lack of bells
in Islam, save two authors who were probably known to
Marlowe. Hugh Gough says that when the Turks capture a
Christian town they remove from the churches all bells and
other musical instruments; [4] and the English epitomist of
Sebastian Munster states that the Turks 'have no belles nor
yet do suffer the Christians abiding amongst them to have
bells.' [5] These statements were probably in Marlowe's mind
when he makes Bajazet, who has been taken prisoner by
Tamburlaine, lament:

> Now will the Christian miscreants be glad,
> Ringing for joy their superstitious bells,
> And making bonfires for my overthrow. [6]

1 Ibid., ix,105.
2 *A new and large Discourse of the Travels of Sir Anthony Sherley*, p.10.
3 Father Castela, having described the call to prayer, goes on: 'Ils n'usent ordi-
nairement que de telles et semblables cria-illeries, au lieu des cloches, . . . des-
quelles on ne scauroit trouver en toute la Turquie'—with the exception, he adds,
of some bells in the houses of European ambassadors (*Le Sainct Voyage de Jerusalem*,
p.113). Des Hayes de Courmenin, having referred vaguely to the *Koran* to explain
the prohibition of bells, adds: 'Ils n'ont point aussi d'horologues publics' (*Voiage du
Levant*, pp.232f.)—a statement which, if true three centuries ago (which is highly
doubtful, for did not Harborne present to the Sultan a clock of rare workmanship?),
is certainly not true today when incongruous occidental 'grandfather clocks' stand
in many of the mosques of Stamboul. In the preliminary editorial matter attached
to the first English version of the *Koran* (1649) it is stated that 'They have no
clocks'—a mistranslation of the French 'cloches.'
4 *The Ofspring of the House of Ottomanno*, Sig.Hvii^v.
5 *Straunge and Memorable Thinges*, folio 35^r.
6 *1 Tamburlaine*, III,iii,236f.

As noticeable in Mohammedan countries as the absence of the sound of church-bells were the prevalence and sanctity of the colour green. The gay and garish colours of Levantine costume were not so conspicuous to the European traveller of that day as they are in ours, because occidental costume was not then so sober a livery as it has since become; but the European traveller had reason to be impressed with the characteristic green worn by certain privileged individuals. According to Sir Richard Burton the wearing of this colour by persons claiming to be of the family of the Prophet is an innovation in Islam and appears to be of Turkish origin, not Arabic.[1] If this is so, the costume may have been more often noted three hundred years ago in Constantinople and Anatolia than in provinces of the Ottoman Empire that had a high percentage of population of non-Turkish race. At all events, the colour was probably especially remarkable in the capital of the empire. Christians who had travelled in Mohammedan countries had good reason to remember the colour, for, as William Lithgow notes, they were punished if they wore it.[2] When Fynes Moryson was on his travels he congratulated himself upon the possession of a certain taffety-lined doublet which he wore day and night because lice will not breed in taffety. But he had to conceal it carefully, for its lining was green and had it ever been seen by the Moslems he would have been in great danger because the colour can be worn only 'by the line and stock of Mahomet (of whom I could challenge no kindred).' Sir Edward Barton, who entertained Moryson at Constantinople, afterwards told him of the case of a poor Christian who was beaten with cudgels 'because ignorantly he wore a paire of green shoo-strings.'[3] Biddulph has several similar anecdotes:

> Greene they account Mahomet's colour; and, if they see any Christian wearing a garment of that colour, they will cut it from his back, and beat him, and ask him how he dare presume to wear Mahomet's colour, and whether he be kin to God or not: this I have

1 *Personal Narrative of a Journey to Mecca and El-Medina*, ii,4. Compare E.W.Lane, *Modern Egyptians*, i,43.
2 *Rare Adventures*, p.146; *A Most Delectable and True Discourse*, Sig.I.
3 *Itinerary*, i,451.

known put in practice upon Christians, not acquainted with the custom of the country, since my coming. One, for having but green shoe-strings, had his shoes taken away. Another wearing green breeches under his gown (being espied) had his breeches cut off, and he reviled and beaten.[1]

These and other passages which might be cited [2] illustrate a passage in Massinger's *Renegado*. 'Take you heed, sir,' says Gazet to his master (a Venetian in disguise) as they stand together in a street in Tunis:

> What colours you wear. Not two hours since, there landed
> An English pirate's whore, with a green apron,
> And, as she walked the streets, one of their muftis,
> We call them priests at Venice, with a razor
> Cuts it off, petticoat, smock and all, and leaves her
> As naked as my nail; the young fry wondering
> What strange beast it should be. I 'scaped a scouring—
> My mistress's buskpoint, of that forbidden colour,
> Then tied my codpiece; had it been discover'd,
> I had been capon'd.[3]

The colour green is still of religious significance today and the wearing of it still limited to members of the family of the Prophet.[4]

1 *The Travels of Certaine English Men*, p.64.
2 In Alexander Ross's brief but in the main accurate account of the Meccan *Haj* it is said that the velvet cloth which covers the Ka'aba (erroneously described as the Prophet's tomb) is green (*A View of all Religions*, pp.155f.). Elsewhere (Hakluyt, v,352) we find the erroneous statement that all the inhabitants of Mecca wear green clothes.
3 *The Renegado*, I,i.—In 1814 a Jew was banished from Constantinople because his daughter was seen through the open window sitting on a green sofa (William Turner, *Tour in the Levant*, 1820, iii,398).
4 Two of the present writer's most vivid memories of Islam have to do with the holy colour. One is of a Friday afternoon at the *Tikiyet el-Mawlawîya* in Cairo, the monastery where the Mewlewi Dervishes dance most beautifully and solemnly. One who was with the writer on that occasion recorded in her diary: 'Twirling and whirling as lightly as thistledown among his white-clad brethren was a little man clothed all in green, like a fair emerald among pale moon-stones. His eyes were closed and on his face an expression which proved that in the intoxication of the dance he had found God. "Him very holy man," our dragoman whispered to us; "him of Mohammed's family."' . . . The other memory is of a return at evening to the Nile steamer when a dignified Egyptian passed by, riding upon a stalwart donkey and wearing a green turban of extraordinary size. He gave a cordial salaam, upon which the donkey-boy, who had hitherto evinced no knowledge of English, said with startling suddenness: 'Ain't he a bloody fool!' Why the exclamation? Was the portly Egyptian wearing a colour, and thus making a claim, to which he was not entitled? Or had modern scepticism contaminated the donkey-boy to the point of making him contest not the validity but the value of the claim?

For books supplying information on the Sultan, his court and his government there was a ready market throughout our period. The most important of those dealing seriously with the political aspects of the Ottoman problem have been considered in our third chapter; others whose emphasis is upon the religion of Islam will be examined in Chapter IX. Some account of one of the most ambitious popularizations of this kind of knowledge [1] may appropriately round out the present chap-

---

1 Here may be noted several continental books not unknown in England and one which in English translations had a long vogue. Giovanni Antonio Menavino was captured when a boy by Barbary pirates who gave him to Bajazet II. He was placed in the famous 'school of pages' at Constantinople to be educated for the public service, but after about ten years made his escape in 1514. His *Trattato de' Costumi et Vita de' Turchi* (Florence, 1548, and other editions) was for long authoritative. Christopher Richer, a groom of the chamber of Francis I, is the author of *De rebus Turcarum*, Paris, 1540, a series of treatises on the origins of the Turks, on Tamburlaine, on Ottoman rule, and so forth—a sort of Mohammedan miscellany. Richer himself made a French version of the first of these monographs: *Les Coustumes et Manieres de vivre des Turcs*, Paris, 1540. An encyclopaedic compilation made by a Dutch scholar which in two English versions was read for many years is Johannes Boemus's *Mores, Leges et Ritus Omnium Gentium ex multis clarissimis rerum scriptoribus collecti*, Lyons, 1561 (and earlier editions). There is a French translation, *Receueil de diverses histoires touchant les situations de toutes regions et pays*, Paris, 1553. William Watreman's English translation is entitled: *The Fardle of Facions concerning the aunciente maners, customes, and Lawes of the peoples enhabiting the two partes of the earth, called Affricke and Asie*, [colophon, 1555]. A later version, identical in substance with Watreman's but, it would seem from the fact that the phrasing generally differs from his, made independently, is Edward Aston's *The Manners, Lawes and Customes of all Nations. Collected out of the best Writers by Joannes Boemus Aubanus, a Dutchman. With many other things of the same Argument* [a long analytical title follows], 1611. In both versions Turkey is discussed in Book ii, chapter 11. The account of Mohammedanism in this treatise will concern us in a later chapter of the present work. When the religious issue is disposed of, Boemus has much to say that is creditable to the Turks. They are praised, as usual, for the military virtues of celerity in action, constancy, and perseverance; for their frugality, their patient endurance of poverty, and so forth. Many customs—their prohibition of the use of bells; their removal of shoes before entering houses; their abstinence from gambling and from swine's flesh and from wine; their fashions of apparel—are noted as curiosities rather than for the purpose of holding them up to scorn. Occasionally there is perhaps a tinge of Protestant sympathy with Islam, as when their renunciation of all pictures and images is mentioned or the fact that they make no marked distinction between priests and laity. It is not made clear whether the paradox that despite the *Koran*'s command to 'prosecute their adversaries in Religion' there is no forcing of their faith upon other peoples is regarded as commendable or not. There is an unmistakably warm commendation of the strict enforcement of justice in Moslem lands. The reappearance of this old book in the seventeenth century is significant of the continuing interest in the subject.—Of an early English book to which we have already referred several times (see p.113, note 1, above), Hugh Gough's *Ofspring of the House of Ottomanno*, some further notice may be taken here. Beginning with an exposition of the manner in which 'the Turkes do use to make warres,' it passes on to an account of the duties of no less than twenty-three officials of the Great Turk's court; then to Moslem religious rites and ceremonies, the form of their temples, their prayers and preaching, their 'Lent' (Sig.C$_{10}$^{v}; with the mistaken notion that Ramadan comes one year in January, the next in February, and so on through the year), their hunting and other sports. At the close of this survey there is a naïve

ter in which our attention has been centered upon Constantinople. This elaborate work is Edward Grimestone's English
version of Michel Baudier's *Histoire Generalle du Serrail*.[1]

In its opening pages statistics impress upon the reader the
size, importance, and magnificence of Constantinople, with its
more than three hundred 'carravasserails,' its two thousand
mosques, its forty-eight thousand shops (each trade in a separate quarter), its bazaars, slave-market, mints, colleges, hospitals, granaries, and arsenals. Then follows a description of
the courts and gardens and apartments of the Seraglio. The
long remainder is devoted to an account of the Sultan's way

little dialogue between a Turk and a Christian, given in Turkish with an English
translation, and ending with this complacent comment: 'These few wordes of the
turkyshe language, I have here added for the[e], most gentil reader, not of neces-
sitie, but for delectations sake: that thou maist understand, how grosse and barbarous
they be. The ever living God grant, that they maye have more neede of our speche,
then we of thers' (Sig.G$_{iii}$^{r}f.). A narrative follows of the 'affliction of captives'
(Sig. G$_v$^{r}.) and the little book concludes with the story of the murder of Mustapha
which will occupy our attention in Chapter XI.—Another book that had a long
vogue is Pierre de la Primaudaye's *L'Academie* (1577) of which the first part was
translated into English by T.Bowes and published in 1586. Other parts followed
and the complete work appeared in 1618: *The French Academie Fully Discoursed
and finished in foure Bookes*. Into a chapter 'Of divers kinds of Monarchies, and of
a Tyranny' (Book i, chapter 58, pp.259f.) a brief discussion of Turkish rule is introduced. The Great Turk commands, it is said, 'in rigorous fashion,' using the services
of 'runegate slaves.' Sultan Solyman's execution of a 'Bascha' who had dared
to claim authority almost equal to his master's is given as an example of Turkish
ruthlessness.—It is surprising that there was no English translation of the Byzantine
History of Chalcondylas. The two fine folio volumes of the definitive French version
(*Histoire de la Decadence de l'Empire Grec*, Paris, 1650) have no less than sixty-four
copperplates picturing the Sultan on his throne, different types of officers and soldiers, peasants, Greek villagers, a Jewish physician, a self-mortifying Calender, a
pilgrim from Mecca, different types of women, and so forth; the whole series forming
an invaluable supplement to the travel-literature. Chalcondylas was a learned refugee
who taught Greek in Milan and other Italian cities in the earlier sixteenth century.
1 *Histoire Generalle du Serrail, et de la Cour du Grand Seigneur Empereur des Turcs. Ou
se void l'image de la grandeur Otthomane, le tableau des passions humaines, et les exem-
ples des inconstantes prosperitez de la Cour. Ensemble l'Histoire de la Cour du Roy de
la Chine. Par Le Sr Michel Baudier de Languedoc*, Paris, 1624. The quaint title-page
is adorned with cuts showing the Great Turk with a retinue of horsemen, the Great
Turk bathing in a garden, and another garden-scene where ladies of the Seraglio
dance. The English translation (which omits the Chinese section of the original)
has two title-pages. The first is: *The History of the Imperiall Estate of the Grand Seigneurs: Their Habitations, Lives, Titles, Qualities, Exercises, Workes, Revenews, Habit,
Discent, Ceremonies, Magnificence, Judgements, Officers, Favourites, Religion, Power,
Government and Tyranny. Translated out of French by E.G.S.A.*, 1635. The second
title is: *The History of the Serrail, And of the Court of the Grand Seigneur, Emperour
of the Turkes. Wherein is seene the Image of the Othoman Greatnesse, A Table of humane passions, and the Examples of the inconstant prosperities of the Court. Translated
out of French by Edward Grimestone Serjant at Armes*. In a dedication to his nephew
Grimestone describes his book as 'a verball Legacie, the last of my fruitlesse labours.'
In his translation of P.d'Avity's *The Estates, Empires, and Principalities of the World*,
1615, Grimestone had already dealt summarily with the Ottoman Empire.—For the
history and architecture of the Seraglio see N.M.Penzer, *The Harem*, 1937.

of life. This begins, quite logically, with the order of ceremonies for his coronation: how on his father's death he returns secretly to the capital from whatever distant province he has made his home while heir-apparent; receives the sceptre from the chief 'Bassae'; takes an oath upon the *Koran*; is seven times blessed by a 'priest'; and having ridden out to show himself to his people, returns to the Seraglio for the strangling of his brothers in order that the saying 'One God in Heaven, One Emperour upon Earth' may be fulfilled.[1] Chapters or parts of chapters follow on the Sultan's titles, his food and drink, his exercise and amusements with jesters and women, his hours of prayer and of sleep. All night watchers with torches are near him. 'Thus he rests which troubles all Europe, disquiets Asia, and afflicts Affrica and the shoare of the Mediteranean with his Fleet.'[2] The gravity and frowning dignity of the potentate make his slaves fear and adore him. Conforming to religious custom, each Turkish emperor does some manual labour: Mahomet II was a gardener and sent the fruit he raised to market; another sultan made little knives; others have ploughed the land.[3] A long chapter follows on the Sultan's many loves.[4] So jealous is he to keep his concubines from profane eyes that 'when they say the Emperour is in the Garden with his women every one flies as farre as hee can,' for 'the contagion of these faire creatures is dangerous; some die for that they have beene seene, and others for that they have seene them.'[5] These women are accustomed to sell secretly the presents which the Sultan lavishes upon them, so that they may accumulate gold against the day when they shall have lost his favour. Incontinence among them is punished by their being sewn in a sack and thrown into the sea.

A catalogue of gifts sent to the Sultan includes a clock which strikes the hours to the accompaniment of music; and we wonder whether this may not have been Dallam's organ.

---

1 Grimestone, op.cit., p.29.   2 Ibid., p.38.
3 Ibid., Book i, chapter 9. Compare the account of the Sultan's handicrafts in Robert Withers, *Description of the Grand Signor's Seraglio*, p.78; and for a modern discussion of this matter see B.Miller, *Beyond the Sublime Porte: The Grand Seraglio of Stamboul*, New Haven, 1931, pp.68f. See also A.J.Toynbee, *A Study of History*, iii,22f.
4 Grimestone, Book i, chapter 10.   5 Ibid., p.55.

Particularly interesting is the description of certain festivities when the Sultan was entertained with a display of artificial combats representing his victories over the Christians. There is a nice irony in the fact that at the very time when (as we shall see in a later chapter) there were water-festivals on the Thames in which Christian victories over the Turks were represented, similar shows were being presented by the Turks. In one of them the Turks stormed a mimic castle held by the Franks, whose 'counterfeit heads' were lifted above the walls. 'The contempt they make of us'—that is, which the Turks make of Christians—'ended the triumph. They let slip into the place about thirty Hogs . . . and ranne after them crying and howling in mockerie.' [1] Another spectacle was of an island 'admirably well made of boords and pastboord' which represented Cyprus. The Turkish assault thereof, the siege of Famagusta, sallies, skirmishes, batteries, mines, and breaches, 'and whatsoever the furie of Warre could invent' were enacted. On this occasion there were also minor exhibitions and displays of strength and skill; tame elephants; a boy who was rolled about naked in a hogshead filled with live serpents and came out whole and sound; and a troop of 'wretched Greciens' on their way to become Mohammedans.

The Great Turk's revenues and expenditures; the organization of the various departments of his government; the juridical procedure; his officers; arsenal supplies; his manner of going to war, to sea, to the hunt; the sexual perversions and scandals of the court; the violence of lust and the extremes of cruelty— these and similar subjects are described and sometimes illustrated with brief anecdotes. 'Thus these people live farre from the light of true Faith, in the darknesse of Mahometan ignorance, which have carried them to the excesse of all sorts of vices.' [2] After much else in like vein, there is an account 'Of the Death, Mourning, Funerall, and Burying of the Grand Seigneurs'; [3] and the book closes with these words:

1 Ibid., p.85.   2 Ibid, p.167.
3 Ibid., Book ii, chapter 20. Various travellers describe the Turkish cemeteries which, with the turban-topped tombs of men and the flower-topped tombs of women, were so different from Christian sepulchral monuments. See, e.g., the detailed description in Sir Henry Blount, *Voyage into the Levant*, p.107.

Thus they shut him up in sixe foot of ground whom all the World could not containe, and whose unrestrained ambition aspired to more Empire than the Earth containes: And after that he had bin a terrour to Men, and the cruell scourge of many Nations, he is made the subject of Wormes, and their ordinary food. In this manner passeth and ends the glory of the World.

CHAPTER FIVE

THE SOPHY AND THE SHI'A

I

UNTIL the second half of the sixteenth century no Englishman had ever visited Persia, that distant country of which the wealth and luxury were fabulous and where men adored the sun. Italians forestalled them there as in other parts of the Near and Middle East. The missions of the Venetian representatives, Josafa Barbaro (in 1471) and Ambrogio Contarini (in 1473), had had a double objective: to secure concessions for a trade from the further East and to persuade the Shah to attack the Sultan in order to relieve Turkish pressure upon Europe.[1] Presently there was established such a trade as they had aimed at (subject to vicissitudes from Turkish hostility), which came from India through Mesopotamia to Aleppo and Tripoli and hence into the Mediterranean; and by the middle of the sixteenth century the Venetians possessed a practical monopoly of this sea-borne traffic.[2] Moreover, so early as 1520 the route into Persia through Muscovy, down the Volga and across the Caspian, had been used experimentally by the Genoese, following a course along which the Vikings had raided and which had been used by Scandinavian traders from early times.[3]

English merchants saw that if they were to establish profitable trade-relations with Persia and the more distant Orient it would be necessary to circumvent the Venetians. The strictly

1 *Viaggi Fatti da Vinetia alla Tana, in Persia, in India, et in Constantinopoli*, Venice, 1545; *Travels to Tana and Persia by Josafa Barbaro and Ambrogio Contarini*, Hakluyt Society, 1873. See also *A Narrative of Italian Travels in Persia in the Fifteenth and Sixteenth Centuries*, Hakluyt Society, 1873.
2 One of Antonio's argosies was 'bound for Tripolis,' that is, Tripoli in Syria, along the Italian trade-route (*The Merchant of Venice*, I,iii,18; compare III,i,108).
3 T.J.Arne, *La Suède et l'Orient*, Stockholm, 1914; T.D.Kendrick, *A History of the Vikings*, 1930, pp.158f. A memorial of the contact of ancient Scandinavia with the Arabic world is Ahmed ibn Fudhlan's description of a cremation which he witnessed on the Volga in the year 921. See the translation by Charles Waddy in 'A Scandinavian Cremation-Ceremony,' *Antiquity*, viii (March 1934), 58f.

Persian trade was unquestionably subordinated in the minds of the original projectors to the more ambitious quest of a passage to Cathay; but the promise held out by the route through the Persian Gulf must have been apparent to Richard Chancellor who before his first journey into Muscovy had already participated in a voyage into the eastern Mediterranean.[1] With the story of the expedition whose goal was China we are concerned only in so far as it touches upon the story of the penetration into Persia. After consultation with Sebastian Cabot and having obtained a charter from Edward VI,[2] a group of London merchants fitted out three ships in 1553 under the command of Sir Hugh Willoughby with Chancellor as pilot-general. Two of the vessels were frozen in the Arctic Ocean with the loss of Willoughby and all hands; but the third, under Chancellor's command, made land near the mouth of the Dvina. News of their coming travelled southward and they were encouraged to visit Moscow. The Czar Ivan Vasilovich gladly extended trading privileges to these Englishmen, for at that time he had no outlet to the West by way of the Baltic. As for Chancellor, though the expedition had failed to discover a north-east passage to China, he had reason to be satisfied, for not only did Russia provide certain commodities for which there was a demand in England but—what was more important—its climate rendered it a promising market for English woollens.

As a result of this initial success Queen Mary in 1555 granted a charter to 'The Mysterie and Companie of the Merchant Adventurers for the Discoverie of regions, dominions, islands and places unknown'—or the Muscovy Company, as it soon came to be called.[3] Chancellor immediately made his second voyage to Russia, taking with him several merchants who were to remain there as factors in charge of trading-posts. The

1 Foster, *England's Quest of Eastern Trade*, p.15, note 1.
2 For the Muscovy Company see Foster, op.cit., chapter 1; W.R.Scott, *Joint-Stock Companies*, i, chapters 2–6, and ii,37f. Documents are in Hakluyt, ii. See also Purchas, xi,595f. The grant of the charter has not been traced but its existence is deduced from the instructions for the voyage given in Hakluyt. Sir William Foster suggests (p.8, note 1) that though drafted it may not have been completed before the death of Edward VI and hence is absent from the Patent Rolls.
3 It seems never to have been called the Persian Company even during the years when the attention of the merchants was concentrated upon the Persian trade.

Czar was now so well impressed that when Chancellor returned to England he dispatched with him an emissary—the first Muscovite ambassador to an English sovereign. Their ship was wrecked on the coast of Scotland; Chancellor was drowned; and the Russian envoy was among the few survivors. In London he was welcomed by Queen Mary and King Philip and lavishly entertained by the merchants of the Muscovy Company.[1]

The later fortunes of the strictly Russian trade may be briefly summarized. The original understanding with the Czar certainly promised the Company a monopoly of the Anglo-Russian trade in both directions; but their exclusive rights were only by way of the North Cape, and when the Czar captured Narva on the Baltic this shorter route was promptly used by independent English traders ('interlopers') to the serious loss of the Company. Moreover, the route to Riga had for long been practically pre-empted by the Hanseatic League, and the Dutch were also formidable competitors in those waters.

Competition in Muscovy served to stimulate the original intention (which had never been forgotten) to seek out new markets in the further East; and in 1557 the Company appointed Anthony Jenkinson Captain-General of a new fleet.[2]

1 The memory of the curiosity with which this exotic stranger was greeted in London was perhaps still alive when Shakespeare introduced his courtiers disguised as Muscovites into *Love's Labour's Lost*.

2 On Jenkinson see the article in *D.N.B.* and Foster, op.cit., chapters ii and iii. 'The Voyages of Persia, traveiled by the Merchauntes of London' in 1561-67-68 are in Richard Eden, *The Historye of Travayle*, 1577, folios 321f. Jenkinson's voyage is at folio 322ᵛ. Eden's original work, *The Decades of the newe worlde*, 1555 (translated from the Latin of Peter Martyr Anlegrius, with some additional material from other sources) has a good deal about Muscovy, giving an idea of the knowledge of that country at the time of Jenkinson's first visit. The volume of 1577 was 'newly set in order, augmented, and finished' by Richard Willes. Most of the narratives of Jenkinson's voyages were collected by Hakluyt, ii,413f.; iii,15f. Purchas relates the first voyage, xi,623f.; xii,1f. The Hakluyt material (collated with Jenkinson's manuscripts) and other documents are in *Early Voyages and Travels to Russia and Persia by Anthony Jenkinson and other Englishmen*, ed. E.D.Morgan and C.H.Coote, Hakluyt Society, 1886. Morgan's introduction is of especial value for questions of geography. Texts are also in John Harris, *Navigantium atque Itinerantium Bibliotheca: or, a compleat Collection of Voyages and Travels*, 1705, i, Book iv, chapters 3-9. Adam Olearius, *The Voyages and Travels of the Ambassadors . . . to . . . Muscovy and . . . Persia*, translated by John Davies, 1672, though of a date long after Jenkinson's visits, is of interest for its account of the route from Moscow via the Volga and Caspian into Persia. At p.150 there is a large map of the Volga region. See also Jonas Hanway, *Historical Account of the British Trade over the Caspian Sea: with the Author's Journal of Travels from England through Russia into Persia*, 1753. Conditions along this route had changed but little between Jenkinson's day and Hanway's,

Jenkinson, an explorer of an energy and intrepidity which marked him out even in that age of daring and resourceful merchant-adventurers, had already travelled extensively in the Levant,[1] where his observation of commercial conditions in Syria seems to have convinced him that the way eastward through Aleppo into Mesopotamia was shut to English traders and that their future lay along the Russian route. The terms of his commission make it evident that his objective was far beyond Moscow. That city he reached in December 1557; and in the following spring, supplied with recommendations from the Czar, he and two English companions and an interpreter set out eastward. Travelling mainly by the rivers, they came to Astrakhan on the delta of the Volga [2] at the top of the Caspian Sea.[3] The party surveyed the northern coasts of the Caspian but did not proceed far south, and Jenkinson's map [4] proves that he failed to grasp its shape, size, and axis. It is possible that reports of the disturbed condition of Persia dis-

and that little was mainly for the worse. See further G.N.Curzon, *Persia and the Persian Question*, 1892, ii,533f.; Sir Percy Sykes, *History of Persia*, third edition, 1930, ii,166f.

1 Jenkinson had witnessed the entry of Solyman the Magnificent into Aleppo in 1553; see Hakluyt, v,105f.; Morgan and Coote, op.cit., i,1f.

2 When John Fletcher wrote of 'Volga, on whose face the North wind freezes' (*Valentinian*, V,ii,32) he may have had in mind not only descriptions in *The Russ Commonwealth* by his relative Giles Fletcher the Elder but the experiences of these early explorers. Jenkinson reported that 'Volga hath seventie mouthes or fals into the sea' (Purchas, xii,8). Marlowe writes of 'the fifty-headed Volga' (*1 Tamburlaine*, I,ii,103) where 'heads' obviously means mouths in the delta, as in the medieval use of *caput* by geographers. When, however, Fletcher (*The Loyal Subject*, IV,v,70) refers to the seven heads of Volga he probably intends its branches. Dekker has:

> Swift Volga . . . whose curld head lies
> On seaven rich pillowes

(*Londons Tempe*, 1629; *Dramatic Works*, ed. Pearson, iv,120).

3 Horace (*Odes*, II,ix) refers to the stormy Caspian. In the imagination of English poets the classical heritage combines with the Renaissance experience. Spenser draws a simile from the hardships of those 'who swelling sayles in Caspian sea [do] cross' (*The Faerie Queene*, II,vii,14). Marlowe writes of 'the ever-raging Caspian Lake,' 'the craggy rocks of Caspia,' and especially of the

> Christian merchants, that with Russian stems
> Plough up huge furrows in the Caspian sea

(*1 Tamburlaine*, I,i,168; II,iii,48; I,ii,193f.). The last two lines occur with the change of one word in *The Taming of a Shrew*. Milton likens the meeting of Satan and Death to that of two storm-clouds over the Caspian (*Paradise Lost*, ii,716). Milton's *Brief History of Muscovia* (*Works*, ed. Mitford, viii,469f.) introduces some of the early English explorers. There is a theory that this *History* was compiled from notes originally intended for an epic of English exploration of the East.

4 Reproduced in Morgan and Coote, op.cit., i,cxx.

couraged him from proceeding further south but it is likelier that such an excursion was never part of his plan, for his goal was not Persia but Cathay. With a caravan of Persian and Tartar merchants he and his associates went eastward and arrived at Bokhara in December 1558, eight months after their departure from Moscow. They were the first Englishmen, and for two centuries and a half the last, to visit that swarming mart of Chinese and Indian traffickers with Persians, Turkomans, and Muscovites.[1] He arrived at an inopportune time when turmoil further east had cut off all intercourse with China. Another disappointment was the information that the remaining distance to Cathay was far greater than he had supposed and that another nine months would be required for the journey, even granting that it was possible to make it at all. The oriental traders would hold out no promise of a profitable trade even so far as Bokhara; and though he had been received with decent courtesy by the Khan he was cheated out of payment for some of the goods which he had managed to sell. It was therefore with no vision of fabulous oriental wealth but with a distinct impression of authentic mid-Asian poverty that he and his companions, having retraced almost exactly their outward route, arrived in England early in 1560. He described his journey as 'so miserable, dangerous, and chargeable . . . as my penne is not able to expresse the same.'[2]

His pessimism led to the abandonment of the idea of opening up trade with India and China by way of Central Asia. There remained the alternative route by the Caspian into Persia. What Jenkinson had learned of the poverty and unrest of that country might have deterred a less hardy man; but in that very unrest a promise was discernible. Ever since Shah Ismail I, the founder of the Safavi dynasty, had ascended the throne of Persia more than half a century before, wars had been intermittently in progress between the Shi'a Mohammedans of Persia and the orthodox Sunni Mohammedans of the Ottoman Empire. Advantage might well be taken of the stagnation

---

1 'The people of Bohare' are characters listed in the 'plot' of the lost play of *Tamar Cam (Henslowe Papers*, ed. Greg, p.148).
2 Hakluyt, ii,400.

of trade between these two states to introduce English goods into Persia by way of Muscovy. And could not the commerce which came from India be tapped at the head of the Persian Gulf for the benefit of English trade? The experiment seemed worth while. Consequently in the spring of 1561 Jenkinson set out again, bearing letters from Queen Elizabeth to the Sophy.[1] There were long delays in Moscow, and not until October 1562 did the expedition reach Casbeen (Kasvin) in northern Persia.[2]

He arrived at an unpropitious moment when there was a truce with the Turks and the Shah's policy was to avoid giving offence to his dreaded neighbour, while his merchants were anxious that there should be no disturbance of the newly revived trade with Turkey. Furthermore, Jenkinson, in calculating upon the Shah's hatred of the Turks, had not reckoned with his hatred of Christians. The Persians believed, or affected to believe, that Jenkinson was a Portuguese spy; and courtiers counselled his dismissal or arrest or even that he—or his head— be sent as a present to the Great Turk. Thus were commercial interests intertwined with religious fanaticism. When at last

1 The Elizabethans usually called the Shah the Sophy or the Great Sophy. The title derives from Safavi, the surname of the Persian dynasty from c.1500 to 1736, which is from the Arabic cafi-ud-din, 'Purity of Religion,' given to an ancestor of Ismail I. The word is not related to Sophia, wisdom, nor to Sufi. The latter is the name of a member of a sect of Mohammedan mystics and derives from an Arabic word meaning 'man of wool,' i.e., clothed in woollen garments. This meaning was not unknown to the Elizabethans; see, for example, Washington's translation of Nicolay's Navigations, III,ii,108. Greaves, in his Seraglio, 1653, has the marginal gloss 'Puritan' opposite Sufi. But in the 'Table' appended to Hartwell's translation of Minadoi's History of the Warres Betweene the Turkes and the Persians, 1595, the definition is: 'Soffi and Sofito, an auncient word signifying a wise man, learned and skilfull in Magike Naturall. It is growen to be the common name of the Emperour of Persia.' See ibid., p.47, and the English version of Soranzo's Ottoman, folio 39ᵛ. Those who confounded the words Sophy and Sufi risked the offence of lèse majesté. Geoffrey Duckett writes (Hakluyt, iii,158): 'The king of Persia (whom here we call the great Sophy) is not there so called, but is called the Shaugh. It were there dangerous to cal him by the name of Sophy, because that Sophy in the Persian tongue, is a begger, and it were as much as to call him The great begger.' (Compare Eden, The Historye of Travayle, folio 324ᵛ.) The association of Sophy and Sophia suggests to Giles Fletcher the fine epithet for the Wise Men who came to Bethlehem: 'The kingly Sophies' (Christ's Victorie and Triumph, i,82). The same false etymology provides William Strode with a play on words: 'This Persian cydaris [a jewelled turban] hath made some Sophies that scarce were wise before' (The Floating Island, II,iv). See further O.E.D. for early uses of Sophy, from 1539; and the commentators on the allusions to the Sophy in Twelfth Night. On Sufism see R.A.Nicholson, The Mystics of Islam, 1914; P.K.Hitti, History of the Arabs, pp.432f.

2 En route they paused on the western side of the Caspian where they were so lucky as to win the friendship of the Khan who governed the province under the Shah. This petty ruler was of assistance to later English visitors and his death was a serious blow to the Anglo-Persian trade.

received in audience by Shah Tahmasp—'Shaw Thomas,' as the English generally call him—Jenkinson was required to wear 'basmackes' (a kind of over-shoes) because, being a giaour, it was thought that he would contaminate the imperial precincts. The suggestion that this fancied insult was merely the Englishman's misunderstanding of the Persians' method of keeping clean the carpets they sat on [1] does not explain away Jenkinson's further statement that when he was dismissed from the Shah's presence, 'after me followed a man with a basanet of sand, sifting all the way that I had gone within the said palace' [2]—as though covering something unclean. This humiliating incident is introduced into William Warner's narrative of Jenkinson's adventures:

> When a Christian (who they call an infidel because
> He not beleeves in Mahomet nor Mortezalie's lawes)
> Is cal'd to audience, least the same prophaine where he doth stand,
> Must doffe his shoes, and to and fro treade on new-sifted sand. [3]

Geoffrey Duckett, who visited Persia some years later, was subjected to an even more grievous mortification. Not only was he forced to don the prophylactic shoes but before he entered the courtyard where the audience was held, a causeway was heaped up from the entrance to the Shah's throne and along this temporary path the infidel Englishman had to walk. 'When the Christian departs,' says Duckett, 'the causey is cast down and the ground made even again.' [4]

Later, through the good offices of a friendly official, Jenkinson obtained somewhat better treatment, and though he accomplished little in the way of a trade agreement he had reason to consider his long journey not altogether fruitless. For one thing, he had managed to get into touch with certain Indian merchants who held out hopes of trade. For another, he was greatly impressed with the splendour and lavish display of the Shah's court: his pavilion and throne, robes and jewels, carpets and concubines; and notwithstanding the evidence of general

---

1 Sir John Malcolm, *History of Persia*, i,513.
2 Hakluyt, iii,30f.
3 *Albion's England*, 1586, Book xi; Chalmers' *English Poets*, iv,638f.
4 Eden, *Historye of Travayle*, folio 324ᵛ; Hakluyt, iii,159.

poverty in the country, he concluded that if the Shah were persuaded to look with more friendly eyes upon the English a profitable trade might be developed. Consequently on his return to Moscow in August 1563 he arranged for another expedition into Persia under the leadership of two of his factors. He then returned to England.

Jenkinson was now elected a member of the Company which hitherto he had served as an agent. He made two more visits to Moscow: in 1566, when he obtained further commercial concessions, and in 1571, when he found the Czar intractable because of Elizabeth's refusal to conclude a military alliance, and the privileges which the English merchants had enjoyed were withdrawn. Once more at home, 'wearie and growing old,' as he described himself, he resolved to travel no more. But he lived for another twenty years, a person of honour and renown, 'than whom no man had more perfect knowledge of the North part of the World,' [1] often consulted as one who could speak with the authority of long and wide experience. [2] William Warner celebrated his exploits along with those of Willoughby, Chancellor, and other hardy travellers; and the old explorer's heart must have warmed when he read Warner's hearty peroration:

> Rest may thy honorable Bones, good old Man, in sweet Peace:
> Nor have thy Phoenix-Ashes since beene barren on increase:
> But late had we a Fowle like rare, us'd oftener Sea than Shore,
> Ofte swam hee into golden Strands, but now will so no more,
> For, though he were a dyving Fowle, to Heaven did he sore.
> In England, not Arabia, now the Phoenix Birdes be bread,
> And evermore shall theare revive, when shall the olde be dead. [3]

Drayton includes Jenkinson among the explorers whose achievements he celebrates in *Poly-Olbion*. Jenkinson, he says,

> Adventured to view rich Persias wealth and pride,
> Whose true report thereof, the English since have tride. [4]

1 William Camden, *History of England*, ed. 1688, p.216.
2 Foster, *England's Quest of Eastern Trade*, p.34. For the elder Hakluyt Jenkinson wrote a 'Memorandum' of all the countries through which he had travelled (Hakluyt, iii,195f.).
3 See p.211, note 3, above. The other 'Fowle' is Sir Francis Drake.
4 xix,226f.; *Works*, ed. J.W.Hebel, iv,403.

When Jenkinson died in February 1611, Sir Robert Sherley (as we shall see) was about to return to England from Persia as the ambassador of the Sophy. It is not on record whether these two men, the chief links between England and Persia in their respective generations, ever met.

II

WE have now to follow the fortunes of the English who 'tried' Jenkinson's 'true report.' [1] In the summer of 1564 the expedition which he had organized at Moscow before his return to England started out under the leadership of Thomas Alcock and Richard Cheney (or Cheinie). Though Alcock was murdered and though those members of the party who managed to return to England brought home a tale of harrowing perils and hardships, Cheney was sanguine about the prospects of importing silk profitably from the provinces of Persia nearest the Caspian.[2] Consequently a third expedition went out in 1565-7 under the leadership of Richard Johnson who had been Jenkinson's companion on the journey to Bokhara. Johnson remained in the district west of the Caspian (then part of Persia) and sent Arthur Edwards south. Edwards found Shah Tahmasp in a tolerant and even friendly mood; and for good reason, for new troubles were brewing between Persia and Turkey and it was likely that the frontier would soon be closed, thus depriving the Shah of an inlet for European woollens and an outlet for Persian silk. In these straits he now looked propitiously upon the project of a trade through Muscovy. The report which Edwards submitted to his employers was naturally highly optimistic. He found that London cloths were in great request and that there was also a ready demand for tin and copper. The Shah had personally supervised the negotiations, helping to compile a list of commodities to be sent from England and specifying, among many other things, 'ten or twelve good shirts of male being very good or else none, that may abide the shot of an arrowe'; also a quantity of 'hand guns' and 'dags' (a kind of pistol). His thoughts were

1 See, in addition to the texts in Eden, Hakluyt, and Purchas, Foster, op.cit., chapter 3.
2 Hakluyt, III,40f.; Morgan and Coote, i,150, note, and ii,378f.

upon the approaching campaign. Edwards reported also that Persia offered for export pepper, ginger, nutmegs, cloves, brimstone, rice, yew for bow-staves, and, most important of all, silk. He noted carefully those localities where silk of good quality might be procured cheap.[1]

A scheme which Edwards meditated, to proceed in disguise through Persia to Ormuz in order to spy out the feasibility of tapping the Aleppo-bound spice-trade, came to nothing because, Richard Johnson having returned to Moscow, Edwards had no one to whom he could entrust his goods en route to Russia. But on his return to England his suggestion about Ormuz was not ignored by his employers, and the instructions for a fourth expedition included methods of making contact with the trade through the Persian Gulf. This expedition was again under the leadership of Edwards, but the narrative of it was written by Lawrence Chapman, one of his associates. Of all the Company's agents Chapman is the most outspoken on the matter of hardships. He draws a lamentable picture of the inconveniences and privations of travel in Persia; the miserable quarters assigned to the English traders; the scarcity of water; the perpetual peril from the Moslems 'who do account it remission of sins to wash their hands in the blood of one of us.' 'Better it is therefore,' he concludes, 'in my opinion to continue a beggar in England during life than to remain a rich merchant seven years in this country.'[2] The inference from this remark, however, that though life in Persia might be uncomfortable and precarious it was possible for an Englishman to amass a fortune there, is valid, for this fourth voyage brought rich returns.

This success accounts for the elaborate preparations for the fifth expedition which was more ambitiously conceived than any that had been undertaken hitherto. The leader was Thomas Bannister, a merchant of London who accompanied to Moscow an envoy from Queen Elizabeth to the Czar. That large hopes of gain were entertained is shown not only by the fact that

---

1 Eden, *Historye of Travayle*, folio 333: 'The prosperous voyage of Arthur Edwards'; Hakluyt, iii,53f.; Morgan and Coote, ii,382f.
2 Hakluyt, iii,136f.; Morgan and Coote, ii,412f.

three other important English factors were with Bannister and that their retinue numbered a dozen English sailors and about forty Russians but by the fact that they descended the Volga on a vessel especially built to their order. Bannister died not long after their entrance into Persia and the command was assumed by Geoffrey Duckett who later wrote the narrative which it was customary to submit to the Company.[1] His long residence in Persia, his visits to widely separated localities in search of trade, and his consequent familiarity with the country account for the greater detail of his story as compared with earlier reports. A supplementary narrative was composed by Lionel Plumtree, one of his colleagues. Plumtree tells of an incident during negotiations with Shah Tahmasp which, if reliance may be placed upon the story, shows how changed was that potentate's attitude towards Christians in general and English merchants in particular since the days when with gross insults he had dismissed Jenkinson from his presence. By way of indicating the value which the Shah placed upon the reputation of Englishmen for honest dealing, Plumtree says that when Tahmasp wished to make an offering at Mecca he purchased from the merchants a quantity of English coin, saying that their money 'was gotten by good deeds and with a good conscience, and was therefore worthy to be made an oblation to their holy prophet, but his own money was rather gotten by fraud, oppression and unhonest means, and therefore was not fit to serve for so holy a use.'[2] That the Shah ever had such a thought or made such a remark seems a shade incredible.

This fifth expedition was away from England nearly seven years, from 1568 to 1574. When the merchants at last set out upon their homeward voyage on the Caspian they had with them a vast stock of commodities, estimated in value at between thirty and forty thousand pounds—or many times that amount in the terms of today. At sea they were set upon by Cossack pirates; and in a desperate battle all the English were wounded and the pirates got away with all their goods.

1 Eden, folio 324f.; Hakluyt, iii,159f.; Morgan and Coote, ii,261f.,423f.
2 Hakluyt, iii,152.

Part of the booty was subsequently recovered; but this mis-adventure was undoubtedly a decisive factor in the long delay before another expedition went to Persia. Another cause of the five-year interruption of the Persian trade was the shifting of interest towards the North-West while Frobisher was attempting to discover a route to China in that direction. With the failure of his efforts came a renewal of intercourse with Persia.

The sixth voyage was once more under the leadership of Arthur Edwards. The party should have known that the political and economic confusion resulting from the war with Turkey rendered unpromising the prospects of trade in Persia. Yet they were dumbfounded when on their arrival at Astrakhan they learned that provinces along the Caspian where in former years their trade had flourished were now in Turkish hands. Edwards remained at Astrakhan and sent a party under the conduct of Christopher Burroughs further south. Burroughs found the country in a chaotic state and could not effect a penetration into Persia. Consequently he was constrained to sell or barter his goods to the Turks for what they would bring; and then he returned to Astrakhan only to discover that Edwards had died during his absence. The report which Burroughs submitted particularized the perils through which he had passed and was, not unnaturally, discouraging as to the future.[1]

This expedition (1579–81) was the last sent by the Muscovy merchants through Russia into Persia. In view of the fact that the six 'voyages,' despite vicissitudes and disasters, had brought large profits (a dividend of 106 per cent was declared in 1581[2]), the unpropitious outlook discerned by Burroughs is scarcely sufficient to account for the abandonment of the trade. Conditions in Persia certainly provided no warrant for optimism. Since Shah Tahmasp's death in 1576 there had been confusion during the reigns of two weak monarchs, and the glories of Shah Abbas the Great still lay hidden in the future. The merchants were in fact confronted with a dilemma. When

1 Purchas, xii,32f.; Morgan and Coote, ii,441f.
2 Scott, *Joint-Stock Companies*, ii,46; Foster, *England's Quest of Eastern Trade*, p.43.

Persia was at peace with Turkey she was reluctant to affront her powerful neighbour by countenancing a trade which drew off profit from the Ottoman Empire. When, on the other hand, she was at war and was anxious to develop the Caspian-Volga trade, the turmoil was such that the trade was unprofitable. The laxity of the Company's administration at home and the dishonesty of some of their factors in Russia, together with the confusion entailed by conducting two distinct enterprises at once—the Russian and the Persian—were other grounds for discouragement. Moreover, the trade's success depended in large measure upon the favour or disfavour of the Czar, who could at any moment sever their communications or cancel their privileges and who had in fact already caused them serious difficulties and losses when the whim seized him. But the fundamental reason for the abrupt change in the Company's policies and fortunes was that the enormous distances involved charges that made it impossible to compete with a direct Levantine trade through the Mediterranean; and it is highly significant that the Russian route was abandoned in the very year when, as we have seen, the Levant Company obtained commercial concessions from the Porte.

Twenty years later a warning of the difficulties of gaining access to the East through Muscovy and Persia was published in *The Travellers Breviat*; and the information and counsel here given, though originally addressed to Italians, were doubtless applied by the merchants of London to their own circumstances. The Duke of Muscovy, it is said, will not suffer strangers to pass through his territories; the Caspian Sea is very dangerous and unfrequented; Persia presents difficulties in the way of lofty mountains and vast deserts; only ambassadors are permitted to enter and even they are not allowed to travel freely or to converse with the natives at their pleasure.[1] If this extreme pessimism is not confirmed by the actual experiences of some travellers (English merchants were still at Moscow and there were those who urged the reopening of the Volga trade-route), it is at any rate indicative of certain currents of sentiment at the beginning of the seventeenth century.

1 *The Travellers Breviat*, pp.101f.

III

THE beginnings of English trade with the further East by way
of the Mediterranean and Mesopotamia, which influenced the
decision to abandon the Russian route into Persia, concern us
here because travellers along this southern route penetrated
into parts of Persia not frequented by the agents of the Muscovy Company and because the adventures and projects of
the Sherley brothers, which will occupy our attention in the
two following chapters, cannot be understood without some
knowledge of the circumstances which brought about the
formation of the East India Company.[1] We shall, however,
overstep as little as possible the geographical limits set in this
volume and shall not involve ourselves in the story of the
English penetration into India.

While the last expedition of the Muscovy Company was
still in Persia and while negotiations which led to the establishment of the Levant Company were in progress at Constantinople, a merchant of London named John Newbery made in
1579 his first journey into the East, impelled in part, it seems,
by a desire to visit the Holy Land and in part to see for himself
the conditions and prospects of trade in those parts. He was
absent from England for but a few months; but in the following
year he set out upon a much more ambitious journey. This
took him by sea to Tripoli and thence overland to Aleppo and
to Bir on the Euphrates which he descended to a point opposite
Baghdad. From there he struck across Mesopotamia to the
Tigris which he descended to the Persian Gulf and so to Ormuz.
This river-route had been long known to Venetian traders, but
Newbery was the first Englishman to follow it and, with the
possible exception of an obscure renegade whose very name is
unknown,[2] he was the first Englishman to visit the famous
mart whose name was almost legendary as a synonym for

1 See Sir W.W.Hunter, *A History of British India*, 1899, chapter 6; W.R.Scott, *Joint-Stock Companies*, ii,98f.; Foster, *England's Quest of Eastern Trade*, chapters 8–18; *The Dawn of British Trade in India*, ed. Henry Stevens, 1886; *The Register of Letters . . . of the Governour and Company of Merchants of London trading into the East Indies*, ed. G.Birdwood and W.Foster, 1893. Original narratives, drawn for the most part from Purchas, are in *Early Travels in India*, ed. Foster, Oxford, 1921.
2 Foster, *England's Quest of Eastern Trade*, p.41.

fabulous wealth.[1] With the Portuguese, who then permitted merchants of other nations to trade freely at Ormuz, Newbery got into no sort of difficulty at this time; but his coming aroused the jealousy and suspicions of an Italian merchant who later caused him trouble. Newbery remained six weeks at Ormuz and then returned westward through southern Persia, visiting both Shiraz and Isfahan. He was, so far as is definitely known, the first Englishman who had ever seen either of these famous cities. He then crossed Persia and Asia Minor; came to Constantinople; and returned home through Rumania and Poland.[2]

This very remarkable journey—an exploit the more notable since beyond Aleppo he was not accompanied by any other Englishman—led to Newbery's appointment as leader of an expedition which was now organized by Sir Edward Osborne and Richard Staper. Persuaded by Newbery's glowing description of the wealth of Ormuz and his confidence that a trade with India could be developed, these merchants in consort with others supplied funds for a mission to the potentates of India. Newbery's chief associate was the celebrated Ralph Fitch, who,

1 On the wealth of Ormuz see Marco Polo, Book i, chapter 19; Friar Odoric, *Journal*, chapter 2; *Travels of Sir John Mandeville*, chapter 19; Richard Eden, *Historye of Travayle*, folio 331. The famous Italian traveller Cesare Federici, who completed well-nigh two decades of wandering in the East just at the time that Newbery set forth on his second voyage, describes the 'very great trade' of Ormuz in spices, drugs, silk, brocade, 'and divers other sorts of marchandise' (*Viaggio*, 1587; English translation by Thomas Hickocke, 1588; reprinted in Hakluyt, v,365f.). The equally famous Dutchman Jan Huyghen Van Linschoten, whose path crossed Newbery's, devotes an entire chapter to the great island-mart (*Voyage*, Hakluyt Society, i,46f.). These reports are reflected in imaginative literature. Ben Jonson speaks of a ship coming from Ormuz laden with drugs (*The Alchemist*, I,iii,59f.). Fletcher says that 'diamonds of Ormuz, bought for little' have in London 'vented at the price of princes' ransoms' (*Women Pleased*, I,ii). Jasper Mayne describes the wreck of two ships returning from Ormuz with the loss of cargoes worth forty thousand pounds (*The City Match*, V,iv; Hazlitt's Dodsley, xiii,303). Milton describes Satan's throne as far outshining the wealth even of Ormuz (*Paradise Lost*, ii,2). Andrew Marvel says that the pomegranates of Bermuda enclose 'jewels more rich than Ormuz shows' (*Bermudas*; *Poems and Letters*, ed. H.M.Margoliouth, i,17). Ormuz never recovered from the pillaging which followed the combined Persian and English onslaught upon the Portuguese in 1622. Sir Thomas Herbert, who visited it a few years afterwards, describes it as 'a poor place, now not worth the owning,' though formerly the stateliest city of the Orient and once deserving the proverbial tribute:

If all the world were but a Ring
Ormuz the Diamond should bring

(*Relation of Some Yeares Travaile*, 1634, p.46). This couplet, by the way, occurs, with or without its Latin original, with tiresome frequency in descriptions of Ormuz.
2 Foster (*England's Quest of Eastern Trade*, pp.87f.) believes that the narrative of this journey in Purchas, viii, was compiled by Purchas himself from the roughest notes.

because (as Sir William Foster has lately noted with proper emphasis) he chanced to survive and return home while his chief perished on the way, has been called 'England's pioneer to India,' a title which by right belongs to Newbery.[1] The third important member of the party was John Eldred. They took with them an expert in jewelry; and a painter named James Story was permitted to accompany them at his own expense. Story had the strange fortune to be engaged by the Jesuits at Goa to adorn their church. He disappears afterwards from the narrative and it is thought that he perished at sea on the return-voyage to England by way of the Cape of Good Hope.

Newbery's expedition left England in February 1583. Their ship was the *Tiger*; their immediate destination Aleppo. When the Witch in *Macbeth* refers to the wife of the 'master o'the *Tiger*' who had 'to Aleppo gone' we have evidence that Shakespeare had read the narrative of this voyage in Hakluyt and that the exploit was still, twenty years afterwards, well enough remembered to warrant an allusion to it on the popular stage.[2] By the Mesopotamian route they came to Baghdad, where two factors remained; and Eldred was left at Basra at the head of the Persian Gulf. The business of these subordinates was to dispose of their stock, make new purchases, and at a later date return home. Newbery and Fitch sailed on down the Gulf. Of their experiences and of the misadventures of some of their successors an audience in the London theatres would be reminded many years later when Massinger alluded to 'a noble captain who, in his voyage to the Persian Gulf, perished by shipwreck.'[3]

1 J.H.Ryley, *Ralph Fitch: England's Pioneer to India*, 1899. See also Foster, *Early Travels in India*, pp.1f. and *The Travels of Pedro Teixeira*, translated by W.R.Sinclair, Hakluyt Society, 1902, pp.xxviif. The Portuguese traveller Teixeira was at Goa at the same time with Fitch though it is not certain whether the two men ever met.
2 With the development of the Syrian trade the fame of Aleppo as a mart spread in England. The expression 'I would not, for Aleppo' (Fletcher and Massinger, *The Knight of Malta*, V,i) is equivalent to I would not do such-and-such for great riches. In Dekker, *Lanthorn and Candlelight* and in Davenant, *The Wits*, IV,i, there are allusions to merchants who have been to Aleppo.
3 *The Guardian*, V,iv.—Fitch and Eldred were the first Englishmen to bring home stories of the thievish propensities of the denizens of the banks of the Euphrates, Tigris, and the upper waters of the Persian Gulf. Fitch says (Hakluyt, v,466, and compare vi,1f.) that 'in the night when your boats be made fast, it is necessary that you keep good watch. For the Arabians that be thieves will come swimming

The details of Newbery's and Fitch's adventures at Ormuz must be read elsewhere. Suffice to say that they got into trouble through the machinations of the same Italian who had threatened Newbery on his first visit; and but for the kind offices of some Jesuits they 'might have rotted in prison.' [1] They nourished a reasonable grievance, holding that it was 'contrary to all justice' that the Portuguese should permit all other nations to trade with them and except Englishmen alone from this amicable treatment.[2] From Ormuz the governor sent them to Goa to be dealt with by the Portuguese viceroy.[3] The scenes of their further adventures lie definitely beyond our limits. Newbery presently set his face towards home and from the time of his separation from Fitch was never heard of again. He may have been murdered on the way or more probably died of disease. Fitch proceeded into further India, Cochin China, Burma, and other parts of the East.[4] He returned to London in 1591 after an absence of nine years.

Fitch's personal narrative of his travels was published in the second edition (1598–1600) of Hakluyt's *Voyages*.[5] He had probably kept no journal, for the discovery of such a document might have landed him in difficulties among enemies and the sheer bulk of adequate memoranda of so lengthy a journey would have been inconveniently large. He relied upon memory,

and steal your goods and flee away.' Cesare Fererici (ibid., v,367f.) found that these marsh-dwellers were 'theeves in number like to ants.' Cartwright bears similar testimony in *The Preachers Travels*. The habits of the Marsh Arabs have not altered during the past three centuries; in the Great War the British, bringing up supplies by the railway close to the marshes, had to sling iron nets over the open cars to prevent Arabs, hidden in the reeds, from hooking articles from passing trains. (See *Haji Rikkan, Marsh Arab*, by 'Fulanain,' 1927. A photograph facing p.38 of this pleasant book suggests better than any description the wild waste of reeds and waters through which Newbery and Fitch passed and the type of people they encountered on the way to Ormuz.)

1 Morgan and Coote, op.cit., ii,441f.
2 Hakluyt, v,458f.
3 The English Jesuit, Father Thomas Stevens, who laboured long as a missionary at Goa and who was the first of all Englishmen to set foot on Indian soil, used his good offices in their behalf. On Stevens, see Foster, *England's Quest of Eastern Trade*, p.91, note.
4 Fitch's journey 'to view those parts, to us that were the most unknowne' is celebrated by Drayton (*Poly-Olbion*, xix,237f.; *Works*, ed. J.W.Hebel, iv,403). Drayton mentions Eldred's visit to Persia but is silent about Newbery.
5 The elder Hakluyt had been in touch with members of this expedition before they left England and had commissioned Newbery to procure for him a certain Arabic *Cosmography*, which, however, Newbery, despite 'earnest inquirie,' could not find. See Newbery's letter from Aleppo, Hakluyt, v,452.

supplemented where possible with material drawn from Hic-kocke's translation (1588) of the *Viaggio* of Cesare Federici. This mode of composition accounts for the want of proportion be-tween parts of his story; when he has to do with parts of the East unknown to the Italian traveller he becomes at once vague and meagre. With Fitch's narrative Hakluyt published a shorter report by Eldred, adding six letters from Newbery and one from Fitch.

Fitch's account of India as an inexhaustible treasure-house was presently supplemented by the similar impressions of the Dutch traveller J.H. Van Linschoten, whose narrative appeared in English translation in 1598.[1] The organization of the East India Company owed much to the incentive provided by these two explorers. But other influences were also at work. After Spain absorbed Portugal in 1580, the growing tension between Spain and England threatened to close to the latter country the spice-market of Lisbon. In 1587 a great Spanish ship, the *San Filipe*, was captured, and its immensely valuable cargo furnished concrete proof of the rumoured value of Indian com-modities. Shortly after Fitch's return from India came the famous capture of the *Madre de Dios* on which was found, be-sides astonishing riches in goods of many sorts, a register of the Spanish government which contained more evidence.[2] Then, in 1595–6, came the initial successes of the Dutch ventures by way of the Cape of Good Hope. The difficulties in which, as we have seen, the Levant Company became involved in 1599 made London merchants see that the time had come to organize a direct trade with India by the Cape. Preliminary organization, in which several merchants of the Levant Company took part, was rapidly effected; and in 1600 a charter was granted to 'the Governor and Company of Merchants of London trading into the East Indies.'[3] The first voyage under the auspices of the

---

1 *John Huighen Van Linschoten His Discourse of Voyages into the Easte and West Indies*, 1598. The translator was William Phillip. The first book, dealing with the East Indies, is reprinted in the *Voyage of . . . Linschoten*, ed. A.C.Burnell and P.A.Tiele, Hakluyt Society, 1885. In the same year, 1598, from the pen of the same translator and from the same publisher came Bernardt Langenes's *The Description of a voyage made by ships of Holland into the East Indies.*
2 John Bruce, *Annals of the East India Company*, 1810, i,119.
3 W.R.Scott, *Joint Stock Companies*, ii,92f.; in full in Purchas, ii,366f.

new Company was undertaken in 1601.[1] This was the final blow to any hopes of reopening trade down the Volga and through the Caspian. Yet in that same year Sir Anthony Sherley was unfolding his grandiose and impracticable designs in first one and then another of the European courts and his brother Robert Sherley was a hostage at the court of Shah Abbas the Great.

IV

THE reports which the English factors in Persia submitted to their employers were not always limited in scope to the problems and prospects of commerce. Their aim to establish cordial or at least workable arrangements between English and Persian merchants led some of them to take note of any characteristics of Shi'a Mohammedanism that appeared to link it with Christianity and separate it from the orthodox Sunni Mohammedanism of the Turks. This tendency was perhaps strengthened by the idea, intermittently present in the minds of European statesmen, that an alliance might be effected between Persia and Christendom against the Ottoman Empire. Of all the English agents the one who took most interest in the religion of the Persians was Geoffrey Duckett. To this subject he de-

---

1 The most interesting of the early narratives is *The Last East-Indian Voyage. Containing much varietie of the State of the Severall kingdomes where they have traded, . . . begun by one of the Voyage: since continued out of the faithfull observations of them that are come home*, 1606. This has been reprinted as *The Voyage of Sir Henry Middleton*, Hakluyt Society, 1855. Narratives by Midnall, Hawkins, and Withington are in *Early Travels in India*, ed. Foster, pp.49f.,60f.,188f. See also *A true and large discourse of the Voyage of the Fleet to the East Indies*, 1603. The new interest stimulated by the Company's activities gained an audience for Edward Grimestone's translation of Joseph de Acosta's *Natural and Morall Historie of the East and West Indies*, 1604, and for Edmund Scott's *An Exact Discourse of the subtilties, fashishions* [sic], *pollicies, religion and ceremonies of the East Indians, as well Chyneses as Javans*, 1606. Visitors to India opened up new sources of material for tales of wonder. An example is: *A True Relation, without all Exception, of strange and admirable Accidents, which lately happened in the Kingdom of the great Magor, or Mogul, who is the greatest Monarch of the East-Indies . . . Written and certified by Persons of good Import who were Eye-witnesses of what is here reported*, 1622; reprinted in *Harleian Miscellany*, 1744, i,251f. The anonymous authors refer to Sir Thomas Roe and the Reverend Edward Terry as men who will vouch for the truth of what they write. They tell of the Mogul's greatness; of the magnificence of his court; and so forth. They do not neglect to edify as well as to amuse; and tell a long tale of a prince who died of a gangrene caused by a fester in his breast where a hair had been pulled out by a concubine at the very moment when he was flouting and jesting at the Deity. On his death-bed this *Rasa* abjured atheism, and assembling his followers solemnly pointed out to them the lesson of his shameful death.

voted a long section of his narrative.[1] He observed the ceremonial turning in prayer towards Mecca. He tells how the
Mohammedans watch for the new moon which signals the beginning of Ramadan and of how during that month they fast
'until the day be off the skie' and then eat and drink all night.
It is odd that he commits the error of fixing the occurrence of
Ramadan just after Christmas; for even if he was never told
that the Moslem year is lunar and that consequently all feasts
and fasts pass gradually through the cycle of the seasons, the
shift in date during the five or six years of his residence in
Persia was sufficiently considerable for him to have observed it.
But perhaps he did not have access to a Christian calendar and
lost his reckoning.

Duckett watched the departure of the annual pilgrimage to
Mecca [2] and says that on their way the pilgrims pause at
Jerusalem to visit reverently the tomb of Christ. Similar erroneous statements may be met with elsewhere; thus, Laonicus
Chalcondylas says that Moorish pilgrims returning from Mecca
visit Christ's tomb [3] and an anonymous English writer says the
same of Turkish pilgrims.[4] These writers were certainly misinformed. It is true that the cult of Hussein with its memorial
of martyrdom gave to the Shi'a Persians a sympathy with the
dogma of the Atonement that is altogether lacking among the
Sunnis; but the Shi'ites deny as emphatically as do the Sunnis
the truth of the Gospel narrative of the death of Christ. This
fact was known to some writers of the period. Father Gabriel
de Chinon, who was a missionary among the Persians, discusses
the difficulties in the way of making converts to Christianity;
and one of the three major obstacles he mentions is the Chris-

---

1 'Of the religion of the Persians,' Hakluyt, iii,159f.
2 See the annex on 'The Schism in the Iranic World' in A.J.Toynbee, *A Study of History*, Oxford, 1934, i,347f. Toynbee says that Shah Ismail I and his successors discouraged the custom of making pilgrimages to the Holy Cities of Arabia because
they were in Sunni territory; but he fails to note that travellers of the late sixteenth and early seventeenth centuries refer frequently to Persian pilgrimages
to Mecca. It is conceivable that they were misinformed but more likely that by
their time the prohibition was relaxed. See also in general D.M.Dwight, *The
Shi'ite Religion. A History of Islam in Persia and Irak*, 1933; P.K.Hitti, *History
of the Arabs*, pp.439f.
3 *L'Histoire de la Decadence de l'Empire Grec et Establissement de celuy des Turcs*,
Paris, 1650, ii,28.
4 *The Policy of the Turkish Empire*, 1597, folio 57ᵛ.

tian doctrine of the Crucifixion and Resurrection.[1] This had been for centuries a commonplace of European knowledge concerning Islam. Even the author of *The Travels of Sir John Mandeville*, in the sympathetic account of Mohammedanism which is grounded in his scepticism, is constrained to admit that for all the resemblances between Christianity and Islam the two religions differ fundamentally on the one point of Christ's death. Such citations could be multiplied, for in the pages of many Christian writers the denial of Christ's Death and Resurrection is referred to as a crowning example of the blasphemies of Islam.[2] Christian pilgrims in Jerusalem were, as we have seen, often scoffed at by the Moslems during their devotions at the Holy Sepulchre.

The authoritative basis for the Mohammedan denial of the Crucifixion and the insuperable barrier between Christianity and Islam is the passage in the *Koran*: 'They slew him not nor crucified, but it appeared so unto them; . . . they slew him not for certain. But Allah took him up unto Himself.'[3] This docetism or illusionism—the belief that Jesus was not crucified but that there was some form of deception or a phantasm or the substitution of someone else—dates from very early times, long before the foundation of Islam, and appears in one form or another in early Christian heretical literature.[4] It is worth noting that to a statement by the seventeenth-century writer Robert Chambers that Moslems believe that Christ 'ascended up into a heaven, putting another man in his place to be crucified' there is a marginal gloss: 'Judas is the man who they say was crucified insted of Christ: which error might grow of this,

1 *Relations Nouvelles du Levant; ou Traites de la Religion, du Governement, et des Coûtumes des Perses, des Armenians, et des Gaures*, Lyons, 1671, p.180.
2 Thus Robert Withers (*A Description of the Grand Signor's Seraglio*, 1650, p.188) says: 'When they go to Jerusalem, they go not to visit Christ's sepulcher; for they say, he did not die.' The Moroccan traveller Ibn Battúta is a representative of the Mohammedan point of view. He characterizes the Holy Sepulchre at Jerusalem as 'the church of which [the Christians] are falsely persuaded to believe that it contains the grave of Jesus' (*Travels in Asia and Africa*, translated by H.A.R.Gibb, *Broadway Travellers*, 1929, p.57).
3 Surah iv,157f. (Marmaduke Pickthall's translation). There are other passages in the *Koran*, especially Surah xix,33, which appear to contradict this statement. The question is too complex to be more than suggested here. See, among innumerable authorities, the recent discussion in Emile Dermenghen, *The Life of Mahomet*, pp.113f.
4 For example, *Acts of John*, §97; *The Apocryphal New Testament*, ed. M.R.James, Oxford, 1924, p.254. St. Ignatius reproves docetism (*Epistles*, Smyrna, ii).

that Simon Sireneus carried his cross.'[1] This anticipates the opinion of modern scholarship that the words in Saint John's Gospel (xix,17): 'Jesus . . . bearing his own cross' were intended to controvert a current docetical interpretation of the narrative in the Synoptics that Simon of Cyrene was 'compelled to bear the cross.'

Christian writers of the Renaissance who report the Moslem belief that someone else was crucified in Christ's stead do not always name Judas Iscariot. Quite often the substitute is left unidentified or it is said (in closer accord with the words of the *Koran*) that there was an illusion or deception. Fryer tells of a Moslem with whom he discussed various questions of religion and who 'would not have Christ Crucified but another so like him that he could not be distinguished.'[2] Joseph Pitts quotes the Mohammedans as saying that 'our Saviour was not crucified in Person but in Effigy or one like him.'[3] According to another report of the Mohammedan belief, there was no deception but Jesus was rescued by angels and snatched up into heaven, and the Jews, 'astonished and extreamly vexed,' crucified another in his place.[4]

But a natural craving for ironic justice made Judas the favourite protagonist of this strange perversion of the Gospel story. The most elaborate narrative of the crucifixion of Judas is the so-called *Gospel of Barnabas*.[5] This forgery has but little direct bearing upon English literature and that little at a date long subsequent to the period in which our interest centres, but because it is perhaps the strangest document of Islamic-Christian relations produced during the Renaissance it deserves

1 *A True Historicall Discourse of Muley Hamets Rising*, 1609, Sig. H₃ᵛ. Compare Michel Baudier, *Histoire Generale de la Religion des Turcs*, Paris, 1625, p.302. 'Judas loco eius crucifixus sit,' says Sebastian Munster (*Cosmographiae universalis Libri VI*, Basle, 1550, p.1038). The Judas story is told at length in *Nouveau Voyage du Levant* by le Sieur D.M., The Hague, 1694, letter xx. See also Cornelis Bruin, *Voyage au Levant*, 1700, chapter xvii.
2 *A New Account of East India and Persia*, ed. William Crooke, Hakluyt Society, 1909, iii,76.
3 *A True and Faithful Account of the Religion and Manners of the Mohammetans*, Exeter, 1704, chapter viii.
4 Robert Withers, *A Description of the Grand Signor's Seraglio*, p.174.
5 For what follows the writer is under great obligations to the introduction by Lonsdale and Laura Ragg to their translation of *The Gospel of Barnabas*, Oxford, 1907. The Italian manuscript is in the Imperial Library at Vienna.

a brief notice here. It was not in print nor probably even in circulation in manuscript in the sixteenth and seventeenth centuries; and the news of its discovery was first announced in 1709 by the English deist John Toland.[1] It is probable that the Moslem world first became acquainted with it through the writings of George Sale. No version earlier than the Italian text has ever been discovered; and though that text claims to be a translation from the Arabic, Mohammedan controversialists, challenged now for more than two centuries, have failed to produce the original. The Arabic version, entitled *Injîl Barnâba*, which at the present day still sells widely in Egypt and Syria,[2] is really, despite the assertion that it is the original, a translation from the Italian.

Mysticism, universalism, and asceticism are strains in the *Barnabas* at variance with orthodox Mohammedan interpretations of the *Koran*. There are various characteristically medieval and Italian touches in it, especially in the verbal echoes of Dante. The writer has made use of the Vulgate and of Rabbinical legends, and when he uses the *Koran* he sometimes expands mere hints, as in his elaborate angelology. He betrays ignorance of the relations between the Synagogue and the Roman authorities in Judea and is markedly ignorant of Palestinian topography, as when he speaks of a voyage by sea from Nazareth to Jerusalem. The conclusion to which the editors of the English translation come with regard to the book's authorship is that it was composed by an Italian who was familiar with Christian doctrine but knew little about Islam, who wished to damage Christianity and exalt Islam, and who was probably a convert to Mohammedanism. The idiom makes it probable that the writer was a Venetian using Tuscan without complete mastery. Of the date of composition it is not possible to speak with entire

1 *Nazarenus: or Jewish, Gentile, and Mahometan Christianity, containing the history of the ancient Gospel of Barnabas and the modern Gospel of the Mahometans, attributed to the same Apostle*, 1718; reprinted in Toland's *Miscellaneous Works*, 1747. See Ragg, op.cit., pp.lxvf.
2 Eldon Rutter, *The Holy Cities of Arabia*, pp.401f. (one-volume edition). Mr. Rutter errs in saying that the *Barnabas* was written originally in Latin or Spanish.—A century ago Sir John Malcolm made inquiries about the book in Persia but never saw a copy (*History of Persia*, ii,324). See also 'Abn-Ul-Ahan and W.H.T.Gairdner, *The Gospel of Barnabas: An Essay and Inquiry*, London, Madras, and Colombo, The Christian Literature Society, 1908. In this refutation of the book's authenticity Mohammedans are upbraided for stooping to make use of such a manifest forgery.

assurance. The surviving manuscript is certainly of the sixteenth century but the language points to the fourteenth; and
the probability is that it is a sixteenth-century work deliberately archaized.

But though as a polemic the *Barnabas* is a malignant fraud
it is possible to rate it higher as a work of the imagination. In
the course of the narrative Jesus several times names Mahomet
and foretells his coming as the Messiah or Messenger of God.
This conception is in line with that of the schools of Moslem
theology in which the Prophet is identified with the *Logos*.[1]
The most interesting portion [2] tells how Judas, miraculously
transformed to resemble Jesus, is arrested, tried, and crucified.
His trial, at which he vainly protests that an error is being committed, is told at great length and with remarkable dramatic
power. After Judas has been crucified, rumours of the Resurrection get abroad, and Jesus obtains from God permission to
descend from the Third Heaven to his mother and his disciples,
whom he comforts with the assurance that he has not been put
to death nor will die till the end of all things is near at hand.
In conformity with the Moslem belief that Jesus is destined to
judge the world at the last day, the *Barnabas* contains an elaborate description of the Signs of Judgment.[3]

The *Koran* declares that all the People of the Scripture will
believe in Jesus 'before his death' and that 'on the Day of
Resurrection he will be a witness against them.' [4] This verse is
the authority for the Moslem tenet that Jesus will return to
judge the world which is occasionally referred to by Christian
writers of the Renaissance; [5] and associated with it is the *hadith*,
firmly rooted in the Moslem mind, that he is destined, after his
return, to live out the appointed term of his life to three score
years and ten and then will die. But no Elizabethan writer
refers to the empty tomb close by the tomb of Mahomet at
El-Medina which is prepared for the body of Jesus.[6] A confused
and vague statement by Varthema may possibly refer to this

1 See R.A.Nicholson in *The Legacy of Islam*, p.225.   3 Chapters lii[b]f.
2 Chapters ccxvf.   4 Surah iv,159.
5 Once at least (Cornelis Bruin, *Voyage au Levant*, chapter xvii) in the fantastic form
   that if Jesus judges rightly Mahomet will give him his daughter in marriage.
6 Compare Guillaume, *The Traditions of Islam*, p.158, and for a recent description of
   the tomb prepared for Jesus see Rutter, op.cit., p.505.

tomb,[1] but the earliest description by an Englishman seems to
be that by Joseph Pitts.[2]

It is evident that Christians reported the Mohammedan
denial that Christ was crucified as a mere blasphemous curiosity of infidelity without any understanding of the basic doctrinal significance of this docetism in which the reality of the
Atonement is denied. Since the two religions differed on this
central dogma, the resemblances which the Elizabethans noted
were so much froth and smoke, quite valueless. The agents of
the English merchants who sought to establish commercial relations, and possibly looked for a political alliance, between
England and Persia would naturally welcome any signs of
sympathy with Christianity. The cult of Hussein offered the
closest point of contact. It may therefore appear surprising
that neither Geoffrey Duckett nor any of his fellows touches on
the analogy between Jesus and Hussein. But it must be remembered that the Shi'ites had been an obscure minority in Persia
for hundreds of years till the beginning of the sixteenth century
when the persecutions of the Sunni majority, deportations, and
forcible conversions initiated by Shah Ismail I resulted in the
establishment of the Shi'a as the national religion. Not until
two or three generations had passed and the faith had become
firmly fixed, was it possible for the cult of Hussein with its
elaborate ceremonial to emerge and expand. The silence of the
English factors was, then, probably due not so much to fear of
committing a blasphemy by comparing Hussein to Christ as to
the fact that the rudimentary form of the cult was in their day
not so like Christian ceremonial as it became at a later date.

At this point a digression may be introduced both because
the subject is of interest in itself and because of the analogy
between the development of the so-called 'Persian Passion-
Play' and the development of liturgical drama in medieval
Christian Europe.[3] The tragedy of the house of 'Ali was not

1 *Itinerary*, Argonaut Press, p.16.
2 *A True and Faithful Account*, chapter viii.
3 The Persian religious plays, of intolerable length to European taste (for their performance extends over many days) but of extraordinary power to move Shi'a spectators, were first described in English by James Morier in his *Journey through Persia*
(1812), pp.194f. The Count de Gobineau gave a much more elaborate account of
them (*Les Religions et les Philosophies dans l'Asie Centrale*, Paris, n.d., chapter xiii,

dramatized till quite recently, probably towards the close of the eighteenth century or even in the first years of the nineteenth.[1] But the semi-dramatic ceremonies out of which the miracle plays later developed were performed annually in the seventeenth century and were witnessed by several European travellers. Their descriptions, set out in chronological order, enable us to trace the growth of the ceremonies to the verge of drama.[2] When Sir Anthony Sherley was in Isfahan in 1599 he witnessed the annual Shi'a ceremony of the burning of effigies of the three false caliphs; and Sherley's follower, William Parry, describes a related ceremony:

> The Persian [he writes] praieth only to Mahomet, and Mortus Ally, the Turks to those two, and to three other that were Mahomets servants. Against which three the Persian still inveighs, and hath in al townes, men that carry axes on their shoulders, challenging them to rise againe, and they are there prest [ready] to incounter them by force of armes.[3]

Pietro della Valle, who was in Persia in 1618, passed near Kierbela, 'the place of the Martyrdom of Hhussein,' and gives

pp.369f.). Upon this Matthew Arnold based the essay which first made them widely known to English readers ('The Persian Passion-Play,' *Essays in Criticism*, First Series, 1865). Sir Lewis Pelly collected from oral tradition in Persia no less than fifty-two of the plays, and of these, with the help of A.N.Wallaston, he published thirty-seven in English translation (*The Miracle Play of Hasan and Husain*, 1879). Edward G.Browne describes a performance which he attended in Persia (*A Year among the Persians*, Cambridge, 1926, pp.602f.), and in his *Literary History of Persia* (iv,188f.) he gives a somewhat meagre notice of them with a few specimens in the original and translated. There is a sympathetic account of them in Stanley Lane-Poole's *Studies in a Mosque* (second edition, 1893, chapter vii). Here the character of Hussein is not idealized as it is in Arnold's better-known essay. The classical narrative in English of the death of Hussein is Gibbon's (*Decline and Fall of the Roman Empire*, chapter 50; ed. Bury, v,415f.). But Gibbon knew nothing of the dramatic memorial of the tragedy. See also Sir Percy Sykes, *History of Persia*, i, chapter xlvii.—The resemblances between Persian and European religious drama are perhaps not simply fortuitous. Be it noted that the former originated at a date long subsequent to the appearance of Christian missionaries in Persia. Dramatic representations, repugnant to the Arabian Semites, would be agreeable to the Aryan Persians.

1 E.G.Browne, *A Literary History of Persia*, iv,29.
2 Only one of these descriptions (that by Olearius; see p.231, note 2, below) is quoted by E.G.Browne (op.cit., iv,28); and other writers pass over these early accounts altogether.
3 *A New and Large Discourse*, p.25.—With the burning of the false caliphs in effigy one may compare another annual custom of the Shi'ites. Effigies of Abu Bakr, Omar and Osman are fashioned out of dough; the dough is filled with honey; the effigies are 'stabbed'; and the honey is drunk from the 'wounds.' See Malcolm, *History of Persia*, ii,239; Hughes, *Dictionary of Islam*, p.138.

a long and striking description of the annual mourning ceremonies, with no indication that anything like a formal drama or cycle of plays then existed.[1] In 1637 Adam Olearius passed a month at Ardabil, a sacred city of the Shi'a, and brought away vivid memories of the rites of mourning. He saw camels led through the streets burdened with coffins 'to represent those of Haly, and his two sons, Hassan and Hossein.' Later these coffins were interred amid loud wailings and lamentations while the mourners lacerated their own flesh.[2] We have here clearly a religious rite on the verge of drama. The French missionary Father Gabriel visited a Persian city during 'un dueil et un tems de tristesse' when 'la pompe funebre de cet Heussen' was celebrated by men and women with their bodies blackened. 'Cette trouppe de diablotins vont ainsi pêle mêle dans la place royale, hurlans comme des loups.'[3] The great French traveller Tavernier witnessed a celebration of the Feast of Hassan and Hussein. He saw effigies of the martyrs borne upon biers to the accompaniment of loud lamentations; and when the procession halted, a 'Moulla' delivered a discourse upon the circumstances of Hussein's death.[4] Tavernier is the first observer to remark upon this ceremonial sermon. If, as it is permissible to assume, in it was the germ of later drama, then the parallel is very striking between its delivery and the delivery of the pseudo-Augustinian sermon out of which, according to a well-known theory, arose the Old Testament plays of the medieval church. Finally, the Italian traveller Giovanni Francesco Gemelli saw the images of the martyrs carried through the streets of a Persian city to the accompaniment of mournful melodies.[5]

The Shi'ites, with the exception of a few sects of extremists (ghulah), do not elevate 'Ali, the Prophet's son-in-law and the father of Hussein, to a position so exalted as that of Mahomet; but it was natural that the controversy over the claim of his

---

1 *Viaggi*, Rome, 1652, ii,139f.; *Travels*, anonymous English translation, 1665, p.263.
2 *The Voyages and Travels of the Ambassadors Sent by Frederick Duke of Holstein to the Great Duke of Muscovy and the King of Persia*, translated by John Davies, 1662, pp.217 and 235.
3 *Relations Nouvelles du Levant*, pp.101f.
4 *Les Six Voyages*, Paris, 1676, i,425f.
5 *Voyage around the World*, in Churchill's *Collection of Voyages and Travels*, 1732, iv,144. (The Italian original is of 1693.)

family to the caliphate should be misunderstood by ill-informed English visitors. Consequently they returned home with the notion that the Persians revered two prophets. In Anthony Jenkinson's early narrative we find the phrase: 'Their false and filthie prophets Mahomet and Murtezallie.' [1] Of the muezzins Duckett says that 'they use to goe up to the tops of their churches, and tell there a great tale of Mahumet and Mortus Ali.' He shows an acquaintance with the fact that the Persian schismatics repudiate the succession from Mahomet through the first three caliphs and claim that the true succession is from 'Ali, the fourth caliph. The scurrilous style of medieval controversialists survives in Duckett's tale of a council held after Mahomet's death to which there came 'a little Lizard, who declared that it was Mahumet's pleasure that Mortus Ali should be his successour.' (At this point in the narrative Hakluyt adds the ironical editorial gloss: 'A godly and well grounded religion.') Where Duckett picked up this ignoble anecdote is not apparent; but the fact of interest is that neither he nor any contemporary Englishman who refers to the claims of 'Ali shows any awareness of the point at issue in the controversy over the caliphate, which was nothing less than the principle of Divine Right (through 'Ali) against the principle of succession through democratic election (through the first three caliphs).

That in England it was actually believed that the Persians ranked 'Ali even above Mahomet is shown by Thomas Nashe's likening of his quarrel with Gabriel Harvey to that of the Sunnis and Shi'ites. 'Harvey and I,' he writes, 'take upon us to bandie factions . . . as the Turkes and Persians about Mahomet and Mortus Ali, which should bee the greatest.' [2]

We may pause to examine another passage in Nashe's writings because his learned editor, Dr. McKerrow, has for once failed to supply the requisite elucidation. Nashe writes of

the Ismael Persians Haly or Mortus Alli, they worship, whose true etymologie is *mortuum halec*, a dead red herring, and no other, though by corruption of speech, they false dialect and misse-sound it. Let any Persian oppugn this, and, in spite of his hairie tuft or

1 Hakluyt, iii,29; Morgan and Coote, op.cit., i,145 and cf. p.154.
2 *Have with You to Saffron-Walden, Works*, iii,19.

love-locke he leaves on the top of his crowne, to be pulld up or pullied up to heaven by, Ile set my feet to his, and fight it out with him, that their fopperly god is not so good as a red Herring.[1]

Dr. McKerrow suggests that the word 'Ismael,' used as an adjective, is an allusion either to one or another of the two Shahs named Ismail or else to the belief that the Arabs in general and Mahomet in particular are descended from Ishmael. The latter explanation may be rejected; there is nothing peculiarly appropriate to Persia in a belief shared with all Islam. Shah Ismail II is also out of the question; his memory was not held in special honour. The memory of the great Shah Ismail I was, however, cherished by the Persians, not only because he was the founder of the Safavi dynasty but also as the establisher of the national Shi'a faith. Persians deemed him a saint and made use of his name in their prayers. Even so, the reference is fundamentally more appropriate if it points to Ismail the seventh Iman who initiated what is known as the Isma'ili movement which strongly influenced the development of the Shi'a.[2] The derivation of Mortus Ali from *mortuum halec* is one of those grotesque philological feats which Nashe, like Rabelais, enjoyed. *Halec* or *alec*, a word sufficiently rare but used by Plautus and Ovid, means a pickled fish and is therefore translated with reasonable accuracy as red (or salted) herring; it is, indeed, a cognate form of herring. The epithet 'Mortus,' apparently regarded as a proper name and sometimes (as in several passages already quoted in this chapter) joined in one word with 'Ali, occurs with various spellings in early English narratives of travel in Persia and in plays whose scene is laid in that country. Explanations of it are seldom offered by our old writers.[3] It is a corruption of a Persian word, one of the many titles of honour which the Persians bestow upon the Prophet's son-in-law, the meaning being 'One agreeable to God' or 'He in whom God is well pleased.' [4] As for the 'love-

1 *Lenten-Stuffe, Works*, iii,195.
2 E.G.Browne, *A Literary History of Persia*, i, chapter xii; P.K.Hitti, *History of the Arabs*, p.441.
3 But see Richard Eden, *Historye of Travayle*, folio 325; and the long note on 'Mortys Ally' in Robert Baron's tragedy of *Mirza*, n.d., pp.167f.
4 *Encyclopaedia of Islam*, article 'Ali'; Pelly, *The Miracle Play of Hasan and Husain*, i,66, note.

lock,' Nashe seems to be indebted for this derisive detail to Geoffrey Duckett, who writes:

> Although they shave their heads . . . twise a weeke, yet leave they a tuft of haire upon their heads about two foote long. I have enquired why they leave the tuft of haire upon their heads. They answer, that thereby they may easilier be carried up into heaven when they are dead.[1]

The mode and the belief that prescribed it in Islam were not limited to Persia; other writers noted the same fashion among the Turks.[2] This mode of wearing the hair was popular in the London world of fashion, as is indicated by Dekker's remark that 'the Persian lock' is one of 'the most essential parts of a Gallant.'[3]

V

THE Elizabethan conception of the luxury, gorgeousness, and voluptuousness of Persian life was part of their heritage from the classical past. Cicero and Horace were among the authors who had borne testimony to this life of pleasure, ease, and splendour. Spenser describes Persia as 'the nurse of pompous pride' and likens to a Persian mitre the headgear of Duessa, which is garnished with 'crowns and ouches.'[4] It was probably from Spenser that Thomas Campion derived the idea of personifying the continent of Asia as a Persian lady who wears a crown.[5] It is true that there was classical authority for the sim-

---

1 Hakluyt, iii,162; Morgan and Coote, op.cit., ii,436.
2 See, for example, Father Castela, *Le Sainct Voyage*, 1612, p.115; Robert Baron. *Mirza*, p.179.—Two points of minor importance may be consigned to this note, Englishmen commented upon the Persians' disregard of the Koranic injunction against the use of wine; but the English visitors failed to grasp the doctrinal significance of this disobedience. The lifting of the ban against wine was an early step in the development of allegorical interpretation of the *Koran*, the wine which Mahomet prohibited being, it was said, the intoxication of spiritual pride.—Of Persian origin is the story which came into the *Koran* (ii,102) of the rebellious angels Hârût and Mârût. This legend is occasionally referred to in English books; see, for example, *The Ofspring of the House of Ottomanno*, Sig. D$_{VII}$^{r}. It indirectly influenced William Basse's poem *The Woman in the Moon* (c.1610). See further E.Kölbing, 'Die Engel Harut und Marut in der Englischen Dichtung,' *Englische Studien*, xxxvii,461f.
3 *The Gull's Horn-Book*, chapter vi.
4 *The Faerie Queene*, I,iv,7, and I,ii,13.
5 *Maske at the Marriage of the Earl of Somerset, Works*, ed. P.Vivian, Oxford, 1909, p.152. Compare Philippe Galle's engraving in which Asia is personified as a woman wearing a turban, reproduced in R.Van Marle, *Iconographie de l'Art Profane*, The Hague, ii (1932), 324.

plicity and abstinence of Persian military discipline; and remembering this, Nashe remarks that 'the Persians were satisfied with breade, salt and water'; [1] and Lyly repeats the old
anecdote that 'the Persians to make their youth abhorre
gluttonie would paint an Epicure sleeping with meate in his
mouthe, and most horribly overladen with wine, that by the
view of such monsterous sightes, they might eschewe the meanes
of the like excesse.' [2] But the opposite notion was the prevailing
one, partly because it was substantiated by some of the reports
brought home by English travellers. To say of any sort of
luxury that the Persians might envy it was as much as to say
that it was unparalleled. So Massinger's Calipso describes the
'retiring bower' to which she invites Laval.[3] Again in Massinger
there is promise of 'such a feast as Persia in her height of pomp
and riot did never equal.' [4] Sir Epicure Mammon intends to
wear such raiment 'as might provoke the Persian' to envy him
when he has obtained an unlimited supply of gold from the
alchemist.[5] Greene's Prince Edward, wooing the fair Margaret,
promises her 'frigates overlaid with plates of Persian wealth.' [6]
That Greene was thinking not only of the traditions of Persian
splendour preserved in classical authors but also of the actual
observations of modern traders is shown by another passage
in the same play, where Friar Bacon, promising a miraculously
gorgeous banquet, declares that

> Persia [shall] down her Volga by canoes
> Send down the secrets of her spicery.[7]

In the fairly frequent allusions to Persian silks and tapestries
and hangings which we find in the drama the classical tradition

1 *The Anatomy of Absurdity, Works,* i,39.
2 *Euphues: The Anatomy of Wit, Works,* i,188.
3 *The Guardian,* II,iv.
4 *The City Madam,* V,i.
5 *The Alchemist,* II,ii,90f. So Volpone promises Celia: 'I will have thee . . . attired
like . . . unto the Persian Sophy's wife' (*Volpone,* III,vii,226f.).
6 *Friar Bacon and Friar Bungay,* III,i.
7 Ibid., III,ii. Greene's editor, J.Churton Collins, summarily disposed of this allusion as sheer ignorance on the dramatist's part; but Greene was not wholly ignorant;
he was thinking of the Volga route and confused the direction in which the river
flows. Elsewhere (*Greenes Orpharion,* 1599; *Works,* ed. Grosart, xii,34), still thinking
of the Muscovite trade, he writes of 'Volgo, a River that leadeth into Persia.' This
is not due to ignorance but to careless phrasing.

has been confirmed by the evidence of actual imports. In one play on a classical subject the reins of Croesus's horses are made of Persian silk [1] and in another the command is given to cover the pavement with Persian tapestries (that is, carpets).[2] Elsewhere Mars is said to have 'wrapped his battered limbs in Persian silks.'[3] In other cases the allusions are evidently to the contemporary trade, though rather to the trade through the Mediterranean than to that through Russia in which an elder generation of merchants had been engaged. The argosy of Barabas is laden with 'exceeding store of Persian silks.'[4] Lady Loadstone lies on a feather-bed 'under a brace of your best Persian carpets.'[5] Massinger describes 'the costliest Persian silks, studded with jewels'[6] and the walls of a room which are adorned with 'Persian hangings wrought of gold and pearl.'[7] Similarly, the walls of a bridal-chamber in one of Fletcher's plays are hung with 'rich Persian arras';[8] and Davenant refers to the 'rich hangings of the antick Persian loom.'[9] Even had no records survived we should be able to infer from these and other [10] passages in the dramatic literature of the time that the chief commodities imported from Persia were silks and carpets.[11]

1 The Wars of Cyrus, I,i (anonymous); Tudor Facsimile Texts.
2 Thomas Nabbes, Hannibal, II,iv.
3 Henry Glapthorne, Argalus, I,i.
4 Marlowe, The Jew of Malta, I,i.
5 Jonson, The Magnetic Lady, IV,iii.
6 The Roman Actor, II,i.
7 The Bondman, I,iii.
8 Love's Cure, or the Martial Maid, I,ii.
9 The Unfortunate Lovers, III,iv. Compare The Just Italian, I,i, where a lover promises his lady that 'the soft entrail of the Persian worm shall clothe [her] limbs.'
10 Revenge for Honour, I,i, where the anonymous playwright associates Persian silks with 'costly Tyrian purples.'
11 Here may be gathered together a few notes on three or four points connected with Persia. (1) Lyly's unnatural natural history contains two items from the flora of that country. He likens Love to 'the Apple in Persia, whose blossome savoreth lyke Honny, whose budde is more sower then gall' (Euphues: The Anatomy of Wit, Works, i,208). This characteristic of the Persian apple is not mentioned by Pliny (Historia naturalis, xv,11). Lyly is probably thinking confusedly of the Apple of Sodom or Dead Sea Fruit. Again, with no discoverable authority, Lyly states that 'the Palme Persian Fig tree beareth as well Apples as Figs,' but when it is transplanted to Rhodes it bears no fruit at all (Euphues and His England, Works, ii,22).—(2) From classical sources, especially Plato, came the association of Persia with magic and esoteric wisdom. This notion was strengthened by the common belief that the Magi, the 'star-led wizards,' were Persians. Caxton writes of 'the Royame of Perse, where as a science called Nygromancie was first founden; which science constrayneth the enemye, the fende, to be taken prisoner' (The Mirrour of the World, p.81, and Prior's note on Caxton's sources for this statement). Bacon refers to 'Persian magic, which was the secret literature of their kings' (A Brief Discourse Touching the Happy

With luxury is associated idleness [1] and with idleness libidinousness and jealousy; whence comes Nashe's quaint analogy between the perils of a guest at a Persian banquet and the dangers attending the life of a man of letters in London.

> Writers and Printers in these days [he writes] are like to Men placed at the Persian banquets; if they rowle theyr eye never so little at one side, there stands an Eunuch before them with his hart full of jealousie, and his Bowe readie bent to shoote them through because they looke farther then the Lawes of the Country suffer them. [2]

Nashe's authority for this statement has not been discovered; but bearing in mind that the earliest English visitors must have brought home with them more impressions and anecdotes than ever got into print, one may guess not too rashly that one of these travellers was Nashe's informant. Later visitors told similar stories. Sir Thomas Herbert, for example, tells how one night he mounted to the roof of his house and looked out over the city.

Union, Works, iii,257).—(3) From classical and medieval sources came vague notions of Zoroastrianism. Hence the occasional allusions to Persian fire-worship, as when Furnace, the cook in Massinger's *A New Way to Pay Old Debts*, II,ii,100, swears 'By fire,' adding, 'for cooks are Persians and swear by it.' Hence, too, the surprising notion that Mohammedans worship the sun, as when Eleazer the Moor in the anonymous play *Lust's Dominion*, III,iv (Hazlitt's Dodsley, xiv), swears 'by heaven's great star, which Indians do adore.' Mully Mumen, the Moor in William Rowley's *All's Lost by Lust*, II,iii, addresses the sun as 'thou burning Diety' and as his father because he is 'stampt with thine owne seale.' Both these Moors are Moslems. Caxton had written (op.cit., p.71): 'Toward the eest is another maner of peple that worshyppe the sonne only, and taketh it for their god.' But he did not identify this people with Mohammedans.—(4) Sugden has collected the references in the drama to Cyrus, Darius, and Xerxes. One allusion may be noted here for its association of ancient Persian prowess with modern Turkish fame in warfare. Duarte, boasting of his own feats of war, says:

> Were the Persian host, that drank up rivers, added
> To the Turk's present powers, I could direct,
> Command and marshal them

(Fletcher, *The Custom of the Country*, II,i). Marlowe (*1 Tamburlaine*, II,iii,15f.) had already taken from Herodotus the tradition that the hosts of Xerxes drank 'the mighty Parthian Araris.'

1 Lyly has the puzzling statement that 'the Persian kings sometimes shaved sticks' (Prologue to *Campaspe*) or, as he puts it more definitely elsewhere: 'The Kings of Persia . . . did nothing els but cut stickes to drive away the time' (*Euphues and His England, Works*, ii,213). The source of this odd notion has not been discovered. Perhaps with his thought that whittling sticks was an idle pastime appropriate to lazy luxurious monarchs there was crossed a dim reminiscence of the report that had come to England that Mohammedan potentates were under a religious obligation to perform some sort of manual toil.

2 *Pasquil of England, Works*, i,63.

Every housetop was spread with Carpets, whereon each night slept the master of the house and his Seraglio. . . The curiosity . . . might have cost me dearly, the penalty being no lesse than to shoot an Arrow into his braines that dares to doe it.[1]

There were some protests against the importation of Persian luxuries into England and the imitation of luxurious oriental modes of life. In a rough hearty song on the manners of different nations Thomas Heywood had contrasted the homely 'English beaver' with the linen with which the Turk 'wraps his head' and the lawn used as headgear by the Persians.[2] But presently we find George Wither, in the course of a satire on the increasing luxury of English life, complaining that

> We, that once did feed
> On homely roots and hearbs, doe now exceed
> The Persian Kings for dainties.[3]

And William Harrison, lamenting the alteration in the character of Englishmen, who were formerly 'oak' and now are 'willow,' ascribes the change to the intrusion of 'Persian delicacie' into England.[4]

---

1 *Relation of Some Yeares Travaile*, 1634, p.193. John Fryer (*A New Account of East India and Persia*, iii,130) says that 'if they [the Persians] observe any peeping upon them, or their Wives, an Arrow drawn up to the head is let fly.' With Herbert's and Fryer's testimony may be compared what Sir Richard F.Burton says of a like violence of feeling throughout Moslem countries. He tells of bullets flying about the heads of Europeans who have been seen gazing from house-tops, and reports that muezzins have sometimes in some places been appointed from among blind men (*The Thousand Nights and a Night*, ii,330, note).
2 *A Challenge for Beauty, Dramatic Works*, ed. Pearson, v,65.
3 *Abuses Stript and Whipt*, Book ii, Satire i; *Poems*, Spenser Society, p.218.
4 *Description of England* (reference from Sugden).

CHAPTER SIX

'A GREAT PLOTTER AND PROJECTOR IN MATTERS OF STATE'

I

WE have already met with the eldest of the three Sherley brothers, and have now to follow the fortunes and misadventures of the second brother, Anthony, who though not an attractive figure is one of the most arresting personalities in the history of the relations between England and Islam.[1] Anthony's energy and resilient self-reliance, had they been directed into practicable channels, might have carried him to high office. He dreamt dreams and saw visions, nourishing vast designs of complex statecraft which bore little or no relation to the realities of international politics. He had a way with him; he could impress people, often the most influential people in Europe—almost everyone save the imperturbable Sir Robert Cecil. His impudence was colossal, his self-conceit fantastic; on occasion he showed himself a

[1] The most important contemporary accounts of Sir Anthony Sherley are five in number: (1) the anonymous *True Report of Sir Anthony Shierlies Journey*, 1600. (2) William Parry, *A New and Large Discourse of the Travels of Sir Anthony Sherley*, 1601. (3) George Manwaring, *A True Discourse of Sir Anthony Sherley's Travel into Persia*. This was written about 1601. It was communicated to John Cartwright who used parts of it in *The Preachers Travels*, 1611. These excerpts reappeared in Purchas, viii. Parts of the narrative were published in *The Retrospective Review*, ii (1820), and the work in entirety in an anonymous compilation *The Three Brothers*, 1825. (4) *Sir Antony Sherley His Relation of His Travels into Persia*, 1613. (5) Abel Pinçon, 'Relation d'un Voyage faict es annees 1598 et 1599,' in *Relations Veritables et Curieuses*, Paris, 1651, pp.101f. Pinçon's authorship has been convincingly demonstrated by Ross (see below). E.P.Shirley, *The Sherley Brothers*, 1848, has not been entirely superseded by later research, and the same author's *Stemmata Shirleiana*, second edition, 1873, chapter ix, is of genealogical value. Franz Babinger, *Sherleiana*, Berlin, 1932, has to do chiefly with Anthony Sherley's wanderings from court to court in Europe. Sir E.Denison Ross, *Sir Anthony Sherley: His Persian Adventure*, 1933 (in *The Broadway Travellers*), appeared after the first draft of the present chapter was written. Ross's interests are almost exclusively oriental and topographical; he says nothing of the many points at which Sherley's career touches upon the literary history of the period. He reprints entire items 1,2, and 3, above; gives two excerpts from 4; and a complete translation of 5. His introduction is of value and to it the present account is indebted for some particulars; but it is imperfect in many respects and much material of importance is omitted altogether.

liar and a trickster; he seems to have been unable to remain loyal to any of his masters, more than one of whom he sometimes served simultaneously. His deportment was often that of a *miles gloriosus* who has stepped down from the stage into real life.

A clue to his character may be found on the opening page of his autobiographical *apologia*, where he says: 'In my first yeares, my friends bestowed on mee those learnings which were fit for a Gentlemans ornament, without directing them to an occupation.' Born in 1565, he was in the prime of manhood when he enters our story in 1598. He had already seen much of the world and had experienced many a rude buffet of fortune.[1] After Oxford and perhaps the Inns of Court, he had served, like his father and elder brother, in the Low Countries; had been employed in a confidential capacity by the Earl of Leicester; and had been a colonel in Essex's expedition to Normandy in 1591. Already he was passionately devoted to the fascinating favourite of the Queen. 'I desired,' he wrote afterwards, 'to make him the patterne of my civill life, and from him to draw a worthy modell of all my actions.'[2] In France he committed the grave indiscretion of accepting knighthood from Henry of Navarre; whereupon Queen Elizabeth fell into a passionate rage, crying: 'I will not have my sheep marked with a strange brand; nor suffer them to follow the pipe of a strange shepherd!'[3] Sherley was forced to renounce his French title formally; and he never received an English title; yet he continued to style himself 'Sir Anthony.' The wheel of fortune, upon which he was destined to revolve incessantly, had brought him for the first time to the ground, and he described himself as 'exiled from all hope of recovering . . . grace in the Court.'[4] It was probably with the hope of recouping himself that he now contracted a marriage of

1 The account of Sherley's early life in Ross, op.cit., should be supplemented by L.P.Smith, *Life and Letters of Sir Henry Wotton*, i,242; Thomas Arundel's testimony in *Hatfield MSS*, vi,105; Sir Thomas Sherley the Elder's letter of complaint against Anthony in ibid., vii,526. Ross omits details regarding the circumstances of Anthony's departure from England and his journey through Germany into Italy.
2 *Relation*, p.2.
3 J.Briggs, 'A Short Account of the Sherley Family,' *Journal of the Royal Asiatic Society*, First Series, vi,80.
4 *Hatfield MSS*, v,176.

convenience rather than of love with Frances Vernon, a cousin of the Earl of Essex. Rumours were soon abroad that the union was an unhappy one; [1] and Lady Sherley's only influence upon her husband's career was, it would seem, that she acted as an incentive to far wandering. After his departure from England in 1598 he never saw her again. This connection by marriage with the Earl of Essex was later one of the chief causes of the disfavour with which Elizabeth continued to look upon him. [2]

We cannot follow Anthony through the extreme hardships and bitter disappointments of his expedition to America [3] nor recount his undistinguished share in Essex's fruitless and unlucky 'Island Voyage' to the Azores. [4] At the end of 1597 we find him in debt and in trouble, having borrowed money from his own father which he failed to repay. [5] His financial difficulties doubtless influenced his decision to take command of a party of English volunteers dispatched by Essex to the aid of Don Cesare d'Este, the claimant to the duchy of Ferrara. [6] Leaving England without obtaining permission from the Queen, [7] he passed through Germany and the Alps in the dead

1 Rowland Whyte to Sir Robert Sydney, 7 November 1595, in Arthur Collins, *Letters and Memorials of State*, 1746, i,359. Compare *C.S.P.,Dom., 1598–1601*, pp.35 and 130.
2 Presently we find the governor of Zante explaining to the Venetian authorities that the Sherleys' espousal of Essex's cause led to their disgrace and exile from England (*C.S.P., Venetian*, ix,550). As a matter of fact, the disgrace of Essex came as a surprise and bitter blow to Sherley who was thousands of miles away from England during the last eight months of the Earl's life. Thomas Birch (*Memorials of Queen Elizabeth*, 1754, i,456) says that Sherley accompanied Essex into Ireland; this is certainly not so.
3 In his account of English explorers in *Poly-Olbion* (xix,383f.; *Works*, ed. J.W.Hebel, iv,407) Drayton devotes more space than the achievement warranted to the American voyage of 'Sherley (since whose name such high renowne hath won).'—See Irene A.Wright, 'The Spanish Version of Sherley's Raid on Jamaica,' *Hispanic-American Historical Review*, v (1922), 227f., from material in the Archives of the Indies at Seville. The narrative of the expedition, written by one of Sherley's companions, is in Hakluyt, x,266f. There is other material in Purchas, xvi. See also *Hatfield MSS*, vii,159 and 265.
4 See Sir Arthur Gorges, *Relation of the Island Voyage*, 1607; Purchas, xx,43; *Hatfield MSS*, vii,346,352f.,369; *C.S.P.,Dom., 1592–1597*, p.482; and Sir William Brown's letter to Sir Robert Sydney, 24 July 1597, in Arthur Collins, op.cit., ii,58.
5 See the father's despairing letter to Sir Robert Cecil, 30 December 1597, *Hatfield MSS*, vii,526.
6 *Cambridge Modern History*, iii,397. So long before as 1592 Francis Bacon had foreseen the dispute regarding the succession (Spedding, *The Letters and the Life of Francis Bacon*, i,171). Fynes Moryson, who visited Ferrara, gives an account of the dispute (*Itinerary*, i,198f.).
7 That he left England without permission was one of the charges later brought against him. Such leave was not easily obtained; and Italy, because of the peril of lapsing

of winter, and reached Italy only to find that Don Cesare had abandoned his claims and that Ferrara had been incorporated into the States of the Church.

What was he to do with himself and his company of volunteers? He went to Venice in the hope of obtaining military employment under the Republic but could find none. Upon an observer he made at this time the impression of a dissipated boaster, and his reputation was not of the best.[1] Many years later Anthony claimed that the expedition to Persia upon which he now set out was proposed to him by Essex after 'a small relation' which he made to the Earl. His patron was, says Sherley, unwilling that the company of volunteers should return to England after the Ferrara fiasco and there be mocked for 'this vain expense of time, money and hope.'[2] This is far from the truth of the matter. In deciding upon the Persian adventure he was doubtless swayed by what he learned of Persian relations with Venice. Of long duration, these relations had been during recent years, till lately, less intimate than of old, because anxiety lest the Turks be offended and uncertainty as to the military and political situation in Persia had made Venice hold aloof. But the accession of Shah Abbas gave a new vitality to the old friendship. Venetian consuls in Syria and *baili* at Constantinople had reported favourably on the character of the new Shah, on the reforms instituted in his state, on the condition of his armies, and so forth; and these agents explained how the pressure of the Tartars upon his flank handicapped the Shah's efforts in his thrusts against the Turks.[3] From about 1596, then, sentiment in Venice had been again strongly pro-Persian and must have influenced Sherley. Moreover, encounters with two individuals set his

into Roman Catholicism, was often specifically excepted (Clare Howard, *English Travellers of the Renaissance*, pp.86f.; L.P.Smith, op.cit., ii,482). There was a special form entitled 'Queen Elizabeth's Letter of Recall for those who have gone abroad without her leave' (Ellis, *Original Letters*, iv,46). Anthony's offence was double: he travelled without a licence and he went to Italy.

1 This impression comes from a Frenchman or someone writing in French, in March 1598, to a friend in Frankfort. An English merchant there saw the letter and obtained a copy which he sent to George Gilpin, Essex's agent at the Hague. Gilpin forwarded it to Essex but it fell into the hands of Cecil's secret agents. See *Hatfield MSS*, viii,116f. and 151.

2 *Relation*, pp.4f. Compare Purchas, viii,377.

3 Guglielmo Berchet, *La Repubblica di Venezia e la Persia*, Turin, 1865, pp.41f.

thoughts towards Persia. One of these was a Persian merchant who was buying English cloth in the Venetian market. The other was Angelo Corai, a Levantine Christian, a great traveller and accomplished linguist, newly come from the court of the Sophy, who acquainted Sherley with the opportunities for advancement offered by a visit to Persia. With Angelo Anthony had many conferences and subsequently he engaged him as his guide and interpreter.[1] This goes to show that the proposal for the expedition did not come from Essex. If further proof is needed, it is found in the fact that Sherley thought it expedient to send home a messenger to justify his new enterprise. From Lyons, where he was delayed, this messenger dispatched a letter in lieu of a verbal report.[2] In it he offered Sherley's excuses for departing 'without special order, and perhaps disagreeing with some letters received at Venice.' Before deciding to go to the East Sherley 'had left no stone unmoved or means untried to find employment in the state of Venice'; but the authorities would entertain no proposals for 'new actions or instruments of war.' 'All things appertaining to innovations or tumults in Italy lay dead'—a sentence which casts a lurid light upon the mentality of the professional military adventurer. In sum, Sherley had found 'all propositions answer his expectations weakly save only that of the Levant.' He hoped to accomplish there something which would benefit all Christendom, transfer war into another part of the world, make head against the Portuguese, and open the Red Sea to commerce. 'He held him happy that should by this good and lawful means immortalize his name forever.' The letter concludes: 'By this time I hope that Sir Anthony Sherley is arrived at his desired parts, where his intent is to attempt nothing without warrant from England.' From all this we gather that Anthony was at loose ends, that he had failed to obtain military employment at Venice, and that the expedition to Persia offered the prospect of adventure, fame, and large rewards. The precise objects he had in view will appear in the sequel.

1 Manwaring, *True Discourse*, Ross, p.176.
2 Thomas Chaloner to Anthony Bacon, 2 June 1598, *Hatfield MSS*, viii,188.

II

SHERLEY and his company sailed from Venice towards the end of May 1598.[1] They numbered altogether some twenty-six or twenty-seven souls. Among the half-dozen Englishmen of some standing was their leader's younger brother, Robert. Of the other English followers the most important was Thomas Powell, who was destined to have a military career of some distinction in Persia where he remained with Robert Sherley after Anthony's departure. Powell later accompanied Robert on his return to England and was knighted by James I. Returning to Persia, he died on the way. George Manwaring and William Parry are noteworthy because they afterwards wrote narratives of the expedition; and it is possible that two other members of the party, shadowy figures who remain anonymous, were responsible for the first story of the expedition to get into print. Then there was a Frenchman named Abel Pinçon who also wrote a narrative, and Angelo Corai, the interpreter. Besides all these there were nineteen servants of whom most were Englishmen and some few Persians (probably hired at Venice).

They had not been long at sea when a quarrel arose. One of the Italian passengers uttered scurrilous words against Queen Elizabeth, and Anthony 'caused one of his meanest sort of men to give him the bastinado.' A riot threatened, but some Armenian merchants intervened and restored order. Bad feeling lingered, however, and the captain decided to rid his ship of these adventurers. Consequently when at Zante Anthony and his men went ashore for fresh food, their luggage was sent after them and the ship sailed away. Thus they lost their passage-money and found themselves in a quandary. Sherley dispatched a letter to Henry Lello, the English ambassador at the Porte, requesting a passport on the ground that he was en route to the Red Sea on business for Queen Elizabeth.[2]

---

1 Sherley (*Relation*, p.5) gives the date of his departure as 24 May 1599—a year out. The error is repeated in many modern books: Curzon, *Persia and the Persian Question*, ii,537; *D.N.B.*, art. 'Sherley, Sir Anthony'; *Shakespeare's England*; even by various editors of the publications of the Hakluyt Society and the *Broadway Travellers*.
2 Lello to Cecil, 26 August 1598; E.P.Shirley, *The Sherley Brothers*, p.17.

This brazen falsehood, when discovered, prejudiced his case at home and caused him anxieties and delays after his arrival at Baghdad.

From Zante they made a dangerous passage in an open boat to Crete, and thence to Paphos in Cyprus, where Anthony noted that the monuments of antiquity were defaced by 'the barbarousness of the Turks and Time.'[1] In Tripoli in Syria they had the ill luck to encounter the Italian crew who had abandoned them on Zante. On an accusation brought by these vindictive sailors they were arrested by the Turkish authorities and were suffered to proceed only after the payment of a large sum of money. A great gale then struck them and they ran short of provisions; but they managed to reach Scanderoon (Alexandretta) whence they sailed up the Orontes to Antioch. Here they received such ill treatment from the Turks that many years later Anthony still nourished bitter memories of them.[2] Parry's impressions were similar. The Turks' 'behaviours,' he wrote,

> in point of civilities (besides that they are damned Infidells and Zodomiticall Mahomets) doe answer the hate we christians doe justly holde them in. For they are beyond measure a most insolent superbous and insulting people, ever more prest [ready] to offer outrage to any christian, if he be not well guarded with a Janizarie.[3]

In Aleppo, whither the adventurers went across the mountains from Antioch, George Manwaring had to endure just such a humiliating outrage as Parry remembered, for a Turk took him by the ear and marched him up and down the street while the bystanders threw stones at him and spat upon him.[4] Is it possible that Shakespeare had heard of Manwaring's experience and had it in mind when he made Othello tell how in

1 *Relation*, p.6. This is one of several passages which show that William Lithgow made use of Sir Anthony Sherley's narrative. Compare: 'In all this country of Greece I could finde nothing to answer the famous relations given by auncient Authors, . . . the barbarousness of Turkes and Time having defaced all the Monuments of Antiquity' (*A Most Delectable and True Discourse*, 1614, Sig. E₃ᵛ). Lithgow's first narrative appeared the year after Sherley's *Relation*.
2 *Relation*, pp.10f.
3 *A New and Large Discourse*, pp.10f.
4 Manwaring, in *The Three Brothers*, 1825, pp.27f.

Aleppo a malignant turban'd Turk beat a Christian? No Othello was at hand to defend poor Manwaring, but he obtained some sort of redress from the English consul. Racial and religious clashes must have been of frequent occurrence in this great city where Christians of the East and West met with Turks, Jews, and Arabs.

During a sojourn of some six weeks, while they awaited the assembling of the caravan with which they were to travel, the party had ample opportunity to observe the manners and customs of Aleppo. Of the mosques and Orthodox churches, the lack of bells, the muezzins' call to prayers, the coffee-houses, the carrier-pigeons, and other matters we read in the narratives of Sherley's followers. As for their leader, he had weightier affairs to claim his attention. He was engaged in raising money, as we learn from a report which reached England in December 1598.

> Sir Anthony Sherley hath ben at Constantinople, and there wrounge out of our merchants 400 *l.* and from thence he went to Aleppo, and there scraped together 500 *l.* more, wherewith he hath charged the Lord of Essex in his billes, and so is gon on God knowes whether to seeke his fortune.[1]

Sherley had not been at Constantinople; but the rest of the story is likely enough. It would be quite in character for him to charge his borrowings against Essex.

From Aleppo the party, enlarged by the presence of merchants of various nationalities and conducted by two Turkish officials, travelled by the short caravan route to Bir on the Euphrates. There they had to wait till a fleet of about a dozen boats had been collected. Then for three weeks they sailed down the river, often annoyed by volleys of stones thrown from the banks by Arabs whom it was necessary at times to frighten off by firing muskets into the air. One day a chance shot killed an Arab, and this accident caused several days' delay while conferences were held with the local 'king,' whom Manwaring describes as 'a man of goodly presence, exceeding black and very grim of visage.' [2] A settlement of damages was effected,

1 John Chamberlain, *Letters*, p.32.   2 Ross, op.cit., p.190.

'which being paid,' says Parry, 'and wee discharged, we held on our course from thence some two or three days passage, where we were eftsoones stayed by the King of the Arrabs there living by the rivers side in Tents.' [1] This ruler, whose name was Aborisci, Sherley characterizes as 'a poore king with a ten or twelve thousand beggarly subjects, living in tents of blacke haire-cloth' [2]—precisely as the bedouin live today. The strangers were brought before him, kissed his hand, informed him that they were English merchants, and were permitted to go upon their way.

Farther down the river they passed the petroleum wells. Parry describes one of them as 'a lake or poole of very pitch, which in their language they call, the mouth of Hell. It swelles in the middest thereof to the bignesse of an hogshead, and so breaketh with a great puffe, falling flat, and thus continually it worketh.' [3] Manwaring adds that the Jews call the place Sodom and Gomorrah. [4]

---

1 *A New and Large Discourse*, p.14. With Parry's account it is interesting to compare Pietro della Valle's narrative of his reception by an Arab 'Sceich' dwelling in a hair-tent (*Travels*, 1652, pp.264f.).

2 *Relation*, p.19.

3 *A New and Large Discourse*, p.14. The naphtha-pits of the Euphrates area had been a commonplace of geographers ever since Plutarch told of Alexander's astonishment on seeing them after the battle of Arbela. Marlowe's allusion to 'Asphaltis,' the bituminous lake near the ruins of Babylon (*2 Tamburlaine*, IV,iii,5), may derive from Plutarch or from Sebastian Munster (*Cosmographiae universalis Libri VI*, ed. cit., p.1030: 'De asphalto Babylonico') or from some other cosmographer; or he may have heard returned travellers tell of it. John Eldred had seen near Heit in Mesopotamia a number of wells 'throwing out abundantly at great mouths a kind of black substance like unto tarre . . . Every one of these springs,' he says, 'maketh a noise like unto a smiths forge in the blowing and puffing out of this matter . . . The people of the country call it in their language *Babil gehenham*, that is to say, Hell door' (Hakluyt, vi,8). Medieval writers mention the pitch-wells of Persia, and from them, through the *Image du Monde*, knowledge of them came to Caxton, but quaintly perverted because of his misunderstanding of the French. He writes (*The Mirrour of the World*, E.E.T.S., p.81): 'In this contree groweth a pese whiche is so hot that it skaldeth the handes of them that holde it, and it growyth with encreasyng of the mone, and wyth wanyng it discreceth at eche tyme of his cours. It helpeth wel to them that ben nygromanciers'—as well it might, for mistaking *la poiz* meaning 'pitch' for *le pois* meaning 'pea' Caxton has invented a vegetable unknown even to Pliny! Geoffrey Duckett's ample narrative of his long sojourn in Persia (Hakluyt, iii,159f.) contains a description of a well which he saw at Baku on the shores of the Caspian. He observed 'a marvellous quantity of oil' issuing out of the ground, a black variety called 'nefte' (naphtha) and a white called petroleum. The natives told him that Persians came from the farthest bounds of their country to fetch this

---

4 Ross, op.cit., p.191. Manwaring may have confused reports about the Dead Sea ('the Asphaltic Pool') or Mesopotamian Jews may have transferred the names from the Moabite shore to the banks of the Euphrates.

At Phaloughe (Felluja) the company landed, near the ruins of Old Babylon. Parry, Manwaring, and Pinçon have nothing to say about these antiquities; but they impressed Sherley, though in his *Relation* he could not find room to expatiate upon them and with characteristic haughtiness wrote:

> To tell wonders of things I saw, strange to us, . . . is for a traveller of another profession than I am, who had my end to see, and make use of the best things; not to feed myself and the world with such trifles, as either by their strangeness might have a suspicion of untruth: or by their lightness add to the rest of my imperfections, the vanity or smallness of my judgement.[1]

From Felluja they struck across the Land-Between-the-Rivers and so came to Baghdad on the Tigris.[2] There new troubles met them. The rapacious Turkish viceroy confiscated the richly jewelled cups and other articles which Anthony had purchased in Aleppo as presents for the Shah. Fortunately, before his luggage was ransacked a sympathetic and honest Turk had accepted the custody of his jewels and other personal belongings, and these were returned to him before he left the city. An order arrived from Constantinople that the Englishmen were to be arrested and sent thither. This had probably been issued at the instigation of Lello who must have been indignant on discovering that Anthony's claim to an official status on requesting a passport was false. In this crisis Sherley

---

stuff to burn in their houses. John Cartwright saw a similar well and described it (*The Preachers Travels*, p.105; Purchas, viii,508) as 'a very strange and wonderful fountain under ground, out of which springeth and issueth a marvellous quantity of black oil which serveth all the parts of Persia to burn in their houses and they usually carry it all over the country upon kine and asses, whereof you shall oftentimes meet three or four hundred in a company.' According to Professor A.J.Toynbee (*A Study of History*, ii,278f.), 'a few conspicuous natural gushers were imprisoned in towers that the rising jet might minister to the Zoroastrian cult of Fire by feeding a perpetual flame at the summit,' but when Zoroastrianism gave way to Islam 'these perpetual flames ceased to burn and the sole use which Man had so far made of Mineral Oil became obsolete,' until its economic potentialities were realized by Peter the Great. That oil was used for fuel in houses at a much earlier date than Toynbee gives is shown by the accounts of Duckett and Cartwright; and the latter implies a very considerable trade in it all over Persia.

1 *Relation*, p.20.
2 Sherley and his followers conform to the Elizabethan usage of calling Baghdad Babylon; but Sherley himself is careful to note that he intends the modern city, not the ruins some miles away.

had the good luck to meet a merchant—a Florentine, he says, but Manwaring says an Armenian—who acted with extraordinary generosity. Sherley's record hitherto warrants the surmise that he inveigled this kind man into helping him by boasting of his military prowess, social status, and diplomatic importance. At all events, the Englishmen were indebted to his solicitude for a large loan, fresh presents for the Shah, and an opportunity to join a caravan en route to Persia. Sherley says that this caravan was of Persian pilgrims returning from Mecca; Manwaring that they were Persian merchants. Evading the soldiers sent out to arrest them, our adventurers departed secretly from Baghdad early in November.

For a month they 'wandered with that company of blind pilgrims through the deserts.' 'My frailtie,' says Sherley, 'gave mee a continuall terrour during those thirtie dayes.' The hardships and anxieties and perils that would have afforded a Palgrave, a Doughty, or a Blunt matter for a volume are compressed into those few words. According to a Persian writer (who could, however, have had this only on hearsay), the Englishmen were disguised as Turkish merchants;[1] but since they spoke neither Turkish nor Persian the oriental costumes which they may have assumed could not have been very effectual. When warning came to them of the tyrannical cruelty of a provincial governor named Cobatbeague (Qubat Beg), 'it had beene an easie matter,' says Parry, 'to have found a company of poore hearts neere their maisters mouthes';[2] but by making a detour through the territory governed by one Heyderbag (Hayder Beg),[3] who did not mistreat them, they managed to circumvent this peril. On the frontier of Persia they were stopped for a time, but presently they were received into a band of Persian merchants journeying towards the capital, and with them they pursued their way through the arduous country of Kurdistan and Ardelan until they came to Casbeen (Kasvin). This was their goal. They arrived there in December 1598.

1 *Don Juan of Persia*, p.227. (See p.262, note 2, below.)
2 *A New and Large Discourse*, p.16. Compare Sherley, *Relation*, p.28.
3 Ross, op.cit., p.15, says that they made a detour to avoid the territory of Hayder Beg; but Parry, Manwaring, and Pinçon all expressly mention its crossing.

III

WHAT object had Sherley in mind in thus penetrating into Persia? It was twofold: to promote commercial relations with Persia which had languished during the past two decades; and to persuade the Sophy to make common cause with Christendom against the Turks. This was of course the old program of the first English traders in the country, but it was now opposed to the English policy of friendship with the Porte and direct trade with Turkey through the agency of the Levant Company. Of the two schemes the political was nearer than the commercial to Sherley's heart. There was a considerable weight of tradition behind the design to effect an alliance between Christendom and Persia. Throughout the sixteenth century there had been European statesmen whose intrigues were directed towards the maintenance of Turko-Persian hostility which would deter the Sultan from aggressive operations in Europe. In particular, for more than twenty years after 1525 the Emperor Charles V had been in communication with Persia, and there is ground for the belief that the Persian effort of 1551 to recover the territories lost to Solyman the Magnificent in 1534–6 was due in part to the Emperor's instigation.[1] After his accession to the Persian throne Shah Abbas made new overtures to Christian princes, inviting them to form an alliance with him against the Turks.[2] Europeans were, as we have seen in the last chapter, informed about the enmity existing between the orthodox Sunnis and the heretical Shi'ites. 'As Papistes and Protestants doe differ in opinion, concerning the same Christ: so doe the Turkes and Persians about their Mahomet: the one pursuing the other as hereticks with most deadly hatred.'[3] A popular chronicle of this century-long intermittent struggle was the *Historia della Guerra fra Turchi et Persiani* (1588), by Giovanni Thomaso Minadoi, an Italian physician who had lived for seven years in Constanti-

1 *Cambridge Modern History*, iii,113 and 121.
2 His predecessor had made similar overtures. See *Copie des Lesttres du Grand Sophy, Roi des Perces, envoies au Roi tres Catholique Despaigne et de Hongrie, auquelz ilz promet aliance perpetuelle, et les exorte et admonneste a aller combatre avec luy contre le grand Turc*, Paris, 1580.
3 George Abbot, *A Briefe Description of the Whole World*, 1599, Sig. Bₘⱼʳ.

nople and Syria. Abraham Hartwell's version of this book, the *History of the Warres betweene the Turkes and the Persians* (1595), was, one may assume, known to Anthony Sherley. The leading thesis of Minadoi's work, propounded on its opening page, is that the long and bloody wars between these two peoples have been 'very commodious and of great opportunities to the Christian Commonwealth.' There was nothing new in this point of view. Busbecq, the Archduke Ferdinand's ambassador at the court of Solyman the Magnificent, had long since given as his considered opinion that ' 'Tis only the Persian stands between us and ruin. The Turk would fain be upon us, but he keeps him back.'[1] In like fashion George Whetstone wrote of 'the Empire of Sophy: who is to this day a bridle to the Turke and a hinderer of dammage to the Christians.'[2] The infrequent successes of the Persians were welcomed as auguries of the decline of Ottoman power and as such announced to Europe.[3] All this accounts for the popularity of the Persians in Christian countries; they are often contrasted favourably with their opponents; Nicolas de Nicolay, for example, says that they are 'sans comparison plus nobles, plus civils, plus liberaux, et de meilleur esprit et jugement que ne sont les Turcs.'[4]

Properly to understand not only the situation at the time of Sherley's visit but also allusions to that situation in Elizabethan literature, the course of the Turco-Persian wars must

---

1 C.T.Forster and F.H.B.Daniell, *The Life and Letters of Ogier Ghiselin de Busbecq*, 1881, i,221f. See also Sir Edward S.Creasy, *History of the Ottoman Turks*, 1877, p.171f.; E.G.Browne, *A Literary History of Persia*, iv,11 and 93.

2 *The English Myrror*, 1586, p.75. Whetstone goes on to explain the hostility between Turk and Persian on the ground that the Persian Empire 'began by one Ismael, that named himselfe a Prophet, and published an Alcoran contrary to Mahomet.'

3 Even in the midst of Solyman the Magnificent's victorious campaign of 1535 German news-sheets hailed reports of Persian victories. One such (*Newe Zeyttung von Kayserlicher Maiestat, von dem Turcken, und von dem grossen Sophi*, [etc.], 1535) reports the prevalence of sickness among the Turkish troops in Persia and a terrible disaster to them at the hands of the Persians. The reliability of this may be estimated from the fact that the pamphlet goes on to tell how the imperial German army is moving towards Constantinople whose fall is expected daily. There were similar pamphlets in 1536. Seventy years later Europe was greeting with like satisfaction news of Shah Abbas's successes against the Turks. See, for example, De Sallignac, *Avis et Relations de Turquie*, Paris, 1608, p.8; René de Lucinge (*Beginning, Continuance and Decay of Estates*, translated by Sir John Finett, 1606, p.128.

4 *Les Navigations, Peregrinations et Voyages*, Antwerp, 1576, p.216; *Navigations*, Washington's translation, 1585, folio 117^r.

be briefly outlined. The Sultan Bajazet II (1481–1512), hard
pressed in Europe, had been forced to maintain nominal
peace with Shah Ismail I who, however, repeatedly violated
Ottoman territory. Hence Bajazet's complaint in a play:

> The Persian Sophi, mighty Ismael,
> Took the Levante clean away from me.[1]

This is an exaggeration; but the inevitability of war with
Persia was one cause of Bajazet's abdication, forced by his
son Selim the Grim in 1512. Selim at once began the task of
extirpating the Shi'a from his dominions and then extended
to Persia this campaign against heresy. In 1515 he inflicted
a great defeat upon Shah Ismail, wresting from him the
province of Kurdistan. His conquest of Syria and Egypt
followed, victories which secured for a time the eastern frontiers of the Ottoman Empire and left Selim's successor, Solyman the Magnificent (1520–66), free to campaign in Europe,
with the consequent fall of Belgrade and Rhodes, the defeat
of Hungary, and the two sieges of Vienna. Meanwhile Ismail
died and was succeeded by Tahmasp, the Shah to whose court
came the earliest English visitors to Persia. Tahmasp (1524–76),
after biding his time, took advantage of Solyman's preoccupa-
tions in Europe. The author of *Soliman and Persida* fumbles
in the effort to suggest the historical situation when he makes
a councillor of the Sultan give his master the cautious advice:

> I hold it not good policy to call
> Your forces home from Persia . . .
> Strive not for Rhodes by letting Persia slip.[2]

The chronology is here at fault, for war with Persia did not
break out till eleven years after the fall of Rhodes; but the
essential element in the military situation—the threat of
Persia upon Solyman's rear—is grasped. In 1533, while Solyman was heavily engaged in Hungary, Tahmasp began war.
He captured Tabriz, near the borders of Kurdistan, and
overran the country to the north of that city. The great
Sultan was, however, equal to the task confronting him:

1 *Selimus*, l.46 (the play is of uncertain authorship).
2 *Soliman and Persida*, I,v,23f. (the play is perhaps by Kyd).

promptly arranging a truce in Hungary, he directed his energies eastward. The lost provinces were recovered, border fortresses surrendered without resistance, Baghdad was reached, and in certain parts a frontier was established that despite subsequent vicissitudes endured practically unchanged until 1919. Tahmasp was compelled to retire far into the interior of his country. It is to this discomfiture that Milton alludes in the famous passage describing the retreat of the Sophy from the horns of the Turkish crescent.[1] Hostilities continued intermittently during the next two decades. Fortunes fluctuated. The Turks suffered severely from the climate and from the necessity of campaigning in difficult mountainous country. The Persians, on the other hand, were unable to prevent their enemies from repeatedly ravaging their lands. At length a treaty, of peace was concluded in 1555 which endured with only minor interruptions till the accession of Shah Abbas the Great (following two weak and insignificant Shahs who each reigned but a few years) in 1587.

The Prince of Morocco, Portia's suitor in *The Merchant of Venice*, had taken part in these wars. Commending himself to the Lady of Belmont, he exhibits a scimitar

> That slew the Sophie, and a Persian Prince
> That won three fields of Sultan Solyman. [2]

Doctor Johnson's comment on this is not one of his happiest efforts as an annotator. 'Shakespeare,' he says, 'seldom escapes well when he is entangled with geography. The Prince of Morocco must have travelled far to kill the Sophy of Persia.' Of course the Prince had travelled far; but Sultans of Turkey had in their armies various leaders who were natives of the Barbary States. There is a close analogy in one of Massinger's plays, where Princess Donusa commends Mustapha, who lives in Tunis, for his valour in the Turkish wars against the Persians.[3] On the other hand, one of the claimants to the throne of Portugal, who had lived in Morocco, travelled to Persia, where for several years he served the Sophy as a

---

1 *Paradise Lost*, x,432f.   2 *The Merchant of Venice*, II,i,25f.   3 *The Renegado*, I,ii.

commander against the Turks.[1] The obvious difficulty in the
passage, a difficulty which no emendation can remove, is that
no Sophy was slain by anyone in any of the Turco-Persian
wars. It is conceivable that Shakespeare, remembering this
and counting on his audience to remember it, intended to
portray Morocco as a mere braggart; but he is not otherwise
so portrayed. It is more likely that Shakespeare was 'entangled'
with history. Other difficulties are perhaps not incapable of
solution. As the passage stands, the Persian Prince whom
Morocco slew had won three victories over Solyman. The
natural inference is that the Turks were discomfited in these
wars, and this is the inference drawn by the Shakespearean
commentators.[2] But the campaign of 1534–6 was a triumph
for the Turks, and though there were later vicissitudes the
balance of victory remained heavily on their side. It was
perhaps with a view to eliminating this objection that Rowe
long ago (followed only by Halliwell-Phillipps among later
editors) essayed an emendation by placing a comma after
'Persian Prince.' The sense then runs that the scimitar, besides
slaying the Sophy and the Prince, also won three fields from
the Sultan. In other words, Morocco fought on both sides—
which is silly. Let Rowe's comma be retained, the comma
after 'Sophie' omitted, and 'for' substituted for 'of.' The
lines then read:

> This Symitare
> That slew the Sophie and a Persian Prince,
> That won three fields for Sultan Solyman.

The commentators have failed to note the striking parallel
in *Soliman and Persida*; Brusor the Turkish knight is speaking:

> Against the Sophy in three pitched fields,
> Under the conduct of great Soliman,
> Have I been chief commander of an host
> And put the flint-heart Persians to the Sword.[3]

---

1 [Anthony Munday], *A Continuation of the Lamentable and Admirable Adventures of Don Sebastian*, 1603, p.42. Sherley met this claimant in Persia.
2 Thus we find references to Solyman's 'unfortunate' or 'unsuccessful' campaign of 1535 and to his defeats by the Persians. See the notes on the passage in the Furness *Variorum* edition, the *Arden* edition, and so forth.
3 *Soliman and Persida*, I,iii,51f.

The doughty deeds performed by Brusor with his sword are identical with those performed by Morocco with his scimitar: service under the same Sultan, Persians slain, three fields won for the Turks.

From this digression, justified if it has resulted in a reasonable emendation of the text of Shakespeare, we return to history. Immediately upon his accession Shah Abbas found himself under the necessity of defending his north-east frontier against the Uzbegs; and Sultan Amurath III took advantage of this distraction to make inroads into Persia with such success that in 1590 he forced upon the Shah a treaty of peace whereby Persia lost Tabriz and other districts. This inauspicious opening of the new Shah's reign gave no promise of the triumphs soon to come.[1] Before the death of Amurath III (1595) Abbas had renewed war against Turkey with some success; but fighting in that direction languished while he conducted a formidable campaign in Uzbegistan. This campaign had reached a victorious conclusion at the moment of Anthony Sherley's arrival at Kasvin at the close of 1598.

IV

WE now continue our narrative of Sherley's adventures. Angelo Corai, the Italian interpreter, and John Ward, one of the most faithful of Anthony's followers, pushed on four days in advance of the main party to announce their coming and arrange for their lodgings in Kasvin. During the journey northward Sherley and his company had been hospitably received in various towns along the way, and now the governor of the capital city welcomed them on behalf of the absent Shah. They had to wait some time before the victorious potentate returned from the wars, bringing the heads of two thousand Uzbegs upon poles.[2] Anthony had reckoned upon the Shah's well-known tolerance of Christians; and the fact that two of the royal wives were themselves of that faith doubtless was of benefit in securing him a favourable reception.

1 These defeats may have prompted Shah Abbas's temporary abdication in 1591 concerning which something will be said in connection with William Cartwright's drama *The Royal Slave*. See p.516, below.
2 Parry, op.cit., pp.19f.; Sherley, *Relation*, p.63.

But it was not merely tolerance that induced Abbas to receive him graciously. He was flattered by the arrival of this embassy from afar, rightly interpreting it as evidence of his renown—the more so because it arrived opportunely to congratulate him on his victory over the Uzbegs. On their formal presentation the two Sherley brothers were richly dressed in cloth of gold and wore turbans; Angelo was in cloth of silver, and the rest in cloth of silver or velvet taffety or damask gowns according to their rank.[1] Sherley made a formal address beginning: 'If it may please your Majestie to accept the consecration of [my] poore Carcas unto you.'[2] He presented to Abbas six pairs of emerald pendants, a gold-enameled cup, a salt-cellar, and a fair ewer of crystal in the shape of a dragon covered with silver-and-gilt 'cut-work.' The emeralds were those he had successfully secreted when his luggage was pillaged at Baghdad; the other gifts he had obtained from the merchant who had befriended him there. John Cartwright the preacher gives a glowing account of Sherley's reception:

> To this great monarch came Sir Anthony Sherley, Knight, with six and twenty followers, all gallantly mounted and richly furnished; whose entertainment was so great that the Persians did admire that the King should vouchsafe such high favour to a mere stranger without desert or trial of his worth. Of whose bounty the world may judge, since within three days after his first arrival the king sent him forty horses furnished with saddles and very rich trappings; four of them fit for the proper use of any prince, twelve camels for carriage, together with six mules, four and twenty carpets, most of them rich and fair, three tents or pavilions, with all other necessaries of house; and lastly six men laden with silver.[3]

Sherley's first meeting and early conferences with the Shah took place at Kasvin; but early in January 1599, the court removed to the new capital, Isfahan. The horses, beasts of burden, and pavilions were appropriate and convenient gifts, doubtless intended for immediate use in the journey to that city. While still in Kasvin the Shah conferred upon his guest the title of Mirza or Prince. There were sports and military

1 Manwaring, in Ross, p.204.　　　3 *The Preachers Travels*, pp.67f.
2 *A True Report of Sir Anthony Shierlies Journey*, p.1.

parades and banquets with music and fire-works and dancing-women. At one banquet Sherley was 'placed in the king's place' and entertainment was provided by sixteen women, gallantly attired, who did halloo 'much like the wild Irish.' [1] Parry gives us a lively picture of the revels in the town by night:

> The king continued in that towne about some thirty dayes, where many nights the people entertained him with spectacles and shewes in their Basars, which we doe call shoppes, all covered over head, as the Royal Exchange. At which alwayes we must meete the king. Their manner is to make the greatest shew of those weares they have, in foure long streetes, in the middest whereof is a round kinde of stage, covered with costly carpets, whereon is layde all kinds of fruites, confections, and wine for the king to banquet withall. After that he hath seene all the shewes, towards night, they set up as many lights as possible can stand one by another, consisting all of lamps; so that, by estimation, there burneth at once in those four streetes a hundred thousand lampes, so close upon and round about their stalls upon the ground, that a man can hardly put his hand betweene each lampe. After which sights, he goeth to that place appointed for the banquet, where banqueting till midnight, being solaced all the while with all kinds of musicke, of instruments, and voice, with boyes and Curtezans, dauncing strange kinds of Jigges and Lavoltaes: without which Curtezans, no banquet, be it never so costly, hath any rellish with them.[2]

These revels, needless to say, were to celebrate the military triumph; the only special honour done Sherley was that he was accorded a conspicuous position among the Shah's guests.

Once established at Isfahan, Sherley settled down to the important business that had brought him to Persia. At the moment a Turkish ambassador was at the Shah's court, making extravagant territorial demands as the price of the renewal of the peace treaty of 1590. This circumstance strengthened Sherley's position. One may be sure that he was neither slow nor reluctant to make known his prowess on European battlefields; and it would seem that his brother Robert, for all his youth, had already had some experience or at any

1 Manwaring, in Ross, p.206.   2 Parry, op.cit., pp.21f.

rate instruction in the art of war. Shah Abbas was quick to see that he could make use of the brothers to reorganize and train his armies upon occidental lines. He had long confer-ences with Anthony on problems of arms and fortresses and artillery. He desired Sherley to send to him from England men skilled in the casting of great ordnance.[1] He displayed great interest in the books on the science of fortification which Sherley had brought with him.[2] Sherley does not say what books these were, but it is a valid surmise that among them was Paul Ive's treatise on the *Practice of Fortification* (1589) from which Marlowe had derived technical information on the subject.[3] These conferences bore some fruit later. During his comparatively short stay Anthony probably accomplished little; but Robert, who remained behind, gave Persia her first practical initiation into the military science of Europe, forming her first regiments of infantry in place of the irregular loose cavalry which had previously been her mainstay.[4] Even so—to have done at once with this subject—the Persians did not prove very proficient pupils; and the English at Ormuz in 1622 were astonished at the backwardness of the military technique of their Persian allies.[5]

But Sherley had not come to Persia to be a drill-master. To foster his fantastic projects it was necessary to maintain the pretence that he was an official envoy of Queen Elizabeth, though he was in fact not only without any governmental authorization whatsoever but was the proponent of an alliance at variance with English policy. That both the Queen and Sir Robert Cecil were indignant because of this arrogant and dishonest assumption of ambassadorial rank the East, how-ever, could not know; and rumours were afloat as to possible changes in English policy adumbrated by his mission.[6] The well-informed were sceptical as to the practicability of his project to expand trade with Persia and through Persia with

1 Cartwright, op.cit., p.69.   2 *Relation*, p.66.
3 F.C.Danchin, 'En Marge de la seconde partie de Tamburlaine,' *Revue Germanique*, 1912; cited by Miss Ellis-Fermor, *Tamburlaine, Arden* edition, p.45.
4 G.N.Curzon, *Persia and the Persian Question*, ii,533f.; Sykes, *History of Persia*, ii,176.
5 Edward Monoxe, 'Relation of the late Ormuz business,' Purchas, x,348.
6 *C.S.P., Venetian*, iv,446.

the further East. Richard Colthurst, the English consul at Aleppo, wrote to his employers, the merchants of the Levant Company, in March 1599:

> For the matters written unto you out of percia concerning Sʳ Anthony Sherley and his proceadinges. Wee concurre with you in opinion therein expecting little good of ther event wishing them better successe then wee by anie probabylyty cann hitherto conjecture.[1]

The tinge of irony in this remark foreshadows the later open hostility of the Levant Company to the Sherleys. On the other hand, Anthony let his friends in England know of the esteem shown him by the Shah; and certainly the royal favour was not minimized in the telling. An old friend, Sir Francis Vere, sent him a congratulatory letter, expressing the gratification of Sherley's 'wellwyshers,' his own envy of Sherley's chance to distinguish himself in warfare, and his desire to see for himself 'the number and discyplyne' of the armies of 'thatt famous Kyngedome of Persia.'[2] One must remember that though it ran contrary to the course of action adopted by the government, there was a strong anti-Turkish sentiment in England.

Sherley was encouraged by the Shah's policy of tolerance towards Christianity, and probably still more by a misunderstanding of the attitude of the Shi'a towards Christianity, to broach to the potentate the project of a league against the Turks. Among the Shah's ministers, however, there were men seasoned in statecraft, shrewd and suspicious, who warned their master that the Englishman was trying to advance the power of Christendom by embroiling true believers with one another. That the second point in Sherley's proposals—the plan to reopen the old Caspian-Volga trade-route—was of greater moment to Shah Abbas than the highly speculative anti-Ottoman league is probable; but the alliance against Turkey formed the chief subject of discussion at conferences at which the Grand Vizier tried to dissuade his master while a certain Persian general (who naturally saw the advantages of the scheme from the military point of view) sided with Sherley.

1 *The Dawn of British Trade to India*, p.272.   2 E.P.Shirley, *The Sherley Brothers*, p.21.

The length at which Sherley records the substance of these conversations in his *Relation* becomes tolerable when we realize that an ageing and disappointed man is recalling the great days when he helped, or thought he was helping, to shape the destinies of empires.

A powerful argument on Sherley's side was the fact that the Emperor Rudolph II was already at war with Turkey, thus weakening the eastern Ottoman frontier against a Persian invasion. At length Shah Abbas yielded to his guest's solicitations and dismissed the Turkish ambassador with a message to Sultan Mahomet III presaging the renewal of war. That he had much to gain and little to lose by coming to an agreement with the Christian powers and yet hesitated so long is evidence that he was not entirely satisfied with Sherley's credentials.

In the intervals of conferences and entertainments Anthony had opportunities to accumulate impressions of the country and people and his royal host; and many years later he set them down along with a detailed and extraordinarily well-informed history of the reign of Shah Abbas.[1] He is lavish in his praise of the 'true virtues' of this wise and mighty prince; and if we are inclined to think his terms extravagant we must remember that the sovereign under whom the Safavi dynasty reached the zenith of its glory was a man who impressed his personality and power and grandeur not only upon Sherley but upon all Europe. When confronted with the need to make some reference to the crimes against his own children which (at a date after Sherley's visit but before the publication of the *Relation*) stained the annals of the Shah's reign, Sherley was in a predicament and offered a curious apology. He admits that the necessity to prepare against the civil dissentions which might otherwise arise among rival claimants to the throne after the Shah's decease compelled Abbas to incapacitate all his sons save the first-born. The eldest remains unharmed; 'the rest,' says Anthony, 'are not inhumanely murdered, according to the use of the Turkish government, but are made blind with burning basons; and have otherwise all sort of contentment and

1 *Relation*, pp.31f.

regard fit for Princes' children.' [1] Barbarity is relative; and if this remark seems to us shockingly complacent we must recall that in 1599, while the Sherleys were in Persia, Sultan Mahomet III had had nineteen of his brothers strangled. But the inference which Sherley wished his readers to draw, that the Shahs were never guilty of executing their brothers, is not warranted; for when Ismail II succeeded to the throne in 1576 he had caused his eight younger brothers to be beheaded—'imitating the Turkish manner,' says Minadoi.[2] In 1616, three years after Sherley published his *Relation*, came the horrible tragedy of the death of Shah Abbas's son Khudabanda, of which something will be said in a later chapter.

V

ANTHONY now prepared to return to Europe. It was decided that Robert Sherley with some of the English retinue should remain behind in Persia, the Shah declaring, says Anthony, that 'the company of my brother should give him great satisfaction in my absence.' [3] This statement is disingenuous, for beyond question Robert was detained, as was reported in Venice,[4] as a hostage for Anthony's good faith, and Cartwright is correct in saying that he was a 'pledge' of his brother's return.[5] The subsequent adventures of Robert Sherley, thus left at a tender age in a strange country, will be the subject of our next chapter.

According to his own account, Sherley expressed the desire to have some Persian of rank accompany him as an assistant on his diplomatic mission.[6] It is more likely that Shah Abbas wished to send along a representative whom he could trust. The nobleman appointed was Husayn 'Ali Beg.[7] His rank and

1 Here again (compare p.245, note 1, above) Lithgow echoes Sherley: 'The Persians differ much from the Turks, in nobility, humanity, and activity . . . Neither are the Sonnes of the Persian Kings, so barbarously handled as theirs; for all the brethren (one excepted) are onely made blind, wanting their eyes, and are always afterward gallantly maintained, like Princes' (*Rare Adventures*, pp.151f.).—On the blinding of the Shah's sons see also Linschoten, *Voyage to the East Indies*, Hakluyt Society, i,46; Pedro Teixeira, *Relaciones*, 1610, p.40.
2 *History of the Warres betweene the Turkes and the Persians*, Hartwell's translation, p.9.
3 *Relation*, p.127.   4 *C.S.P., Venetian*, ix,428.   5 *The Preachers Travels*, p.70.
6 *Relation*, p.119.
7 This personage is referred to by European writers under a bewildering variety of approximations to his name. In Venetian dispatches he is sometimes called Has-

status relative to his English *confrère* were later the subject of acrimonious disputes; and in after years Sherley professed to believe that God punished him (Sherley) for the pride which this 'great and glorious business' had 'swollen' in him by selecting as the instrument to bring all his labours to nought the very colleague for whom he had himself asked.[1]

In Husayn's retinue was a very romantic person, one of his secretaries, a man named Uruch or (more probably) Uluch Beg who was afterwards converted to Roman Catholicism in Spain. There he remained when his master returned to Persia; and in 1604 he published at Valladolid the *Relaciones de Don Fuan de Persia*,[2] in part controversial, in part narrative. Based upon diaries, it was composed in Spanish with much assistance from a priest. The reason for this clerical fostering becomes apparent towards the close where there is a long and edifying account of the author's conversion and baptism. Much of the book has to do with the geography and history of Persia, and in various places the author controverts the assertions of the Italian historian Minadoi. But in other parts he is more personal, tells about his own travels, and provides us with some information about Anthony Sherley.

Husayn and Sherley were provided with separate credentials the discrepancies between which later caused trouble. In what purports to be a literal translation of the document carried by Sherley, Shah Abbas recommends the bearer with a fervour that is truly oriental, declaring, 'Daylie, whilst he hath bin in thiese partes, we have eaten togither of one dysh, and drunke of one cup, like two breethren.'[3] As the source of this document is open to question and as it is totally different from the translation of Sherley's credentials made at Rome and preserved

---

san Nabrech, once Usein Alibri. Antonio de Gouvea, *Relation des Guerres de Cha Abbas*, 1646, p.105, calls him Usseum Alibeg. In Purchas, viii,439, he is Assan Chan. His portrait made to commemorate his entry into Rome in 1601 (reproduced in Ross, facing p.52) is labelled Cucheinollibeag. Other variants are Assan Halevech and Seane Olibeg. One may compare the difficulty which Italian agents had with Sherley's name. It appears in their dispatches as Syhirle, Scherlei, Cherle, Giarlee, Sciarner, and Ciarles.

1 *Relation*, p.125.
2 See the lively translation of this curious and entertaining book, *Don Juan of Persia: A Shi'ah Catholic*, ed. Guy Le Strange, *Broadway Travellers*, 1926.
3 *A True Report of Sir Anthonie Shierlies Journey*, Sig. B.

among the Venetian archives, it may be a fabrication.[1] Sherley
also carried with him the Shah's *firman* conceding commercial
privileges and religious freedom to all Christians desiring 'to
trade and trafique into Persia.' It promised protection of life
and property and the unmolested exercise of their religion.[2]

Sherley tells us that as a parting gift to his young brother he
handed him a paper of 'instructions and advice.' This tediously
rhetorical exercise gives us a glimpse of a mind filled with
lofty abstractions and vague generalities concerning the deportment proper to an envoy of state. Master Robert Sherley
is instructed in the decorous conduct of negotiations with
princes; he is warned to beware of rumours and factions at
courts and to avoid inconstancy and lightness of spirit; and
he is urged to develop the qualities of Counsel, Force, and
Reputation.[3] One may doubt whether such a paper was ever
given to Robert; possibly it is founded upon recollections of
conversations between the brothers, but in all likelihood its
composition dates from later days of enforced idleness in Spain.

Shortly before his departure from Isfahan Sherley sent
Angelo Corai, the interpreter, through Turkey to Venice to
announce to the government there that his mission was on its
way. Angelo's knowledge of languages probably enabled him
to traverse Turkish territory unmolested, and it is noteworthy that at Constantinople he kept his identity secret and
remained in seclusion at the residence of the Persian ambassador. At Venice he gave the Signory some information about
Sherley's movements and intentions and about the condition of
affairs in Persia. Coincident with his arrival came a Persian,
who gave out that he was a merchant in quest of Venetian
commodities but acknowledged privately that he was a secret
agent of the Shah commissioned to report upon the actions
of the official plenipotentiaries.[4]

1 E.P.Shirley, apparently accepted it as genuine. See also Malcolm, *History of Persia*,
  i,534, and Ross, p.95. For the Italian translation of the undoubtedly genuine credentials see p.273, note 3, below.
2 The Coppie of the free Priviledges,' *A True Report*, no pagination or signature;
  reprinted in Ross, pp.96f.
3 *Relation*, pp.132f.
4 The records of Angelo's visit to Venice and of his examination there were first printed
  by Guglielmo Berchet in *Raccolta Veneta*, 1866; translated by Ross, pp.25f. See
  also Berchet, *La Repubblica di Venezia e la Persia*, p.43.

These plenipotentiaries with some two score persons in their
train set out from Isfahan at the beginning of May 1599.[1]
With them travelled two Portuguese friars, a Franciscan and an
Augustinian, who were returning home from Ormuz. These
men later caused Sherley much trouble, the root of the difficulty being that Sherley's commercial designs were in part
directed against the trade of their country.[2]

The way taken was that traversed in earlier days by Anthony
Jenkinson and his successors. On the Caspian they encountered
such terrifying storms that only fear of the Shah's wrath kept
the Persian members of the party from turning back. September
was half gone when they reached Astrakhan; and there they
had to wait for the arrival of yet another Persian envoy especially accredited to the Czar Boris Godunoff. (It should be
noted that Sherley's and Husayn's credentials were not addressed to the Czar and that to him they presented only letters
requesting a safe-conduct through his territories. The lack of
diplomatic standing probably accounts in part for the scant
courtesy with which Sherley met in that country.) At length
the two missions, now increased to the enormous number of
five or six hundred men (including the galley-rowers), started
again on their way, provided with a military guard by the
governor of Astrakhan. They mounted the Volga to Nijni-
Novgorod whence they proceeded on sleighs to Moscow where
they arrived towards the end of November.

As a fellow-countryman of the special Persian envoy to
Muscovy Husayn was received honourably by Boris; but
Sherley's reception fell far short of his expectations and of
what he doubtless considered his deserts. It is possible that, as
Anthony himself thought, one of the friars prejudiced officials

1 There is contradictory testimony about the date; that given in the text is intentionally vague but approximately correct (see Ross, pp.22 and 26). The date 24 May 1599,
in C.S.P., Venetian, ix,428, is about right for Sherley's departure from Gilan, not
from Isfahan. Uluch Beg's date, 9 July, is much too late (Don Juan of Persia, p.234).
On 26 July, Colthurst had 'instantly received' word at Aleppo from Sherley announcing his departure for England (John Sanderson, Travels in the Levant, p.176).
2 Parry recounts the quarrel at great length (op.cit., pp.27f.). It is the subject of a
long and confused letter from Sherley to Anthony Bacon, dated from Moscow,
12 February 1600 (E.P.Shirley, op.cit., pp.23f.). Uluch Beg (a prejudiced witness)
says (op.cit., p.258) that Sherley not only robbed one of the friars but had him
done away with in Moscow. See further Ross, p.35.

against him. Or the Persians, with whom his relations were already none too cordial, may have betrayed him behind his back. Or the Czar may have had letters from England denouncing him as a charlatan. For whatever reason, the Persians were preferred before him and he was subjected to various mortifications, forbidden to hold communication with the English merchants in Moscow, and even, it seems, put for a while into prison. At length, when the English merchants protested against this treatment of their fellow-countryman and vouched for his credit, he was released. Between him and one of the friars there was a violent scene in the Czar's presence, and Anthony struck the friar, knocking him down. Thereafter, says Parry, the Czar 'used him better' and when the time came for his departure Sherley was dismissed courteously.

Since their destination was Prague one would have expected the envoys to go westward overland.[1] That they did not do so was probably due to the fact that their heavy luggage made it advisable to go by water as much of the way as possible. By the middle of June 1600, they were on the shore of the White Sea, preparing to embark. There Sherley found time to write a long letter to Sir Robert Cecil, attempting to conciliate the Queen and to obtain permission to return to England. 'I upon the knees of my heart acknowledge,' he wrote, 'the greatness of my fault in departing from her Majesty without the blessedness of her gratious favour'; and he went on to plead that his motive had been to 'bring generall profitt to my Country, and disburden myself of the spread ignomyny which wass allso by soome of my best frendes daily passed over me.' [2] By the Arctic route they sailed to Stode at the mouth of the Elbe. On the voyage Anthony had word of the disgrace of his patron Essex following the return from Ireland; we have a

1 Concerning Sherley's travels through Europe before his arrival at Rome only so much is said here as has some bearing upon our subject or sheds additional light on his character. For his itineraries and sojourns in Central Europe see Babinger, *Sherleiana*, i,8f. There are errors in most accounts of the itinerary followed after the departure from Moscow. The contemporary narratives are careless in their indications of routes and places. The dispatches of foreign agents are often based on mere rumour (see, for example, *C.S.P., Venetian*, ix,427f.). One report had it that he had crossed India and come 'by sea round the whole of Africa' (*The Fugger News-Letters*, ed. Victor von Klarwill, translated by Pauline de Chary, [1924], pp.230f.).
2 10 June 1600; E.P.Shirley, op.cit., pp.28f.; Ross, Appendix ii.

glimpse of him on shipboard hastily destroying a mass of letters which, one surmises, were incriminating.[1] From Stode William Parry took ship for England, the bearer of official and private letters from his master.[2] He arrived in London about the middle of September 1600.

VI

BEFORE following Sherley's fortunes further we must see what came to pass after Parry's arrival home. Whether intercepted or voluntarily surrendered by the bearer or the recipients, the letters entrusted to him came into the archives of Sir Robert Cecil.[3] In one addressed to his father, Anthony recommends the bearer (unnamed but of course Parry) as 'a gentleman, my friend, who is the true witness of my whole pilgrimage.' A similar recommendation to the Earl of Essex contains indiscreet expressions of passionate loyalty. 'The last words which your Lordship spake unto me were the star that guided me,' he exclaims; and he assures the Earl that 'so rare and excellent a virtue as your Lordship's can but receive a momentary eclipse.' In another letter to Essex, sent (it is important to note) by a second messenger, he describes himself as 'plunged in grief to hear of your Lordship's misfortunes' and assures him of his undeviating devotion. Parry handed a packet of letters to Anthony Bacon who wrote of them to Essex, praising Sherley's 'gallant, rare and resolute spirit' which 'base carping spirits and envious idle brains' calumniate. This letter was intercepted by Cecil's agents.[4] Letters addressed to Sherley from his father and from Thomas Dudley of the Essex faction were likewise intercepted.

Elizabeth's government was in fact closely watching the movements of this impudent and inconvenient adventurer who, having arrogated to himself the title of English envoy to Persia, now claimed to be an ambassador of the Grand Sophy to the European courts.[5] Cecil found it advisable to instruct

1 Anthony Bacon to Essex, 19 September 1600; *Hatfield MSS*, x,318.
2 *A New and Large Discourse*, pp.38f.
3 *Hatfield MSS*, x,180,190,227,30,3,318 (in the order of citation).
4 See Sir Nicholas Parker's report of intercepting letters, ibid., x,149.
5 For reports of Sherley's movements on the continent see *C.S.P.,Dom., 1598–1601*, pp.130,371,372,477.

Lello to calm Turkish suspicions by informing the Sultan that no matter what sinister practices Sherley had been guilty of there was no ground for questioning the Queen's friendliness; she was grateful to the Sultan 'for his just usadge of her subjects' and she 'did foresee how dangerous it might have been to her Merchants trade with the Grand Signor yf any such fond practise should have ben sett on fote'—that is, if Sherley had succeeded in effecting a Persian-European combination against Turkey. The project of opening up trade through Muscovy and Persia Cecil dismissed contemptuously: 'There is no man of any sense, that would imagine . . . that there should be any great Commodity had by it.' He went on to inform Lello that Sherley's friends in England reproved him for his folly.[1] This communication reached Lello at an opportune time, enabling him to refute the French ambassador's charge that Sherley was an authorized English agent stirring up trouble against the Porte. Lello was at pains to speak openly against him at Constantinople, characterizing him as a rebel.[2]

Meanwhile, in October 1600, there was published *A True Report of Sir Anthonie Shierlies Journey overland to Venice, from thence by sea to Antioch, Aleppo, and Babilon, and soe to Casbine in Persia: his Oration: his letters of Credence to the Christian Princes: and the Priviledg obtained of the great Sophie, for the quiet passage and trafique of all Christian Marchants, throughout his whole Dominions.* The title accurately summarizes the contents of this black-letter pamphlet. On the title-page is the device of a clenched fist with the motto 'Ex Avaritia Bellum'—which seems unhappily chosen but not inappropriate. At the beginning of the report is the claim that it is 'by two Gentlemen who have followed [Sherley] in the same [journey] the whole time of his travails, and are lately sent by him with Letters into England, September 1600.'[3] The pamphlet was suppressed and on 22 October 1600, R.Blore and J.Jaggard, the printer and bookseller, were fined 'for printing without

1 E.P.Shirley, op.cit., pp.3of., from the original draft of the letter.
2 *C.S.P.*, *Venetian*, iv,458.
3 In Ross's reprint (op.cit., pp.91f.) of the *True Report* this opening statement as to authorship is omitted; and in his introduction, p.xiv, Ross attributes the statement solely to the Catalogue of the British Museum.

license, and contrary to order, a little book on Sir Anthony
Sherley's voyage.' They were ordered to bring all copies to
Stationer's Hall to be destroyed. The order seems to have been
ineffective, for it had to be repeated on 7 September 1601.[1]
The documents printed in this pamphlet may have been pur-
loined from Parry; but since, as we have noted, the bearer of
one of Sherley's letters to Essex was someone else than Parry
the claim advanced concerning the pamphlet's authorship may
be true; moreover, the narrative refers to Anthony's arrival
at Prague which occurred after Parry had separated from
him.

From whatever source it came, its unauthorized publication
doubtless prompted Parry to publish his own fuller narrative:
*A new and large Discourse of the Travels of Sir Anthony Sherley,
Knight, by Sea, and over Land to the Persian Empire. Wherein
are related many strange and wonderful accidents: and also, the
Description and conditions of those Countries and People he
passed by: with his returne into Christendome. Written by William
Parry, Gentleman, who accompanied Sir Anthony in his Travells*
(1601).[2] Appended to it is a commendatory sonnet by John
Davies of Hereford, in which the idea, struggling through
laborious conceits, is that most travellers lose rather than gain
by their wanderings; 'they gather not but rather scatter';
whereas Parry has brought home 'Wisdom and Experience.'[3]
This estimation is not mere flattery, for even today the book
has a value and interest independent of its connection with
Sherley. Parry was a discerning traveller and had his individual
comments to make on Turks, Persians, and Muscovites. His
narrative has already been drawn upon so freely in this chapter
that nothing need be added except that he had acquired a low
opinion of the intellectual attainments of the Persians, pro-

---

1 See Ross, pp.xivf., for miscellaneous memoranda from the *Stationers' Register*. Professor E.E.Willoughby believes that the censor objected to the pamphlet because by
defending Sherley it inferentially attacked the English government (*A Printer of
Shakespeare*, New York, 1935, p.58). But since the censor did not suppress Parry's
subsequent narrative it is more likely that Jaggard was guilty of publishing matter
to which he had no legal right.
2 Reprinted in part by Purchas, viii,442f. and in part in *The Three Brothers*, 1825;
entire in J.Payne Collier, *Illustrations of Early English Popular Literature*, 1864,
ii, and in Ross, pp.98f.
3 Reprinted in Davies, *Works*, ed. Grosart, 1878, ii, *Commendatory Poems*, p.7.

nouncing them ignorant of 'liberal arts and learned sciences' and crediting them only with craftsmanship in harness-making, carpet-weaving, and the manufacture of silken stuffs.[1]

His book combined with the gossip circulated by these Englishmen newly arrived from Persia to arouse interest in the brothers. 'I am haunted with the spirit of the Sherleys,' wrote Lord Thomas Howard to Sir Robert Cecil,[2] meaning that he was thrilled with the thought of their exploits. Cecil probably smiled sardonically. Another Englishman contemplated these exploits with coldly satiric detachment. In Ben Jonson's *Volpone* the character of Sir Politic Would-Be is generally recognized as a caricature of Sir Henry Wotton;[3] but a portrait may have more than one model, and apparently Jonson had Anthony Sherley also in mind. At one point in the play it is suggested that Sir Politic Would-Be might be shipped away 'to Zant or to Aleppo' 'and ha' his Adventures put i' th' *booke of voyages.*' No editor of Jonson has identified a 'book of voyages' connected with Wotton; two such books had lately appeared about Sherley. Wotton was never in Zante or Aleppo; Anthony had had memorable experiences in both places. If Jonson had heard of Wotton's association with Sherley in Italy (a matter to which we shall come in a moment), it becomes the more likely that he intended to combine traits of both men in his satiric portrait. Surely to no man could the name Sir Politic Would-Be be applied more appropriately than to Anthony Sherley.

VII

THAT would-be politician and his colleague arrived at Prague on 11 October 1600. They were received 'in very fine fashion,'

1 *A New and Large Discourse*, p.23.
2 *Hatfield MSS*, x,444.
3 See the discussion of the problem in *Volpone*, ed. J.D.Rea, Yale University Press, 1919, pp.xxxf. For the passage quoted see *Volpone*, V,iv,4f.—It is tempting, in view of the date and especially of the slight but significant change in the title, to guess that the lost 'tragedie called the ij brothers' (presently called 'the playe of the iij brothers') for which Henslowe paid 'Mr. Smythe' (Wentworth Smith) in October 1602, was on the subject of the Sherleys. The difficulty is that Henslowe also records payments for properties for this play, and they include 'a devells sewte,' 'a wiches gowne,' 'a tabell and a coffen.' A dramatization of the adventures of the Sherleys would not, one supposes, have afforded occasion for the use of such accessories. See *Henslowe's Diary*, ed. W.W.Greg, i,182f.

the Fugger correspondent reported, adding that 'the head of the Embassy is an Englishman and he is short and dressed in English fashion.' [1] An account of the reception accorded them by the Emperor, published some years later, perhaps exaggerates the splendour of the occasion; [2] but it was something of an achievement to secure a reception at all, for at this time Rudolph II was sinking into melancholia, neglecting business, and often refusing to admit ambassadors to his presence. [3] He proved well disposed towards the Shah's proposals for an alliance and sent a formal reply to this effect by a special mission. [4] News of Rudolph's goodwill reached England, and the Levant Company, increasingly alarmed lest Sherley's activities work damage and perhaps ruin to their factories and merchandise in Turkey, implored Queen Elizabeth to prevent his further progress through Europe; whereupon she dispatched an agent post-haste to Prague 'to discredit the ambassador by some sinister representations'; but no more is heard of this messenger who, it was guessed, met with some disaster upon the way. [5] Foreign political intelligencers were puzzled by Sherley's mission and programme; they could not 'make out the object of this journey, for the Queen is an ally of the Turk.' [6] Distorted gossip—for example, that Anthony was leaving his brother 'Andrew' at Prague [7]—was afloat; and there were grotesque rumours that the Shah had become, or was about to become, a Christian. [8]

Notwithstanding the initial promises inferred from his flattering reception, things did not go well with Anthony at

1 *The Fugger News-Letters*, p.230. Compare *C.S.P., Venetian*, iv,427. Regarding Anthony Sherley's personal appearance, compare Uluch Beg's description: 'A man of great parts, although short of stature' (*Don Juan of Persia*, p.261). The arrogance and pomposity of Anthony's bearing and literary style were perhaps 'compensations' for this physical defect.

2 Anthony Nixon, *The Three English Brothers*, 1607, pp.108f. For some notice of this book see below, p.287.

3 *Cambridge Modern History*, iii,697.

4 For an account of this mission, which was met at the southern limits of the Caspian by Robert Sherley, see *Iter Persicum*, ed. Charles Schefer, Paris, 1877, cited by Ross, pp.43f. Compare *C.S.P., Venetian*, iv,438f.

5 *C.S.P., Venetian*, iv,450. This, the preceding, and the three following excerpts from the dispatches of Pietro Duodo, Venetian ambassador at Prague, are given with their contexts in Charles Schefer's edition of Father Raphael du Mans, *Estat de la Perse en 1600*, Paris, 1890, pp.277f., and are quoted by Ross, pp.39f.

6 *C.S.P., Venetian*, iv,432.

7 Ibid., iv,428.   8 Ibid., iv,431.

Prague. He was an irascible man, opinionated, truculent, and turbulent. Trouble had long been brewing between him and Husayn 'Ali Beg. Perhaps there had been reciprocal jealousy even before their departure from Isfahan; and the contrasting receptions accorded them by the Czar had wounded Sherley's pride. Now at the imperial court each advanced his claim to precedence. The Englishman's vanity and the Persian's caution were in conflict; and gossip had it that Rudolph, with his own ends in view, was planning to send the Persian ambassador in the company of an envoy of his own to the different courts of Europe, while he packed Sherley off to Persia again. Anthony resisted this plan to the uttermost.[1]

It is now time to note that Sherley had become a Roman Catholic. It is not possible to determine exactly when this happened. So long before as 1594, when he accepted an order of knighthood from Henry of Navarre, he had 'taken the whole oath,' which included a defence of the Mass,[2] but he was certainly not formally received into the Roman Catholic Church at that time. It is possible that his recusancy took place at Venice in 1598, before his departure for the East; he was then loud in praise of Spain and of the Pope.[3] Furthermore, Father Parsons, the head of the English College at Rome, wrote: 'He denyeth himselfe to have been a Protestant ever since his first being at Venice for that there he was reconciled.'[4] On the whole, however, this early date is unlikely for this reason, that his younger brother would probably have been converted along with him, and we know definitely that Robert's conversion took place in Persia, after Anthony's departure.[5] By the time of the visit to Prague he had certainly gone over to Rome. He

1 The uncertain status of the two emissaries is amusingly indicated in an extant letter in which Sherley is described as ambassador: the word 'ambassador' has been stricken out of the text and then reinserted in the margin. See *Hatfield MSS*, xi,147.

2 Philip Gawdy wrote to his brother in 1594: 'The Queene is very angry with Sir Anthony Sherley and Sir Nicholas Clyfford for taking the Order of St. Michel, and hath commanded that they shall send the order backe again; First, bycause they tooke it without her pryvyty; next bycause they toke the whole othe, and one part thereof is to defende the masse while they lyve' (*Royal Commission on Historical Manuscripts*, Seventh Report, Part i, 1879, Appendix, p. 523). Sherley's father was for a time in the Roman communion.

3 This is reported of him in the French letter of March 1598; see p.242, note 1, above.

4 E.P.Shirley, op.cit., p.33.

5 Anthoine (Antonio) de Gouvea, *Relations des Grandes Guerres et Victoires obtenues par le Roy de Perse Cha Abbas contre les Empereurs de Turquie*, Rouen, 1646, p.107.

spoke boastfully of his good relations with the Curia and received a snub from the Papal Nuncio, who sent him word that the Holy Father did not relish vaingloriousness. It was generally believed, however, that the Pope was awaiting Sherley's coming with eager interest.[1]

Negotiations dragged on at Prague and it was not till February 1601, that the two envoys set out for Rome. Sherley had intended to visit Venice, but the Signory refused to permit his coming lest his presence give offence to a Turkish mission which was expected.[2] In Florence he met an old acquaintance and relative by marriage, Sir Henry Wotton, who travelled with him to Rome.[3] At Siena a bitter quarrel broke out between Sherley and Husayn. While they were in Moscow the Persian had entrusted to Anthony some thirty-two chests of valuables with the understanding that they were to be sent by ship from the White Sea to Rome. It now turned out that Anthony had sold or bartered away the contents of these boxes and it was recalled that 'our pieces of brocade and cloths had . . . been publicly sold by the English merchants in Muscovy.' The quarrel was composed after a fashion, but bad blood remained between the two men.[4]

They reached Rome on 5 April 1601, and were received with great pomp, the guns of Sant' Angelo thundering a salute as they rode across the bridge leading to Saint Peter's.[5] They were

1 C.S.P., Venetian, iv,431 and 447.
2 Don Juan of Persia, p.282.
3 Wotton's uncle had married Sherley's aunt. The two men had probably seen something of each other in earlier years, especially during Essex's 'Island Voyage'; and in 1590 they may have met in Germany. See L.P.Smith, Life and Letters of Sir Henry Wotton, i,242 and 430. Their encounter in Florence had an important effect upon Wotton's career, for it was Sherley who introduced him to the Grand Duke of Tuscany who later in the same year entrusted him with a secret message to James VI of Scotland regarding a Spanish plot against his life. In Rome Sherley handed him an 'account of his [Sherley's] proceedings' to be delivered to Sir Robert Cecil. This seems to have miscarried; and the secrecy with which Wotton travelled via Norway to Scotland is shown by Anthony's fear lest, having heard nothing further from him, he had perished on the journey (Sherley to Cecil, 3 March 1602, C.S.P.,Dom., 1601–3, p.159).
4 Don Juan of Persia, pp.283f. Uluch Beg enters into many details regarding the journey through Italy.
5 Of an Italian pamphlet narrating their arrival and reception no printed copy seems to be extant but there is a transcript in the Vatican Library (Babinger, Sherleiana, i,27; Ross, p.46). It was translated into French as L'Entrée Solemnelle faicte à Rome aux Ambassadeurs du Roi de Perse le cinquieme Avril, 1601, Paris, 1601. Other editions appeared at Lyons and Rouen the same year, a fact testifying to the interest roused

lodged splendidly in the Palazzo della Rovere, and there the old quarrel over precedence broke out anew; 'the Englishman insisted upon forcibly occupying the best apartment.' [1] 'They have armed themselves with daggers,' a correspondent reported.[2] Husayn submitted his credentials to prove that he was the only genuine Persian ambassador. The document was translated and appeared to substantiate the claim, whereupon Sherley roundly declared that the translator did not know Persian. This was pretty shameless, considering that he had but a smattering of the language himself. (In Persia he had employed an interpreter and a few years later his brother Robert had to translate for him the substance of a document written in Persian.) Husayn, bewildered foreigner, requested a private interview with the secretary of the Venetian embassy. To him through the medium of an interpreter he bitterly denounced his English colleague who was, he said, taking advantage of his ignorance of any European language. Sherley, he went on, had robbed him of costly jewels and was so deep in debt that 'his sole object now was to extract money from princes.' Husayn asked the secretary to convey to the Signory the suggestion that when Sherley reached Venice he should be placed under arrest.[3]

We have three glimpses of Sherley on Easter Sunday. From the window of Cardinal Borromeo's residence he watched before dawn 'a procession of the Resurrection' performed by Spanish priests, and admired 'the number of lamps and artificial lights which faded into the distance on either side of the piazza.' Later he witnessed the entry of the Pope into Saint Peter's, and

by the event. Henri IV had reason to watch the Persian mission anxiously since the policy of France was pro-Turk. The French brochure is reprinted by Ross, Appendix iii.

1 *C.S.P., Venetian*, iv,451.
2 *Fugger News-Letters*, Second Series, pp.331f.
3 *C.S.P., Venetian*, iv,451 and 456. Copies of the credentials of both parties to the dispute were obtained by the Venetian embassy and are still in the archives at Venice. In them Husayn is styled 'ambassador' and Sherley 'supreme commissioner' (ibid., iv,439 and 445). Additional evidence of the falsity of Sherley's claim to ambassadorial rank is in a letter from Shah Abbas to the King of Spain in which he speaks of two English brothers (unnamed but of course the Sherleys) in his employ, of whom one is in Persia while the other is in Spain 'au service de Vostre Majesté en la compagnie de mon Amb[a]ssadeur.' See Father Antoine Gouvea, *Histoire Orientale des Grans Progrès de l'Eglise Cathol[ique]*, Antwerp, 1609, p.747.

as the Holy Father passed by, Sherley made him a profound reverence.[1] He dined at the English College, and, says Father Parsons, 'was in conversation after dinner among the fathers where he did so well discourse . . . concerning [the] likelyhood of casting religion in Persia, that many of our fathers were very much enclined to be imployed there.' [2]

After a few days, during which it had been arranged that in order to keep the peace Anthony and Husayn were to be received on separate days, the former had an audience with the Pope. Sherley prostrated himself and then, retiring three paces, 'seated himself on his heels Turkish-fashion.' [3] He spoke glowingly of the Shah's favour to Christians, adding that 'God had so touched the heart of his master that he and all his kingdom might be converted.' His Holiness displayed great satisfaction to hear this.[4]

But no agreement was reached and the discussions dragged on for many days. In these negotiations Father Parsons seems to have taken part. One day Sherley had a violent altercation with Thomas Wilson, one of Cecil's intelligencers. Anthony accused him of having attempted his assassination, a charge which Wilson indignantly repudiated, though he expressed his willingness to apprehend Sherley, if Cecil so desired, and to bring him to England for examination before the Privy Council.[5]

VIII

A more pleasant encounter was with Will Kemp, the picturesque and popular dancer and comedian. This meeting is not mentioned in any of the contemporary narratives of the Sherleys but it forms a scene (set, however, in Venice, not in Rome) in a play founded on their adventures of which some account will be given in a later chapter.[6] In this scene Anthony asks

1 *Hatfield MSS*, xi,171f. (an unsigned letter written in Italian).
2 From a letter intercepted and sent to Cecil, 30 April 1601; E.P.Shirley, op.cit., p.33.
3 From the letter referred to in note 1, above.
4 *C.S.P., Venetian*, iv,459.
5 *Hatfield MSS*, xii,322f. Wilson was the informer who afterwards helped to bring about the downfall of Sir Walter Ralegh.
6 *The Travailes of the Three English Brothers*, by John Day, William Rowley, and George Wilkins. See John Day, *Works*, ed. A.H.Bullen, ii,55 (separate pagination for each play).

Kemp: 'What play of note have you?' 'Many of name; some of note, especially one,' replies the actor and proceeds to refer briefly to a theatrical hoax entitled *England's Joy*. We need not pause over this allusion, which has nothing to do with our subject.[1] The significance of this bit of dialogue for us is that it apparently indicates that Sherley was known to dramatists in London as a gentleman who even in exile interested himself in theatrical affairs at home. It thus presents him in a new and unexpected light. It is unlikely that he would have been shown hobnobbing with Kemp if in earlier days he had not at least occasionally associated with actors in London. Can it be that Kemp was a relation by marriage? Anthony's mother's maiden name was Kempe.[2] This would account for the familiarity of the actor's bearing towards one who was his social superior.

That Kemp's meeting with Sherley is not an invention of the playwrights but really took place—or at any rate that Kemp said it had taken place—is proved by an entry (dated 2 September 1601) in a contemporary diary to the effect that a certain actor named Kemp who after wandering through Germany and Italy had returned home had much to tell about Sir Anthony Sherley, the Persian envoy, whom he met in Rome.[3] No imagination is required to picture the welcome accorded him by his friends, because it is on record in a play of the period: 'God save you, Master Kemp; welcome, Master Kemp, from dancing the morris over the Alps!' [4] The voluble mime doubtless poured

1 See Sir Edmund Chambers, *The Elizabethan Stage*, iii,500f. Though it is almost certain that Sherley and Kemp did meet at Rome, *England's Joy*, which is of November 1602, could not have been the subject of a conversation in the spring of 1601.

2 This possibility had occurred to the present writer before he discovered that it is the keystone of the argument in a fantastic and little-known book by the Reverend F.Scott Surtess: *William Shakespeare of Stratford-on-Avon. His Epitaph Unearthed and the Author of the Plays run to Ground*, Hertford, privately printed, 1888. The theory is here advanced that Anthony Sherley was the author of the plays ascribed to Shakespeare! The argument is that Kemp, whose company produced the play on the Sherleys, was his cousin; that Sherley is thus shown to have had a close confidential connection with the theatres; that he possessed the wide experience of men and affairs exhibited in the plays; that at Venice he had financial difficulties with a Jew; and so forth.

3 The Diary of William Smith of Abington (Sloane MS.414,f.56): 'Kemp, mimus quidam, qui peregrinationem quandam in Germaniam et Italiam instituerat, post multos errores et infortunia sua reversus: multa refert de Anthonio Sherly equite aurato, quem Romae (legatum Persicum agentem) convenerat.' This excerpt was first printed by J.O.Halliwell-Phillipps in a note on Kemp in the *Ludus Coventriae*, Shakespeare Society, 1841, p.410.

4 2 *Return from Parnassus*, IV,iii; Hazlitt's Dodsley, ix,195. Kemp, who had danced

forth to a circle of wondering theatre-folk his impressions and anecdotes of the romantic adventurer who claimed to be the envoy of the mighty oriental despot, the Grand Sophy. Kemp's auditors would spread his stories through London; the printed narratives already on the market would confirm them.

These tales—perhaps from Kemp's own mouth—came to the ear of Shakespeare, who echoes the current gossip in *Twelfth Night.* Fabian, spying with heartless glee upon Malvolio's antics, exclaims: 'I will not give my part of this sport for a pension of thousands to be paid from the Sophy!' [1] The topical allusion would have gained pathetic and ironic point had Shakespeare and his audience known that at the time the play was produced (1602) Sherley, far from enjoying 'a pension of thousands,' was discredited and falling into poverty.[2] If, through Kemp or another, reports of Robert Sherley's military exploits in Persia had reached England by 1602, added point would be given to another passage in the same comedy where Sir Toby, by way of mock encouragement to Sir Andrew Aguecheek, who is about to fight a duel with the disguised Viola, exclaims: 'They say he hath been fencer to the Sophy!' [3] Professor J.Dover Wilson has adduced evidence for a revision

his way from London to Norwich, had gone to the continent with the announced intention of dancing his way across the Alps.

1 *Twelfth Night*, II,v,197f. The passage has caused much confusion to the commentators. Thus, the Furness *Variorum* edition leaves uncorrected and without comment an old explanation that the allusion is to Sir Thomas Sherley, ambassador from Persia. Sir Thomas was never in Persia and never an ambassador. Sir Edmund Chambers, following without verification a note in the *Arden* edition, says that 'Sir Robert Shirley, returning enriched from Persia in 1599, perhaps inspired the allusion' (*William Shakespeare*, i,406). The Sherleys of Wiston did not spell their name with an *i*; Robert was not a knight in 1599; the mis-dating 1599 for 1601 or 1602 blunts the point of the allusion; Robert Sherley did not leave Persia till 1608 nor arrive in England till 1611; his brother Anthony never returned to England at all; neither of them was, properly speaking, 'enriched.' A remarkable number of errors in one sentence to come from a scholar who has often rebuked other scholars caustically for mistakes.

2 That the allusion belongs to the 1602 version of the play and not to the revision (if there was a revision) of 1606 is evident, for by the latter date Sherley's discredit was notorious.

3 *Twelfth Night*, III,iv,310. This, on the other hand (see previous note), may have been added in 1606 by which time Robert Sherley's achievements in Persia were certainly known in London.—If Kemp aroused his interest in the Sherleys, it is likely that Shakespeare read Parry's account of their adventures; he might have done so anyway. In it occurs the fine phrase: 'Those resplendent crystalline heavens over-canopying the earth' (*A New and Large Discourse*, p.2) which G.B.Harrison (*Shakespeare at Work*, pp.277f.) thinks suggested Hamlet's 'This most excellent canopy the air' (II,ii,317). Shakespeare's indebtedness to Parry is, thus, more likely than J.Dover Wilson is willing to admit (note in the *New* Cambridge edition, p.175).

of *Twelfth Night* about 1606 and on the basis of various parallels between the two plays associates that revision with the composition of *King Lear*.[1] In 1606 an allusion to the Sherleys had not the timeliness of the references of 1602, for Anthony was by then lost to sight in Africa and Robert had not yet appeared above the eastern horizon. Yet such an allusion occurs in *King Lear*. 'I do not like the fashion of your garments,' says the mad king. 'You will say, they are Persian attire; but let them be changed.'[2] This coincidence with *Twelfth Night* has not been remarked by Professor Wilson in his argument for a revision of that play. It would seem that the reperusal of the comedy recalled to Shakespeare's mind the fantastic English adventurers with the consequent insertion of the topical reference to their oriental dress in *Lear*.

IX

WE now rejoin Anthony Sherley, whom we last saw at Rome in the spring of 1601. How he kept himself going it is difficult to guess. Rumour had it that he 'one day ebbs and another day

1 *Twelfth Night*, *New* Cambridge edition, pp.96f.

2 *King Lear*, III,vi,84f. Here again the commentators go quite regularly astray. The allusion is usually said to be to a Persian embassy which came to England early in the reign of James I. But what is the record of this embassy? The only Persian mission reported in London before the arrival of Sir Robert Sherley in 1611 is that which, according to the Venetian ambassador in Madrid (*C.S.P.*, *Venetian*, ix,445), was received by Queen Elizabeth in February 1601. This embassy is a very shadowy affair. We know nothing of it save this dispatch from Madrid, which is obviously based upon distorted rumours of Anthony Sherley's movements. The editor of the *State Papers,·Venetian*, says that the ambassador received by Queen Elizabeth was Anthony Sherley—which is absurd. In the early months of 1601 Sherley was in Prague or on the road between Prague and Rome. Queen Elizabeth would certainly have refused to see him. Moreover, he never returned to England at all! Nor could the envoy in question have been Husayn 'Ali Beg, who was with Sherley at this time. There is no evidence or likelihood that Shah Abbas's special envoy to Czar Boris or his secret envoy to Venice (both of whom we have met with) were commissioned to go to England or anywhere else save their immediate destination. And no other Persian envoys are on record at this time. In any case, it does not seem likely that in 1605-6, the date of *King Lear*, a reference to an embassy of 1601 would have had much point to it. Nor was this embassy, if it ever came at all (which it almost certainly did not), an embassy to King James.—In a note on the *Lear* passage in their so-called *First Folio* edition Miss Porter and Miss Clarke fell into a whole series of errors, to wit: 'The first English embassy to Persia was sent in 1598 under Sir Roger Sherley and his brother Anthony.' It was not an embassy; it was not sent; it was not under Sir Robert Sherley; his name was not Roger; and he was not then knighted. The Furness *Variorum* edition of *Lear* reproduces without comment or correction a note by Moberley explaining the allusion as suggested by the death of the secretary of the Persian embassy. Ineptitude could not go farther: this death, as we shall see later, occurred two decades after *Lear* was written, a decade after Shakespeare died!

flows with money,' [1] and after his departure the current gossip was that 'he has done many out of much money, and loud are the lamentations.' [2] The negotiations with the Pope proved fruitless. Clement VIII had reason to distrust the plausible politician if, as is likely, he chanced to recall the part Anthony had planned to play in the Ferrara business three years earlier; and he soon lost whatever initial enthusiasm he may have had for the design of a coalition against the Turks. For whatever cause, at the end of May 1601, he dismissed him abruptly; and the disgruntled envoy left Rome without so much as bidding adieu to his late Persian companions. [3]

Before accompanying him further we must trace briefly the subsequent fortunes of Husayn 'Ali Beg. The Pope remained well disposed towards him. When finally he took his departure (26 May 1601), his retinue had been reduced by three; the butler, the barber, and a secretary had become Roman Catholics. Husayn had reasoned with them, but finding them steadfast in their new convictions he left them behind at Rome. [4] Provided with funds from the Pope, the remainder of the party of Persians proceeded overland to Spain. What happened there in the course of negotiations with King Philip III has no bearing on our subject. When Husayn sailed from Lisbon for Persia in 1602 it was with a retinue reduced by one more convert to Roman Catholicism—Uluch Beg, henceforth to be known as Don Juan of Persia. No trustworthy record has come down of the remainder of Husayn's career. Anthony Nixon's story of his miserable fate is almost certainly a fabrication. It is to the effect that Husayn brought before the Shah accusations against Anthony Sherley which Robert Sherley convincingly refuted, whereupon Abbas commanded that Husayn's hands be lopped off and his tongue cut out; and when this was done and the Shah asked Robert 'what he would have more done unto him,' Robert replied that 'that which was already done, was more than he was willing or consenting to' and entreated for the poor

1 *Hatfield MSS*, xi,264.
2 *C.S.P., Venetian*, iv,462.
3 *Don Juan of Persia*, p.286.
4 Ibid. For details of their further wanderings in Europe see Uluch Beg's narrative.

wretch the boon of a speedy death. The Shah then had Husayn's head chopped off.[1]

On quitting Rome[2] about the beginning of June 1601, Anthony travelled incognito for fear of assassination by some Turk or Levantine Jew. 'Except the Pope himself, no man knoweth whither I am gone,' he wrote. With but four gentlemen accompanying him he crossed Italy in haste and at Ancona prepared to embark upon a frigate provided for him by the Pope. His destination was Persia, as he wrote to Anthony Bacon. During his absence 'certain Portugals' had been attempting to supplant him in the Shah's favour, an untoward development 'which hath drawn me back thither with all speed.' His letter is a pathetic one: he mourns for his 'dear and unhappy Lord' (Essex); he has 'infinite burdens' upon him; the failure of England to appreciate the opportunity he has won by opening Persia to commerce astonishes him.[3]

He crossed the Adriatic to Ragusa but returned to Ancona, nor did he sail for the Levant or ever see Persia again. The change in plans was perhaps due to fear of the Turks, or perhaps he had warning from his brother Robert that he was no longer *persona grata* in Isfahan. The following September he was reported to be at the Spanish court with a Persian colleague. Had he rejoined Husayn 'Ali Beg? It seems unlikely, and our doubts are increased when the informant adds: 'He is come concerning a treaty of peace with the Turk'—an inconceivable errand for Anthony to be upon.[4] For the next year and a half his movements are difficult to trace. On 3 March 1602, he was at Venice, whence he dispatched a letter of warm appeal to Sir Robert Cecil, repudiating the slanders of 'merchants' (that is, the Levant Company or the old Muscovy Company) for whom he claims to have opened 'so great a way of profit.' 'If I have deserved punishment,' he continues, 'I will

1 [Anthony Nixon,] *The Three English Brothers*, 1607, Sig. I₃.
2 Sir E. Denison Ross, who has not utilized in his *Sir Anthony Sherley* the sources of information regarding the sojourn in Rome upon which the present account is in part based, quotes (pp.47f.) from the *Lettres* of Cardinal d'Ossat to Henri IV and M. de Villeroy (Paris, 1624) five interesting passages on the quarrel of the envoys, the audiences with the Pope, and gossip about Sherley's projects.
3 *Hatfield MSS*, ix,215f.
4 *C.S.P.,Dom., 1601–3*, p.100.

lay myself at the feet of Her Majesty's ministers to receive it. I am reported to be banished, and proclaimed traitor.' 'I will not,' he assures Cecil, 'beg for myself the reputation of disclosing the counsels of men about things which are now acted' —a cryptic sentence which appears to mean that he will not claim merit on the score of having communicated to the English government the secret plots of foreign states.[1] Possibly the disclosures to which he refers had to do with the Spanish landing in Ireland in 1601, of which he may have heard from the Jesuits in Rome. If so, the fact that the information was derived from the Jesuits would count more heavily against him than the fact that it was communicated to the English ministers would weigh in his favour; he was judged by the company he kept. This is probably the reason why he told his nephew Anthony Tracy, whom he met at this time, that he was 'much disturbed to hear that his honest endeavours should be so sinisterly judged.'[2] His great concern at the moment seems to have been to refute the allegation of being an agent of Spain.

This accusation was now brought against him by Thomas Wilson, the secret agent with whom he had had an altercation at Rome. Wilson's charge was that Sherley had written to King James of Scotland about plots against his accession which were being fomented in England, and that Sherley had urged James to come to an understanding with Spain in order to secure the succession to the English throne. Wilson added that he had urged the Venetian authorities to arrest Sherley for plotting against Elizabeth but that they had refused to do so. His own belief was that Sherley was working with 'the viper of Rome' (by which he intends Father Parsons) to form a conjunction between James VI and King Philip of Spain.[3]

At this time Anthony was going in danger of his life. In June 1602, he was assaulted one midnight and fell over a bridge into a canal.[4] Who attacked him—whether Turkish agent or English intelligencer or Italian bravo—is not clear. In July he wrote a pitiable letter in which he complains alliter-

1 Ibid., p.159.   2 Ibid.
3 E.P.Shirley, op.cit., p.40, citing three letters from Wilson, 23 June, 3 July, and 9 August 1602.
4 Ibid.; reported by Simon Fox, an English intelligencer.

atively of 'the manifold miserys which my fortune and mallyce multipliethe uppon me'; of the indigence and defamations from which he has suffered; and especially of the persecutions of 'a fellar of a vyle occupation one wyllsonne anne Intelligencer.' He protests against the rejection of his 'humillyty,' the disregard of his 'beseetching,' and the 'intollerable injurys' which may at length drive him into disloyalty.[1]

In the following spring his troubles reached a climax. On 5 March 1603, there arrived at Venice a magnificent Persian mission headed by a certain Fethy Beg.[2] Their object was to revive and strengthen the commercial alliance between the two states; and as usual fine gifts were presented, among them a piece of embroidery which the Senate ordered to be displayed in Saint Mark's on feast-days and which is still, though now in a ruined condition, preserved in the sacristy of the Duomo. To commemorate further this embassage the Senate commissioned Gabriele Caliari to paint a picture of the reception of the Persians by the Doge Marino Grimani. This painting is still on the wall of the Sala delle Quattro Porte in the Ducal Palace.[3]

Shortly after the arrival of this mission the Venetian authorities placed Sherley under arrest 'for the insult to the Persian merchant's house.'[4] The nature of the offence and the precise occasion of it are not in the record, but the incentive is obvious, for the coming of these Persians and the reception accorded them must have mortified and enraged Anthony because they cast discredit upon his claim to represent the Shah. Since his health was bad it was judged consonant with mercy to allot him ample quarters in a new prison, but he was held *incommunicado*, so out of reach of inquiry, indeed, that English residents did not know whether he was alive or dead.[5] The pernicious activities of his brother Thomas (which have been related in Chapter IV) strengthened prejudice against him, and

1 Ibid., pp.38f.
2 Berchet, *La Repubblica di Venezia e la Persia*, pp.44f.
3 The merchants and officials in the foreground of this painting are examining not a sample of Persian stuff, as one might expect, but a piece of Italian velvet. Either the artist made a blunder or else, for the greater glory of Venice, he intentionally depicted the orientals admiring the beauty of occidental workmanship and material.
4 The records upon which is based this account of Sherley's experiences in Venice, March 1603–December 1604, are in *C.S.P., Venetian*, x,1,2,8,23,29,34,72,88,100,195.
5 Reported by Simon Fox, 27 April 1603; E.P.Shirley, op.cit., p.41.

the possibility was investigated that he had shared in Thomas's booty got by robbing a Venetian ship. Apparently he was found innocent of all specific charges, yet an undesirable alien, for it was ultimately voted to release him under orders to leave Venetian territory within eight days; 'nor is he ever to return upon pain of our indignation.' Upon receiving this decree of expulsion Anthony wrote to Cecil re-affirming his innocence; [1] and 'from a heart full of anguish' he poured out an impassioned *apologia* to Chief Justice Popham. 'I am now in the utmost extremity,' he wrote. [2]

And then his fortunes took a turn for the better. A physician's certificate that he was suffering from the stone and that travel would be fatal to him won for him permission to remain in Venice another three months. Just at this time Queen Elizabeth died and James I ascended the English throne. As a member of the Essex faction who continued to support James's claim to the succession after their leader's execution, Anthony enjoyed the new monarch's favour. It was probably in response to a request from Sherley that in 1601 James had addressed a Latin letter to Shah Abbas in which he outlined the state of English politics, explaining that the Shah could count on no aid from England at the moment and that he had advised Sherley to stay quietly abroad, and hinting that on his own accession international policy might change. [3] This well-meant letter could not have helped Sherley with the Shah. Why await the death of a Queen whose ambassador he had claimed to be before he could bring his labours to fruition?

Sherley could not know that after the death of Essex James had entered into secret communication with Sir Robert Cecil, the late Earl's arch-enemy. From Cecil the King of Scotland had received warnings to distrust Sherley's pretensions and machinations, Cecil being inclined to suspect him of conspiring with Spain regarding the English succession. James's response to Cecil came indirectly in the form of a letter from Edward Bruce, one of the Scotch envoys in London, to Lord Henry

1 *C.S.P.,Dom.*, *1601-3*, p.159. See also *Hatfield MSS*, xii,442.
2 *C.S.P.,Dom.*, *1601-3*, pp.223f.,236. In E.P.Shirley, op.cit., p.36, the letter to Popham is misdated 1601.
3 E.P.Shirley, op.cit., pp.105f., from the original draft in the Advocates' Library.

The Reception of the Persian Ambassadors
PHOTO. ALINARI

Howard. 'What you wreat of sir anthnie scheurly may well be trewe in a man so ambitius, so much crossed in the way to hes preferment and honor'—that is, it would not be surprising if disappointments led him into desperate courses. Nevertheless Bruce saw no grounds for suspecting him of taking part in any plot with Spain. Far from conspiring about English affairs, Sherley was absorbed in Persian politics:

> It is all percian he hes spoken unto us, and all papers from him to m. antonie [Anthony Bacon] during hes abood in persia were farsed wyth no thing but occurrants in that great kingdome, all utterly unprofitable to this poor state.

The bewilderment of a Scotch official who knew nothing of oriental affairs is discernible in this sentence. Then Bruce says that King James has heard again from Sherley, whose letter was

> the image of hes ouen fortune and what disasters had happened unto hem in hes jowrnay, but of the state of england or Spaine we never had advertisement frome hem.

By way of final assurance Bruce says that King James 'had never so muche accompte of hem as yow suppose' and did not believe that he was employed by Spain, which had 'many fitter agents.' [1] The allusion in this carefully guarded language is evidently to Spanish efforts to advance the pretensions of the Infanta to the English succession; James refuses to believe that Sherley is involved in that intrigue.

The new sovereign, then, was well disposed towards Anthony even though he did not accept his own estimate of his worth. To old Sir Thomas Sherley he granted an audience, and the father went down upon his knees and begged the King to use his influence on behalf of his two sons: Thomas, a prisoner in Constantinople, and Anthony living in Venice under the shadow of a decree of expulsion. The result was that, as we have seen in Chapter IV, James secured from the Porte the release of the younger Sir Thomas Sherley; and he bestirred himself on

1 *Correspondence of King James VI of Scotland with Sir Robert Cecil*, ed. John Bruce, Camden Society, 1851, pp.40f. The letter is undated but is of 1601 or 1602. King James is referred to by a code number.

Anthony's behalf. Though Cecil urged the Italian envoy in London to speak candidly to his Majesty about Anthony's behaviour in Venice, James assured this envoy that he held Anthony in high esteem, that he had been wrongfully persecuted by the anti-Essex faction, and that he would consider it a favour to himself if the Venetian government dealt mercifully with him.[1] Whereupon the Signory revoked the decree of expulsion. The King's interest did not stop here. Sherley now won a somewhat less ambiguous status on the continent. Hitherto he had travelled as the Shah's emissary. Now he received a document from King James styled 'a license to remain beyond the seas,' roughly equivalent to a passport except that it did not carry permission to return home. If not a full endorsement, it was at any rate a *carte d'identité* and served to show that he was not without some protection from his own country.[2]

Till the close of 1604 he seems to have remained in Venice. What brought him again into difficulties with the Venetian government is not in the record; it is a safe guess that he was still meddling with affairs of state.[3] What is known is that in December 1604, 'for important public reasons' his expulsion from Venetian territory was peremptorily decreed, 'upon pain of death, never to return.'[4]

And so his wanderings began again. In June 1605, on an invitation from the Emperor, he was in Prague to assist in negotiations relative to Persia. This visit brought him into contact with a part of the Mohammedan world not hitherto

---

1 *C.S.P., Venetian, 1603–5*, p.34.   2 *C.S.P.,Dom., 1603–10*, p.76.
3 Sherley's relations with the Jesuits had become very intimate and confidential. In 1604 rumours were current on the continent that King James was intending to declare his adherence to the Roman Catholic Church. There was a certain English priest, a Doctor Whorwelle, Canon of Vicenza, who claimed to have authority from England to negotiate on questions of religion and who obtained an audience with the Pope. It is probable that conversations with his Holiness had to do with the report of James's coming conversion. Clement seems to have placed no credence in him (*C.S.P., Venetian*, x,306). For this priest Sherley tried to obtain from Cecil a guarantee of safety during a proposed visit to England for the purpose of communicating secret information to King James (E.P.Shirley, op.cit., pp.46f.). The secret had probably to do with one of the various rumoured Jesuit plots to overthrow the English government. Sherley's motive in this activity was doubtless to ingratiate himself at home; but on such matters Cecil was well informed by his own agents and he ignored Sherley's request.
4 *C.S.P., Venetian*, x,195.

known to him, for the Emperor employed him on a mission to Morocco. In line with his old anti-Turkish policy, Sherley's intention was to observe conditions in the Barbary States and report upon the feasibility of stirring up a movement there to cast off political allegiance to the Porte (thus foreshadowing what actually came about some twenty years later). That King James approved of this scheme is shown by the fact that he provided Anthony with a letter authorizing him to collect funds from English merchants in Morocco. With a characteristic ability to serve several masters at once, Sherley carried with him fourteen thousand ducats furnished by Austrian horse-dealers for the purchase of Arab horses.[1]

Having embarked at Genoa, Sherley was forced by storms to put into Alicante. There he abandoned his much damaged ship and travelled overland to Cadiz [2] whence he sailed to Saffee on the Atlantic coast of Morocco, arriving there on 2 October 1605.[3]

At this time Muley Bu Faris, or Muley Boferes as he was known in England, was head of the Sa'adian dynasty and Sharif of Morocco. He was engaged in a civil war against his brothers Muley Sheck (Shaykh) and Muley Zedan (Zidan). Of that struggle we shall hear more in a later chapter. There is a vividly circumstantial account of Anthony's bearing and behaviour in Morocco in the *True Historicall Discourse of Muley Hamets Rising* (1609), by 'Ro.C.' (Robert Chambers), a black-letter quarto whose long title includes the promise of *the Adventures of Sir Anthony Sherley, and divers other English Gentlemen, in those Countries.* [4] Anthony's retinue impressed this writer as 'better than a private man' but scarcely worthy of an imperial ambassador. He had with him, however, 'thir-

---

1 Henri de Castries, *Sources inedites de l'histoire du Maroc. Première Série*, II, i (Paris, 1906), i,275 (quoting a letter from the representative of the Low Countries in Morocco).

2 'What the Intention of their Journey is I cannot learne, but thought first instantly to advertise it.' Thus Sir Charles Cornwallis, the English ambassador to Spain, to the Earl of Salisbury (Cecil). See *Memorials of Affairs of State in the Reigns of Elizabeth and James I . . . from the . . . Papers of Sir Ralph Winwood*, 1725, ii,143 [hereafter referred to as *Winwood Memorials*].

3 Letter (in Italian) from Sherley to the Emperor Rudolph, dated Saffee, 5 October 1605, *C.S.P.,Dom., 1598–1601*, p.371.

4 Chapter xi, Sig. E₂f. In condensed form in Purchas, vi,81f. The book is reprinted in full by H.de Castries, op.cit., *Première Série*, III (Paris, 1925), ii,318f.

teen persons, of every Christian language one, because he would be fitted for interpretation of tongues.' He spent lavishly, his munificence and prodigality making a great impression on the Moors. He kept open house where Christian merchants were made welcome daily. But he also behaved with much arrogance and on one occasion went so far as to ride on horseback through the council-chamber of the palace—an indiscretion which stirred up much trouble.

Sherley urged upon Muley Boferes the desirability of a league against the Turks; but the Sharif was sufficiently occupied with the task of coping with his own brothers, and nothing was accomplished.[1] The Sharif may, however, have said something which awakened in Sherley the hope of negotiating a commercial treaty between Morocco and Spain, for not long afterwards we find him engaged in this business. Before leaving Morocco in September 1606, he redeemed from captivity two Portuguese whom he took with him to Lisbon. There were those who believed that his story of their redemption was false, a mere hoax to obtain money; the two men denied the debt; and Sherley, having failed to persuade the authorities in Lisbon to reimburse him for the outlay, spent much time later in Spain in efforts to obtain redress. It is pleasant to note that the English consul in Lisbon commended his 'honourable carriage' and his kindness to his fellow-countrymen; specifically, his labours to procure the enlargement of an English merchant who had been imprisoned by the Inquisition.[2] Such favourable notices by English agents abroad are rare in the history of Anthony's career.

It now becomes increasingly difficult to disentangle the confused web of his fortunes. The plunges from high to low estate and the sudden rebounds occur with bewildering frequency. But the periodical elevations in his luck are gradually less and less high and the general trend is a sinking in the scale of consequence. Often almost exactly contemporary evi-

1 A letter from Sherley to the Emperor Rudolph's secretary, dated from Saffee, 10 December 1605, fell into Salisbury's hands; see E.P.Shirley, op.cit., pp.51f. In language so pompously rhetorical as to be almost incomprehensible it reports his progress, or rather his failure to make progress.
2 Hugh Lee to Salisbury, 8 September 1606; E.P.Shirley, op.cit., p.53. The episode of the English merchant is also mentioned by Nixon, op.cit., Sig. Kf.

dence is contradictory. Thus, on 14 March 1607, it is reported from Madrid that he is 'in great credit and reputation' and expecting 'more gifts and honours,' [1] while on 31 March the English ambassador writes that he is supported only by the Jesuits at whose college he is living while his attendants have not sixpence for their support.[2] Of his close affiliation with the Jesuits there can be no question. Significant is a document, undated but certainly of this period, sent to Anthony by a Jesuit, unnamed but assuredly Anthony Creswell, which contains instructions as to how to comport himself in the difficult task of adjusting his religious to his political loyalty.[3] Ultimately loyalty to England was sacrificed. His position in Spain was a curious one, for while the English ambassador tried to discredit him with the Spanish government the latter was naturally suspicious of English representations and inclined to regard favourably an English Catholic out of favour with his own government.

In this year, 1607, Anthony Nixon, a pamphleteer who was probably hired by the Sherleys to write in their interest, published his *Three English Brothers*.[4] He pictures Anthony in Spain as 'not desirous to bury his thoughts in the delights of the Court' but earnest to promote his public policies, exerting himself, indeed, to 'redeem' his brother from Persia (which shows that Robert was definitely regarded as a hostage) but anxious chiefly, as ever, 'to restore Religion to those unhappy conquered kingdomes by the Turkes, where now the holy Churches and sanctified Temples of our Saviour are changed to be idolatrous places of the blasphemous Synagogue of Mahomet.' Somewhat disingenuously, since he must have known that Anthony was forbidden to re-enter England, Nixon wonders how he has been able to restrain the natural desire to return home; but he explains that Sherley refuses to sacrifice his public work to private feeling and therefore continues to labour to make good his promise to the Sophy to stir up the

---

1 E.P.Shirley, op.cit., p.65.   2 Ibid., p.67.
3 *C.S.P.,Dom., 1598–1602*, p.372. This document is incorrectly calendared, the editor dating it 1598 with a query. It commends Sherley for liberating the Portuguese and is therefore of 1606 or 1607.
4 See p.174, note 4, above.

minds and powers of kings against the House of Ottoman. 'There is a great hope and expectancie,' Nixon concludes, 'in short time to see a sodain darkning and eclipse of that glaring beautie and outstretched bounds of the Turkish Empire.' [1]

Cornwallis, the English ambassador at Madrid, provides us with a contrasting portrait.[2] Sherley, fresh from North Africa, seems to have relegated to the background his old design of an anti-Turkish league and to have concentrated his efforts upon the limited but more practicable plan of obtaining for Spain a port of entry into Morocco. 'He came,' wrote Cornwallis, 'to offer projects for Barbarie'; but Spain, having her hands full elsewhere (that is, with the Dutch), 'gave no ease to these Overtures.' Sherley therefore turned to another project; or, as Cornwallis, resorting somewhat surprisingly to a metaphor from the *Decameron*, puts it: 'Instead of Shewing forth the Feathers that the Angell Gabriell had in his Wings when he was sent to salute our Lady, he offereth now for as holy a Relique, the Coales whereon St. Lawrence was broyled.' In other words, Anthony, no more trustworthy than a pedlar of relics, became 'very earnest . . . to intrude himself' in the business of the proposed 'French marriage.' We need not follow him into this intrigue; it has nothing to do with our subject and he played no part of importance in it.

Successive dispatches to Venice repeat gossip about his activities. The Spanish government temporizes, their policy being to 'feed him on fair promises.' He is living 'in great splendour,' though who furnishes the wherewithal is a mystery. 'He goes on taking everyone in.' He has been forced to reduce his style of living and 'not much attention is paid to him.' The Venetian ambassador is doing everything possible to discredit him.[3]

But Anthony's persuasiveness and plausibility had not yet abandoned him. At an opportune moment came a message from Shah Abbas guaranteeing Sherley's good faith;[4] and what helped him even more was the news that his brother Robert,

---

1 *The Three English Brothers*, Sig. I₄f.   2 *Winwood Memorials*, ii,273f.
3 *C.S.P., Venetian*, xi,498,437,478,458,418 (in the order of the quotations).
4 Ibid., x,413 and compare xi,32.

provided with credentials of unimpeachable authenticity, had set out as the Shah's new ambassador to Europe. On 20 March 1607, Anthony received a commission from Philip III to be 'general of all his Commands' because of his experience in marine service; was directed to 'infest the common enemies of Christendom, the Turks and Moors'; and was authorized also to employ his forces against the Dutch but not against the English or Venetians.[1] He was granted an increase of salary and on him was conferred the title of Count (henceforth he is often referred to as Count Sherley); and he was appointed 'General of the Galleons of the Kingdom of Naples.'[2]

Anthony à Wood says that Anthony's 'greatness' after receiving these honours and appointments aroused the jealousy of King James, who 'sent for him to return; but he refused to come, and therefore was numbered among the English Fugitives.'[3] It is unlikely that James summoned him home, but his acceptance of a foreign naval command marks his complete severance from his native country.

With his new title—equivalent to that of admiral—Sherley set about his new business. He sent a faithful follower, one Jeremy Lawrence, into England for the purpose (it was said, but this may have been an idle rumour, for nothing more is heard of the matter) 'to drawe Shipps out of England to serve . . . in the Levant Seas against the Turks and Hollanders.'[4] Plans hung fire for a long while; and Cornwallis wrote satirically of the repeated postponements. Sherley's 'harvest,' the ambassador remarked, 'proves not suitable to his spring . . . A cunning Juggler tarries not long upon his Tricks, least Tyme and Visibility discover what Legerdemaine seeks to drawe into Obscurity and Marvayle . . . I suppose,' he adds, 'Cresswel many times wisheth, that he had not meddled with the Scrutiny of such a Conscyence.'[5] A few weeks later Cornwallis again wrote:

1 E.P.Shirley, op.cit., p.65. The report implies that Sherley held supreme command, which is of course an exaggeration.
2 C.S.P., Venetian, xi,31.
3 Athenae Oxonienses, i,551.
4 Cornwallis to Salisbury, 3 May 1607; Winwood Memorials, ii,307.
5 Ibid., ii,308.

Creswell with much labour and sweate of his Browe, hath in Conclusion cleared his Ghostly Childe Sir Anthony Sherley out of this Towne; though with so great an Aspertion of evil Fame, as much of the same hath fallen upon his own Clothes.[1]

After Anthony's departure frauds committed by him—or perhaps one should say more fairly (for the report is from a hostile source), frauds charged against him—were exposed and his arrest was ordered.[2] These accusations may have been baseless; at all events they were hushed up or let drop.

In July 1607, Sherley was at Naples. There he got into communication with the notorious English pirate John Ward, sending 'letters unto him to disswade him from this detestable life'; but Ward was a desperate man and refused to trust any assurances.[3] This exchange of messages was, however, the beginning of negotiations with the object of inducing some at least of the Barbary corsairs to take part in an attack on Turkey. In this same summer Anthony addressed a request to the Venetian Signory for permission to pass, en route to Prague, through their territories (from which, it will be remembered, he had been excluded by decree).[4] The request was granted and Sherley arrived; but Sir Henry Wotton, now English envoy at Venice, protested vigorously, warning the Signory that it was 'to be presumed that Sherley nourishes some evil designs' because of his association with the Jesuit Anthony Creswell. The Signory took alarm and ordered Sherley to depart at once. What he accomplished at Prague is not on record. Later he was in Milan; and then at Genoa he was supposed to be organizing a squadron with the design to ferret out the English and Dutch pirates from their lairs on the Barbary coast.[5] To recruit his forces he is said to have offered bribes and promised booty to English sailors of the mercantile marine if they would desert to him.[6] That he was not

---

1 Ibid., ii,312. See ibid., ii,318f. for Sherley's suspicious efforts to see the exiled Earl of Bothwell before leaving Madrid.
2 C.S.P., Venetian, xi,21.
3 Newes from Sea, Of two notorious Pyrates Ward the Englishman and Danseker the Dutchman, 1609, Sig. C.
4 C.S.P., Venetian, xi,25,31,35,40.
5 Ibid., xi,51,206.   6 E.P.Shirley, op.cit., p.67.

entirely cut off from communication with his own country is proved by references, in a letter to his sister Lady Tracy, to meetings with friends and relatives travelling on the continent.[1] He returned to Spain in the summer of 1608. At this time, through an emissary whom the King of Spain sent to Persia, Sherley had some success in persuading Shah Abbas to divert the annual consignment of silk for the European markets from the land-route via Aleppo to the way by sea from Ormuz to Lisbon.[2]

But in general his projects became ever more fantastic. The sardonic Cornwallis reported that, 'finding his first projected inventions not of Strength to draw Money out of so dry a Purse'—that is, being unable to extract funds from the Spanish treasury for an expedition against the corsairs, he had 'lately made much discourse of the King's [James I's] planting in Virginia, and [had] given many Reasons of the evile Consequences like to follow it, yf by this Estate [Spain] it be not prevented.'[3] This is evidence of open hostility to his native country. A few weeks later Cornwallis writes that there are 'many larks in his net' but 'as yet none come to his hand'; and in January 1609, the same writer reports that Sherley has in his employ a cunning counterfeiter of jewels, so that when other resources fail him he can still by these means keep himself in greatness[4]—probably irresponsible slander but casting a sinister light upon Anthony's reputation.

Meanwhile communications of some sort had been maintained with Captain Ward; and Father Creswell had been in touch with the Dutch buccaneer Simon Danziker, Ward's partner at times and at times his rival, trying to persuade him to serve at sea under Sherley. The depredations of the Barbary corsairs were at their worst in this year, alarming the English government greatly; and it must have given Cornwallis much satisfaction to be able to announce in April that 'the ayerye Hopes that Sir Anthonie Sherley and his Confident Cresswell the Jesuite have given here of reducing these Rovers to his

1 Ibid., pp.67f. The letter is signed 'Il Conde Don Antonio Sherley.'
2 Ross, op.cit., pp.69f., citing the Portuguese edition of Antonio de Gouvea's *Relation*, 1611.
3 *Winwood Memorials*, ii,439.   4 E.P.Shirley, op.cit., p.70.

Servyce . . . are much cooled yf not whollie quenched.' In the same letter he informs the Privy Council that the real fear is that Ward and Danziker will make an alliance not against but with the Turks. With this letter went a copy of an intercepted communication from Creswell to Danziker which declared that if any Christian prince whose subjects have been despoiled by Danziker complain that this pirate was 'entertayned and patronized' by Spain, the Spanish King was prepared to excuse himself by saying that the thing was done 'without his Privity' by Sherley.[1] In other words, Sherley's Spanish employers were ready to repudiate him if and when international complications made it politic to do so.

The story of the Spanish attack upon the pirates belongs to a later chapter; here we are concerned only with Sherley's part in this affair. Though he seems to have reckoned upon being given the supreme command of the Spanish fleet, his actual share in the enterprise was slight and disappointing. The truce with Holland (April 1609) enabled Philip III to embark upon a more active program to suppress the corsairs. The galleons of the main ocean squadron were sent into the Mediterranean in June 1609, with the intention of effecting a combination with the squadron which Sherley was then assembling in Sicily.[2] But the main Spanish fleet, under Admiral Fijardo, by some mischance failed to make this contact; and equally by accident met with some French privateers commanded by the Sieur de Beaulieu. In the subsequent combined attack upon La Goletta in Tunis, which resulted in the destruction of more than thirty vessels belonging to Ward and other pirates, Sherley had no share of fighting or booty or reputation. Beyond doubt this was due not to cowardly reluctance but to bad luck and mismanagement.

His mortification can be imagined, and the rage and restiveness of the cut-throat crews lured to his ships by promises of plunder. He maintained headquarters for some months at Messina, his fleet undisciplined and 'very badly commanded,'

---

1 *Winwood Memorials*, iii,15, and compare ibid., iii,39; see also *C.S.P., Venetian*, xi,385.
2 J.S.Corbett, *England in the Mediterranean*, 1904, i,19f.; *Cambridge Modern History*, iii,54. See p.358, below.

himself regarded as little better than a pirate.[1] He enlarged his fleet in a high-handed manner, seizing ships without re-munerating their owners.[2] In the autumn he came to a new decision: since he had lost the opportunity to take part in the attack on the Barbary pirates, he would wage war on his own account against his old arch-enemy, the Turk. 'Yf I dy I will dye welle,' he wrote to his father.[3] He was destined neither to die well nor to live well. Sailing eastward with eight galleons and some smaller ships, he was reported in the Ægean towards the close of the year ruthlessly harrying the poor Greeks of the islands.[4] As we discern his temper through the mists of three centuries it seems a compound of mortified pride, wounded self-esteem, and something akin to despair.

Early in 1610 he returned westward and was at Barcelona, apparently without ships or followers. There a fresh humilia-tion awaited him. For some months he had been in communica-tion with his younger brother, now a famous ambassador, and he seems to have planned to meet him at Barcelona; but, if the report be true, Robert 'did not stay to see him.' [5] When they met in Madrid in 1611 it was to quarrel bitterly, as we shall see in the next chapter.

'Extreme poor both in purse and reputation,' he returned to Madrid. The description is from the pen of Francis Cotting-ton, the new English envoy, who adds: 'These people do begin much to despise him.' [6] Then he sojourned for a time at Gra-nada, consorting with the Earl of Bothwell and other exiled English malcontents.[7] It must have been about this time that he occupied himself with the composition of his *apologia*, the *Relation of his Travels into Persia*.[8] The manuscript of this

1 *C.S.P.*, *Venetian*, xi,417,435.
2 Francis Cottington to Salisbury, 3 November 1609, E.P.Shirley, op.cit., p.71. Cottington was the successor of Cornwallis at Madrid.
3 From Palermo, 9 September 1609, ibid., p.71.
4 *C.S.P.*, *Venetian*, xi,440,466.
5 Cottington, 10 January 1611, *Winwood Memorials*, iii,250.
6 22 February 1611, E.P.Shirley, op.cit., p.75.
7 Digby to Salisbury, 9 August and 2 October 1611, ibid., p.87.
8 *Sir Antony Sherley His Relation of his Travels into Persia. The Dangers, and Distresses, which befell him in his passage, both by sea and land and his strange and unexpected deliverances. His Magnificent Entertainment in Persia, his Honourable imployment there-hence, as Embassadour to the Princes of Christendome, the cause of his disap-pointment therein, with his advice to his brother, Sir Robert Sherley, Also, A True Relation of the Great Magnificence, Valour, Prudence, Justice, Temperance, and other*

work was probably taken to London by Sir Robert Sherley in 1611, and there it was published in 1613. When reprinted in abridged form by Samuel Purchas, the editor introduced the narrative with an amusing gloss:

> This summary is . . . in his own words, but many things which pertain rather to his mind than body's travels, in discourse of causes, etc., are left out not for want of worth but of room: this work [the *Pilgrimes*] looking another way. The studious may read the Author himself; the History we have extracted.[1]

The author puts a somewhat severe strain upon the studious, for his book is difficult and dull reading. As would be expected, a large amount of space, more than half the book, is devoted to a history of the reign of Shah Abbas and to the project of an alliance between Persia and the Christian states. What Purchas deleted is that which Sherley doubtless reckoned the most valuable portion of his book. In its complete form the 'relation of travel' is interrupted from time to time with arguments to justify his procedure in every crisis of his career and with sententious disquisitions and aphorisms on kingship, on the principles of statecraft, on the causes of the downfall of princes and ambassadors, on the interrelation of nations, on the virtues necessary to him who would take part in public life, and on similar matters. To emphasize the importance of these observations they are often printed in italic type. Most of them are commonplaces elaborately phrased. They obscure the narrative sadly. But the sympathetic reader will remember that the book was composed in forlorn circumstances by a proud man whose armour of self-esteem had been dinted by the buffets of fortune.

Spain had little further use for him.[2] A pension of two or three thousand ducats a year was allowed him, but the greater

---

manifold vertues of ABAS, now King of Persia, with his great Conquests, whereby he hath inlarged his Dominions. Penned by S^r. Antony Sherley, and recommended to his brother, S^r. Robert Sherley, being now in prosecution of the like Honourable Imployment.—The portrait of Sherley which serves as the frontispiece had been issued separately in 1612 and does not occur in all copies of the *Relation*.

1 Purchas, viii,375f.

2 It has been thought that he was perhaps employed in the rough and ignominious task of aiding in the expulsion of the Moriscos from Spain (Corbett, op.cit., i,20); but there seems to be no contemporary evidence to support this conjecture and in

LEGATVS ✳ ANTON ✳ SCHERLEYNS ANGL ✳ EQ ✳ AVRAT ✳ MAG ✳ SOPH ✳ PERSAR ✳ AD ✳ CÆSAREM ✳ &

ANTONI *Orator Persæ, Angliæ, regis, ad istud*
Excelso munus peruenis ingenio.

Sir Anthony Sherley

part of it was applied to his debts, 'some small portion being assigned unto him to keep him only from starving.' [1] In 1619 the design was on foot to persuade or force him to live in the Canary Islands so that the Spanish government 'would be free of his daily begging and importunities.' Cottington, who reports this, describes Anthony at that time as 'a very poor man, and much neglected, sometimes like to starve for want of bread.'

> The poor man comes sometimes to my house, and is as full of vanity as ever he was, making himself believe that he shall one day be a great Prince, when for the present he wants shoes to wear.[2]

There is another picture of him about this time in James Wadsworth's curious book *The English Spanish Pilgrime*. Wadsworth came to Spain after he had been redeemed by a French merchant from slavery in Morocco. He became a Jesuit and moved freely in the circle of English Roman Catholics living in exile. In later life, 'newly converted into his true mothers bosome, the Church of England' (as his title-page announces), he wrote his book to 'lay open' the Jesuits and to depict 'the state and demeanour of the English fugitives.'

> First and formost [he writes] S. Anthony Shurley, who stiles him-selfe Earle of the sacred Roman Empire, and hath from his Cath-olick Majesty a pension of 2000. duckets *per annum*, all which in respect of his prodigality is as much as nothing. This S. Anthony Shurley is a great plotter and projector in matters of State, and undertakes by sea-stratagems to invade and ruinate his native country, a just treatise of whose passages would take up a whole volume.[3]

any case such an activity would have been at a somewhat earlier stage in his career. He is not mentioned in *Newes from Spaine. The King of Spaine's edict for the expulsion of Moores*, 1611. That his advice was still occasionally sought is shown by a document lately brought to light in which we learn that he was consulted as to the means to thwart Sir Walter Ralegh's plans in Guiana. In a letter commenting upon this document Sherley offered his 'life and labour' to carry out 'the plan that I wot of' (V.T.Harlow, *Ralegh's Last Voyage*, 1932, p.141. Compare Ross, op.cit., pp.82f.).

1 Archbishop Abbot to Sir Thomas Roe, 20 January 1617, *C.S.P.,Dom., 1611–18*, p.429.
2 12 December 1619, E.P.Shirley, op.cit., p.87.
3 *The English Spanish Pilgrime, or, A New Discoverie of Spanish Popery, And Jesuiticall Stratagems. With the estate of the English Pentioners and Fugitives under the King of Spaines Dominions*, 1630, p.62. On Wadsworth see further pp.381–2, below.

There are one or two indications that Anthony was not completely forgotten in England. Ben Jonson may have had him in mind when he wrote his harsh epigram on 'Captain Hungry,' a *miles gloriosus* who even while eating a meal provided by public charity boasts of his influence with the Emperor, of his travels, of the states he has gulled, and of his public pension. He has done service and gone on embassies to countries so far away that

> there must more sea and land be leap'd,
> If but to be believed you have the hap,
> Than can a flea at twice skip in the map.[1]

It is conceivable that the anonymous author of *Two Wise Men and All the Rest Fooles* (1619) had Sherley in view as one of his models when he drew the character of the far-travelled Seigneur Antonio.[2]

But little remains to be told. When Robert Sherley visited

1 Epigram cvii, *Works*, ed. Gifford, viii,209f.
2 In 1619 there appeared anonymously, without printer's or bookseller's name, a semi-dramatic piece or series of dialogues, with hardly a trace of plot but quite witty characterization, entitled: *Two Wise Men and all the Rest Fooles: or a Comicall Morall, Censuring the follies of this age, as it hath beene diverse times acted: Anno, 1619* (Reproduced in *Old English Drama, Students' Facsimile Edition*, 1913.) In it there is a character named Anthony, otherwise 'Segnieur Antonio' or 'Sir Antonio.' Fleay argued (*Biographical Chronicle of the English Drama*, ii,333) that this is a satiric portrait of Anthony Munday. Ward (*English Dramatic Literature*, ii,447) thought this probable; but Schelling (*Elizabethan Drama*, ii,257) is doubtful and advances strong arguments against the identification. That the anonymous author knew about the Sherleys is proved by the following passage (pp.22f.,6): 'This Ladie yesterday hath received a book from a friend of hers that went over with Sir Robert Sherley into Persia.' The book is described as having been 'written by a learned Physician decorated by the magnificent order of the Mountebanks there.' We need not bother about the book and its connection with a ribald joke. There is no obvious reason for dragging in Robert Sherley's name. Antonio (pp.2f.) is described as 'a man of extraordinary action and faction . . . hath been beyond seas some leven or twelve yeeres . . . We call him Segnieur Antonio, by reason of his travailes in Italy and other places . . . This Sir Antonio or Anthony . . . hath seene many countries, and learned many strange qualities.' Before he went abroad he was 'very honest, and of good expectation' but now covetousness and the devil have got into him. He lives meagrely; 'his dinners are for the most part ordinary, except foure dayes in the weeke he visits his housekeeping friends.' He is a great quarreller; he 'cavils and wrangles with any man that he deales withall.' He associates with grooms at court, and 'if from them he learne any newes, . . . this carries him scot-free to all the gentlemens houses of his acquaintance.' When subsequently (p.13) Antonio appears on the scene, he is portrayed as unscrupulous in getting money, full of stratagems, and a secret papist. If it be argued that in 1619 Anthony Sherley was living obscurely in Spain, it must be remembered that his brother Robert was then a conspicuous figure in international politics. Ridicule of one brother might be used to discredit the other.

Spain in 1617 on his second diplomatic mission Anthony again quarrelled with him. He was still plotting and projecting in 1625 and 1627.[1] So late as 1636 he was reported to be living privately and in retirement.[2] Then he drops out of sight. The date of his death and his place of burial are alike unknown.

1 E.P.Shirley, op.cit., pp.98f.
2 Ibid., p.100.

CHAPTER SEVEN

'THE GREATEST TRAVELLER IN HIS TIME'

I

MASTER ROBERT SHERLEY, a hostage at the court of Shah Abbas, was in a perilous position where tact and discretion were needed if he was to conserve the goodwill of the capricious despot. He was then in but his twentieth year;[1] but men matured rapidly in those days, and he was soon to distinguish himself on the field of battle, where his valour probably did much to advance his position at Isfahan. His first two years in Persia are a blank; but in 1601 his opportunity came. Shah Abbas then reopened warfare against the Turks who, led by the feeble voluptuary Mahomet III, were defeated in a series of engagements. In one of these, a decisive victory which regained for Persia many districts and towns and especially the sacred city of Kierbela, Robert was wounded.[2] Tales of his prowess lost nothing in the telling by the time they reached England. Anthony Nixon relates how Robert offered to exchange a batch of prisoners for his brother Thomas, then lying in prison in Constantinople. The offer was rejected by the Turkish commander, whereupon Robert delivered a rousing 'Oration to his Soldiers' (which Nixon gives *verbatim*!) and forthwith they plunged into battle, defeating the Turks with great slaughter.[3] Samuel Purchas informs us that in one engagement where Robert was thrice wounded only two thousand Turks remained to fly the field out of a hundred

---

1 The precise date of Robert Sherley's birth is unknown. The engraved portrait described p.306, note 1, below is dated 28 September 1609, and in the thirtieth year of his age. This puts the date of his birth in 1578 or 1579. Father Gouvea (*Relation des Grandes Guerres*, p.102) describes him in 1602 as 'un jeune homme . . . aage de vingt ans ou environ,' probably a slight underestimate. According to Thomas Herbert's reckoning (p.334, note 5, below) Robert was many years older; but either Herbert was misinformed or used the words 'grand clymacterick' in a loose incorrect sense.

2 Sykes, *History of Persia*, ii,178.   3 *The Three English Brothers*, Sig. K₂ᵛ.

and sixty thousand who had issued forth to battle.[1] The numbers are quite incredible, but there is no reason to question the traditions of young Sherley's bravery. Shah Abbas showed his confidence in his guest by placing him in command of a fortified position which dominated the route from eastern Persia to Isfahan. How long he remained there and what he accomplished is uncertain; but the name of Sherley was for long associated with the place, for many years later the traveller John Fryer passed that way and took note that

> here a countryman of ours is remembered to be Governor of a Castle (whose Ruins are still extant) for Shah Abbas the Great, in the beginning of King James the First's Reign; viz. Sir Anthony Sherley, who took Pay under the Emperor to defend this Pass.[2]

(Fryer of course confused Robert with Anthony Sherley; the latter never held any military office in Persia.)

Robert obtained the Shah's approval of his betrothal to a lady who, says Nixon, had 'entered into liking of his worthiness.' According to Nixon, she was a niece or 'cousin Germaine' of the Sophy. More accurately, she was a relative of one of the Shah's wives. Teresa Sanpsonia was of noble Circassian family and a member of the Orthodox Church. The Carmelite missionaries with whom her fortunes were to be so strangely connected remembered and placed on record her beauty and accomplishments, her attainments as a linguist, her courage and robust endurance, her skill in javelin-throwing, and her feats in the hunting field.[3] Thomas Fuller says quaintly of her that 'she had more of Ebony than Ivory in her Complexions; yet amiable enough and very valiant.'[4] There is other testimony to her intelligence and charm. Whatever the claims of the Sherley brothers to be remembered as heroes, there can be no doubt that in Lady Teresa Sherley we have a heroine.

Nixon tells an incredible story of two children by this marriage, born and baptized in Persia, 'the King himselfe

1 'Brief Memoriall of the Travelles of . . . Sir Robert Sherley,' Purchas, x,376.
2 *A New Account of East India and Persia*, Hakluyt Society, ii,231. The fortress was near Ossipus (Asupas) to the north of Persepolis.
3 R.P.Petro-Andrea [Father Pierre de Saint-André], *Historia Generalis Fratrum Discalceatorum Ordinis B.V.Mariae de Monte Carmelo*, Rome, 1668–71, ii,374f.
4 *Worthies*, ii,393.

beeing a witnesse to one of them in Baptisme.' [1] This crass invention forms an incident in the drama on the Sherleys of which an account will be given later, is laughed at by Francis Beaumont, perhaps glanced at by Shakespeare,[2] and is referred to by John Cartwright who, reproving Nixon, writes:

> That he [Robert Sherley] should have a child in Persia, and that the King . . . should bee the God-father; this certainely is more fitte for a Stage, for the common people to wonder at, then for any mans more private studies.[3]

Many years later it was still matter for a joke. Signior Medico Campo, the quack doctor in Randolph's *Aristippus* (1630), boasts:

> I cured Sherley in the grand Sophy's court in Persia, when he had been but twice shot through with ordnance, and had two bullets in each thigh: and so quickly that he was able at night to lie with his wife, the Sophy's niece, and beget a whole church of Christians.[4]

From Nixon came also the tale of how he roused the jealousy and envy of the Persian lords by giving quarter to captives who craved it. There was no such merciful code among the Persians. The combination of 'much Courage and more Mercy' won for Robert the love of the ladies and consequently the envy of the lords. This rivalry forms an incident in the play of *The Travailes of the Three English Brothers*.[5]

There were more serious reasons than this rivalry (if it existed) for making Robert's position in Isfahan increasingly difficult and even dangerous. Months and then years passed with no satisfactory news of the progress of his brother Anthony's negotiations at the European courts; and it was but natural that the Shah should come to look with suspicion and unkindness upon the younger brother, especially after he heard that the elder was excluded from his own country which he had claimed to represent as ambassador. Moreover,

---

1 *The Three English Brothers*, Sig. K₄ᵛ.
2 See p.508., below.
3 *The Preachers Travels*, p.70.
4 Thomas Randolph, *Poetical and Dramatic Works*, ed. Hazlitt, p.29.
5 It is also recounted by Thomas Fuller; see p.299, note 4, above.

though the Shah had been planning a renewal of war with Turkey before Anthony's arrival in Persia, the prospect held out by the latter of a European alliance had confirmed him in his warlike resolve. And now it seemed likely that he would have to fight alone, that, as Cartwright put it, 'the whole war was like to lie upon his own neck.' [1]

Anthony Sherley sent letters to his brother when he could arrange for their transmission, but some of them were intercepted [2] and, for all his ability to put a fair complexion upon circumstances, those that reached their destination could not have been very reassuring. Two of Robert's letters to Anthony survive, documents of poignant interest in which is audible a cry of loneliness from this young stranger in a strange land. The first is from Tabriz, 22 May 1605:

> I am almost distracted from the thought of anie helpe for my delivery out of this Countrye . . . I knowe you have likewyse suffered discomodytie in those parts you live in, though they cannot be compared unto myne, consythering I live amongste turkes, infidells, and enymies to the Christian name . . . He [the Shah] publisheth to the world the hatred he bears to the name of Christians . . . He giveth me still the same meanes he was wont: but God knowes yt is in such a Scurvie fashion that I cannot possibly meynteine myself with yt, and it is every yeare *da mal in peggio*.

He goes on to say that long since he would have solicited friends in England for his delivery except for his awareness that Anthony had extolled to the skies the generosity of the Shah's hospitality and the warmth of his regard; and he is unwilling to embarrass Anthony by telling the truth about his circumstances. 'I would rather chose to die coupped up in my myseries, then make a contrarie report.' But, he concludes, if things are not better within a year he will be compelled 'to seeke [his] passadge from hence by some meanes.' He did not carry this warning into execution. Sixteen months later, 10 September 1606, he wrote despairingly, telling Anthony that his large promising 'hath made me be estimed a common

1 *The Preachers Travels*, p.70.
2 On 7 May 1603, Henry Lello forwarded to Cecil letters from Anthony to Robert Sherley which his agents had intercepted (E.P.Shirley, op.cit., pp.56f.).

lyar.' 'Brother,' he exclaims, 'for Gods sake, eather perform, or not promis any thinge!' [1]

And now comfort arrived from an unexpected quarter. In the autumn of 1607 Robert Sherley and his wife, quite out of favour with the Shah, were living precariously in retirement at Kasvin when there came to Persia a party of missionaries of the Carmelite order.[2] Robert's statement about the Shah's hatred of Christians to the contrary, there is this much of truth in Nixon's anecdote, that Abbas exhibited during the earlier part of his reign a sympathetic tolerance of Christianity. Sherley was able to be of assistance to the missionaries by procuring them an audience with the Shah, who received them graciously, interpreting their visit as a direct indication of the Pope's friendliness towards him. Doubtless Robert was quick to put a political complexion upon a mission whose purpose was in reality chiefly, if not wholly, religious; and one surmises that he advanced the argument to his royal host that the coming of these priests was a proof that, for all his delays and unfulfilled assurances, Anthony Sherley's embassage had not been a failure. The Carmelites later affirmed that they arrived on the scene in the nick of time to reinstate Sherley in the Shah's graces. The obligation was, however, not all on one side, for Sherley was probably influential in winning for them permission to proselitize without molestation and to build the mission-church of Jesu e Maria at Isfahan.[3]

1 Both Robert's letters are printed in full in ibid., pp.56f.
2 Pierre de Saint-André, op.cit., ii,374; Berthold-Ignace de Sainte-Anne, *Histoire de l'Etablissement de la Mission de Perse par les Pères Carmes-Deschaussés*, Brussels [1885], pp.219f.
3 B.-I.de Sainte-Anne, op.cit., p.253. Pietro della Valle (*Viaggi*, Rome, 1652, ii,192) says that Shah Abbas permitted the Christians to build as many churches as they desired. He adds, however, that it must be admitted that there were but few Christians in Persia to avail themselves of these privileges; when he attended mass in a Persian city on Palm Sunday, 1618, he found but twenty or thirty people in the congregation.—An interesting memorial of mission-work in Persia during this period is the cope woven for a Christian community in that country, with representations of the Annunciation and Crucifixion, which is now in the Victoria and Albert Museum. Of somewhat earlier date is the chasuble of Persian brocaded silk in the Musée des Arts Décoratifs in Paris; but its design contains no Christian elements and it is likely that a piece of silk imported from Persia was fashioned into a liturgical vestment in France.—The policy of tolerance towards Christians suffered reverses in the later years of Shah Abbas and native converts were persecuted. See *A brief Relation of the late martyrdom of five Persians*, Doway [Douai], 1623.

Among their first converts were Sherley himself (who abjured the errors of Anglicanism), his wife, and seven or eight of his followers. They were received into the Roman Catholic Church and admitted to the sacraments on the Feast of the Purification (2 February) 1608.[1]

II

His long years of exile were now magnificently atoned for by an appointment as the Shah's ambassador to the European courts. This time the credentials were of unimpeachable authenticity. Among the letters he carried was one to King James I in which he was recommended as a worthy gentleman, dear and beloved, in whom the Shah's confidence reposed. Abbas went on to urge that 'the Turcke ought to be assaulted by dyvers wayes' and to outline a plan of campaign 'to ruyne hym and to blott out his name.'[2]

Cracow, the capital of Poland, was Robert's immediate objective.[3] Accompanied by his wife and Thomas Powell and a handsome retinue he left Persia in February 1608.[4] The

1 The precise date is in the Carmelite archives; see B.-I.de Sainte-Anne, op.cit., pp.253,257. Father Antonio de Gouvea, who had met Sherley in Persia in 1602, tells how having disputed with the missionaries the errors with which he had been 'infected' in England, Robert cast off these heresies and received that divine light from which he had been farther separated in his own country than he was among infidels where he had the comfort of the sacraments (*Relation des Grandes Guerres*, p.107). Pietro della Valle (*Viaggi*, ii,135) writes: 'Don Roberto Sherley, quando venne giovanetto la prima volta in Persia co'l suo fratello maggiore, ci venne Heretico; ma poi, dimoratoci molti anni, con la lunga pratica, e buona conversatione de' Religiosi Agostiniani, ci si fece Cattolico.'

2 E.P.Shirley, op.cit., pp.60f., from S.P.Royal Letters, xxx,171, a contemporary translation with the endorsement that it was presented by Robert Sherley at Hampton Court, 1 October 1611.

3 An Italian translation of a letter from Shah Abbas to King Sigismond III of Poland is in the Vatican archives. For a photostat of this document and of others in the Vatican acknowledgment is due to the Reverend Father Marcellino Dorelli. Beginning 'In the name of God and of great Ali,' the letter to Sigismond passes through the customary florid compliments to a recommendation of Sherley who is described as in the Shah's service and confidence and entrusted with a proposal of great political importance. The Italian version provides us with an interesting example of the devious ways of the Sherleys. It is highly unlikely that the original Persian letter invoked God and 'Ali with no mention of Mahomet. The omission of the name of the Prophet was probably due to Robert Sherley's desire to emphasize the distinction between the heretical Persians and the orthodox Turks.

4 Some months after Sherley's departure an Englishman returning home from India arrived at Isfahan. This was Robert Covert. 'Heere I made enquiry,' he writes (*A True and Almost Incredible Report*, p.54; see below), 'of Master Robert Sherley, thinking to have had some assistance, and better directions from him, or by his procurement, in my Journey, but it was told me directly that he was departed some

party, travelling by the Caspian and through southern Russia, reached Cracow without misadventure. On the basis of information supplied by a certain Master Moore whom Robert sent to England in the spring of 1609, there was published in that year a curious account of Sherley's reception: *Sir Robert Sherley, Sent Ambassadour in the Name of the King of Persia, to Sigismond the third, King of Poland and Swecia, and to other Princes of Europe. His Royall entertainement into Cracovia, the chiefe Citie of Poland, with his pretended* [that is, proposed or intended] *Comming into England. Also, the Honourable praises of the same Sir Robert Sherley, given unto him in that Kingdome, are here likewise inserted.*[1] This pamphlet exists in two issues: one with an unsigned dedication to Sir Thomas Sherley the elder, the other with a dedication to Sir Thomas Sherley, Jr. signed by no less a person than Thomas Middleton. The most likely explanation of this is that Middleton dedicated the pamphlet to the father but that the son, who was probably behind its publication, insisted upon the substitution of a dedication to himself. He, rather than the old man, would gain by the reflected glory of his brother's reputation. The tract adds nothing to Middleton's reputation, for it is a laboured and incoherent rhapsody, as tedious as it is brief; but there is no reason to question his authorship. Middleton urges the English people to prepare a welcome for their countryman who comes 'laden with the trophies of war and the honours of peace.' 'The Turk hath felt the sharpness of his sword, and

seven months before for England, and had his way by the Caspian Seas . . . That is to say, himselfe, and his wife, being a woman of great esteeme in that Country, with Camels and Horses to carry his treasure, stuffe, and provision, and many attendants both men and women. And in his Company was one Captaine [*sic*] and sixe or seven Englishmen more.' The blank in the text was obviously to be filled in when Powell's name was learned, and Covert forgot to do so. Concerning Covert's voyages to the Indies, the final total loss of the ship of which he was master, and his further adventures see Sir William Foster, *England's Quest of Eastern Trade,* and Covert's own narrative. This is: *A True and Almost Incredible report of an Englishman, that (being cast away in the good ship Assention in Cambaya in the farthest part of the East Indies) Travelled by Land through many unknowne Kingdomes, and great Cities . . . With a Discovery of a Great Emperour called the Great Mogoll, a Prince not till now knowne to our English Nation,* 1612. The statement that the Great Mogul had been hitherto unknown in England is of course absurd. One of Covert's companions, Joseph Salbancke (or Salbank), wrote a narrative of the same voyage; see Purchas, iii,82f.

1 Reprinted in *Harleian Miscellany,* iii,87f. and in Middleton's *Works,* ed. Bullen, viii,87f.

against the Turk he is now whetting the swords of Christian princes.' 'Greater tales are likely hereafter (and that very shortly) to swell the true report of his actions.' The propaganda then descends to turgid rant. There is a complicated anagram on Robert Sherley's name. Next comes a fable of how Mercurius, the messenger of the gods, resigned his office to Sherley so that the Shah's messenger, fittingly exalted, could effect, going from court to court, 'an honourable, a pious and inviolable league' against the common enemy. Mercurius in a long discourse prophesies that 'the hell-hound brood of Mahomet' shall be confounded. A sketch of Persian religion and manners follows. Then comes an encomium 'uttered as it were by the whole body of the Polish court' to welcome Sherley; and finally a so-called 'sonnet' in Latin, composed, it is stated, by a Polish scholar in Sherley's honour.

From Cracow, where he left his wife (whom he did not rejoin till the winter of 1610–11 in Spain), Robert passed on to Prague, where he presented to the Emperor Rudolph a letter from the Shah of similar content to that addressed to Sigismond. In the imperial city the old story repeated itself: his stay (April–July 1609), despite his flattering reception, accomplished nothing of practical importance. The Emperor knighted him and made him a Count Palatine of the Holy Roman Empire.[1] He was also supplied with a letter of recommendation to King James which later probably helped to smooth his diplomatic path in England. In August of the same year he was in Florence. He impressed the citizens with the exotic splendour of his costumes and he 'put his household in silks of various colours'; but the Venetian envoy who provides these details adds ominously: 'He gets the stuff but does not pay.' He was, this observer thought, living beyond his means, reckoning on a substantial present from the Grand Duke of Tuscany. 'The whole court wishes him away.' When at last a present was forthcoming it was smaller than he had calculated it would be. All this gossip comes, it is fair to note, from sources hostile to Anthony Sherley and consequently prejudiced against Robert.[2]

1 The Imperial Grant is quoted in Purchas, x,378f. 2 C.S.P., Venetian, xi,330 and 341.

Arriving in Rome on Sunday, 27 September 1609, he made a solemn entry through the Porta del Popolo on the following day.[1] In oriental dress and wearing a turban to which was affixed, in lieu of the Mohammedan crescent, a huge golden crucifix (a gift from the Pope), he was presented to His Holiness Paul V. This crucifix-adorned turban afforded matter for excited comment to intelligencers, diplomats, and gossips for years to come. James I, when he heard of it, remarked bluntly that Sir Robert Sherley was a humbug (*una fintione*).[2] Wotton wrote to Salisbury: 'His habit, and half his train, and most of his language is merely Persian, except a jeweled crucifix (given him by the Pope) which he carrieth in the top of his turbant.'[3] The *crocifisso* is among the papal gifts enumerated in a contemporary Italian pamphlet describing Sherley's reception in Rome.[4] From the same account we learn that the members of his retinue who were of Persian nationality wore their turbans in the presence of the Pope.[5] On the occasion of this first audience with the Holy Father, Sherley, after many genuflections and kissings of the papal feet, made an oration in which he assured His Holiness that 'when the Turk was defeated and Constantinople taken . . . his master intended to become a Christian and to render entire obedience to the Apostalic See.' So a Venetian agent reported the substance of his words, but this may be nothing but malevolent misrepresentation.[6] There is no such assurance or promise in the letter from the Shah to the Pope of which an Italian translation is in the Vatican archives and which with high-flown compliments asks for friendship and an alliance.

1 The date is on the rare engraved portrait of Sir Robert wearing turban and crucifix (reproduced in John Nichols, *Progresses of King James the First*, ii,430). Beneath the portrait is the scene of his reception by the Pope. Sir Robert kneels bare-headed, his turban resting on the step of the papal throne. The original copper-plate *incisione* from which the print was made is still in the possession of the Carmelite fathers of S.Maria della Scala in Rome. The painting of Sir Robert, darkened, damaged, and never very good, which is at S.Maria della Scala, is not from the life (it is dated 1663, long after his death) but is copied from this engraving of 1609.
2 *C.S.P.*, *Venetian*, xi,431.
3 L.P.Smith, op.cit., i,477.
4 *Vera Relatione della solenne Entrata Fata in Roma da Don Roberto Scerlei*, Bologna, 1609, p.7. Of this tiny pamphlet of four leaves the only copy known to the present writer is in the Greville Library of the British Museum (G. 6677).
5 Ibid., p.4: 'Sua Beatitudine . . . li diede la beneditione, come fece à tutti li altri, non ostante, che li Persiani tenessero il turbante in testa, conforme alla lor legge.'
6 *C.S.P.*, *Venetian*, xi,361.

At a later interview Sherley presented a written address. Of this a copy, dated 4 October 1609, and signed 'Per me il conte Roberto Sherley,' is in the Vatican. In it, after assuring the Pope of the Shah's love, he submits a genealogy exhibiting Shah Abbas's descent from 'Ali—apparently as evidence of his hostility to the Turks. Acknowledgments are made to 'i padri Carrimillitani' for their assistance to Sherley in Persia. Arguments are advanced for an alliance against the Ottoman Empire, and the Pope is respectfully urged to use force or persuasion to make all Christian peoples break off relations with the Turks. There are suggestions as to military strategy and as to financing an alliance. The Pope is requested to send an ambassador to Persia and to exercise especial care in the choice of missionaries to be sent there. In a postscript Robert asks for a personal boon: that when his brother Anthony is free to do so he be permitted to return to Persia.[1] This is the only indication we have that Anthony had any such design at this time when he was, as we have seen, in desperate straits; papal permission would be necessary if he planned to sail from Ancona or some other port in the States of the Church.

Paul V gave Robert his blessing, created him a Count of the Sacred Palace of the Lateran, and, it is said, bestowed on him the curious right or power to legitimize bastards.[2] Altogether the visit was, or appeared to be, a success. But there were those who jeered at the impracticability of Robert's plans. Wotton wrote that the idea of maintaining war between the Emperor and Turkey 'maketh wise men much sport' when everybody knew that Rudolph was not able even to impose his will upon the burghers of Prague.[3]

Sherley arrived at Barcelona in December 1609, and after a wearisome delay went on to Madrid the following February. His wife had now rejoined him, and in his company for a while

1 Other related documents in the Vatican archives are letters from the Shah to the Spanish ambassador in Rome and to the General of the Carmelites.
2 Purchas, x,378f. Purchas, however, says that this power was conferred on Sherley by the Emperor, and adds amusingly: 'Many thousands at Goa were suitors to him (such is the Portugall dissoluteness in those parts).' Archbishop Abbot wrote to Sir Thomas Roe that it was the Pope who conferred this 'power' on Sherley (E.P.Shirley, op.cit., p.64).
3 L.P.Smith, op.cit., i,477. The allusion is to the edict of 1609 granting religious toleration in Bohemia.

was the picturesque and charming English Roman Catholic Sir Toby Matthew.[1] During protracted negotiations that were often at a standstill for weeks together Sherley remained at Madrid till well into the year 1611. He seems to have set aside the old scheme for an anti-Ottoman alliance and was now concentrating his efforts upon the definite object of negotiating a Hispano-Persian treaty to regulate the silk trade through Ormuz. But Spain was dilatory, and gradually Robert came to the decision to withdraw his offer and to propose to his 'natural sovereign,' King James, the advantages of the Ormuz trade. Cottington, the English envoy, a man by no means prejudiced in favour of the Sherleys, was impressed with the practicability of the plan and recommended his government to accept it. He closed his dispatch with this personal estimate:

> Mr. Sherley hath here gotten very great reputation through his wise and discreet carriage; he is judged both modest and moreover brave in his speech, diet and expenses, and in my poor opinion to those vices which in Sir Anthony do so abound, in this man may be found the contraries.[2]

Robert's relations with his brother, from whom he had been separated for a decade, were both mortifying and inconvenient. Anthony was, says Cottington, 'so extreme poor, as if his brother did not relieve him he would doubtless suffer much misery.' Robert gave him the hospitality of his residence in Madrid, an act of charity that made subsequent difficulties all the greater. For Anthony—entirely under the control of the Jesuits, ashamed of his own failures, excluded from England, poor, and in ill repute—heartily disapproved of Robert's overtures to the English government and went so far as to communicate to Prada, the Spanish minister, a plan to prevent his brother's proposed departure for England. Prada's reply, addressed to Anthony at Robert's house, fell into the latter's hands. In great agitation he hastened to the English embassy and laid the letter before Cottington, expressing his fear that his brother intended to poison him. He said, furthermore, that he had been refused permission to leave Madrid and thought

1 *Winwood Memorials*, iii,98,104,128.   2 E.P.Shirley, op.cit., pp.72f.

that he would be able to get away only by stealth. Cottington soothed him and temporized, being, as he put it, 'very retired in [his] fashion towards him.' The ambassador was in fact uncertain whether Robert would be *persona grata* to the English government, and while awaiting advice from Salisbury contented himself with assuring Robert that if the necessity arose it would not be difficult to escape secretly from Madrid.[1]

This alarm subsided; the need for secrecy disappeared; and at the beginning of June 1611, Sir Robert and Lady Sherley with their retinue left Madrid and in due course arrived in England.[2] There is an immediately contemporary allusion to him in John Cooke's play, *Greenes Tu Quoque*, in which a courageous character is commended as 'the Captain of brave citizens, . . . a Sherley for his spirit.'[3] The Reverend John Cartwright chose this appropriate time to publish the narrative of his travels with an account of the Sherleys in Persia. 'We cannot denie,' he writes

> but that both the Embasseies of Sir Anthony Sherley, and also of M. Robert his brother, are of great importance, and that a combination of so great forces together would soone have delivered many poore Christians of their miseries, the world of it ignominy, and mankind of that monster of Turkish tyranny that hath too long raigned and laid the earth desolate.[4]

In England Robert Sherley could count on a measure of sympathy with his adopted country, for it was recognized that Persian attacks on the Ottoman Empire had lessened the latter's pressure upon Europe. 'Twixt Turkes and Christians now no Trumpets sound,' the Earl of Stirling wrote a little later, because, he adds, the Persians are bounding the Turkish conquests.[5]

1 Ibid., pp.75f. This long dispatch from Cottington to Salisbury, 10 April 1611, gives further particulars of the quarrel between the two brothers.
2 On Sherley's arrival in England see Edmund Howes's 'augmentation' of John Stow, *Annales*, 1631, pp.1002f.
3 *Greene's Tu Quoque, or The Cittie Gallant*, 1614; Hazlitt's Dodsley, xi,113. The play is definitely of 1611; it satirizes Coryat's *Crudities*, published in that year, and was acted in December 1611.
4 *The Preachers Travels*, p.71.
5 *Doomes-Day* (1614), Fifth Hour, stanza 84; ed. cit., ii,192. It may be noted, however, that long after the Sherleys' day Francis Osborn cautioned England against a too great reliance upon Persian successes against the Turks. Events had taught him,

But King James's advisers had no confidence in the proposals for an alliance, and such little interest as they had in the Persian mission was commercial rather than political. Robert was kept for weeks awaiting an audience. This interval was spent in the family home, Wiston Manor. It must have been a mournful reunion after so long a separation. The father was broken in health and fortune; the eldest son was in a debtors' prison; thoughts must have gone out to the second son, an exiled pensioner of Spain. Robert was obliged to write to Salisbury begging him to countermand orders for the collection of arrearages of rent.[1] In these sad circumstances contemplation of Robert's dignities may have afforded some solace to his family, and his Persian wife doubtless provided exciting distraction. Some notion, albeit farcically exaggerated, of the interest and gossip roused in London by the arrival of an exotic and picturesque lady may be had from Davenant's play *The Wits*, which though of much later date (1634) may preserve some tradition if not of Lady Sherley's first then of her second visit to England. In this drama some gossips report the presence in London of the niece of the Grand Mogul, and we remember that Anthony Nixon and others had said that Lady Sherley was the Sophy's niece. The gossips say that the strangeness of this foreigner's bearing proves that she is of 'great blood.' She reposes upon a rich ermine quilt. Her maids brush her ermine clothes. Her pages, 'cloath'd like the Sophy's sons' (note the Persian reference), dice for extravagant stakes. Her grooms quaff sherbets and juleps.[2] In all this there may be reminiscences of the sort of chatter once current about Robert Sherley's wife.

Not unnaturally King James at first associated Robert with Anthony and was inclined to regard him as an outlaw. He was, moreover, annoyed by a subject's claim to be the envoy of a foreign potentate. Then there was the seemingly trivial but none the less awkward problem of Robert's oriental costume. It is uncertain what decision was arrived at; some say that he wore

he says, that Turkish soldiers fight more courageously against Christians than against Persians, 'a people looked upon as too near of kin to them in Religion, to warrant their Murdering' (*Political Reflections upon the Government of the Turks*, 1656, p.69).

1 E.P.Shirley, op.cit., p.77.   2 *The Wits*, III,iii; *Works*, ii,176.

English dress when received in audience, others that James suffered him to wear his oriental clothes but required him to doff his turban for a moment. English officials would not know —or if informed by Sherley would be indifferent to the fact— that Moslems do not doff their turbans either in their mosques or in a royal presence, so that for Robert to remove his turban in the presence of King James, thus singling him out for unique homage, would be an affront to Islam and to the Shah which the Persian members of his retinue would undoubtedly report to Isfahan. 'They never uncover their heads or take off their turbants,' James Howell was to write some years later, 'so that in the rough of their fury the greatest Execration they use to rap out is, "God send thee as much trouble as a Christians hatt," which is almost in perpetuall motion.' [1] Robert had, then, anxious practical reasons for wearing his turban. On the other hand, he might have made a better impression upon English officials and merchants if his appearance had been less outlandish. 'When a traveller returneth home,' Bacon had counselled in his essay *Of Travel*, 'let his travel appear rather in his discourse than in his apparel or gesture; and in his discourse let him be rather advised in his answers, than forward to tell stories; and let it appear that he doth not change his country manners for those of foreign parts.' Robert followed this advice in no respect. [2]

At last, on 1 October 1611, he had an audience with the King at Hampton Court; and throwing himself on his knees he implored pardon for having accepted office under a foreign monarch, pleading that he had done so at the Shah's express command whom in the circumstances he could not disobey. King James granted him forgiveness, listened graciously to his proposals, and when Sherley had withdrawn commended his 'prudence, eloquence and modesty.' Lodgings were provided for the ambassador and his suite; the sum of £666. 13sh.

1 *Instructions for Forreine Travell*, ed. Arber, p.86.
2 Three centuries later history repeated itself. Colonel T.E.Lawrence, accompanying King Feisal to Buckingham Palace, wore Arab dress; and he received this rebuke: 'Is it right, Colonel Lawrence, that a subject of the Crown, and an officer too, should come here dressed in foreign uniform?' (Liddell Hart, *Colonel Lawrence: The Man behind the Legend*, New York, 1934, p.313).

4d. was allotted him as a 'free guifte and reward' from the King; £1888. was allowed for the embassage's diet; and for house-rent £300.[1] That James defrayed these expenses is remarkable, for his policy had been to abolish the old custom of providing free food and lodging for ambassadors and their suites.[2]

On 12 October four merchants of the Levant Company were appointed to consult with Sherley. It is difficult to determine just what his designs were and with what degree of sincerity they were urged. What is obvious is that the Shah was actuated primarily by the desire to obtain purchasers for his silk (which was a royal commodity) and to divert the silk export-trade from its usual but now hazardous channel through the dominions of his enemy the Turk. Two alternative routes were possible, at least in theory. There was the old Caspian-Russian route now abandoned these many years. It is perhaps not insignificant that in this very year 1611 Cartwright reopened discussion of the likelihood of profitable trade between England and Persia by way of the Volga and Caspian. 'I am perswaded,' he wrote, 'that any honest factor residing in Casbin may vent a thousand cloathes yearly.'[3] Is it not probable that Cartwright was in touch privately with Sherley and was advancing his interests in writing thus? But the English merchants possessed too bitter memories of distances, storms, hardships, Muscovite treachery, and the peculations of their factors to harbour any notion of reopening this route. The alternative was the long sea way through the Persian Gulf, the Indian Ocean, and round Africa. But traffic in the Gulf was controlled by the Portuguese from Ormuz, Goa, and other settlements. The obvious course was to come to terms with Spain which ruled Portugal, for if the English decided to use the Gulf route they must either drive the Portuguese from their points of vantage or else make an arrangement for both countries in Persia tantamount to what we call the policy of the open door.

In these conferences an important part was played by Sir

---

1 E.P.Shirley, op.cit., p.108. But John Nichols, op.cit., ii,430, gives the item of £666 odd as the sum total granted Sherley.
2 E.R.Adair, *Extraterritoriality of Ambassadors in the Sixteenth and Seventeenth Centuries*, 1929, pp.266f.
3 *The Preachers Travels*, pp.54f.

Thomas Roe, who put the weight of his long experience of the East and his knowledge of conditions in the Persian Gulf in the scales against Sherley. Roe's opinion of him was that 'as hee is dishonest, soe is hee subtile.' [1] One of Roe's letters, though of later date (1617, when Robert was on his second mission to Europe), is applicable to conditions in 1611 and probably represents the arguments he advanced at that time. He warns the merchants that Sherley's proposals will advantage only the Portuguese and advises them to discard all hope that these schemes will advance English trade. There must be no agreement between the two nations. We must trust to ourselves and 'our owne honest wayes.' Not, he goes on, 'that wee will take Ormus and beate the Portugall out of those seas; these are vanityes. The Company entend a trade, not a warre.' [2] Roe proved to be a bad prophet; within five years after these words were written the English had captured Ormuz and had driven out the Portuguese.

Robert submitted samples of Persian silks for the Levant Company's inspection, but these realistic merchants found them not good enough.[3] There were other reasons for their scepticism; and John Chamberlain sums up their point of view in a sentence: 'I doubt his projects are to little purpose, for the way is long and dangerous, the trade uncertain, and must quite cut off our traffick with the Turk.' [4] The last was the essential consideration; a bird in the hand was worth two in the bush— the bush so distant and the birds therein perhaps imaginary. It is probable that word from Spain increased the hopelessness of Sherley's situation, for now that he had withdrawn his mercantile projects from that country and was offering them to England, his Spanish connections sought to disparage and discredit him. Sir John Digby, the new ambassador at Madrid, wrote that Sir Robert's former friends now did not spare 'to give him the name of a Cosener and of a Counterfeit.' [5] Another thing calculated to harm his reputation was the report current

1 *The Embassy of Sir Thomas Roe*, ed. Foster, Hakluyt Society, i,xlvii, note 1.
2 Ibid., ii,406.
3 *C.S.P., Venetian*, xii,253.
4 Letter to Sir Dudley Carleton, 13 November 1611, E.P.Shirley, op.cit., p.78.
5 19 January 1612, ibid.

in England that he had distributed to his co-religionists papal indulgences obtained in Rome. 'When called in question for it,' the record runs, he 'laid the fault on his wife.' [1]

But though he failed with the hard-headed merchants he was by no means out of favour with the King. Long years of friendship with the Sherley family account in part for James's personal benignancy. He took the trouble to institute inquiries as to whether 'the objecttions made by the marchantts were of mallis or truthe,' though what conclusion this inquiry led to is not in the record. Looking at the Persian question from the political as well as the economic point of view, James could see more clearly than the merchants the advantages of the Shah's offer of the right of entry into his ports ('Plases for Landin on,' as Robert expressed it) for English shipping—a concession of obvious value in the event of new trouble with Spain. [2]

III

THE royal condescension was evinced that autumn when the Prince of Wales consented to stand godfather to Sir Robert and Lady Sherley's infant son. Sir Robert expressed to the Prince his 'londginge' (longing) to do him 'som segnniolated servis.' 'I have not the pen of Sissero,' he wrote (and indeed he had not!), 'yet wontt I not means to sownde your highnesses worthy prayses in to the ears of forran nattions and migtey Prinses.' This, he believed, would be a welcome service because the Prince's 'highborne sperritt thirsts after fame, the period of great Princes ambissions.' [3]

The child was christened Henry after his royal godfather. When, early in 1613, Sir Robert and his wife left England for Persia, they left their little son, then fourteen months old, behind them, 'bequeathing him to the Favour and Care of the Queen.' [4] The fate of this boy is obscure, and what little we know of him is confused with our information regarding his first cousin, another Henry Sherley, the second son of Sir Thomas Sherley, Jr., by his first wife, Frances Vavasour.

1 C.S.P.,Dom., 1611–18, p.429.
2 Sherley to Salisbury, 2 March 1612, E.P.Shirley, op.cit., p.80.
3 4 November 1611, ibid., p.79; Nichols, op.cit., ii,431.
4 John Chamberlain to Sir Ralph Winwood, Winwood Memorials, iii,428.

The date of the birth of Henry, the son of Thomas, is un-known. Henry, the only son of Robert, was born, as we have just seen, about 1 November 1611. Lady Sherley, the widow of Sir Thomas Sherley the elder, and grandmother of the two Henrys, in her will dated 19 February 1623 (proved 1 April 1623), left an annuity of forty pounds to her grandson Henry Sherley. Her executor, Sir Thomas Bishop, in his will, proved 14 February 1626, charged this annuity on a certain farm.[1] Which Sherley received this annuity?

E.P.Shirley, citing the manuscript pedigree of the Sherleys compiled by one of the family in the later seventeenth century,[2] records that 'Henricus Shirleius,' the second son ('secundo natus') of Sir Thomas Sherley, Jr., died without offspring ('sine obole occisus est'); and he adds, on the authority of the parish register, that he was buried on 5 March 1606, at Foot's Cray in Kent.[3] But elsewhere we have record that in February 1618, Henry Sherley, the son of Sir Thomas Sherley, Jr., escaped from prison in the King's Bench and was reported to be planning to attempt to transport himself beyond the seas.[4]

On 31 October 1627, a Henry Sherley came to the lodgings of Sir Edward Bishop, M.P., the son of the Sir Thomas Bishop who had been the executor of Lady Sherley's will. Of Sir Edward this Henry Sherley demanded an annuity of forty pounds due him. There was an altercation, and Bishop ran Sherley through with a sword, slaying him. This 'foul murther' is recorded in a letter a few days thereafter.[5] It is also mentioned by William Prynne, the puritanical opponent of the theatres, as an example of 'the sudden and untimely ends of all those ancient play-poets' and as 'a caveat to our moderne [poets] to deter them from their ungodly profession.' In a marginal gloss Prynne offers as a specific instance: '——— Sherly, slaine suddenly by Sir Edward Bishop, whiles hee was drunke, as most report.'[6] The murdered Henry Sherley was, then, a dramatist, and the

1 E.P.Shirley, op.cit., p.85, note 13.
2 *Genealogica Historia Domus de Sherley*, MS. Harl. 4023, p.125b.
3 Op.cit., p.100; see also Daniel Lysons, *The Environs of London*, 1792-6, iv,425.
4 *Acts of the Privy Council, 1617-19*, pp.33 and 61.
5 Mr. Beaulieu to Sir Thomas Puckering; transcript by Birch in the British Museum (Add. MSS. 4177), printed by E.P.Shirley, *Notes and Queries*, First Series, xii,27.
6 *Histriomastix*, ed. 1633, p.554.

provocation was a quarrel over Bishop's refusal to pay him the annuity bequeathed him by his grandmother. Yet E.P.Shirley says that the grandson provided for in the will was the son of Robert. (Obviously the grandmother might have left annuities to both grandsons of the same name; but only one is mentioned in her will and in her executor's will.) It is quite incredible that Henry, the son of Robert, was a dramatist in 1627, the author not only of *The Martyr'd Soldier*, a play that has come down to us, but of four other plays (if the attribution to him is not an error) licensed in 1653 but now lost.[1] The murdered playwright must have been the son of Sir Thomas. Yet E.P.Shirley, as we have seen, states on good authority that this son died in 1606. This must be an error both because this young man, and not his cousin, must have been the dramatist and also because he was reported to the Privy Council to have escaped from prison in 1618. So much being granted, it is obvious that he it was who was the beneficiary under old Lady Sherley's will. It follows that E.P.Shirley is again in error in citing this will as evidence that Robert's son was alive in 1623. In fact, it leaves us with no knowledge at all of the fate of the baby whom Robert and his wife left in England when they returned to Persia in 1613.

The Martyr'd Soldier, first published eleven years after the death of its ill-fated author, is of some interest if of little merit.[2] The original edition concludes with an address to the reader in which it is admitted that 'this play's old.' The piece is not only old but old-fashioned. Of its plot all that need be said is that two Vandal kings persecute the Christians; a Vandal general and his wife turn Christian and suffer martyrdom; one of the kings is struck dead and the other is converted to Christianity. Such interest as the play offers to the student of the drama lies not in its wild perversions of Roman history[3] but in certain

1 F.E.Schelling, *Elizabethan Drama*, i,430.
2 *The Martyr'd Soldier. As it hath been sundry times Acted with a generall applause at the Private house in Drury Lane, and at other publicke Theatres . . . The Author H.Shirley, Gent.*, 1638; reprinted in *Old English Plays*, ed. A.H.Bullen, 1882, i,165f.
3 The historic Genseric was not a pagan but an Arian; and Belisarius, who is introduced as one of Genseric's generals, really appears in history more than fifty years after the latter's death and was, moreover, not himself a Vandal but a conqueror of the Vandals.

belated survivals of elements from the miracle plays. Its nearest seventeenth-century analogues are *The Virgin Martyr* by Massinger and Dekker and *The Two Noble Ladies; or The Converted Conjuror*, an anonymous piece; but its resemblance to these dramas is remote. Angels make their appearance; miracles abound; stones are transformed into soft and harmless sponges when they are cast at a holy bishop; saintly persons are cured supernaturally and enabled to sustain torture without suffering; a persecuting pagan king is struck dead by a thunderbolt. In one scene some iniquitous camel-drivers who are about to ravish a holy matron are rendered mad, blind, deaf, or impotent. In all this it is not fanciful to detect sympathy with Roman Catholic hagiology; and it is what one might expect from a nephew of Anthony and Robert Sherley. In particular the episode of the camel-drivers [1] (without parallel in the drama of the period) is singularly appropriate as coming from the pen of one who in childhood must have heard from his Uncle Robert and Aunt Teresa anecdotes and descriptions of deserts and caravans and lawless bedouin. In another scene there is what seems to be a more intimate allusion to Sir Robert and Lady Sherley. The Clown says (never mind the context): 'You that are borne Pagans both by father and mother, the true sonnes of Infidelity.' [2] Lady Teresa Sherley must have seemed in the eyes of her husband's English relatives little better than a pagan, and one may suppose that Sir Thomas Sherley's children taunted their little cousin Henry with his mother's outlandish nationality and upbringing. But they had to admit that their Uncle Robert was English, and therefore his son, the dramatist's cousin, was not a 'true son of infidelity.' The point is a small one; it concerns a clownish phrase in a stupid play. But it prompts the question of how many personal allusions might not be brought to light in the works of the great dramatists if we knew more about their childhood.

In the dedication of the play to Sir Kenelm Digby it is said that it was received with applause and favour on the stage;

1 IV,iii; Bullen's edition, pp.235f. (there are no scene-divisions in the original quarto).
2 I,iii; ibid., p.198.

and in the concluding address to the reader it is said that it drew 'even the Rigid Stoicks of the Time, who, though not for pleasure yet for profit have gathered something out of his [the dramatist's] plentiful Vineyard.' The modern reader will endorse the qualification 'not for pleasure' but will not gather much 'profit' from *The Martyr'd Soldier*.

And now, having closed this digression into which we were led by the confusion between the two young Henry Sherleys, let us return to the dramatist's Uncle Robert.

IV

INDEPENDENTLY of Sir Robert Sherley the Levant Company effected a compromise between Turkey and Persia permitting goods to be sent westward through Syria. This arrangement was tantamount to a rejection of Sherley's project which was tied up with the Portuguese and the Cape route. He realized that the game was up and prepared to return to his adopted country.[1] He weighed the possibility of making the journey through Muscovy and sought the advice of one who had formerly been a factor there—we do not know his name but he must have been a survivor of one of the early expeditions. This man gave him 'litel hope of any passinge that way.'[2] The Mediterranean route was out of the question because of the Turks. Hence his design to go by the Cape of Good Hope. He drew up articles of agreement with Sir Henry Thynne, owner of the ship *Expedition*, for conveying the embassage to Persia: the ship to remain eight months at a Persian port while Sherley busied himself to obtain a cargo for the return voyage. The ship's master was Christopher Newport who had already had experience in eastern waters. Thynne, the owner, sailed in her, and his companion Henry Mainwaring, who had the honour of receiving a sonnet of farewell from John Davies of Hereford.[3] On board in an unascertained capacity was Walter Payton who

1 *C.S.P.,Dom., 1611-18,* p.140.
2 Sherley to Salisbury, 2 March 1612, E.P.Shirley, op.cit., p.80.
3 'To my most deare and no lesse worthily-beloved Frend and Pupill, Henry Main-warring Esquier, with the truly noble and venterous Knight Sr Henry Thynne, accompanying into Persia, the meritoriously farre-renowned Knight, Sr Robert Sherley, Englishman, yet Lord Ambassadour from the great Persian Potentate, to all Christian Princes, for the good of Christendome,' *The Muses Sacrifice*, 1612, folio 171.

afterwards wrote a narrative of the voyage.[1] In Sherley's retinue were Sir Thomas and Lady Powell, Captain John Ward (not to be confused with the corsair), a secretary, a barber and a 'musitioner' (all English), a Persian woman, a Dutch goldsmith, an old Armenian, three Persian men, and one or two nondescript attendants.

The *Expedition* left Gravesend on 7 January 1613. There was anxiety in England and Spain lest she 'take to piracy' at sea; [2] merchants had already suffered from the depredations of the two older Sherley brothers and were fearful lest the third follow their example. They did Robert an injustice, for there is no record of any buccaneering on the way. The long voyage was uneventful till they approached their destination. After some eight or nine months at sea they reached the Persian Gulf and attempted a landing on the coast of Baluchistan. Walter Payton gives a lively account of the misadventure that followed. The Baluches captured the Sherleys' luggage which had been put ashore; but some of these perfidious people were enticed on board and a message was sent that unless the luggage was restored within two hours these hostages would be put to death. A 'running-glass' was put up in plain sight of the shore; and before its sands had run out the threat proved effective, the luggage was returned, and the *Expedition* sailed away from that inhospitable place.[3]

In September 1613, Sherley and his company landed at Lari Bandar at the mouth of the Indus.[4] The Portuguese settlers, who had heard that he had 'come forth of England . . . into the Indies of purpose to steal,' [5] gave him a hostile reception, instigating an attack by the natives upon the Englishmen. In this scuffle Captain Ward was slain. Presently Sir Thomas Powell and another follower died of disease. Then an attempt was made to burn the house in which Sherley was living. A little later that sorely tried diplomat tried to escape from the

---

1 Purchas, iv,202. For the articles of agreement see E.P.Shirley, op.cit., p.81.
2 *C.S.P., Venetian*, xi,393,435,494.
3 Purchas, iv,192f.
4 Changes in the delta of the Indus have made the site now unidentifiable with any certainty; see *The Embassy of Sir Thomas Roe*, ed. Foster, i,123, note 2.
5 Purchas, iv,202.

town by night, but was caught, imprisoned and 'hardly used.'
At length, after suffering many indignities, he and his party,
now much reduced in number, were permitted to go upon their
way. They journeyed to Surat, where the Great Mogul held
his court. Jahangir received them graciously. Ten years later
Robert painted in such glowing colours his position at Surat
that one might suspect exaggeration but that Purchas's narrative [1] is, generally speaking, confirmed by independent witnesses. Thomas Aldworth and William Biddulph allude to the
Mogul's favour towards Sherley as a matter of common
knowledge; [2] and—what is more striking—when Sir Thomas
Roe wished later to indicate how welcome he was at Surat he
could find no stronger way of putting it than to say that the
ruler had placed him in 'the place given to Sir Robert Sherley
and indeed above all his subjects.' [3] But this condescension had
its disadvantages, for when the Great Mogul offered Sherley a
large salary if he would leave the Shah's service for his, and
Sherley declined to do so, Jahangir spoke 'too liberally' in
disparagement of the Shah, whereupon Sherley's loyalty to his
master forced him to retort in kind. This quarrel 'eclipsed the
Mogolls benevolence towards him'; but nevertheless when the
time came to depart Sherley received gifts of elephants and
'huge massie Coines.' [4]

They had not gone far upon their journey when plodding
along the road towards them came that indefatigable traveller
Thomas Coryat. Thus he described the encounter to his friends
at home:

> About the middle of the way, betwixt Spahan and Lahore, just
> about the frontier of Persia and India, I met Sir Robert Sherley,
> and his Lady, travailing from the court of the Mogul . . . so gal-
> lantly furnished with all necessaries for their travailes, that it was a

1 Ibid., x,377f.
2 Aldworth and Biddulph were agents of the East India Company. In a letter of
   19 August 1614, they told their employers of the perils Sherley had undergone among
   the Portuguese and of his reception by the Great Mogul (E.P.Shirley, op.cit., p.83).
   For another account of Sherley at this time see Nicholas Withington in Purchas,
   iv,170. (Withington's narrative was compiled from his journal after his return home;
   it is much condensed in Purchas; a fuller text appeared in 1735. See also *Early Travels
   in India, 1583–1619*, ed. Foster, pp.188f.)
3 *The Embassy of Sir Thomas Roe*, i,151.
4 This disagreement and its outcome are related by Purchas.

great comfort unto me to see them in such a flourishing estate. There did he shew me to my singular contentment, both my Bookes neatly kept; and hath promised me to shew them . . . to the Persian King . . . to the end, I may have the more gracious accesse unto him after my returne thither . . . Both he and his Lady used me with singular respect, especially his Lady, who bestowed forty shillings upon me in Persian money; and they seemed to exult for joy to see mee.[1]

The two books to which Coryat refers are the *Crudities* and the *Crambe*; this chance meeting gave him the only opportunity he ever had to see them. He expressed the hope that the Shah, that 'jocund Prince,' would be pleased with his 'facetious heiroglyphicks' if Sherley found an opportunity to expound them to him. And so they parted, Coryat continuing on his way eastward to his death, Sherley westward to Isfahan which he reached in June 1615, two and a half years after his setting forth from England. During this period he had lost by death or desertion every one of his English followers.

To Shah Abbas he brought as a gift two magnificent Indian elephants. The only recorded expression of the Shah's appreciation of his services was the confidence in him implied in the command to set out forthwith upon a second mission to Europe. The summer passed in preparation and in consultation with one Richard Steele, an agent of the East India Company then in Isfahan.[2] Then, in October 1615, Sherley and his wife started for Europe again, taking with them as chaplain 'a Friar of the Bare-foot Order,' that is, a Carmelite. But the Shah held as hostages six friars, vowing, says Steele, to cut them to pieces if Sherley did not return.[3] That Abbas had some ground for the suspicion that his envoy might elect to remain safely in Europe is shown by a report which came to the East India Company:

Sir Sherley's [*sic*] poor reward from this King, after so many years spent for his service, and return from his last Embassage, may persuade him of little better at his second return. I am told by a

1 *Thomas Coriate Traveller for the English Wits*, 1616, pp.14f. There is a brief allusion to the encounter in *Mr. Thomas Coriat to his friends in England sendeth greeting*, 1618, Sig. C^v. Compare also John Taylor the Water-Poet, *Works*, Spenser Society, 1869, p.246; and Purchas, iv,471.
2 E.P.Shirley, op.cit., p.36, note 3.   3 Purchas, iv,276f.

bosom friend of his, that he intends his abode in Christendom, if his invitation, (especially in his own Country), could but afford him the small means of a poor gentleman.[1]

The *Expedition* had long since sailed for England. When Sherley reached Goa he found that the only ship departing thence for Europe during the autumn of 1615 was already gone; and consequently he was compelled to wait at Goa for three months.[2] It is difficult to reconcile the fact of this delay with Richard Steele's statement that Sherley took with him to Spain forty-five Portuguese prisoners in order to impress upon the Spanish government the might of the Grand Sophy and to demonstrate that it would be the part of wisdom to accept Persia's terms for an understanding about the silk trade. Where were these captives all the while that Sherley waited at Goa and what was to prevent their rescue by the Portuguese?

Robert reached Madrid in May 1617, and there he remained for no less than five years. It was at this time that his path and Anthony's crossed for the last time. 'The two brothers are much fallen out,' wrote Cottington, 'and both by word and writing do all the harm they can in defaming each other, but I must needs confess that the Ambassador is the discreeter of the two.'[3] It is probable that poor Anthony had little influence upon the course of negotiations in which Robert was engaged. These dragged on even more slowly than others we have recorded in this chapter. The correspondence of Sir Thomas Roe during this period betrays his anxiety lest their successful termination cause the English factors to be shut out of the trade in the Persian Gulf. Actually two agents of the East India Company—Edward Connock and Thomas Barker—were in Persia endeavouring to extract concessions from the Shah while Robert was in Spain.[4] That he was not a mere fantastic visionary like his brother Anthony is proved by the fact that these agents were pursuing a policy very similar to that which Robert had urged on the London merchants in 1611–12; only they were

1 E.P.Shirley, op.cit., p.84, from East India Company records.
2 Purchas, iv,365; *The Embassy of Sir Thomas Roe*, ii,310,347,354,356.
3 12 December 1619, E.P.Shirley, op.cit., p.87.
4 There are many allusions to these agents in Roe's correspondence; see the Index to the *Embassy*.

pursuing it without his mediation. This policy now led to violent action. There had been various earlier disputes and clashes between the English and Portuguese traders; [1] but in 1620 matters came to a head when the efforts of the East India Company to open up trade with Persia were vigorously opposed by their Portuguese rivals at Ormuz. The English, beaten off at first, returned with superior forces and established a station at Jask on the Gulf. Shah Abbas now saw an opportunity to obtain English aid for an attack upon the Portuguese and refused to permit the English factors to obtain cargoes unless they first joined him in an onslaught on Ormuz. With genuine or feigned reluctance the Englishmen consented. Ormuz soon capitulated. This was in 1622. In the various narratives of the capture and siege published by Purchas emphasis is laid on the fact that the English were not responsible for the attack but that under the pressure of Persia they made a virtue of necessity. This explanation was officially adopted as an apology to Spain, where the taking of Ormuz made, as James Howell (who was in Madrid at the time) records, 'a great noise' and Digby, the English envoy, had to explain that 'it was no voluntary but a constrain'd act.' [2] But England kept Ormuz. [3]

It was just as well for Robert Sherley that before this event took place he had left Spain and was in Rome, presenting to Pope Gregory XV the old project of a league between Christendom and Persia against the Turk. It was during this sojourn that the portraits of Sir Robert and Lady Sherley now at Petworth were painted by the young Anthony Vandyke. [4]

1 Such as those narrated by Sir Henry Middleton in *The Last East-Indian Voyage*, 1606; reprinted as *The Voyage of Sir Henry Middleton*, Hakluyt Society, 1855.
2 James Howell, *Familiar Letters*, i,157.
3 See Purchas, vi,332f., and Andrew Shilling, *The true relation of that worthy Sea Fight in the Persian Gulph*, 1622; and among modern authorities Bruce, *Annals of the East India Company*, i,229; S.R.Gardiner, *History of England from the Accession of James I*, ed. 1908, v,237f.; and Malcolm, Sykes, and other historians of Persia.
4 A seventeenth-century biographer of the artist writes: 'Nel qual tempo, essendo venuto a Roma D.Roberto Scherley Inglese, che andava per la Christianità Ambasciadore di Abbas Re di Persia, da esso inviato principalmente a Gregorio Decimoquinto, per la mossa dell' armi contro 'l Turco suo nimico, Antonio ritrasse questo Signore e la moglie nell' habito persiano, accrescendo con la vaghezza de gli habiti peregrini la bellezza de' ritratti' (Giovanni Pietro Bellori, *Le Vite de Pittori, Scultori et Architetti Moderni*, Rome, 1672, p.255).—An eighteenth-century water-colour copy of the Vandyke portrait of Sherley is in the British Museum and is reproduced in E.D.Ross, *Sir Anthony Sherley*, facing p.225. Another portrait, from an engraving based on a miniature by Peter Oliver, faces p.50 of Sir William Foster's *John Company*, 1926.

In January 1624, the Persian embassage arrived in England. Their coming was, it would seem, unexpected in London society, for John Chamberlain wrote: 'Sir Robert Sherley and his lady is come hither again, out of the clouds, I think, for I cannot learn where he hath been all this while.' [1] The interest and excitement occasioned by his coming are communicated to us by Samuel Purchas, that stay-at-home admirer and chronicler of far wanderers, who in 1624 was preparing his *Pilgrimes* for the press. 'Who ever since the beginning of things and men,' he exclaims, 'hath beene so often by Royall Employment sent Embassadour to so many Princes, so distant in place, so different in rites?' To review Sherley's accomplishments is 'to read a Geographicall Lecture in one man's travells.' His journey to the East was 'a noble attempt to goe meete the Sunne.' Breaking into Latin, Purchas asks: 'Quae regio in Terris Sherlii non plena laboris?' 'The mighty Ottoman,' he continues, 'terror of the Christian World, quaketh of a Sherly-Fever' because 'the prevailing Persian hath learned Sherleian Arts of War' and having been taught the use of artillery, 'they which at hand with the Sword were before dreadfull to the Turkes, now also in remoter blowes and sulfurian Arts are growne terrible.' Purchas goes on to say that he had the opportunity to meet Sherley personally and hoped to obtain from him some relation of his experiences which he might put into the *Pilgrimes*; but 'much and weightie businesse, which hee hath beene forced to attend' left the ambassador no leisure for autobiography. Purchas did, however, dine with him and derived from 'his humanitie and conference' information which he afterwards used in his narrative. He sets forth the Sherley policy, with an undiplomatic frankness which must have disconcerted the Shah's envoy, as being 'to kindle a fire betwixt the two most puissant of both Asian and Mahumetan Princes, that by their division and diversion of Turkish invasions, Christian Princes, Countries, and States might bee indebted to their [the Sherleys'] private undertaking.' He even goes so far as to describe this policy as a 'Jasonian sowing the Dragons teeth . . . whereby Mahumetans have killed each other, while Christen-

1 17 January 1624, E.P.Shirley, op.cit., p.88. Compare *C.S.P.,Dom., 1623-5*, p.150.

Teresa, Lady Sherley

dome might have gotten the Golden Fleece, the usuall fruit of peace.' 'Let mee admire,' he exclaims, 'such a Traveller, which travells not of and for some vaine discourse, or private gaine or skill, but still travelleth and is delivered of the publicke good!' So with a characteristic play on words Purchas concludes his encomium.[1] His summary of the policy of Sir Robert Sherley (with which he associates to some extent that of his brother Anthony) distorts the truth, for while on the one hand it was not so disinterested as he makes out, on the other it was never deliberately and guilefully anti-Persian; and while this summary may have enhanced Robert's popularity in England it was bound to amaze and enrage Shah Abbas if any report of it came to Isfahan.

When the time came for an audience with King James Robert's turban again caused trouble. 'He much affected to appear in foreign vests,' says Thomas Fuller, 'and as if his Clothes were his limbs, accounted himself never ready till he had something of the Persian Habit about him.' [2] As on the occasion of his first return to England, Robert was faced with a dilemma: to remove his turban would be an offence to the Shah; not to remove it would be an offence to King James. The duty of reconciling these conflicting points of etiquette lay upon Sir John Finett, the Assistant Master of Ceremonies at court. After Sherley had told Finett that 'he had kept it always on in the Presence of the Emperour and the King of Spaine,' the citation of these precedents satisfied King James, who 'in regard to his [Sherley's] naturall Subjection'—that is, considering that he was by birth a subject—had at first been disinclined to permit him to remain covered in his presence, but in view of the circumstances made 'allowance' and accepted a compromise: Sherley removed his turban, laid it at the King's feet, and donned it again. The punctilious orientalism of his behaviour at these royal audiences was not only a matter of costume; Finett describes how he bowed low, touching the ground first with his right hand and then with his head.[3]

1 Purchas, x,374f.
2 *Worthies*, ii,393.
3 *Finetti Philoxenis: Som choice Observations . . . touching the Reception and Precedence, the Treatment and Audience, the Punctillios and Contests of Forren Ambassadors in England*, 1656, pp.136f.

The conferences, which began promptly, at first went well. The recent attack on Ormuz had emphasized the common interests existing between England and Persia, and King James was personally inclined to come to a commercial understanding.[1] But the Levant Company was as stubbornly opposed as ever to an arrangement that would reduce their trade with Turkey. The interlocking membership between that Company and the East India Company served to strengthen opposition on the part of the latter organization. While they acknowledged that in theory Sherley's proposals were advantageous, the India merchants declined them, 'thinking the trade too great for them.'[2] That is, they did not want the raw silk trade diverted from its ancient route through Turkey and could not guarantee to accept more silk than, they reckoned, the market could absorb. (In earlier years they had had repeated and bitter experience of the difficulty of disposing of too great quantities of commodities from the East.) The trade of the Company was at this time declining on account of the fierce competition of the Dutch;[3] some of the shareholders were urging that their affairs be wound up and the organization disbanded; and even the most hopeful were in no mood to undertake new and costly commerce in Persia. But Sherley was probably encouraged by the criticism of the East India Company's monopoly uttered in the House of Commons during this year.[4] Furthermore, James, whose interest in the English silk-weavers had already led him to disappointing experiments in the acclimatization of the silk-worm in England, was willing to consider the import of raw silk. A tentative arrangement was made with the King to charter four or five vessels independently of the East India Company and send them to

---

1 C.S.P.,Dom., 1623-5, p.381.   2 Ibid., p.349.
3 The rivalry with the Dutch became acute in 1622 and is reflected in the following publications of that year: The Hollanders Declaration of the Affaires of the East Indies, Amsterdam [really London], 1622; An answere to the Hollanders Declaration, 1622; A courante of newes from the East India, 1622; A second courante of newes from the East India, 1622. None of these four pieces contains a proper imprint indicating printer or bookseller; the third and fourth do not even reveal the place of publication (which was of course London). These irregular meagre imprints point to difficulties with the censorship. In the following year, 1623, came the Dutch outrages against the English at Amboyna; see p.332, note 3, below.
4 W.R.Scott, Joint-Stock Companies, ii,106.

Persia. For the moment nothing came of this; but the three 'Persian Voyages' of 1628–29–30, though organized by the Company's own agents, were in effect a posthumous recognition of the practicability of Sherley's designs.[1]

The death of King James (27 March 1625) brought these negotiations to a standstill. In April Sherley was granted an audience by King Charles, but there was opportunity for only 'some few words of condoling compliment.'[2]

Then suddenly all Sir Robert's hopes and expectations crashed round him. Probably persuaded by the agents of the East India Company who were intriguing in Persia against Sherley, Shah Abbas sent to England another ambassador, a native Persian, named Naqd 'Ali Beg. His appointment was a grave reflection upon Sherley, implying that the Shah lacked confidence in him and warranting the suspicion that he was a charletan. The events which followed the new envoy's arrival are narrated by Sir John Finett, whose pleasant phraseology, appropriate to such a tragi-comedy, is retained so far as possible in the following much abbreviated account.[3]

The East India merchants exerted themselves to do signal honour to the new ambassador, going so far as to defray the expenses of his board and residence. In so acting their motive was to belittle Sherley. Accompanied by Finett (in his official capacity as a master of diplomatic ceremonial) and by several noblemen, Sherley presented himself at the envoy's house. Naqd 'Ali Beg, sitting 'on his legs doubled under him after the Persian Posture,' afforded 'no motion of respect' to any of the party until an interpreter informed him of Lord Cleaveland's rank, when 'he let fall his trust-up leggs from his chaire, and made a kinde of respect to his Lordship.' The object of the visit was to exhibit Sir Robert's credentials; but when Sherley produced the document, kissing it and touching it to

---

1 Ibid., ii,109f. A character in Thomas Randolph's *Hey for Honesty* (*Poetical and Dramatic Works*, ed. Hazlitt, p.455) boasts that his credit with the London merchants is so good that he can

>　　borrow money ne'er to be repaid
>　Till the return of my silver fleet from Persia.

2 Finett, op.cit., p.145.
3 Ibid., pp.172f.

his eyes, the Persian 'snatched his Letters from him, toare them, and gave him a blow on the face with his Fist.' Some of the company intervened and 'remonstrated . . . the danger and insolencie of the Fact.' Sir Robert seems to have been dazed; he offered no resistance and was afterwards criticized by his English acquaintance for suffering the buffet without returning it in kind. Naqd 'Ali Beg declared that Sherley's letters were forged and explained his own violence as the result of his anger that 'so meane a fellow and an Imposter should presume to say he had married the King his Masters Neece.' (Evidently the envoy had picked up gossip founded on Nixon's pamphlet or on the play about the Sherley brothers.) Sherley, 'who in the meane time retyred behind the company, amazed and confounded with his blow and treatment,' declared that he had never said any such thing; his wife was a kinswoman of the Persian Queen. He also disproved to the satisfaction of the Englishmen present the charge that his credentials were counterfeit.

This shocking scandal caused much excitement. Naqd 'Ali Beg's audience with King Charles was postponed; and when at length he was admitted to the royal presence he behaved with extreme arrogance and insolence, scarcely bowing to his Majesty and turning his back on him when he was dismissed. But though Sherley had the sympathy of the court, the Lords in Council failed to reconcile the differences between the rival envoys and at length decided that the only course to follow was to pack them both off to Persia so that their master might adjudicate between them and send whichever he pleased to England again.

V

WHILE this controversy raged and the problems growing out of it were debated, Naqd 'Ali Beg suffered the loss of a member of his retinue. With him there had come to London a Persian merchant named Khwaja Shahsuwar, a man evidently of some importance since in 1613 and again in 1621 he had been in Venice on missions from the Shah.[1] His son was in London

1 Berchet, *La Repubblica di Venezia e la Persia*, pp.48f.,210f.

with him. In August 1626, Khwaja Shahsuwar died. The East India Company arranged for his burial in the lower church-yard of Saint Botolph's Bishopsgate, not within but just without London wall, in ground not consecrated for Christian burial. There is a brief account of his death and funeral in Anthony Munday's expanded edition of Stow's *Survey of London* (1633) and additional details are furnished in Strype's edition of Stow (1720) from which the following is quoted:

> In Petty France, out of Christian Burial, was buried Hodges [Hajji] Shaughsware a Persian Merchant, who with his Son came over with the Persian Ambassador, and was buried by his own Son, who read certain Prayers, and used other Ceremonies, according to the Custom of their own Country, Morning and Evening, for a whole Month after the Burial: For whom is set up at the Charge of his Son, a Tomb of Stone with certain Persian characters thereon; the Exposition thus, *This Grave is made for Hodges Shaughsware, the chiefest Servant to the King of Persia, for the space of twenty Years, who came from the King of Persia and dyed in his Service. If any Persian cometh out of that Country let him read this and a Prayer for him; the Lord receive his Soul, for here lyeth Maghmote Shaughsware, who was born in the Town of Novoy in Persia.*

The chronicle continues with an account of the funeral, which was attended by the ambassador and many other Persians. The rites were performed for the most part by the dead man's son who sat cross-legged at the head of the grave, reading and singing, 'intermixed with sighing and weeping.' For a month the mourners returned twice a day for further funerary devotions; 'and had come,' says the chronicler, 'the whole time of their abode here in England, had not the rudeness of our People disturbed and prevented their Purpose.' [1] There is

1 John Stow, *A Survey of London and Westminster*, ed. John Strype, 1720, Book ii, pp.93f. This contains an illustration of the 'Persian Tomb' which is reproduced in Smith's *Antiquities of London*, 1791, and again in Sir William Foster's *John Company*. The monument disappeared long since, probably about 1862 when the churchyard was converted in part into a public recreation-ground while on other parts offices were erected. What became of it is unknown; it was probably destroyed by ignorant workmen. This curious and now lost antiquity was not, it may be added, analogous to the old Turkish tomb-stone surmounted with a sculptured turban which was found in some gardens adjoining the Middle Temple in 1852 (see *Notes and Queries*, Third Series, ix,36,109; *Journal of the Royal Asiatic Society*, xiii,Part ii). That object seems to have been brought to England as ballast or else as a curiosity and set up in the gardens as an ornament.

unconscious pathos in this simple narrative. The Persians, till interrupted and driven off by the jeers and perhaps the missiles of a crowd of London roughs, were performing the obsequies in the fashion of their country. When Sir Thomas Herbert was in Persia a short while afterwards he remarked that after a burial 'the next of kin watches to keep the evill Angell from his Tomb,' warbling meanwhile 'Elegiac Threnodies, as the last expression of love he can show him.' [1] A French traveller observes of a Persian funeral: 'Le deuil dure une année, et pendant ce tems on vient tous les jours faire des prieres sur le tombeau.' [2]

VI

WE come to the last phase of Sir Robert Sherley's restless life. Having reached their decision to send the two envoys back to Persia, the Lords in Council decided further to dispatch for the first time an ambassador to the court of the Shah. The ill-fated person chosen for this position was Sir Dodmore Cotton, a gentleman well known to King Charles.[3] Cotton hoped that the East India Company would pay him a large salary as they had done to their agent, Sir Thomas Roe, at the Great Mogul's court. But the merchants refused to risk any money in this Persian mission nor could they be persuaded by the King, who was forced to grant Cotton £1000 to furnish his expedition together with an allowance of two pounds per day for expenses on the way. It was reckoned that after the mission reached Persia the Shah would defray the costs. Cotton's official instructions are extant: to tell the Shah of the clash between Sherley and Naqd 'Ali Beg; to inquire whether the Shah was prepared to abide by Sherley's proposals; and, if the answer was in the affirmative, to promise that King Charles would endeavour to meet his wishes so far as possible.[4]

Among the gentlemen who accompanied Cotton was Thomas

---

1 Thomas Herbert, *Relation of Some Yeares Travaile*, ed. 1638, p.236.
2 Père Gabriel de Chinon, *Relations Nouvelles du Levant*, Lyons, 1671, p.118.
3 See Sir William Foster's introduction, pp.xixf., to his abridged edition of Thomas Herbert's *Relation* which under the title *Travels in Persia* is in the *Broadway Travellers* Series, 1928.
4 Ibid., p.xxi, from a manuscript at All Souls' College.

Herbert, a young man who had lately obtained from his distant kinsman the Earl of Pembroke an 'allowance to defray his charge' for travel and who, not satisfied with the customary grand tour, sought this larger experience of the eastern world. On his return to England he composed a narrative of his adventures and observations which is the principal source of information about Sir Robert Sherley's last days.[1]

1 Of this the first edition, 1634, has two title-pages, one engraved and beginning *A Description of the Persian Monarchy*, the other printed and beginning *A Relation of Some Yeares Travaile*. In subsequent editions, 1638, 1639, 1665, and 1677, only the second title (with trifling variations) was employed, as follows: *A Relation of Some Yeares Travels into Divers Parts of Asia and Afrique. Describing especially the two famous Empires, the Persian, and the Great Mogull: weaved with the History of these later Times. As also, many rich and spatious Kingdomes in the Orientall India, and other parts of Asia; Together with the adjacent Iles. Severally relating the Religion, Languages, Qualities, Customes, Habit, Descent, Fashions, and other Observations touching them*, 1638. There are changes in each later edition and very considerable enlargements, the new material being drawn not from Herbert's own memories of his experiences but at second-hand from other writers and often about countries and peoples he had not himself visited. (For example, his long disquisition on two religious sects owes much to Henry Lord, *A Display of Two forraigne sects in the East Indies, viz!: The Sect of the Banians the Ancient Natives of India and the Sect of the Persees the Ancient Inhabitants of Persia, together with the Religion and Maners of each sect*, 1630). Herbert's narrative stands in need of shortening, as Jonathan Swift remarked long ago; but Foster's abridgement, mentioned p.330, note 3, above, is too drastic.—The most interesting pages of Herbert's book have to do with his visit to Persepolis. He was perhaps the first Englishman to visit the famous ruins. True, Lionel Plumtree says that Geoffrey Duckett had been there, finding the ancient city 'now altogether ruined and defaced' (Hakluyt, iii,154), but Sir William Foster gives good reasons for believing that Duckett did not actually visit the site (*England's Quest of Eastern Trade*, p.40). Be that as it may, Plumtree's report, whether founded upon observation or hearsay, is of interest in relation to Marlowe's celebrated line about the city. Commentators upon Tamburlaine's ambition 'to ride in triumph through Persepolis' (*1 Tamburlaine*, II,v,24 and 49) have generally remarked upon Marlowe's apparent ignorance of the fact that after its destruction by Alexander the Great Persepolis remained in utter ruin; but Miss Ellis-Fermor, the latest editor of the play, affirms that it 'was not actually at this time a ruin' but 'was presumably to some extent rebuilt as it figures in ancient and medieval history.' This defence of Marlowe's accuracy seems unjustified, for the modern Shiraz was sometimes identified by travellers with Persepolis (for example, *The Travellers Breviat*, p.150; Cartwright, *The Preachers Travels*, p.84) and the historians to whom Miss Ellis-Fermor alludes either refer to Shiraz or perhaps to the small town of Mardash near the ruins, which may have been called by the great name much as Baghdad was commonly called Babylon. Later visitors support Plumtree's assertion that the site was an utter ruin. Sir Thomas Herbert so describes it (*Relation*, 1634, pp.58f.), and an illustration in his book shows nothing but a group of columns standing upon a platform to which a flight of steps leads up—very much as it is today. Herbert notes that the inhabitants of Mardash 'so little know or value memory, that they daily teare away the monument, for Sepulchres or benches to sit on.' Fryer, too, gives a careful description of Persepolis and reports it in ruins and uninhabited (*A New Account of East India and Persia*, ii,221; a footnote at this reference discusses the puzzling problem of the name and identity of Mardash). One may also compare the description with an accompanying illustration in Gemelli's *Voyage around the World* (Book ii, chapter ix; Churchill's *Collection of Voyages*, iv,164). It is evident from all this that Marlowe was relying upon his imagination, not upon geographical knowledge, when he made his hero aspire to ride in triumph through Persepolis.

Sherley took with him many presents for the Shah, some purchased in England, others on the continent, including a vast quantity of Venetian glass, fifty sword-blades, and more else than there is space here to enumerate.[1] He carried also a personal letter from King Charles to Shah Abbas which shows that royal sympathy was with him in his quarrel with Naqd 'Ali Beg. Charles explains that the only way to solve 'soe strange a contradiction' of claims was to send both envoys home, but goes on to declare that the Persian's conduct in striking Sherley and tearing up his commission 'could not have been passed over in his Majesty's just and civill governement but for respect to the King of Persia, whose ambassador he was.'[2]

The East India merchants upon whom devolved the obligation of sending these diplomats to Persia feared lest Sherley might turn pirate en route and ruin their commerce or might confiscate the goods stored in their factories on the Persian Gulf in revenge for their rejection of his proposals. They therefore refused to provide him with an escort of several ships, which had been originally intended as a precaution against a possible attack by the Barbary corsairs who were then committing many outrages, and they limited him to a single vessel in which he voyaged with Cotton, Herbert, and other Englishmen. So intense was the bitterness between Sherley and his Persian rival that it was out of the question to send them home together. Consequently a separate ship was assigned to Naqd 'Ali Beg and his retinue. Arrangements were made to land them at separate Persian ports. The merchants displayed their partisanship by 'richly accomodating the Persian' in a brand-new ship, the *Mary*,[3] while on the other ship, the *Star*,

---

1 See the interesting list of articles which accompanies his petition for permission to take them out of England without paying export duty, E.P.Shirley, op.cit., pp.92f.
2 Ibid., p.96.
3 The *Mary* had been launched the previous October. This is the subject of part of the plot of Walter Mountfort's curious drama *The Launching of the Mary or the Seamans honest wyfe*, the last item in the batch of fifteen manuscript plays in Egerton MS. 1994 (folios 317–349); ed. J.H.Water, Malone Society, 1933. (This edition is erroneously called a reprint on the title-page; the play had never been printed before.) It is in part a defence of the policy of the East India Company, in part a refutation of the belief that seamen's wives, in the absence of their husbands, were no better than they should be. References to Dutch outrages against the English at Amboyna in 1623 got the piece in trouble with the censor and connect it with an anonymous ballad called *Newes out of East India of the cruell usage of our English merchants at*

they provided quarters for Sherley and Cotton that are described as 'kennels.' Furthermore, they made an allowance to Naqd 'Ali Beg for wine on the voyage but none for Sherley.[1]

The *Mary* and the *Star* with other ships bound for the East Indies sailed from Dover on 23 March 1627. Sherley's vessel was seen labouring down the Channel in such a storm that it was feared lest the voyage end in a wreck ere it was well begun.[2] We may pass over the tedious and on the whole uneventful weeks at sea[3] and come at once to Swally, near Surat, where Naqd 'Ali Beg, fearing the wrath of his formidable master and with a desperate gesture tacitly acknowledging that he had been in the wrong in the quarrel with Sherley, committed suicide by swallowing an overdose of opium. His body was conveyed ashore and entombed, says Herbert, 'not a stones cast from Tom Coryats grave, knowne but by two poore stones, there resting till the resurrection.'[4] Many years later John Fryer came to Surat and noted that 'this way was all strewed with Moor-men's Tombs, and one of especial Note of a Persian Ambassador, who returning from England with Sir Anthony Sherley, is reported to poyson himself here, rather than answer some ill Management of his Office to his Master.'[5]

In the early summer of 1628 Sherley and his party reached Ashraf, the Shah's summer retreat on the shores of the Caspian. Abbas was a grimmer and more world-worn despot than he had been when Sherley left Persia eleven years before. He was tortured with memories of his barbaric cruelty to his son Khudabanda (Mirza)—of whose unhappy fate Herbert gives an account in his book. The prospect of an audience with the tyrant could not have been an agreeable one. However, the

Amboyna [1625] and more distantly with Dryden's drama *Amboyna*. The author of *The Launching of the Mary* was an official of the East India Company and a very poor dramatist. For an elaborate study of the play from various angles see F.S.Boas, *Shakespeare and the Universities*, Oxford, 1923, chapters viii-x.

1 For these arrangements see *C.S.P.,Dom., 1623-5*, p.309; ibid., *1625-6*, p.345; ibid., *1627-8*, pp.27f.,98f.

2 Some tradition of this storm may have been passed down to Thomas Fuller who says, oddly, that Sherley died at sea (*Worthies*, ii,394).

3 Four extant manuscript journals of this voyage are summarized in Sir William Foster, *English Factories in India, 1624-29*, pp.183f.

4 *Relation*, 1634, p.35.

5 *A New Account of East India and Persia*, i,252. Here as elsewhere William Crooke, the Hakluyt Society's editor, does not correct Fryer's error of Anthony for Robert Sherley.

two English envoys were received civilly, and the Shah even went so far, says Herbert, as to remove his turban as a token of respect to Sir Dodmore Cotton.[1] It was soon obvious, nevertheless, that he was disappointed to learn that Cotton's mission was one of tentative inquiry only.[2] It was also obvious that Sherley's position at court was insecure, for a certain favourite, one Mahomet 'Ali Beg, an old enemy of Robert's and, in Herbert's words, 'a most pragmatical pagan,' was intriguing against him. This courtier undertook to show King Charles's letter to the Shah and then with deliberate deceit suppressed the document. It was believed that Mahomet had been bribed; Herbert does not reveal by whom but hints that agents of the East India Company had a hand in the affair. Whatever the cause, the Shah turned upon Sherley with sudden violence, wishing him 'to depart his kingdome, as old and troublesome.'[3] This treatment of one who had served him for nearly thirty years confirms Sir Thomas Roe's characterization of Shah Abbas as 'one who will eate upon any man . . . and when hee hath left you empty will not know you.' Roe says also: 'The disposition of the King [Abbas] is to bee very familiar with strangers if they be in Cash. In hope to gett, no man can escape him; when he hath suckd them, hee will not knowe them.'[4] Alas! Sir Robert Sherley had been sucked and was empty.

To Sherley this disgrace was a shattering blow; and at Kasvin less than a fortnight later, on 13 July 1628, 'he gave,' says Herbert, 'this miserable and fickle world an ultimum vale in his great clymacterick,[5] and (wanting a fitter place of burial) we intombed him under the threshold of his own house in this city without much ceremony.' Herbert adds his own encomium and estimate of Sherley, in prose and verse:

1 This episode is referred to by Robert Baron in his long note on 'Tulipant' (that is, turban) in *Mirza*, pp.179f.
2 Malcolm, *History of Persia*, i,549; Sykes, *History of Persia*, ii,196f.
3 Herbert, op.cit., p.124.
4 *The Embassy of Sir Thomas Roe*, ii,433 and 419.
5 Herbert was misinformed about Sir Robert's age. The grand climacteric is the sixty-third year; Sherley was forty-eight or forty-nine when he died. In later editions Herbert says more cautiously that his age 'exceeded not the great clymacterick.' Sir William Foster is certainly mistaken in accepting (in his abridgment of Herbert, p.324) Herbert's first categorical statement.

Hee was the greatest traveller in his time, and no man had eaten more salt than he, none had more relisht the mutabilities of Fortune. He had a heart as free as any man: his patience was more Philosophicall than his Intellect, having small acquaintance with the Muses: many Cities he saw, many hills climb'd over, and tasted many severall waters; yet Athens, Parnassus, Hippocrene were strangers to him, his Notion prompted him to other employments: hee had tasted of sundry Princes favours: . . . and from the Persian Monarch had enricht himselfe by many meriting services: but obtained least . . . when he best deserved, and most expected it. Ranck mee with those that honour him: and in that he wants the guilded trophees and hyeroglyphicks of honour to illustrate his wretched Sepulchre (his vertue can out-brave those bubbles of vanitie, *Facta ducis vivunt*: and till some will doe it better) accept this *Ultima amoris expressio* from him, who so long traveld with him, that so much honour'd him.

> After land-sweats, and many a storme by Sea,
> This hillock aged Sherleys rest must be.
> He well had view'd Armes, men, and fashions strange
> In divers Lands. Desire so makes us range.
> But turning course, whilst th' Persian Tyrant he
> With well dispatched charge hop'd glad would be;
> See Fortunes scorn! under this Doore he lyes,
> Who living, had no place to rest his eyes.
> With what sad thoughts, mans mind long hopes do twine,
> Learn by anothers losse, but not by thine.[1]

Of Naqd 'Ali Beg, Shah Abbas had said that it was well for that envoy that he had killed himself, for otherwise 'I had cut him in as many pieces as there are dayes in a yeare, and burnt them in the open market with stincking dogs turds.' But of Sherley he said, now that it was too late, that he had 'done for him more than any of his native subjects.'[2]

Ten days after Sherley's death Sir Dodmore Cotton died of 'a deadly flux,'[3] the victim of the unhealthy climate of northern Persia which had carried off many of the English factors of the old Muscovy Company.[4]

The disquieting position in which the remaining Englishmen

1 Herbert, *Relation*, ed. 1638, p.203. 3 Ibid.,p. 204.
2 Ibid., p.170.   4 Curzon, *Persia and the Persian Question*, i,387.

now found themselves may be easily imagined. 'We have small joy to stay here any more,' wrote Herbert; 'three Ambassadors wee have buried.'[1] The greatest hardships were borne by Lady Sherley. After her husband's death a Flemish artist named Cole,[2] under pretence of an old unpaid loan to Sherley, conspired with Mahomet 'Ali Beg and obtained a warrant to seize the widow's goods. Getting wind of this, she entrusted her jewels to Master Hedges, one of Sherley's men. When (in Herbert's words) 'the Pagan serjeants with John the Fleming' came to her house, they rifled it of whatever was valuable or vendible: 'horses, camels, vests, turbans, a rich Persian dagger, and some other things'; but 'finding no jewels (for . . . it was for them they had worried in their ostrich appetites), mad, angry, and ashamed, they departed unsatisfied.'

Now that Cotton was dead, the pecuniary allowance from the Shah upon which he had reckoned was cut off. The chaplain of the party, Doctor Gooch, assumed charge. All that they could do was to set out for home as best they could. Leaving Lady Sherley behind them, they made for the coast and sailed from Swally in April 1629. They arrived in England the following January.[3]

Meanwhile Lady Sherley had taken refuge with the Carmelite fathers in their mission at Isfahan. The death of Shah Abbas, who notwithstanding his recent unfriendliness had after all relied upon her late husband for many years and was her own

1 Op.cit., p.205.
2 E.F.Shirley (op.cit., p.99) had in his possession a portrait of Sir Robert in oriental costume which he believed to be the work of this artist. To the right of the head was an inscription in Persian running: 'The Protector of the Universe has graciously condescended to cast his light upon the portrait of his Ambassador to Frangistan.' In the *Journal of the Royal Asiatic Society*, 1838, p.214, is described another portrait, then in the possession of Lord Western and by some attributed to this same Fleming. Sir John Malcolm, in his *Sketches of Persia from the Journals of a Traveller in the East*, 1828, ii,124, tells us that when in 1800 an English envoy was preparing to make his official entry into Teheran there was shown to him as a pattern for an envoy's court dress a miniature which the Persians said was of 'the English Representative.' It was in Elizabethan costume. It is more likely that it was a portrait of Anthony Sherley than of Robert; certainly of one or the other. See further E.P.Shirley, *Stemmata Shirleiana*, p.274.
3 Herbert's narrative is supplemented, especially for the return voyage, by the fragmentary but interesting diary of another member of Cotton's suite, lately discovered in the Bodleian; see *The Journal of Robert Stodart*, ed. Sir E.Denison Ross, 1935. In this volume Ross prints also Dr. Gooch's account of the mission (chiefly a defence of Sherley and complaints of the 'sordid entertainment' provided by the Shah); see the *Calendar of the Clarendon Papers*, 1872, i,32.

connection by marriage, occurred in January 1629. As a consequence she found herself in a critical position, because Abbas's grandson, Sufi Mirza who now ascended the throne as Shah Sufi, was a religious bigot. To him Lady Sherley was denounced as a Christian, and when brought before him she made, according to the Carmelites' narrative, a courageous profession of her faith.[1] This is the scene, painted in grisaille, below the portrait of Lady Sherley painted long afterwards in Rome. It depicts a young woman who, bearing upon her shoulder a large cross, stands before an enthroned monarch who is garbed in the classical toga but wears a turban, while turbaned soldiers stand round. What was the immediate outcome of that ordeal is uncertain; but eventually she managed to escape from Persia, travelled by way of Anatolia and Constantinople, and reached Rome at the end of 1634. She installed herself in a house in Trastevere near the church of Santa Maria della Scala—a house which is still standing in that quiet backwater of the city. The long remainder of her life she devoted to good works under the direction of her spiritual advisers the Carmelites. In 1658 [2] she effected the translation of her husband's bones from Isfahan to Rome and buried them in the church with which she had been associated so long. In 1663 she had a portrait of Sir Robert painted, copied from the engraving of 1609. Her own portrait, painted at the same time, of an old and care-worn woman, shows little trace of the exotic beauty which distinguishes the Vandyke portrait of forty years before; but the high-bridged nose and elongated eyes are recognizably the same. Five years later, in 1668, she died at the age of seventy-nine and was buried in the same grave with her husband.

The tomb is in the floor of the nave of Santa Maria della Scala, just outside the second chapel on the right coming from the west door. It is a great stone slab upon which the heraldic bearings of Sir Robert Sherley are displayed in inlaid coloured marbles. A proud inscription in Latin recites the titles and

1 B.-I.de Sainte-Anne, *La Mission de Perse*, pp.263f.
2 This is the date on the tomb; the Carmelites' *Historia Generalis*, ii,384, gives the date as 1662–3.

honours bestowed upon him by 'Scia Abas,' by the Emperor, by popes and many kings, and records that his bones were brought *in urbem e Perside* by his wife.[1]

As a more general epitaph not only upon Sir Robert but upon Sir Thomas and Sir Anthony, Archbishop Abbot's comment may serve: 'All venture on great things and come to beggary.' [2]

VII

THERE remains the question why the memory of these three brothers, picturesque and romantic personalities, proud and energetic, stubborn and sometimes truculent, scheming and ambitious and yet ineffectual, is not more plainly stamped upon the English imagination. They were the theme of pamphlets and gossip in their own day, admired, pitied, jeered at, and sometimes feared. But no great drama or poem or romance was ever founded upon their deeds. Perhaps it was because, though venturing on great things, they all came to beggary; they were not successful. More likely it was because their reputations were tinged with suspicions of disloyalty; they were prototypes of what at a much later date came to be called 'rogue Englishmen.' Their fame, moreover, has been obscured by the glory of greater men—Grenville and Frobisher, Ralegh and Drake, and others of a gallant company. Only occasionally does one come across anyone, even among those well versed in Elizabethan life and letters, who has any accurate knowledge of their careers; and it is no exaggeration to say that there does not exist an account of them that is not either inaccurate or incomplete or both. Travellers in successive generations who followed them into Persia—Fryer and Malcolm and Curzon, for example—picked up and handed on traditions of the brothers. Horace Walpole accumulated many notes on them, his intention having been, it is said, to compose a monograph which would clear up the confusion existing about them.[3] The Romantic Period, notwithstanding its char-

1 The epitaph is quoted in full in B.-I.de Sainte-Anne, op.cit., p.272, and in E.P.Shirley, *Stemmata Shirleiana*, pp.285f.
2 Letter to Sir Thomas Roe, *C.S.P.,Dom.*, *1611-18*, p.429.
3 *Letters of Horace Walpole*, ed. Toynbee, Oxford, 1904, iv,84, and vi,24.

acteristic interest in the Levant, passed them by, save for the anonymous compilation called *The Three English Brothers*, a dainty little book, typical of its decade, valuable for its text of Manwaring's narrative, but not altogether reliable and far from complete. In lively fashion but not without many errors General Briggs retold their story to the Asiatic Society in 1841. Three years later it was revamped for popular consumption and amazingly sentimentalized by an anonymous writer who depended in the main and quite uncritically upon Manwaring and Nixon.[1] Family pride and antiquarian enthusiasm impelled E.P.Shirley to explore the letters and other documents in the old 'State Paper Office,' the British Museum, and the East India archives. Upon his researches the later investigator depends in part; but many documents bearing upon the Sherleys have been calendared since his time.

1 'The Three Shirleys' [*sic*], *The Gentleman's Magazine*, New Series, xii (November and December 1844), pp.473f.,594f. For further references see p.239, note 1, above.

CHAPTER EIGHT

'THE THRONE OF PIRACY'

I

THE heroic or golden age of Mediterranean piracy (if such epithets may be applied to such a calling) covers the first three quarters of the sixteenth century, or, to be more precise, from 1492, when Ferdinand and Isabella drove the Moors from southern Spain, to 1571, the year of the battle of Lepanto. Depredations in the Mediterranean had been growing in frequency and seriousness ever since the Crusades and especially since the establishment of Venetian and Genoese commerce in the Levant. But the danger increased suddenly when the exiled Moors, thirsting for revenge against the country which had thrust them out and seeking compensation for their lost property, came to terms with the local Beys and other leaders along the north-west coast of Africa and in return for a percentage of their booty were permitted to make use of the harbours of Morocco, Algiers, and Tunis. Gradually the chief corsairs came to dominate the Barbary Coast, and as religious fanaticism fanned the flames of desire for vengeance sporadic spoliation of Spain developed into something like a *Jihad*.

In 1519, at the conclusion of a seven-years' war of conquest, Algiers was added to the Ottoman Empire. Kheyr-ed-din, the most formidable of all the pirates, then offered his services to the Sultan, declared himself his vassal, and received from the Porte the title of Viceroy or Governor-General of Algiers. But the Turkish conquest did not extend to Morocco on the westernmost fringe of the Islamic world. Consequently at a later period, when the Porte was heeding the remonstrances of European ambassadors and attempting, or at any rate pretending to attempt, to suppress piracy, the centre of the activity of the corsairs was shifted from the harbours of Tunis and Algiers to remote Sallee on the Atlantic coast of Morocco.

The story of Kheyr-ed-din and of his elder brother Arouj (both known to Europe as Barbarossa) and of their able lieutenants and successors Dragut (slain at Malta in 1565), Murad, and the rest, has been often told;[1] and our concern here is with later phases of these pernicious activities when, after Lepanto, the corsairs were in large measure deprived of the protection which Turkish prestige had previously afforded them. An age of petty piracy followed. Depredations were no longer undertaken upon a large scale. In their place were quick sudden raids with, if possible, an avoidance of fighting and a swift escape with captives and plunder. Where the corsairs had been sea-highwaymen, so to speak, they now became sea-sneak-thieves. But they remained none the less a formidable nuisance and a constant menace to merchantmen.

These raids, from which the chief sufferers were the Spaniards, were often tacitly encouraged by France as a means of weakening the power of Spain. There was also, during the last two decades of Elizabeth's reign, an informal understanding between the Barbary pirates and the English privateers. England had a long tradition of buccaneering; vessels engaged in lawless enterprise had put out for many years from West Country ports such as Plymouth and especially Bristol.[2] The privateers whom Elizabeth encouraged to attack Spanish shipping had a bond of sympathy with the Moors and renegades of Africa. English sailors occasionally visited the ports of Barbary; Hakluyt records the voyage of the *Lion* in 1551 and the mission of Edward Hogan in 1577.[3] When the news of the defeat of the Spanish Armada reached Barbary, we are told, 'the Englishmen that were there, hadde . . . leave of Mahamet [that is, the Sharif Muley Hamet] to espresse their joy in Bone-fires and other triumphs.'[4] It must

---

1 See in general R.L.Playfair, *The Scourge of Christendom*, 1884; Stanley Lane-Poole, *Barbary Corsairs*, 1890; J.S.Corbett, *England in the Mediterranean*, i, chapter ii; and Philip Gosse, *The History of Piracy*, 1932.
2 C.L.Kingsford, *Prejudice and Promise in Fifteenth Century England*, Oxford, 1925, chapter iv: 'West Country Piracy.'
3 Hakluyt, vi,136f. and 285f.
4 George Wilkins, *Three Miseries of Barbary: Plague, Famine, Civill warre. With a relation of the death of Mahamet the late Emperour: and a briefe report of the now present Wars betweene the three Brothers* [1604], Sig. B^v.

not be supposed, however, that a common hatred of Spain sufficed to protect English merchantmen from the depredations of the corsairs. From surviving records it is not always possible to tell whether lost ballads and news-sheets on the subject of brushes with pirates had to do with those of Barbary or Spain or even with the Knights of Malta. What was the fight 'in the passage of the straits' in 1586? [1] What was the subject of a 'Ballad of Tripoli'? [2] Or of a 'Dittye of the fight upon the seas . . . in the straytes of Jubraltare.'? [3]

Outlaws of different strata of European society, from gentlemen-adventurers to the lowest ruffians, flocked to Barbary in search of gain. 'La plus part de ceux qu'on appelle Turcs en Alger,' says Nicolas de Nicolay, 'sont Chrestiens reniez et Mahumetizez de toutes nations, . . . tous addonez à paillardise, Sodomie, larrecins et tous autres vices detestables ne vivans que des courses, rapines, et pilleries qu'ils font sur la mer et Isles circonvoisines.' [4] It is an exaggeration to say that most of these scoundrels were renegade Christians; but there were many such among the pirates and several of the most notorious leaders, including the two brothers Barbarossa, were among the number. Nicolas de Nicolay adds that most of them were Italians, Spaniards, or of Provence; he does not mention Englishmen; and as a matter of fact not only at the time when he wrote but at a later date English cut-throats were not so numerous among the corsairs as were the off-scouring of the Latin nations.

The Barbary coast offered ideal bases for piratical operations, a succession of natural shallow harbours with lagoons protected

---

1 'A true report of the Late woorthie fight performed in the voyage from Turke [*sic*] by fyve shippes of London against xi gallies and ii fregates the strongest of Christendom in the passage of the straightes the 13 of Julye 1586 by Thomas Ellis marryner,' *Stationers' Register*, 10 November 1586 (Arber's *Transcript*, ii,459).

2 Ibid., 19 June 1587 (Arber, ii,472).

3 Ibid., 31 July 1590 (Arber, ii,557).—Of writers who celebrated the exploits of English privateers one of the most vociferous was Henry Roberts (or Robarts). See his *Newes from the Levan[t]e Seas. Describing the many perrilous events of . . . Edward Glenham Esquire. His hardy attempts in honorable fights, in great perrill. With a relation of his troubles, and indirect dealings of the King of Argere in Barbarie. . . Written by H.R.*, 1594. See further L.B.Wright, 'Henry Robarts: Patriotic Propagandist and Novelist,' *Studies in Philology*, xxix (1932), 176f. and the same author's *Middle-Class Culture in Elizabethan England*, pp.515f.

4 *Navigations*, Antwerp, 1576, pp.16f.; T.Washington's English translation, 1585, folio 8ʳ; Purchas, vi,114.

by sandy islands from the sea within which the swift currents were navigable only by expert pilots in galleys of light draught.[1] These bases were well adapted both for defence and for swift escape if necessary. The securest harbour was Algiers[2] but many of the pirates, notably Captain Ward, used to operate from Tunis.

The policy of peace with Spain, initiated by James I and pursued till near the end of his reign despite popular opposition, was directly responsible for making the Barbary ports nests of desperate English outlaws. 'After the death of . . . Queen Elizabeth,' says Captain John Smith, 'our Royall King James . . . had no employment for those men of warre,' that is, for the buccaneers who, protected by Elizabeth's letters of marque, had thriven on Spanish plunder. 'Those that were rich,' continues Smith, 'retired with that they had; those that were poore and had nothing but from hand to mouth, turned Pirats.' These desperadoes did not confine their activities to raids against Spanish commerce but plundered French, Venetian, and even English shipping, and 'because they grew hatefull to all Christian Princes, they retired to Barbary.' These outlawed Englishmen were expert in seamanship and the ablest of them won positions of authority. But not everyone made a fortune. Among them there were poverty-stricken blackguards and wastrels. Smith paints an appalling picture of the factions among them: 'So riotous, quarrellous, treacherous, blasphemous, and villanous, it is more than a wonder they could so long continue to doe so much mischiefe; and all they got, they basely consumed it amongst Jewes,

1 'There be not many good Harbours,' John Smith remarked in his *True Travels*, but 'there are convenient Rodes, or the open sea, which is their chiefe Lordship' (*Travels and Works of John Smith*, ed. Arber and Bradley, ii,914).

2 In 1617, when he was a member of the Commission to determine measures for the suppression of Barbary piracy, Francis Bacon drew up a memorandum one of whose points was that 'the only harbour and receptacle of the Pirates is Argiers' and that though they made use of Tunis 'and other wild roads' yet if threatened with a fleet they would certainly retire to that one secure harbour (James Spedding, *The Letters and the Life of Francis Bacon*, ed. 1892, vi,175f.). Bacon's meditations on this problem are further illustrated in the same year in his correspondence with Sir John Digby who was in Spain negotiating for the Spanish marriage. Among the 'noble effects' of the proposed union between the royal houses of England and Spain Bacon notes that 'it will be a means utterly to extinguish and extirpate pirates, which are the common enemies of mankind, and do so much infest Europe at this time' (ibid., vi,158).

Turks, Moores, and whores.' They were accustomed to put to sea only when, having squandered their previous gains, necessity urged them to seek more plunder. Their preference was to remain ashore in riot or lethargy; and there 'they became so disjoynted, disordered, debawched, and miserable, that the Turks and Moores beganne to command them as slaves.' [1] Against this testimony must be set the fact that even in later years when hard blows had been struck against the pirates, there was no lack of energetic and resourceful leaders; but that the general run of them were squalid desperadoes there is other testimony besides that of John Smith. William Lithgow, who visited Tunis, calls them 'discontented castaways,' 'driven to the servitude of Infidells' and wearing 'the double yoake of dispaire and condemnation.' The terrors of a guilty conscience in these men who have denied Christ produces in them, says the same observer, 'a torment of melancholy' which is 'a torturing horror.' [2] A contemporary chronicler pictures them as weighed down with offences that are 'unpardonable by law and nature' because they have become Runagates and have 'wilfully submitted themselves unto Mahometisme, . . . exercising all manner of despites, and speaking of blasphemy against God, their King, and Country.' [3] The thought of them moved Samuel Purchas to unwonted vehemence. He describes Algiers as 'the Whirlepoole of these Seas, the Throne of Pyracie, the Sinke of Trade and the Stinke of Slavery; the Cage of uncleane Birds of Prey, the Habitation of Sea-Devils, the Receptacle of Renegadoes of God, and Traytors to their Country. . . As for Ward,' he adds, 'and other English, infesting the World from that Hel-mouth, I was loth to blot these Papers with so rotten Names.' [4]

Sycorax, the mother of Caliban, was born in Argier (Algiers) and banished thence; [5] Shakespeare's audience would think of the pirates' nest as a suitable birthplace for so damned a witch.

1 Loc.cit., p.343, note 1, above.
2 *Rare Adventures*, p.169.
3 Stow, *Annales*, augmented by Edmund Howes, 1631, p.893.
4 Purchas, vi,108f.
5 *The Tempest*, I,ii,263f. The vague allusion to some mitigating circumstances which led to her life being spared has never been satisfactorily explained.

Even in Elizabeth's reign, when the English privateers against Spain were national heroes, the Barbary pirates, whether Moors or renegades, were dreaded and detested,

> the cruel pirates of Argier,
> That damned train, the scum of Africa,
> Inhabited with straggling runagates.[1]

At the beginning of the seventeenth century King James's efforts to suppress piracy were impeded by English sympathy with their fellow-countrymen who attacked and plundered Spain. The link between English privateers and the English navy (if what were once practically indistinguishable may be said to have been linked) was not yet broken. Since English merchant vessels went armed for defence and could when occasion invited commit acts of piracy on their own account, it was sometimes difficult to draw a legal distinction between their crews and the professional corsairs. Moreover, various members of the King's Council shared in the profits of English buccaneering; the pirates even sent booty, and money realized from the sale of booty, to the Lord High Admiral. The problem steadily grew more critical, and piracy was at its worst about 1608 at which time John Ward, the most notorious of all the English corsairs, was at the apex of his criminal career. But far down in the reign of Charles I no solution of the problem had been reached. At that time the merchants' dread of the Barbary corsairs gave point to a simile which Abraham Cowley employs in the Prologue to *The Guardian* (the original version of *The Cutter of Coleman Street*):

> As when the Midland Sea is no where clear
> From dreadful Fleets of Tunis and Argier,

and merchant vessels dare not venture out of port, and trade decays; so of late, says Cowley, timorous wits have hesitated to put forth upon the stage, affrighted by the 'Critiques of Argier' who shoot with 'Wind-gunns, charg'd with Air.' Cowley advises these corsairs of criticism to permit his play, a 'little Forlorn Hope,' to pass, for if it is unharmed the glad

1 Marlowe, *1 Tamburlaine*, III,iii,55f.

news of its safety will encourage others to send their plays forth and they will be rich prizes for the critics. On the other hand,

> All these, if we miscarry here today,
> Will rather till they Rot in th' Harbour stay.

To this Prologue Cowley added some lines on the occasion of the performance of his comedy at court. Charles is, he says, the sovereign of 'these Narrow Seas of Wit'; and if we the actors please him we shall obtain a passport and shall 'fear no little Rovers of the Main.' [1] How wide of the mark was Cowley's ingenious analogy will appear in the sequel. For the moment we must return to an earlier period.

The recruiting-grounds for these bands of ruffianly renegades were the slums and purlieus of London and other English ports. There was poetic justice in the choice of Wapping as the place where captured pirates were hanged, because it was from Wapping that many a corsair had set out at the outset of his lawless career. Sturdy vagabonds were often recruits, as were discharged soldiers and sailors and deserters from the mercantile marine. Many an adventurer down on his luck meditated the possibility of joining up with the corsairs. Staines, a character in *Greenes Tu Quoque*, had been so poor, 'so far gone,' he says, 'that desperation knocked at my elbow, and whispered news to me out of Barbary.' [2] This does not mean, as has been suggested, that he proposes to enlist as a soldier against the Moors but that he meditates the possibility of restoring his fortunes by turning pirate. So with the adventurers in *Lady Alimony* who 'have resolved, for want of better supplies, to hazard the remainder of their broken fortunes upon a desperate adventure for Tunis.' [3] These bravos sing a sea-catch:

> To Tunis and to Argiers, boys!
> Great is our want, small be our joys.
> Let's then some voyage take in hand
> To get us means by sea or land. [4]

---

1 *The Cutter of Coleman Street, Works*, ed. Grosart, i,178.　　3 III,i; ibid., xiv,326.
2 Hazlitt's Dodsley, xi,215.　　4 III,iii; ibid., xiv,328.

II

OF such desperados the most notorious was Captain John Ward.[1] The date of his birth is unknown, but since he was, it would seem, already a man of middle age in 1602 and was described in 1608 by one who had seen him lately as a man of about fifty-five,[2] it is a valid guess that he was born about 1553. He was a native of Faversham in Kent, 'a fellow, poore, base and of no esteeme,' says a contemporary writer;[3] 'as base in Birth as bad in Condition,' says another.[4] In youth he was a fisherman.[5] He entered the Royal Navy, served in the wars with Spain, was a member of some semi-piratical expeditions in the West Indies, and rose to the grade of a petty officer or its equivalent.[6] There is no evidence that in these early years his service on privateers brought him into any intercourse or connection with the Barbary corsairs. Shortly before the death of the Queen, Ward found himself in bad circumstances, out of employment; and in desperation he re-enlisted in the Navy, shipping aboard the pinnace *Lion's Whelp*. Surly and insubordinate, he spread discontent among his fellow-seamen, lamenting the old days 'when the whole sea was our Empire where we robbed at will.' One who knew him in 1602 pictures him thus: 'He would sit melancholy, speake doggedly, curse the time, repine at other mens good fortunes, and complaine of the hard crosses attended his own.' He was 'welcome into any tap-house, more for love of his coyne, then love of his company.' He spent his days in drinking and swearing.[7]

One day, as the pinnace was lying at anchor in Plymouth harbour,[8] Ward saw his opportunity; and obtaining leave to

1 His given name has been thought doubtful or unknown; but he is called John several times in the State Papers and never by any other given name.
2 *C.S.P.*, *Venetian*, xi,140.
3 Andrew Barker, *A True and Certaine Report of . . . Captain Ward*, 1609, p.2.
4 *Newes from Sea*, *Of two notorious Pyrats*, 1609, Sig. B[r].
5 The anonymous *Newes from Sea* contains a woodcut of 'Wards Skiffe when he was a Fisherman.'
6 This is Sir Henry Wotton's statement to the Venetian Signory, *C.S.P.*, *Venetian*, xi,140.
7 Barker, op.cit., p.3.
8 J.S.Corbett, op.cit., ii, chapter ii; Gosse, op.cit., p.135, and the *D.N.B.* all say that this event took place at Portsmouth; but Barker, op.cit., p.2, and Wotton (see note 6, above) say Plymouth; and Sir Julius Caesar sent an officer to Plymouth, not Portsmouth, to apprehend Ward (*Hatfield MSS*, xii,374).

go ashore he gathered round him in a public-house a crew of rascals as ruffianly as himself and to them unfolded his design. He had heard that a certain gentleman, a Catholic recusant, had hired a small bark to convey him and his family over to France. 'Hee hath imbarked above two thousand pound in ready chinkes, besides plate and household provision,' Ward told his mates.[1] This vessel was lying close by in the harbour, easily accessible to plunderers. But in some way the intended victim got wind of Ward's design and secretly disembarked all his belongings. That night the confederates boarded the ship and put to sea; and not till the next morning did they discover that the expected booty had vanished. The rage of the ruffians who had been persuaded into the venture may be imagined, and also the quandary in which their leader found himself. He dared not return to harbour; he must appease his crew. Somewhere in the Channel he attacked and captured a French vessel of eighty tons and five guns. After transferring himself and some of his crew to this new prize, which he renamed the *Little John*, he headed for the Mediterranean, capturing other prizes on the way. Finally he sought shelter at El Arisch (Alaraca) on the Atlantic coast of Morocco. He had no cordial reception from the Dey, for though in general anyone who pillaged the Spaniards was welcome in Barbary, at the moment there was a special prejudice against Englishmen because of the action of a certain Captain Gifford who in a sudden raid had set fire to shipping in the harbour of Algiers.[2] Accordingly Ward sailed through the Straits and eastward to Tunis where he entered into a compact with Kara Osman,[3] a powerful Turk grown rich from plunder, who behind the back of the feeble basha was the real ruler of the city and neighbouring country. In return for permission to use Tunis as a base Ward agreed to share his booty with this unprincipled adventurer.

At El Arisch Ward had fallen in with two English sea-captains named Bishop and Michael. The latter soon returned

1 Barker, op.cit., p.5.
2 Corbett, op.cit., ii,12.
3 *Cambridge Modern History*, iii,541. Kara Osman is the Osman Bey of Wotton's report to the Venetian Signory; the 'Crosomond' of *C.S.P., Ireland, 1608–10*, p.279; the 'Crossyman' of Barker's narrative; and the 'Crosman' of Daborne's play *A Christian Turn'd Turke*.

to England after assigning to Ward his crew and his lieutenant, Anthony Jackson. Bishop's ship was in bad condition and presently rotted, and he joined forces with Ward. He is often mentioned in dispatches and rumours as one of Ward's ablest and most dangerous colleagues.

It is important to remember that Ward absconded from England at a time when Elizabeth was still living and before the initiation of the definite policy of peace with Spain. There is no evidence of unimpeachable authenticity that he had ever held a commission from Elizabeth, but he must have shared the consternation of those whose commissions were revoked by James and who were proclaimed outlaws. The shutting of the home ports against them helped to make these men desperate. Their old renown as despoilers of Spain no longer counted in their favour and there was a mounting indignation against them not only because they preyed on English commerce but because they consorted with Moslems and were reported to have 'turned Turk.' The narratives of the miseries of captivity circulated by redeemed Christian slaves, among whom were various Englishmen, enhanced the public anger excited by their misconduct.

The range and volume of acts of piracy committed by Ward and his associates expanded; and from 1605 or 1606 they had the formidable co-operation or competition of another desperado, a Dutchman variously called Simon Danzer, Dansker, Dansiker, or le Danseur, who generally operated from Algiers as Ward did from Tunis and who, at first Ward's colleague, was afterwards frequently his rival. A growing grievance in England was that these two 'taught the infidels the use and knowledge of navigation, to the great hurt of Europe.' [1] John Smith goes so far as to say that until Ward and Dansiker first established their 'marts' in Barbary 'the Moores knew scarce how to saile

1 Stow, *Annales*, ed. cit., p.893.—The Moors and the Turkish governing class of north-west Africa were, like the Turks of Stamboul and the ports of Asia Minor, not expert in seamanship. It is significant that in the sixteenth century the official language of the Ottoman fleet was Italian. The Turks have, indeed, always been dependent to a great degree upon other nations and particularly upon the Greeks for their sea-borne trade. Sir Henry Blount notes (*A Voyage into the Levant*, 1636, p.73) that they are 'ill supplyed with sea-men; for beside Renegadoes they have but few skilfull Saylers.'

a ship' and that these two 'were the first that taught the Moores
to be men of warre.' [1] Lithgow declares that if it had not been
for 'our Christian Runnagates' who cast cannon for them and
became their 'chiefe Cannoniers' the Moors would have been
as inexpert in handling ordnance at sea as were the 'silly
Æthiopians' on land.[2] The responsibility for having taught the
Moors new methods of ship-construction, navigation, and naval
warfare appears to rest more heavily upon Dansiker than
Ward, and undoubtedly this instruction was chiefly in navigation; he taught them the use of swift sailing vessels instead of
the galleys which were dependent for rowers upon a supply of
slaves which because of cruel usage had constantly to be re-
plenished. This innovation proved of immense value after 1610
when the expulsion of the last Moriscos from Andalusia deprived the North Africans of sympathizers in Spain upon whom
they had hitherto depended as guides on raids into the interior.
After 1610 the pirates tended to limit land-operations to swift
descents upon the Spanish coast. The use of sailing vessels released many fighting men who otherwise, when galley-slaves
were scarce, would have had to expend their energies at the
oars.

In 1605–6 the French government sent a mission to Algiers
and Tunis to protest against the piracies, to try to persuade the
Berber authorities to chase the corsairs from their harbours,
and to arrange for the redemption of French slaves. Some sort
of agreement was reached, but it was soon a dead letter, for the
Berbers reaped too rich a profit from the slave-markets not to
connive at piracy. The head of this French mission seems to
have met Ward at La Goletta in Tunis.[3] There is a story that
this envoy appealed to him to show special favour to the
French. 'I favourable to the French?' quoth Ward; 'I tell you
if I should meet mine own father at sea, I would robb him, and
sell him when I had done.' There is another story that when
Mustapha, the Turkish *Cha'usch*, encountered Ward on his
way to England and asked him whether he could do anything

1 *Travels and Works*, ii,914.
2 *Rare Adventures*, p.169.
3 Father Pierre Dan, *Histoire de Barbarie et de ses corsaires*, Paris, 1637, p.228. The
  pirate whom Father Dan calls 'Captain Wer' is almost certainly Ward.

towards procuring him a pardon and permission to return home, Ward 'answered that he would never see England againe but would be buried in the Sea.' [1]

About this time there occurred an incident that almost cost Ward his life. Having taken a French ship he hastily and secretly transferred himself and some chosen companions from his own vessel, which was rotten and leaky, to the new prize. On the old ship he left some Englishmen and almost all his Moslem sailors. These wretches all went to the bottom. Andrew Barker tells this tale, which is confirmed by Wotton's report to the Venetian Signory that on Ward's return to Tunis he was almost torn to pieces by the enraged 'Turks' (that is, Moors) but succeeded in pacifying them. A little later, disaster overtook some of his ships in a storm, and he also suffered in an encounter with a Venetian squadron. These misfortunes may have influenced his decision in the summer of 1607 to make overtures to King James to procure a pardon and leave to return to England. It was to the advantage of England to stop his plundering even at the heavy cost of giving him a pardon; but because of the large depredations which he had committed against Venetian commerce it was necessary to win the approval of Venice before James could act. Sir Henry Wotton was charged with this task while the Venetian envoy in London consulted with Salisbury. This business dragged on for several months.[2] Wotton told the Venetians frankly that Ward was 'beyond doubt the greatest scoundrel that ever sailed from England' but that it would be a great public benefit if he retired from his nefarious activities and his three hundred followers were dispersed. As it appeared increasingly likely that a pardon would be forthcoming the pirate insolently began to impose conditions. At first Wotton was able to report that Ward was offering full restitution to Venice; then, partial satisfaction; then: 'Ward wants to return home and also keep his plunder, but the king will never assent to that.' The Signory expressed their trust that there would be no pardon for

[1] Both these anecdotes are in a letter to Sir Edward Hoby, Ellis, *Original Letters*, First Series, iii,88.
[2] C.S.P., *Venetian*, xi,49f.,54f.,58f.,62f.,73,94f.,103,107f.,117,121,140f.,166,172,183,189. These references carry the Venetian records of this affair to the close of 1608.

'Guart' before restitution was made and an indemnity paid. Wotton suspected that there was an intrigue in England working for the pardon; and a report came to Venice that the pirate, being enormously rich, counted on his gold to overcome all opposition; and it was said that there were people who deliberately exaggerated his power so as by inspiring terror to bring about a leave for his return home. These people reckoned on a reward from him for having exerted their influence in his behalf. Venice continued to withhold her approval save on the conditions already set forth; and James sent word that though Ward was offering large sums as ransoms or bribes he would issue no pardon without Venetian consent. Two years later, in February 1610, when all this discussion had come to nothing, James, entertaining the Venetian envoy at dinner, told him that one of the pirates (unnamed, but certainly Ward) had offered him £40,000 for his pardon.[1]

Meanwhile conditions became worse and worse. The Signory gave orders that all merchant ships should be convoyed by men-of-war. From England came alarming reports of the increase in the buccaneering spirit; lawless men were 'incited not merely by their natural instinct towards it,' wrote the Venetian envoy, 'but also by the rumours of Ward's riches.' An English sea-captain who landed at Venice told Wotton that he had hailed Ward at sea; the corsair had shouted threats against the Venetians, 'who have been the occasion that I am banished out of my country. Before I have done with them I will make them sue for my pardon!' [2] It was in this mood of ferocious despair, in the summer of 1607, that, as we have already seen, Ward conducted his brief correspondence with Sir Anthony Sherley. Sherley wrote to 'disswade him from this detestable life' but Ward 'made answere that he would give no credit to any fayre promises, or hazard his life on the hope of words, but would rather venture himselfe amongst the Turks, then into the handes of Christians.'

During 1608 wild and often contradictory rumours of Ward's activities flew about. There were reports that he had been wrecked and drowned off the coast of Crete; that he was in

1 Ibid., xi,430.   2 L.P.Smith, *Life and Letters of Sir Henry Wotton,* i,415.

Constantinople; that he had obtained his pardon and had arrived in London; that his followers were haunting the Irish coast; that he had been seen making East through the Straits of Gibraltar; that Lord Danvers was under arrest for giving him shelter in Ireland.[1] In June 1608, an English sailor [2] who had seen Ward in Tunis gave Wotton some impressions of him which the ambassador communicated to the Signory. Ward, according to this informant, was about fifty-five years old, very short of stature, with little hair and that quite white, swarthy of visage. He spoke little and that little almost always swearing. He was usually drunk from morning to night. He slept a great deal when his ship was in port, preferably on board. He was 'a fool and an idiot out of his trade.' The following October Wotton submitted to the Signory the offer of an English sea-captain who claimed to know the pirate's habits and where-abouts, to go to Tunis, kill him, and burn his ships. All this captain asked was that Venice defray the expenses of the ex-pedition. But though Wotton recommended the acceptance of the offer nothing came of it because the Doge believed, prob-ably rightly, that Ward was not then in Tunis. A raid there by the Spanish fleet some months earlier (July 1608) had resulted in the destruction of a score or so of ships; [3] but Ward had been ashore at the time and had made his escape; and though it was optimistically reported that 'his greatest strength, with much riches of his and his confederates perished in the fire,' by the autumn he was as redoubtable as ever.[4] Yet another proposal for the capture of Ward was laid before Wotton in January 1609.[5] It came from an English gentleman who said he had been one of Ward's captains before Ward took to piracy, though he must have been lying since in his career in the Royal Navy Ward certainly did not rise high enough to have captains serve under him. This new visitor outlined to Wotton a plan of

1 Lord Danvers did give shelter to some pirates though Ward was not among them; see his plea (*C.S.P., Ireland, 1606–8*, pp.550f.) that they were in far stronger force than he and that he had to come to terms with them.
2 Probably Henry Pepwell; see ibid., p.279.
3 This raid is mentioned in the *Cambridge Modern History*, iii,541. The *History* is in error in the statement that Sir Francis Verney was one of the pirate-captains at the time. Verney was still in England when the raid took place.
4 *Verney Papers*, ed. John Bruce, Camden Society, 1853, p.99.
5 *C.S.P., Venetian*, xi,220,225,228,246.

attack; but he wanted 'anticipatory rewards' and these the ambassador refused to advance, urging him to be 'satisfied with a remuneration after the execution of the design.' Negotiations and solicitations continued for a couple of months. The adventurer suggested the compromise of a fixed sum payable on the delivery of the pirate in London. Wotton temporized, and by March the discussion had languished. Apparently this unnamed adventurer set out upon his dangerous enterprise, for Wotton's last note on him is: 'Pray God that if he does not succeed he take not himself to piracy.'

III

This unidentified Englishman, whom Wotton expressly calls a gentleman, may have been Sir Francis Verney, the most memorable of all Ward's recruits.[1] Verney,[2] born in 1584 of an ancient family, passed through an undisciplined youth into a wild and unhappy manhood. When we first hear of him, in 1604, he was living in the disreputable region known as Alsatia on the western fringe of London. At that time he was involved in a law-suit regarding his inheritance brought against his stepmother. The immediate result was a compromise, but family dissensions continued; and in 1606 a mounting sense of injustice and an increasing burden of debt heaped on him by reckless living led to his eccentric and desperate action of ordering the instant sale of all his property. This was accomplished at a ruinous loss. Verney then made a pilgrimage to the Holy Land, and thereafter visited Spain where he had the portrait of himself painted which still hangs in Claydon Hall in Buckinghamshire.[3] It shows a man of distinguished bearing, handsome and very tall, wearing the peaked beard of the current mode, and fashionably dressed.

Verney was in England again and for the last time in the summer of 1608. Some months later he was in the Barbary

---

1 See, however, p.355, note 2, below.
2 Lady Frances Parthenope Verney, *Memoirs of the Verney Family*, 1892, i,60f.; *The Verney Papers*, pp.93f.; Gosse, op.cit., pp.130f.
3 The portrait was for long ascribed to Velasquez but is of too early a date; see Lady F.P.Verney, op.cit., i,66. Other belongings of his that are still preserved at Claydon Hall are two pairs of Turkish slippers and a turban.

States, and it may have been on his way there that he proposed to Wotton his scheme to capture John Ward. If it was indeed he who is referred to by Wotton, the shrewd ambassador's fears lest his visitor turn pirate were well founded. Somewhat more than a year earlier, in November 1607, a certain Captain John Giffard (or Gifford), who was a relative by marriage of the Verney family, and who with some two hundred followers had joined the army of Muley Sidan, one of the claimants to the throne of Morocco, had been slain in battle.[1] It is possible that news of his relative's death may have drawn Sir Francis into Barbary. Under what circumstances he came to associate with Captain Ward is not known. Nor is much known about his subsequent exploits as a corsair. His name occurs occasionally in dispatches along with the names of other pirates.[2] In December 1610, the Venetian envoy in London sent word home that 'the pirate Ward and Sir Francis Verney, . . . an Englishman of the noblest blood, have become Turks, to the great indignation of the whole nation.'[3] A modern historian of the Verney family has interpreted the phrase 'turned Turk' in its political, not its religious, sense, and from the fact that after his death Sir Francis was found to have retained his pilgrim's staff, a Christian relic of his journey to Jerusalem, has argued that 'he did not commit the unnecessary and improbable offence of becoming a renegade.'[4] But there was nothing improbable in the offence, which was committed by many corsairs and more cap-

---

1 Seeing the hopelessness of victory, Muley Sidan sent Giffard 'a good horse to save himself. The English returned word, that they came not thither to run, but rather to die an honourable death. Captain Giffard encouraged his men, telling them, there was no hope of victory, but to prepare and die like men, like Englishmen' (*A True Historicall Discourse of Muley Hamets Rising*, 1609, Sig. G^v; Purchas, vi,94). Gosse, op.cit., p.131, seems to confuse this John Giffard with Philip Giffard the pirate. The Captain Giffard or Gifford who set fire to the shipping in the harbour of Algiers in 1602 seems to have been a third person. None of the three is to be confused with the Signor Robert Gifford, an English Roman Catholic whom Pietro della Valle encountered several times in the East and whom he describes as 'amico mio di molto tempo' (*Viaggi*, iii,335).

2 Stow, *Annales*, ed. cit., p.893; C.S.P., *Venetian*, xi,225. These refer to an English proclamation against piracy dated 8 January 1609, in which Verney's name is included in a list of desperate men banded together under Ward's leadership. The date perhaps invalidates the suggestion that the man who consulted with Wotton at Venice at just that time was Verney; but the insertion of his name among proscribed outlaws may have been due to an erroneous report.—Later in the same year came a report from Madrid that Verney had captured five merchantmen (Lady F.P.Verney, op.cit., i,65; *Winwood Memorials*, iii,91).

3 C.S.P., *Venetian*, xii,100.   4 Lady F.P.Verney, op.cit., i,63,68.

tives in Barbary; nor was it unnecessary if a man sought to establish himself in a Mohammedan state. The existence of the pilgrim's staff is no evidence that Verney did not embrace Islam, for whether he was a renegade or not it is highly improbable that he carried into Barbary a souvenir so challenging to Moslem sensibilities.

William Lithgow transmits to us the story that Verney was captured by Sicilians and for two years was a slave rowing in the Sicilian galleys. This, too, has been questioned, but for the tale there is some slight independent confirmatory evidence.[1] What is definitely known is that on 25 August 1615, Verney applied for admission to the hospital of Our Lady of Pity at Messina, and there he died on 6 September.[2] Lithgow was in Messina at the time and from him we have the pathetic story:

> Here in Messina I found the (sometimes) great English Gallant Sir Frances Verny lying sick in a Hospitall, whom six weekes before I had met in Palermo: Who after many misfortunes in exhausting his large patrimony, abandoning his Country, and turning Turk in Tunneis; he was taken at Sea by the Sicilian Gallies: In one of which he was two yeares a slave, whence hee was redeemed by an English Jesuite, upon the promise of his Conversion to the Christian faith: When set at liberty hee turned common Souldier, and here in the extreamest calamity of extreame miseries, contracted Death: Whose dead Corpes I charitably interred in the best manner, time could affoord me strength, bewailing sorrowfully the miserable mutability of Fortune, who from so great a birth, had given him so meane a Buriall; and truly so may I say, *Sic transit gloria mundi.*[3]

Where Sir Francis was buried is not known. An English merchant, one John Watchin, gathered the dead man's effects together and sent them to his family in England. His pilgrim's staff, inlaid with crosses of mother-of-pearl, hangs to this day beneath his portrait at Claydon Hall.

---

1 This evidence is in the form of a belated and distorted report of Verney's death 'at the galleys in Sicily' which reached London in January 1617. See *C.S.P.,Dom., 1611–18*, p.425.
2 The entry in the hospital register is quoted in *Verney Papers*, p.101.
3 *Rare Adventures*, pp.348f.

IV

WE return now to Captain Ward who was, as we have seen, newly proclaimed an outlaw in January 1609. In March of the same year the English Admiral John Rander struck a blow at him by taking prisoner two of his chief associates, Longcastle and Taverner.[1] A little later the masters of certain ships sent to their owners in London a narrative of an encounter with Ward from which they had extracted themselves with difficulty. This wordy and bombastic story was rushed to press and forms the principal item in an anonymous black-letter quarto entitled: *Newes from Sea, Of two notorious Pyrats Ward the Englishman and Danseker the Dutchman. With a true relation of all or the most piracies by them committed unto the sixth of April 1609.* A cut on the title-page shows two ships engaged in combat; one flies the cross of Saint George; the other, three flags each displaying the crescent moon. On the deck of the Moslem vessel are two men wearing turbans, and at her mast-head hang two corpses. The pamphlet provides a hasty sketch of Ward's career by way of introduction to the aforesaid letter from the ship-masters.[2] There is very little about his Dutch partner Dansiker. Undated but probably of about the same time as this pamphlet is an execrable ballad entitled: *The Seamans Song of Captain Ward, the famous Pyrate of the World, and an Englishman Born.* A single stanza will serve as a sample of its quality:

> Men of his own Countrey,
> He still abused vilely,
> Some back to back are cast into the waves,
> Some are hewn in pieces small
> Some are shot against a wall,
> A slender number of their lives he saves.

Ward's gallant palace in Tunis is described; but despite his wealth and fame it is prophesied that disaster will surely overtake him; his honours will 'prove like letters written in the sand.' It will suffice barely to mention a similar ballad of the same time: *The Seamans Song of Danseker the Dutchman, his robberies done at sea.*[3]

1 *C.S.P., Venetian*, xi,259f.
2 Sig. D^r.   3 These two ballads are reprinted by A.E.H.Swaen, *Anglia*, xx,180f.

In June 1609, occurred the combined Franco-Spanish attack on La Goletta in Tunis in which, as we have seen, Sir Anthony Sherley planned but failed to take part. The credit for initiating and accomplishing this raid belongs to the French commander rather than to the Spanish admiral. Admiral Fijardo, while awaiting contact with the squadron which Sherley had assembled at Naples, encountered a French galleon and pinnace under the command of the Sieur de Beaulieu. The gallant Frenchman incited Fijardo to make a dash upon Tunis, to which the latter consented reluctantly.[1] The outcome was a success beyond all expectations; a large number of ships were fired in the harbour and the corsairs received the heaviest blow in their experience.[2] An allusion to this raid is probably combined with memories of an earlier battle with the Moslems in Fletcher's lines:

> Here's a goodly jewel;
> Did you not win this at Goletta, captain?
> Or took it in the field from some brave bashaw?[3]

The Spaniards, however, failed to follow up the victory. Swift action might have rid the Mediterranean of the pirates; but Spain turned vindictively on the Moriscos of Andalusia and employed the armada she had assembled to deport tens of thousands of these unfortunates to North Africa. These ill-used exiles gave a new impetus to the activities of the predatory denizens of the Barbary sea-ports. Fifteen years later Bacon remarked that 'the Moors of Valentia expulsed, and their allies, do yet hang as a cloud or storm over Spain.'[4]

News of the destruction of the pirates' ships prompted a certain Anthony Barker, an English ship-master who had been captured and detained some time by Ward, to publish a brief popular biography of the notable salt-water thief. This is a black-letter quarto of about thirty pages entitled: *A New and*

---

1 Father Dan, op.cit., p.169; Corbett, op.cit., i,19f. Corbett notes that the Spanish accounts are silent on the French ships and give all the credit to Spain.
2 *C.S.P.*, *Venetian*, xi,319,325,346,360.
3 *Rule a Wife and Have a Wife*, IV,i. The Turks had captured La Goletta from Don John of Austria in 1574. Compare *Don Quixote*, Part I, Book iv, chapter xii.
4 *Considerations Touching a Warre with Spain* (1624); Spedding, *The Letters and the Life of Francis Bacon*, 1874, vii,501.

Nevves from Sea,

Of two notorious Pyrats

Ward the Englifhman and *Danfeker*
the *Dutchman*.

VVith a true relation of all or the moft
piraces by them committed vnto the firſt of
April. 1 6 0 9.

Printed at London for *N. Butter* and are
to be fold at his ſhop, at the Signe of the

An Encounter with the Barbary Pirates

Certaine Report of the Beginning, Proceedings, Overthrowes, and now present Estate of Captaine Ward and Danseker, the two late famous Pirates, 1609. Upon this not too sensational narrative we have drawn occasionally in the foregoing pages. It contains a list of ships captured by Ward, an account of Simon Dansiker, and a report of the recent destruction of many ships in the roads of Tunis. If this report is true, says Barker, then Ward and his confederate 'are at length deprived of most of their strength.'

At the time of the Franco-Spanish raid the danger had seemed so great that no merchantmen were venturing out of English harbours and it was impossible to procure insurance save at prohibitive rates.[1] But Ward now suffered another heavy blow in the defection of Simon Dansiker. Whether it is true or not that, as one report had it, he openly revolted and freed three hundred slaves, at all events, wearying of his perilous life and perhaps yielding to the counsels sent him by Father Creswell, Dansiker landed in Marseilles and petitioned for pardon from Henry IV, offering his services against other pirates. This desertion 'was expected to be the utter ruin of Ward.' But Dansiker did not live long. According to one story, he was murdered in Paris; according to another, having been enticed to land in Tunis while in the French service, he was made prisoner and put to death.[2]

Ward, the old rascal, displayed admirable resiliency. Diplomatic agents continued to record rumours of his activities.[3] That these formed a subject of conversation in London might be guessed even if an allusion in one of John Donne's *Elegies* did not enable us to overhear a fragment of such talk. The poet, attracted to the personable wife of a citizen whom he chanced to meet, got into conversation with her husband as a means to approach the woman, and tactfully adapting his discourse

1 *C.S.P., Venetian,* xi,282.
2 Ibid., xi,375; Corbett, op.cit., i,18, note 1; Gosse, op.cit., p.52.
3 For example, that he was negotiating with Tuscany for permission to reside at Leghorn where he could be employed in an offensive against the Turks; that he was going to Ireland where he could find friends and shelter; that he had put to sea with six galleys; that his depredations were countenanced by the Sultan's Grand Vizier and that a Constantinopolitan Jew acted as a middleman for the receipt and disposition of goods stolen by Ward. For these reports see *C.S.P., Venetian,* xi,301, 309,380; xii,173,308.

to suit the man's interests, chatted of this or that: the affairs of the Virginia venture, the latest bankrupts, the reconstruction of Aldgate, and the report that Ward 'the traffique of the inland seas had marred.' [1]

In 1612 no less than twelve captured pirates were hanged on the same day at Wapping. The trial and execution of these men must have stirred up much excitement in London; and it was probably this event that suggested to Robert Daborne the idea of composing a play on the subject of John Ward, *A Christian Turn'd Turke*, which belongs to this year. Some account of this piece will be given later. All that need be said here is that its ending with the sentencing of Ward to be torn to pieces and thrown into the sea is a wild departure from the truth, for the pirate continued to live prosperously among the Moors. Contemporary with the play are two satirical poems by Samuel Rowlands which undoubtedly refer to Ward. These are 'The Picture of a Pirat' and 'To a Reprobate Pirat that hath renounced Christ and is turn'd Turke.' [2] In the former the pirate himself is imagined speaking; he describes his dwelling on the raging waves, his ship 'man'd with incarnate devils,' his 'crew of theevish Knaves,' his lawless nature and atheistical heart. At the end of his life he must, he says, expect 'to Anker at the Gallowes.' The second poem (in which Ward is definitely named in the final punning play on words) denounces that 'wicked lumpe, of onely sin and shame,' that Hellish Beast

> That hast liv'd cursed Theife upon the Seas,
> And now a Turke, on shore dost take thine ease,

who has denied Christ, and to whom the satirist sends 'this warning from thy native land,' that God's judgments are at hand, devils attend, hell fires are prepared, and 'perpetuall flames is reprobates Re-Warde.'

From this time on we hear no more of Ward at sea, but he continued to live in entire comfort (so far as we know) at Tunis.

1 *Elegy* xiv,ll.23f.; *Poetical Works*, ed. Grierson, i,106. Grierson dates this after 1609, probably in 1610. The word 'inland' is Grierson's emendation for 'iland.'
2 *More Knaves Yet? The Knaves of Spades and Diamonds* [1612], pp.8 and 9; *Complete Works*, Hunterian Club, 1880, vol.ii.

In 1615 William Lithgow, journeying through the Barbary States, was entertained by the old corsair. He has left us this circumstantial description:

> Here in Tunneis I met with our English Captayne, generall Waird, once a great Pyrat, and Commaunder at Sea; who in despight of his denied acceptance in England, had turned Turke, and built there a faire Palace, beautified with rich Marble and Alabaster stones. With whom I found Domesticke, some fifteene circumcised English Runagates, whose lives and Countenances were both alike, even as desperate as disdainful. Yet old Waird their maister was placable, and joyned me safely with a passing Land conduct to Algiere; yea, and diverse times in my ten dayes staying there, I dyned and supped with him, but lay aboord in the French shippe.[1]

With desperate and disdainful runagates infesting Ward's palace, it was a wise precaution to sleep on shipboard. But Ward treated Lithgow courteously, one day sending two of his servants to guide him to a place where he could see the curious phenomenon of chickens being hatched in an oven.[2]

When Captain Ward died is unknown; the inference from an allusion in one of James Howell's letters is that by 1622 he was dead and gone. Howell writes of Ward and Dansiker as 'two of the fatalest and most infamous men that ever Christendom bred, . . . the chief raisers of those Picaroons to be Pirates, who are now come to that height of strength, that they daily endamage and affront all Christendom.'[3]

Ward's memory was still green so late as about 1680 when there appeared a lusty and quite unhistorical ballad entitled *The famous Sea-Fight between Captain Ward and the Rainbow.*[4] According to this, Ward offered 'full thirty Tun of Gold' to King James in return for permission to come home; but the King said: 'To yield to such a rover my self will not agree.'

1 *Rare Adventures*, p.315.
2 Ibid., p.334.
3 *Familiar Letters*, i,110.—In an *Epithalamium* among Thomas Randolph's *Poems*, 1638, (*Works*, ed. Hazlitt, p.571) the bridegroom, who is named Ward, is compared, as the rifler of his bride's treasure, to 'that other Ward' who 'awed the seas' and plundered merchants.
4 British Museum Roxburghe Collection, ii,56-7 (various broadsides); *Bagford Ballads*, i,65; Child, Number 287. The ballad was sung 'To the Tune of Captain Ward'; this may imply an earlier ballad now lost or a tune especially written for the extant piece.

He sent the *Rainbow* (which had been one of Drake's ships)
to attack the pirate.

> Ile tell the[e] what says Rainbow,
> Our king is in great grief,
> That thou shouldst lye upon the Sea
> And play the arrant Thief.

This challenge was followed by a battle in which, though the
shooters of the *Rainbow* proved themselves 'brass,' Ward was
'steel.' All their shots were in vain and they returned home
empty-handed. Whereupon King James expressed his regret
for the three lost 'jewels'—Lord Clifford, Lord Mountjoy,
and the Earl of Essex—who would have brought 'proud Ward'
a prisoner to England. The ballad displays a curious perverse
pride in an outlaw whose doughty deeds showed that he remained an Englishman even if he had yielded to the temptation
to belong to another nation and had turned Turk.

V

THE retirement of the old buccaneer about 1612 [1] did not free
the sea from pirates of English nationality. In January 1617,
the ship *Dolphin* was attacked by six Turkish (that is, Moorish)
vessels, and it is recorded that 'the Captaines of three of their
ships were Englishmen who tooke part with the Turkes thus
to rob and spoyle upon the Ocean.' The *Dolphin* effected her
escape and John Taylor the Water-Poet celebrated her deliverance.[2] We may look ahead a quarter of a century to notice
another valiant fight and fortunate escape which Taylor celebrated. The ship *Elizabeth* encountered three Turkish vessels
at the very entrance to the English Channel. The Englishmen
drove off the Turks who 'discontented shrunk away, making
their moanes to Mahomet.' 'In a mery or jeering way' the

---

1 Ward is not mentioned in *A famous victorie atchieved by the christian gallies of Sicilia,*
 1613.
2 *The Dolphins Danger and Deliverance*, 1617; John Taylor, *Works*, Spenser Society,
 1869, p.519. An anonymous narrative of the same encounter is: *A Fight at Sea fa-
 mously fought by the Dolphin of London against five of the Turkes Men of Warre*, 1617.
 Of this same period is an undated pamphlet by H.R. (Henry Roberts) entitled:
 A True Relation of a most worthy and notable Fight [etc.], narrating the battle between
 two small English ships and 'sixe great Gallies of Tunes.' See L.B.Wright, op.cit.,
 pp.523f.

English held up some slaughtered hogs and showed them to the Turks 'to invite them to come aboard of their Ship to eate some Porke.' From this exploit Taylor extracts a parable. The Ship is the Church; the three Turkish vessels are the World, the Flesh, and the Devil; Christ is the Anchor; and so forth.[1] This parable is an interesting late survival of a figure used frequently in medieval sermons, homilies, and iconography.[2]

We return to 1617. In that year, in consequence of a series of depredations of quite alarming audacity, active preparations were begun for an attack upon the corsairs. Many state papers of about this time have been calendared relating to acts of piracy, proceedings against piracy, the capture of pirates, and so forth. Thus, in October 1617, a Turkish—that is, as always, a Moorish—pirate vessel was taken in the very estuary of the Thames.[3] The inhabitants of Swanwich, Isle of Purbeck, in Dorsetshire, appealed to the government for a supply of ordnance and for funds to repair their block-house as a protection against pirates; and another sea-port suffered so much from depredations that it was necessary to erect a fort and to repair a bridge and a church which, one infers, had been damaged or destroyed by corsairs.[4] Steps were now taken to levy assessments towards the expenses of an expedition to Algiers; and the communities and commercial organizations upon which the levies were laid began with one accord to make excuse, promising at most only a percentage of the sums required of them. Exeter merchants argued that they had but little trade to southern parts; the combined Merchant Adventurers of London insisted that a large fraction of their total assessment should be contributed by the parties chiefly interested in the southern trade; Plymouth merchants admitted that their trade was injured by pirates but said it was more seriously damaged by competition from London; Bristol, Southampton, York,

---

1 *A Valorous and Perillous Sea-fight. Fought with three Turkish Ships, Pirats or men of Warre, on the coast of Cornwall . . . by the good Ship . . . Elizabeth*, 1640; reprinted in Taylor's *Works . . . not included in the Folio volume of 1630*, Spenser Society, 1877.
2 On the symbolic Ship see G.R.Owst, *Literature and Pulpit in Medieval England*, Cambridge, 1933, pp.68f.
3 *C.S.P.,Dom., 1611–18*, p.427.   4 Ibid., p.607.

Weymouth, Yarmouth, and the Cinque Ports all made difficulties of one kind or another. The Levant Company pleaded that their commerce with Turkey was of late so much shrunk that they could not meet necessary expenses and that their commerce with India had been taken from them; their tall ships were, moreover, enjoined to keep company at sea and consequently did not fear the corsairs. It is unnecessary to pursue further this story of lack of public spirit; it can be pieced together from entries in the *Calendar of State Papers*.[1] So late as 1623 a list was compiled of those companies and communities which had not yet completed their contributions; in 1625 certain ship-owners petitioned against the continuance of impositions laid on them; and even in 1628 some contributions were still the subject of disputes.[2] The decision arrived at in April 1619, to postpone the expedition, was probably due to delays in collecting funds.[3]

Concerning the expedition something can be gathered from the *State Papers*,[4] but our principal source of information is the narrative 'written by one employed in that Voyage' to be found in Purchas.[5] Under Vice-Admiral Sir Robert Mansell, a commander of long experience,[6] it consisted of six ships of the Royal Navy, ten merchantmen, and two pinnaces. The precise date of departure is uncertain, either in August or October 1621, the contradictory testimony being reconcilable on the assumption of a false start and delay because of storms.[7] The expedition resolved itself into two phases: the first diplomatic, when after negotiations under a flag of truce some forty poor captives of Algiers were delivered to the English ships; the second openly hostile, when after delays, hesitations, divided counsels, much sailing about the Mediterranean, and occasional brushes with Moorish vessels in the open sea, Mansell at last attempted

1 Ibid., p.475f.; ibid., *1619–23*, pp.12,25f.; ibid., *Addenda, 1580–1625*, p.599.
2 Ibid., *1619–23*, pp.37 and 296 (and see the Index, *sub* 'Pirates, expeditions against'); ibid., *1623–5*, p.142.
3 Ibid., *1619–23*, p.37.
4 See the Index to *C.S.P.,Dom., 1619–23*, under appropriate headings.
5 'A large Voyage in a Journall or briefe Reportary of all occurrents,' etc., Purchas, vi,131f.
6 So long before as 1602 he had published his *True Report of the Service done upon certaine gallies*.
7 *C.S.P.,Dom., 1619–23*, p.175, says 28 August; Purchas, vi,133, says 12 October.

to set fire to the pirates' ships in the harbour of Algiers either anchored in the roads or made fast to the mole. The undertaking was a daring one. Two small captured Moorish vessels were filled with a 'great store of fireworks'—'dry Wood, Wood of Acham, Pitch, Rozen, Tarre, Brimstone, and other Materials fit to take fire.' The ships were equipped with chains and grappling-irons and with boats to bring off the men charged with the perilous duty of taking these fire-ships into the harbour, securing them, and starting the conflagration. Contrary winds caused disappointments and delays; and when at length the attempt was made it was a flat failure—'wanting wind to nourish or disperse the fire, the fire-workes took no effect at all.' So runs the narrative in Purchas; but Thomas Porter, one of the officers of the expedition, told James Howell that a sudden downpour of rain quenched the fires.[1] The raid served only as a warning to the Algerines to guard themselves against a repetition of the attempt. They 'boomed up the Mould [mole], so that it was not possible . . . to get in to fire the ships' a second time, and they set a stout guard upon their fleet. Consequently Mansell was compelled to return to England with nothing accomplished of an importance proportionate to the outlay for the expedition.

The prompt result of this failure was a new outbreak of piracy, 'the late expedition having done nothing but irritate' the corsairs.[2] The merchants of several trading companies, who had been less than half-hearted in their support of Mansell, now thought it impossible to raise funds for a new expedition and advocated the redemption of captives by treaty. Sir Thomas Roe, who was now ambassador at the Porte, attempted to secure the suppression of piracy through diplomatic representations to the central Ottoman government. In this he was unsuccessful, but he did succeed in obtaining, partly at his own cost, the liberation of some English captives; and a treaty with Algiers, arranged in November 1624, led

---

1 *Familiar Letters*, i,100. Here is Howell's facetious summary of Porter's 'relation' to him: 'It seems their Hoggies, Magicians, and Maribots were tampering with the ill Spirits of the Air, . . . which brought down such a still Cataract of Rain-water suddenly upon you, to hinder the working of your Fire-works.'
2 *C.S.P.,Dom., 1619–23*, p.301, and compare p.393.

to the liberation of many more, though its provisions were before long ignored.[1]

Meanwhile acts of piracy took place with as much impudence as ever. In October 1621, a Bristol ship which had been taken by 'the Turkish Pirats of Argier' was recovered by four intrepid English youths who slew thirteen of the 'Turks' and sold nine others to Spain as galley-slaves.[2] The fortunes attending another Bristol ship are well summarized in the title of a contemporary narrative: *The Famous and Wonderful Recovery of a ship of Bristol, called the Exchange, from the Turkish Pirates of Argier. With the Unmatchable attempts and good success of John Rawlins, Pilot in her, and other slaves: who, in the end (with the slaughter of about forty of the Turks and Moors), brought the ship into Plymouth, the 13th. of February last, with the Captain a Renegado, and five Turks more; besides the redemption of twenty four men and one boy from Turkish slavery,* 1622.[3] Rawlins, the author of this lively narrative, tells of the 'violent rages of piracy' of the Turks and of their cruelty to prisoners. He and his fellows were 'hurried . . . like dogs into the market' with 'prices written in [their] breasts.' He was sold into slavery, but with some companions managed to escape and regained his own ship. The five Turkish sailors and Henry Chandler, the renegade Englishman whom he captured, were at the time of writing in Plymouth gaol.

To 1623 belong the most sensational exploits of Captain John Nutt, one of the most insolently daring of all rogue Englishmen.[4] In the spring of that year Sir John Eliot, Vice-Admiral for Devon, was in charge of the business of pressing men for the Royal Navy; and to escape this hateful service several hundred West Country men got away to Newfoundland in the fishing fleets. Under the command of Nutt, who had been a gunner, some of these refugees seized a French ship and took

1 *Negotiations of Sir Thomas Roe in his Embassy to the Ottoman Porte,* 1740, i,pp.14, 117,140. See also *C.S.P.,Dom., 1623–5,* p.13.
2 Purchas, vi,146f.
3 Reprinted in *Stuart Tracts, 1603–1693,* ed. C.H.Firth, pp.247f. Compare Purchas, vi,151f.
4 *C.S.P.,Dom., 1619–23,* pp.597f.,603,605f.,611,619; ibid., *1623–5,* pp.29,44,54,69. John Forster, *Sir John Eliot,* i,24f., has the story of Nutt in great detail from the point of view of Eliot, his captor. See also Gosse, op.cit., pp.131f.

to piracy. Within a few weeks Nutt was terrorizing the Devon-shire coast, attracting numbers of discontented seamen to him, and even putting into Dartmouth to visit his wife and children. He had the effrontery to appear on the streets in the fine clothes of one of his plundered victims. Upon Sir John Eliot devolved the task of apprehending him. Force failed but wiles succeeded. By means of an old pardon which, unknown to Nutt, had been cancelled, he was enticed to Torbay where he and his accomplices were soon under lock and key. He was put on trial in London; but he had influential friends (among them Sir George Calvert, afterwards Lord Baltimore) who plotted for his release. They managed to get Sir John Eliot, the principal witness against him, imprisoned on a trumped-up charge, and while he was out of the way the pirate's pardon was secured. The government paid dearly for this favouritism. Nutt soon returned to his old activities and was presently in command of no less than twenty-seven vessels of Barbary. Then for several years he disappears from the record. Apparently he retired from his wicked trade and seems even to have obtained a second pardon. When he reappears a decade later we find him entrusted with a pardon for his brother, Captain Robert Nutt, also a pirate. At that time there was fear lest while at sea he would join his brother in 'that devilish trade.'[1]

In 1624 Algiers and Tunis renounced their allegiance to the Porte with the consequence that the situation became more acute than ever,[2] for the Turkish government, heeding the representations of Sir Thomas Roe, had hitherto made feeble efforts to curb piracy. Of about this time or a little later is an undated petition from the 'distressed wives' of almost two thousand poor English mariners held in miserable captivity at Sallee on the Atlantic coast of Morocco, a port which had become the notorious centre of the slave industry. Their hus-

---

1 *C.S.P.,Dom.*, *1631-3*, p.333. Gosse, op.cit., p.134, seems to confuse somewhat the two brothers.

2 In August six 'Turkish' men-of-war were reported off the Scilly Islands (*C.S.P., Dom.*, *1623-5*, p.329). In September eleven pirate ships sailed right up the river Severn and captured prizes; and the East India Company was compelled to protest to the government that unless they were afforded better protection they could not subsist (ibid., p.334).

bands, these petitioners declared, were so wretched that they were almost forced to 'convert from their Christian religion.' [1] In June 1624, letters patent were issued for a general collection throughout the kingdom for the relief of fifteen hundred English captives in Algiers, Tunis, Sallee, and other places.[2] The ill success of Mansell's expedition had discouraged further attempts to raid the pirates in their lairs, and during 1624–5 activities against them were limited to the Channel, the Irish Sea, and other home waters.[3] Shortly after Mansell's return an English consulate had been established in Algiers, a step which shows that England differentiated between the corsairs and the citizens of Barbary who were themselves more or less at the mercy of the pirate-gangs infesting their harbours. John Frizell, the consul, was active in the work of ransoming and exchanging prisoners. Another agent energetic in the prosecution of this work of redemption was John Harrison, who made no less than seven visits to Barbary, where he was occupied also with the task of settling terms of peace.[4] With this purpose in view a Moslem envoy came to London in the spring of 1625, bringing presents of horses, tigers, and lions to the King. He had several audiences with Charles; but though he remained till the following autumn with his costs defrayed by the Turkey Company he departed dissatisfied.[5] These negotiations probably account for the numerous estimates of English captives made about this time, ranging from six or eight hundred in Sallee alone up to some 4500 for the entire Barbary States.[6]

Two episodes of 1626 are examples of the sort of experiences which Englishmen underwent. In February Thomas Duffield and Hendrick Henderson with three other Englishmen were slaves on a Sallee man-of-war. They revolted and, according to the record, slew no less than sixty-two 'Turks.' One would like to have details of this victory at odds of more than twelve to one. The victors brought the ship to Crookhaven in Ireland; and there officers of the King's fleet seized her and packed off the five Englishmen who had captured her, with no reward

1 Ibid., *1625–6*, p.516.
2 Ibid., *1623–5*, p.287. These unfortunates had petitioned parliament for their relief.
3 Ibid., pp.146,282,296,328.
4 Ibid., *1629–31*, pp.60,350.   5 Ibid., *1625–6*, pp.82,113.   6 Ibid., pp.54,79,167,343,414.

whatsoever. They petitioned to the authorities in London for redress and compensation. As usual, the case dragged on for some time; the action of the naval officers was approved; the ship was put up for sale; and in the end a reward of three pounds ten shillings was paid to each of two unnamed sailors— probably Duffield and Henderson—who had captured the prize.[1]

A couple of months later a similar case involved the problem of the disposition of some Moorish prisoners, for on this occasion not all the pirates were slain. William Harrys and other Englishmen brought into Saint Ives in Cornwall a warship from Sallee. These men had been slaves in Barbary, but had revolted on the ship where they were rowers, slew the 'Turks' who were on deck, and kept thirty-two others under hatches. The authorities of the Cornish naval station requested a prompt trial of these prisoners. Orders came from London that they were not to be put to death. Delays followed, and the Cornish officials, impatient because of the heavy charges for diet and guards, turned the prisoners over to the civil authorities. In consequence a petition of Cornishmen was presented for relief from the burden of the captives and it was requested that they be exchanged for English prisoners in Barbary. The final settlement of their fate does not appear in the record.[2]

During the later 1620's the long lull in piracy reflects the efforts to arrive at an understanding with the corsairs. The visit of another emissary from Sallee in 1628 was followed promptly by royal proclamations to forbear hostilities towards Barbary.[3] The temporary agreement presently reached involved humiliating terms for England, for a portion of the ransom of captives was paid not in money but in munitions of war which the corsairs soon employed against the English. In 1631 there was a new outbreak, so violent that it becomes impracticable to cite even typical instances of these outrages; the *Calendar of State Papers* records them by the score.[4] In June

1 Ibid., pp.257,427.
2 Ibid., pp.339,356,439
3 Ibid., *1628-9*, pp.260,328,256.
4 For example, in the summer of 1631 'Turks' seized a vessel in the harbour of Baltimore in Ireland (ibid., *1631-3*, p.285) and a year later chased two English ships within the Needles (ibid., p.388). It is not always possible to tell whether the pirates were Moors or Europeans; the pirates of Dunkirk were very active at this time.

1634, Secretary Coke, in the course of a gloomy survey of the unsatisfactory relations existing between England and foreign countries, reported to King Charles that of the many English sailors enslaved in Tunis a large proportion had turned Turk, while at Sallee and elsewhere in Morocco the spoils taken from English vessels were the chief source of wealth.[1] The demoralization of trade by September 1636, is apparent in a petition of the merchants of half a dozen seaside cities who declared that the pirates of Sallee, numerous, strong, and nimble, and piloted by English and Irish renegades, so infested the Channels that ships dared not put to sea and fishermen refrained from taking fish.[2] The anxious care with which the testimony of certain captured Moorish and Dunkirk pirates was taken is a further indication of the strain and stress of the problem.[3] Yet some minds were sufficiently detached to consider the advisability of pardoning two young Moorish captives of not above fourteen years of age in order that they might be converted to Christianity.[4]

Even a government so lethargic and inefficient as that of Charles I was compelled at length to rouse itself to action. In the summer of 1636 various consultations were in progress.[5] It was calculated that within the past six months men, women, and children to the number of a thousand had been taken by the Moors. Captain Thomas Porter, who had been on Mansell's expedition, was recommended as the man fittest because of his valour and his knowledge of languages to be employed in the 'pious work' of 'surprisinge' the heathen Moors of Sallee. Another man who possessed intimate knowledge of conditions in Morocco and whose counsel was particularly valued was Captain Giles Penn. A decision, based upon his advice, was reached to collect provisions, funds, vessels, and crews for an

1 Ibid., *1634–5*, pp.68f.
2 Ibid., *1636–7*, p.111.
3 Ibid., pp.141,145f.
4 Ibid., p.177. Reports of conversions from Islam were occasionally made the theme of edifying pamphlets. See, for instance, Meredith Hanmer, *The Baptizing of a Turke. A Sermon*, Edinburgh [1586?], and T.Warmstry, *The Baptized Turk, or a Narrative of the Happy Conversion of Signior Regeo Dandulo*, 1658.—In 1605 an allowance of sixpence per diem was made to John Baptista, a Turkish captive who had been converted to Christianity. (*C.S.P.,Dom., 1603–10*, p.216.)
5 *C.S.P.,Dom., 1636–7*, pp.86,212,253,449,484,498.

attack upon Sallee, the most dangerous 'nest' of the corsairs. Both Porter and Penn were passed over and Captain William Rainsborough was appointed commander of the expedition.

By the end of March 1637, the fleet was blockading Sallee, having had the good fortune to arrive before the pirates' ships had put to sea for the annual summer raids upon English commerce.[1] Attempts to set fire to shipping in the harbour were frustrated;[2] and the heavy draught of the English war-ships made an attack upon the castle, which dominated the town, difficult. The English were, however, much assisted in their operations by the circumstance that a revolt was in progress against the Emperor of Morocco and the town was divided into two hostile factions. It was not merely by coincidence that the expedition had been undertaken at this propitious moment; Giles Penn had argued that the civil war would weaken the enemy. The governor of New Sallee (as one section of the town was called) was the leader of this revolt. The governor of Old Sallee, who was loyal to the Sharif, permitted the English forces to land and occupy his part of the city. They joined him in the civil war, and as a result were able to arrange terms of peace with Morocco and to redeem about three hundred Christian captives.[3] These negotiations were conducted by a certain R. Blake who is described as an English merchant trading with Morocco.[4] It is probable that this man was he who afterwards became the great admiral; in early life Robert Blake is supposed to have made mercantile voyages, and it would certainly be in character if it was he who accomplished this settlement.[5]

In a poem whose ecstatic adulation of Charles I was scarcely

1 Ibid., *1637*, p.87.
2 Ibid., p.524.
3 See the summary of Rainsborough's log or 'Journal of Sallee,' ibid., p.475. John Dunton, the commander of one of the English ships, wrote: *A True Journall of the Sally Fleet, With the Proceedings of the Voyage. . . Whereunto is annexed a List of Sally Captives names, and the places where they dwell, and a Description of the three Townes in a Card*, 1637. Dunton had already had more than his share of adventures, for some time earlier he had been taken by Moorish pirates and compelled to serve in their vessel. This was captured by the English and Dunton was tried for piracy. He convinced his judges that his presence on board the pirate ship was involuntary, and doubtless accepted with satisfaction his appointment to a command.
4 *The Arrivall . . . of the Embassador*, 1637, pp.23,27.
5 The *D.N.B.* says that Admiral Blake, like other pushing merchants, made voyages oversea, but does not mention these negotiations for the redemption of captives.

warranted by the actual circumstances Edmund Waller celebrated the victory. King Charles, 'the sovereign of the sea,'
'the injured world's revenger,' has triumphed over the 'hungry
wolves,' 'pest of mankind,' who infest that den of monsters,
Sallee.[1] Waller takes occasion to note the presence in London
of 'the chief among [the] peers' of Morocco. Rainsborough had
in fact brought back to England an envoy from the Sharif.
When this personage arrived in London he was accorded a
ceremonious reception.[2] He was a native of Portugal who had
been captured by the Moors in childhood, had been 'distes-
ticled,' and had grown up in favour with the Emperor.[3] The
Earl of Shaftsbury now lent his coach to draw him in a stately
procession from the landing-stage through the streets of London
and beyond Temple Bar along the Strand. There were trump-
eters on horseback, a company of 'Redeemed Captives,' a
crowd of 'voluntary Gentlemen all bravely acountred,' and the
ambassador's personal retinue. The anonymous purveyor of
news who tells all this takes the opportunity to sketch the
history of Morocco and its ruling dynasty and to give some
account of Mohammedanism. He has something to say of the
wretched existence led by the Christian slaves of Barbary who
were constantly enticed by their masters to forsake their faith
and embrace Islam.[4]

The repatriation of quantities of these unfortunate renegades
rendered acute the problem of 'how they, having renounced
their Saviour and become Turks, might be readmitted into
the Church of Christ'; and Bishop Hall, in consultation with
Archbishop Laud, devised *A Form of Penance and Reconciliation
of a Renegado, or Apostate from the Christian Church to Turcism.*[5]

---

1 'Of Salle[e],' *Poems*, ed. G. Thorn Drury, 1893, pp.13f.
2 *The Arrivall and Intertainements of the Embassador, Alkaid Jaurar Ben Abdella, with
his Associate, Mr. Robert Blake. From the High and Mighty Prince, Mulley Mahamed
Sheque, Emperor of Morocco, King of Fesse, and Sussi. With the Ambassadors good
and applauded commendations of his royall and noble entertainments in the Court and
the City. Also a Description of some Rites, Customes, and Lawes of those Affrican Nations. Likewise Gods exceeding Mercy, and our Kings especiall grace and favour manifested in the happy Redemption of three hundred and two of his Majesties poore subjects,
who had beene long in miserable slavery at Salley in Barbary,* 1637.
3 Ibid., pp.5f.
4 Ibid., p.27.
5 Joseph Hall, *Works*, ed. 1833, xii,346f.—In this same year, 1637, Father Dan
published his *Histoire de Barbarie et de ses Corsaires*, a work of over five hundred

This involved private admonition and public reproof. On a Sunday the penitent, clothed in a white sheet and holding a white wand, stood in the porch of his parish church, imploring of the faithful as they passed in to worship, prayers for a poor renegade. The next Sunday he was admitted so far as the font, whose base he kissed with expressions of contrition and prayers for forgiveness. On the third Sunday he was brought near the minister's pew where still clothed in his sheet he publicly asked pardon. The minister addressed the congregation, and then welcomed the contrite sinner into the company of the faithful, saying 'I absolve thee from this heinous crime of renegation' and promising to receive him at Holy Communion when next it should be administered.

To pursue further the story of the Barbary corsairs and their outlawed English associates would carry us beyond the temporal limits of this book. The triumph of 1637 proved to be no more than a temporary truce; the pirates were soon at their old pernicious practices again; and not until the strong arm of Oliver Cromwell, through the instrument of Admiral Blake's fleet, inflicted severe punishment upon them did their power in the open ocean begin to decline.

VI

WHEN we come to inquire into the conditions in which Europeans, whether Christians or renegades, lived in Mohammedan countries a distinction must be drawn between the so-called 'Levantines' who sought in the Ottoman Empire an asylum from religious persecution in Europe and prisoners of war or piracy who found themselves there without the exercise of their own choice. Many of the former became Moslems to escape the penalization of social and political inferiority. Renegades were to be met with all over the Islamic world. Some, like Thomas Dallam's dragoman in Constantinople, 'a Turk but a Cornishman born,' or like the 'old blind Portigall renegado' whom John Jordain encountered so far away as

pages. He was a Redemptionist, sent into Barbary to ransom and negotiate for the release of captives. His book is in part a record of his experiences. He left in manuscript an account of the most illustrious captives; this was first published in 1892.

Aden,[1] were quite possibly contented with their lot; and there is no reason to doubt the sincerity of the confession of faith made by some converts to Islam. Reports of proselytizing among Christian captives occur with a frequency that is somewhat puzzling because, except when and where fanaticism has been peculiarly fierce, it has not been the usual policy of Mohammedans to make forcible converts of vanquished peoples. Some observers went so far as to praise this forbearance. Sir John Chardin, for example, commends the Persians for 'leur tolérance pour les religions qu'ils croient fausses et qu'ils tiennent même pour abominable.'[2] There is little recognition among writers of the Renaissance of the social and economic incentive to this policy, namely that a cool spirit of calculation has found it profitable to tolerate Christianity and Judaism and to collect penalties in the form of services or fines. Without questioning the fact that this has been one motive in formulating this policy we must also acknowledge that the humanitarian spirit of Islam, at its best, has also been a guiding force in treating these other 'Peoples of the Book' with more forbearance than Jews ever enjoyed in Christian Europe or than Protestants enjoyed in Catholic, or Catholics in Protestant, countries. There were of course cases of bloodthirsty bigotry. Take, for example, the story told by Thomas Saunders who was one of a ship's company captured by Tripolitan pirates. A Frenchman in the crew 'protested to turne Turke, hoping thereby to have saved his life. Then saide the Turke, If thou wilt turne Turke, speak the words that thereunto belong: and he did so. Then said they unto him, Now thou shalt die in the faith of a Turke, and so he did.'[3] But this was immediately after the heat of battle; it is unlikely that Moslems often slew such convertites, and it is noteworthy that save one valiant Englishman who refused to embrace Islam no one else was slain and Saunders himself

---

1 *Journal, 1608–1617*, ed. Sir William Foster, Hakluyt Society, 1905, pp.96f. The renegade whom Jordain describes had turned 'witch,' that is, wizard or sorcerer, and was thought by the foolish people of Aden to be a saint 'because he could doe a fewe of the Divells myracles.'—In Crete Lithgow met 'an English Runagate named Wolson' who, because he cherished a sworn hatred of Scots, planned to murder him; but Lithgow escaped (*Rare Adventures*, pp.81f.).

2 *Voyages en Perse*, Paris, 1686, iv,101.   3 Hakluyt, v,292f.

and the rest of his companions were not subjected to proselytizing by violence. The most terrible of such rare cases is
reported from Constantinople by John Sanderson—the case
of a Christian captive, unnamed but described as 'princely,'
who was told that his life would be spared if he became a
Mohammedan.

> Wheruppon he turned [that is, 'turned Turk'], and uttered to such
> effect the wourds, beinge content, rather then die, to be Turke . . .
> which done, this cruell dogge tould him that he was glad he would
> die in the right beliefe, and therfore wheras he should have bine
> gaunched, nowe he shalbe but hanged by the necke; wherat the
> poore soule presentlie repented and cried often and alowde uppon
> Christ.[1]

The general impression in England that Moslems practised
forcible conversion was probably founded upon the reports
of escaped or ransomed captives who hid under the plea of
compulsion their voluntary lapse from Christianity for the
sake of ameliorating their condition. What was doubtless a
typical case—of later date than the period with which we have
to do but worth citing because conditions in Barbary in his
day were much the same as fifty or a hundred years earlier—
was that of Joseph Pitts of Exeter. Algerine pirates captured
this young sailor in 1678. When sold at auction in the city of
Algiers he remained cool and detached enough to observe in
that extremity that the slave-dealers were 'extremely addicted
to Cozening and Cheating.' His successive masters (for he

1 *Travels in the Levant*, pp.89f.—Gaunching or ganching was a kind of impaling, the
victim being hurled from a high place upon spears, spikes, sharp hooks, or pointed
stakes either projecting from a wall or set in the ground. The punishment was
witnessed by various European visitors to Constantinople. See, for example,
Peter Mundy's sketch of 'Punishments used in Turkie, Stakeing, Gaunching, Drub-
bing or Beating on the Feete,' and the accompanying description in *Travels of
Peter Mundy*, ed. Sir Richard C.Temple, Hakluyt Society, 1907f.,i,54f. Dryden
refers to ganching in *Don Sebastian*, III,ii. Elkanah Settle introduced into *The Empress of Morocco*, 1673, a sensational episode in which one of the characters 'appears
cast down on the Ganches, being hung on a Wall set with Spikes of Iron.' In the
original edition of this tragedy there is a plate illustrating this scene. Nevil Payne
attempted to surpass Settle in horrible sensationalism. In the last scene of his *Siege
of Constantinople*, 1674, a stage-direction reads: 'A great Number of Dead and Dying
men in several manner of Deaths. The Chancellor, Lorenzo and Michael Empal'd.'
See Montague Summers's note to Dryden's allusion in his edition of Dryden's *Dramatic Works*, vi,528. See also Allardyce Nicoll, *History of Restoration Drama*, p.120.
There is a horrible picture of 'One Impaled on a Stake' in Captain Robert Knox's
Historicall Relation of the Island Ceylon, 1681, facing p.39.

changed hands three times) were cruel to him and he suffered beatings and bastinadoes till at last after many torments and overcome with terror he apostasized. 'I being then but young,' he wrote long afterwards, 'could no longer endure them and therefore turned Turk to avoid them.' In his narrative this confession is followed by the ejaculatory prayer, printed in large capital letters, 'God be Merciful to Me a Sinner!' Not until he had paid the great price of making the pilgrimage to the Holy Cities of Arabia did Pitts regain his freedom; but when once he was a Hajji he received regular wages as a servant, not a slave.[1]

The adoption of Islam did not carry with it the assurance of freedom, for though Moslem canon law forbade a believer to enslave his co-religionist it did not promise liberty to an alien slave who became a Moslem. However, many masters freed slaves who were converted.

The fate of renegade ex-slaves was miserable; they were outcasts from Christendom and despised by their new co-religionists.[2] The ceremony to which they were forced to submit when they renounced Christianity was humiliating in the extreme. Among Arthur Edwards's notes of his observations in Persia is one on 'the maner how the Christians become Busormen and forsake their religion.' (Edwards, who had recently been in Muscovy, uses the Russian word for Mohammedan.) The renegade is, he says, forced to curse his father and mother.[3] William Davies furnishes us with some details of the ceremony. The ex-Christian convertite is placed on horseback,

1 *A True and Faithful Account of the Religion and Manners of the Mohammetans*, Exeter, 1704, p.181.
2 Nicolas de Nicolay paints a pathetic picture of the state of the renegades of Algiers; see his *Navigations*, Washington's translation, 1585, folio 8ʳ. So does George Wilkins, of the people whom he calls 'elkes (that is to say, a Christian turned Moore)'; see *Three Miseries of Barbary*, Sig. A₄ᵛ. On the same page Wilkins uses the expression 'Elkes or Regadoes' (*sic*, for renegados). In Edmund Hogan's relation of his mission to Morocco in 1577 he describes the king of that country as sitting 'with his Counsell about him, as well the Moores as the Elchies' (Hakluyt, vi,288). Hogan does not explain who the latter personages were; but from their differentiation from the Moores one infers that they were Turks and perhaps official representatives of the Porte. The earliest use of the word 'Elchee' meaning ambassador (from the Turkish word for 'tribe'; hence a representative of the tribe) given in the *O.E.D.* is dated 1828. Hogan's use of the word and Wilkins's use and meaning are not recorded in the *O.E.D.*
3 Richard Eden, *The History of Travayle*, 1577, folio 335; *Early Voyages and Travels to Russia and Persia*, ed. Morgan and Coote, Hakluyt Society, 1886, ii,420f.

his face towards the tail, and thus mounted is led through the streets. In his hands are a bow and arrow which he aims at a picture of Christ which a Moslem, following him, carries upside down. So, cursing aloud his parents, his kindred, and his country, he rides to the place of circumcision.[1] We shall observe in a later chapter Robert Daborne's attempt to represent this ceremony in dumb-show in his play on the life of Captain Ward. Edward Grimestone gives at second-hand a description of a ceremony in a public square in Constantinople when a large number of 'wretched Grecians ran by troupes in this place to make themselves Mahometans.'

> This detestable troupe of Rascals went to shew themselves before the Grand Seigneur, their Bonnets under their feet, in signe that they did tread their law and honour under foot: There a Turkish Priest did cause them to lift up the demonstrative finger of the right hand, in signe that they did not beleeve but one God in one person, and to say with a loud voice, La illa ey alla Mehemet resoul alla.

Having thus professed their faith they were led away to be circumcised.[2] Grimestone also informs us that most of the fair women destined for the pleasure of the Grand Seigneur are by birth Christians who have been made to embrace the Turkish religion, and this they do 'by lifting up the second finger of the hand, in signe that they beleeve but one God only in one only Person, and they speake this word Mehemet.'[3] The special ceremony required of converted Jews is described by several writers. The Mohammedans 'preferre Christianity so farre,' says Francis Osborn, 'as no Jew can turne Turke till he hath been Christened.'[4] Henry Blount notes, more accurately, that

1 *True Relation of the Travailes and most miserable Captivitie of William Davies,* 1616, Sig. B₃ᵛ.—One of the many charming colour-plates in A.L.Castellan, *Moeurs, Usages et Costumes des Othomans,* Paris, 1812, six volumes, illustrates the ceremony of a Christian's conversion to Islam much as it is described by our early English writers.
2 *The History of the Imperiall Estate of the Grand Seigneurs,* 1635, pp.93f. The transliteration of the Arabic is fairly accurate. The Moslem profession of faith is: 'Lâ ilâha illa'llâh; Muhammadan rasûlu'llâh'—'There is no god but Allah; Mahomet is the Prophet of Allah.'
3 Ibid., p.57f.—There is an exceptionally interesting account of the ceremony of receiving a convert into Islam in Cornelis Bruin, *Voyage au Levant,* 1700, chapter xxxii.
4 *Politicall Reflections upon the Government of the Turks,* 1656, p.79.

Jews who embrace Islam 'must first acknowledge Christ as farre as the Turke does, that is, for a great Prophet, and no more.' [1]

Christians were held in captivity in many parts of the Ottoman Empire; but after the establishment of commercial relations between England and the Porte there were few English slaves in Constantinople and of these, apart from renegades who remained more or less of their own volition having become through long stay more at home there than in Christendom, most were either ransomed or else set free unconditionally in a short time. But diplomatic representations that were efficacious at the capital carried far less weight in the Barbary States where the policy of the central government was often disregarded and Turkish control was never absolute. With the growth of piracy the number of captives increased. Estimates vary, some running so high as twenty thousand for Algiers alone. No calculation is reliable because exact figures were unobtainable, the total must have varied from year to year and decade to decade, and there was a natural tendency on the part of those engaged in the work of redemption to appeal to Christian charity by exaggerating the number of these unfortunates. But that it was very large is beyond question. 'Avec leur art piratique,' wrote Nicolas de Nicolay, '[ils] ameinent journellement en Alger un nombre incroyable de pouvres Chrestiens qu'ils vendent aux Maures.' [2] In most countries of Europe were published narratives of the adventures and sufferings of men who had been held in captivity and had been ransomed or had made their escape. We shall now pass in review the principal English narratives of this sort, for though the subjects of them had not all been prisoners in Barbary their experiences were similar whether they had been slaves in Algiers or Tunis or Stamboul or Alexandria or elsewhere.

On his third visit to Moscow (1566–8) Anthony Jenkinson had in his service a twelve year old boy, Edward Webbe, who was destined to undergo amazing adventures and hardships. Jenkinson left him behind in Moscow with the English factors, and Webbe was there when the city was taken and sacked by

1 *A Voyage into the Levant*, p.122.   2 *Navigations*, 1576, p.17.

the Tartars in 1571. They carried him as a slave into the Crimea where he obtained his ransom. Returning to London, Webbe set forth again immediately, joined the forces of Don John of Austria, and was present at the capture of Tunis from the Turks in 1572. When the Turks retook La Goletta in 1574 he fell into their hands and became a galley-slave. For no less than twelve years he endured the miseries of the painful oar, subjected to the cruelty of the taskmaster who with his lash goaded the rowers to the limit of their strength. Later Webbe was a prisoner in Constantinople. He attempted to escape but was caught, and his condition after his recapture was worse than before. In 1588 his case came to the attention of Sir William Harborne through whose influence his freedom was procured. Webbe has left on record his gratitude to this ambassador, who 'did behave himselfe wonderfully wisely, and was a speciall meanes for the releasement of me and sundrie other English captives.'[1] After his liberation Webbe got into trouble in Italy but his luck held and he managed to reach England in May 1589. Nor were his adventures yet over. An ardent Protestant and rendered the more so because of his recent uncomfortable experiences in Italy, he enlisted under Henry of Navarre and was a master-gunner at the battle of Ivry in 1590. After the victory some French gunners, jealous, he says, of the favour shown him by his superiors, tried to poison him; but a dose of powdered unicorn's horn proved an effective antidote, and he was in England again before the end of the year. He immediately wrote and published *The Rare and Wonderful Thinges which Edward Webbe . . . hath seene and passed in his Troublesome Travailes*.[2] Webbe apologizes for his halting story 'for that my memory faileth me, by meanes of my great and greevous troubles.' His narrative is indeed somewhat confused, and it is naïve and credulous and some of its pages are doubtless too highly coloured; but it forms an impressive picture of an indomitable spirit.

John Fox was another adventurer of like temper. He was a

---

1 *Rare and Wonderful Thinges*, ed. Arber, p.28 (see next note).
2 The original edition is undated but appeared in 1590; a 'newly enlarged edition' appeared in the same year. Reprinted by Arber, 1868.

sailor aboard the English ship *The Three Half Moons*—ominous name for a Christian ship!—which was set upon in 1563 by no less than eight Turkish galleys. The Englishmen put up a valiant resistance but were at last overcome, their vessel being pulled down, says Fox, as the stag is by the hounds. The prisoners were taken to Alexandria and placed in the gaol where Christian galley-slaves were housed when bad weather kept them ashore. There Fox remained for fourteen long years. He won the confidence of his gaoler and was permitted to practise the trade of prison barber. A fellow-prisoner was a Spaniard who had passed so many years tranquilly in captivity that he was the last person to rouse suspicions. The two men concocted a plot word of which was passed circumspectly among the captives. At a given signal there was a sudden outbreak. The prisoners in overwhelming numbers set upon the gaoler and warders and slew them. A quantity of Spanish ducats was discovered in a hiding-place and appropriated. The prison was close by the harbour, and before the alarm was raised in the city it was possible to stock a galley with provisions. A few of the captives lost their lives in the gaol-delivery; the rest now put to sea, passing out safely between the two fortresses guarding the entrance to the port. A month of agony followed, for there were dreadful storms and food ran short and several men died of starvation. At length the survivors reached Candia where Greek monks fed and cared for them, so that they were strengthened to continue their voyage. At Taranto the company scattered, each group journeying to their own land. Of two hundred and sixty-six escaped prisoners the great majority reached their homes in safety. There were but three Englishmen, of whom Fox was one. These adventures were fashioned into a lively and vigorous narrative by Anthony Munday and published in Hakluyt's collection.[1] In 1608, when piracy and captivity in Barbary had centred public attention upon the miseries of Christian slaves, Munday reprinted the story with little change except that Fox's name was altered to Reynard.[2]

1 Hakluyt, v,153f. There is a brief narrative in Purchas, vi,149.
2 *The Admirable Deliverance of 266. Christians by John Reynard Englishman from the Captivitie of the Turkes, who had been Gally slaves many yeares in Alexandria*, 1608. Reprinted by Arber, *English Garner*, 1877, i.

Another of Hakluyt's narratives of the distresses of captive Englishmen is that of the voyage of the ship *Jesus*—challenging name considering its destination!—to Tripoli in Barbary in 1583. The story is told by Thomas Saunders, one of the ship's company.[1] We have seen that he escaped the fate alike of the Frenchman who professed Islam and of the Englishman who scorned to deny Christ. Saunders and the remainder of the company were sent to the galleys where, 'chained three and three to an oare,' 'naked above the girdle,' and cruelly lashed, they rowed about the sea. Later he was transferred to land and became a slave in Tripoli, fetching wood and carrying stone. Finally Queen Elizabeth sent letters (afterwards published by Hakluyt) to the Porte demanding the restitution of the *Jesus* and her crew and through the persistent efforts of Sir Edward Osborne and the agents of his company in Constantinople this was accomplished.

At the beginning of the seventeenth century James Wadsworth, whom we have already met with as a witness of the latter days of Sir Anthony Sherley, was captured by the Moors and sold into slavery in Sallee. He did not suffer the extreme hardships of the galleys but was subjected to miserable and humiliating treatment ashore. His account of the state in which he and his wretched companions lived makes painful reading even after three hundred years. 'Our beds,' he says, 'were nothing but rotten straw laid on the ground, and our coverlets peaces of old sailes full of millions of lice and fleas.'[2] So sick and feeble did he become that his master gave him leave to attempt to persuade a French merchant to purchase his redemption. In this he was successful. He does not make it clear whether his 'perversion' to Roman Catholicism was the price he paid for his liberation by this benefactor or whether he changed his creed after obtaining his freedom. At all events he proceeded from Morocco to Spain,

---

1 Hakluyt, v,292f. The narrative had previously appeared as *A true Description of a Voiage made to Tripolie in Barbarie*, 1587. This had been licensed as 'a booke of a voyage into Turkye intytuled *a most lamentable voyage made into Turkye* Compiled by Thomas Saunders Captyve. 1584' (*Stationers' Register*, 22 March 1587; Arber,ii, 467).
2 *The English Spanish Pilgrime*, 1630, p.41. Chapter v is on Wadsworth's experiences in Morocco.

and there found unusual opportunities to consort with people of importance, rising at length to the post of tutor to the Infanta Maria. On his return to England he was 'newly converted into his true mothers bosome, the Church of England' and published the account of the English Catholic exiles in Spain to which reference has been made in an earlier chapter.[1] This contains also an exposure of Jesuitical stratagems and other sinister activities in the Church from which he had relapsed.

The True Relation of the Travailes and most miserable Captivitie of William Davies[2] (1614) is the record of sufferings undergone a few years after Wadsworth had been redeemed from captivity. Like him Davies experienced adventures among 'Papists' as well as among Moslems. Captured by pirates of Tunis, Davies was a galley-slave for nearly nine years save for intervals of servitude ashore. He is one of the earliest English writers to report the Turkish punishment of an unfaithful wife by sewing her in a sack and throwing her into the sea.[3] He witnessed, as we have noted, the ceremony of receiving a convert into Islam. One day the galley in which he rowed was set upon by the galleys of the Duke of Florence and he was taken prisoner. Instead of being set at liberty he was forced to pull an oar in the Tuscan galleys. This hard fortune is an instance of the fact that when a Protestant prisoner was rescued from the Turks by Roman Catholics he frequently found himself in as bad a predicament as before.[4] Davies's comments on his Italian experiences, though of some little interest, are

1 See p.295, note 3, above.
2 This is but a fraction of the immensely long title. Davies's narrative is reprinted in Osborne's *Collection of Voyages*, 1747, vii.
3 *True Relation*, Sig. B₂ᵛ.
4 That a Protestant who fell into the hands of the Spaniards might be worse off than when in Moslem lands is shown by the experiences of William Lithgow who though courteously treated when he passed through Barbary was mercilessly tortured in Spain, and by the experiences of Richard Hastleton who became a victim of the Inquisition. (See *Strange and Wonderfull Things happened to Richard Hastleton in his ten yeares travailes in many forraine countries*, 1595; reprinted in *An English Garner: Voyages and Travels*, ed. E.R.Beazley, ii,151f.) We have already noted that the Knights of Malta were not above practising piracy in intervals of warfare with the Turks, and their victims were by no means always Moslems; and the Christian inhabitants of southern Greece were notorious for seizing Christian voyagers whom they sold to the Turks. (See Corvel's 'Diary' in *Early Travels in the Levant*, Hakluyt Society, p.133.)

without bearing on our subject. Nor have we to do with his subsequent voyage to the West Indies and the Amazon. He indulges in no anecdotes in the series of rather dry little chapters in which he describes the places he has seen and the manners of strange peoples. His purpose in writing was, he says, partly to keep fresh in mind his gratitude to God for his escape from such wretchedness, partly to induce thankfulness in his readers who live in a country not subject, as are most nations, to such miseries and thraldoms.[1]

The desire to draw an edifying lesson from their experiences was a motive natural to those who had endured the harrowing hardships of the galley-benches and the squalid suffering of life in a Turkish prison. These unfortunates, restored to their homes, were not awake to the comic possibilities inherent in the exploit of escaping from beneath the watchful eyes of Mohammedan gaolers. But those men of letters who, having been spared the sight of any Turk in the flesh, pictured him as a ridiculous figure, might have grasped this opportunity. However, no English writer did so, not even Thomas Nashe, who certainly possessed the gusto requisite for the subject. To fill this lacuna one must turn to the greatest humourist of the Renaissance; and the reader may like to be reminded briefly of the adventure of Panurge among the Turks. It will serve by way of a comic interlude.[2]

Panurge had been a member of the French expedition which in 1502 made an ill-fortuned attempt to capture Mytilene from the Mohammedans, and he was one of the soldiers taken prisoner. Shortly after Pantagruel took him into his service Panurge told how he escaped from the Turks. These rascals broached him on a spit, greased with strips of bacon because otherwise his lean body would have been unappetizing. The *roustisseur* by divine mercy fell asleep; and Panurge, contorting his body, grasped between his teeth the unlit end of a blazing

---

1 Of many similar narratives of later date the best known is that by Joseph Pitts. Here may be mentioned J.B[utton], *Algiers Voyage in a journall*, 1621; Francis Knight, *A Relation of seaven yeares slaverie under the Turkes of Argeire*, 1640; and *The Adventures of (Mr.T.S.) an English Merchant, Taken Prisoner by the Turks of Argiers . . . Written first by the Author, and fitted for the Publick view by A.Roberts*, 1670.
2 Rabelais, *Pantagruel*, i, chapters ix and xiv.

faggot and managed to toss it into the cook's lap. 'Fire, fire!' cried the startled cook (in Turkish of dubious authenticity).[1] In rushed the master of the house who, enraged at the cook's carelessness, seized the spit from which Panurge was hanging and with it stabbed the menial so that he died instantly. This impulsive act saved Panurge's life, for when the spit was withdrawn he tumbled to the floor, the bacon larded round him breaking his fall. The basha cried aloud upon a hundred devils, whereupon Panurge, fearing lest the devils come, made the sign of the Cross and no devils appeared. The failure of his invocation drove the basha to despair and he tried to commit suicide by stabbing himself with the spit. 'You're wasting your time,' said Panurge; 'you'll never kill yourself that way; you'll merely hurt yourself and spend the rest of your life in the surgeon's care. If you like I'll kill you outright; I'm an expert at that sort of thing.' 'Ah, my friend,' said the basha, 'if you would, you may have my purse.' So Panurge strangled him with an old pair of Turkish drawers. Then he escaped from the burning house; and people in the street poured water over him, and pitying him offered him refreshment; but he could not eat much, for they gave him only water to drink, *à leur mode*. Meanwhile the fire was spreading terribly; more than two thousand houses were aflame; and the people cried '*Ventre Mahom*, all the town's burning and we are idling here!' and dashed off to their own houses. Panurge made his way down to the port; and turning like Lot's wife he almost disgraced himself for joy to see the burning city. But while he was watching the destruction with great content, more than six, in fact more than thirteen hundred and eleven dogs swarmed around him, attracted by the odour of roast meat. They would have devoured him had he not thought of the bacon, which he pulled in strips off his body and threw to

1 With this fragment of dubious Turkish compare the 'Turkish' which astonishes and delights Monsieur Jourdain ('Ah! que je suis amoureux d'elle! Voila une langue admirable que ce turc!') in Molière's *Le Bourgeois Gentilhomme*, IV,iii–v. Compare the English version of Molière's farce, Edward Ravenscroft's *The Citizen Turn'd Gentleman*, V,i. Dryden hits at this episode in the Prologue to *The Assignation*, 1672:

> Sure there's some spell our Poet never knew,
> In hullibabilah da, and Chu, chu, chu.
> But Marabarah sahem most did touch you.

them; and while they snarled and fought over it he made his escape. *Ainsi eschappé gaillard et de hayt, et vive la roustisserie!* [1]

VII

WHEN at Morning Prayer on the thirteenth day of the month in the cycle of the Psalms appointed for the daily offices of the Church, Englishmen praised God 'Who bringeth the prisoners out of captivity; but letteth the runagates continue in scarceness,' [2] the words must have borne a weight of associations now lost to us after three hundred years. Worshippers meditated upon the miserable lot of apostates in this world and the next, and rendered thanks for the mercy shown unto thousands of slaves redeemed out of captivity in Mohammedan lands. In England there was no organization analogous to the Order of Redemptionists founded in France for the express purpose of collecting funds for the ransoming of captives and of sending agents into Barbary to arrange for their deliverance. In England this pious work was entrusted to private charity, and collections were occasionally authorized in individual dioceses or throughout the country. Marlowe's mind was upon the circumstances of his own time when he made his Tamburlaine announce his intention to liberate 'those Christian captives . . . that naked row about the Terrene sea' and that suffer the 'bastones' of the 'cruel pirates of Argier' as they lie panting on the galley's side.[3] Spenser, too, seeks to rouse pity for these wretches. In the House of Holiness there are seven Bead-men, personifications of the Seven Works of Mercy. The fourth Work of Mercy is the visitation of prisoners. Spenser associates this charitable office with the particular need of his own age; and he describes thus one of these Bead-men:

---

1 The allusion to the famous dogs of Constantinople is obvious and has been noted by the commentators, who, however, miss the fact that in Panurge's story there is evidence that Rabelais was acquainted with the especial peril of the great city, its liability to conflagrations. (Panurge, by the way, does not say that his adventure happened in Constantinople, but the inference is indisputable.)
2 Psalm lxviii,6.
3 *I Tamburlaine*, III,iii,46f.

The fourth appointed by his office was
Poore prisoners to relieve with gratious ayd,
And captives to redeeme with price of bras
From Turkes and Sarazins, which them had stayd.[1]

1 *The Faerie Queene*, I,x,40. Compare the inspection of slaves and chaffering in ibid., VI,ix,9f. In Heywood's *A Challenge for Beauty* (*Dramatic Works*, v,23f.) an English sea-captain is ransomed at the 'Male Market.' The slave-market in Marlowe's *Jew of Malta*, II,iii, is conducted by Christians for the sale of Moslem captives. Compare Fletcher's brilliant scene of the slave-market in *A Very Woman*, III,iv, which Dryden probably had in mind in the opening scene of *Don Sebastian*. In both these scenes the slaves are made to run through their paces to prove their strength and soundness of limb and wind. For such tests the dramatists had the warrant of eye-witnesses; compare, for example, Nicolas de Nicolay, *Navigations*, English translation, 1585, folio 8ʳ (Purchas, vi,124); Captain John Smith, *True Travels*, ed. Arber and Bradley, 1910, ii,853 (Purchas, viii,321f.). In Davenant's *The Fair Favourite*, III,i (*Works*, iv,235) one of the characters has redeemed slaves 'from the gallies of Algiers.' Compare the scene in Massinger's *The Guardian*, V,iv, in which the King of Naples persuades the outlaw Severino to contribute redemption-money. This episode, which in itself has nothing to do with the plot of the play, was strikingly topical at a time when 'gatherings' were being made among the charitable for the redemption of captives. In John Day's *Law-Tricks*, V,i, there is a story of a lady whose freedom from concubinage in Turkey is purchased by her friends.

CHAPTER NINE

THE PROPHET AND HIS BOOK

I

IF we would account for, and place in their proper perspective, the legends and lies which passed current in Shakespeare's England about Mahomet and Mohammedanism, some knowledge of medieval ideas on these subjects is necessary, for the Renaissance inherited a confused and contradictory mass of grotesque notions concerning the Founder of Islam, and so long-lived are prejudices that, even when the scholarly and the curious had rendered accessible sources of information that at least approximated to the truth, these notions persisted almost unchallenged, were indeed fortified by new prejudices against the Ottoman conquerors of the Levant.[1]

A few early writers possessed some genuine information on these subjects. William of Malmesbury—to cite a solitary instance—writes definitely and emphatically: 'Saraceni et Turchi Deum creatorem colunt, Mahumet non Deum, sed eius prophetam aestimantes.' [2] Nothing could be clearer or more exact, so far as it goes; but William of Malmesbury's writings still reposed in manuscript, practically unknown, when Spenser

---

1 Much learning has been expended upon the occidental legend of the Prophet in the Middle Ages but the ideas that survived into the period of the Renaissance and were more or less familiar to the Elizabethans have not hitherto been inquired into. For an analytical list of studies of the occidental legend see Victor Chauvin, *Bibliographie des ouvrages arabes ou relatifs aux arabes, publiés dans l'Europe chrétienne de 1810 à 1885*, xi (1909), 212f. The fullest study is that of Allesandro D'Ancona, 'La Leggenda di Maometto in Occidente,' *Giornale storico di letteratura italiana*, xiii (1889), 199f., reprinted in *Studii di Critica e Storia Letteraria*, Bologna, 1912, ii,165f. References to this monograph in the present chapter are to the reprint. D'Ancona's edition of the *Tesero* of Brunetto Latini (*Atti della Reale Academia dei Lincei*, iv [1888]) contains a collection of medieval texts illustrating the legend. Some similar texts are assembled without commentary in H.de Castries, *L'Islam*, Paris, 1896. Ernst Renan, 'Mahomet et les origines d'Islamisme,' *Etudes d'Histoire religieuse*, Paris, n.d., pp.222f., contains some brief but suggestive remarks on the subject. See also E.Dumeril, *Poésies populaires latines du moyen âge*, Paris, 1847, pp.374f.; Gustave Soulier, *Les Influences orientales dans la Peinture toscane*, Paris, 1924, especially Part I, chapter vi; D.C.Munro, 'The Western Attitude toward Islam during the Period of the Crusades,' *Speculum*, vi (1931), 329f.
2 *Gesta regum Anglorum*, Book ii, §189; Migne, *Patrologia Latina*, clxxix,col.1170.

and Shakespeare were alive; and there are few parallels to this accurate statement; and they were without influence in forming popular opinion. The general notion was that Mohammedans were mere pagans, which explains the curious confusion in the *Chansons de Gestes* between Saxons and Saracens and the fact that, as everyone knows, in old days the great rude monoliths of Stonehenge and other remnants of neolithic civilization in Britain were popularly known as Sarsen—that is, Saracen—stones.

The truth, that Moslems revered Mahomet as the Prophet of God, obtained no currency and little credence during the centuries when Christendom believed either that he was an idol or false god or else that he was a heresiarch, the founder of the most scandalous of schisms in the history of Christianity. Since the notion that he was an idol or false god springs from a greater depth of ignorance than the idea that he was a heretic or schismatic, it may be of earlier origin, at least in the West; but what we are confronted with seems to be not so much an earlier conception succeeded by a later as a popular point of view opposed to an ecclesiastical. Renan's formula 'A l'idole Mahom succède l'hérésiarque Mahomet' is an over-simplification. The two notions existed side by side.

In the *Chanson de Roland* King Marsilies, in flight from Charlemagne, arrives at Saragossa bleeding from his wounds. He and his followers vent their desperate rage upon their own gods who have failed them in their need.

> They hurl themselves upon their god Apollin who is in a grotto;
> They heap upon him a thousand reproaches, a thousand insults.
> 'Ah, wicked god, why hast thou done us such shame?
> And our king, why hast thou suffered him to be confounded?
> Ill dost thou requite those who serve thee!'
> Then they took from Apollin his sceptre and his crown, . . .
> They beat him with sticks and broke him to pieces.
> Tervagan, also, lost his carbuncle.
> As for Mahumet, they threw him into a ditch
> Where the swine and the dogs trod upon him and devoured him.

Unkes mais Deu ne furent a tel hunte!—'Never were gods put to such shame!' [1]

1 *Chanson de Roland*, ccxvii,2570f.

It has sometimes been supposed that in the popular mind of medieval Christendom the three gods here mentioned— Mahomet, the chief divinity of the pagans, Apollo, representative of the fallen Olympians, and Termagant, chief of devils— composed an unholy Saracenic trinity blasphemously analogous to the Christian Trinity. But for this there is little evidence, for Mahomet often appears not as one of three but as the most conspicuous figure of an entire pantheon. Besides Apollin and Termagant, there were Jubiter and Jovin and Ascarot and Alcaron and more rarely ten or a dozen other divinities and demons.[1] Even more frequently Mahomet stands alone.

1 P.Casanova holds that the names of three of these deities associated with Mahomet are corruptions of Arabic religious words or phrases; see 'Mahom, Jupin, Apollon, Tervagant, dieux des Arabes,' *Mélanges Hartwig Derenbourg*, Paris, 1909, pp.391f. The forms Jubiter and Jovin and Apollin suggest confusion with the Olympian gods; Ascarot is probably from Ashtaroth; and Alcaron seems to be Alkoran, the *Koran*, the book transmuted into a god. Of the lesser divinities with whom the medieval Christian imagination surrounded Mahound the only one who survived down to the period of the Renaissance was Termagant, a mysterious and elusive being. Layamon refers twice to Tervagant, once as a god of ancient Rome, afterwards as a god of the pagan Saxons (*Brut*, ll.5353 and 16427). More commonly he is a god of the Saracens and as such is often referred to in the metrical romances. The characteristic oath of Sir Olifaunt, Chaucer's giant, was 'By Termagaunt' (*Sir Thopas, Canterbury Tales*, B.2000); and the paynim in Spenser 'oftentimes by Turmagant and Mahound swore' (*The Faerie Queene*, VI,vii,47; compare ibid., II,viii,30). Joseph Hall, with what seems to be a satiric fling at Spenser, writes of those who

> fright the reader with the pagan vaunt
> Of mighty Mahound and great Termagaunt

(*Satires*, I,i). Massinger's disguised Venetians in Tunis believe that in order to pass for Mohammedans they must learn to swear 'by Mahomet and Termagant' (*The Renegado*, I,i,8). Marston employs the names Mahomet and Termagant as equivalents of devil (*The Insatiate Countess*, V,ii,182). Florio in *The Worlde of Wordes* defines the Italian Termigisto as 'a great boaster, . . . child of the earthquake, . . . brother of death.' 'I'll march where my Captaine leads,' says a character in Heywood's *The Royal King and the Loyal Subject* (*Works*, vi,23), 'wer't into the Presence of the great Termagaunt.' Taylor the Water-Poet carries this conception of the demon to the grotesque length of imagining that 'Acheron and Termagant did sing' when Pluto kissed Proserpine ('Sir Gregory Nonsense,' *Works*, Spenser Society, p.164). Thomas Randolph has the queer fancy that Termagant was one of the familiars attending upon Doctor Faustus (*Hey for Honesty, Poetical and Dramatic Works*, pp.458f.). 'He lies like a Termagant,' says one of Shirley's characters (*The Maid's Revenge*, IV,i; *Works*, i,157). Elsewhere in the drama we find swaggering soldiers who swear not by but like Termagant (Beaumont, *A King and No King*, IV,ii,152; Lodowick Barry, *Ram Alley*, Hazlitt's Dodsley, x,322). Various etymologies of the name have been suggested; the O.E.D. does not record them all. An old derivation is from a supposed Anglo-Saxon *tyr* meaning 'very' and *maegan*, 'main' or 'strong'; hence the Very Mighty, the hypothetical title of a pre-Christian Saxon god, then of any idol, and finally of an idol worshipped by the Saracens. (This was suggested to Bishop Percy by 'the learned editor of Junius'; see *Reliques of Ancient English Poetry*, ed. 1860, p.75.) Attractive but quite fantastic is the theory that the name derives from Ramadan—that is, that Christendom perverted reports of the Mohammedan Lent into a notion that the Moslems worshipped a god named Ramadan or Termagan (see the note on *Hamlet*, III,ii,16, in the Furness *Variorum*). Another

Extravagantly picturesque are the ramifications of the conception of the idol Mahomet. When Tancred entered the temple at Jerusalem, which had been converted into a mosque, he discovered therein a silver statue of Machumeth decorated with gold and gems and placed upon a high throne.[1] The *Chronicle* attributed to Bishop Turpin tells of an idol of Mahound worshipped at Cadiz, 'an image of the finest gold, cast in the shape of a man, and standing on its feet on a lofty stone pedestal.' Christians did not dare to approach it and Charlemagne himself feared to destroy this image because of the legion of devils that guarded it.[2] Cervantes tells us that Don Quixote, devotee of old romances, admired Rinaldo best of all men in the world and praised most that feat 'when he carried off the idol of Mahomet, which was all of gold.'

That pagans in general worship Mahomet is unquestioningly assumed by the anonymous authors of the English Cyclical Plays. Pharaoh exhorts his followers to 'heave up their hearts to Mahownde' who will help them in their need. Caesar Augustus swears by, and prays to, the same god. Herod swears by him and his bones and threatens to destroy anyone who does not believe in 'sant Mahowne, our god so sweet.' The idols of Egypt which, according to the beautiful legend, fell down at the

untenable suggestion is that Termagant is from *Ter Magnus*, a Latinized form of Trismegistus. The usual French and Italian forms, Trivigant and Trivigante, point to the much more likely derivation from *Trivagans*, Diana wandering as a threefold divinity (this is doubtfully endorsed by the *O.E.D.*). But the matter may be simpler still. The second element in the name—Magant or Magaunt—may be merely a variant of Mahaund, with the first element added as an intensitive; that is, Mahomet himself may be concealed behind the personality of his fellow-god. This explanation had occurred to the present writer before he saw the note on *The Faerie Queene*, II,viii,30, in the *Variorum* edition, 1933. The only surviving use of the word termagant is in the sense, now literary and perhaps becoming obsolete, of a shrewish, scolding woman. This meaning, which is rare in Elizabethan usage (see Fletcher, *Rule a Wife and Have a Wife*, V,v,138), is said to exist in no language save English. The shift in gender is curious, but compare the ungallant limitation of the epithet 'scold' to the female sex.

1 *Historia peregrinorum euntium Jerusalymam*, cited by H.de Castries, *L'Islam*, pp.278f. The Roman Emperor Sir Adrian built a temple of Moumetes on Mount Calvary. See *Legends of the Holy Rood*, ed. Richard Morris, E.E.T.S., Original Series, xlvi,35 and 90.

2 *De Vita Caroli Magni et Rolandi Historia Joanni Turpino*, ed. A.S.Ciampi, Florence, 1822, Book i, chapter xxviii. For this tradition there is some foundation in the fact that there existed at Cadiz a statue of Hercules which was destroyed in the twelfth century by an emir who hoped to discover treasure inside it. See René Basset, 'Hercule et Mahomet,' *Journal des Savants*, July 1903, pp.391f. Basset gives the Latin and French passages in pseudo-Turpin.

coming of the infant Christ, are called 'Mahomets' or 'mau-
mets.' Just before the crucifixion one of the executioners declares that not all Christ's 'mawmentry'—His idols or idolatry—shall save Him.[1]

More interesting than these casual and conventional allusions
is the part taken by the idol Mahound in the play of *Mary
Magdalene*.[2] In this play the King and Queen of Marseilles [3]
worship various gods, among them 'Mahond that is so mykyll
of myth [might].' In a temple on whose altar is an idol of
Mahond they attend a service conducted by a heathen priest
and his acolyte. The latter recites a nonsensical, confusedly
obscene, dog-Latin liturgy entitled 'Leccyo mahowndys viri
fortissimi sarasenorum.' Rex Mercell makes an offering with the
prayer to 'sweet Mahound' to suffer not his soul to be lost.
The priest exhibits relics of the god, his neck-bone and his
eyelid. In a later scene the King conducts Mary Magdalene
to Mahomet's temple at Marseilles. He beseeches the god to
condescend to address words to her, but the priest declares
roundly: 'He woll natt speke whyle Chriseten here is.' Then
Mary makes her prayer to the true God: 'Dominus, illuminacio
mea.' What follows is set forth in an elaborate stage-direction,
beginning: 'Here xal [shall] the mament tremyll and quake.'
A cloud from heaven sets the temple on fire. The priest and his
clerk sink into the ground.[4] The King and Queen are converted

---

1 *York Plays*, xix; *Towneley Plays*, ix,xiv,xvi; *Chester Plays*, i,viii,x. Oaths 'by Mahounde full of mighte' and the like occur with special frequency in the *Chester Plays*;
  in that on Doomsday two of the devils swear by Mahounde. Jonathas the Jew in
  The Play of the Sacrament prays to Machomet (ll.69f.).—In the *Cursor Mundi* (ed.
  E.E.T.S., ii,675,ll.11753f.) it is told how the Egyptian folk offered sacrifice to their
  'maumet'; but when Mary carried her Son into the church all these devils (or idols)
  fell grovelling to the ground.
2 *Digby Mysteries*, ed. F.J.Furnivall, E.E.T.S., Extra Series, lxx,ll.1140f.,1539f.
3 Mercyll is of course Marseilles, the city near which Mary Magdalene and her companions landed; but in making Rex Mercyll a worshipper of Mahomet the anonymous
  author may have had some confused memory of King Marsilies in the *Chanson de
  Roland*.
4 The situation owes something to the contest between Aaron and the Egyptian wizards
  and to the story of Saint Francis and the Soudan of Egypt; but its special resemblance
  is obviously to the story of Elijah and the priests of Baal. When in the metrical romances a Saracen upbraids, or a Christian knight derides, Mahomet or other heathen
  deities for sleeping too long or too soundly, there is an echo of Elijah's taunt 'Peradventure he sleepeth.' Hence Bajazet's invocation 'O Mahomet, O sleepy Mahomet!'
  (Marlowe, *2 Tamburlaine*, III,iii,269). Compare also the description of a sea-fight
  when the defeated Turks 'howled' to 'their sleepy prophet' in Fletcher and Massinger, *The Knight of Malta*, II,i.

to Christianity and start together for the Holy Land to be baptized by Saint Peter.

In the metrical romances of the wars of Charlemagne and his Twelve Peers against the Saracens similar perverted notions of Mohammedanism are often turned to dramatic account. Thus, when the Soudan Laban, in the course of his war with Rome, was repulsed in battle,

> He cryede to Mahounde and Apolyne
> And to Termagaunte, that was so kene,
> And said 'Ye goddes, ye slepe to longe,
> Awake and helpe me nowe.'

Later, wrathful in defeat, he smote a golden image of Mahounde to the ground, at which desecration the heathen bishops howled and wept and persuaded the Soudan to kneel before the idol and beg forgiveness. But before long another defeat caused the Soudan to give orders to cast Mahounde and four other gods into a fire of pitch and brimstone. Again a bishop interceded 'and charged him by the hye name Sathanas' to save his gods.[1] The idols did not always get off so easily, for it was an established custom for discomfited paynim leaders to berate and beat them. In one romance a counsellor says to the Soudan, his master: 'To tell the truth, our gods hate us. Thou seest, neither Mahoun nor Apolin is worth a pig's bristle.' The Soudan, sulking in his tent, gave orders for his gods to be brought before him. 'Sorrow ye do us and no good,' he said reproaching them. 'Fye upon thee, Appolyn. Thou shalt have an evil end. And much sorrow shall come to thee also, Termagant. And as for thee, Mahound, Lord of all the rest, thou art not worth a mouse's turd.' He took a stout stick and beat his gods on back and belly and threw them on the ground so that their arms and legs were broken. 'No more goodness was ever found in you than in a dog,' he said, and he dragged them by the feet out of his tent.[2] When Roland defeated the paynim giant Vernagu the latter cried out, 'Help, Mahoun and Jubiter of

1 *The Sowdone of Babylon*, ed. Emil Hausknecht, E.E.T.S., Extra Series, xxxviii, ll.2105f.,2507f.,2761f.
2 *The Romance of Guy of Warwick*, ed. Julius Zupitza, E.E.T.S., Extra Series, xlii, xlix,lix,ll.3675f.

gret renoun!' but Roland mocked him and cut off his head.[1]
On another occasion, however, when the same Christian champion urged a Saracen to forsake Mahoun and offered him a
duchy and a fair wife as inducements to turn Christian, the
Saracen, though he recked nought of such bribes, was convinced of the goodness of his enemy's God and did embrace
Christianity.[2] He acted wisely; for dreadful was the fate of the
Soudan Arabas. During the siege of Milan Roland and three
of his fellows were made prisoners and led before this Soudan.
Roland pleaded with him to become a Christian, but he laughed
him to scorn, saying that he had no more faith in the Christian
God than in a rotten tree. 'Go, fetch in one of their gods,' he
commanded. A Rood (Crucifix) was brought in and cast into
the fire where it was not consumed though the Saracens heaped
brimstone and pitch upon it. Then fire burst forth from the
Rood and blinded the Saracens, whereupon the knights slew
the Soudan, threw the other Saracens into the fire, and made
their escape.[3] The episode is a little disappointing; one expects a
contest in miracle-working; but Arabas makes no allusion to
the power of Mahound nor attempts to work wonders by him.

More elaborate and more entertaining is another incident.
Once upon a time the Twelve Peers of France were shut up,
by a strange trick of fortune, in a tower belonging to an emir
named Balan. The emir's daughter Floripas was secretly
betrothed to Sir Guy. She heard the prisoners' complaints that
they were short of food and reproached them, saying that had
they worshipped her gods they would have had an abundance
to eat. Roland asked her to show them her gods and she conducted them to the 'maumerye.' She drew back the curtain
from before the shrine, and they saw the mametes of bright
gold, powdered with precious stones. Incense burned sweetly
and there was an odour of balm and spicery. Floripas besought
them to pray to these idols; but said Oliver, 'They are so sound

---

1 *Roland and Vernagu*, ll.851f. This fragmentary romance is included in the volume
mentioned in the next note. With Vernagu's despairing cry to Mahoun the editor
compares the episode in pseudo-Turpin (ed. cit., p.49) when Gigas in battle with
Roland invokes his god: 'Mahumet, Mahumet, Deus meus, succurre mihi, quia
morior!'
2 *The Taill of Rauf Coilyear*, ed. S.J.H.Herrtage, E.E.T.S., Extra Series, xxxix,ll.891f.
3 *The Sege of Malayne*, ed. S.J.H.Herrtage, E.E.T.S., Extra Series, xxxv,ll.385f.

asleep they cannot hear us. I will awaken them!' He drew his sword and smote Sir Mahound to pieces; Ternagan he dashed against the wall; another knight hacked Jubiter and Appolyn to bits. Floripas forthwith declared that never again would she worship gods that tolerated such destruction, and she began to pray to Him who died on Rood. Later in the story, her father Balan, defeated and a prisoner, was urged by Charlemagne to become a Christian, with the promise that if he did so his possessions would be restored to him. But Balan, sweating for rage, declared that he would never forsake Mahoun; and he spat into the font. Ferumbras his son (who long since had been converted) endeavoured to persuade him to submit to baptism; but when Bishop Turpin told him he must renounce Mahoun the gallant old emir smote Turpin so hard that he nearly broke his jaw-bone; and again he spat into the font. Ferumbras implored him to change his mind; but Balan replied, 'Son, by Mahoun, thou art a foolish man to counsel me to believe on one who was put to death for his own misdeeds. I defy him and all his people. By Mahoun, I would not give a pea for Christ or all his might.' Charlemagne then saw that to dispute further would be of no avail, and he gave permission to Ogier to strike off Balan's head. Afterwards Floripas stripped herself stark naked and had herself baptized—a sight that pleased Charlemagne and his barons.[1]

Without lingering to search out other such incidents in the metrical romances we return now to the early drama to note that with the exception of the idol in *Mary Magdalene* Mahomet does not appear in any extant English miracle or mystery play and it is not easy to see where he might have been introduced. When John Skelton wrote:

> As ferce and as cruell
> As the feende of hel
> His servauntes meniall
> He doth revile and brall;
> Lyke Mahound in a play
> No man dare him withsaye,[2]

1 *Sir Ferumbras*, ed. S.J.H.Herrtage, E.E.T.S., Extra Series, xxxiv,ll.2533f. and 5720f.
2 *Why Come Ye Not to Court?*, Chalmers' *English Poets*, ii,275.

the awkward phrasing of the simile is, it may be suggested, due to a combination of two associations with Herod in the mysteries, for Herod swears by Mahound and reviles and threatens his menials. Similarly, when John Bale described the papist magistrates who threatened his wife as 'grennyng upon her lyke Termagauntes in a playe,' [1] the simile may be nothing more than a confused recollection of the idol which Mary Magdalene saw at Marseilles. In all probability there never existed any now lost early English drama having among the *dramatis personae* either Mahound or Termagant. Hamlet's comment upon the ranting actor: 'I could have such a fellow whipped for o'er-doing Termagant' is significantly like his 'out-Heroding Herod.' [2]

The tradition of the idol Mahomet survived into Elizabethan times. When the philosophical Fulke Greville, a scholar notably attracted to the manners and thought of the East, wrote:

> Mahomet himself an idol makes,
> And draws mankind to Mecha for his sake, [3]

it is doubtful whether he intended to imply the existence of any actual material image of the Prophet. But in two plays—Robert Greene's *Alphonsus King of Arragon* and Robert Daborne's *A Christian Turn'd Turke*—an image or 'head' of Mahomet plays a conspicuous part; and such a 'head' was among the properties belonging to the Admiral's Company. [4] The strength of prejudice and the difficulty with which truth makes its way are illustrated in these dramas, for in a period when enlightenment was to be had for the asking the credulity was deep-seated which continued to fasten the charge of idolatry upon the rigid iconoclasts of Islam. John Selden, one of the three most learned Arabists of seventeenth-century England, protested against this Christian libel. 'They call'd Images Mammetts,' he said, 'and the adoration of Images Mammetry, that is Mahometts and Mahometry, odious names,

---

1 *Actes of English Votaryes*, 1550, Part ii, folio 83. 2 *Hamlet*, III,ii,15f.
3 *A Treatise of Monarchy*, stanza 518; *Works*, i,185.
4 See pp.483–5, below.

when all the world knowes the Turkes are forbidden Images
by their Religion.' [1]

Equally defamatory but not so crassly uncouth as the
theatrical device of the 'Mahomet's Head' is the view of
Mohammedanism displayed in John Mason's play *The Turk*.[2]
Here the sinister villain Muleasses prays thus to Mahomet:

> Eternal substitute to the first that mov'd
> And gave the Chaos forme, thou at whose nod
> Whole Nations stoop, and hold thee still a God, . . .
> Thou God of Mecha, mighty Mahomet,
> . . . mew not up my soule
> In the pent roome of conscience.
> Make me not morall, Mahomet, coopt up
> And fettred in the fooles phylosophy,
> That points our actions unto honesty.

The inappropriate Machiavellianism of this prayer is, like some
of the sentiments uttered by Marlowe's Tamburlaine, grounded
upon the prevalent conviction that Mohammedans were
peculiarly treacherous; but for a writer with Mason's pretensions to philosophy to ascribe to the unitarian Moslems a belief
in a second deity, proceeding from, partner with, substitute for,
or altogether superseding God, is indeed a curious error. It is
noteworthy that Mason attributes to Mahomet the power and
desire to lead men to dishonesty and to destroy their con-
sciences. This thought is in line with the idea in Greene's
Alphonsus that the 'god' of the Turks is in reality a juggling
fiend who by false promises lures his followers to destruction.
Thus the Founder of Islam becomes a devil; and as such he is
mentioned by John Marston [3] and by Edgar in *King Lear*,
where the foul fiend Mahu is recognizably Mahon or Mahound.[4]
Only very rarely, however, is the Prophet exalted by Christian
prejudice to the terrifying position of the Antichrist, for he
does not fulfil an essential condition of Saint Paul's prophecy—

1 *Table Talk*, ed. Sir Frederick Pollock, pp.99f.
2 *The Turke, A Worthie Tragedy*, 1610 (*Stationers' Register*, 1609); ed. J.Q.Adams,
Bang's *Materialien*, 1913. The passage quoted is ll.688f. Compare ll.880f.
3 *The Insatiate Countess*, V,ii,182.
4 III,iv,148. The identification, though obvious, is strangely ignored by the editors;
the Furness *Variorum* has no note on the name and the *Arden* editor merely offers
a parallel passage where Moho is a 'general of the infernal furies.'

he is outside, not within, the Church. The Earl of Stirling emphatically refutes such attempted identifications:

> That spirituall plague which poysons many Lands
> Is not the Turke, nor Mahomet his Saint,

for, he explains, Antichrist must be one who has authority in the Church, 'no foe confess'd, but a professor faint.' [1]

II

WE now turn to the conception of Mahomet as a great heresiarch. In the Middle Ages it was widely held that Islam was a heretical form of Christianity and that Mahomet was a perverse instrument of schism operating by diabolical inspiration. The conception of Christianity as the one universal religion, opposed only by barbarous paganism destined soon to be converted or destroyed, carried with it the conviction that any self-styled religion that had arisen since the founding of Christianity must necessarily be nothing other than a bastard and treacherous offshoot from the true faith. Hence Dante dooms Mahomet and his son-in-law 'Ali to that *bolgia* in hell in which are placed the sowers of scandal and schism, 'seminatori di scandalo et di scisma.' [2] From this point of view it is but a step to that whence Mahomet is regarded as the enemy of all religion. Thus, in an early fifteenth-century fresco of the Inferno in the church of San Petronio in Bologna he appears as one of a group of three whose other members are Julian the Apostate and Nicholas, the founder of the Nicolaitan heresy: [3] that is,

1 *Doomes-Day*, Second Hour, stanza 42. Compare p.101, note 1, above.

2 *Inferno*, xxviii,23f. D'Ancona, *Leggenda*, pp.225f., summarizes the interpretations of the commentators. Some of the older commentators detected another allusion to Mahomet in the weird incident during the Triumph of the Church (*Purgatorio*, xxxii) when a Dragon fixes his wasp-like tail in the Chariot of the Church and drags off part of the bottom (*il fondo*) of it. Modern criticism is inclined to see in this an allusion to heresy in general or Arianism in particular; or, interpreting *fondo* in the sense of basis or foundation, considers the Dragon Worldliness which has deprived the Church of its basic ideal. But it remains at least possible that Dante had Mahomet in mind.

3 See the commentaries on Revelation, ii,6f. This Nicholas was identified in the Middle Ages with the Nicholas of Antioch who was elected one of the seven deacons of the primitive Church. The heresy associated with his name was a species of Quietism which taught that spiritual calm was to be had through the gratification of sensual passion. Hence his association in the fresco with Mahomet who was thought to have permitted unrestrained carnality to his followers. Dante makes Mahomet send from hell a message of warning to a certain friar who was accused of advocating plurality of wives.

Mahomet is numbered among the heretics; but in the celebrated fresco of the Inferno in the Campo Santo at Pisa Mahomet's companions are Averroës and Antichrist: that is, he is counted among the scorners of all religion.[1] It was difficult for Christian piety to conceive any sincere non-Christian or non-orthodox belief; and the more clearly Christians realized Islam's claim to be a separate and distinct creed the stronger grew the belief that the Founder of Islam must have been a deliberate impostor. The development of the conception of Mahomet is, then, from that of a heretic to that of a fraud.

Before tracing this development we may pause to examine the earliest extensive account of the Prophet's character and career written by an English poet. This is the story 'Off Machomet the fals prophete and how he beyng drunke was devoured among swyn' which is told by John Lydgate in the last book of *The Fall of Princes*.[2] This portion of the poem was probably composed about 1440. Lydgate says that he took the story from 'bookis olde'; actually some deviations from his principal source indicate that either he dared invent for himself or else that he had at hand some authority in addition to the second, expanded, French version by Laurent de Premierfait of Boccaccio's *De casibus virorum illustrium*. Boccaccio narrates the history of Mahomet with remarkable brevity; Laurent, greatly enlarging his original, derives his additional material from Vincent of Beauvais.[3] If the following condensed paraphrase of Lydgate's narrative appears to move sluggishly, let the reader be assured that it is not so stagnant as Lydgate's verse.

Machomet, 'a fals prophete and a magicien,' was born in Arabia of low kindred. He was an idolater. He was the first person to use camels as a means of locomotion. In Egypt he

1 But Dante places Averroës in Limbo with Saladin and the pagan philosophers (*Inferno*, iv).—Mahomet sometimes appears in paintings of hell in which, because of the artist's indifference to matters of doctrine or because of the small scale on which he worked, it is impossible to determine the particular offence of which the Prophet was considered guilty. Thus, in the Metropolitan Museum, New York, there is a 'Christ's Descent into Hell' of the school of Hieronimus Bosch in which, in the lower right-hand corner among devils, is a tiny figure in a green gown wearing a large turban. This is undoubtedly Mahomet.
2 Book ix,ll.50f.; ed. Henry Bergen, E.E.T.S., 1924, iii,920f.
3 See ibid., iv,342f., for the relevant passages in Boccaccio and Laurent.

fetched merchandise. He studied the Bible. He married in Corozan a lady named Cardigan whom he attracted by 'his sotil false daliaunce,' for 'he koude riht weel flatre and lie.' He proclaimed that he was the Messiah, thus by his false teaching bringing the people into great error. He suffered from the falling-sickness; and this shameful affliction he explained away by telling how when Gabriel appeared to him, sent by the Holy Ghost to instruct him, so dazzling was the angel that 'to stand upriht he myghte nat susteene.' Milk-white doves were often seen on his shoulders picking grain out of his ears. These, he declared, came by grace of the Holy Ghost,

> Hym to visite, to shewe and specefie
> He was the prophete that callid was Messie.

Claiming to be 'a prophete of most excellence,' he hung pots of milk and honey on a bull's horns, deceiving the people by interpreting the milk and honey as symbols of the abundance that would come to them by the merit of his ghostly works. A clerk of his, named Sergius, wrote down his laws and also wrote down 'thes myracles thre.' (Lydgate, it may be remarked, has mentioned but two miracles, stupidly running together two of the false marvels of Laurent's narrative. In the French text there are three: that of the dove which pecked from Mahomet's ear; that of the bull between whose horns the *Koran* was hung; and that of the pots of milk and honey which Mahomet hid in the ground and of which he claimed to know the location by divine inspiration.[1]) Mahomet became the governor of the Arabians, Sarsyns, and Turks with the folk of Persia and Medea. He gathered the people together, 'gan to wexe a werreiour,' and conquered Alexandria 'with many mo cities.' Being 'lecherous of corage,' he caused an image of Venus to be set up. He made the Sarsyns perform their acts of worship on Fridays. He got drunk with wine, but like the false prophet that he was he bade the people drink water. Bochas (Boccaccio) did not tarry over

---

1 In the famous Munich manuscript of Laurent's *Des cas des nobles hommes et femmes* the miniature at the head of Book ix shows in the foreground the people unearthing a bee-hive and a dish of milk; in the middle distance Mahomet preaches from a pulpit while a dove sits on his shoulder and nearby is the bull with the *Koran* between its horns. See Paul Durrieu, *Le Boccace de Munich*, Munich 1909.

the errors of this 'nigromacien' whose doctrines vary from those of Holy Church. He was a 'foon [foe] to our faith.' Anyone who lists may read his laws 'as they be set in his Alkeroun,' every one of them grounded on falseness.

> Lik a glotoun deied in dronknesse,
> Bi excesse of mykil drynkyng wyn,
> Fill in a podel, devoured among swyn,
> This was the eende of fals Machomeete,
> For al his crafftis of nigromancie, . . .
> Whom Sarsyns so gretli magnefie.

In this deplorably jejune narrative are many features and incidents that we shall meet with in Elizabethan writers.

The conception of Mahomet as a fraudulent heretic is the distorted development of one of the most beautiful of the almost numberless traditions of the Prophet which accumulated during the first two centuries of the Hegira.[1] This is the *hadith* or tradition of the monk Bahîrâ, the annunciator or forerunner of the Prophet. The story exists in various forms. In one, the scene is laid at a Christian monastery in Syria. Bahîrâ, a pious monk, saw an approaching caravan above which a cloud hovered, shading it from the scorching sun. When the travellers came to rest beside the monastery the branches of a palm-tree gathered themselves together to form a parasol over a young camel-driver who reclined in their shade. This miracle was observed only by Bahîrâ. The members of the caravan were invited to refresh themselves in the refectory; and as they sat down to eat Bahîrâ asked the guests whether all their company were assembled. 'There lacks no one fit to present unto you,' was the reply; 'only a lad whom we have left outside.' 'Call him, call him in,' said the monk. They summoned the camel-boy, and Bahîrâ embraced him and made him sit at meat; and as he ate, the monk watched him narrowly and recognized on his person

---

1 What follows in the next three paragraphs is in the main a drastic condensation of D'Ancona's account of the medieval development of this tradition in his erudite monograph on the occidental legend of Mahomet.—On the genuine Mohammedan *hadith* (traditions) see in general Alfred Guillaume, *The Traditions of Islam*, Oxford, 1915. On the science of *hadith* see also P.K.Hitti, *History of the Arabs*, pp.393f. Bahîrâ's recognition of Mahomet is the subject of an illustration in an Arabian manuscript of the fourteenth century in the Edinburgh University Library; it is reproduced in Hitti, op.cit., p.421.

The False Miracles of Mahomet

the evident signs by which the Prophet of God should be known.

This legend found its way into Byzantium where it received a Christian colouring. In a version sprung from Jacobite Christianity we have a monk who was driven from his monastery because of his heretical opinions concerning the Crucifixion. He wandered a great way and came at length to Yathrib (El-Medina) in Arabia, and there he encountered an aged man named Bahîrâ who for the space of forty years had seen no Christian. Bahîrâ told the new-comer that long before, he had seen coming toward his cell a youth whom by the nimbus of light round his head he recognized as the fore-ordained Prophet of God. So far there is nothing in this story that might not derive from Islamic sources, but the Christian prejudice is revealed in what follows. For Bahîrâ goes on to tell how he taught Mahomet to proclaim that he had received his doctrines from the archangel Gabriel; and to further this deceit Bahîrâ gave Mahomet a certain book, with instructions to fasten it to the horns of a cow which, having been secretly trained, would bring the volume, fixed upon its horns, to the Prophet in the sight of all the people. Whereupon Mahomet should proclaim that it was the Word of God, miraculously sent to him from heaven.[1]

There is another Mohammedan tradition which in Christian redactions became confused with that of the monk Bahîrâ. Reduced to its simplest outlines and with various subsidiary elements omitted, the story is as follows. Waraqah, a pious Arab in the days of the Ignorance, was scandalized by the idol-worship of the people of Mecca and by the particular adoration which they offered to a certain black stone (the meteorite set in the corner of the Ka'aba). He studied diligently the Hebrew Scriptures and the Evangelists and translated portions of the latter into Arabic. Through these studies he became more or less Christianized, and gradually the conviction grew in him that a new Prophet was about to appear among his own people. Word came to him of a young man named Mahomet to whom

---

1 It has been suggested that this story of the cow had its origin in the fact that the second Surah of the *Koran* is called 'The Cow.' This is ingenious but unconvincing.

came visions which at times he thought were vouchsafed him by Gabriel while at other times he feared lest they were temptations of the devil. Waraqah sought out the youthful seer and assured him that he was indeed the chosen Prophet of God; and he expounded to him the Sacred Books of the Jews and Christians.

There are thus two traditions: that of Bahîrâ the Forerunner and that of Waraqah the Teacher of the Prophet. The former is strictly Moslem in origin; the latter lent itself easily to anti-Mohammedan propaganda. (The charge that Mahomet was taught by some nameless 'outlandish' person was, in fact, made by contemporary opponents; he refers to it twice in the *Koran* and repudiates it.) [1] Sometimes the two traditions combine in one. The original names attached to them disappeared from Christian rehandlings of the legends and for one or the other of these personalities, or for both, there was substituted that of Sargis or Sergius, possibly with a confused recollection of a monophysite heretic of that name. The problem before the Christian narrators was to account for the action of the monk Sergius in treacherously abandoning his faith and in saluting, associating with, and instructing Mahomet. The favourite explanation was that he abjured Christianity in disappointed rage when he failed to obtain preferment in the Church. This idea was transferred, by a process familiar to the folklorist, from the secondary to the principal character in the tale; and as a consequence there arose the grotesque legend that Mahomet was a cardinal residing at Rome who failed to obtain the election to the papacy and who avenged himself by seceding from the Church and establishing a rival religion. [2] It has been suggested, on no very good grounds, that the story is an invention of Ghibelline malice against the papacy. Rather it is an outgrowth of the age-long experience that heresies and schisms

---

1 Surah xvi,103 and xxv,4–5. Compare Alfred Guillaume, 'The Influence of Judaism on Islam' in *The Legacy of Israel*, Oxford, 1928, pp.133f., and Richard Bell, *The Origin of Islam in its Christian Environment*, 1926.

2 See E.Doutté, *Mahomet Cardinal*, Chalons-sur-Marne, 1889, an edited excerpt (with brief comments) from a fifteenth-century French poem. In the first Italian redaction in verse (end of the thirteenth century) of Brunetto Latini's *Tesoro* (159ʳ; D'Ancona, op.cit., p.167), Mahomet is made a member of the great family of Colonna in Rome.— A typical medieval rendering of these phases of the Prophet's career may be found in the rapid narrative introduced digressively into the French romance *L'Entrée d'Espagne*, ed. Antoine Thomas, S.A.T.F., 1913, i,ll.2450f.

have been often inspired and led by men high in the ecclesiastical hierarchy. Hence was deduced the notion that Mahomet the heresiarch had himself been a prince of the Church. Whether because they had discarded the extremes of credulity or for some other reason, the Elizabethans quite ignored this legend of Mahomet the Cardinal. A vestige of it, in distorted form, was accessible to them in the translation of Ludovico di Varthema's *Itinerario* (1510) which Richard Willes included in the 1577 edition of Richard Eden's *History of Travayle*.[1] Varthema says baldly that 'Babacher'—that is, Abu Bakr, the first Caliph—'was cardinal and wanted to be Pope.' Save for this scarce recognizable scrap of misinformation the medieval tradition makes no appearance in Elizabethan literature.

The legend of Sergius, on the other hand, was still very much alive in Shakespeare's England. It is repeated times beyond number in the anti-Mohammedan controversial literature of the later Middle Ages and the Renaissance.[2] Our interest lies in some specimens from English sources. In *The English Myrror* (1586) George Whetstone offers as a warning to his fellow-countrymen a series of narratives of the disasters wrought by Envy upon commonwealths. This theme allows ample room for moral discourses upon many famous examples drawn from history. A chapter is devoted to 'the envy of Sergius a monke of Constantinople, who being banished for heresie, fledde into Arabia, unto Mahomet; by divelishe policies, ambitious Mahomet forced the people to holde him for a Prophet, which damnable sect, until this day hath beene nourished with the bloud of many thousandes.'[3] This train of disasters followed

1 'The Navigations and vyages of Lewes Vertomannus,' *History of Travayle*, folio 354f.
2 D'Ancona gives the medieval variants. The tale was one to appeal to the once celebrated Swiss philologist and controversialist Theodorus Bibliander (Theodore Buchmann); see his *Confutationes Legis Machumeticae* (1543?), p.23. Father Crespet introduces the story into the commentary accompanying his translation of Pope Pius II's famous letter to Sultan Mahomet II; see *Instructions de la Foy Chrestienne*, Paris, 1589, folio 224ʳ. Johannes Boemus, Feyerabend, Des Hayes de Courmenin, Michel Baudier, and many other writers tell, or refer to, the story.
3 *The English Myrror*, Book i, chapter vii, pp.55f. A curious variant of the story of Mahomet's relations with Sergius tells that while the Prophet lay in a drunken slumber the monk was murdered. Awakening to discover the crime, Mahomet in remorse forbade the use of wine. The tale of the murdered Sergius does not occur in the early English narratives, but it is the subject of a magnificent engraving (1508) by Lucas Van Leyden, reproduced in Max J. Friedländer. *Lucas Van Leyden*, Leipzig [1925], plate 1. See ibid., p.8.

from Sergius's desire 'to be revenged of the clergy that banished him Constantinople.' The moral is forcefully brought home. The Reverend Henry Smith, the preacher whose eloquence attracted crowds of listeners to Saint Clement Danes, attacked Mahomet and Mohammedanism with quite exceptional ferocity. The monk Sergius, an unnamed Jewish magician, and a certain John of Antioch are reviled as Mahomet's fellow-conspirators in concocting the *Koran* to delude the ignorant.[1] The accusation is characteristic of much controversial literature, for the desire was not only to demonstrate that Mohammedanism is grounded in imposture and apostasy but to expose the *Koran* as a patchwork of various creeds. For this blasphemous amalgam Sergius is often held especially responsible because he had been educated as a Christian. English travellers, home from the Levant, are wont to introduce accounts of Mohammedanism into their narratives of far wanderings; and it is seldom that such books do not include the story of Sergius and his evil colleagues. William Lithgow, for example, handles the subject in his usual violent and vigorous style:

> About this time there was one Sergius, an Italian borne, banished from Constantinople, because he allowed of the Arian sect; who afterwards came to Palestine, and . . . fell in acquaintance with the young man Mahomet; and this Frier perceiving the aspiring quicknes of his braine, bore a great affection to his naturall perfections. . . [Mahomet] consulted with this Sergius, a Nestorian Monk, and Atodala another Thalmudist, a diverted Jew; hereupon these two helhounds, and the other perverst Runagate, patched up a most monstrous, and divellish Religion to themselves, and to their miscreant beleevers; partly composed of the Judaicall law, partly of Arianisme, partly intermixed with some points of Christianity; and partly of other fantasticall fopperies, which his own invention suggested unto him.[2]

At Agra Thomas Coryat addressed to a Mohammedan some very candid remarks about the deceits and 'profane fooleries' of the false prophet, telling his auditor, among other things,

---

1 *Gods Arrowe against Atheists*, 1593, chapter iiii, Sig. J^rf. By 1637 a dozen editions of this celebrated sermon had appeared. It may have aided materially to spread anti-Mohammedan prejudice in England.
2 *A Most Delectable and True Discourse*, 1614, Sig. I^vf.; *Rare Adventures*, pp.130f.

that Mahomet 'was not able to make [the *Koran*] without the helpe of . . . a certaine Renegado Monke of Constantinople called Sergius.' Proud, apparently, both of his boldness and of his command of a foreign language, Coryat sent home a 'Copy of a Speech that I made to a Mohematan in the Italian tongue.' He admits that had he said so much in Turkey or Persia he would have been roasted on a spit; but in the dominions of the Grand Mogul one may speak one's mind more freely.[1] Other travellers, when safely home, wrote in much the same strain. William Biddulph modulates from the tale of Sergius into a series of comments upon the many sources of Mohammedan doctrine.[2] George Sandys repeats the tale with no novel variation.[3] Thomas Herbert says that Mahomet wrote the *Koran* 'by the Devills prompting, and with the help of Sergius an Italian (a neast of uncleannesse, a Monck, a Sabellian, a discontented wretch for missing worldly preferment).'[4] John Fryer concludes his telling of the story with the remark: 'By their joint perverting the Holy Bible sprang up this Motley of Blasphemous Dotages.'[5] Many other such denunciations of the renegade monk might be quoted;[6] the Christian animus against this fictitious person was extreme.

Towards the close of the sixteenth century rumours were afloat about a certain scandalous treatise entitled *De Tribus Impostoribus Mundi*. The 'three impostors' who had deceived the world were, it was said, Moses, Jesus Christ, and Mahomet. The blasphemous charge against the Saviour and the association of Him with the Arabian impostor roused general indignation. There were various attributions of authorship, the blame being attached to Erasmus, Rabelais, Pietro Aretino, Giordano Bruno, or anyone else in sufficient disrepute to bear the responsibility appropriately. It was even said that the docu-

---

1 *Mr. Thomas Coriat to his friends in England sendeth greeting*, 1618, Sig. Df.
2 *The Travels of certaine Englishmen*, 1609, pp.47f.
3 *A Relation of a Journey*, 1615, p.53.
4 *A Relation of Some Yeares Travaile*, 1634, p.253.
5 *A New Account of East India and Persia*, iii,75.
6 See, for example, the anonymous *Policy of the Turkish Empire*, 1597, Chapter i; Edward Terry, *A Voyage to East-India*, 1655 (ed. 1777, p.243); and as instances of the late survival of the legend: Jeremy Collier, *Great Historical Dictionary*, 1701, article 'Mahomet'; George Sale, *Koran*, pp.223f.; J.H.Grose, *A Voyage to the East Indies*, 1757, p.283.

ment had come down from the Middle Ages and had been composed by the Emperor Frederick II. Thomas Nashe controverts Gabriel Harvey's assertion that Pietro Aretino was its author.[1] Nashe writes as though there were no doubt of the existence of this treatise; but the fact is that neither he nor anyone else had ever seen a copy of it. There was, in a word, no such book. How reports of it became current nobody knows. In the eighteenth century there was a renewal of interest in it and it was discussed in circles of free-thinkers in different countries. The Empress Catherine the Great is said to have offered a large reward to anyone who should furnish her with a copy. Such discussions were naturally an instigation to forgery and more than one *De Tribus Impostoribus* were manufactured to meet the demand.[2] The incident is of interest to us because it illustrates further the popular belief that Mahomet was an impostor. His reputation even suffered from the fact, for which Moslems were obviously not to blame, that Moses and Jesus were placed in the same category with him.

The most popular example of Mahomet's impostures and deceits—far more popular than the tale of how he tricked a wealthy widow into marriage (which perhaps was not beyond the range of ordinary Christian experience)—is the story of how he 'accustomed and taught a Dove to be fedde, and fetche meate at his eares, the which Dove his moste subtile and craftye maister called the holy Ghost.'[3] This story is sometimes found along with that of the bull or camel to whose horns or neck, as the case might be, he fastened the *Koran*; but more often it occurs by itself. Vincent of Beauvais seems to

---

1 *The Unfortunate Traveller, Works*, ii,265, and McKerrow's note. Burton denounces *De Tribus Impostoribus* as 'that pestilent book' (*The Anatomy of Melancholy*, III,iv, ii,1).

2 See 'Philomneste Junior' (a pseudonym may be suspected), *De Tribus Impostoribus MDIIC. Texte Latin . . . Augmenté . . . d'une notice philologique et bibliographique*, Paris, 1861. See also Charles Nodier, *Questions de littérature legale*, Paris, 1828; and George T. Buckley, *Atheism in the English Renaissance*, Chicago, 1933.

3 *Straunge and memorable thinges gathered out of the Cosmography of Sebastian Munster*, 1574, Sig. 63ᵛf. Compare Munster, *Cosmographiae universalis Libri VI*, ed. Basle, 1550, p.1038. The English traveller Andrew Borde tells the story quaintly: 'Macomyt, a false felow, . . . sedused the people under thys maner: he dyd bryng up a dove and would put ii or thre pesen in his eare, and she would every day come to his eare and eate the peason, and then the people would thynke the holy ghost or an Angell, did come and teache him what the people should do' (*The fyrst boke of the Introduction of Knowledge* [1548]; ed. cit., p.214f.).

have been the first writer to spread it abroad.[1] The suggestion for it came probably from the old conception of
Saint Gerome inspired by the Holy Ghost in the likeness
of a dove or from some similar idea. The anecdote served
as a weapon in the hands of anti-Mohammedan controversialists such as Henry Smith,[2] and we find Thomas
Coryat, in his Italian address to a Mohammedan, speaking
scornfully of the tame pigeon by means of which Mahomet
cozened 'the sottish people of Arabia.'[3] When Hugo Grotius
made use of this pretended miracle in his *De Veritate Religionis
Christianae*, Edward Pocock, the greatest of seventeenth-
century English Arabists,[4] who was engaged in translating
Grotius's work into Arabic for the purpose of proselytizing,
inquired of him his authority for the story and Grotius was
compelled to admit that it was unknown to the Moslems. 'Lest
it should provoke their indignation and laughter,' says Gibbon,
who narrates the incident, 'the pious lie is suppressed in the
Arabic version; but it has maintained an edifying place in the
numerous editions of the Latin text.'[5] Pocock, for all his learning, himself gave the tale further currency in his own writings.[6]

1 *Speculum historiale*, Book xxiii, chapter xxxix. Invariably a compiler, not an orig-
inator, Vincent must have found the legend somewhere; but his source has not been
discovered.
2 *Gods Arrowe against Atheists*, Sig. J^{r}f.
3 *Mr. Thomas Coriat to his friends in England*, Sig. Df.
4 Edward Pocock (or Pococke) was guided in his early studies of Semitic languages
by William Bedwell. His specialized learning won for him the appropriate appointment to the chaplaincy of the Levant Company's agency at Aleppo. There he resided
from 1629 to 1636. He achieved nothing of note in the way of travel or exploration
but he made good use of his opportunities, associating on friendly terms with Moslems
and Jews, acquiring many oriental manuscripts (some of them on commission from
Archbishop Laud), and accumulating a vast amount of first-hand knowledge of
eastern customs and the temperament and character of orientals which stood him
in good stead when he applied it to the interpretation of the Old Testament. He
returned to England in 1636 and became Professor of Arabic at Oxford (the cedar
in the garden of Christ Church was, it is said, brought by him from Lebanon).
Between 1637 and 1640 he was again in the Levant, residing at Constantinople.
One of his minor works is the translation of the tiny Arabic treatise on coffee quoted
in Chapter IV, above. He also edited the Arabic text of the philosophic romance of
Ibn Tufayl, *Hayy ibn-Yaqzan*; and his son provided a Latin version of it under the
title *Philosophus Autodidactus*, 1671, of which an English version, *The Self-Taught
Philosopher*, appeared in 1708. This has been thought to be the chief source of
Robinson Crusoe and certainly influenced the 'Autodidactus' type of philosophic and
speculative romance in the eighteenth century. On Pocock see further the *D.N.B.*
and authorities there cited; and compare *The Legacy of Israel*, Oxford, 1928, pp.353f.
5 *Decline and Fall of the Roman Empire*, chapter 50; ed. Bury, v,400, note 166.
6 In a note on p.186 of *Specimen Historiae Arabum, sive Gregorii Abul Farajii Malatien-
sis, de Origine et Moribus Arabum succincta Narratio, in linguam Latinam conversa* . . .

Later, dispassionate scholars took the trouble to refute it; Humphrey Prideaux, for example, dismisses it along with the tale of the bull as 'idle fables not to be credited,' arguing that the Arabians would have easily seen through such tricks.[1] Yet so late as the eighteenth century it was still to be met with along with other ancient fables.[2]

The author, whether Shakespeare or another, of *1 Henry VI* was acquainted with the tale. When La Pucelle has fought with and subdued the Dauphin Charles, she tells him that it is her mission to be the scourge of the English; and in admiration of her prowess he exclaims:

> Was Mahomet inspired by a dove?
> Thou with an eagle art inspired then![3]

That is, Joan in comparison with even so great a warrior as Mahomet, is as an eagle in comparison with a dove. In the course of a discussion of the various devices by means of which tricksters, claiming to be sorcerers, cozen the unwary, Reginald Scot gives the example of Mahomet's pigeon,

> which would resort unto him being in the middest of his campe, and pick a pease out of his eare; in such sort that manie of the people thought that the Holie-ghost came and told a tail in his eare: the same pigeon also brought him a scroll, wherein was written, *Rex esto*, and laid the same in his neck.[4]

Opera et Studio Eduardi Pococki, Linguarum Hebr. et Arab. in. Academia Oxoniensi Professoris, Oxford, 1650. This book, which is a corner-stone of Arabic scholarship in England, contains the original Arabic text and a Latin version of the *Dynasties* of Gregorius (Abu Al-Faraj) which is an account of Arabian manners and customs before and after Mahomet with a sketch of the Prophet's life. The text and translation occupy only 31 pages; Pocock adds over 350 pages of philological, historical, and theological notes.

1 *The True Nature of Imposture Fully Displayed in the Life of Mahomet*, 1697, p.48. This book, originally composed as a biography of Mahomet, Prideaux adapted to the purpose of vindicating Christianity from the charge of imposture brought against it by the Deists.

2 In the eighteenth century bird-fanciers gave the name 'Mahomet' to a kind of pigeon. This was doubtless a reminiscence of the old tale. It forms an odd conclusion to the history of a legend that began in the pages of Vincent of Beauvais. See *O.E.D.*, *sub* 'Mahomet.

3 *1 Henry VI*, I,ii,140f.—Robert Baron finds a place for the legend in the voluminous notes to his tragedy *Mirza*, p.199. Compare also Dryden, *Don Sebastian*, Act IV, and *The Hind and the Panther*, iii,1095f.

4 *The Discoverie of Witchcraft*, 1584, Book xii, chapter xv, p.252. Compare Book ix, chapter iii, p.171. Scot certainly knew the account of the dove-deception in Johannes Wierus, *De praestigitis daemonum*, Basle, 1568, i, chapter xviii.

As Scot connects the dove with the general subject of animals trained to deceive the ignorant, so Sir Walter Ralegh relates it to Banks's celebrated performing horse which was one of the sights of Elizabethan London. He likens the horse to Mahomet's dove 'which he had used to feed with wheat out of his ear; which dove, when it was hungry, lighted on Mahomet's shoulder, and thrust his bill therein to find his breakfast.' [1] Thomas Nashe twice refers to the tradition, each time in an individual way. In a discussion of familiar spirits he says that 'Socrates' Genius was one of this stampe, and the Dove wherewith the Turks hold Mahomet their Prophet to bee inspired.' [2] Moslems of course hold no such belief, the legend being a purely Christian fabrication; but it is noteworthy that Nashe emphasizes by implication Mohammedan credulity, not Mahomet's deceitfulness. Elsewhere, in his customary satiric vein, Nashe says that 'idol Mahomet' is believed to be in heaven,

whence, with his Dove that he taught to pecke Barley out of his eare, and brought his Disciples into a fooles paradise that it was the holy ghost in her similitude, he is expected every minute to descend. [3]

Here the dove has become the faithful companion of the Prophet, accompanying him even into heaven; just as in one much earlier form of the legend (apparently unknown in England) it had been transmogrified into a magical bird on whose back Mahomet flew from place to place. [4]

In this story of the magical bird there is obvious contamination with traditions of the Prophet's miraculous translation from Mecca to Jerusalem. The *Koran*'s vague allusion to such a supernatural journey is doubtless the record of a vision or a dream; [5] but subsequent Mohammedan tradition elaborated

1 *The History of the World*, 1614, Book i, chapter ix, section 6.
2 *The Terrors of the Night*, 1594, *Works*, i,351. So also there is no implication that Mahomet was a deceiver in this matter when Fulke Greville writes of 'the sacred dove whisp'ring into his ear' (*A Treatise of Monarchy*, stanza 58, *Works*, i,25). But the Earl of Stirling dismisses it as a 'show prepost'rous' (*Doomes-Day*, Fifth Hour, stanza 40).
3 *Lenten-Stuffe*, 1599, *Works*, iii,192.
4 This form of the legend appears in *La Vengeance de Jésus-Christ*. See Arturo Graf in the *Giornale storico della Letteratura Italiana*, xii,204, and D'Ancona, op.cit., p.269.
5 Surah xvii,1: 'Glorified be He Who carried His servant by night from the Inviolable Place of Worship to the Far Distant Place of Worship' (Marmaduke Pickthall's version).

upon the Koranic text, and there came to be distinguished the
cycle of an infernal voyage and the cycle of an ascension into
heaven.[1] The genuine Mohammedan tradition of the Prophet's
temporary abode in Paradise—the legend of Mirach, as it is
called [2]—is occasionally referred to by Christian writers of
the Renaissance. Michel Baudier, for example, a serious student
of such matters, speaks of it; [3] and Robert Burton, a scornful
investigator of the aberrations of the human mind, says:
'In the Turks Alcoran Mahomet is taken up to heaven, upon
a Pegasus sent a purpose for him, as he lay in bed with his
wife, and, after some conference with God, is set on ground

[1] The problems presented by the analogy to the *Divine Comedy* are so interesting and
have recently engaged the attention of so many scholars that a brief digression may
be permitted. Earlier inquiries such as E.Blochet, *Les Sources orientales de la Divine
Comédie*, Paris, 1901, and that in A.de Gubernatis, *Su le orme de Dante*, Rome,
1901, were largely superseded by Miguel Asín y Palacio, *La Escatologia Musulmana
en la Divina Commedia*, Madrid, 1919; English translation (condensed, with the
omission of the Arabic texts and the parallels in Dante) by Harold Sunderland,
Islam and the Divine Comedy, 1926. The flood of comment occasioned by this book
was summarized by the author in 1924 in an article which he broadcast through
Europe in the pages of four separate journals; see 'L'Influence musulmane dans la
Divine Comédie: Histoire et Critique d'une Polemique,' *Revue de littérature comparée*,
iv (1924), 160f.,369f.,537f. Noteworthy discussions are T.W.Arnold, 'Dante and
Islam,' *Contemporary Review*, August 1920, and the appendix on 'Sources arabes'
in H.Hauvette, *Etudes sur la Divine Comédie*, Paris, 1922. There is a brief but excellent summary of the discussion in Gustave Soulier, *Les Influences orientales dans la
Peinture toscane*, Paris, 1924, pp.153f. The case against Asín y Palacio is put con-
cisely and moderately by C.H.Grandgent, 'Islam and Dante,' *Studii Medievali*,
Nuova Serie, iii (1930), 1f. See also the latest (1935) revision of Professor Grandgent's
edition of the *Divine Comedy*. On the other hand Asín y Palacio's thesis has the
almost unreserved approval of so high an authority as R.A.Nicholson who believes
that the number of resemblances in Dante to the Arabian sources are of 'a closeness
that can scarcely be fortuitous' (see Nicholson's chapter on Mysticism in *The Legacy
of Islam*, Oxford, 1931, p.227). To some extent criticism has divided along national
lines, Italian scholars being especially reluctant to abandon traditional views.
Criticism has not, however, disposed of some of the closer parallels between Dante's
journey through the Other World and the picture of the World beyond the Tomb
in the eschatology of Islam. The question is still at issue but it is perhaps safe to say
that the general opinion is that while it is hardly likely that Dante knew at first-
hand any of this large corpus of Arabic literature, there were demonstrable points
of contact (particularly through Spain) and he could have known derivatives, more
or less direct, to be found in the Latin world. Nevertheless the sixth book of the
Aeneid remains his primary source and he was also influenced by the apocryphal
accounts of Saint Paul's supernatural journeys, by Voyages of western origin (such
as Saint Brendan's), and by medieval Christian iconography.—This note may be
loosely attached to our subject by means of a reference to Robert Burton who
thought that Mahomet's picture of Paradise was as 'ridiculous' as Dante's (*The
Anatomy of Melancholy*, III,iv,i,3).

[2] Founded on such texts as *Koran*, xvii,60, whose mysterious vagueness stimulated
the imagination. On the origins of the Mirach see A.A.Bevan, 'Mohammed's Ascension into Heaven,' *Studien Wellhausen*, Giessen, 1914; J.Horovitz, 'Muhammeds Him-
melsfahrt,' *Der Islam*, ix (1919), 159f.

[3] *Histoire generale de la Religion des Turcs*, p.22.

again.'[1] There is of course nothing of all this in the *Koran*; it is a peculiarly flagrant distortion of the tradition that Mahomet was caught up from the Temple at Jerusalem through the seven heavens into the presence of God. This tradition of a temporary assumption, half-understood and often deliberately misrepresented, became curiously crossed with hearsay about beliefs in the coming of the Mahdi, and created the occidental idea that Islam awaits a return of the Prophet. We have just noted Nashe's statement that Mahomet is 'expected every minute to descend' from heaven. William Parry is more detailed and explicit. He writes:

> Some priest three times in the day mounts the toppe of their church, and there, with an exalted voyce cries out, and invocates Mahomet to come in post, for they have long expected his second coming. And if within this six yeeres (as they say) he come not (being the utmost time of his appoyntment and promise made in that behalfe) they have no hope of his coming. But they heare (according to a prophecie they have) the Christians at the end thereof shall subdue them all, and convert them to christianitie.[2]

Parry was probably misled through the similarity of names of Mahomet the Prophet and Muhammad (or Mahomet) the son of Al-Hasan al-'Askari, the twelfth Iman for whose Second Coming the Shi'ites do pray.[3] The phenomena of Mahdi-ism seem not to have been set forth by an English writer until the second decade of the seventeenth century.[4]

1 *The Anatomy of Melancholy*, II,ii,3.
2 *A New and Large Discourse of the Travels of Sir Anthony Sherley*, 1601, p.10.
3 See the striking account of the daily ceremony at the Sanctuary of the Master of the Age at Hillah, in H.A.R.Gibb's introduction to Ibn Battûta, *Travels in Asia ana Africa*, 1929, pp.38f. Compare A.J.Toynbee, *A Study of History*, Oxford, 1934, iii,463f.; P.K.Hitti, *History of the Arabs*, pp.440f.
4 Muley Om Hamet ben Abdela, one of the three brothers involved in the Moroccan civil war, claimed to be a 'saintish king' or Mahdi. In 1609 Muley Zidan, one of the warring brothers, had won the upper hand and begun his long reign, but in 1612 Muley Om Hamet inflicted on him a defeat which temporarily deprived him of his throne. The 'saintish king' promised his people to restore Mohammedanism in Granada and throughout Andalusia. An English merchant residing in Morocco sent news of these events to England, signing his letter 'R.S.' and heading it: 'Laus Deo in Saphia [that is, Saffee], the 9 of September, 1612.' This letter was published with the title: *Late Newes out of Barbary. In a Letter . . . from a Merchant there . . . Containing some strange particulars of this new Saintish Kings proceedings: as they have been very credibly related from such as were eye-witnesses*, 1613. Having told of the promised conquest of southern Spain, this narrator proceeds: 'And having gayned these countries, he must raigne forty yeeres, and then must com Christ, whom they

III

WE now turn [1] to another portion of the western legend of Mahomet, that concerning his death, his place of burial, and his sepulchre.

The orthodox tradition that the Prophet was poisoned was known, as we shall see, to the Elizabethans in a perverted form; but the medieval Christian legend was that having died of a sudden seizure [2] his body was eaten by swine. The tale, which afforded a facile explanation of the Mohammedan law against the eating of swine's flesh, was sometimes expanded with circumstantial details of revolting filthiness. There is a reminiscence of it in the *Chanson de Roland* where swine and dogs trample upon and devour the idol Mahumet when it has been tumbled into a ditch; but it first appears in anything like complete form in an eleventh-century Latin poem by Hildebert Archbishop of Tours. [3] In the twelfth century it was retold in

call Sidie Nicer: and he must surrender all to him; for he must judge the world, and then all must end' (Sig. B₃). The signs by which 'their Fatamie, that is, a Saviour' is to be known are particularized: a wart over his eye, a black front tooth, and so forth; all these signs the new king possesses. Here—in the promise to re-establish the Faith; the signs; the reign of forty years; the subsequent coming of Jesus to judge the world—are all the phenomena of Mahdi-ism. In this little pamphlet Englishmen read for the first time in any detail of the Moslem belief in the predestined coming of the Guided One whose reign is to usher in the last brief period of the world. Like other claimants to Mahdiship, before and since, this Moorish king did not for long make good his pretensions; his reign was soon over and Muley Zidan regained his throne.—Included with the letter from 'R.S.' is a second letter signed 'G.B.' A general preface is signed 'J.H.' An alternative title of the pamphlet reads *The New Prophetical King of Barbary*.—That Robert Burton confused Mahomet with the Mahdi is shown by his remark that Mohammedans 'look for their Prophet Mahomet as Jewes do for their Messias' (*The Anatomy of Melancholy*, III,iv,i,3).

1 What is to us one of the most familiar of all anecdotes of the Prophet occurs only once, or possibly twice, in Elizabethan literature. This is the tale of Mahomet and the mountain which Bacon tells in his essay 'Of Boldness' (*Essays Civil and Moral*, xii). Apparently it was from Bacon that it passed into popular proverbial use. What may be an earlier garbled form of the story is in Robert Wilson's *Three Lords and Three Ladies of London* (Hazlitt's Dodsley, vi,410), where Dissimulation asks how 'it comes to pass that we are thus fortunate to meet' and Simony replies: 'I'll tell thee why we met: because we are no mountains.'—On John Mason's recondite allusion in *The Turke* (ll.1727f.) to the Mohammedan tradition of the bull Kujuta see J.Q.Adams's edition of the play.—On possible reminiscences of the story of Mahomet's first miracle in *Cymbeline*, III,iii,2f. and Webster's *The Duchess of Malfi*, IV,ii,239f., see F.L.Lucas's note on the latter passage in his edition of Webster.

2 Mahomet's epileptic fits and his deceitful explanation of them are often referred to by Christian writers. Thus, Francis Osborn says that he professed to hold daily commerce with angels and pretended that the seizures incident to his disease were 'holy extasies, in which God did mind him of the way and means, how to lead his people' (*Politicall Reflections upon the Government of the Turks*, p.4).

3 D'Ancona, op.cit., pp.184f., from Migne, *Patrologia Latina*, clxxi.

Latin verse by a certain Gualterius [1] whose poem is the direct source of Alexandre du Pont's *Roman de Mahomet* [2] (thirteenth century). It is safe to say that Christian prejudice against Islam never went to greater extremes than in this French poem. Mahomet is portrayed as a sort of feudal lord (for the point of view is purely European) who took orders, became a cardinal, and failing in the election to the papacy revenged himself by inventing a new heresy. The poet makes him out to have been an infamous debauchee, a thief, and a sorcerer. As in several other French romances, [3] so here there are explicit allusions to the devouring of his body by swine. We have already noted Lydgate's abrupt, uncouth words: 'Fell in a puddle, devoured among swine.' The nasty story occurs but rarely in Elizabethan literature.

A tradition occasionally met with in Renaissance writers [4] is that the Prophet was poisoned by his own disciples who were eager to put to the proof his prophecies of his resurrection. (Here, as in other circumstances, the Christian imagination invented blasphemous analogies to the life of Christ, sometimes going to the extreme of citing a prophecy about rising on the third day.) George Whetstone does not mention the accusation of poisoning but tells how the Prophet's followers, expecting his resurrection,

> kept him above the ground untill his bodie stuncke as badde as his soule, which was then closed in iron, and by his sayde disciples was carried into the Citie of Meque in Persia, where he is worshipped of all the people of the East, yea of the greater part of the worlde. [5]

Henry Smith, in the violent and vituperative sermon to which we have already referred, revives one of the foulest forms of the medieval story, in which Mahomet dies on a dunghill. Thereafter, the preacher goes on, the body was kept for thirty days till it stank. Then Mahomet's companions, despairing of his resurrection,

1 Dumeril, *Poésies populaires latines du moyen âge*, pp.368f.
2 Edited by Reinaud and Francisque Michel, Paris, 1831, with a preface, still of some value, on medieval ideas of Mahomet with special reference to Vincent of Beauvais.
3 Passages from five romances are quoted by D'Ancona, op.cit., pp.238f.
4 See, for example, Michel Baudier, op.cit., p.35.
5 *The English Myrror*, p.59.

chest him in an iron coffin (saith Sabellicus and Nauclerus [1]); they
bring him unto the famous Temple at Mecha (in which Citie he
was borne) with great solemnitie, as if he had never been scared
upon the dunghill with swine: they convey to the roofe of the
Temple mighty loadstones, they lift up the iron Coffin, where the
loadstones according to their nature drawe to them the iron, and
holde it up, and there stands Mahomet on high.[2]

Here we have the most famous of all Christian traditions of
Mahomet—one that has given a proverbial simile to the English language.[3] No trace of this tradition is discoverable among
the Mohammedans themselves. It is, says J.L.Burckhardt,
'unknown in the Hedjaz: nor have I ever heard [of it] in other
parts of the East.'[4] Sir Richard F.Burton's testimony is to the
same effect.[5] Yet in Christendom it is at least as old as the
eleventh century, for it appears in the Latin poems on Mahomet
mentioned above, and in the *Roman de Mahomet* we read:

> Ains dist que Mahons par miracle
> Se soustient en son abitacle.[6]

That the notion of the suspended coffin was widespread will
surprise no one who recalls the popularity of stories of magnetic
phenomena such as the Rock of Adamant which drew to it
the nails and other iron-work of passing ships. But what was
the origin of this notion of the suspended coffin?

Several possible answers have been, or may be, suggested,
none of them entirely convincing. There are literary analogues
that may have fostered belief in the suspended tomb. Martial
describes a certain tomb which was supported by pillars so
slender that it seemed to be floating in the air.[7] Pliny tells of the
device, designed for one of the Ptolemies by Dinocrates, for

---

1 Smith's authorities are the *Chronica* of Nauclerus (1516 and later editions) and the
  Enneades of Marcus Antonius Coccius (Sabellicus).
2 *Gods Arrowe against Atheists*, Sig. J₃ᵛ.
3 Sir Henry Wotton uses the expression in a manner suggesting that it was already
  proverbial, at least among the Italians. Reporting rumours of an attack by the Turks
  on Poland in 1589 he writes: 'The Polonians are sospeti in aria come l'archo di Macho-
  meto, and know not what to do' (L.P.Smith, *Life and Letters of Sir Henry Wotton*,
  i,231).
4 *Travels in Arabia*, ed. 1829, ii,168f.
5 *Personal Narrative of a Pilgrimage to Mecca and El-Medina*, ed. 1857, i,312.
6 Ed. cit., p.78,ll.1900f.   7 *Liber Spectacularum*, i,5.

roofing the dome of a temple at Alexandria with loadstones so that an image of Arsinoë, made of iron, might hang without visible support.[1] This analogy from Pliny was cited long ago by Humphrey Prideaux in the course of his discussion of Mahomet's tomb.[2] It is cited also by Sir Thomas Browne, who notes similar contrivances by means of which an iron chariot was reported to be suspended in a temple of Serapis and an iron image of a horse in yet another temple.[3] According to a Mohammedan writer, the corpse of Aristotle was suspended by the same means in the great mosque of Palermo.[4] A similar report came into the West concerning the tomb of Saint Thomas, the Apostle to the Indies, whose coffin hung in the air between four great loadstones, two above and two beneath. Moreover, from far-off Kashmir there may have been brought into the Levant and thence by travellers into Europe the tradition of a king who about the year A.D. 700 set up an image between two loadstones.[5] It is more likely that the tradition of Mahomet's coffin arose from confusion with other stories of the Prophet. There is, for example, the tale of the stone at Mecca upon which Mahomet slept. When in sleep he was conveyed on a heavenly steed to Jerusalem this stone started to follow him; the Prophet forbade it to rise further and it remained in air.[6] Then there is the tradition attaching to the great rock immediately under the dome of the so-called Mosque of Omar—the Dome of the Rock—in Jerusalem. To this day the visitor is told that when Mahomet ascended into heaven from this site the rock essayed to follow him and was thrust back into place by Gabriel; the enormous foot-print where the archangel gave it a mighty shove is still pointed out. Centuries ago Christian pilgrims (who never saw the interior of the mosque nor were so much as permitted to enter the temple-area) were told that this rock hung supported in mid-air. But these instances are all parallels and not explanations unless we assume that one place

1 *Historia naturalis*, xxxiv,14.
2 *The True Nature of Imposture*, pp.134f.
3 *Vulgar Errors*, Book II, chapter iii.
4 Cited by D'Ancona, op.cit., p.241.
5 *Notes and Queries*, Ninth Series, viii,80.
6 Monconys, *Journal des Voyages*, Lyons, 1665, Part i, pp.464f.

and object were confounded with another place and object. It has been suggested that the idea arose from a misinterpretation of some rude ground-plan of the mosque at El-Medina. If a copy of this plan, brought away by some pilgrim, fell into the hands of someone who had never visited Mahomet's sepulchre, it might be mistaken for an elevation, in which case the tomb, more or less in the centre of the design, would appear to be floating unsupported in mid-air.[1] This explanation is too neat to be convincing. We must leave the question open, with the weight of probability on the side of confusion with some bit of folklore, perhaps reinforced with reports about the rock at Mecca or the rock at Jerusalem or both.

An error of great vitality, and one often linked with the tradition of the suspended coffin, is that Mahomet was buried at Mecca. The association of ideas which probably accounts for this is that the widespread fame of Mecca as the goal of the *Haj* was coupled with the Christian experience of pilgrimages to a Holy Sepulchre. In the next section of the present chapter we shall see that Arabia Deserta was well-nigh a *terra incognita* to Renaissance Europe, and the Holy Cities of Arabia had been visited by fewer Europeans than might be counted on the fingers of one hand. Few travellers came nearer them than Palestine or Syria. At Damascus in 1432 Bertrandon de la Brocquière, the French diplomatic agent, was told by a renegade Bulgarian that Mahomet was buried at Mecca, and he accepts this piece of information unquestioningly.[2] Nearly two centuries later William Biddulph saw the pilgrims gathering in the same city to go, he says, on their journey to Mahomet's tomb at Mecca.[3] At Tripoli in Syria Father Castela met a band of Mohammedan pilgrims 'qui vont visiter à la Meque le corps de leur faux prophete.'[4] How credulous and uncritical were these old travellers! A pointed question or two would have elicited the truth. What the pious pilgrims really told these

---

1 Cited from Carsten Niebuhr, the eighteenth-century oriental traveller, by Burton, *Personal Narrative*, i,312, note 1. See also Burton, *The Guide-Book to Mecca*, 1865, reprinted in his *Selected Papers on Anthropology, Travel and Exploration*, ed. N.M.Penzer, 1924, p.61.
2 *Travels*, translated (from a version in modern French) by Thomas Johnes, 1808, p.132.
3 *Travels of certaine Englishmen*, p.95.
4 *Le Sainct Voyage*, second edition, Paris, 1612, p.108.

Europeans was that they were on their way to Mecca and to the Prophet's tomb. That stay-at-home compilers of geographical information [1] should complacently repeat the error is not surprising in the face of its evident vitality when even visitors to the Holy Land,[2] with the means at hand to obtain correct information, preferred to cling to the old mistake.

Of particular interest is the information gathered by Brother Felix Fabri who was in Palestine in 1481–3. He says that in 'the town of Mecca, the city of the cursed Mahomet,' there is 'the temple of his sepulchre, which it is said is so subtly suspended by mechanic art that those who know not how it is done believe that it hangs in the air by some Divine power.' The truth is that it hangs between loadstones 'placed in the ground below and in the vaulted roof above.' He records sorrowfully that some Christians, infirm in their belief, have renounced their faith and embraced Mohammedanism, so much impressed have they been by the supposedly miraculous entombment. But divine vengeance has of late been wreaked upon the ingenious contrivers of this imposture, for in 1480 fire and hailstone from heaven 'drove the temple and tomb of that accursed seducer into the earth, or rather into hell. . . Thus the Saracens have been deprived of the relics and body of their false prophet.' [3] Martin Baumgarten, who travelled in the Levant about 1507, tells the same story except for a change of date to 1470,

> for at that time a violent storm of Lightning and Hail falling upon part of that profane Temple, did so shake it, and dash'd the Coffin with the wretched Body to pieces, that it was all beat to ashes, and sunk into the Earth so as it could never be found or seen again.[4]

1 For example, Sebastian Munster, *Cosmographiae universalis Libri VI*, Basle, 1550, p.972; George Abbot, *A Briefe Description of the whole World*, 1599, Sig. C₂ᵛ. Johannes Boemus (*Recueil de diverses Histoires*, Antwerp, 1540, folio 101ᵛ) adds the wildly extravagant statement that 'tous Sarrasins sont tenuz de aller une fois l'an au temple qui est au lieu qu'on appelle Mecha.'
2 Even Bartholomeus a Saligniaco, whose *Itinerarii Terre sancte* (1525) was, as we saw in Chapter II, a recognized authority, writes (folio xxʳ): 'Hec est Arabia magna: in qua Mecha est: ubi spurcissimi Mahumeti sepulchrum.'
3 *The Wanderings of Brother Felix Fabri* (Palestine Pilgrims' Text Society), ii,577f. and 668f.
4 Churchill's *Collection of Voyages and Travels*, 1732, i,433. Another account of the destruction of the coffin by lightning is in Sigmund Feyerabend, *Reyssbuch dess Heyligen Lands*, 1584, folio 78ʳf.

It is possible that this rumour of the destruction of Mahomet's coffin by lightning flowed down through some channel to the Elizabethan dramatist Samuel Rowley and became associated in his mind with some confused recollection of the story that the Prophet's body was eaten by swine. Rowley has a scene in which Will Summers, the licensed fool, narrates various bits of fantastic news to King Henry VIII. Summers tells him that the French ambassador has arrived. 'What doe they say he comes for, Will?' asks the King.

> Marry they say hee comes to crave thy aide against the greate Turke that vowes to over-runne al France within this fortnight, he's in a terrible rage belike, and they say, the reason is, his old god Mahomet that was buried ith top on's Church at Meca, his Tombe fell downe, and kild a Sow and seven Pigges, whereupon they thinke all swines flesh is new sanctified and how it is thought the Jewes will fall to eating of Porke extreamely.[1]

In compensation for this ignoble foolery we may note that there are finer allusions to the suspended tomb in Elizabethan drama. The idea was one to appeal to Marlowe's imagination and he writes of Mahomet

> Whose glorious body, when he left the world,
> Closed in a coffin mounted up the air,
> And hung on stately Mecca's temple roof.[2]

Beaumont has the rather fine hyperbole:

> Mecca shall sweat and Mahomet shall fall,
> And thy dear name fill up his monument.[3]

A tinge of scepticism may perhaps be discerned in these lines by an anonymous dramatist:

> In midst of Mecca's temple roof, some say,
> He now hangs, without touch or stay at all.[4]

---

1 *When You See Me You Know Me*, 1613, Sig. B^r.
2 *2 Tamburlaine*, I,ii,64f.
3 *The Scornful Lady*, III,ii.
4 *Diana*, IV,v (reference from Sugden, *Topographical Dictionary*).—Nashe writes of 'the temple of Maecha, where Mahomet is hung up' (*The Unfortunate Traveller*, *Works*, ii,249). In Simon Baylie's little known play *The Wizard* (ed. Henry de Vocht, *Materials*, Louvain, 1930, ll.763f.) we read:
> I would have sworn by my Pendant Prophet
> To make her Empresse of the heathen world.
The editor of this drama confesses that he is puzzled by the epithet 'pendant' and

But the only dramatist of the period who rejects the old tradition unreservedly was that young and self-consciously erudite disciple of Ben Jonson, Robert Baron, the author of *Mirza*. 'The vulgar tradition,' he says in one of the notes to his tragedy, 'that he hangs in an Iron Chest attracted to the roof of a Mosque by a loadstone there placed, I find approved of by few good Authors, therefore wave it.' [1]

Who some of these 'good authors' were we shall see in a moment, but first it may be noted that the very unlikelihood of the phenomenon of the hanging tomb, far from turning men's minds from belief in its actuality, was itself an argument in credulous days when it was expected that marvels would happen in the East. Christians sometimes accepted the physical fact of the magnetized coffin as another proof that the Mohammedans fabricated their miracles: that is, there are writers who describe the tomb not in order to expose the absurdity of the report that it hangs in mid-air but to show that something which the cursed infidels use as a miraculous proof of the truth of their doctrines can really and readily be accounted for on purely natural grounds. That this was Brother Felix Fabri's state of mind we have just seen. Richard Brathwayte puts the responsibility for the fraud not upon the Prophet's followers but upon Mahomet himself. The passage about to be quoted has at its beginning the marginal gloss: 'How Mahomet the first deluded his credulous posterity with an opinion of his miraculous Sanctity, in that very Monument which hee had caused to be erected in his Memory.' The text runs as follows:

> In the discourse of the Ceremonies of Mecha, we shall find a rare device there recommended to our view, in the perpendicular placing of that Sepulchre of Mahomet: meerely contrived by that cunning Projector to delude the Mahometans, by making them beleeve that to be a miraculous object, which to more approved and refined judgements appeared only a native [natural] experiment. Those that write of that Subject describe it thus: There is an *Adamant*

suggests that it describes a full flowing beard; but the allusion is plainly to the tomb. The suspended lover in William Haughton's *English-Men for My Money*, 1616; ed. W.W.Greg, Malone Society, 1912,ll.2111f., is likened to Mahomet's sepulchre.

1 *Mirza*, p.169.

placed in the Roofe above, and a *Magnet* fixed in the pavement by an equall or direct line below; now the Sepulchre of Mahomet made of solid iron, hangs in a Diametrall manner betwixt these two: without stay or supportance of either. This begot in those bewitched people a wonderful amazement, honouring that Monument with their yearely Processionall visits; offering rich presents to that Mahometan shrine: never understanding those occult vertues of the two stones fixed above and below; who by their naturall opposition and enmity (as one maligning the others attractive quality) would not suffer that heavy ponderous body either to ascend or descend; but to retaine an equall site or location betwixt them both. This it was that confirmed these Mahometans in the Strength of a deluded opinion, that their Mahomet was a great and powerful Prophet, shewing such high proofes and demonstrations of his extraordinary abilities living; and leaving such a Miracle for all posterity to admire in his departing.[1]

How gradually the truth makes its way against credulity and prejudice is shown by those writers who hesitate between the venerable tradition and the testimony even of eye-witnesses. In the mind of that stout sceptic William Lithgow the struggle between tradition and testimony resulted in a quaint compromise. Mahomet, he says, was indeed entombed in Mecca in an iron coffin 'which betweene two Adamants hangeth to this day (as I have been informed of sundry Turkes, who saw it).' But of late the Turks, 'understanding the derision of Christians concerning their hanging Tombe,' and also because pilgrims 'were often suffocate to death, with a fabulous desart in going to Mecha,' have transported the body to Medina where it is now set in a mosque upon the ground.[2] William Bedwell, who as an Arabist should have known better, accepts the old report that Mahomet is buried at Mecca; but he is puzzled by El-Medina and in the glossary attached to the dialogues of which something will be said later in this chapter he says of the latter city: 'Whether it be Iethrab, or Mecha, or a third city different from both, I dare not for certain affirme.'[3] Michel Baudier accepts the report of the suspended coffin but trans-

---

1 *A Survey of History: or, a Nursery for Gentry*, 1638, pp.210f.
2 *Rare Adventures*, p.133.
3 *Mohammedis Imposturae*, 1615, Sig. M4ᵛ. (On this book see pp.435–7, below.)

fers the phenomenon from Mecca to El-Medina.[1] Christoph
Fuerer, the German traveller, remarks that he has heard it
said that Mahomet is buried at El-Medina, but, he says, this
contradicts the more usual opinion that he is buried at Mecca;
consequently he goes on to report on various descriptions of
the Meccan tomb.[2] These four writers exemplify the efforts to
arrive at a compromise in the face of conflicting testimony.

Yet authoritative testimony was available, had it been
heeded, to the falsity of the report. Ludovico di Varthema,
who visited both the Holy Cities of Arabia, wrote:

> Some who say that the body of Mahomet is suspended in the air at
> Mecca must be reproved: I say it is not true. I have seen his sep-
> ulchre in this city, Medinathalnabi [3]. . . And you must know (I
> tell it you for a truth) there is no coffin of iron or steel, nor load-
> stone.[4]

This explicit statement was accessible to English readers in the
1577 edition of Richard Eden's *History of Travayle* and it
reappears in Purchas's abridged extracts from Varthema.[5] Other
continental travellers are equally precise. Giovanni Antonio
Menavino, the Genoese authority on Mohammedanism, describes the *Haj* in some detail, placing the Prophet's tomb at
El-Medina and not referring to the magnets.[6] Pierre Belon,
one of the best-informed of Renaissance travellers, devotes a
brief chapter of his book to the Moslems' 'voiage de devotion'
to the Holy Cities and distinguishes between them, not, however, without some geographical confusion:

> Les Turcs allants à la Mesque, font deux voiages, l'un en Almedine,
> ou gist le corps de Mahomet: l'autre à la Meque pour traffiquer et
> marchander: Car ils en rapportent grande quantité de drogues et
> marchandises. C'est celle que les anciens autheurs ont nommé
> Petra.[7]

1 *Histoire Generale de la Religion des Turcs*, p.35f.
2 *Reis-Beschreibung in Egypten, Arabien, Palestinam, Syrien* [etc.], Nuremberg, 1646,
pp.87f. This is a version of the same author's *Itinerarium Ægypti* [etc.], Nuremberg,
1620, from which Purchas took material about Mount Sinai.
3 That is, Medinatu'n-n-Nabi, 'the City of the Prophet.'
4 *Itinerary*, translated by J.W.Jones, *Argonaut Series*, 1928, pp.15 and 17.
5 Purchas, ix,64.
6 *Trattato de costumi et vita de' Turchi*, Florence, 1548, Book II, chapters xivf.,pp.82f.
7 *Les Observations de plusieurs singularitez et choses memorables*, Paris, 1553, chapter liii,
folio 121ʳ.

The Byzantine historian Laonicus Chalcondylas dismisses as fables the reports that Mahomet's sepulchre was made of precious stones and hung in the air in the midst of a temple; and at this point in his book his French translator adds a marginal gloss: 'Tout cecy est faux, car c'est une sepulture fort simple, en une petite tour dans une mosquee à Medina Talnabi.' [1] There is a fairly accurate description of the tomb-mosque in the *De nonnulis orientalium urbibus* of Gabriel Sionita and John Esronita (1619) of which a version appeared in Purchas. There, following an account of the 'chapel' in a stately temple at El-Medina, we read:

> Within this . . . Mohameds carkase was placed, and not lifted up by force of Loadstone or any other Art; but that stone-Urne lyeth on the ground. [2]

These two authorities are cited by Sir Thomas Browne as witnesses against the suspended coffin; 'which conceit,' says Browne, 'is fabulous and evidently false, from the testimony of oculor testators.' [3] Finally, it may be noted that Edward Pocock says roundly that Moslems laugh at this fable propagated by Christians. [4]

---

1 *L'Histoire de la Decadence de l'Empire Grec, et Establissement de celuy des Turcs*, translated by Blaise de Vigenare, Paris, 1584, p.166.
2 Purchas ix,110f. The treatise *De nonnulis orientalium urbibus* is attached to the *Geographia Nubiensis*, an inaccurate Latin version of a geographical work by Al-Idrisi, a twelfth-century Spanish-Arab at the court of Roger II of Sicily. See P.H.Hitti, *History of the Arabs*, p.609.—Sandys (*Relation*, p.125) places the tomb at El-Medina, 'not hanging in the aire.'
3 *Vulgar Errors*, II,iii.
4 *Specimen Historiae Arabum*, p.180: 'Unde igitur nobis Mohammedes cistae ferrae inclusus et magnetus vi in aere pendulus? Haec cum Mohammedistis recitantur, risu exploduntur, ut nostrorum in ipsorum rebus inscitiae argumentum.'—As a curiosity of scholarship it may be noted that towards the end of the seventeenth century the problem of the tomb of Mahomet was made the subject of a doctoral dissertation at Marburg written in the most solemnly Teutonic style: *Disquisitio Historico-Physica de Sepulcro Muhammedis*, Marburg, 1680. The disquisitor, Samuel Andreas, begins his discussion with this contemptuous remark: 'Nam quamvis nostra nihil intersit, quomodo ille et Pseudo-propheta cubet, aerem an terram occupet, qui nec aere nec terra dignus; tamen cum sepulcrum peregrinantium superstitione quotannis hoc tempore verno frequentetur, ipsaque traditio recepta sit, veritatem eruere conabimur.' Citing an abundance of authorities, among them Varthema, Breydenbach, and Linschoten, for and against the pendant tomb, Andreas discusses the physical possibility of such a phenomenon. He reaches the conclusion that it is physically possible; that there are analogous cases well authenticated; but that Mahomet is not so buried.

IV

BEFORE proceeding further along the path we have been pursuing in this chapter, we may pause to inquire as to how much was actually known of the country in which Mahomet was born and whence Islam went forth to conquer much of the world. Our inquiry may begin with a passage from George Sandys's *Relation of a Journey*. That Sandys was a poet as well as a traveller is a fact not often apparent to the reader of the narrative of his travels, for his book is distinguished by an ostentation of learning rather than by any notable beauty of style; but in his account of the denizens of the Arabian desert he reaches heights of eloquence perfectly in keeping with his subject:

> They dwell in Tents, which they remove like walking Cities, for opportunitie of prey, and benefit of pasturage. They acknowledge no Soveraigne, not worth the conquering, nor can they bee conquered, retyring to places impossible for Armies, by reason of the rolling sands and penurie of all things. A Nation from the beginning unmixed with others, boasting of their Nobilitie, and at this day hating all Mechanicall Sciences. They hang about the skirts of the habitable Countries; and having robbed, retyre with a marvellous celeritie. Those that are not detected persons, frequent the neighbouring Villages for provision, and trafficke without molestation, they not daring to intreat them evilly. They are of meane stature, raw-boned, tawnie, having feminine voyces, of a swift and noyselesse pace, behind you ere aware of them. Their Religion Mahometanisme, glorying in that the Impostor was their Countriman; their Language extending as farre as that Religion extendeth.[1]

Few European travellers of the Renaissance penetrated into 'the vasty wilds of wide Arabia,'[2] that is, into Arabia Deserta.

1 Purchas, vi,217. The resemblance to the austere cadences of Doughty's prose will be evident to the reader. Sandys is, in fact, among the authors whom Doughty is known to have read.—Jeremy Taylor offers a curious explanation of the nomadic life of the bedouin: 'All the inhabitants of Arabia the desert are in continual fear of being buried in huge heaps of sand, and therefore dwell in tents and ambulatory houses, or retire to unfruitful mountains, to prolong an uneasy and wilder life' (*The Rule and Exercise of Holy Dying*, I,iv,1).—No early English writer displays any understanding of the economic necessity which compels the steppe-dwellers to move in a seasonal cycle, driving their flocks from place to place in search of pasturage.
2 *The Merchant of Venice*, II,vii,41.

A considerable number had crossed the Sinai desert from Egypt into Palestine and had passed along the edge of the Hauran on the way from Damascus to Jerusalem. The route from Aleppo to the nearest point of embarkation on the Euphrates had been followed, as we have seen, by various Englishmen. But the overland way into Mesopotamia by the desert route to the south of the Euphrates was scarcely known; [1] and even so, it was far to the north of the Hedjaz. For ages pilgrims from Europe had looked across the Jordan towards the mountains of Moab and some hardy travellers had gone for a considerable distance round the eastern shore of the Dead Sea; but few had reached the further side of the mountains where the *Haj* road runs southward and fewer still had gone any distance along that road. No Elizabethan traveller visited Petra, which, as we have just seen, Belon confused with Mecca. The pilgrim-way leading to the mysterious Holy Cities was, beyond a certain point, absolutely forbidden to non-believers. What, then, and how much was known to Renaissance Europe about the Holy Cities of Arabia? [2]

Not to repeat the mere rumours which came to medieval Europe, we may begin our answer with Bertrandon de la Brocquière who at Damascus about 1432 made inquiries about the pilgrimage and heard tell of the beautiful traditional belief

1 The first Englishman to traverse the desert-route was Richard Steele in 1614 (Purchas, iv,217,279). Ten years later Pietro della Valle travelled through the desert from the head of the Persian Gulf to Aleppo (*Travels*, 1665, pp.257f.). It was again followed by J.B.Tavernier in 1638 (*Les Six Voyages*, Paris, 1676, Book ii, chapters iii, iv, and vii. Tavernier discusses the four routes from Aleppo into Mesopotamia: 'la route du grand desert'—that here in question; the water-way by the Euphrates; the desert-route between the rivers; and the water-way by the Tigris. See further R.Campbell Thompson, 'Tavernier's Travels in Mesopotamia,' *Scottish Geographical Magazine*, March 1910, pp.141f.). The less arduous river-route was almost always followed by Englishmen until the eighteenth century when conflicts with the Dutch made the Persian Gulf dangerous. The way through the desert was then again opened; but in the nineteenth century it was once more abandoned and remained practically unknown, though crossed at several points by Gertrude Bell and other explorers, till our own day. See further *The Desert Route to India*, ed. Douglas Carruthers, Hakluyt Society, 1929, p.xix. The first English traveller in Yemen was John Jourdain, a factor of the East India Company, who, leaving his ship, the *Ascension*, at Aden, penetrated into the interior as far as Sana. Meanwhile the *Ascension*, under the command of Alexander Sharpeigh, passed through the Bab el Mandeb and entered the Red Sea—the first English vessel in that part of the world. Jourdain rejoined her at Mocha, whence she sailed to India. This was in the spring of 1609. See Jourdain's *Journal, 1608–1617*, ed. Foster, Hakluyt Society, 1905.
2 See D.G.Hogarth, *The Penetration of Arabia*, 1904, Augustus Ralli, *Christians at Mecca*, 1909, and R.H.Kiernan, *The Unveiling of Arabia*, 1937.

that if in any year the *Haj* does not contain seven hundred thousand pilgrims God sends his angels to make up the required number.[1] The same traveller saw 'two young men who had got their eyes thrust out at Mecca after having seen the tomb of Mahomet.'[2] This appalling practice of religious fanatics was reported fairly often in the seventeenth century. William Biddulph says that many 'Hogies' pull out their own eyes after seeing the tomb of their Prophet.[3] William Lithgow writes:

> I have seene sometimes two thousand Turkes travelling to Mecca, in Pilgrimage; . . . where many in a superstitious devotion, having seene the Tombe of Mahomet, are never desirous to see the vanities of the World againe: For in a franticke piety they cause a Smith to pull forth their eyes: And these men are called afterwards Hoggeis, that is, Holy Men.[4]

Des Hayes de Courmenin says that he had heard this custom attributed only to pilgrims from India and he declines to vouch for the truth even of this qualified report.[5]

If we set aside the case of Johannes Schiltberger who claimed to have visited Mecca about 1425 but whose credibility has been generally impugned,[6] the first European to visit the Holy Cities (other perhaps than some nameless renegade of whom no record has come down to us) was the astonishing Italian traveller Ludovico di Varthema whose *Itinerario*, published in Rome in 1510, was translated from a Latin version (inaccurate in some particulars) into English by Richard Willes

1 *Travels*, translated by Thomas Johnes, p.134. The belief that God uses angels to fill the ranks of the Hajjis is noted by various early writers, for instance by Adam Olearius, *Voyages and Travels of the Ambassadors*, translated by John Davies, 1662, p.231.
2 *Travels*, p.171.
3 *Travels of certaine Englishmen*, p.96. Sandys (*Relation*, p.124) says that some pilgrims blind themselves with hot bricks.
4 *Rare Adventures*, p.135. Lithgow is of course in error in thus limiting the meaning of 'Hoggeis,' for the title Hajji belongs to anyone who has made the pilgrimage.
5 *Voiage du Levant*, 1624, p.242.
6 Schiltberger, a prisoner of war from Germany, was a slave of Sultan Bajazet I with whom he was taken prisoner by Tamburlaine. For a quarter of a century he was a slave holding important offices under Tamburlaine. Finally he escaped and made his way home. The authenticity of his narrative in general has not been questioned, merely the claim to have visited the Holy Cities. See *The Bondage and Travels of Johannes Schiltberger . . . 1396–1427*, translated by J.B.Telfer, Hakluyt Society, 1879; and for the German editions see the Catalogue of the British Museum.

and included in the 1577 edition of Eden's *History of Travayle*.[1]
From this version Elizabethan Englishmen obtained their first
reasonably accurate impressions of the Haj and of the Holy
Cities. Of the authenticity and credibility of the story Sir Richard C.Temple has given proofs which settle this vexed question
once and for all. Varthema, who was at the time of his journey
a professing and possibly convinced Mohammedan, joined
the Damascene *Haj* in April 1503. The pilgrim-route was
approximately that of the modern Damascus-Medina railway.
Of El-Medina Varthema's description is quite accurate and
reasonably full. Of Mecca and of the pilgrim ceremonies performed there and in the neighbourhood his description is
very detailed and surprisingly accurate. The confusion in the
order in which he gives these ceremonies does not tell against
his credibility, for it is what we should expect from one who
could not risk taking notes on the spot and had to rely upon
his memory. His account of the Ka'aba and of the Tawaf or
circumambulation of the Holy House; the drinking of the
water from the well Zemzem; the sacrifice at Mecca; the
Sermon on Mount Arafat; the stoning of the devil on the return
from the Mount—the accuracy of these and many other particulars can be tested by the narratives of subsequent visitors.[2]
Two or three details may be noted. We have already remarked
upon his statement that Abu Bakr had been a cardinal and
'wanted to be Pope' as a vestige of an old legend of Mahomet.
Another instance of the contamination of fidelity of observation
with medieval Christian tradition is his explanation of the
fact that the Meccans never molest the flocks of doves in the
sacred enclosure because the birds were held sacred in memory
of 'that dove which spoke to Mahomet.' It is noteworthy

1 *Itinerario de Ludovico de Varthema Bolognese nello Egypto, nella Surria, nella Arabia
deserta e felix, nella Persia, nella India, e nella Ethiopia*, Rome, 1510. A copy of this
original edition, a delightful little book and very rare, is in the Greville Library of
the British Museum. On English translations of Varthema see Henri Cordier, *Les
Voyageurs dans L'Extrème Orient au xvᵉ et aux viᵉ Siècles*, Leiden, 1899, pp.22f., and
the introduction, p.xviii, to J.W.Jones's translation of the *Itinerary*, *Argonaut Series*,
1928. (This is reproduced from the edition of the Hakluyt Society, 1863.)
2 See, in addition to Burckhardt, Burton, and other nineteenth-century visitors discussed by Hogarth, Ralli and Kiernan, Eldon Rutter, *The Holy Cities of Arabia*, 1928.
(The one-volume edition, 1930, is more desirable because of the many fine illustrations.)

that he says nothing about the requirement that ordinary dress be discarded and the pilgrim-garb donned on approaching Mecca, for this rule (which still holds) was already in force in his day.[1] Very curious is his definite statement that he saw two unicorns in the temple at Mecca. These, he says, had been presented to the Sultan of Mecca by the King of Ethiopia. He describes them as of dark bay colour with head like a stag's and slender legs like a goat's, 'a very fierce and solitary animal.' [2]

Till we come to the narrative in Hakluyt all other sixteenth-century accounts of the *Haj* and the Holy Cities are at second-hand, deriving either from Varthema or from hearsay picked up in the Levant or from a combination of these two sources of information.[3] Hakluyt's collection contains 'A Description of the yeerely voyage or pilgrimage of the Muhamitans, Turkes and Moores unto Mecca in Arabia.' [4] Whence he obtained this anonymous account of the *Haj*, which despite some mis-statements and exaggerations is in the main astonishingly accurate, is an unsolved problem. Varthema is not the source, for not only does Hakluyt's narrative contain details that are not in the *Itinerario* but his narrator started on the pilgrimage from Cairo with the western *Haj* whereas Varthema travelled from Damascus. The most likely supposition is that the nar-

---

1 The Moroccan Moslem traveller, Ibn Battûta, describes the donning of the pilgrim-garb; see his *Travels* (1325–1354), translated by H.A.R.Gibb, *Broadway Travellers*, 1929, p.75.

2 *Itinerario*, Rome, 1510, folio xx^r: 'Cap. delli Unicorni nel tempio della Mecha non molto usitati in altri lochi.' Following Varthema, other writers (for example, Sebastian Munster, op.cit., p.1035) mention the unicorns at Mecca.

3 Vincent Le Blanc claimed to have visited Mecca about 1568. It is far from certain that his narrative is not fictitious; and in any case its posthumous publication was at too late a date to influence English writers of our period. See *Les Voyages fameux de Sieur V.Leblanc . . . le tout recueilly de ses memoires par le Sieur Coulon*, Paris, 1648; *The World Surveyed; or the famous Voyages and Travailes of V.Le Blanc or White . . . Rendered into English by F.B.Gent.* [Francis Brooke], 1660. Compare Ralli, op.cit., pp.29f.—For early specimens of summary descriptions of the pilgrim-age see Pierre Belon, *Observations*, chapter liii, folio 121^r; *The Ofspring of the House of Ottomanno*, Sig. D$_{vi}$^{v}; Richer, *De rebus Turcarum*, Paris, 1540, p.70; Menavino, *Trattato de costumi et vita de' Turchi*, Florence, 1548, pp.82f.; Nicolas de Nicolay, *Navigations*, Antwerp, 1576, p.203. This last is illustrated with a cut showing Moorish pilgrims returning from Mecca bearing banners each of which is surmounted with a crescent. A fine large copperplate in the French translation of Chalcondylas with the supplement by F.E.de Mezeray, Paris, 1650, ii,28, shows pilgrims returning from Mecca.

4 Hakluyt, v,329f. Neither Hogarth nor Ralli nor Kiernan mentions this narrative.

rative is an amalgam of earlier accounts, including, it may be, information imparted by Hajjis to some English traveller in the Levant who in turn communicated to Hakluyt what he had gathered concerning the pilgrimage.

'This wicked fact'—that is, the pilgrimage—'purgeth them from a multitude of sins,' says this anonymous writer. The company of pilgrims left Cairo with eight pilots going before them through the desert. In the midst of the caravan was borne a covering for 'a little house in Mecca' and a similar covering for the tomb at El-Medina. The caravan started each morning at two o'clock, rested from sunrise till noon, and was on the way again from noon till nightfall. As they neared Mecca 'a little drumme' was heard upon the mountains; 'they say the sayd drumme is sounded by the angels.' (This was probably the phenomenon of the 'singing sands' [1]). The people of Mecca were clad in green. 'The women of the place are courteous, jocund, and lovely, faire, with alluring eyes, being hote and libidinous, and the most of them naughtie packes.' The great Mosque is described as resembling a cloister—which is sufficiently accurate, though the statement that each side of it is half a mile in length is a wild exaggeration. The Holy House in the wall of which the sacred stone is set is not named but it is described in great detail, it being noted not only that it is black and that pilgrims kiss it and encircle it seven times but that the entrance into it is small in the manner of a window. (This last small particular, which is precisely true, certainly suggests that the writer had himself seen what he records.) The pond 'Zun Zun,' the sermon at Jebel Arafata, and the ceremony of stoning the devil are all described. Of the mosque at El-Medina this writer says that 'in the midst thereof is buried the body of Mahomet, and not in a chest of yron cleaving to the adamant, as many affirm that know not the truth thereof.' (This, too, sounds like the words of an eye-witness.)

Ben Jonson had doubtless read about the Holy Cities in the pages of Eden and Hakluyt as well as in the writings of con-

[1] See Bertram Thomas, *Arabia Felix*, 1932, p.169; H.St.J.B.Philby, *The Empty Quarter*, 1933, pp.204f.

tinental scholars and travellers. Of the knowledge thus acquired he made use in his *Masque of Augurs*.[1] Here there is a
character named Vangoose, an Englishman that 'hath learn'd
to misuse his own tongue in travel, and now speaks all languages
in ill English.' He is an itinerant showman and quack and
possesses a catoptric, an instrument or apparatus for producing
fantastic effects by reflection.[2] Here is his promise to provide
entertainment for a company assembled to witness his performance:

> Ich sall bring in de Turkschen, met all zin bashaws, and sin dirty
> towsand Yanitsaries met all zin whooren, eunuken, all met an
> ander, de sofie van Persia, de Tartar cham met de groat King of
> Mogull, and made deir men, and deir horse, and deir elephanten,
> be seen fight in the ayr, and be all killen, and aliven, and no such
> ting. And all dis met de *ars* van de Catropricks, by de refleshie van
> de glassen. I vill show yow all de brave pilgrim o' de world: de
> pilgrim dat go now, now at de instant, two, dre towsand mile to de
> great Mahomet, at de Mecha, . . . and shew all de brave error in
> de world.

There follows an Antimasque 'which was a perplexed Dance
of straying and deformed Pilgrims taking several paths.' Jonson
was aware of the esoteric and pseudo-mystical experiments for
which the catoptric was employed and though the language
which he puts into his showman's mouth is uncouth and repellent he intends a serious underlying symbolism of the mazes
of error in which humanity is prone to wander; and for all its
grotesqueness there is something strangely impressive in this
symbolic interpretation of the Meccan *Haj*.

A like sad consciousness of the disposition of the mind of
man to err may be detected between the lines of the comments
on Mohammedanism which Robert Burton introduces into his
analysis of the symptoms of religious melancholy. Moslems,
says Burton,

> go as far as Mecha to Mahomets tombe, which journey is both
> miraculous and meritorious. The ceremonies of flinging stones to

1 *Works*, ed. Gifford, vii,418f.
2 The instrument was a sort of *camera obscura* with glasses which distorted images
grotesquely. See Rabelais, *Tiers Livre*, chapter xxv; Burton, *The Anatomy of Melancholy*, I,iii,3; John Evelyn, *Diary*, 8 November 1644.

stone the divel; of eating a camel at Cairo by the way; their fastings, their running till they sweat, their long prayers, Mahomets temple, tombe, and building of it, would aske a whole volume to dilate: and for their paines taken in this holy pilgrimage, all their sins are forgiven, and they reputed so many saints. And divers of them with hot bricks, when they return, will put out their eyes, that they never after see any profane thing, bite out their tongues, etc.[1]

Thus, with an impatient *et cetera*, as though unwilling to devote further thought to such irrational enthusiasm, Burton breaks off, referring his readers for further information to the writings of Lonicerus, Breydenbach, Leo Africanus, Busbecq, Sabellicus, and Theodore Bibliander (authors and travellers familiar, at least by name, to readers of the present volume).

With Burton's contemptuous picture of the extravagances of fanaticism performed at Mecca this subject might conclude; but it is better to pass beyond the not very strict temporal limits of this study and devote a few words to Joseph Pitts, the first Englishman (exception being again made of some unrecorded renegade) to visit the Holy Cities. His experiences as a slave among the Moors have already been touched on,[2] and we have here to note only his impressions of the *Moggarib Haj*, that is, the band of pilgrims from north-west Africa, and of the Holy Cities. The company of devotees with whom he travelled sailed from Suez down the Red Sea to Jidda where they were instructed in the ceremonies to be performed at Mecca. Of that city Pitts's long and conscientious description corrects earlier writers on some points and supplements them on others. 'I am not fond,' he says, 'of contradicting Authors, especially such as are thought to be Great Men; but I speak by Knowledge, they only by Hearsay.' He had the alertness to observe and the intelligence to record many small details of the life at Mecca. He watched the arrogant effendis, and the fanatic dervishes, and the swarms of beggars who accosted the pious with the plea that 'Whatsoever thou givest, that will go with thee'—that is, with thee after death and be meritorious

1 *The Anatomy of Melancholy*, III,iv,i,3.
2 See pp.375–6, above. His book, *A True and Faithful Account of the Religion and Manners of the Mohammetans*, Exeter, 1704, is discussed by Hogarth, Ralli and Kiernan. Pitts deals with Mecca and El-Medina in chapters vii and viii.

at the Judgment. From him we learn that little models of the mosque at Mecca were sold to pilgrims as souvenirs. He was much moved by the reverent behaviour of the pilgrims.

> I could not choose but admire to see those poor Creatures so extraordinary devout and affectionate, . . . and with what Awe and Trembling, they were possessed; insomuch, that I could scarce forbear shedding of Tears, to see their Zeal, tho' blind and idolatrous. . . It is a matter of sorrowful Reflection to compare the Indifference of many Christians, with this zeal of these poor, blind Mahometans.

But the immorality of Mecca scandalized him; it 'comes short of none for Lewdness and Debauchery . . . and they'll steal even in the temple itself.' El-Medina was quite as bad. As his master stood at his devotions by the tomb of the Prophet he 'had his silk Handkerchief stole out of his Bosom.' Equally vivid are Pitts's swift little sketches of life in the *Haj*—the sense of fellowship, the charity bestowed by the more fortunate upon the poorer pilgrims, the danger from marauding bedouin, the night-marches when the caravan was guided by lights fastened to the top of tall poles. He did not consider the tomb-mosque at El-Medina beautiful; there were only about a hundred hanging lamps in it, not three thousand as had been reported. 'I speak what I know and have been an eye witness of,' he says firmly. In reading his book we feel that we have passed beyond the ages of credulity.

To a more credulous age we must now return to ask what conception of the country of the Prophet was in the minds of the Elizabethan poets. In half a dozen lines Spenser draws a memorable picture of just such travellers as we have met with:

> A silly man, in simple weeds forworne,
> And soild with dust of the long dried way;
> His sandales were with toilsome travell torne,
> And face all tand with scorching sunny ray,
> As he had traveild many a sommers day
> Through boyling sands of Arabie and Ynde.[1]

---

1 *The Faerie Queene*, I,vi,35. But when Spenser alludes to the 'wines of Greece and Araby' (ibid., I,v,4) he has the supposed luxury of Arabia in mind.

Here there is no illusion as to the realities of travel through the desert; Arabia is not painted in the voluptuous colours of a poet's fancy. But to the minds of most Elizabethan poets the country was associated with images of luxury and wealth strangely in contrast with the actual barren desolation of most of the great peninsula. Marlowe's Barabas exclaims:

> Well fare the Arabians who so richly pay
> The thing they traffic for with wedge of gold! [1]

Such thoughts were suggested partly by general associations of the East with riches and by accounts in classical authors of the wealth of Arabia but particularly by the problem of the localization of Ophir, the mysterious city whence Solomon fetched his gold. A long treatise on Ophir serves as an appropriate prologue to Purchas's *Pilgrimes*; and Robert Burton in fancy set himself the task of discovering where the city lay.[2] There is a somewhat similar association of Sheba or Sabaea with ideas of spices and perfumes, as in Chapman's beautiful lines:

> Haste thee where the grey ey'd Morn perfumes
> Her rosy chariot with Sabaean spices.[3]

From the time of Herodotus the notion had been prevalent that the winds of Arabia passed out to sea laden with balmy odours; and the conception was an attractive one to the poets who dwelt in noisome London.

> The sweetness of the Arabian wind, still blowing
> Upon the treasures of perfume and spices,

says Fletcher,[4] the thought lending an additional sweetness

---

1 *The Jew of Malta*, I,i. Lyly (*Euphues and His England, Works*, ii,85) writes of 'the river of Arabia which turneth golde to drosse and dust to silver'—rather pointless feats for a river to perform. Where Lyly got the notion is unknown.

2 *The Anatomy of Melancholy*, II,ii,3. Milton (*Paradise Lost*, xi,400) refers to the theory identifying Ophir with Sofala in Mozambique.

3 *Bussy d'Amboise*, V,iv,100f. Massinger twice expresses the thought that a small offering of pure devotion is preferable to Sabaean spices or gums that are 'offer'd in ostentation' (*The Bashful Lover*, I,i; *The Bondman*, IV,iii).

4 *The Bloody Brother*, V,ii. Elsewhere in Fletcher a perfumed gallant suggests the image of Sabaea and Arabia (*The Fair Maid of the Inn*, I,i). Massinger likens the sweetness of Lidia's breath to the 'smooth gales that glide O'er happy Araby' (*The Great Duke of Florence*, II,iii) and Beaumont uses the same simile with more voluptuous ardour (*Philaster*, III,i). Elsewhere a lover compares his lady's breasts to two 'lemons of Arabia'—a less happy fancy (John Cumber, *The Two Merry Milkmaids*, 1661).

to his characteristic cadence. Conversely, a most drastic image of contamination is that of a foulness which cannot be sweetened by 'all the perfumes of Arabia'; [1] and Lady Macbeth's thought is echoed by Fletcher when he writes:

> All the gums in sweet Arabia
> Are not sufficient, were they burnt about thee,
> To purge the scent. [2]

Robert Davenport's description of

> the Indian winds,
> That blow from off the coast, and cheer the sailor
> With the sweet savour of their spices [3]

anticipates in a measure the most beautiful passage in English poetry inspired by the perfumes of Arabia, where Milton compares the pure air and gentle gales of Eden to the perfumes which greet those who having sailed around the Cape of Good Hope voyage northward:

> Off at sea North-East winds blow
> Sabaean odours from the spicy shore
> Of Araby the blest; with such delay
> Well pleas'd they slack their course, and many a league
> Cheer'd with the grateful smell old Ocean smiles. [4]

The idea of Arabia as a land of perfumes points to Arabia Felix, the high lands of the extreme south of the peninsula, bordering

1 *Macbeth*, V,i,56.
2 *The False One*, III,ii,73f. This is the balm or gum from which frankincense is made. In Florio's *World of Words* 'rasin' is defined as 'a tree in Arabia' upon which the phoenix sits. The name Rasis which Ben Jonson gives to his 'great Arabic doctor' (*The Tale of a Tub*, IV,i) is probably intended to suggest rasin (rosin) with an added thought of medicinal virtue. The rapidity and abundance with which the liquid flows makes Othello liken his weeping eyes to the Arabian trees which let fall 'their medicinable gumme' (*Othello*, V,ii,349f.)—a thought which is expressed with tasteless bombast in the anonymous play *Tiberius* (l.2248): 'Mine eyes shall drizel down Arabian mirrhe.'—The contrary of the thought that Arabian perfumes are specifics against foulness is the idea, deriving from Pliny, xii,38, and Strabo, XVI,iv,19, that 'the Arabians being stuffed with perfumes, burn Hemlock, a ranck poison' (Lyly, *Sapho and Phao*, Prologue, *Works*, ii,372). Nashe says that the 'overcloyed' Sabaeans 'refresh their nosthrilles with the unsavourie sent of the pitchy slime that Euphrates casts up, and the contagious fumes of Goats beards burned' ('To the Gentlemen Students,' *Works*, iii,313).
3 *The City Night-Cap*, V,i; Hazlitt's Dodsley, xiii,193.
4 *Paradise Lost*, iv,159f. Compare *Paradise Regained*, ii,362f.

on the Indian Ocean, wooded, watered, fertile. Even so, distance has lent its customary enchantment. 'The splendid colouring of fancy and fiction,' says Gibbon of Arabia Felix, 'has been suggested by contrast and heightened by distance.' [1] The contrast is with the stark and barren North—Arabia Deserta, the land of the Prophet.

V

So much for the Prophet and his country; now for his Book. The Latin version of the *Koran* which was known in Christendom, or if not known at any rate accessible, during the period of the Renaissance was that which had been prepared under the direction of Peter the Venerable, Abbot of Cluny, about A.D. 1143. [2] During a journey through Spain Peter observed the growing power of Mohammedanism and became convinced of the need for better instructed propaganda against Islam. If Christian scholars were no longer to attack blindly a body of doctrine with which they were acquainted only through ill-report they must have a first-hand knowledge of that whereof they spoke. To supply the want Abbot Peter engaged three Christians who knew, or claimed to know, Arabic to translate the *Koran*. They were assisted by an Arab. The mood in which this heavy task was undertaken did not encourage accuracy nor was the state of scholarship such as to insure it. The resulting version is notoriously full of errors of translation and reveals no effort to reproduce sympathetically the stylistic features which in any case can be rendered only approximately and with difficulty in a European language. Supplementary to the text Peter composed a refutation of Mohammedanism. Not all of this is extant but what survives shows that it included biographical and theological material apparently drawn from Arabic sources. The portions of this controversial material that survived were gathered together, edited, and amplified by Theodorus Bibliander who issued this amalgam of arguments and diatribes together with a revised Latin version of the

1 *The Decline and Fall of the Roman Empire*, ed. Bury, v,334.
2 D'Ancona, op.cit., pp.193f.; D.C.Munro, in *Speculum*, vi,337. Much later (*c*.1475) Bishop Guglielmo Raimondo, a Sicilian, translated parts of the *Koran* into Latin. The *Koran* in Arabic was first printed at Venice between 1485 and 1499.

Koran.[1] The words with which this version closes—'Explicit Liber Legis Diabolicae Saracenorum, qui Arabice dicitur Alchoran'—indicate the tone and temper of these Islamic studies. Even so and despite the rancorous contempt expressed in his other controversial writings (particularly the *Confutationes Legis Machumaticae*), Bibliander suffered notoriety and discredit and was in danger of prosecution for tampering with, and offering to the Christian public, these damnable doctrines. His writings were widely read not only on the continent but in England; Burton numbers him among his authorities; and often where in other writers no acknowledgment of indebtedness is made it is possible to detect his influence upon phraseology. His books contain immensely detailed arguments against the heresies of Islam. In the *Confutationes* he gathers together excerpts from many Christian controversialists; and in his *Historiae Saracenorum* he presents a compilation of Byzantine and Italian historians, reprints Luther's attack upon the Turks,[2] and offers to the curiosity of his readers a discourse on the iniquities of Mahomet composed in Turkish. This discourse may have suggested to Lazaro Soranzo and René de Lucinge their scheme to disseminate in the Ottoman Empire books exposing the 'mad fooleries' of the *Koran*, whereby the faith of the Moslems might be undermined.[3]

To the type of propaganda proposed by Soranzo and Lucinge there is something roughly analogous in William Bedwell's remarkable little book *Mohammedis Imposturae* (1615), an English translation of an anonymous Arabic original which had been published at an unascertainable place and at an uncertain date a few years earlier.[4] The translator, who has

---

1 *Machumetis Sarracenorum Principis Vita et Doctrina omnis,* edition without place or date (1543?); the translation of the *Koran* occupied pp.8–188. D'Ancona, op.cit., p.262, mentions a Basle edition of 1547. See also Bibliander's *Machumetis . . . eiusque successorum vitae, doctrina ac ipse Alcoran . . . Haec omnia in unum volumen redacta sunt opera,* Zurich, 1550.

2 That is, the preface by Luther in *Libellus de Ritu ac Moribus Turcarum,* Wittemberg, 1530. (The anonymous author of this book was a European slave in Ottoman families from 1436 to 1453. On the great vogue of the book see A.H.Lybyer, *The Government of the Ottoman Empire,* Cambridge, Massachusetts, 1913, pp.309f.)

3 See pp.111 and 116, above.

4 *Mohammedis Imposturae: That is, A Discovery of the Manifold Forgeries, Falshoods, and horrible impieties of the blasphemous seducer Mohammed: With a demonstration of the insufficiencie of his law, contained in the cursed Alkoran: Delivered in a conference*

often been described as 'the father of Arabic scholarship in England,' was led into these studies through his interest in mathematics, astronomy, and theology. He won a continental reputation as one of the most learned orientalists of the day, becoming the correspondent and then the friend of Isaac Casaubon and Scaliger. It was from Leyden that he imported the first fount of Arabic type to be brought to England; on his death he bequeathed this fount to Cambridge where a chair of Arabic had been lately established by Sir Thomas Adams. The *Mohammedis Imposturae* consists of three dialogues between two pilgrims returning from Mecca where they have worshipped at 'the Alkaaba.' One of these pilgrims, Sheich Sinan, has become a Christian—which is somewhat odd in the circumstances. The other, Doctor Ahmed, is anxious to learn the truths necessary to salvation. Sinan demonstrates to him that the essential points of faith set forth in the *Koran* are in the Gospels; and that the *Koran* merely adds personal anecdotes of Mahomet together with a quantity of legends and lies. Moslem morality and precepts of devotion are borrowed or stolen from the teaching of Christ. Ahmed's criticism of points of Christian doctrine are controverted by Sinan, who lays special emphasis upon the homage which Islam pays to Jesus. In the end Ahmed, it is implied, is won over by his friend's arguments. Marginal numbers refer to the Surahs of the *Koran* supporting statements made in the text. The book,

betweene two Mohammetans, in their return from Mecha. Written long since in Arabicke, and now done into English by William Bedwell. Whereunto is annexed the Arabian Trudgman, interpreting certaine Arabicke termes used by Historians, 1615. In the same year Bedwell's etymological work was issued in a separate edition: *The Arabian Trudgman, that is, certaine Arabicke termes, as names of places, titles of honour . . . expounded according to their . . . etymologie . . . By W.B.* This includes also a catalogue or index of all the Surahs or chapters of the *Koran.* Bedwell's use of the form 'Mohammed' instead of the current erroneous 'Mahomet' is well-nigh unique in English books of the period but is what we should expect from his knowledge of Arabic. His 'Trudgman' (that is, dragoman, interpreter) is often far in advance of its time. One may compare his definition of 'Mesgied' or mosque as a church or temple 'where they meete and performe all their superstitious service unto their idoll' (*Mohammedis Imposturae,* Sig. N) with the quaint etymology of 'Moschee' from the Latin *mosca,* a fly, because the Turks worship 'Bahalzebuf, Idole of Flies' in Hartwell's translation of the *Ottoman of Lazaro Soranzo,* 1603, folio 97ʳ.—Bedwell, like many of the great Arabists, English and continental, of the earlier seventeenth century, was drawn to the language because of its importance for his mathematical studies. Much interesting information on the connection between Hebrew and Arabic studies and on the dependence of mathematicians and astronomers upon Arabian learning may be found in *The Legacy of Israel,* Oxford, 1928.

though simple in style, is genuinely learned in substance, and though polemical, is by no means so fantastically hostile to Islam as the epithets of its catch-penny title would lead one to expect.

The tradition of such debates between Christians and Mohammedans in the Levant is an old one and is even today hardly extinct.[1] From time to time during our period reports came to Europe of discussions of this character, sometimes ending disastrously. Thus, in 1539, there was published in Germany a letter from Constantinople recording an alleged dispute between Sultan Solyman and his priests as to whether Mohammedanism or Christianity was the superior religion. The priests investigated the *Koran* and the New Testament and after comparing the two reached the conclusion that the Christian religion was the better, the purer, and the more logical. Whereupon Sultan Solyman had them beheaded.[2] In Christendom hopes were cherished and occasionally expressed that the Sultan and his subjects could be converted to Christianity. It was with this object in view that Pope Pius II composed his letter to Sultan Mahomet II, promising the Conqueror that when he had embraced Christianity and made his obedience to the Holy See he should be recognized as Emperor of the East.[3] A century and a half later the rumour spread abroad that the reigning Sultan had actually been converted.[4] The prevalence of this sort of fantastic gossip gave substance to the assurances given the Pope by the Sherley brothers that the conversion of the Shah of Persia was imminent. Of somewhat similar tenor were the popular prophecies coupling the

---

1 A *disputatio* between a Christian and a Mohammedan was attached to the Latin version of the *Koran* made under the auspices of Peter the Venerable. This reappears in Vincent of Beauvais. It is possible that this debate was an Arabic composition, or at any rate was based upon one, for it resembles an Arabic text translated by Sir William Muir: *The Apology of Al Kindy . . . in Defence of Christianity*, 1882. On Al-Kindy and the custom of debates on religion between Christians and Moslems see P.K.Hitti, *History of the Arabs*, p.354.

2 *Abschrifft eines brieffs, von Constantinopel, auss wellichem man zuuernemen hat welcher gestalt der Gross Turck, seine Priester . . . hat lassen vmbbringen* (no place), 1539.

3 This letter is probably merely a rhetorical exercise. See *The Cambridge Modern History*, i,78.

4 *Les Prodigieuses et admirables visions apparues a Achmeth, Grand Seigneur des Turcs, le 3 aout 1614 . . . traduites de la langue turque en francoise par un gentilhomme estant a Constantinople ou la conversion du dit Grand Seigneur du Mahometisme au Christianisme*, Paris, 1614.

downfall of Turkish military power with the conversion of the Turks.[1]

No legend of the Prophet is too extravagant, too apocryphal to be attributed to the *Koran*, even though totally unwarranted by the text. Thus, Nashe writes of 'Mahomet's angels in the Alchoran, that are said to have eares stretching from one end of heaven to the other,' and declares scornfully that in the same book 'it is written that 250 Ladies hanged themselves for the Love of Mahomet.'[2] There is nothing in the *Koran* about either of these matters; their origin is to be sought among the fantastic traditions concerning Mahomet; they appear to be far-off echoes of one or another fanciful *hadith*. Burton offers as an instance of the sottish absurdities of the book the stories of beasts and stones saluting Mahomet and of the moon descending from heaven to visit him.[3] It contains no such stories. The currency of these and other fables shows that hostile writers seldom troubled to acquaint themselves with the Latin text; and if they did so their prejudices blinded them to the beauty and grandeur which would else surely have glimmered, albeit obscurely, through the unworthy rendering of the original. Even a man of such wide literary sympathies as Ben Jonson, one so little moved by merely religious prejudice, exhibits by implication in his poem on the burning of his library his contempt for the book. Had he been aware, he says, of Vulcan's desire for a feast of fire he would have offered the deity whole reams of 'proper stuff' if by doing so he could have redeemed his own manuscripts. Of such 'stuff' he gives a list, and it is headed by the *Talmud* and the *Koran*.[4] There were other famous men of letters who nourished a like antipathy. Burton, as we have seen, introduces a fairly long account of Mohammedanism into the section of his great

1 *Declaratio oder Erklarung. Eines Furtreffenlichen Turcken Propheceyung. Von der Turcken Vndergang vnd bekehrung zum Christlichen Glauben . . . auss Turckischer Sprach Transferirth . . . Durch Wilhelmum Eo: Neuheuser*, Erffordt, 1594. This 'prophecy' is given in Turkish, German, and Latin.
2 *Have with You to Saffron-Walden, Works*, iii,33 and 111.
3 *The Anatomy of Melancholy*, III,iv,i,3.
4 'Execration upon Vulcan,' *Underwoods, Works*, ed. Gifford, viii,401. Compare: 'These are the books of the black art; I hate them worse than Bellarmine, the Golden Legend, or the Turkish Alcoran' (Thomas Randolph, *Aristippus*, 1630, *Poetical and Dramatic Works*, ed. W.C.Hazlitt, 1875, p.25).

treatise devoted to religious melancholy. He describes Islam as an absurd and sottish 'compound of Gentiles, Jewes, and Christians,' and 'their Alcoran' as 'a gallimaufrie of lyes, tales, ceremonies, traditions, precepts, stole from other sects, and confusedly heaped up, to delude a company of rude and barbarous clownes.' [1] In like tone is Sir Thomas Browne's estimate of the *Koran*, 'an ill-composed Piece,' he says, 'containing in it Vain and ridiculous Errors in Philosophy, impossibilities, fictions, and vanities beyond laughter.' [2] So, in the 'cursory survey' of Mohammedanism which James Howell introduces into one of the letters on religion addressed to a friend, Islam is characterized as 'this fatal sect, . . . most mischievous and destructive to the Church of Christ.' Arabia was, Howell adds, 'the Nest where that Cockatrice Egg was hatched.' [3] Robert Baron, for all his oriental erudition, describes the *Koran* as 'a Fardel of Blasphemies, Rabinical Fables, Ridiculous Discourses, Impostures, Bestialities, Inconveniences, Impossibilities and contradictions.' [4]

It must not be supposed, however, that comment upon the *Koran* is limited to such immoderate and ill-informed diatribes as these; for while it is too much to expect from any writer of the time an entirely dispassionate and non-partisan criticism and analysis of the book, there are some authors who even when most denunciatory do show some knowledge of the work, even occasionally some sympathy with its religious and ethical ideals. This is markedly true of some of the writers who have travelled in the Levant and introduce accounts of Mohammedanism into their narratives. Pierre Belon is an early instance of a traveller concerned to understand the religious ideas of the people among whom he had dwelt. He shows a particular interest in Mohammedan eschatology, describing, not without some signs of appreciation of the conception, the Bridge of Judgment over which the Souls of the Dead must pass, the Faithful accomplishing the perilous crossing while

1 Loc.cit., p.438, note 3, above.
2 *Religio Medici*, Part I, section xxiii. John Fryer (*A New Account of East India and Persia*, iii,114) cites Browne's opinion and endorses it.
3 *Familiar Letters*, ii,391f.
4 *Mirza*, pp.197f.

the Wicked fall into hell.[1] In line with Christian writers from
the beginnings of controversy with Islam, he lays emphasis
upon the sensuality of the Mohammedan conception of Paradise.[2] This is declared by many writers to be the chief attraction to converts to Islam. Similar summaries of the religious
and moral teaching of Islam are found in various English
travel-books. Thus, William Biddulph introduces into one of
his letters a history of the religion of the Turks, beginning
with the broad statement that 'the first Author thereof . . .
was (no doubt) the divell, who used that false Prophet Mahomet as his instrument to broach it abroad.' Biddulph's interest is chiefly ethical. He enters into considerable detail regarding
the eight commandments of the Mohammedan law, giving a
summary of each followed in nearly every instance by comments upon how badly Mohammedans observe the commandment in question. The second, for example, 'Obey thy parents,'
is followed by this comment: 'How badly this duty is performed
among them I know by experience: for I did never reade or
heare of more disobedient children to their parents, either in
word or deed.' The commandment to give to the poor inspires
the curt and unjust comment: 'Turks are more merciful to
birds, cats and dogs then to the poore.' The commandment
regarding the marital relationship offers Biddulph an opportunity to contrast the low lot of women in Turkish countries
with that of the 'more blessed women' of England. And so
forth.[3] George Sandys was of two minds about the creed of
Islam.. On the one hand he characterizes it as a 'damnable
doctrine, . . . a hodge-podge of sundry religions,' but on the
other he was much impressed with the reverence which the
Turks show to the *Koran*: 'They kisse it, embrace it, and
sweare by it, calling it the booke of glory.' Sandys gives a
summary of Islamic doctrines and practices, dwelling on their
ideas of heaven and hell and showing some appreciation of
their piety.[4] Such expressions of admiration for the reverence

1 *Observations*, folio 173ʳf. Bridges similar to the Mohammedan Bridge of Judgment
  are to be found in medieval romances as one form of the folklore theme of the Perilous
  Passage.
2 Founded on such texts as *Koran*, lii,20; lv,46f.; lxxviii,33.
3 *The Travels of Foure Englishmen and a Preacher*, pp.40f.
4 *Relation of a Journey*, pp.53f.

and devoutness of the Moslems are not uncommon and are sometimes connected with rebukes addressed to Christians who are guilty of unbecoming frivolity in their devotions. This contrast is drawn not only by travellers but by authors who have never seen a Mohammedan. Thus, Robert Wilson writes:

> Of the Gospel we do boast, and do it professe,
> But more honest fidelitie is among Turkes.[1]

George Wither makes the same point more elaborately:

> Our cursed Pagan unbeleeving foe,
> I meane the Turke, more reverence doth show
> In those his damn'd erronious Rites than we
> In the true Worship: for 'tis knowne that he
> Will not so much as touch his Alcharon,
> That doth containe his false Religion,
> With unwasht hands: nor till he hath o'erwent
> All that his vaine and confus'd rabblement
> Of Ceremonies us'd much lesse dares looke
> On the Contents of that unhallowed Booke.[2]

We may now examine somewhat more closely a group of writings in which attention is directed to Mohammedan doctrine rather than to the scandals of Mahomet's career. (The two subjects are, however, seldom if ever entirely separated.) The earliest thing of the sort to appear in English is a brief, jejune tract published in 1515 by Wynkyn de Worde: *Here begynneth a lytell treatyse of the turkes lawe called Alcaron. And it also speketh of Machamet the Nygromancer.* This counterblast to the *Koran*, set forth in ten pages, is of so general a character and is so lacking in individuality that it is impossible to ascertain whence the anonymous author derived his material. His 'treatise' is of very little interest save for its early date.

In another connection we have already examined Johannes Boemus's *Mores, Leges et Ritus Omnium Gentium* (1536) of

---

1 *The Pedlars Prophecie*, 1595 (anonymous but probably by Wilson); ed. W.W.Greg, Malone Society, 1914, ll.916f.
2 *Abuses Stript and Whipt*, 1622, Book II, Satire iv; *Poems*, Spenser Society, 1871, pp.311f.

which there are two English versions: William Watreman's
Fardle of Facions (1555) and Edward Aston's *The Manners,
Lawes and Customes of all Nations* (1611).[1] The chapter on the
Turks in this compilation, though, as we have seen, by no means
entirely hostile, must on the whole have reinforced the prejudices of Christians against Islam. Beginning with a review
of the geographical situation of the Ottoman Empire, it passes
on to an account of Mahomet who framed and invented 'a
religion most dangerous and pernicious to all mankinde.' There
follows a long account of the errors and heresies of Islam, with
particular emphasis upon the Moslems' denial of the dogma
of the Redemption and upon their opinions concerning Christ.
The 'incredible allurement' that has drawn countless men to
Mahomet has been 'his giving people free liberty and power
to pursue their lustes and all other pleasures, for by these
meanes this pestilent religion hath crept into innumerable
Nations.' In consequence the number of true believers is few
in comparison with the multitude of misbelievers who have
accepted Mahomet and 'his accursed religion.'

The English abridgment of Sebastian Munster's *Cosmography*
contains a chapter on 'Howe the Turkes do beleeve, and howe
they worship God.' This is quite accurate so far as it goes
and is not without a touch of sympathetic admiration for the
austere religious discipline to which Moslems subject themselves. Here the Elizabethan reader could learn of the five
obligatory periods of daily prayer; the ceremonial ablutions;
the requirement that shoes be put off before entering a mosque;
the Friday sabbath; the prohibition of images; the separation
of men and women during religious services; the rigidly imposed obligation to fast from sunrise to sunset during Ramadan;
the multitude of lamps burning in every mosque; and many
similar matters.[2] A separate section is devoted to 'the Opinion
of the Turkes upon the world to come'[3]—everlasting pleasure
in a paradise of sensual delights being the reward of those
who keep the law.

In the sermon from which we have quoted several times

1 See p.200, note 1, above.
2 *Straunge and memorable thinges*, folio 35ᵣf.
3 Ibid., folio 39ᵣ.

already Henry Smith advances a variety of arguments to prove the vanity and falsehood of a religion that is little if at all better than atheism. Its newness proves that it is false. It is shot through with carnality. Its law is tyrannical, dependent upon the sword. It was patched together from many sources and is maintained by wiles and deceit. No miracles manifested Mahomet's vocation.[1] This last point is worth a moment's further consideration, for it is of very ancient origin. From the earliest times the absence of miracles occasioned taunts by Christian controversialists against Islam. Mahomet himself did not profess to work miracles other than the supreme miracle of the revelation of the *Koran*. But Mohammedan apologists could not afford to let him labour under the disadvantage apparent when his everyday mundane life was compared with the mighty works attributed to Jesus Christ. Consequently there grew up in the *hadith* or traditions the representation of him as a miracle-worker.[2] Our preacher, ignoring the traditions, fixes his attention upon the silence of the *Koran* on this matter.

In 1597 appeared the most elaborate of Elizabethan accounts of Mohammedanism. This is an anonymous work entitled *The Policy of the Turkish Empire*. The title-page bears the words 'The first Booke'; but only this thin quarto was published. Apparently civil and military life and affairs were to be considered in later instalments, for the published portion deals exclusively with matters of religion and ethics. It is not so bigoted in point of view as the opening sketch of the life of Mahomet—'this monster of mankind'—would lead one to expect. Of the *Koran* it is said that the version in use among the Turks is not the same as that originally invented and written down by Mahomet, a curious misstatement which seems to be a distortion of the Moslem opinion that only the Arabic text is inspired and that all that a translation can do is to convey the general meaning of the original. The eight commandments are explicated in a series of separate chapters: Belief in God and Mahomet; Honour due unto Parents; the

1 *Gods Arrowe against Atheists*, chapter iv.
2 Guillaume, *The Traditions of Islam*, pp.135f.

Golden Rule; Prayers in Mosques; the Month's Fast; Alms-giving; Marriage; Against Murder.[1] The devices used to per-suade or compel a Christian to 'turn Turk' form the subject of a chapter. The rite and method of circumcision are ex-plained—a subject to which almost all English travellers in Mohammedan lands recur with prurient curiosity. The Turkish doctrine regarding each of the Seven Deadly Sins is expounded.[2] The pilgrimage to Mecca is touched on briefly, with some vague generalities about the *Haj*. The Turks' 'Meschits' (mosques) and hospitals are described, and their hostility to images and bells is noted. Then, following a description of their manner of burial and their sepulchres, we come to Mohammedan ideas of heaven and hell and find one of the earliest allusions in English literature to Israphill, the Angel of Death. The enormous bridge that hangs between two mountains in the Other World is described: 'The Bridge of Justice: upon the which, all the sinfull Soules are to passe with the weightie burthen of their sinnes upon their shoulders.'[3] The last two chapters have to do with Mohammedan 'priests' of different ranks and functions and with the religious orders, the begging 'friars' and 'darvisses.' From this treatise the Elizabethan reader could obtain a good deal of quite accurate information about Islam.

In 1607 the Reverend Joseph Hall sent to a friend an epistle on the subject of 'the trial and choice of the true religion.'

---

1 Biddulph seems to have obtained from these chapters his material on the command-ments.

2 The discussion of the Seven Deadly Sins, while descending from medieval sources, seems to owe a good deal directly to Menavino's *Trattato de costumi et vita de' Turchi*, 1548.

3 *The Policy of the Turkish Empire*, 1597, folio 69ᵛ. Compare the description of the Bridge of Judgment in Thomas Herbert, *Some Yeares Travels*, ed. 1638, p.239. It was from such descriptions as these that Addison obtained the idea of the 'Vision of Mirza.'—The doctrine of the 'immediate judgment' of the dead, founded upon such Koranic texts as iv,97, and much elaborated by commentators, is referred to appropriately in the *Hydrotaphia*, chapter i, where Sir Thomas Browne writes: 'The Musselmen believers will never admit this fiery resolution [that is, the cremation of the dead]. For they hold a present trial from their black and white angels in the grave; which they must have made so hollow, that they may rise upon their knees.' It is the function of the Black Angel to interrogate the dead; if satisfied, he departs, and the White Angel keeps the dead company till the Final Judgment. This impres-sive idea is referred to occasionally by English travellers; see, for example, Sandys's account of Turkish funerals (*Relation*, p.71; Purchas, viii,153) whence Browne seems to have derived his information save that Sandys mentions two Black Angels and two White. Compare Bruin, *Voyage au Levant*, 1700, chapter xix.

Having quickly dismissed as negligible certain heresies, Hall considers the merits and defects of the five religions which 'stand in competition for truth,' the Jewish, Turkish, Greekish, Popish, and Reformed. This is what he has to say about Islam:

The Turk stands out for his Mahomet, that cozening Arabian; whose religion, if it deserve that name, stands upon nothing but rude ignorance and palpable imposture. Yet, lo here a subtle devil in a gross religion; for when he saw that he could not by single twists of heresy pull down the well-built walls of the church, he winds them all up in one cable, to see if his cord of so many folds might happily prevail: raising up wicked Mahomet, to deny, with Sabellius, the distinction of persons; with Arius, Christ's divinity; with Macedonius, the Deity of the Holy Ghost; with Sergius, two wills in Christ; with Marcion, Christ's suffering. And these policies, seconded with violence, how have they wasted Christendom! O damnable misture, miserably successful! which yet could not have been, but that it meets with sottish clients, and soothes up nature, and debars both all knowledge and contradiction. What is their Alcoran but a fardel of foolish impossibilities? Whosoever shall hear me relate the stories of angel Adriel's death, Seraphuel's trumpet, Gabriel's bridge, Harroth and Maroth's hanging, the moon's descending into Mahomet's sleeve, the litter wherein he saw God carried by eight angels, their ridiculous and swinish paradise, and thousands of the same brand; would say that Mahomet hoped to meet either with beasts or madmen. Besides these barbarous fictions, behold their laws, full of license, full of impiety: in which revenge is encouraged, multitudes of wives allowed, theft tolerated; and the frame of their opinions such as well bewrays their whole religion to be but the mongrel issue of an Arian, Jew, Nestorian, and Arabian: a monster of many seeds, and all accursed. In both which regards, nature herself, in whose breast God hath written his royal law, though in part by her defaced, hath light enough to condemn a Turk, as the worst pagan. Let no man look for further disproof. These follies a wise Christian will scorn to confute and scarce vouchsafe to laugh at.[1]

There is a similar diatribe in Joseph Wybarne's erudite book *The New Age of Old Names* (1609), where a contemptuous account of Mahomet—a 'Mungrell born'—introduces a sum-

---

1 Joseph Hall, *Works*, ed. Philip Wynter, Oxford, 1863, vi,193f.

mary of the teaching of the *Koran* in which exaggerated emphasis is laid upon the doctrines that hostile sects are to be destroyed with fire and sword and that polygamy is lawful. The survey winds up with the remark that 'thus from a mungrul Mahomet came a mungrull Religion, compilde of shadowes and impostures.' [1]

Almost half a century passed before another significant account of Mohammedanism and the *Koran* was published in England; [2] and to bridge over this long solution of continuity we may glance for a moment into France where in 1625 appeared a well-informed work which became known in England—Michel Baudier's *Histoire Generale de la Religion des Turcs*. The delightful engraved title-page points the contrast between Christianity and Islam: a vision of the Trinity enthroned upon the clouds amidst adoring angels is set over against a celestial banquet where turbaned Turks carouse with naked women; Christian baptism is contrasted with Mohammedan ceremonial ablutions; the luminous sign I.H.S. with the Cross is the proper foil to the inconstant moon. The book is lengthy and contains an astonishing amount of miscellaneous information: on Mahomet's life (with all the old errors and prejudices); the *Koran*; the *Haj*; rites and prayers; ablutions and circumcision; alms and charities; the eight commandments; Turkish morality as evidenced by their attitude towards each of the Seven Deadly Sins; the prohibition of wine and swine's flesh; the muftis and religious orders; and so forth. There is a fairly accurate, though incomplete, survey of the heresies and schools of Mohammedanism with particular reference to the hostility of the orthodox Sunni Turks to the Shi'a Persians. In Book iv there is a long examination of the 'depraving' in the *Koran* of various stories in the Old Testament; and in Book v an

---

1 *The New Age of Old Names. By Jos. Wib.*, 1609, chapter xviii, pp.94f.
2 In 1637 was published *The Life and Death of Mahomet, The Conquest of Spaine together with the Rysing and Ruine of the Sarazen Empire*. This was ascribed to Sir Walter Ralegh. The publisher, addressing a dedicatory epistle to Carew Ralegh, declared that he had found it 'by the stile thereof, and my good intelligence, to be natively derived from your Fathers worth.' Actually it is one of several posthumous pieces that are apocryphal imitations of Ralegh's style. The biographical sketch of Mahomet occupies pp.1–25. There is nothing of novelty or interest in it.—The diatribe in Thomas Beard's *Theatre of Gods Judgements* (pp.104f., of the revised edition of 1631) offers nothing new.

QVÆ SVNT SPIRITVS SAPIVNT.

QVÆ CARNIS SVNT SAPIVNT.

HÆC LAVAT.

INQVINAT ILLA.

IHS

LVX CERTA SALVTIS.

MVTANDA SEQVNTVR.

HISTOIRE
GENERALE
DE LA RELIGION
DES TVRCS.

AVEC LA NAISSANCE,
la vie, et la mort, de leur
Prophete Mahomet, et
les actions des quatre
premiers Caliphes
qui l'ont suiui.

Celles du Prince Mahumas

Et les rauages des Sarra-
sins en Europe aux trois
premiers siecles
de leur loy.

Ensemble le tableau de toute
la Chrestienté a la venue
de Mahomet

Par le Sr MICHEL BAVDIER
de Languedoc.
A PARIS.

En la Boutique de L'Angelier
Chez CLAVDE CRAMOISY
au premier Pillier de la grande
Salle du Palais. 1625

Christianity and Islam: A Contrast

account of the impieties of Mohammedanism against Jesus
Christ with many arguments intended to convince Moslems
of Christ's Divinity. Book vi is devoted to eschatology and
contains a fine description of the Bridge of Justice.

The principal subject of Francis Osborn's *Political Reflections
upon the Government of the Turks* (1656) has already been discussed in Chapter III, and we have here to note that interspersed among the author's thoughts on the causes of Turkish
victories are many remarks upon the religion of Islam. Osborn's
prejudices are directed against Rome, not Islam, and his
efforts are persistent to draw analogies between Roman Catholicism and Mohammedanism. Nevertheless he exhibits an
understanding of Islam that is altogether unusual and is perhaps due to the fact that, as we shall see presently, there
was available to him what had been lacking to his predecessors,
an English version of the *Koran*. That he had had some difficulty in mastering the book is perhaps implied in his quaint
remark that Mahomet 'sinned' in 'swelling his Alcoran to so
large a volume' but that he modified the inconvenience by
'prohibiting the reading of it, to any but the Priests.' [1] This
observation is in line with the comment frequently met with
in books of our period, that Moslems are ignorant or actually
illiterate. Apparently Renaissance writers had no realization
of the fact that the use of the Arabic script in Turkish was a
grave deterrent to learning and even to ordinary literacy
among the Turks. In his comment on this matter of keeping
the sacred volume from the laity Osborn's hostility to Rome
is implied. It may be discerned in other parts of his treatise.
Thus, in view of the fact that Mahomet did not hold that any
merit resided in voluntary 'maceration or persecution of our
Bodies,' Osborn contends that the 'putting out of their eyes
before the Tombe of their Prophet to prevent the sight of
anything after, and the wearing of such huge and painfull
Rings in the most tender parts of their bodies,[2] grew not from

---

1 *Political Reflections*, p.13.
2 Calenders or mendicant dervishes who wear a large ring thrust through the genitals
are described by Nicolas de Nicolay, *Navigations*, 1576, p.182. Father Crespet
(*Instructions de la Foy Chrestienne*, folio 75ʳ) writes: 'Ces faux moynes se percent le
membre viril, et y pendent un anneau de fer.' One of the illustrations in the volume

any Institute of his, but are rather Bastards of that Church reputed for nothing more justly, the Whore of Babylon' [1]— in other and more seemly words, ascetic practices in Islam are borrowings from Roman Catholicism. Again, Osborn approves of the subjection of the ecclesiastical to the civil power among the Turks. 'The Turk [that is, the Sultan] in this is happy, that the Mufty his Pope, no lesse then Mecca his Rome, are within the reach of his power . . . Though the Turkish Court no lesse then the Common People do afford the Gaudy plumage of Honour to the Mufty, the highest Bird in this earthly Paradise, yet if he but offers to tune his note contrary to the true Dialect of State, he is straight unperched.' [2] His approval of Islam is not limited to those points of doctrine and manners where he draws a parallel or a contrast to Rome. He suggests that 'perhaps the cause why Sacrifice is not taken in, amongst the number of things borrowed from the Jews' is because Moslems think it 'incongruous with a Divine Essence, to be appeased or delighted by the losse and blood of poor Creatures, incapable of the Will or Power to transgresse.' [3] His admiration goes out to the Mohammedans for their reverence to God. 'The awfulnesse the Turks beare to the Name of God is so great, that they dare not employ the paper wherein they find it written, to any base office, but leave it hid in a hole to the farther disposal of the Owners Providence.' [4]

VI

IN 1649 the Sieur du Ryer, who for many years had represented France as consul at Alexandria, published his translation of the *Koran* into French. [5] In a preliminary address to the

supplementary to Chalcondylas, Paris, 1650, shows a calender wearing this ring (ii,22).
1 *Political Reflections*, pp.23f.
2 Ibid., pp.31f. Osborn, like other European writers, merely betrays his ignorance when he writes about the 'ecclesiastical' system of Islam.
3 Ibid., p.23. The injunction regarding sacrifice at Mecca (*Koran*, xii,33) is overlooked by Osborn and is in any case only an apparent contradiction, for this slaughter of animals is not propitiatory but commemorative of Abraham's sacrifice.
4 Ibid., p.18. Osborn misses the point, which is that Moslems treat reverently any piece of writing for fear lest the name of Allah be written on it. That they count it a sin to be careless of any 'scroll' is noted in *The Ofspring of the House of Ottomanno*, Sig. Diiii.
5 *L'Alcoran de Mahomet. Translate d'Arabe en Francois, par le Sieur du Ryer, Sieur de la Garde Malezair. Iouxte* [sic. ?] *la Copie imprimée à Paris*, 1649.

reader he describes the book and justifies the publication of his version:

> Ce Livre est une longue conference de Dieu, des Anges, et de Mahomet, que ce faux Prophete a inventée assez grossierement. . .
> Il a esté expliqué par plusieurs Docteurs Mahometans, leur explication est aussi ridicule que le texte. . . Tu serras estonné que ces absurditez ayent infecté la meilleure partie du Monde, et avoueras que la connoissance de ce qui est contenu en ce Livre, rendra cette Loy meprisable.

It may be questioned whether the man who carried to completion the heavy task of this translation sincerely held an opinion so unqualifiedly condemnatory; but it was necessary to say as much in order to obtain permission to issue his work and to guard himself and his printer from prosecution for publishing blasphemous matter.

In the same year there appeared across the Channel: *The Alcoran of Mahomet, Translated out of Arabique into French; by the Sieur du Ryer, Lord of Malezair, and Resident for the King of France, at Alexandria. And now newly Englished, for the satisfaction of all that desire to look into the Turkish vanities. London Printed, Anno Dom. 1649.* No printer's or bookseller's name appears on the title-page and there is nothing to indicate the name of the translator: circumstances which point to the need to issue so dangerous a book surreptitiously. After various brief preliminaries, including a summary of Turkish religion (translated from the French), comes the English version of the *Koran*, occupying 394 pages. Then, after a short biography of Mahomet, there follows 'A needful Caveat or Admonition for them who desire to know what use may be made of, or if there be danger in reading the Alcoran, by Alexander Ross.' [1] Ross begins his warning with these words:

> Good reader, the great Arabian impostor, now at last, after a thousand years, is, by way of France, arrived in England, and his Alcoran, or Gallimaufrey of Errors (a Brat as deformed as the Parent, and as full of Heresies as his scald Head was of scurf) hath learned to speak English.

[1] *The Alcoran of Mahomet*, pp.409f. Professor Hitti (*History of the Arabs*, p.126) says that Ross was himself the translator.

Such was the fashion in which the book which has exercised the minds, moved the hearts, and shaped the destinies of countless millions of human beings was introduced to the English public. Certain hints which follow confirm the suspicion aroused by the lack of imprint on the title-page, that there had been some question as to the propriety of licensing this translation for publication. Ross argues that it is no more dangerous to read the *Koran* than to read the writings of heretical Christian sects or to read books on palmistry, astrology, or necromancy. Such books are allowed publication; why not the *Koran*? It is not, he says, as though the *Koran* were beautiful and seductive as are the Christian Scriptures; but who would abandon a much loved mistress to seek the embraces of a baboon? The book is already accessible in French and Italian and has often been quoted and summarized in English; therefore a complete English text can do no harm. Moreover, it is needful to acquaint ourselves with evil in order that we may the better appreciate our own blessings.

> While they [the Moslems] heare the voyce of Satyres, Ostrages and Scrich-Owls, we hear the voice of the Turtle, and the Songs of Sion: . . . whilst they feed on husks with swine and drink the corrupted puddles of Mahomets inventions, we are fed with Angels food . . . and drink of the pure river of life.

There is, furthermore, gold in this dunghill (Ross concedes): Christians will find edification in the piety, devotion, and charity of Mohammedans which should make us blush for our own coldness and negligence. But the *Koran* is not for all men to read; it is not for ignorant, inconstant, or disaffected minds but for the pious and learned. Queasy stomachs must avoid food which to the strong will do no harm.[1]

The anonymous English translator (was he Ross himself?) has followed the French version with close fidelity; and the French is reasonably faithful to the literal sense of the original. But though there is no ground for suspecting any deliberate intentional falsification, there is an all-pervading vulgarizing

---

1 Ross returned to the subject of Mohammedanism in his ΠΑΝΣΕΒΙΑ: *or, A View of all Religions of the World*, 1653, pp.144f. Here he characterizes the *Koran* as 'Fables, Lies, Blasphemies, and a meer hodg-podge of fooleries and impieties.'

of the spirit and style of the book. This is due in part to a lack
of literary tact and skill and in part to congenital racial and
religious antipathy. The strange perversions of biblical stories
and characters [1] irritated and alienated Christian readers, who
ascribed to deliberate malice and calculated blasphemy what
was due to misunderstanding or ignorance. The soaring eloquence which moves Arabs to tears or to shouts of joy becomes
in French, and still more in English, tasteless extravagance
and bombast; the passages of homely wisdom and good counsel
seem merely tedious platitudes, especially when this pedestrian
version is set in contrast to the majestic language of the
Authorized Version of the Bible; the figurative style, natural
to the Semites, required for the transmission of something of
its beauty a literary art beyond the reach of Le Sieur du Ryer
and his English translator; mysteries which to the Moslems
have all the allurement of the sublime unknown become merely
puzzling and distracting; historical and biographical allusions
clear to the Faithful through the exegesis of a thousand years
seem but wearisome digressions. It is only fair to add that the
same strictures apply in large measure to the translation which
in the next century superseded this; for despite the great
learning of George Sale his version [2] fixed in the English mind
the notion that the *Koran* is a stupid, verbose, and extravagant
book. Nevertheless, the eighteenth century accomplished something towards a clearer understanding of its qualities, because
that age saw the development of a philosophical cosmopolitan-
ism that was willing to exert itself to understand the thoughts
and ideals of alien peoples and because with the appearance of
the Deists and later of the Unitarians there developed a bond
of sympathy, even though feeble, with the worshippers of Allah.

1 For example (to cite the most notorious instance), the identification of the Virgin
Mary with Miriam, the sister of Moses and Aaron, who are consequently the uncles
of Jesus (*Koran*, iii,34 and xix,28). But Mohammedan commentators explain away
the confusion.

2 *The Koran, commonly called the Alcoran of Mohammed. Translated into English from
the Original Arabic: with Explanatory Notes*, 1734. The most recent edition of Sale's
translation, with his famous 'Preliminary Discourse,' is that with an introduction
by Sir E.Denison Ross, 1921.

CHAPTER TEN

FESTIVITIES *ALLA TURCHESCA* AND *ALLA MORESCA*

I

THE use of oriental motives, dresses, and accessories in the dances, revels, and other forms of pageantry at the Tudor court does not, at any rate in earlier years, necessarily point to any concentrated interest in Mohammedan peoples, customs, and costumes or to any particular enthusiasm for the Levant, but rather, in the first place, was one result of a persistent search after picturesque and exotic effects, which, ranging widely, was bound from time to time to hit upon Levantine designs for apparel and Mohammedan themes for 'devices,' and, in the second place, was due to the vogue of Italian fashions in aristocratic England. Castiglione, commenting upon the infinite variety of courtiers' clothes, imitating the styles of foreign peoples, remarks: 'Neither want we of them also that will clothe themselves like Turkes.' [1] At a later date Anthony Munday observed in Rome that gentlemen during the carnival were wont to attire themselves 'lyke Turkes.' [2] So also Spenser, alluding not to garb but to bearing, says that a deportment 'alla Turchesca,' dignified, disdainful, and with lofty looks, is characteristic of 'newfangledness.' [3] Of the Masque we know that, in the oft-quoted phrase, it was performed 'after the manner of Italy'; and the pervasive influence of Italian spectacles upon various forms of English pageantry has been demonstrated by various investigators. [4] It seems probable, therefore, that the emphasis which Florentine designers of pageants put upon Levantine elements had an influence upon similar, though

1 *The Book of the Courtier*, translated by Sir Thomas Hoby, 1561, Book ii.
2 *The English Romayne Lyfe*, ed. G.B.Harrison, p.95.
3 *Mother Hubberds Tale*, ll.675f.
4 See especially Enid Welsford, *The Court Masque*, Cambridge, 1927.

less elaborate and generally less appropriate, shows in England. There is extant an early fifteenth-century poem describing the celebration of the Feast of Saint John the Baptist at Florence.[1] In the procession on this occasion women wore clasps whose devices were derived almost exclusively from the oriental bestiaries, and there were also to be seen 'Teste di Saracini che parean vivi'—the very device which was to be used as an inn-sign and house-sign in Tudor England. Some of the *Sacre Rappresentazioni* contain motives or material of an oriental kind;[2] but over these we need not linger nor over the problem of the presence of eastern motives in Italian painting,[3] for another sort of orientalism at Florence has a closer connection with our subject. The jousts, tournaments, processions, *trionfi*, and other festivities sometimes have a more or less eastern colouring and magnificently anticipate their somewhat pale reflections in the court revels of Henry VIII and his successors. Thus, so early as 1406 there was held in the Piazza Santa Croce a tournament in which the combatants were garbed as Saracens, and though this was obviously inspired by traditions of the Crusades, an awareness of the Turkish threat in Asia Minor whose shadow was beginning to fall over Europe must have sharpened interest in the spectacle. More important is the direct historical link with the Levant when in 1439 there met at Florence representatives of East and West to consider the question of the reunion of the Latin and Greek Churches. Contemporaries record the keen curiosity of the Florentines who saw in their midst the Emperor John Palaeologus and a Russian bishop, Jacobites and Mongols (of one of whom Pisanello made a sketch), Armenians and Ethiopians, and envoys from Prester John. (These last were probably Coptic Christians.) Again in 1454, after the fall of Constantinople, Florentines, to whose city refugees flocked, had an opportunity to see Levantines in the flesh. The annual Feast of Saint John the Baptist was conspicuously orientalized in this year, for the Prophets of the Old Testament who rode in

---

1 *Le Feste di San Giovanni Battista in Firenze*, ed. D'Ancona, Pisa, 1882.
2 D'Ancona, *Origini del Teatro Italiano*, i,574f.; Soulier, *Les Influences orientales dans la Peinture toscane*, Paris, 1924, p.307.
3 Soulier, op.cit., pp.158f. See also F.Gilles de la Tourette, *L'Orient et les Peintres de Venise*, Paris, 1923.

procession wore turbans and there were many other participants in eastern costumes. Such garments reappear in later
festivities, as when at the wedding of Lorenzo the Magnificent
in 1469 the bridegroom wore at a jousting a coiffure *alla Turchesca*.[1] The *Canti Carnascialeschi*—descriptive commentaries
upon the allegorical *trionfi* drawn in chariots through the streets
of the city—contain some evidence as to the stimulus which the
Orient gave to the Florentine imagination; there is a 'Song of
Levantines,' a 'Song of a Moor of Granada,' and a *Canto di
mercanti tornati in Firenze richi* from the East. Florence entertained actual authentic Turks in 1483 and again in 1487 (a
hundred years and more before a *Cha'usch* was seen in England)
when ambassadors of the Sultan Bajazet II arrived and offered
gifts to the Grand Duke. No records of similar festivities are
extant in the archives of Siena, but the presence of oriental
motives in Sienese painting makes it likely that there was an
abundant orientalism in the pageantry of that city. Venice had
special reasons and unrivalled opportunities to observe Levantines close at hand. Memorials of the influence survive not only
in paintings of great splendour but in some records of entertainments. Thus, in 1498 certain merchants organized a *momaria*
or masquerade in which many of the participants were dressed
as Moors with blackened faces. Again, in 1526 there was a
'most beautiful *momaria*' in the courtyard of the Ducal Palace
when the Doge and the Council of Ten witnessed a dance performed by twelve people *vestidi da Sarasini*.[2]

The earliest surviving record of this kind of display in England is of a banquet held on Shrove-Sunday 1510, in the Parliament Chamber at Westminster, when King Henry VIII, 'with
the Erle of Essex, came in appareled after Turkey fasshion, in
long robes of Bawdkin, powdered with gold, hattes on their
heddes of Crimosyn Velvet, with great rolles of Gold, girded
with two swordes called Cimeteries.' At this banquet two ladies
had their heads 'rouled in pleasauntes and typpers, like the
Egipcians' and their faces, necks, arms, and hands were covered with fine black 'pleasaunce' 'so that the same ladies

1 This *giostra* is described in a poem by Luigi Pulci, 1572; ed. Carocci, Bologna, 1899.
2 Molmenti, *La Storia di Venezia nella Vita Privata*, 1925, ii,399f.

seemed to be nygros or blacke Mores.' [1] What circumstances on this occasion rendered these comparatively modest efforts to achieve an oriental colouring appropriate we do not know; but that to don these particular fancy costumes was a novelty may be inferred from the chronicler.

The fashion, once introduced, reappeared from time to time. The surviving accounts and inventories of the Office of the Revels during the last three Tudor reigns give us some tantalizing glimpses of Turkish and Moorish masques. At Shrovetide in 1548 there was a 'Masque of Young Moors' in which King Edward VI took part. Among the charges for that entertainment are sums for black leather gloves for the torchbearers, 'nether stockes of lether black for mores' (evidently tights or fleshings), timber from which were made darts for the Moors, 'Belles to hange at the skyrtes of the mores garments,' and so forth.[2] At the Christmas festivities of 1552–3 the Lord of Misrule was bothered by the need to provide for 'one to plaie uppon a kettell drom with his boye and a nother drome with a fyffe whiche must be apparelled like turkes garmentes according to the patornes.' [3] Whether these exotic costumes for the musicians were procured does not appear in the record. Lists of 'maskyng garments' afford some faint notion of the gorgeousness of these royal entertainments: 'hedpeces of sarcenet' of various colours 'turkes ffassyon,' 'cootes for turkes of clothe of golde,' and the like. One list is of 'olde garments for turkes' which were no longer 'servisable.' [4] Another list is of 'Remnanttes and odde Stuff Remayenying in a cheest in the stoorhouse to be Cutt and made into garmentts from tyem to tyeme at the masters Commaundement.' Among these oddments was 'cloth of golde Crymsyn Tyssewe' which might be used for 'capes for turckes,' and purple velvet 'strypped with silver' from which 'buttons to the Turckes' could be fashioned, and striped lawn of orange colour with white silk which was suit-

1 Hall's *Chronicle*, ed. 1809, pp.513f. There was a 'King of the Moors' in the Midsummer Pageant of 1522; see Robert Withington, *English Pageantry*, Cambridge, Mass., 1918, i,40. At the installation of the Mayor of Norwich in 1556 there were in the pageant several figures of naked Moors (ibid., ii,16).
2 A.Feuillerat, *Documents relating to the Revels at Court in the Time of King Edward VI and Queen Mary*, pp.26,29f.,33.
3 Ibid., p.89.   4 Ibid., pp.11,13.

able for 'hedpecssys and turckes gyrthells.' [1] There is a memorandum of the loan of half a dozen Turkish costumes, 'upper
shorter garmentes,' and 'hedpeces' to an official of the Household [2]—perhaps for an entertainment at his own residence.

More details are available about a 'Masque of Turkish
Magistrates' which was designed by Nicholas Udall and performed at Shrovetide 1555, at the court of Queen Mary.[3] The
performers included eight magistrates, eight torchbearers,[4] sixteen 'men turkes maskers' and sixteen 'women maskers god-
desses huntresses.' The juxtaposition of the oriental and the
classical, Turks dancing with divinities, is characteristic. This
masque must have been a gorgeous affair. The neckcloths,
girdles, headpieces, and tassels worn by the men were of red
and gold sarcenet. The 'Karver or propertie maker' supplied
'viii fawchons'—imitation swords probably of wood—for the
magistrates; and it was also his task to make 'hedpeces of
Asshen hoopewood in queynte and strange fasson'—evidently
for turbans so huge that some sort of framework was required
to support them.[5] In the same list there are buskins, scabbards,
'turky bowes,' 'turky quevers of arrowes,' and other costumes
and properties, and quantities of rich and gaudy stuffs.

The first revels of an oriental cast in the reign of Queen
Elizabeth was a 'Masque of Moors' performed in 1560.[6] Of

---

1 Ibid., pp.190f.
2 Ibid., p.251.
3 Ibid., pp.172f. and compare pp.181f.
4 The entry reads 'vi Turkes magistrates with vi turkes Archers their torcheberers,'
but 'vi' seems to be a slip of the pen for 'viii,' for eight falchions are presently provided for the magistrates and eight for the torchbearers and the number eight
accords better with the sixteen male and female dancers than six would have done.
5 Compare the enormous turbans depicted in some Italian paintings of the period.
Actual turbans, equally huge, may be seen in the military museum at Constantinople.
See the *O.E.D.*, *sub* 'turban,' for an illuminating series of quotations illustrating the
various early forms of the word.
6 A.Feuillerat, *Documents relating to the Office of the Revels in the Time of Queen Elizabeth*, pp.20,26. G.M.Sibley, *The Lost Plays and Masques*, p.194, catalogues a 'Masque
of Turks' performed at court in 1559; but the record of that date (Feuillerat, op.cit.,
p.19) is only of certain cloths and 'hed peces' which had been used for various purposes, including a 'Maske of Turkes' of unspecified date. As these were worn and
ruined by damp and no longer serviceable, the masque may have been performed
some years earlier. This same list mentions some white velvet for 'Morisshe ffryers'
and some wallets to be carried by palmers. Another list of the same year (1559–60)
contains such items as 'gounes' for Turks, 'corled hed Sculles' for Moors, and 'hedpeces of crimsen sattan whiche did serve for the ffryers that were torchberers to the
Moores' (ibid., pp.39f.).

this we have no details. The Levantine colouring of the revels ·
of the season of 1571–2 was probably suggested by the desire to
celebrate the victory of Lepanto and patterned after the
elaborate Venetian celebrations of that triumph.[1] The accounts
for this season show expenditures for 'Turkes vizards,' 'one
Turky Bowe and iii arrowes,' 'Bumbast to stuf Rowles for the
Turkes heades,' 'yolow garding Imployed on the mores heades,'
and so forth.[2] In 1579 charges were recorded for 'the mores
maske that should have served on Shrovetuesday'; apparently
this was not presented.[3] During the Christmas revels of 1584–5
there appeared among those who performed 'dyvers feates of
Actyvytie' two people clad in 'sutes of canvas' and described
as 'Ianes.'[4] The meaning of the word is obscure. Up to this
time no English traveller had brought home any report of the
Jains of India; consequently Professor Feuillerat's suggestion
that the word may be an abbreviation for Janissaries is perhaps
the solution.

Following a chronological order and filling the wide gap before we meet with other orientalized festivities in London, we
may now glance at the record of the celebration of the baptism
of Prince Henry, the son of James VI, at Edinburgh in 1594.[5]
Among the events on this occasion was an 'action' in 'the valey
neare the castle' in which three Christians, three Turks, and
three Amazons took part. Originally it was intended to include
also three Moors, but they were omitted because it was uncertain whether the gentlemen designated for these parts would be
present. King James himself was one of the Christian knights.
The Turks were enacted by noblemen 'very gorgeously attired.' The Amazons likewise were played by men, one of them
being the Abbot of Holyrood-house (Lord Robert Stewart). Devices were carried by pages, one of those assigned to the Turks
being 'the moone farre opposite the sunne.' The action con-

1 See pp.125–6, above.
2 Feuillerat, op.cit., p.144 and the accounts compiled in June 1572, p.158.
3 Sir Edmund Chambers, *The Elizabethan Stage*, iv,96, reads this entry as 'Morris
Mask.'
4 Feuillerat, op.cit., p.365.
5 *A true reportarie of the baptisme of Frederick Henry, Prince of Scotland*, Edinburgh,
n.d., (1594?); new edition, London, 1603; reprinted in John Nichols, *Progresses . . .
of Queen Elizabeth*, 1823, iii,353f. See also Withington, op.cit., i,218.

sisted of the ever-popular contest of running at the ring. The appropriateness of the Levantine colour of the day's festivities becomes apparent when we remember that James had written a narrative poem on the battle of Lepanto.

James took with him to London his liking for oriental festivities. At one of the Christmas revels at court early in his reign Queen Anne and some of the noblest ladies blackened their faces and arms so as to resemble Ethiopians. But Sir Dudley Carleton, who disapproved of those goings-on, thought that they looked like 'a troop of lean-cheek'd Moors.' [1]

We have next to note that in Thomas Campion's *Maske* at the marriage of the Earl of Somerset in 1613 there were personifications of the Four Parts of the Earth. Asia wore 'a Persian Ladie's habit, with a crowne on her head' and Africa appeared 'like a Queene of the Moores with a crown.' [2] The point of interest about these brief descriptions is that the costumes worn are closely analogous to those worn by allegorical figures representing the continents in contemporary engravings. [3]

Of the brilliant masques at court during the reign of Charles I only two fall within our survey. Both are by Sir William Davenant. In *The Triumphs of the Prince d'Amour*, 1635, some of the Venetian courtesans appear 'in a Turkish dress.' [4] This is nothing more than picturesque exoticism of small importance. *The Temple of Love*, produced in the preceding year, is much richer in oriental costumes and motives. The setting was designed by Inigo Jones who wrote the description of it. On the stage was

> an ornament of a new invention agreeable to the subject, consisting of Indian trophies: on the one side, upon a basement a naked Indian

---

1 *Winwood Memorials*, ii,44.
2 *The Description of a Masque*, 1614; Campion, *Works*, ed. Percival Vivian, Oxford, 1909, p.152; Nichols, *Progresses . . . of King James I*, 1828, ii,707f. In Spenser's description of the marriage of the rivers (*The Faerie Queene*, IV,xi,28) the Thames wears a diadem 'with hundred turrets, like a Turribant' (that is, a tulibant or turban).
3 See p.234, note 5, above.
4 Davenant, *Dramatic Works*, ed. Maidment and Logan, Edinburgh, 1872, i,334. Davenant's not very scintillating fancy occasionally plays elsewhere with oriental imagery. Thus we have the simile: 'Sneake through a tavern with Remorse, as we had read the Alcoran' (*The Wits*, I,i) and 'As many night-caps as would make sick Mahomet a turban for the winter' (ibid., II,i) which is sadly pointless since Mohammedans wear turbans winter or summer, sick or well.

on a whitish elephant, his legs shortening towards the neck of the
beast, his tire and bases of several coloured feathers, representing
the Indian monarchy: On the other side, an Asiatique in the habit of
an Indian borderer, riding on a camel; his turban and coat differing
from that of the Turks, figured for the Asian monarchy: over these
hung shield-like compartments. In that over the Indian was
painted a sun rising, and in the other a half moon In this over the
Indian lay the figure of an old man, with long white hair and beard,
representing the flood Tigris; on his head a wreath of canes and
sedge, and leaning upon a great urn, out of which run water; by
him, in an extravagant posture, stood a Tiger. At the other end of
this freeze lay another naked man, representing Meander, the
famous river of Asia, who likewise had a silver urn, and by him lay a
unicorn.[1]

The masque gently satirizes the current vogue of so-called
Platonic love and develops at the close into a triumph of chaste
love. Among those who took part in it were nine young noblemen and gentlemen representing Persian youths. Their costumes were sea-green embroidered coats with wide elbow-length
sleeves and close-fitting under-sleeves of white satin; short
skirts; and 'Persian turbans silver'd underneath and wound
about with white cypress, and one fall of a white feather.' A
Persian Page, 'leaping in,' announces that he is 'a brisk Ambassador from Persian Princes' whose beauty and amorous
disposition he describes. These Princes make their entry and
perform a dance; and then the scene changes to an Indian landscape by the sea where the action proceeds to its conclusion.

II

A NOTABLY picturesque sort of entertainment, so sensational,
elaborate, and costly as to be suitable only for regal occasions
and the royal purse, was the 'Water-Fight' or 'Sea-Fight' on
the Thames. This kind of pageantry, the naumachia, was a
development from the stately processions in barges from the
City to Westminster or Greenwich of which various descriptions have come down to us from Tudor times. It was influenced

---

1 Davenant, *Dramatic Works*, i,281f.

also by motives drawn from the allegorical 'triumphs' and 'devices' staged and drawn on chariots on land. Though descriptions of simpler forms of water-jousts survive from the reign of Henry VIII, Water-Fights seem to have been characteristic of Jacobean rather than of Elizabethan London. Thus, in May and June 1610, the citizens of London celebrated the entry of Henry Prince of Wales into the city with a spectacle on the river which must have been magnificent. One of the events was a Water-Fight. The reader of the following contemporary description must bear in mind the appropriateness of this superb show at a time when the depredations of 'Turkish'—that is, Moorish—pirates were at their height. This is what the citizens witnessed as they crowded to points of vantage along the banks of the Thames:

A Turkish pirate prowling on the seas, to maintaine a Turkish castle (for so their armes and streamers described them both to be) by his spoyle and rapine of merchants and other passengers, sculking abroade to finde a bootie, he descried two merchant's shippes, the one whereof bearing to winde somewhat before her fellowe, made the pirate wafte her to strike sayle and come in, which the merchant either not regarding or no way fearing, rode still boldely on. The pirate, with drawen weapons and other menaces, wafts her againe to vayle her bonnet; but, the merchant answered againe, encouraged therto by her fellowe merchant, who by this time was come neere her, and spake in like language with her to the pirate. When he perceived his hope defeated and this bold resistance returned, he sent shot upon shot very fiercely, wherto they replyed as resolvedly; so that betweene them grewe a verie fierce and dangerous fight. Wherein the merchants waxing to be somewhat distrassed (by reason that the castle likewise often played upon them) two men of warre happening then to be neere, made in to helpe and releeve their hard detriment. And now the fighte grewe on all sides to be fierce indeed, the castle assisting the pirates very hotly, and the other withstanding bravely and couragiously; divers men appearing on either side to be slayne and hurlled over into the sea, as in such adventures it often comes to passe, where such sharpe assaultes are used indeed. In conclusion, the merchants and men of warre, after a long and well-fought skirmish, prooved too strong for the pirate, they spoylde bothe him and blewe up the castle, ending the whole batterie with verie rare and admirable fire-workes, as also a worthie peale of chambers.[1]

Even more elaborately realistic was the naumachia of 1613 which was one of the 'Fire and Water Triumphs' manifesting England's joy at the marriage of the Princess Elizabeth to Frederick Count Palatine. Of this we have a description, far too long to quote entire, from the pen of John Taylor the Water-Poet.[2] No less than thirty-eight vessels were engaged in this mimic battle. Lists or bounds were defined within which, to obviate confusion, 'boats and wherries and other perturbatious multitudes' were not permitted to intrude. An artificially contrived haven was supposed to belong to a 'Turkish or Barbarian Castle of Tunis, Algiers, or some other Mahometan fortification' from which Turkish galleys sallied forth and into which they retired. A beacon fired by the 'Turks' warned the castle of the Christian attack. The engagement between the fleets lacked little of absolute verisimilitude 'but that which was fit to be wanting, which was ships sunk and torne in pieces, men groning, rent and dismembered.' There were thunders of artillery, numberless volleys of muskets, and an 'imaginary hurley-burley'; and in the end a retreat was sounded on both sides with 'all victors, all triumphers.' In the *Epithalamia* composed by George Wither for this royal marriage there is an allusion to the god Mars who showed his fury in 'a bloudlesse fight' which a marginal gloss explains as referring to 'the Seafight, and taking of the Castle on the water, which was most artificially performed.' [3]

1 *Londons Love to the Royal Prince Henry, Meeting Him on the River Thames, at His Returne from Richmonde, with a Worthie Fleete of her Cittizens, on Thursday, the last of May, 1610. With a briefe Reporte of the Water-Fight and the Fire-Works,* 1610; reprinted in Nichols, *Progresses . . . of King James I,* ii,315f., especially p.323. Because of 'violent storms of rayne or other appointment of his Majestie' the Water-Fight had to be postponed till the following Wednesday. See also Withington, op.cit., i,232.
2 *Heaven's Blessing and Earth's Joy; or, a True Relation of the Supposed Sea-Fights and Fire-Works as were accomplished before the Royall Celebration of the All-beloved Marriage of the Two Peerlesse Paragons of Christendome, Fredericke and Elizabeth,* 1613; reprinted in Nichols, op.cit., ii,527f. and in Taylor, *Works,* Spenser Society, iv,115f. There is another account of this naumachia in an anonymous tract *The Magnificent Marriage,* 1613; reprinted in Nichols, op.cit., ii,539f.
3 Wither, *Poems,* Spenser Society, p.462.

A similar show but on a less ambitious scale was enacted on the river Severn on the occasion of Queen Anne's visit to Bristol in June of the same year. A single Christian ship was engaged with two Turkish galleys and came off triumphant. After the mock battle 'some of the Turks remained prisoners and were presented to her Majesty, who laughingly said, that they were not only like Turks by their apparell, but by their countenances.' It was estimated that some thirty thousand people witnessed this spectacle.[1] A Bristol poet, one Robert Naile, in an effusion on the Queen's visit, described the entertainment with gusto:

> This Water-fight (by fame divulg'd) full many a thousand drew,
> Both farre and neere for to behold and take a perfect view.

These cursed Turks, Naile goes on, have captured many Christian merchantmen and condemned them to endless bondage as galley-slaves.

> Such deadly rancour stings
> Their cankered hearts, with pride puft up, inflamed with rage and ire,
> That nothing can aswage their wrath, nor quench this burning fire,
> But Christian bloud by their curst hands is poured upon the ground.

The discords of Christendom have given power to the Ottoman whose 'moony standards' are flaunted so insolently; and the poet urges Christian kings to join hearts and hands 'to chase this off-scumme Scithian brood' from Europe. These sentiments, familiar to us, come with particular appropriateness from a writer whose city had suffered severely from acts of piracy. Robert Naile proceeds to describe the 'Water-combat' at portentous length and with violent rhetoric; but we need not quote further specimens of his verses.[2]

---

1 From a description in a contemporary letter quoted by Nichols, op.cit., ii,646f.
2 *A Relation of the . . . royall Entertainment given to . . . Queen Anne at the Renowned Citie of Bristol, . . . in the moneth of June past, 1613. Together with the Oration, Gifts, Triumphs, Water-Combats, and other Shewes there made,* 1613; reprinted in Nichols, op.cit., ii,648f., especially 659f.

III

THE Lord Mayors' Shows, the annual pageants when the new Lord Mayor was inducted into office, sometimes contained Levantine elements.[1]

George Peele devised and wrote the pageant for 1585. The speaker who delivered the introductory address and acted as interpreter of the emblems was 'apparelled like a Moor' and described himself as coming from 'the parching zone' to offer homage to the Lord Mayor.[2] The appropriateness of this exotic figure lay in part in the fact, not indicated in Peele's text but of course well known to the spectators, that through the mediation of the English agent at Constantinople trade with the Barbary States had been recently put upon a somewhat securer basis of agreement than hitherto, and in part in the suggestive symbolism of the Moor's dark skin, since the new Lord Mayor belonged to the Company of Skinners.

More to our purpose and of richer content is Thomas Middleton's *The Triumphs of Truth*, 1613.[3] The new Lord Mayor was a member of the Company of Grocers whose sphere of trade had been much enlarged by the establishment of the East India Company. One of the principal spectacles was a group of five artificial islands 'artfully garnished with all manner of Indian fruit-trees, drugs, spiceries, and the like; the middle island with a fair castle especially beautiful.' The new Mayor and the members of the Corporation went to the river's edge in civic procession to enjoy the sight of these artificial islands as they lay on the 'crystal bosom' of the Thames. Later these islands were removed to a position in Paul's Churchyard. It is not indicated how this shift from water to land was managed; probably the islands were wheeled 'floats' which could be tugged ashore and then trundled to Saint Paul's. When they had been properly grouped, suddenly towards them came a

1 See in general F.W.Fairholt, *Lord Mayors' Pageants*, Percy Society, Part i, 1843; Withington, op.cit., ii, chapter vi.
2 *The Device of the Pageant borne before Woolstone Dixi, Lord Maior of the Citie of London. An. 1585. October 29.*, 1585; Peele's *Works*, ed. Bullen, i,349f.
3 *The Triumphs of Truth. A Solemnity unparalleld for Cost, Art, and Magnificence*, 1613; reprinted in Nichols, op.cit., ii,679f. and in Middleton's *Works*, ed. Bullen, vii,227f. See also Withington, op.cit., ii,33f. *

strange ship (on a pageant or wagon, probably pushed by men underneath it, for horses tugging it would have destroyed the effect) having neither sailors nor pilot but with the words on a white banner: '*Veritate gobernor*, I am steered by Truth.' Within this little vessel [1] were 'a king of the Moors, his queen, and two attendants, of their own colour.' When it had come to rest near the cathedral the King of the Moors recited the following address:

> I see amazement set upon the faces
> Of these white people, wonderings and strange gazes;
> Is it at me? does my complexion draw
> So many Christian eyes, that never saw
> A king so black before? . . .
>   Many wild thoughts may rise . . .
> At my so strange arrival in a land
> Where true religion and her temple stand;
> I being a Moor, then, in opinion's lightness,
> As far from sanctity as my face from whiteness. . .
> However darkness dwells upon my face,
> Truth in my soul sets up the light of grace;
> And though, in days of error, I did run
> To give all adoration to the sun,
> The moon and stars, nay, creatures base and poor,
> Now only their Creator I adore.
> My queen and people all, at one time won
> By the religious conversation
> Of English merchants, factors, travellers . . .
> We all were brought to the true Christian faith:
> Such benefit in good example dwells,
> It oft hath power to covert infidels.

The speech ended, the Moors all bow their bodies to the temple of Saint Paul. Whereupon the allegorical figure of Error speaks from her chariot, expressing her anger and scorn that her 'sweet fac'd devils' have forsaken her. She attempts

1 The phrase 'this little vessel' is Middleton's. The Merchant Tailors' Company possessed an emblematic vessel of a size to take part in water-shows which when not so used was kept hung in the hall of the Company. This ship is introduced into Webster's *Monuments of Honour* (*Works*, ed. Lucas, iii,335). The ship used in Middleton's pageant was a similar large-scale model or perhaps the identical one borrowed from the Tailors by the Grocers for the occasion. On ships in civic pageantry see Withington, op.cit., i,12 and 113; ii,48.

by charms to win them back; but in the end Truth, aided by her father Time, triumphs; and the show terminates with the chariot of Error glowing in the embers after the fireworks made by Master Humphrey Nichols have been set off. This show, which is gracefully written, has more point and substance than most such pageants.[1]

In 1617 the civic authorities again turned to Middleton to devise and write their pageant. The 'first invention' in *The Triumphs of Honour and Industry*[2] exhibits a company of Indians 'attired according to the true nature of their country, seeming for the most part naked.' They are at work on an island, planting nutmegs, gathering fruits, 'making up bags of pepper.' Having thus suggested the profits of the spice-trade, these natives then 'dance about the trees, both to give content to themselves and the spectators.' After the dance 'a rich personage presenting India, the seat of merchandise' appears in 'an illustrious chariot' attended by personifications of Traffic and Industry. A 'Pageant of Several Nations' passes before India. A Frenchman and a Spaniard make pretty speeches, each in his own language; but the representatives of the other nations, among whom is a Turk (doubtless recognizable by his costume), are silent. The remainder of the show centres in a Castle of Fame—the fame of the Company of Grocers of which the new Lord Mayor was a member.

The pageant of 1624 was John Webster's *Monuments of Honour*.[3] Though not very well designed, this is unusually full of suggestions of the East: heroes of the wars against the Turks; Turks and Moors; pilgrims to Jerusalem and knights guarding the way hither; the Agnus Dei which pilgrims received there; a camel, a dromedary, a unicorn, and an

---

1 'A King of the Moores, gallantly mounted on a Golden Leopard' appears in the pageant of 1616, Anthony Munday's *Chrysanaleia*; reprinted in Nichols, op.cit., iii,195f. The chariot in the pageant at the end of *The Triumph of Honour* (by Beaumont or Field) is drawn by two Moors.
2 *The Tryumphs of Honor and Industry. A Solemnity performed through the City*, 1617; Middleton's *Works*, ed. Bullen, vii,291f. See further Withington, op.cit., ii,37, and references there given. Compare the Indians who, representing riches, attend on Plutus in Fletcher's *The Triumph of Time*, Scene iii.
3 *Monuments of Honour. Derived from Remarkable Antiquity*, 1624; Webster's *Works*, ed. Lucas, iii,311f.

elephant. The Lord Mayor of that year belonged to the Company of Merchant Tailors who for centuries had been 'Brethren of the Fraternity of St. John Baptist' [1] and had been associated till its demolition with the ancient London church of Saint John of Jerusalem. Since the Knights of Saint John 'were instituted to secure the way for Pilgrimes in the desert,' Webster explains that he thought it appropriate to present in his pageant 'two of the Worthiest Brothers of this Society,' namely Amadeus V of Savoy 'by whose ayde Rhodes was recovered from the Turkes' (a purely mythical exploit) and Jean de la Valette 'who defended Malta from the Turkes invasion, and expeld them from that impregnable Key to Christendome.' These historical figures are associated in characteristically baroque fashion with symbolic animals and emblematic architecture. The lion and the camel being proper to the arms of the Company of Merchant Tailors, they appear in the pageant: 'On the Camell rides a Turke, such as use to Travaile with Caravans, and [on] the Lyon a Moore or wild Numidian.' An 'Artificiall Rocke' supports four 'Piramids, which are Monuments for the Dead.' (The appropriateness of this memorial to Henry Prince of Wales is not clear, for the Prince had been dead many years.) Of the several Virtues with which this memorial is allegorically adorned we may note a dromedary ('shewing [the Prince's] speed and alacrety in gratifying his Followers'), a unicorn close by Chastity, and an elephant, 'the strongest Beast, but most observant to man of any Creature,' representing Obedience.

The Lord Mayor of 1638 was a member of the Company of Drapers, had been governor of the East India Company, and as a member of the Levant Company had important commercial connections with the Near East. Into *London's Gate to Piety*, the show written and devised by Thomas Heywood for his inauguration,[2] suitable allusions to these oriental

1 Ibid., ll.221f. Compare p.92 note 3, above.
2 *Porta pietatis, or The Port or Harbour of Piety*, 1638; Heywood's *Dramatic Works*, ed. Pearson, v,259f. (*London's Gate to Piety* is the running-title).—In this same year the Merchant Tailors' Company put on a 'fighting-show' in their hall in which Christians engaged with Saracens or Turks. The Saracens bore a banner with the crescent moon and 'a motto in the Arabian tongue and Characters.' In the end they

interests are introduced. In the printed record of the pageant Heywood displays with ingenuous pride the learning which could only be implied in the actual performance. The first spectacle introduced a shepherd as appropriate to the Company of Drapers; and 'because this worshipfull society tradeth in cloth,' Heywood afterwards wrote, 'it is pertinent that I should speake something of the sheepe.' He proceeds forthwith to inform his readers of the characteristics of oriental sheep. The second spectacle was of an Indian riding upon a rhinoceros, 'an Indian beast . . . for the rareness thereof more fit to beautifie a triumph.' The speech of the Indian is in praise of 'the dignity of Merchants' and contains the rather fine couplet:

> When others here at home securely sleepe,
> He ploughs the bosome of each unknowne deepe.

The third spectacle, of a ship, 'in that small modell figuring the greatest vessell,' is an emblem of Traffic which we have already met with in Middleton's and Webster's pageants.

The same ship reappeared the following year in Heywood's second pageant, *London's Peaceable Estate*.[1] Again the new Lord Mayor was a draper; he was governor or member of many commercial companies—a very important person. The pageant is accordingly of an elaborateness suitable to his eminence in the world of trade. 'The first Shew by water' represented the river Nile, in a chariot drawn by two 'weeping' crocodiles, and holding 'a seven-forked Scepter, alluding to the seven heads or as many Channells through which he runnes.'[2] Nilus recites a speech in which the 'seven heads' are interpreted as the Seven Liberal Arts, doubtless in allusion to the old belief that Egypt was the fountain-head of science. Into this speech is introduced the Spenserian notion of a union of rivers: Nilus

cried for quarter, were taken captive, and led about the hall triumphantly. See Withington, op.cit., i,237f.

[1] *Londini Status Pacatus: or, Londons Peaceable Estate*, 1639; Heywood's *Dramatic Works*, ed. Pearson, v,355f.

[2] Heywood seems to differentiate between the Nile's sources and its outlets and is uncertain whether the number seven applies to the one or the other. See p.84, note 1, above.

has formed 'an alliance with his brother Thames.' The whole conception is clumsily baroque. No better is the fourth 'Shew' in which Medea appears in a chariot drawn by two camels on each of which an Indian rides. Allusions to the story of the Golden Fleece were a convention when the Lord Mayor was a draper; they appear in pageants by Middleton and Munday.[1] Heywood's Medea delivers an address in which classical myth is oddly combined with information about the usefulness of sheep which keep many poor men at work 'by carding, spinning, weaving, fulling, shearing,' who else 'might starve for want of livelyhood.' Pointing to the beasts which draw her conveyance and addressing the Lord Mayor personally, she concludes:

> These Cammels though amongst us rarely seene,
> Yet frequent where your Lordship oft hath beene
> In your long Travells: may the world perswade
> The rich Commerce and noblenesse of your Trade.

It is just possible that live camels were employed in this pageant, for not many years earlier King James possessed a herd; but in general the exotic beasts in these pageants were not live animals but were artificially represented. 'Wee see the Pageants in Cheapside,' remarked John Selden, 'the Lyons and the Elephants, but we doe not see the men that carry them.' [2]

---

1 The Golden Fleece was in fact one of the most usual examples of the union of my-thology and trade-symbolism in civic pageantry; it appears as early as 1522. See Withington, op.cit., i,81 and 179; ii,36.
2 *Table Talk*, ed. Pollock, p.60. For surviving records of expenses for 'paynting of the beastes,' for payment of the porters, and so forth see Withington, op.cit., i,45.

CHAPTER ELEVEN

MOSLEMS ON THE LONDON STAGE

I

CHRISTENDOM, threatened by the ever-advancing Ottoman power, invested with glory and romance the figure of Timur the Tartar or Tamburlaine who had long since humbled the pride of the Turkish Sultan, Bajazet the First. Starting from Samarkand in the last years of the fourteenth century, the hosts of the Scythian conqueror had invaded Muscovy, over-run Mesopotamia, and pillaged Syria; and then, turning westward into Asia Minor, Tamburlaine had met and utterly defeated the Turkish army near Angora in 1402. Bajazet was taken prisoner and unable to endure the shame of his downfall died in captivity shortly afterwards. Subsequent legend, elaborated by Byzantine and Latin historians, magnified his humiliation, telling how Tamburlaine caused him to be exhibited in a cage,[1] fed him with crumbs from his table, and used him as a block from which to mount his horse or as a footstool to his throne, till driven to despair Bajazet dashed out his brains against his

---

1 Pope Pius II first gave currency to this story in western Europe in his *Asiae Europaeque Elegantissima descriptio*, 1534. Thereafter it became one of the most popular incidents in European accounts of the Scythian conqueror. Joseph von Hammer-Purgstall argued long ago (*Geschichte des Osmanischen Reiches*, Pest, 1827, i,317f.) that the legend owed its origin to a misunderstanding of the Turkish word 'kafes' which may mean either a litter or a cage. A typical Elizabethan account of the incident is in George Whetstone's *The English Myrror*, pp.78f. Donne has the simile 'Like Bajazet encag'd' (*The Calme*, p.33). Dryden likens a lover's heart to a bird in a cage: ''Tis a meer Bajazet; and if it be not let out . . . will beat out the brains against the Gates' (*An Evening's Love*, II). Tamburlaine's feeding of Bajazet under his table, a story which seems to have originated in Andrea Cambinus, *Libro dell' origine de' Turchi*, 1529, also became an indispensable part of the legend and occurs often in Elizabethan narratives. As late as Dryden we have:

> I'le cage thee, thou shalt be my Bajazet.
> I on no pavement but on thee will tread;
> And, when I mount, my foot shall know thy head

(2 *Conquest of Granada*, V)—an allusion which shows the long-continued popularity of a third part of the legend. See further Louis Wann, 'The Oriental in Elizabethan Drama,' *Modern Philology*, xii (January 1915), 176f., and Miss Ellis-Fermor's introduction to the *Arden* edition of *Tamburlaine*.

bars. More than two score chroniclers and biographers told and retold the story of Tamburlaine's triumph and Bajazet's shame.[1] 'Tamerlanes non homo sed ira Dei' became a figure at once awful and consoling, awful in his ruthless cruelty and ostentation and in the vast extent of his conquests, consoling because he had set an example to Christian Europe by his conquest and humiliation of the Great Turk. He had forced the Ottoman army to abandon the siege of Constantinople, thus leaving to statesmen of the Renaissance a demonstration of the practicability of bringing pressure from the East upon the Turkish rear. Western historians and moralists generally contemplate with satisfaction the downfall of the Sultan. Among poets Thomas Dekker stands quite alone in his sense of the pathos of his hapless situation. In the vision of exalted and debased kings which the goddess Fortune presents to Fortunatus one of the four ruined kings is Bajazet—

> Poor Bajazet, old Turkish Emperor
> And once the greatest monarch of the East.
> Fortune herself is sad to view thy fall,
> And grieves to see thee glad to lick up crumbs
> At the proud feet of that great Scythian swain,
> Fortune's best minion, warlike Tamburlaine:
> Yet must thou in a cage of iron be drawn
> In triumph at his heels, and there in grief
> Dash out thy brains.[2]

In this brief paraphrase we have the essential episodes in the history of the Sultan's downfall as presented in Marlowe's tragedy.

Of *Tamburlaine the Great* little will be said here because we have nothing to add to the large amount of erudition that has accumulated round the most famous of all English dramas upon oriental subjects. Lately the great play has been studied afresh by Miss U.M.Ellis-Fermor in the introduction to her edition in the *Arden* series of Marlowe's plays. She has passed in review

---

1 For these and for their contributions to Marlowe's drama see the discussion in Miss Ellis-Fermor's edition of *Tamburlaine*, Introduction, iv: 'Sources of the Play.'
2 *Old Fortunatus*, I,i. The third line of this passage in both the Pearson edition, 1873, and the *Mermaid* edition is 'Fortune herself is *said* to view thy fall'—obviously a misprint for 'sad.'

the problems, many of them intricate, connected with the early editions, the date of the play, the authorship (for it is not un-questionably ascribed to Marlowe in any contemporary record), the growth of the legend of Tamburlaine, the sources available to the dramatist and those among them that Marlowe certainly used, and the intellectual and spiritual affinity between the playwright and his protagonist. Concerning these fundamental problems it must suffice here to say that Marlowe's authorship is universally admitted; that the generally accepted date of composition is 1587–8 (though Marlowe's demonstrated use of a book not published till 1589 introduces a complication which may be resolved either by arguing that he was acquainted with the work in manuscript or else that he inserted the passage in question into his text at a date subsequent to that of the original composition); that the earliest extant edition is of 1590; that the first records of stage performances date from 1594 (though there is evidence that the play had been performed several years earlier); that of the abundant source-material there are very few books which we may be confident the dramatist used; and that in its power and pride and aspiring temper, its glorification of human achievements and poten-tialities, and in its boldly questioning spirit it is redolent of Marlowe's genius. To cite anew the documentary and biblio-graphical evidence upon which modern scholarship has based its conclusions or to quote illustrative passages and attempt a fresh appreciation of the drama would be a work of superueroga-tion. Miss Ellis-Fermor's introduction and commentary will serve the reader for all ordinary purposes and her references will guide him into the further recesses of scholarship.[1]

But pertinent to our inquiry are several particulars about the play. In a number of circumstances relative to the defeat and captivity of Bajazet Marlowe departs widely from history and legend. He places the conflict with the Turks in Tamburlaine's youth instead of his old age, thus magnifying his hero's achieve-

---

[1] See Appendices C,D, and E of the *Arden* edition. Miss Ellis-Fermor does not mention a ballad entitled *the storye of Tamburlayne the greate* entered on the *Stationers' Register* 6 November 1594 (Arber, ii,664). Of this nothing more seems to be known. The popularity of the theme is also shown by the translation by 'H.M.' of Jean du Bec's *Historie of the Great Emperour Tamerlane*, 1597.

ment, which is further enlarged by picturing the forces under his command as far inferior in numbers to Bajazet's. Prejudice against the Turks has, however, led him to portray the Sultan as insolently boastful before the battle and impotently raging when a prisoner. The greatness of Tamburlaine would have been enhanced, not lessened, had the dramatist conceived his principal opponent as worthy of his steel. For the sake of topical interest and to present more vividly the Turkish peril, Marlowe invents a mythical siege of Vienna, anticipating by more than a century the first historical siege of the city by the Ottomans. In repeated allusions to Mediterranean pirates and galley-slaves his thoughts are upon conditions in his own day rather than upon those of the beginning of the fifteenth century. More fundamental and in direct violation of the Byzantine authorities is his conception of Tamburlaine's thoughts on religion. The historians uniformly make him a devout Mohammedan, some going so far as to say that his long postponement of an attack upon Bajazet was due to reluctance to engage in warfare with a fellow-believer. But the Tamburlaine of Marlowe reflects the audaciously speculative mind of his creator, 'daring God out of heaven' (in Greene's words) and in the famous scene in which he causes 'the Turkish Alcaron and all the heaps of superstitious books' to be burnt, challenging Mahomet to come down and work a miracle.

> Thou art not worthy to be worshipped
> That suffers flames of fire to burn the writ
> Wherein the sum of thy religion rests . . .
> Well soldiers, Mahomet remains in hell;
> He cannot hear the voice of Tamburlaine:
> Seek out another godhead to adore;
> The God that sits in heaven, if any god,
> For he is God alone, and none but he.[1]

The fallen Sultan and his empress upbraid, in the manner of the medieval romances, the Prophet who has deserted them in their need; but they do not abjure their religion as does Tamburlaine in his triumph.

1 *2 Tamburlaine*, V,i,188f.

The situation of devotees chiding the god who has been unable or unwilling to grant them victory reappears in Robert Greene's *Alphonsus King of Arragon*, an imitation of *Tamburlaine* so impudently coarse and rude as to seem almost a burlesque.[1] It depicts the rise to world-power of the son of a deposed and poverty-stricken monarch. The first two acts are European in setting; not till the King of Naples, flying from Alphonsus, lands on Turkish soil, does the Islamic interest appear. The fugitive monarch and various allied sovereigns are received hospitably and with sympathy by the Emperor Amurack, who dispatches messengers to all the lands that owe him allegiance to gather an army with which to oppose Alphonsus. Through the agency of Medea, a sorceress, Amurack has a dream of his coming defeat; and denouncing the 'proud, injurious god, Mahound' whose vain, misleading prophecies have led him to this 'doleful case,' he declares that as soon as by the help of Jove he has escaped from the bondage which threatens him the altars of Mahomet shall be tumbled about the streets and the Turks shall abandon their sacrifices to him and become his mortal foes. Meanwhile he has already advised the King of Naples and his allies to betake themselves to

> the darksome grove,
> Where Mahomet, this many a hundred year,
> Hath prophesied unto our ancestors.[2]

There they are to consult 'God Mahomet.' According to the stage-direction, a Brazen Head is set up 'in the place behind the stage'—that is, at the back of the inner stage, overshadowed by the balcony. From this mysterious place, while flames come forth, Mahomet, speaking from the Head, announces that he will

> prophesy no more to Amurack,
> Since that his tongue is waxen now so free,
> As that it needs must chat and rail at me.

---

1 On the relation, or rather lack of relation, of this play to history see Greene's *Dramatic Works*, ed. J.C.Collins, i,75f.
2 *Alphonsus*, III,ii.

However, the god consents to give counsel to the assembled kings. They have as yet been too slack in action and must now hasten to attack Alphonsus, for if there is more delay both they and all their men 'must needs be sent down straight to Limboden.' [1] The kings are confident of victory because 'God Mahound' is on their side; but in the upshot they are routed by Alphonsus. When Amurack receives word of the allies' defeat he again chats and rails at Mahomet:

> Is this the honour which that cursed god
> Did prophesy should happen to them all? . . .
> Mahound should know, and that for certainty,
> That Turkish kings can brook no injury.[2]

It is an empty boast, for Alphonsus defeats Amurack, takes him prisoner, and marries his daughter Iphigenia. The goddess Venus blesses the nuptials. Such little interest as this play has for us is to be found rather in the belated survival of medieval conceptions of Mahomet as a divinity than in its debased imitation of *Tamburlaine*. We would willingly sacrifice it if by so doing we might have restored to us the next drama which is on our list of oriental plays.

Of the many Elizabethan plays that have not come down to us the loss of no other is more to be deplored than that on the life of the warrior-hero Giorgio Castriota, known as Scanderbeg. Castriota was born in 1403, the year after Tamburlaine's defeat of Bajazet I. He was the son of an Epirote lord and was taken as a hostage by Murad II when Epirus was invaded by the Turks in 1423. He became a Mohammedan and for twenty years was in military service to the Ottomans—a member of the 'warlike bands of Christians renied' of whom Marlowe wrote.[3] As a tribute to his martial prowess the Turks bestowed upon him the name and title of Iskander-Bey, that is Lord Alexander (with reference to the fame of Alexander the Great), which in Europe became corrupted into Scanderbeg. Through these many years of service to the Ottomans he concealed his resentment at the treatment of the subject populations to whom he

1 Ibid., IV,i.
2 Ibid., IV,iii.

3 *1 Tamburlaine*, III,i,9.

was allied by traditions and blood; but in 1443, when Janos Hunyadi defeated the Turks at Nish, Scanderbeg seized the opportunity, effected his escape, rallied the Albanian clans against his late masters, and proclaimed himself a Christian; and for nearly a quarter of a century thereafter maintained a guerilla warfare in the fastnesses of Albania, where he repeatedly defeated Turkish expeditions sent against him. In 1461 Sultan Mahomet I, the Conqueror of Constantinople, found it expedient to recognize him as Lord of Albania and Epirus. Scanderbeg died in 1467 and was buried at Alessio. His unworthy son sold Albania to Venice and Venice in turn sold it to the Turks. When the Janissaries entered Alessio, according to the famous story, they violated the tomb of the great warrior, not to wreak vengeance or to desecrate his memory, but that they might procure pieces of his bones to wear as amulets so as to get for themselves something of his resourcefulness and valour in battle.

> That Soldier Conquest doubted not,
> Who but one Splinter had of Castriot,
> And would assault ev'n death so strongly charmd
> And naked oppose rocks with this bone arm'd.[1]

The first considerable account of Scanderbeg to appear in English is that by Peter Ashton in his *Shorte treatise upon the Turkes Chronicles*, 1546.[2] More noteworthy is the anonymous biography which John Shute translated out of the Italian in 1562.[3] As a small specimen of Shute's somewhat pedestrian

---

1 Richard Lovelace, 'To the Genius of Mr. John Hall,' *Poems*, ed. C.H.Wilkinson, ii,173. Lithgow retells the story of the rifled tomb (*Rare Adventures*, pp.51f.). In the 'Epistle to the Whigs' prefixed to *The Medal* Dryden wrote of their admiration for the Earl of Shaftesbury: 'I believe, when he is dead, you will wear him in thumbrings, as the Turks did Scanderbeg, as if there were virtue in his bones.' Castriota remained for long famous in England. Nashe ranks him with Alexander, Caesar, and Frederick Barbarossa (*Lenten-Stuffe, Works*, iii,191). Sir William Temple ranks him among the seven chieftains in history who have deserved, without obtaining, a crown (*Essay on Heroic Virtue, Works*, iii,385).

2 Folio xxf. For contemporary biographies of Scanderbeg see Bury's bibliographical note to Gibbon, *Decline and Fall of the Roman Empire* (chapter 57), viii,156. Knolles's account (*Generall Historie of the Turkes*, ed. 1687, i,193f.,248f.) derives from various continental sources but chiefly from Marino Barletto (Barletius), *De Vitis et gestis Scanderbegi*.

3 *Two very notable Commentaries. The One of the Originall of the Turcks and Empire of the house of Ottomanno, written by Andrewe Cambine, and thother of the warres of the Turcke against George Scanderbeg . . . translated out of Italian into English by*

style may be quoted the narrative of the incident which made the Albanian hero even more celebrated after death than during his lifetime. The Turks

> soughte for the bodye of Scanderbeg and as sone as they had founde it, althoughe in his lyfe tyme they feared it, and also hated his name, yet being ded they worshypped it . . . Happie was he that coulde gete some pece of his bones, esteming it for a holly relique, and set it in golde or sylver, and hanged it aboute their neckes as thingis of great hollinesse, saying that thereby thei hoped to have alwaie victorie, which is a paganish superstition.[1]

The English translation, 1596, of Jacques de Lavardin's biography of Scanderbeg is much more ambitious in scope.[2] The translator's name is unknown. His book is a handsome well-printed folio of no less than 512 pages excluding the index. It contains a catalogue of about a score of continental authorities upon which it is based. The narrative is preceded by three commendatory sonnets one of which is by Edmund Spenser. Spenser declares that 'the scourge of Turkes and plague of infidels,' 'great both in name and great in power and might,' is 'matchable with the greatest' heroes of antiquity.[3] The translator has command of a grave and sententious style with formal characterizations, elaborate descriptions, rhetorical speeches, addresses, counsels and messages, and with digressions in which he extracts from history political lessons and moral warnings for western Europe. The characterization of Sultan Mahomet II is a favourable example of one of his modes, while his mastery of narrative is exhibited in his account of the

John Shute, 1562. The folios of this black-letter volume are numbered separately for the two commentaries. The two works had already been associated together; they form, for example, the second and third items in *Commentarii delle Cose de Turchi di Paulo Giovio et Andrea Gambini con gli Fatti et la Vita di Scanderbeg*, Venice, 1541.

1 *Two very notable Commentaries*, folio ii[r] (second numbering).— On the 'paganish superstition' see Sir James G.Frazer, *The Golden Bough*, viii,154.

2 *The Historie of George Castriot, Surnamed Scanderbeg, King of Albanie. Containing his famous actes, his noble deedes of Armes, and memorable victories against the Turkes, for the Faith of Christ. Comprised in twelve Bookes: By Jacques de Lavardin, Lord of Plessis Bourrot, a Nobleman of France. Newly translated out of French into English by Z.I.Gentleman*, 1596.—On 12 October 1593 there had been entered on the *Stationers' Register* a 'Historie de Georges Castriot . . . par Jacques Delavardin' (Arber, ii,638). Books to be translated were often registered before the translation was begun.

3 Spenser, *Poetical Works*, Globe edition, p.608.

siege and sack of Constantinople and in the episode of the pillaging of Scanderbeg's tomb.[1] The *Historie* affords ample material for a stately drama in which might be unfolded the story of Castriot's early years, his captivity, his widening renown as a warrior, his secret cherishing of designs to avenge himself upon the conquerors and oppressors of his fatherland, his escape, his battles with the Turks, the comparative serenity of his later years, his death, and his posthumous fame. The narrative is somewhat monotonous, perhaps, confused in its handling of political affairs, and repetitious in its battle-pieces; but alike in its subject and in its best pages it is undeniably impressive.

In July 1601, there was entered for E.Allde on the *Stationers' Register* 'The true historye of George Scanderbeg as yt was lately playd by the right honorable the Earle of Oxenforde his servantes.' [2] Nothing else is known of this drama but something has been surmised. That Marlowe was its author has been inferred on the slender evidence of a sonnet entitled 'The Writer's Postscript' in Gabriel Harvey's *New Letter of Notable Contents*, where occur these rhetorical and somewhat cryptic questions:

> Is that Gargantuan minde
> Conquerd, and left no Scanderbeg behinde? . . .
> Have you forgot the Scanderbegging wight? [3]

Whether or not there is an allusion to Marlowe here, these lines provide no adequate reason for attributing the lost play to him. In the first place, a 'Scanderbegging wight' may mean nothing more than a swashbuckling fellow.[4] Then, Harvey may not have been thinking of any play at all; the play, of which we

---

1 *Historie*, pp.254f.,314f.,496.
2 Arber, iii,187.
3 Harvey, *Works*, ed. Grosart, i,296. The inference is drawn by Fleay (*Biographical Chronicle of the English Drama*, ii,65) and Schelling (*Elizabethan Drama*, ii,606). Contrast Chambers, *The Elizabethan Stage*, iii,420; iv,400.
4 Compare 'Horson scander-bag rogue' (Jonson, *Every Man in His Humour*, I,iii,22); 'Skellum [that is, rascal] Skanderbag' (Dekker, *The Shoemaker's Holiday*, III,i, and compare *Satiromastix*, *Works*, ed. Pearson, i,233); Captain Squanderbeg in Shirley's *Honoria and Mammon*, IV,i; and contrast the use of the name as equivalent to a valiant fighter in Shirley's *The Gentleman of Venice*, III,i; *Works*, v,33. The name, sometimes with the connotation of ruffian, survived into the Restoration period and is used by Dryden and Otway, among others.

have a record dating only from 1601, may not have been in existence in 1593. Furthermore, the implication in the lines is that Marlowe (if Marlowe is indeed referred to) has *not* left a 'Scanderbeg behind.' All that can be said for the theory of Marlowe's authorship is that the subject was one to appeal to him if the mood in which *Tamburlaine* was composed endured (which is doubtful) beyond the time when that drama was completed. It would have been logical (but was Marlowe 'logical' in the choice of successive subjects?) to turn from the career of Tamburlaine, the conqueror of the Turk, to the career of Scanderbeg who held the Turk at bay. These mighty warriors who had triumphed over the Ottomans appealed on like grounds to the Elizabethan imagination. Even at a much later date we find them associated together in a speech by one of Thomas Randolph's characters: 'I will be the Scanderbeg of this company, the very Tamburlaine of this ragged route.' [1] If this lost play was indeed by Marlowe, we are at liberty to suppose that its success upon the stage may have encouraged translator and publisher to proceed with the heavy task of rendering Jacques de Lavardin's biography into English. If, on the other hand, the lost play was of later date, then it seems likely that the biography suggested its theme.

II

MAHOMET II was doubtless an important character in the lost play on Scanderbeg and probably portrayed as the villainous foil to the hero. Tales of the impulsive and ruthless cruelty of the Conqueror of Constantinople spread through Europe in the later fifteenth century and throughout the sixteenth. Christians who escaped from Ottoman territory helped to create this notoriety. As an example of such witnesses one may cite the case of Giovanni Maria Angiolello, a native of Vicenza, who was present at the capture of Negroponte from the Venetians by the Turks in 1472. For fifteen years he was a slave in Constantinople till, having made his escape, he returned to Vicenza

1 *Hey for Honesty*, III,i. Among the characters in *The Dumbe Knight* by Lewis Machin and Gervase Markham there is a Duke of Epire who is described as 'sprung from the line of famous Scanderbeg' (I,i; Hazlitt's Dodsley, x,118).

PLVS TIBI QVAM NVLLI INDVLSIT FORTVNA SED OLIM
HÆSIT IN EPIRO LAVS TVA FACTA MINOR.

SVLTAN MVCHEMET CHAN

EVROPAM ATQVE ASIAM HIC FELICIB OCCVPAT ARMIS
GRÆCVM ET BITHYNVM DVM RVIT IMPERIVM.

Sultan Mahomet the Conqueror

where he died sometime after 1524. He left some memoirs which Donado da Lezze inserted into his *Historia Turchesca*.[1] From him comes the famous story of how Mahomet, who prided himself upon his skill as a gardener, missed a melon from his patch and commanded that his Janissaries be ripped open one after another till the missing fruit was found. One poor wretch was slain in this manner 'e per la fortuna degl' altri, trovo costui haverlo mangiato et gli altri furono liberi.'[2] Since this version of the tale was not sufficiently bloodthirsty to conform to European prejudice against the Turks, the story was soon elaborated into that of the fourteen disemboweled pages which, with minor variations, continued to be told in Europe for hundreds of years.[3] At a suspiciously late date there appeared in print an analogous story to the effect that in order to demonstrate to Gentile Bellini that in depicting the decollation of Saint John the Baptist the artist had committed an error in his rendering of morbid anatomy Mahomet had the head of a slave struck off before the eyes of the horrified painter.[4] Such anecdotes as these, apocryphal though they doubtless are, illustrate Mahomet's reputation and help to explain why the story of Irene

1 *Historia Turchesca di Giovanni Maria Angiolello schiavo et altri schiavi dall' anno 1429 fin al 1513*, edited with an introduction by I.Ursu, Bucharest, 1909. The editor shows that the principal author of this compilation was Da Lezze. See further Dr. Ursu's article 'Uno sconosciuto storico veneziano, Da Lezze,' *Nuovi archivii veneziani*, xix (1910), 6f.

2 *Historia Turchesca*, p.122.

3 See, for example, Theodorus Spanduginus, *De Origine et Moribus Turcarum* or the Italian version of that widely read work: *I Commentarii di Theodoro Spandugino . . . dell' Origine de Principi Turchi, e de' costumi di quella natione*, Florence, 1551, pp.66f.; Francesco Sansovino, *Dell' Historia universale dell' origine et imperio de' Turchi*, Venice, n.d.,ii,folio 61ᵛ. Peter Ashton (*A Shorte Treatise upon the Turkes Chronicles*, 1546, folio xxxiiif.) says that 'upon very lyght occasion' Mahomet II would cause striplings to be put to death, as when he had some boys beheaded because they had drunk a little wine left upon a table, thinking that their master had done with it. Michel Baudier (and Edward Grimestone, his translator) connect the tale of the disemboweled pages with the Islamic law that sultans must perform some manual labour; Mahomet II raised cucumbers for the market; hence his rage when one of the vegetables was missing from his garden (*The History of the Imperiall Estate of the Grand Seigneurs*, 1635, chapter ix). Montaigne (*Essais*, ii,27) comments on the hideous cruelty of punishments inflicted by Mahomet II but he does not refer to the story of the pages.

4 This story first appeared in Carlo Ridolfi, *Le Meraviglie dell' arte, overo le vite de gl' illustri pittori veneti*, Venice, 1648, pp.40f. Compare L.Thuasne, *Gentile Bellini et Sultan Mohammed II*, Paris, 1888, pp.53f. The earliest English notice of Bellini's visit to Constantinople is in Ashton's *Shorte Treatise*, folio xxivᵛ, where it is said that Mahomet II sent to Venice 'for one Belin (which was a paynter . . .) to draw forth his own princelye portrature.'

the Greek slave, once it came into print, became widely popular.

Von Hammer-Purgstall suggested long ago [1] that the origin of the story of Irene may be detected in the story of Anna Erizzo, the daughter of Paolo Erizzo, the heroic Venetian defender of Negroponte against the Turks. Erizzo was among the prisoners taken to Constantinople. Contrary to the promise that his life would be spared, he was put to death. Legend had it that his beautiful daughter Anna rejected the dishonourable proposals of the Sultan, who thereupon slew her. The differences between this story and that of Irene are greater than the resemblances. Angiolello, who, as we have seen, was present at the fall of Negroponte and was a prisoner when Erizzo was put to death, says nothing about Anna. In Donado da Lezze's *Historia Turchesca* there is, however, an anecdote which may be merely a condensed and simplified version of the Irene-saga as subsequently developed but which, on the other hand, may have the value of independent testimony. It is to the effect that Mahomet was so much infatuated with one of the women of his seraglio that for her sake he neglected public affairs; but that, recognizing his error, he slew her and in that manner conquered the love he bore to that lady.[2] There is here no suggestion that the murdered woman was a prisoner or that she had been the unwilling mistress of the despot; there is no mention of the complaints of the soldiers against the voluptuous idleness of their chieftain; and the scene of the murder is the seraglio, not a banqueting-hall.

The tenth story of the first book of Matteo Bandello's *Novelle* is entitled 'Maometto Imperador de' Turchi crudelmente ammazza una sua donna.' [3] Bandello says that he heard the tale from a certain Francesco Appiano, a physician and philosopher. This may or may not be true; it makes very little difference. Whether he heard it or invented it, this classical form of the story won the credence of early historians,[4] influ-

---

1 *Geschichte des Osmanischen Reiches*, ii,99f. Von Hammer-Purgstall seems not to have known that the tale of Anna is itself apocryphal.

2 *Historia Turchesca*, pp.121f.

3 *La Prima Parte de le Novelle del Bandello*, Lucca, 1554, folio 76rf.; *Le Novelle*, ed. Gioachino Brognoligo, Bari, 1928, i,135f.

4 Martinus Crusius, *Turcograeciae Libri Octo*, Basle, 1584, pp.101f.: 'Excerpsi ex Gallica conversione partis operum Italicorum Bandeli'; Joachimus Camerarius,

enced all subsequent versions, and passed by way of Boiastuau
and Belleforest [1] into William Paynter's *Palace of Pleasure*,
1566, where it is told at great length. [2] Mahomet—'not the false
prophet,' the narrator is careful to note, but the Conqueror of
Constantinople—fell in love with a fair Greek named Hyerenee
and became 'a prey to his darling,' neglecting the affairs of
state so that the people murmured against him and sedition
would have arisen but for dread of his cruel rigour. For a long
while the 'bewitched' despot was 'overwhelmed in beastly
pleasure.' Among the courtiers was a frank and courteous gentleman, one Mustapha, who had been since boyhood the Sultan's intimate friend. He ventured to remonstrate with him and
in order to inspire emulation recited to him the heroic deeds of
his ancestors. [3] He warned Mahomet that the Pope was organizing against him a coalition of all Christendom; and if Europe
joined with the power of the Persian Sophy the Ottoman Empire
would be destroyed. Mustapha suggested that if the Sultan
could not overcome his infatuation he could take the lady with
him to the wars. Mahomet was at first angry with his friend but
presently saw the justice of his remonstrances. For a day and a
night he had his pleasure of the fair Greek; and then after a
banquet he commanded her to appear, decked and adorned;
and in the presence of his nobility he caught her by the hair
and with his falchion struck off her head. 'Now,' he exclaimed,
'ye know whether your Emperor is able to represse and bridle
his affections or not!' Thereafter, in order 'to discharge the
rest of his cholere,' he gathered his armies and besieged Bel-

De Rebus Turcicis, Frankfort, 1598, p.60 ('Non potui facere quin adjicerem id quod
in Italicis narrationibus et de hoc Mahometha traditum reperissem'); Richard
Knolles, *The Generall Historie of the Turkes*, 1603, pp.350f. (Knolles follows Paynter's
story in substance and often almost word for word.) The first person to cast discredit
on the story seems to have been Guillet de Saint George who wrote: 'Matheo Bandello, qui a ecrit cette Histoire, et de qui chacun l'a copiée, semble en avoir osté
toute creance par les fautes qu'il y a faites contre l'Ordre des Temps, et contre les
noms et le rang des personnes qu'il y introduit' (*Histoire du Regne de Mahomet II*,
Paris, 1681, i,299).
1 Pierre Boiastuau, *Histoires Tragiques Extraictes des Œuvres Italienne de Bandel et
mises en nostre langue Francoise*, Paris, 1559; Belleforest, *Histoires tragiques*, i,30.
2 *The Palace of Pleasure*, 1566, Book i, Novel 30.
3 The facts, though sketchily narrated, are pretty accurate, with one exception—the
amazing statement that Bajazet 'cut off the head of the great Tamburlain.' Bandello's narrative gave no warrant for such a perversion of history. Did Paynter
intend this as a humorous touch to indicate that the tactful counsellor resorted
even to lies to inspire martial courage in the amorous emperor?

grade, whence in a notable battle he was put to flight by John
Huniades.

From Paynter's story one can reconstruct fairly clearly the
course of a lost Elizabethan tragedy on the same subject: the
capture of Constantinople; the enslavement of Irene; the infatuation of Mahomet to the neglect of politics and war; the
discontent of his soldiers; the counsellor's respectful protests
to his master; the conflict of Love and Honour in Mahomet's
breast; the triumph of Honour over Love when at a banquet he
kills Irene; the departure of the Sultan for the wars. The central
motive—the conflict of Love and Honour—is found in the
anonymous play of *Edward III* where the King gives over the
pursuit of the Countess of Salisbury and goes off to war, and in
Lyly's *Campaspe* in which Alexander the Great relinquishes
the lady whom he loves and returns to his true mistress, military glory. The Alexander-Campaspe romance had, in fact,
probably not been absent from Bandello's mind when he told
the story of Mahomet and Irene. What he did was to substitute
for Alexander's magnanimity the current European conception
of Ottoman cruelty and lust. There may have been a nearer
resemblance to the Alexander story in another lost play, *The
Blacksmith's Daughter*. This play was one of six commended by
Stephen Gosson as 'without rebuke' and it is described by him
as 'conteyning the trechery of Turkes, the honourable bountye
of a noble minde, and the shining of virtue in distresse.' [1]
Professor Schelling says that it was a 'comedy of travel,' a
forerunner of the 'breezy adventure plays' soon to come into
vogue; [2] but how he knows this it is impossible to say. Another
guess may be offered: that this lost play showed the blacksmith's daughter stolen by Turkish pirates (the treachery);
presented to the Sultan and refusing his solicitations (virtue
shining in distress); and magnanimously restored by the Sultan
to her father (the bounty of a noble mind). The story was not
necessarily about Mahomet II. Another Sultan—Solyman the
Magnificent—was involved, according to Christian legend, in

---

1 *The School of Abuse*, 1578; ed. Shakespeare Society, p.30; Chambers, *The Elizabethan
Stage*, iv,204.
2 *Elizabethan Drama*, ii,404.

love-affairs with Christian ladies; and Europe often praised him for his magnanimity.

But what about the lost tragedy of Irene? In *The Merry Conceited Jests of George Peele* there is an anecdote that involves Peele reading to a friend a 'play-book' which he has written. This book is said to be 'the famous play of *The Turkish Mahomet and Hyrin the fair Greek.*' [1] Of this play there is no mention in the extant theatrical and publishing records of the time; but that it was popular is shown by the currency of what was evidently a scrap of dialogue from it which is quoted and parodied by other dramatists. Shakespeare's Pistol exclaims: 'Have we not Hiren here?' [2] In *Eastward Hoe*, among various tags from old plays, we find: 'Hast thou not Hiren here?' [3] Middleton, with a play on words, has: 'We have Siren here.' [4] It is a valid guess that this tag echoes the rhetorical question put by the Sultan at the moment when Irene appears at the banquet where she is presently to be slain; that must have been the crucial point in Peele's play, and the situation most likely to remain for long in popular memory.

In the absence of records efforts have been made to discover the play under another title. The starting-point of this inquiry is a passage in a poem by Peele himself:

> Theatres and proud tragedians,
> . . . Mahomet's Pow, and mighty Tamburlaine,
> King Charlemagne, Tom Stukeley, and the rest.[5]

Whether these allusions are to dramas or to their protagonists, three of the four are easily identifiable; but 'Mahomet's Pow' is a fantastic and unlikely name for a tragedy and an impossible

---

1 Peele, *Works*, ed. Bullen, ii,394. See G.M.Sibley, *The Lost Plays and Masques*, p.166.
2 *2 Henry IV*, II,iv,172.
3 Jonson, Marston, and Chapman, *Eastward Hoe*, II,i,115.
4 *The Old Law*, IV,i:

> *Gnotho*: We have Siren here.
> *Cook*: Siren! 'twas Hiren, the fair Greek, man.
> *Gnotho*: Five drachmas of that. I say Siren, the fair Greek, and so are all fair Greeks.
> *Cook*: A match! five drachmas her name was Hiren.
> *Gnotho*: Siren's name was Siren.

5 *A Farewell . . . to the Generalls*, ll.20f., *Works*, ii,238. The unmodernized text reads 'Poo.' See Sibley, op.cit., p.100.

name for a tragic hero. Fleay suggested that it is not necessarily the title of a play but may allude to a sensationally bizarre stage-property, namely the head ('pow') of the Prophet Mahomet in Greene's *Alphonsus King of Arragon*.[1] Sir Edmund Chambers, on the other hand, believes that Peele may be alluding to his own *Turkish Mahomet*.[2] But what has Mahomet's Head to do with Irene? Does Sir Edmund Chambers intend to imply that the 'pow' is the head which Mahomet cut off— Irene's? Surely not.

In an inventory of properties belonging to the Admiral's Men, taken 10 March 1598, occurs the item: 'owld Mahemetes head.'[3] Mr. W.W.Greg thinks that this property had been used in a lost play entitled *Mahomet* which (with various spellings) is recorded by Henslowe as having been performed eight times between August 1594, and February 1596.[4] Greg is inclined to identify this lost play with Greene's *Alphonsus*. But, granting that it is odd that *Alphonsus* is never mentioned by name in Henslowe's *Diary* and must therefore be discovered, if at all, under another title; granting, too, that Elizabethan titles were not always strictly appropriate; it is difficult to see why *Alphonsus* should ever have had the alternative title *Mahomet*. More promising of a solution are two entries in the *Diary* in August 1601. Here Henslowe records payment for a crown, a 'parell' (that is, a robe), and divers other things to be used in the play of *Mahewmett*; and later in the same month he bought from Edward Alleyn 'the Boocke of mahamett.'[5] Here we may have documentary references to the lost play by Peele. There are two side-issues that must be considered briefly. In October 1594, the Admiral's Men performed *The Love of a gresyan Lady*; in November 1594, and again in October 1595, *The greasyon* (or *Gresyan*) *comedy*.[6] It is generally agreed that the

---

1 *Biographical Chronicle of the English Drama*, ii,154.
2 *The Elizabethan Stage*, iii,327.
3 *Henslowe Papers*, ed. Greg, p.116. Mr. Greg notes the resemblance to the phrase in Peele's poem and increases the resemblance by misquoting Peele's 'Mahomet's Pow' as 'old Mahomet's Pow.'
4 *Henslowe's Diary*, ed. Greg, i,18f.
5 Ibid., i,147.
6 Ibid., i,19,20,25. Mr. Greg is inclined to identify *The Love of a Grecian Lady* with *The Love of an English Lady*, acted in 1584 (ibid., ii,169f.). It is difficult to see how Henslowe could confuse, or his editor identify, an English lady with a Greek.

same play is referred to under these different titles. It has been suggested that this was Peele's lost play; but surely a tragedy on Irene—and Peele's drama must have been a tragedy—could not have been known even to the haphazard Henslowe as 'a Grecian Comedy.' It is even more unlikely that *A Pastoral or a History of a Greek Maid*, acted at Court in 1597,[1] was on the subject of Irene. Irene was not a maid and her story certainly contained no pastoral element.

One must not dogmatize on the basis of these meagre records but one may offer an opinion. The Greek Comedy and the Greek Pastoral had nothing to do with Irene. The *Mahomet* of 1594–5 was more likely about a Turkish Mahomet, a Sultan, than about the Arabian Mahomet, the Prophet. For a drama on the latter there was only a farrago of distorted and disconnected legends. If on a Sultan of that name, then which? Mahomet I was a vague figure of the far past round whom no body of legends had accumulated. Mahomet III did not ascend the throne till 1595. These two being ruled out, Mahomet II remains. For a drama on his career there was an abundance of promising material, and of that material the best adapted to Elizabethan taste and dramatic technique was the story of Irene. Hence it seems probable that the play performed in 1594–5 was Peele's *Turkish Mahomet*. Furthermore, Peele's phrase 'Mahomet's Pow' had nothing to do with his own tragedy but is a humorous reference to *Alphonsus*. The head of Mahomet the Prophet in that play probably also did service as the Brazen Head in Greene's *Friar Bacon and Friar Bungay*. By 1598 it was an old property and was so inventoried. Possibly it served years later in Daborne's *A Christian Turn'd Turke* in which the renegade Captain Ward is shown kissing a head of Mahomet.

That Peele derived his material from *The Palace of Pleasure* is equally indubitable and unprovable. Directly from Paynter or from Paynter through Knolles's *Generall Historie of the Turkes*, with—the guess may be hazarded—suggestions from

1 A.Feuillerat, *Documents relating to the Office of the Revels in the time of Queen Elizabeth*, p.125.—On Jacob Eyrer's possible connection with Peele's lost play see Chambers, op.cit., ii,271.

Peele's play, the story came to the actor William Barksted who published in 1611 his narrative poem *Hiren or the faire Greeke*.[1] Though following Bandello-Paynter in the main, it differs from these earlier versions in one important circumstance, that whereas in them the soldier who captures Irene gives her to the Sultan, in Barksted's poem Mahomet first sees her during the sack of Constantinople kneeling with other Christian virgins before an altar. Whence did Barksted obtain the idea for this situation? His poem is written in so unimaginative and pedestrian a style that it is unlikely that he invented anything himself. The suggestion may be offered that this episode, which occurs in no other version, may derive from Peele's lost play; it is the likelier because Barksted was connected with the theatres. Attracted to the beautiful Greek as she kneels in prayer, Mahomet makes her his prisoner. She and the Sultan indulge in a tedious *débat* on love, religion, and chastity in which she cites many famous examples of the virtue of chastity. Mahomet magnanimously refuses to 'force' his fair captive, and continues to intermingle philosophic discourse with ardent wooing till at length he 'blinds her with Cupids vaile' (that is, she falls in love with him) and, a 'new convertite' to love, yields to him.[2] The remainder of the tragic story is as in Paynter. It must be added that in style and psychology this poem is beneath contempt.

The analogy to the Alexander-Campaspe story, which we have noted, is explicitly drawn in the earliest surviving English play on Irene. This is *The Couragious Turke, or Amurath the First*, 1632.[3] The author was Thomas Goffe, an Oxford clergyman. This play and his other tragedy (to which we shall come later) were performed by the students of Christ Church; so far as is known they were never presented on the public stage. In the Argument preceding the tragedy the Greek captive with whom the Sultan falls in love is called Irene; but in the play

1 *Hiren or the faire Greeke. By William Barksted, one of the servants of his Majesties Revels*, 1611; reprinted in Grosart, *Occasional Issues*, iii, Manchester, 1876.
2 Ibid., stanza lxi.
3 *The Couragious Turke, or Amurath the First. A Tragedie. Written by Thomas Goffe, Master of Arts, and Student of Christ-Church in Oxford, and Acted by the Students of the Same House*, 1632. This and Goffe's other tragedy (see pp.492–3, below) were published posthumously.

itself she is named Eumorphe. Evidently Goffe tried to achieve originality by changing the names of his characters, yet by a stupid oversight retained in his Argument the original name of his heroine. The first two acts show the infatuation of Amurath for Eumorphe and the circumstances of her death. The Sultan's tutor, Lala Schahin, seeking to cure his master of his love for the beautiful slave, causes to be presented before him two contrasting masques, the first portraying the amorous idleness of the gods, the second Alexander's repudiation of love for the sake of military renown. The lesson of these spectacles is not lost upon Amurath; but notwithstanding his compunctions he goes to bed with Eumorphe. Into the bed-chamber enters the resourceful tutor, disguised as the ghost of Orchanes, Amurath's dead father. He upbraids Amurath for sacrificing empire and glory to lust. The Sultan is much disturbed and the pretended ghost departs. Amurath calls his counsellors into the bed-chamber and pulling off the bed-clothes reveals to them the concubine's beauty. Then suddenly he draws his scimitar and strikes off her head.[1] The murder accomplished, they all set out for the wars. Here, crowded into two acts, the Irene story ends; but there is much more matter in the play. Acts III–V have to do with the victory over, and pardon of, Amurath's rebellious son-in-law and with the conquest of Servia and Bulgaria. There is much threatening of the world in high astounding terms. Then, before a pitched battle, Amurath remarks ominous portents, the stage-direction reading: 'The Heavens seeme on fire; Comets and blazing Starres appeare.' Whereupon the Sultan exclaims:

> Who set the world on fire? How now (ye Heavens)
> Grow you so proud that you must needs put on curl'd locks,
> And cloth yourselves in Periwigs of fire? . . .
> Dare ye blaze still? Ile tosse up Buckets full
> Of Christian bloud to quench you [2]—

a fair sample of the style in which the tragedy is written. A stage-direction notes that 'whilst he is in his fury, arise foure

1 In placing the murder in a bed-chamber of the seraglio, not at a banquet, Goffe departs from the tradition. It is scarcely possible that he could have known Da Lezze's narrative in which the murder of the unnamed concubine takes place in the seraglio.
2 *The Couragious Turke,* III,iii.

Fiends, framed like Turkish Kings, but blacke; his supposed Predecessors dance about him to a kind of hideous noyse.' Amurath defies these apparitions. In the battle which follows, a wounded Christian, exerting his last fast-ebbing strength, stabs the Sultan and dies gloating over his accomplished vengeance. Amurath expires. Bajazet ascends the throne; sends for his younger brother and has him strangled; and the tragedy comes to an end—much to the reader's relief.

Much more tolerable is Lodowick Carlell's *Osmond the Great Turk* which was written some time between 1637 and 1642.[1] The hero of this play, though inexplicably called 'the Great Turk,' (a title properly belonging exclusively to the Ottoman sultans), is really a Tartar, the 'noble servant' of Melcoshus Emperor of Tartary. During the pillaging of a captured city which is not named (but Carlell had in mind traditions of the taking of Constantinople) Osmond rescues from the violence of two soldiers a maiden named Despina. With her Osmond falls in love, but his loyalty to his master is greater than his amorous passion and he hands the girl over to the Emperor. The plot then develops as in the story of Irene till at the opening of Act V the Emperor slays the lady, thus showing the triumph of Mars over Venus. Osmond, to avenge her death, assassinates his master and then commits suicide. A subplot deals with the love of the Emperor's son for a married woman. The son violates her; her husband acquaints the Emperor with his wrongs; the Emperor claims that the woman is his bondslave, but in private he reproves his son, and presently causes him to be blinded and later strangled. This subplot resembles a portion of the plot of *Revenge for Honour;* there is also evident recollection of the story of Shah Abbas's blinding of his son Mirza and perhaps of the story of Sultan Solyman's murder of his son Mustapha.[2] Carlell's play is of some interest in the history of taste, standing as it does midway between Beaumont and Fletcher on the one hand and Dryden and Settle on the other. The heightened heroic tone shows that into Fletcherian romance

1 *The Famous Tragedy of Osmond the great Turk, Otherwise called the Noble Servant,* 1657 (the second piece in a volume having the general title *Two New Plays*); ed. Allardyce Nicoll, 1926.
2 See pp.503,509-14,497-502, below.

there is being introduced something of the atmosphere of Cal-
prenède and Scudéry. 'Osmond,' says Professor Schelling, 'is an
. . . impossible and pseudo-romantic Turk [or rather Tartar,
despite the play's title], although the story of his struggle between his passion for the fair captive Despina, and his heroic
loyalty to his master . . . is told with a directness and moderation in no wise ineffective.' [1]

Contemporaneous with Carlell's play is Gilbert Swinhoe's
Unhappy Fair Irene, first published in 1658 but written before
1640.[2] The commendatory verses prefixed to this tragedy emphasize the author's youth; he needed whatever excuse could
be offered for him. The play is written in execrable verse, if
verse it can be called, chopped up into lines ranging from four
to twenty syllables in length. The scene is laid in Hadrianople.
Irene, a captive rescued during the pillaging of Constantinople
from the clutches of a common soldier, is presented to Mahomet
by the captain who has saved her. The Sultan falls in love with
her and summons a Mufty to join her to him in wedlock. Her
plea for a week's respite is granted. She has secretly arranged
with her true-love, a Greek nobleman named Paeologus, to
meet him at the city gate on his return from Hungary and escape with him. In the interim she keeps aloof from the Sultan,
putting him off with fair promises, the while he becomes more
and more infatuated. He neglects his imperial responsibilities.
The Basha of Natolia remonstrates with him and is banished.
The Janissaries mutiny and beat upon the palace door. To
placate them Mahomet kills Irene—or as Swinhoe expresses it:

> The imperious Soldiers high incens't,
> Forc'd his unwilling hand to part her head and body.

Paeologus, returning to effect her escape, finds her corpse and
upon it he commits suicide. His friends declare, somewhat surprisingly, that

> This is a spectacle of like Woe
> To that of Juliet and her Romeo;

---

1 *Elizabethan Drama*, i,449.
2 *The Tragedy of the unhappy Fair Irene. By Gilbert Swinhoe, Esq.*, 1658.

and upon that note the tragedy ends. Swinhoe has ruined the dignity of the story by making Mahomet kill Irene to placate the incensed Janissaries, not (as in earlier versions) to show himself the master of his passions. 'Irene seems to have preserved her chastity inviolate,' says Genest drily, adding: 'It is a poor play, but not a very bad one.' [1]

III

THE circumstances attending the death of Bajazet II, the son of Mahomet the Conqueror, and the accession of Selim the Grim, 'the vilest of the Ottoman brood,' [2] are succinctly set forth on the title-page of an anonymous play published in 1594: *The First Part of the Tragicall raigne of Selimus, sometime Emperour of the Turkes, and grandfather of him that now raigneth. Wherein is showne how hee most unnaturally raised warres against his owne father Bajazet, and prevailing therein, in the end caused him to be poysoned: Also with the murthering of his two Brethren Corcut and Acomat.* [3] The atrocious events here summarized are historically true: the old Sultan Bajazet II did die of poison

---

1 *History of the English Stage*, x,135.—Three versions of later date are beyond the scope of this book. (1) The anonymous *Irena, a Tragedy*, 1664. Here the old story is distorted to suit the current mode. Mahomet is the embodiment of Honour as Irena is of Chastity. Her true-love saves the Sultan when his soldiers rebel. He relinquishes Irena to her lover and marries another woman who is introduced to complicate the plot, serve as a foil to Irena, and make possible a happy ending. The piece is called a tragedy but it is tragic only for a slave who, by the old device of substitution, is slain in Irena's place. (2) Charles Goring's *Irene, or the Fair Greek*, 1708. The author complains that his play was forced to appear 'strip'd of her ornaments of music' (Dedicatory Epistle); that is, the incidental music was prohibited because the Haymarket held the monopoly for opera. Music might have improved the piece; it could not have made it worse. See Allardyce Nicoll, *Eighteenth Century Drama, 1700–1750*, i,80. Genest, op.cit., ii,396f., outlines the plot. The last four lines indicate the motive and are a sample of the play's quality:

> Jealous of Empire and my lost Renown,
> I stabb'd a Mistress to preserve my Crown:
> But had the Fair return'd my generous Flame,
> I'd slighted Empire, and embraced the Dame.

(3) Dr. Johnson's *Irene*, produced by Garrick in 1749, is too well known or at any rate too easily accessible to require comment. See D.N.Smith, 'Johnson's *Irene*,' *Essays and Studies by Members of the English Association*, xiv (1929), 34f.
2 This characterization appears under Selim's portrait in Knolles's *Turkish History*, ed. 1687, i,338. Compare Montaigne, *Essais*, iii,12: 'Selim, le plus cruel conquerant qui fut onques.' No knowledge of Selim as poet and patron of the arts came into western Europe.
3 Modern editions by A.B.Grosart (*Temple Dramatists*); W.Bang, Louvain, 1908; Malone Society, 1908.

almost certainly administered by his youngest son, Selim; and Selim did have both his elder brothers executed.[1] No other events did more to fix in the imagination of Europe the impression of barbarous cruelty and ruthless determination as qualities of the Ottoman emperors. The author of the play may have obtained his material from any one or more of several sources, most likely from Paolo Giovio, whether in the Italian, Latin, or English form of his *Commentaries* on Turkish affairs. Who the author was is still, after much discussion, an open question.[2] The rhetorical style of the piece, its extravagance and bombast, and its construction through a series of sensational climaxes point to an imitator of *Tamburlaine*; but that Marlowe was himself the author is inconceivable. That there are suggestions of Machiavellian philosophy—or what the Elizabethans supposed to be such—is true; but the presence of these notions of unscrupulous and wily statecraft is a characteristic not only of this play and of *Tamburlaine* but also, very markedly, of Mason's *The Turke*; and it consorts with the popular notion of Turkish treachery and ruthlessness and deceit. Six passages from the play are assigned to Robert Greene in the anthology called *England's Parnassus*, 1600. For this reason, and because various proper names are common to *Selimus* and *Alphonsus*, and because of the use of certain words characteristic of Greene and rare elsewhere, Grosart attributed the play to him. But attributions of authorship in Elizabethan anthologies are notoriously inexact; there is no significance in the appearance of the same proper names in two plays on Turkish subjects; and arguments based upon vocabularies are tenuous Grosart's contention has therefore not won general assent. The sheets of the edition of 1594 were re-issued in 1638 with a new title-page on which the author's initials are given as 'T.G.' Grosart argued that this was a misprint for 'R.G.' The initials have also been explained as an effort to palm off the unsold sheets of *Selimus* as the work of Thomas Goffe. But though he published two plays on Turkish history in the 1630's there is

---

1 *Cambridge Modern History*, i,90, and the various historians of Turkey, including Knolles, ed.cit., i,326f.
2 For bibliography of the discussion see Chambers, *The Elizabethan Stage*. iv,46

no evidence that Goffe won a reputation wide enough to make his initials of value to a dishonest bookseller.

There is, however, a connection between *Selimus* and Goffe's play *The Raging Turke, or, Bajazet the Second*.[1] In this, his first play—it is older by a year than *The Couragious Turke*—Goffe deals with the circumstances of the accession of Selim the Grim. It is likely that he had read *Selimus* and was perhaps inspired to go that tragedy one better in the matter of insane wickedness. The extreme prejudice against the Turks which it reveals may reflect popular resentment at a time when the depredations of Moslem pirates against English trade had reached an unparalleled height of bold insolence. Yet to devise his scenes of extravagant cruelty Goffe had only to amalgamate scattered episodes from various reigns which he found in Knolles's *Historie*. *The Raging Turke* presents a series of plots and counterplots, intrigues and counter-intrigues, alliances and betrayals and treacheries in which Bajazet II, his three sons, and a crowd of generals, viceroys, and bashas are involved in a confused welter of blood and hatred. Two scenes are impressive in a way—an absurdly heightened way. In one Bajazet throws a robe of 'mourning black' over a certain general in pursuance of the Turkish custom of bestowing such a robe as a token of the Sultan's distrust and hatred of someone against whom he suspects but cannot prove treason.[2] The other scene shows the aged and discouraged Sultan falling asleep over a book. The ghosts of his murdered victims enter, led by Nemesis, each bearing a sword and a lighted taper. They brandish their swords at him and *exeunt* performing a solemn dance.[3] Bajazet dies; and all other claimants to the Ottoman throne being dead already, Selymus reigns in his father's stead, declaring, rightly enough:

> Our Empire hath been rackt enough with treasons,
> And black sedition, as if no Christians
> Were left to conquer, wee yeeld our Turkish blades
> Against ourselves, imbowelling the state

1 *The Raging Turke, or Bajazet the Second. A Tragedy*, 1631.
2 Ibid., II,vii. Compare the account of this episode of Bajazet II and Bassa Achomet (Achmetes in the play) in Grimestone, op.cit., chapter xiv, pp.97f.
3 *The Raging Turke*, V,ix.

With bloudy discord; by our strength we fall
A scorne to Christians; with our hands we shed
That bloud which might have conquered Christendome.[1]

We return to *Selimus* for a moment to note that the title-page implies, and an Epilogue promises, a second part, displaying the now victorious Selimus—father, brothers, and other rivals and enemies all dead—dividing kingdoms with triumphant sword:

> If this first part, Gentles, do like you well,
> The second part shall greater murthers tell.

From the fact that Tonombey is a character in the fifth act of *Selimus* and from hints in the Epilogue one gathers that an important episode in the sequel thus genially promised was, or was designed to be, the conquest of Syria and Egypt with the downfall of Tuman-Bey, the last of the Mameluke Sultans. Apart from plays on subjects from classical antiquity whose action takes place in Egypt, Egyptian history is seldom a theme in Elizabethan drama. Tamburlaine's invasion of that country is Marlowe's invention or rather his distortion of history; [2] actually Tamburlaine defeated the Mameluke Sultan Farag at a battle in Syria and never entered Egypt at all. The author of *Selimus* is similarly inaccurate when he imagines that 'that great Ægyptian bug, strong Tonombey' came to the aid of Acomat in his struggle against his brother Selim.[3] Actually Tuman-Bey reigned less than a year, was defeated by Selim at the battle of Heliopolis (22 January 1517), and was put to death.

The despairing defence of the Mamelukes against the Turkish aggression, with the loss of Egyptian independence, was a fit theme for an Elizabethan tragedy along the lines of *Tamburlaine*. But the only attempt to fashion this fine subject into a drama is the Latin tragedy by George Salterne of Bristol entitled *Tomunbeius sive Sultanici in Aegypta Imperii Eversio*. This survives in manuscript but has never been printed. From

---

1 Ibid., Sig. O^r.
2 *1 Tamburlaine*, I,i. Zenocrate is the daughter of Farag, the Mameluke Sultan.
3 *Selimus*, l.2418.

the only published account of it [1] one gathers that it is a hopelessly inchoate piece of work, undramatic in structure, Senecan in style, with little action and that little both intricate and obscure, depending upon messengers, intrigues, despairing speeches, debates, and dreams. The Sultan Selim I, who does not otherwise appear, is introduced in a vision of ill-omen. The tragedy is dedicated to Queen Elizabeth, and on this ground, coupled with the fact that the author was a Bristol man, it has been surmised that the play was presented before the Queen when she visited that city during her progress in 1574. For this guess there is no evidence; [2] and it is more reasonable to suppose that the scholarly author attempted to supply the missing sequel to *Selimus*—that is, that his play is of later date than 1594. His dedication almost rules out the possibility that his source was the account of the invasion of Egypt in Knolles's *Historie* [3] which appeared in the year of the Queen's death. Salterne probably depended upon one or another of the Latin chronicles of the Ottoman Empire. The grim vision of the Turkish Sultan, crushing a weak and despairing opponent and adding a great new domain to his vast empire, should have been evoked for the Elizabethans and for us by a dramatist of genius.

IV

THE legend of the love of Selim the Grim for an Italian lady, which had a considerable vogue among the Italian novelists, does not make its appearance in Elizabethan literature. It springs from a confusion of names; for actually Selim II, the grandson of Selim the Grim, did fall in love with a woman of the great Venetian family of Venier, who, captured as a girl by the Turks, was placed in his harem, became a Sultana, and bore him a son who succeeded him as Amurath (Murad) III. She retained a strong affection for her native city and, being a person of strong character who dominated her husband and her

---

1 G.R.Churchill and Wolfgang Kellner, 'Die lateinischen Universitäts Dramen in der Zeit der Königen Elizabeth,' *Jahrbuch der deutschen Shakespeare-Gesellschaft*, xxxiv (1898), 247f.

2 E.K.Chambers, op.cit., iv,279. 3 Ed. 1603, pp.547f.

son (both weaklings), exercised an influence in the Levant favourable to Venice.[1] Amurath III, whose reign (1574–95) coincided with the rise of Elizabethan tragedy, also married a Venetian wife and was much under her influence.

Related to these historical facts and also to the legend of Mahomet and Irene in that it has to do with the love of an Ottoman Sultan for a captive Christian lady is the tragedy of *Soliman and Persida*, of uncertain date between 1589 and 1592.[2] Who wrote it is uncertain. George Peele's claim to authorship rests solely upon an ancient and rather pointless anecdote and may be set aside.[3] A much better case has been made out for Thomas Kyd, for the subject of *Soliman and Persida* is, with certain changes and much enlargement, that of the 'play within the play' in Act IV of *The Spanish Tragedy*, and there are parallels in dramatic construction to *The Spanish Tragedy*.[4] On the other hand, Kyd does not elsewhere exhibit the taste (one cannot say talent) for comedy shown in the subplot of *Soliman and Persida*, and the play's versification differs markedly from his undoubted work. All that can be safely said is that such evidence as there is points to Kyd or Kyd's influence.

The source of the play—the first story in Henry Wotton's *Courtlie Controversie of Cupids Cautels*, 1578, a translation of Jacques Yvers's *Printemps d'Iver*, 1572—has been exhaustively discussed by Professor Boas with indications of the alterations

---

1 Molmenti, *La Storia di Venezia nella Vita Privata*, ii,361f.; Spagni, 'Una sultana veneziana,' *Nuovi Archivii Veneziani*, xix (1910), 241f.

2 *Stationers' Register*, 20 November 1592 (Arber, ii,622). Besides an undated quarto there is a quarto of 1599. See further Chambers, op.cit., iv,46. There are modern editions in Hazlitt's Dodsley, v,253f. and in Thomas Kyd, *Works*, ed. F.S.Boas, Oxford, 1901, pp.161f.

3 *The Merry Conceited Jests of George Peele, Works*, ed. Bullen, ii,389f. Once upon a time at Bristol Peele pretended to have in his possession a 'history'—that is, a historical play—of *The Knight of Rhodes*. He obtained permission to have it performed, got his stage ready, hired his actors, gathered forty shillings at the door, spoke a short prologue, and absconded, leaving the actors to bear the blame. They were excused on the ground that they were as much gulled as the spectators. How in the circumstances Peele had managed to rehearse them does not appear. It is true that *The Knight of Rhodes* might serve as a title, though not a very good one, for *Soliman and Persida*; but the story does not ascribe its authorship to Peele. Chambers is wrong in saying that the play was one which Peele had 'written, or pretended to have written.' In the anecdote Peele does not claim authorship but only to 'have' the piece in his possession. Furthermore, such point as the stupid jest possesses lies in the fact that he did not have any play at all.

4 Kyd, *Works*, ed. Boas, pp.lvif. Professor Boas relies in part upon arguments advanced by Fleay (*Chronicle*, ii,26) and Sarrazin (*Englische Studien*, xv,250).

effected by the dramatist; and there is nothing to add here on that subject. The historical background is the siege and fall of Rhodes in 1522; [1] but the chronology is confused through references to the campaign of Solyman the Magnificent against the Persians, which did not take place till 1534–6.[2] The atmosphere is hopelessly anachronistic, for the tourney of knights of divers nationalities in celebration of the wedding of the Prince of Cyprus, a tourney in which a Turkish knight takes part, is rather reminiscent of the Crusaders' relations with the Saracens than a reflection, however much idealized, of actual conditions in the sixteenth century. Other incidents are suggestive of Italian rather than of oriental tragedy. The coarse comedy of the circumcision of the braggart is not in keeping with the lyric and romantic tone of the play; but this episode resembles similar scenes of rude clowning in later dramas. The Turks are portrayed as of violent temper, and their traditional treachery is exemplified by the Turkish knight's action in taking advantage of Christian hospitality to spy out the

1 The problem of the date when the action of Othello is supposed to take place involves the date of the siege of Rhodes. In a scene in the council chamber at Venice (I,iii,14f.) a Senator argues that Cyprus is of more importance to the Turks than Rhodes, less well fortified, holding the promise of easy capture and of gain. He doubts a report that the Turks are preparing to attack Rhodes. ''Tis a pageant,' he says, 'to keep us in false gaze'—a feint to distract Venice from the real object of attack which is Cyprus. There is of course a gross anachronism here. When the Turks attacked Cyprus in 1570 they had already held Rhodes for nearly half a century. It has been suggested that the period of the play is a little before 1522 when there was some doubt as to whether the Turks would attack Rhodes or Cyprus (compare Hakluyt, v,6). It is conceivable that Shakespeare had in mind these speculations as to the Turkish plan of campaign in 1522; but it is much more likely that he was indifferent to the violation of history and was thinking of the siege and assault of 1570. 'The Turk with a most mighty preparation makes for Cyprus' (I,iii,221). Such a report as that, and the sense of crisis conveyed in the play, and the appointment of Othello to the responsible post of commander of the defence all point to a time very shortly before the fall of Cyprus in 1570 as the period when the events of the play are supposed to occur.—The most ambitious imaginative treatment of the defeat of the Knights and the loss of the island is Sir William Davenant's operatic play The Siege of Rhodes (Dramatic Works, Edinburgh, 1873, iii,231f.; ed. J.W.Tupper, Belles-Lettres Series, Boston, 1909). Of much importance in the history of the theatre, it is of little interest in itself. For his history Davenant depended in the main on Knolles, but he departs widely from the facts and incorporates material from the legend of Solyman and Persida and from other stores of extravagant romance. See Killis Campbell, 'The Source of The Siege of Rhodes,' Modern Language Notes, xiii (1898), 177f.; C.G.Child, 'The Rise of the Heroic Play,' ibid., xix (1904), 166f.; and Tupper, ed.cit., pp.80f. John Webb's designs for the Siege are reproduced and discussed by W.R.Keith, 'The Designs for the First Movable Scenery on the English Public Stage,' Burlington Magazine, xxv (April and May 1914), 29f. and 85f.
2 See especially I,iii,51f. and the debate between Solyman and his counsellors as to the wisdom of recalling armies from Persia and Russia to attack Rhodes, I,v,1f.

fortifications of Rhodes. In the earlier scenes Sultan Solyman is not without those qualities of courtesy and magnanimity with which popular report in Europe was inclined to credit him, and he betrays a sentimentality so much at variance with history as to be amusing in a way not intended by the dramatist; but before the end he becomes the conventional oriental despot gorged with the blood of his victims. His death—the posthumous vengeance of the dead Persida whose lips, 'sawst [sauced] with deadly poison,' he has kissed—at the moment when Rhodes has fallen to him does so great a violence to history that it is difficult to believe that, witnessing it, even an Elizabethan audience, indifferent though it may have been to most such liberties, was undisturbed; for the fact is that forty-four years elapsed between the fall of Rhodes and the death of Solyman.[1]

If we seek atrocities in the annals of Solyman the Magnificent we find that in one instance history surpasses legend. When Sir William Alexander asks the rhetorical question:

> Great Soliman, sole-man by Turkes thought still,
> Whom could he spare, who his owne son did kill?[2]

the allusion is to the crime which more than any other event of his long reign stained the reputation of the greatest of the Ottoman emperors. In 1553, at the instigation of his wife Khourrem, Solyman caused Prince Mustapha, his son by another wife, to be murdered. Khourrem thus secured the reversion of the throne to her own offspring; she died too soon to witness the bloody struggle for it between her own two sons.[3] What is probably the first account of this atrocity to

---

1 In Dekker's *Satiromastix*, 1602 (*Works*, ed. Pearson, i,229) there is what seems to be a cryptic reference to a play on Solyman the Magnificent. Tucca says: 'My name's Hamlet revenge, thou hast been at Paris garden, hast not?' to which Horace replies: 'Yes Captaine, I ha plaide Zulziman there.' Upon this Sir Vaughan comments: 'Then M.Horace, you plaide the part of an honest man.' This bit of dialogue obviously alludes to a play; that it was a 'popular play' is a guess based upon its association with Hamlet and also with 'mad Ieronimoe' in Dekker's text (Schelling, *Elizabethan Drama*, i,447). But it is not included in Chambers's list, inaccurate and incomplete, of lost plays, *The Elizabethan Stage*, iv, Appendix M, or in G.M.Sibley, *The Lost Plays and Masques*.

2 *Doomes-Day*, Fifth Hour, stanza 83; *Works*, ii,192.

3 Knolles, op.cit., ed. 1603, pp.757f.; ed. 1687, i,512f.; William Robertson, *History of the Reign of Charles V*, Dublin, 1788, iii,304f. (a fine piece of narrative); Von Hammer-Purgstall, op.cit., v,538f.; *Cambridge Modern History*, iii,124.

reach western Europe is given in one of the famous letters of
Ogier Ghiselin de Busbecq, the ambassador of the Emperor
Frederick to the Porte, who was in Constantinople at the time
of the murder.[1] To Busbecq Khourrem owes the name by
which she achieved notoriety; mistaking for her real name the
designation of her as 'the Russian' (she was a native of Russia),
he calls her Roxolana.[2] The earliest published narrative of the
crime seems to be that by Nicholas a Moffan: *Soltani Solymanni
Turcorum Imperatoris horrendum facinus*, published at Basle in
1555—two years after the event. This narrative William Paynter translated in *The Palace of Pleasure*. The most ambitious
and detailed English version of the story is in Hugh Gough's
Ofspring of the house of Ottomanno;[3] it is an important early
specimen of the sort of tragic tale of oriental palace intrigue
which became vastly popular in western Europe in the seventeenth century.

Mustapha, the Sultan's son by a slave, was from childhood
popular among the people. But some time after his birth his
father became bewitched by the beauty of another concubine,
named Rosa, by whom he had four sons—Machomet, Baiasith
(Bajazet), Selimus, and Jangir (Tchihanger), the last a hunchback of 'sharpe, prudent and politicke will.' A daughter by
the same union was married to a deceitful man named Rustanus
who as Vizier extorted money from the poor and enriched
himself at his master's expense. Rosa, wishing to do something
'for the health of her soule,' asked a 'Muchti' whether a temple
and hospital erected by her would be acceptable to God; and
he replied that God would indeed accept them but that they

1 *Itinera Constantinopolitanum*, Antwerp, 1581. This contains the first letter only.
All four letters are in the Paris edition of 1589. A German translation appeared in
1596, a French in 1649, and an English not until 1694: *The Four Epistles of A.G.Busbe-
quius, Concerning his Embassy into Turkey*. This racy but inaccurate version was
revised and re-issued as *Travels into Turkey*, 1744, which is not listed in the bibliography in C.T.Forster and H.B.Daniell, *The Life and Letters of Ogier Ghiselin de
Busbecq*, 1881. On Roxolana see this standard biography of Busbecq, i,111f., and for
the murder of Mustapha, i,117f.

2 The Venetian agents refer to her as La Rossa, Gough calls her Rosa, and elsewhere
she is called Rhode.

3 Sig. Jᵛf.: 'The horrible acte, and wicked offence of Soltan Soliman Emperour of the
Turkes, in murthering his eldest sonne Mustapha, the yeare of our Lord 1553.'
Gough's source is Bartholemaeus Georgiewitz, *De Origine Imperii Turcorum*. Another
early English account is in Thomas Newton, *A Notable Historie of the Saracens*, 1575,
folio 139ᵛ.

would redound to the Sultan's credit, not hers, because as a
bondwoman she had no riches of her own and would be using
her master's money. This answer saddened her; but Solyman
made her free and 'Rosa with a great quantitie of treasure
departed to finishe the woorke before mentioned.' Solyman,
longing for her, commanded her to return; but she sent answer
that she was no longer a slave and 'concerning carnall copula-
tion that of all thinges it could not be done, without the
committinge of a most grevous sinne.' The Mufti confirmed
this decision, telling the Sultan that to love her was now not
lawful 'except he had first contracted lawful matrimony with
her.' So great was Solyman's passion that he thereupon wedded
Rosa though this action was contrary to the custom of the
House of Ottoman, for 'to avoyde equalitie in the Empire
they never marye any honest and lawfull wives.' Rosa now
set about securing the succession for her own offspring. She
sent to Mustapha as a present a poisoned robe; but the Prince
prudently had someone else don it and thus was saved from
this attempt on his life. She tried to kindle her husband's
suspicions against Mustapha, going so far as to administer
to Solyman a magic potion to befuddle his wits. But years
passed without success till at length Rustanus, her fellow-
conspirator, received a letter reporting that Mustapha was
secretly betrothed to the daughter of the Sophy. This evidence
the plotters laid before Solyman as proof that the Prince was
conspiring to murder his father and obtain the throne; else
why an alliance with the Persians, Turkey's 'auncient and
deadly enemies'? Convinced by these wiles, Solyman dispatched Rustanus with an army to Syria, ostensibly to repel a
Persian invasion but with secret instructions to seize Mustapha
and bring him in chains to Constantinople or, failing that, to
have him murdered. In this enterprise Rustanus was unsuccessful; forced to flee, he reported to Solyman that open warfare was impossible because of Mustapha's popularity with the
soldiers. Whereupon the Sultan advanced with a large army
into Syria. Mustapha went forth with his followers to encounter
his father, pitched his tents, and dreamt a dream in which
'Machomet appareled with glisteringe robes' appeared, took

him by the hand, and revealed to him the other world. This vision Mustapha recognized as a presage of death, 'for the supersticious Machometists do attribute very much unto the doting toyes of dreames.' He went unarmed to the Sultan's tent to protest his innocence of any wrong against him in thought or deed. But when he had come to the tent, three deaf-mutes appeared. 'Beholde my deathe!' murmured the unfortunate Prince. He strove to fly, but the mutes seized him and while his father looked on strangled him with a bowstring. Then Solyman sent for Jangir the hunchback who though Rosa's son yet greatly loved Mustapha; and 'when he came unto the place, and unhappy strangled brother, and beheld him lyinge on the earthe, it is impossible to bee declared, with what griping gryfes he was pricked at the harte'; and he denounced his father, saying: 'Coulde ther any such thinge take place in that fearce ungodly and mischevous minde of thyne' as to murder so noble a son? 'I will beware therefore, least hereafter, thou triumphe in lyke maner, bragge soo un-shamefastlye over me poor bunched miser.' So saying, Jangir slew himself with his dagger. Thereafter Mustapha's soldiers rebelled and were only appeased when Solyman seemed moved 'to repent hym of that cruell, detestable and beastlye killing of his sonne.' The moral attached to this woeful tale is to abstain from wars and civil dissensions.[1]

Based either upon this version by Gough or upon Gough's original in Georgiewitz is a Senecan drama in Latin entitled *Solymannidae Tragoedia* of unknown authorship which has never been printed but is extant in a manuscript dated 5 March 1582.[2] It opens with a Prologue spoken by the Ghost of Selymus, the father of Solyman, in which is foretold the ruin of his house through the crime of Rhode against her stepson. In Act I a Messenger arrives asking for Mustapha's hand in marriage to the Princess of Tartary. Solyman is perturbed by

---

1 From the foregoing summary many particulars are omitted, including the execution of an honest basha and the disgrace of the wicked Rustanus. The historical facts upon which the story is based are considerably less complicated than the legend which developed from them. Actually Mustapha's half-brother Tchihanger did not commit suicide but died of grief.

2 The synopsis which follows is condensed from Churchill and Kellner, op.cit., p.494, note 1, above.

reports of Mustapha's prowess and popularity. The Chorus comments upon the Sultan's baseless fear of his son. Act II begins with a colloquy between Rhode and her son Selymus. She assures him that she can so direct events as to win for him the succession to the throne. She then consults with a wicked official named Roxanes who advises her not to attempt to poison Mustapha but to inculcate hatred of him in his father's breast. The Chorus discourses on female faithlessness. In Act III Rhode puts this evil counsel into practice, but Solyman, though already suspicious of Mustapha, is reassured by a loyal Vizier. Rhode and Roxanes realize that they must compass the Vizier's death. Consequently in Act IV they bring accusations against him; he is deprived of his offices; but an old vow made by the Sultan is his supposed safeguard against capital punishment. This is of no avail, however, for without Solyman's knowledge the Vizier is poisoned in prison. The Chorus bewails the willingness of sycophants to further the crimes of princes. In Act V Mustapha is urged to make his escape, but he is too proud to fly. A dream in which Mahomet promises that within three days he will be with him in Paradise Mustapha rashly interprets to mean that within three years he will ascend the throne. An interview follows between Solyman and his son; and then the latter, convinced of Mustapha's loyalty and innocence, countermands an order he has given for his execution. But it is too late. A Messenger arrives, telling Solyman that twelve eunuchs have strangled the Prince.

It required considerable ingenuity to compress the essentials of the original episodic story, in which there are many characters and numerous changes of locality, into the rigid mould of Senecan tragedy with strict obedience to the unity of place and (so far as one can make out) the unity of time. There is no violent action; the murders are reported by messengers. In its prologuizing Ghost, foreboding dream, moralizing Chorus, and sententious dialogue the tragedy is typical of its academic and tedious genre.

Fulke Greville's interest in problems of statecraft combined with his meditations on questions of religion and ethics to attract him to the story of Solyman and Roxolana; and from

it he fashioned the tragedy of *Mustapha*.[1] On the grounds of
its relatively simpler style and relatively less obscure manner
of presentation this tragedy is considered to be of later date
than *Alaham*, the companion piece of which something will
be said presently. Even this comparatively expert workmanship does not, however, assist the reader greatly, for the story
of *Mustapha*, unless one is familiar with it in advance, is
glimpsed fitfully through the heavy stylistic ornamentation.
Specific incident and characterization are obscured by grandiose
generalities. A faltering attention is further distracted from
the difficult matter of the play by the metrical eccentricities.
The versification of *Mustapha* is not so badly clogged as is
that of *Alaham* with rhyming lines in couplets or small batches
irregularly arranged and scattered through the blank verse
in accordance with no discernible principle; but it is often
uncouth enough. The gloomy power of the massive choruses—
especially of the famous one beginning 'O miserable condition
of humanity'—must be admitted; and there are impressive
passages and fine single lines throughout. There are even one
or two scenes whose potentialities for drama are not altogether
betrayed by metaphysical or ethical speculation. The story
follows the familiar course, with no change of scene, much
debate, much resort to messengers and counsellors, and with all
violent action withdrawn into the shadows of elaborate narrative. But Greville at once excused and accused himself when
in his biography of Sidney he said: 'I have made [my] Tragedies
no plaies for the stage' and declared that his purpose was not
'to hold the attention of the Reader . . . in the strangeness
or perplexedness of witty Fictions' but 'to trace out the high
waies of ambitious Governours' along which 'they hasten to
their owne desolation and ruine.'

Though the scene of Greville's other play, *Alaham*,[2] is laid
in a wholly imaginary Ormuz it may be mentioned here because in plan it is very similar to *Mustapha*, with a weak
tyrant upon the throne, a virtuous prince, and an intriguing

1 *Stationers' Register*, 1608; unauthorized edition, 1609; in the folio of Greville's *Works*
1633; *Works*, ed. Grosart, 1870, iii,289f. See M.W.Croll, *The Works of Fulke Greville*,
Philadelphia, 1903, chapter ii and authorities there cited.
2 *Works*, ed. Grosart, iii,155f.

woman. The technique is even more fumbling, the versification harsher, the thought more obscure. No certain source has been discovered and one does not have to rate Greville's powers of invention very high to attribute to them the vague generalized orientalism here displayed. The plot, such as it is, seems to have come from his wide reading in Levantine history.

With the story of Roxolana and Mustapha it is usual to associate a play of uncertain authorship entitled *Revenge for Honour*, a poor piece which because of a seventeenth-century misascription to George Chapman has received more attention than it deserves.[1] It is probably of composite authorship, a lost original version by an imitator of Fletcher having been heavily revised by Henry Glapthorne. The scene is Arabia; the background a war with Persia; there are allusions to Moslem conquests in Spain. The intriguing Sultana of the Roxolana story has disappeared from the plot and in her place there is a villainous younger brother, the Sultan's son by a second wife, who is the foil to the magnanimous elder son of the Sultan. There are notable parallels in situation with Greville's *Alaham*: the contrasting characters of the two brothers; the blinding and execution of the father and elder son; the amours of the villain's wife; and his death at her hands—in *Alaham* by means of a poisoned robe, in *Revenge for Honour* with a poisoned handkerchief. The resemblances to the story of Roxolana are but slight.[2] It seems likely that the plot derives from no one source but is an amalgam of typical oriental material out of the chronicles of various reigns, not excluding the story of the blinding and suicide of the son of Shah Abbas the Great.[3]

---

1 Professor T.M.Parrott includes it in his edition of Chapman's *Tragedies* and discusses the problem of its authorship at pp.713f.

2 Later plays on the Roxolana story are *The Tragedy of Mustapha* by Robert Boyle, Earl of Orrery, 1665 (see Genest, op.cit., i,47 and 61f.; Allardyce Nicoll, *Restoration Drama*, pp.98f.); David Mallet's *Mustapha*, 1739 (Genest, iii,574); and versions by W.Jones, 1770, and H.J.Clinton, 1807, on which see Arnold Lehman, *Das Schicksal Mustapha's des Sohnes Solyman's in Geschichte und Literatur*, Mannheim, 1908.

3 The titles of three lost plays complete the roll of dramas in which the Great Turk figured or may have figured on the London stage. On *Vayvode*, the scene of which was probably somewhere in the Balkans, see p.139, note 3, above. *The history of the Soldan and the Duke of* ———— (thus blank in the record) was performed at court by the Earl of Derby's Servants on 14 February 1580 (Feuillerat, op.cit., p.321; Chambers, op.cit., ii,118; iv,157). It is impossible to guess what this play was about; the Soldan may not have been an Ottoman emperor; the subject may have been drawn from the romances of chivalry. On 13 September 1602, the Duke

V

WE now turn our attention to dramas on Persian history and remark at once that whereas in dealing with Turkish history the English playwrights evince knowledge of the events of many reigns, in the case of Persia their interest, save when they have to do with themes from the classical past, is limited to the reign of Shah Abbas. In some plays on Turkish subjects there are incidental references to his predecessors, but not even Shah Ismail I, the founder of the Safavi dynasty, was represented on the Elizabethan stage. Not until the Abbasid period was the theatre-going public interested in Persia. The exploits of the Sherley brothers may have stimulated this interest, and a play dramatizing their adventures is a convenient connecting link between what has gone before in the present chapter and what we have now to say, because its scenes are laid partly in Turkey and partly in Persia.

The unauthentically heroic role which Sir Thomas Sherley, Jr. plays in Anthony Nixon's narrative, *The Three English Brothers*, leads one to suspect that it was written under his auspices. Nixon was a man-of-letters-of-all-work who could produce a quick supply for the market without embarrassingly

of Stettin, who was visiting England, recorded in his journal: 'Den 13 ward eine comedia agirt, wie Stuhl-Weissenburg erstlich von den Turken, hernacher von den Christen wiederum erobert' (Chambers, op.cit., ii,367, from the *Transactions of the Royal Historical Society*, n.s. vi (1892), 6, where the journal was first printed. Compare Herman Hager, in *Englische Studien*, xviii (1893), 315f.). Stuhlweissenburg (in Hungarian, Szekesfehervar) was taken by Solyman the Magnificent in 1543. Nearly sixty years later it was retaken by the Emperor Rudolph on 20 September 1601. Some six weeks later a news-letter translated from the German, entitled *A true Relation of the Takinge of the Cyttye of Stuhl-Weissenburg . . . by the Christian Army against the Turkes*, was entered on the *Stationers' Register* (9 November 1601; Arber, iii,76). The lost 'comedy' was probably founded upon this narrative. Since it dramatized the taking of the city by the Turks and its re-taking by the Christians it must have embraced a wide span of years, and in the earlier scenes Sultan Solyman probably figured. The theme was an appropriate one with which to entertain a visiting German duke. The record affords an instance of the prompt dramatization of very recent history. Actually, when the comedy was performed, the Turks had recaptured the city (29 August 1602) but the news of this Christian defeat had not yet reached London.—From the extant 'plot' it is impossible to deduce anything about the lost play *Frederick and Basilea* which Henslowe registered as 'new' in June 1597 (*Diary*, ed. Greg, i,53). The 'plot' has been several times printed, most recently by Greg, *Henslowe Papers*, pp.135f. Some of the names of characters suggest that the subject was Levantine. Not even so much can be surmised regarding *The famous Tragicall history of the Tartarian Crippell Emperour of Constantinople*, entered on the *Stationers' Register*, 14 August 1600 (Arber, iii,169). Was this a drama, a ballad, or a prose romance?

conscientious scruples as to the accuracy of the information placed at his disposal. His book provided practically all the material for a drama upon which the playwrights employed must have worked at furious speed, for only three weeks after Nixon's narrative was entered on the *Stationers' Register* (8 June 1607) there was entered as by John Day, William Rowley, and George Wilkins a play which was presently published: *The Travailes of the Three English Brothers. Sir Thomas*

Sir Anthony Shirley. As it is now play'd by her Majesties Ser-

Mr. Robert

vants.[1] This piece was performed at the Red Bull, a theatre which made a specialty of coarse, noisy, spectacular plays that appealed to rough folk. The hands of all three playwrights are recognizable here and there throughout the play; that of Day seems to be responsible for the episode of the Sophy's niece, and Rowley's for the episode of the Jew of Venice.[2] A unique or all but unique copy of the original quarto [3] contains a dedicatory letter signed by all three authors and addressed 'To honours favorites and the intire friends to the familie of the Sherleys.' Herein they describe their play as an 'Idea or shape of honour' in which they have attempted to epitomize into a compendious abstract the 'large volume' of the Sherleys' accomplishments. Friends of 'worth and desert' will accept this abstract just as they would cherish the picture of a friend separated from them. A quaint Prologue elaborates an analogy:

> Who gives a foule unto his Cook to dresse
> Likewise expects to have a foule againe;
> Though in the Cookes laborious workmanship

1 Text in John Day, *Works*, ed. Bullen, 1881, second play (separate pagination for each play). In the original quarto there are no divisions into acts or scenes, nor are localities indicated; but divisions and localities are almost always obvious.

2 See Bullen's introduction, ed. cit.; Fleay, op.cit., ii,277; C.W.Stork, *William Rowley*, p.57. W.Carew Hazlitt (*Notes and Queries*, Third Series, viii,203f.) states that the John Day who collaborated on this play was not the same person as the author of *The Parliament of Bees*, but gives no evidence for this assertion. All modern authorities take for granted that he is the same; and the attribution of parts of the *Travailes* to him is on the basis of their resemblance to his other plays.

3 Hazlitt, loc.cit., describes the quarto containing this dedication. The copy in the British Museum lacks it.

> Much may be deminisht, som-what added,
> (The losse of fethers and the gaine of sauce),
> Yet in the back surrender of this dish
> It is, and may be trulie cald, the same.

To present fully the adventures of the three brothers would, they say, occupy at least five days upon the stage; therefore, 'leaving the fethers and some needlesse stuffe,' only 'the fairest of our feast' is offered. Varying the metaphor but slightly, we may say that too many cooks have pretty well spoiled this broth. It is, however, so curious a production and so nearly unique as a dramatization of contemporary events in which people still living are represented on the boards that it is worth a somewhat detailed examination.

The play begins with a dumb show of old Sir Thomas Sherley parting with Anthony and Robert; and young Thomas leads his grieving father home. The scene shifts to the Sophy's court where the brothers are entertained with a demonstration of the manner of Persian warfare, concluding with the execution of prisoners.

> Then are we sure our enemie is dead
> When from the body we divide the head,

the Sophy explains; whereupon Anthony has his followers enact a Christian battle in which mercy is vouchsafed to the vanquished; and Abbas swears 'by Mortus Aly' that he admires Anthony. The Persian courtiers begin to show signs of jealousy. Anthony tells his host of the virtues and puissance of Queen Elizabeth. The Sophy heaps honours upon him and they all set out to attack the Turks. A quarrel between Robert Sherley and a disgruntled Persian nobleman over the disposition of a prisoner sows seeds of future trouble (in this nobleman we recognize faintly our old acquaintance Husayn 'Ali Beg). Meanwhile Anthony has broached to the Sophy the project of a league with Christendom, and it is implied that Abbas is meditating conversion, for his courtiers implore him not to forsake the worship of the sun to kneel to One 'that liv'd and died a man.' In a discussion of theology Anthony has the best of the arguments. He is then appointed ambassador to Europe;

Haly, the villain of the piece, goes with him. The scene shifts to Russia, where Haly behaves treacherously towards Anthony, poisoning the Czar's mind against him. The complexities of the story now transcend the dramatists' technique and they have recourse to a Chorus which tells how Anthony was imprisoned in Russia, released, and journeyed to Rome. There he is shown graciously received by the Pope who sets him above the Persian envoy; whence more bitter jealousy in Haly's breast. The Chorus then requests the spectators to imagine that Anthony has arrived in Venice. Meanwhile (the Chorus continues) young Thomas Sherley has sailed from England, been captured by the Turks, and imprisoned in Constantinople. The scene changes to somewhere on the Turco-Persian frontier. The Persians under Master Robert win a great victory, try to compel their prisoners to join the name of Mortus Aly with that of Mahomet, and when they refuse condemn them to death. But Robert has heard of his brother Thomas's imprisonment and dispatches an offer to exchange thirty prisoners for him. We have then a glimpse of Thomas's sufferings in Constantinople; and then find ourselves in Venice, where Anthony has been expecting a sum of money from the Sophy and reckoning on this has purchased a fine jewel from a Jew named Zariph. But the perfidious Haly has intercepted the remittance and Zariph sees his opportunity to revenge himself upon the hated Nazarenes in a manner appropriate to a degenerate kinsman of Shylock:

> 'Twould my spirit much refresh
> To taste a banket all of Christian flesh.

Anthony entertains his creditor at a banquet at which appears Will Kemp, the London comedian, who chats about the theatres and is presently involved in a coarse comic episode which has nothing to do with the main plots of the play. In the midst of this banquet Zariph has Anthony arrested and thrown into prison. Again in Persia, we find the Sophy wrathful with Robert because of the affair of the exchange of prisoners and because he has presumed to make love to his niece (the truth being that she has made the amorous advances). A tense situation is developing when the scene changes suddenly to Constantinople where Thomas is set in the stocks and, refusing to reveal his identity, is tortured on the rack. For the last time we are in Persia. The Sophy has restored Robert to favour and punished the Persians who accused him falsely. He permits the building of a church and is present at the baptism of the Sherleys' baby. 'A Show of the Christening' provides a grand climax. Then the figure of Fame appears and addresses the spectators, making no doubt that the people of London will heap honours on these noble brethren. How Anthony and Thomas escape from their respective prisons does not appear. The play concludes with a dumb show in which Thomas is in England, Anthony in Spain, and Robert still in Persia. To accomplish this effect the stage, according to the direction, is divided into three parts. Each brother is provided with a 'perspective glass' by means of which he is able to descry the other two. This is without doubt the earliest instance, at any rate in England, of the use of telescopes as stage properties.

The piece is a crude and lively hotch-potch, difficult to summarize. Its popularity with the groundlings is satirized by Francis Beaumont who makes his Citizen call out from the audience to an actor upon the stage: 'Let the Sophy of Persia come and christen him a childe!' to which the actor replies: 'Beleeve me, sir, that will not doe so well; 'tis stale; it has beene had before at the Red Bull.' [1] Stale or not, is it not possible that the spectacular pageant of the christening scene may have suggested to Shakespeare and Fletcher the concluding episode of *Henry VIII*? In the Induction to *Every Man out of His Humour* to the question: 'How comes it then, that in some one Play we see so many seas, countries, and kingdomes, past over with such admirable dexterite?' the reply is: 'That but shewes how well the Authors can travaile in their vocation, and out-run the apprehension of their auditorie.' Ben Jonson's satire is older than *The Travailes of the Three English Brothers* by several years, but his irony is applicable to a play in which the authors neither manage dexterously the passage of their

---

[1] *The Knight of the Burning Pestle*, IV,i,46f.

many seas nor out-run the understanding of their auditory. Thomas Fuller read their piece and pronounced this judgment upon it:

> As to the general performances of these three Brethren, I know that the Affidavit of a Poet carrieth but a small credit in the Court of History; and the Comedy made of them is but a friendly Foe to their memory, as suspected more accomodated to please the present spectators, then inform posterity. . . When abatement is made for poetical embelishments, the remainder will speak them Worthies of their generation.[1]

Sir Anthony Sherley is connected indirectly with the next play we have to examine. His strange commendation of Shah Abbas will be recalled, that it was not his custom to strangle his sons, as did the Great Turk, but merely to blind them; afterwards they were permitted to live in the luxury mete for princes. At a date later than Sherley's visit to Persia, Abbas did instigate the assassination of his eldest son, Safi. A second son escaped the same fate only by dying a natural death. The third and fourth sons were blinded by order of their father. The third son, Khudabanda, half crazed with pain, wrath, and humiliation, murdered his own daughter, Fatima, in vengeance upon Abbas who loved this grandchild devotedly. Another grandchild, Sufi, escaped from his maddened father and lived to succeed Abbas as Shah of Persia. He it was who was on the throne when Sir Thomas Herbert narrated to English readers the atrocious happenings in which the grandfather, father, and sister were involved; and this monarch was represented on the English stage among the *dramatis personae* of two tragedies founded upon this story of oriental palace intrigue and crime. Herbert's narrative, told in his characteristic pompous and heightened style, is, when disentangled from what he has to say of the fate of Abbas's other sons, quite simple. Shah Abbas was jealous of the fame and popularity of his son Mirza (Prince) Cocobanda, and had him blinded. To deprive his father of his beloved grandchild the Mirza slew her.

---

1 *Worthies*, ii,394. Anthony à Wood (*Athenae Oxonienses*, i,col.552) repeats Fuller word for word.

Instead of love and kindnesse, with admirable celeritie and rage, grasping her tender necke with his strong and wrathfull hands, whirling her about, ere shee could begge for pittie or helpe, the cruell father threw starke dead upon the flore his daughter Fatyma.[1]

The blind man then groped about for his son, intending to kill him also; but Soffee escaped. Three days later the miserable Mirza poisoned himself.

In his tragedy *The Sophy*[2] Sir John Denham simplifies Herbert's narrative by ignoring the stories of the Shah's other sons but complicates it and expands it to five-act length by transferring from Herbert's narrative of the last days of Sir Robert Sherley the character of the Shah's jealous favourite Haly who becomes the villain of the piece. A more fundamental change is in the character of Mirza (here the prince's name, not his title) and in the circumstances of his death, whereby Denham at once violates history, softens the tragedy, and retains sympathy for the protagonist. Through Haly's machinations Shah Abbas is prejudiced against his popular son and has him blinded. In his misery Mirza meditates on the idea of murdering his own daughter in vengeance against Abbas; but when Fatima comes to comfort him in prison his own love for her gains the mastery and he dismisses from his mind this terrible design. Shortly afterwards Haly administers poison secretly to the unhappy prince and causes the old Sophy to be arrested. But the soldiers are enraged because of their beloved leader's death and thwart Haly's scheme to obtain the throne for himself. Abbas dies of poison administered by Haly; Soffy, young Mirza's son, is placed on the throne; and Haly and his fellow-conspirators are sentenced to be executed. In the foregoing brief summary various ramifications of iniquitous intrigues are passed over. The judgment of Denham's latest editor that the play is 'an amateurish example of an outworn

---

1 *A Relation of Some Yeares Travaile*, 1634, pp.99.f There are only small verbal changes in the edition of 1638, pp.174f. Herbert undoubtedly heard of this atrocity while he was in Persia, but his narrative may owe something to Pietro della Valle, *Delle Conditioni di Abbas Re di Persia*, Venice, 1628,p.51, or to I.Baudoin's French version of the same, *Histoire Apologetique d'Abbas, Roy de Perse*, Paris, 1631, p.136.
2 *The Sophy*, 1642; reprinted with some alterations in 1668; in Sir John Denham, *Poetical Works*, ed. T.H.Banks, Jr., New Haven, 1928, pp.232f. For the two Prologues of the original quarto another single Prologue was substituted in 1668.

mode' is scarcely just. It is difficult to regard as outworn a mode which was to inspire so many later dramas of palace intrigue; and though Denham was an amateur *The Sophy* is by no means a contemptible performance. The interest is pretty well sustained. The blank verse is loose but not more lax than James Shirley's. The style is competent and lucid. An obvious breach of good taste—the feeble comic episode of a foolish courtier whose loyalty is mistakenly suspected and who is put upon the rack—occupies, fortunately, but little space. Apart from this incident the action is single, without subplot; and in this respect and in its gravely sententious passages the tragedy reveals the influence of Massinger. The most interesting feature of the play is the presence of pointedly topical allusions to contemporary English affairs. In general, there is the situation of an absolute monarch ill-advised by ecclesiastical and lay counsellors. In his characterization of the Caliph who conspires with Haly the dramatist obviously has Archbishop Laud in mind. Even more specific is a brief episode which, found in the quarto of 1642, is significantly omitted from the edition of 1668 when it would have offended Charles II. The Sophy, threatened with an attack by the Turks, gives orders for fresh supplies of victuals and money. One of his ministers reports that the treasury is empty. 'Talk not to me of Treasures or Exchequers,' exclaims the monarch. 'Send for five hundred of the wealthiest Burghers; their shops and ships are my Exchequers.' A courtier murmurs, aside: ''Twere better you could say their hearts.' [1] The reference to 'ship-money' is clear. It is difficult to believe that a play containing these topical allusions was actually performed before Charles I; yet the original quarto contains two Prologues—one for recitation in the public theatre, the other for the court. Perhaps if it was so presented these allusions may have been suppressed; more likely they are afterthoughts safely inserted in the printed version after the outbreak of the Civil War. In its own day the play won a kind of recognition that is rare. So seldom in old plays do we meet with cross-references to other plays that it is worth while to quote the following lines from *Andromena*:

1 Act I, ll.50f.

> Have you but read
> *The Sophy*, you will find that Haly . . . ruin'd
> Great Mirza by his father, and his father by his son.
> That great politician, while all the court
> Flam'd round about him, sat secure, and laugh'd. . .
> He fell at last,
> 'Tis true; but he was shallow in that part o' th' plot.[1]

Yet more rarely do our old travellers reveal an acquaintance, even inaccurate, with imaginative literature. Without parallel in their books is John Fryer's narrative of the blinding and death of Mirza Suffee, for he notes that to that virtuous and unfortunate prince 'our Countryman Dreyden has ventured to give Immortality in his Tragedy called *The Sophy*.' [2]

Several years after Denham's play appeared there was published *Mirza. A Tragedie, Really Acted in Persia in the last Age. Illustrated with Historicall Annotations. The Author R.B.Esq.* (undated but probably of 1647). There is no record that it was ever acted; it could not have been, in public, when it was new, and in Restoration times it seems to have been forgotten. The author's name was Robert Baron.[3] In a preface he writes:

> I am not ignorant that there is a Tragedy abroad of this sub-
> ject, intituled The Sophy . . . I had finished three compleat
> Acts of this Tragedy before I saw that, nor was I then discouraged
> from proceeding, seeing the most ingenious Author of that has
> made his seem quite another story from this. In his neither doth
> the Prince kill any of his Torturers; Nor doth Fatyma die, which
> I take to be one of the most important parts of the story, and
> the compleatest Conquest that ever Revenge obtained over Vertue.
> In that King Abbas dies too, when, 'tis known, that our King
> Charles . . . An. 1626. sent Sir Dodmore Cotton Embassadour
> to the same Abbas, which was some years after this Tragedy was
> really acted there. From a manuscript of which Embassadours
> Letter, to a friend of his . . . I had a hint of this story. . . I have

---

1 *Andromena, or The Merchant's Wife* (anonymous), III,v; Hazlitt's Dodsley, xiv,245.
2 *A New Account of East India and Persia*, Hakluyt Society, iii,50f. The editor lets pass without correction Fryer's confusion of 'Dreyden' for Denham and the entry in the index is under Dryden.
3 He is named in one of several preliminary complimentary poems.—See in general Edmund Beck, *Robert Barons Leben und Werke*, Strassburg, 1915.

also the Authority for the most important passages of it, of Master Herbert, who relates this story in his Travells.

This citation of authorities and scrupulous regard for history remind one of Ben Jonson. Baron is, in fact, his professed disciple, saying of *Catiline* that that 'miraculous Poem I propose as my pattern.' [1] The text of his tragedy, exclusive of eighteen pages of preliminary matter, occupies 160 pages, and this is followed by 103 pages of annotations, historical, archaeological, mythological, theological, classical, and oriental. The slightest excuse afforded by an allusion in his text sets him off in the notes upon disgressions upon such subjects as the Persian worship of 'Ali, the shrine of Mahomet at Mecca, the custom of wearing a turban, the blasphemies of the *Koran*, the Moslem idea of Paradise, the angels Harod and Marod, the wealth of Ormuz, and so forth. Some notes have little or nothing to do with the subject of the tragedy, an enormous note, for example, on soothsaying and divination, and others on Amazons, harpies, and scorpions. Baron was a young man, fresh from the university, not reluctant to make a parade of his erudition—and he had the precedent of his master Jonson whom he faintly resembles alike in the weight of his learning and in the length and ponderousness of his tragedy. In preceding chapters of this book we have drawn occasionally on his copious supply of orientalia.

Mirza, though carefully written with a good deal of dignity in blank verse of stricter form than is usual at its date and though in essentials clearly constructed, is mercilessly verbose with far too much pointless dialogue among subsidiary characters. The four choruses, faintly reminiscent of Fulke Greville, are of some interest metrically. The following is an intentionally brief and unavoidably arid summary of a very long play. The Ghost of Shah Abbas's brother, murdered by him, speaks the Prologue, for vengeance's sake instilling into the despot jealousy of his popular and gallant son. In Act I the Shah's jealousy is enhanced by his concubine and by two evil counsellors. (The presence of the concubine in the play shows a 'contamination'

1 *Mirza*, p.161.

with the story of Roxolana and Mustapha.) One of the counsellors is Mahomet Ally-Beg in whom we recognize an intrusion from Herbert's narrative of the unhappy end of Sir Robert
Sherley. Aided by a mistress to whom he has promised marriage,
this wicked minister of state is plotting to gain the throne.
Abbas acts upon his advice and summons home Prince Mirza,
who is with the army. In Act II Mirza leaves his soldiers, promising to return to them quickly. In Act III executioners attack
Mirza while he sleeps, bind him, and are about to strangle him
when the Sophy intervenes and he is 'merely' blinded. Act IV
shows the devotion of Abbas to his little granddaughter
Fatyma. Mirza accomplishes his vengeance by breaking her
neck. Act V opens with her funeral. Then Mirza takes poison
and dies. The army rebels. Mahomet Ally-Beg's plots are
revealed and he is punished. Shah Abbas in grief and penitence
declares his grandson Soffie his heir.

Francis Quarles, addressing to Baron some complimentary
verses, says:

> Our Isle a Mirz' and Allybeg can give,
> The text and time do suit, and whilst you tell
> Your Tale, we'll easily find a parallel.

This implies that there was intentional topical significance in
the play; but the parallel is not so easily discernible as Quarles
thought. Mirza cannot well be King Charles's son who was
neither ill-treated by his father nor done to death by himself
or an enemy; yet he cannot well be anyone else. And who is the
false counsellor Ally-Beg? Quarles liked enigmas; and perhaps
the conflict of parties in the play suggested to him the opposing
sides in the English Civil War and he had no intention to point
analogies to individuals.[1]

A drama of the Caroline period which has a possible connection with the character and reign of Shah Abbas is William

---

[1] In the Chorus following Act III there seems to be a reference to the English Civil
War:

> 'Tis punishable to speak reason,
> Now reason and loyaltie are out of fashion,
> And Tyranny and Treason
> Have all the vogue in this besotted Nation.

Cartwright's *The Royal Slave*.[1] This was performed before the King and Queen by the students of Christ's Church on the occasion of Charles's visit to Oxford, 30 August 1636. The elaborate scenery, designed by Inigo Jones, included a palace, a wood, a castle, a Temple of the Sun, and a set which showed 'a City in the front and a Prison on the side.' [2] Inigo Jones also furnished the designs for the Persian costumes. There was music composed by Harry Lawes. The performance was 'generally liked' and 'the Lord Chamberlain so transported with it, that he swore mainly he never saw such a play before.' [3] In November it was acted by a professional company—the King's Players—at Hampton Court by special request of the Queen. On this occasion much money was spent on alterations and additions to the scenery, apparel, and properties.[4] The success of the piece was probably due rather to the music, exotic costumes, and elaborate settings than to its merits as drama; but these merits are not quite negligible. There is a certain stiff dignity about it; though stilted it is not ill written; and the sentiments, though extravagantly high-flown, are in keeping with the atmosphere. It anticipates some of the qualities of the heroic drama of the early Restoration period. The action takes place in ancient times. Arsamnes King of Persia has conquered the Ephesians. From among his prisoners he selects Cratander, according to the Persian custom 'after a Conquest, to take one of the Captives, and adorn him with all the Robes of Majesty, giving him all Privileges for three full days, that he may do what he will, and then be certainly led to death.' Cratander is a philosophic warrior of the Stoic school. When he first appears on the scene he is reading 'a discourse o' th' Nature of the Soul' proving that the vicious only are slaves and that the 'well inclin'd' are 'free and their own though conquer'd.' His character is in shining contrast to the other Ephesian prisoners, who sing ribald songs, defy their gaoler, and desire the kingship in order to enjoy three days of ease and pleasure before being

1 Oxford, 1639. Only the author's initials are on the title-page. Second quarto, 1640. Reprinted in Cartwright's *Tragi-comedies with other Poems*, 1651.—See in general R.C.Goffin, *The Life and Poems of William Cartwright*, Cambridge, 1918.
2 The quarto of 1639 is one of the earliest plays to indicate carefully not merely the changes of scene but the actual sets. These are called 'appearances,' a technical use of the word not recorded in the *O.E.D.*   3 *C.S.P.,Dom.*, *1636-7*, p.114.   4 Ibid., p.563.

put to death. Made temporary king, Cratander bears himself regally and philosophically. He is tempted with meats and wines and music. He silences a love-song with the rebuke, 'I did expect some solemn Hymn of the Great World's beginning.' When strumpets are offered him he has them put in gaol. Meanwhile his fellow-prisoners, set at liberty for the nonce, behave themselves outrageously. Cratander surprises them in an attempt to ravish some Persian ladies and orders them away with the warning, 'The next attempt installs you in a Dungeon.' They conspire to assassinate him in order that one of their number may enjoy the three days of pleasure before his execution; but Cratander thwarts their plot. He rejects an opportunity to make his escape from Persia, holding that he has sworn an oath to the Persian sceptre and must not betray the country. The Persian Queen is fascinated by his noble bearing and lofty sentiments.[1] The three-days' grace passes and Cratander is brought to execution at a Temple of the Sun; but as the priests prepare to sacrifice him an eclipse occurs and a shower of rain dashes out the fire upon the altar—theatrical effects which doubtless astonished and thrilled the audiences at Oxford and Hampton Court. These portents convince Arsamnes that heaven is not pleased with the sacrifice of so noble a man. He spares Cratander's life and sends him home as a sort of viceroy of the Ephesians, who are granted a measure of autonomy.

The pre-historic and world-wide custom of the election and execution of a temporary king was not unknown in Persia in the reign of Shah Abbas. In 1591 Abbas was warned by his astrologers that a serious danger impended over him as the occupant of the Persian throne. To avert the omen descried by his soothsayers he went through the ceremony of abdication. An unbeliever named Yusofee (probably a Christian) was chosen to reign in his stead. He was crowned and for three days enjoyed not only the name but the privileges and power of the king. Then he was put to death and Shah Abbas resumed his place.[2] It is inconceivable that Anthony and Robert Sherley,

---

1 This situation affords an occasion for introducing allusions to Platonic love, a subject then fashionable in courtly circles.
2 Malcolm, *History of Persia*, i,527; Sykes, *History of Persia*, ii,174; Sir James G.Frazer,

Powell, Ward, Herbert, and other Englishmen long resident in Persia did not hear of this sensational event, and it is altogether likely that they—or one of them—told the story in England. If so, the tale may have reached Cartwright's ears and furnished him with a suggestion for his play. At all events, the analogy is striking.

The scene of Sir John Suckling's *Aglaura*, 1637 or 1638,[1] is laid in Persia, and though the story is not connected with Shah Abbas it involves the rivalry of a king and his son. Contemporary gossip had it that the author paid heavily for the scenery and costumes; and certainly an outlay for such .accessories must have been necessary if the piece was to succeed at all. For it is a poor play, the plot a tissue of amorous and murderous intrigues not worth the trouble of unravelling.[2] There is no firmness or consistency of characterization; no individuality; no success in arousing sympathy with any of the *dramatis personae*. The King of Persia conspires against his son because they are in love with the same woman. In fact, to put it loosely, pretty nearly everyone is in love with pretty nearly everyone else.[3] In Act V almost everyone is slain, either on purpose or because his identity is mistaken for that of someone else. Suckling wrote an alternative last act in which pardons or banishments are substituted for deaths, a thoughtful provision for readers with a taste for a technically happy ending which leaves the judicious completely indifferent.[4] Not the slightest

The Golden Bough, iv,157. Dryden perhaps had the mock-king in mind when he wrote (*Aureng-Zebe*, IV):

> I'm to die in state.
> They lodge me as I were the Persian King:
> And with luxurious pomp my death they bring.

1 Probably acted in 1637; published 1638; new edition, 1646; in Suckling's *Works*, ed. A.H.Thompson, 1910, pp.77f. The format of the original edition is unusual. Not in the customary shabby quarto in which plays generally appeared did Suckling issue his piece but in a tall, slim, elegant folio on whose pages a rivulet of fine print flows between broad margins. One suspects that the author paid for the production of this pretentious volume.

2 The execrably unskilful exposition in Act I makes matters worse. For a synopsis which leaves the matter almost as confused as ever see Genest, op.cit., x,66f.

3 The laboured would-be comedy of the discussion of Platonism (or rather of what was thought to be Platonism) reflects the current courtly vogue of Platonic love echoes of which we have noted in Cartwright's *The Royal Slave*.

4 The resemblance to the altered conclusion of the version of *The Maid's Tragedy* fashioned to suit the taste and conscience of Charles II is coincidence only, for both Suckling's versions are of earlier date than the revision of Beaumont and Fletcher's tragedy. There are, however, obvious indebtednesses to *The Maid's Tragedy*, but

effort is made to secure any appropriate atmosphere. The king swears by Osiris. He banishes his queen to 'Diana's nunnery.' Lovers meet in Diana's grove. There is an allusion to Delphos. Pepys, who read this play, called it, quite correctly, a 'mean play.' [1]

VI

LEAVING Persia, we have now to direct our attention to the opposite side of the Islamic world—the Barbary States—and must first glance far back into history. Traditions of the conflict between the Christians and Moslems in Spain, of 'the Sarazens whych vext the Spanyards sore,' [2] were revitalized for the Elizabethans by the prevalence of Moorish piracy during the period. The expulsion of the last Moriscos early in the seventeenth century recalled to mind the circumstances in which the Moors had obtained their first entrance into Spain. According to the famous tale, a certain Count Julian, the Christian governor of Ceuta, brought about the Moorish invasion as an act of vengeance upon King Roderick for the violation of his daughter.[3] In 1619, when piracy was at its height, William

Suckling misses the point of the tragic complexity by making Aglaura (the counterpart of Evadne) innocent.

1 *Diary*, 5 September 1664. When Pepys saw it acted, 10 January 1668, he found 'nothing extraordinary in it at all, and but hardly good in any degree.'—A Shah of Persia was a character in the lost play *Tamar Cam*. 'The plott of The First parte of Tamar Cam' was printed in the *Variorum* Shakespeare of 1803. The original manuscript has since disappeared and Greg had to depend for his reprint (*Henslowe Papers*, pp.144f.) upon the 1803-text. Henslowe records the performance of this first part as a new play, 6 May 1594; but Lord Strange's company had already given it, 28 April 1592. Probably, as Greg suggests, it was then performed in rivalry to *Tamburlaine* which was being acted by the Admiral's men. The play belonged evidently, not to Strange's company, but to Edward Alleyn personally and was brought by him when he rejoined the Admiral's men. On 2 October 1602, that company bought the 'Boocke' of the play for two pounds. Henslowe records the performance of a second part on 11 June 1596. (See *Henslowe's Diary*, ed. Greg, i,14f.,30,42,49,171,182; ii,155; also G.M.Sibley, *The Lost Plays and Masques*, p.155.) The 'plot' of the first part is tantalizing in its indication of characters. Besides 'the Persian Shaugh' there was at least one other Persian. Mango Cham and Tamor Cham appear. There were also not only Tartars, Moors, Bactrians, and 'Crymms,' but pygmies, 'Amozins,' 'Canniballs,' and hermaphrodites. The presence of 'spirritts' in several scenes indicates a supernatural element. The performance was doubtless spectacular in character and much was made of the marvels of the East. A Chorus spoke five times. Of the second part nothing is known save the record of performance. What it was all about one cannot guess.

2 John Bale, *King Johan*, l.1301.

3 Some of the early chroniclers say that the woman was not Julian's daughter but his wife. In these versions the story is analogous to that of 'the sin of David,' for Roderick sends Julian to the wars in order to have easier access to his wife. Julian re-

Rowley composed his tragedy *All's Lost by Lust*.[1] This follows the old story fairly closely but with much intermingling of other romantic material. In the absence of his leading general, Julianus, who is waging war against the Moors, Roderigo, the King of Spain, deflowers the general's daughter, Jacinta.[2] She escapes from his castle, manages to reach her father, and informs him of her shame. Julianus enlists the aid of his soldiers and of some captive Moors, and together they attack the King. Roderigo is defeated and escapes alone to 'seek a weary life in Biscany.' The Moors then turn upon Julianus, and when he refuses to give his daughter in marriage to their chief, Mully Mumen, his eyes are put out and Jacinta's tongue cut out. Thinking to wound the Moorish leader, Julianus strikes out blindly, and unwittingly slays his daughter. The play ends with his death and the proclamation of the Moor as King of Spain. By lust all has been lost. A tragic subplot dealing with the bigamous complexities in the love-affairs of a Spanish Don contains no oriental motive.

The arrogantly regal bearing of Roderigo after the ravishing of Jacinta is reminiscent of a similar situation in Fletcher's *Valentinian*; and the circumstances of Jacinta's death point back to classical sources and forward to one of Cartwright's plays.[3] The supernaturalism of the scene in the vault of the king's castle is crudely contrived, but these portents of disasters to come upon the land are part of the Spanish legend. The Moorish leader's prayer to the sun shows that Rowley's mind is upon Persian fire-worship.[4] Confusion of another sort

mained infamous in Spanish story; Juan de Mena, the imitator of Dante, places him in the lowest pit of hell (*El Laberinto de Fortuna*, stanza 91). The history of the ramifications of the story in Spain is beyond the scope of this book and the author's competence. From the time of Voltaire and Gibbon doubts have been cast upon the authenticity of the tale; but modern historians are inclined to see some basis of fact beneath the legend; see *Cambridge Medieval History*, ii,48 and 265; see also P.K.Hitti, *History of the Arabs*, p.494, note 1. When the Peninsula War directed English attention to Spain the Romantic poets were attracted to the theme. See Landor's *Count Julian*, Scott's *Vision of Don Roderick*, Southey's *Roderick the Last of the Goths*, J.G.Lockhart's *Ancient Spanish Ballads*, Byron's *Childe Harold*, i,35, and Irving's *Legends of the Conquest of Spain*.

1 There are two modern editions: by C.W.Stork, 1907, and by E.C.Morris, 1908.
2 In the Spanish chronicles the woman is sometimes called Florinda but more frequently La Cava (the harlot), though the latter name does not appear till the fifteenth century.
3 See Plutarch's *Life of Cymon* and Cartwright's *The Siege, or Love's Convert*, 1637.
4 *All's Lost by Lust*, II,iii,1f.

is seen in the repeated references to the Turks centuries before their appearance in Europe.[1]

Another play on a Hispano-Moorish subject is *Lust's Dominion, or The Lascivious Queen*.[2] The attribution to Marlowe on the title-page of the first quarto, 1657, may rest either upon a Marlovian substratum beneath the extant text or upon its authorship by a contemporary imitator of Marlowe. Though it came so belatedly into print, scholars are agreed that it is of quite early date. On this ground there is, in fact, no objection to Collier's and Fleay's identification of it with *The Spanish Moor's Tragedy* for which Henslowe paid Dekker, Day, and Haughton in February 1600.[3] There is much evidence of Dekker's presence in the play and there are signs of Day's presence here and there. The plot is an amalgam of lusts and murders in which Eleazar the Moor, to whom the Queen of Spain prostitutes herself, is the central character. The scene in which the King of Spain dies owes something to reports of the death of Philip II; but so fantastic are the perversions of fact that it is impossible to say that the play is founded upon history. As in Rowley's *All's Lost by Lust* and Mason's *The Turk*, Moslem beliefs are confused with Zoroastrianism and with reports of the sun-worship practised by the so-called Indians of the New World. Eleazar several times calls himself or is called an Indian.[4] But we learn that his father was King of Fez and had been slain in a battle in which Eleazar was captured by King Philip. For nearly twenty years he nursed his desire for revenge [5] and fought victoriously 'in Spain's defence . . . against

---

1 We have already remarked that the Elizabethans used the word 'Turk' loosely when 'Moor' is intended; but in this play Rowley draws the distinction between the two races. See, for example, II,vi,44: 'Persuade me to turne Turk, or Moore Mahometan' and V,ii,30: 'An army of Moores, of Turkes and infidels.'

2 The sheets of the first quarto, 1657, were re-issued with a new title-page in 1661. Reprinted in Hazlitt's Dodsley, xiv; and ed. J.Le Gay Brereton, Louvain, 1931.

3 *Henslowe's Diary*, i,118. Mr. Greg (ibid., ii,211) thinks this identification 'not un-likely.' Professor Schelling says first that the two plays are 'not impossibly' and then that they are 'assuredly' the same (*Elizabethan Drama*, i,222 and 428). See Chambers, op.cit., iii,467; G.M.Sibley, op.cit., p.151; H.D.Sykes, *Sidelights on Elizabethan Drama*, pp.99f.; and Brereton's review of the problem of authorship in his introduction to the Louvain edition.

4 *Lust's Dominion*, III,iv; IV,iii. Compare Marlowe, *Doctor Faustus*, I,i,122: 'As Indian Moores obey their Spanish Lords,' where 'Moors' seems to be used in the sense of dark-skinned natives of the New World.

5 See especially his speech, too long to quote, in IV,vi.

the Turkish Ottoman.'[1] As a Moorish soldier fighting in the army of a Christian power against the Turks he resembles Othello.[2] In the end he is caught in the toils of his own bloody and complicated revenge. His character is certainly imitated from that of Aaron in *Titus Andronicus*, though he is even more brutal, if possible, than the original; and he bears a general resemblance to those two Moslem slaves in Christian hands, the unnamed Slave in Davenport's *The City Night-Cap* and Mulleasses (a Christian born) in Mason's *The Turk*. In their cruelty and lust both Aaron and Eleazar have evidently served as prototypes for the Moors in *All's Lost by Lust*. Eleazar is described as 'that fiend, that damn'd Moor, that devil, that Lucifer.'

From Spanish hatred of the Moors, reinforced by the general Christian hatred of Mohammedans and by experiences of piratical depredations, came the Elizabethan emphasis upon the cruelty of these people—and upon their blackness. To this matter of their colour we must devote a fairly long digression. Though there is some evidence that the Elizabethans made a distinction between different races that inhabited Barbary, in general they conceived of the Moors as black or at any rate of swarthy complexion. Of this notion there is a striking illustration in Boissard's *Vitae et Icones Sultanorum* (Frankfort, 1596). In the series of portraits by Theodore de Bry which adorn this work the Turkish and Persian potentates are represented as fair-skinned while the rulers of the Barbary States are very dark. Three items in the accounts of the Revels Office bear upon this point. Among the charges for a 'Masque of young Moors' performed in 1548 is an item for 'ii dossend of Black gote skynes for hosin for moores,'[3] evidently black tights to simulate bare legs. Again, in an inventory of 1560 one item is for thirty-two yards of black velvet 'imployed wholie into legges ffeete Armes and handes for a maske of Moores whereof the lords that

1 Ibid., II,iii.
2 Shakespeare does not disclose the circumstances in which Othello came to fight upon the Christian side. Has any commentator remarked in Othello's contemptuous reference to circumcision (V,ii,354) the implication that he was not nor had ever been a Mohammedan?
3 A.Feuillerat, *Documents relating to the Revels at Court in the time of King Edward VI and Queen Mary*, p.31.

masked toke awey parte.'[1] Here again we have to do with fleshings. Another inventory of the same year includes six 'corled hed Sculles of blacke Laune for Moores,'[2] which suggests that the masquers wore wigs of kinky hair to resemble negroes. Undoubtedly Shakespeare intended to picture Othello as a blackamoor, for though it is proper to disregard the remarks on his appearance made by his enemies—'thick lips,' 'sooty bosom,' and the like—there remains Othello's own description of his face as 'begrimm'd and black.' In Rowley's tragedy these 'half-naked infidels' (grotesquely inaccurate phrase!) are called 'swarty' and 'sooty' and 'blacke Africans.' Eleazar is several times called a negro. But elsewhere a distinction is clearly made.[3] It is apparent in the line 'The black-fac'd Africans and tawny Moors'[4] and again in 'The swart West-Indian or the tawny Moore.'[5] In Lithgow's list of the infidel races who inhabit Cairo he specifies 'tawny Moores, white Moores, blacke Moores, or Nigroes.'[6] Among the characters in the lost play of *Tamar Cam* was 'the ollive cullord moore.'[7] There is a 'White Moor' in *The Thracian Wonder*.[8] In the first quarto of *The Merchant of Venice* the stage-direction for the entrance of the Prince of Morocco reads: 'Enter Morochus a tawnie Moore.' It seems, then, that the distinction was often drawn, though not always observed, between the blackamoor or Moor with negroid features and colouring and the 'tawny' Moor, an exact epithet for the sandy-haired freckled Berber. The Prince of Morocco begs Portia not to mislike him for his complexion which 'wears the shadowed liverie of the burnisht sun'; but because he was sun-burnt it does not follow

---

1 A.Feuillerat, *Documents relating to the Office of the Revels in the time of Queen Elizabeth*, p.24.
2 Ibid., p.41.
3 In Thomas's *Italian Grammar*, 1548, the definition of *Ethiopo* is 'a blacke More, or a man of Ethiope.' Sir Walter Ralegh, in the *History of the World*, writes of 'the Negroes which we call the Black-Mores' (these quotations from *O.E.D.*, *sub* 'Blackamoor').
4 *Look About You* (anonymous), Scene xxxiii; Hazlitt's Dodsley, vii,505.
5 George Wither, *Abuses Stript and Whipt*, Book i, Satire i; *Poems*, Spenser Society, p.58. Here the adjectives are clearly differentiated, but how loosely they were sometimes used is shown by Thomas Lodge's phrase 'Swart like a tawny Indian' (*Wits Miserie, Works*, Hunterian Club, iv,33).
6 *Rare Adventures*, p.271. George Sandys says that 'the Maltese are little lesse Tawnie then the Moores' (Purchas, vi,232).
7 *Henslowe Papers*, p.148.
8 V,ii; Webster, *Works*, ed. W.C.Hazlitt, iv,205f. (The play is not by Webster.)

that he was black, still less that he was negroid in features.[1]

The confusion between Berbers and Ethiopians may have been due in part to the African slave-trade. The proverbial expression about the Ethiope changing his skin occurs innumerable times in Elizabethan literature.[2] It gave rise to the saying that they labour in vain who attempt to wash an Ethiope. Zanthia, the female Moor in Fletcher and Massinger's *Knight of Malta*, is called 'My little labour-in-vain.'[3] This grotesque expression became, by an odd twist of thought, the name of a tavern. This is the point of Zanthia's words to her lover:

> When I have serv'd
> Your turns, you'll cast me off, or hang me up
> For a sign somewhere.

In one of his reformatory pamphlets Thomas Dekker deplores the swearing, drinking, roaring, and surfeiting in taverns and ale-houses and then comments: 'I wash an Æthoipe, who will never be the whiter for all this water I spend upon him, and therefore let mee save any further labour.'[4] One can follow his train of thought to the very tavern—the Labour-in-Vain—to which Zanthia refers. The implication in the choice of this

---

1 *The Merchant of Venice*, II,i,1f. With Morocco's plea to Portia compare Eleazar's insistence that he be valued

> Not by my sunburnt cheeks, nor by my birth,
> But by my loss of blood . . . in Spain's defence

(*Lust's Dominion*, III,iv). The long appendix on 'Othello's colour' in the *New Variorum* edition of the play consists mainly of stage traditions, pertinent passages in the text, analogies drawn from *The Merchant of Venice*, and exhibitions of the prejudices of the commentators. Shakespeare's Cleopatra was 'with Phoebus' amorous pinches black' (*Anthony and Cleopatra*, I,v,28). In a play of uncertain authorship she is called 'black Cleopatra' (*The Wonder of a Kingdom*, II). But Massinger, knowing that she was a Ptolomy, a Greek, not an Egyptian, calls her 'fair Cleopatra' and that he is using the epithet in a precise sense is shown by the parenthetical comment: 'An attribute not frequent in this climate' (*The False One*, I,i,26f.— This act is by Massinger, not Fletcher). The reader may like to be reminded that Tennyson's description of Cleopatra as 'a queen with swarthy cheeks and bold black eyes' (*A Dream of Fair Women*) provoked a satirical comment from Thomas Love Peacock (*Gryll Grange*, chapter xxiii). In the famous 'Longleat Manuscript,' a single folio sheet containing a pen drawing representing Tamora, Titus, and Aaron from *Titus Andronicus*, Aaron is shown as coal-black. See Sir Edmund Chambers, 'The First Illustration to Shakespeare,' *The Library*, Fourth Series, v (1925), 326f.; *William Shakespeare*, i,313f.

2 Founded on Jeremiah's question (xiii,23): 'Can the Ethiope change his skin?' The proverb occurs in at least six plays of our period.

3 I,ii.

4 *A Rod for Run-awaies*, 1625; *Plague Pamphlets*, ed. Wilson, p.151.

name for a tavern was that competitors laboured in vain to brew such excellent ale as was on tap there. At a later date certainly, and probably in Jacobean London, the sign of such a tavern showed two women scrubbing a blackamoor.[1]

The problem of the Elizabethan conception of the Moors' complexion has drawn us away from our examination of the plays in which Moorish characters figure to an important degree. To that topic we now return.

Clashes between the Barbary corsairs and the Knights of Malta were frequent; and in the great siege of 1565 not only was Dragut, one of the Sultan's commanders, himself a Barbary pirate but Moorish soldiers made up a large part of the Sultan's forces. The action of Marlowe's *The Jew of Malta* centres in the demand of the Turks for the payment of an annual tribute which is due; this, as the commentators have pointed out, is pure romance, for Malta never paid tribute to the Turks. But by far the most interesting dramatization of the struggle of the Knights with the Moslems is *The Knight of Malta* by Fletcher and Massinger, 1618.[2] The dramatists have made the Moorish woman Zanthia the mainspring of the action of their fine play. She it is who forges the letter yielding Malta to the enemy; and later she gives Oriana the sleeping-potion. She is wicked, but is quite admirably depicted in her unrepentant devotion to the recreant Knight Montferrat.[3]

The imagination and emotions of Englishmen were stirred by the battle of El-Kasrel Kabir, fought on 4 August 1578,

1 One of Dryden's characters (*The Mistaken Husband*, III) says: 'I went in a melancholy humour to the Labour-in-Vain, and condol[ed] your Worship's misfortune over two pots of Ale.' Compare *London's Ordinarie* (*Roxburghe Ballads*, i,212): 'The porters take pain at the Labour-in-Vain.' Early in the eighteenth century there was a tavern of this name in Old Fish Hill Street; whence the street received the alternative name of Labour-in-Vain Hill. The sign showed two women washing a blackamoor, and it being misunderstood, the tavern came to be popularly known as 'The Devil in a Tub.' According to Professor Sugden (*Topographical Dictionary, sub* 'Blackamoor') there is to this day a public-house in Melbourne called the Labour-in-Vain. (Sugden fails to record the evidence for a tavern of this name in Elizabethan or Jacobean London.)

2 The hand of a third author, probably Nathaniel Field, is discerned by some critics in Acts I and V. For the plot of this play see Genest, op.cit., vi,272f.; Schelling, op.cit., ii,220f.

3 She is called a 'Black Beauty,' a 'black jill,' and is said to look 'like the picture of America.' Her name is borrowed from the Zanthia of Marston's *Sophonisba*, another Moorish woman who is, however, not so well drawn. Yet a third is Zanche in Webster's *The White Devil*, Vittoria's waiting-woman.

known in England as the Battle of Alcazar and in popular
Iberian tradition as the Battle of the Three Kings—

> That renowned battel
> . . . of Alcazar, wherein two kings,
> Besides the King of Barbary, were slain,
> Kings of Morocco and of Portugal,
> With Stukeley, that renowned Englishman,
> That had a spirit equal to a king.[1]

The story of Dom Sebastian, King of Portugal, has been so
often told that only a brief reminder of its essential elements
is necessary here. The African adventure of this unfortunate
monarch was prompted by no desire to assist one of the claimants to the throne of Morocco at the expense of the other but
rather was intended to set one against the other in order to
weaken the Moslem power. Relying on the promise of Philip II
that under certain conditions he would render assistance, Sebastian planned his expedition on the side of Mahmed XI who
had been deposed by his uncle Abd-el-Malek. Actually Philip,
who was secretly in alliance with Abd-el-Malek, urged Sebastian
to abandon his undertaking; but Sebastian persisted with stubborn fanaticism. He recruited to his standard an English Roman
Catholic adventurer, Captain Thomas Stukeley, who with his
followers chanced to be in Lisbon on the way from Rome to
Ireland to raise a revolt against Queen Elizabeth. Englishmen,
moved by Stukeley's gallant death in Africa, were inclined to
forget his intended treachery and to remember him as a martyr
to Spanish perfidy. But the battle at Alcazar and the fate of
Dom Sebastian formed a romantic and tragic story apart from
the fact that Stukeley was slain on that fatal day. George Whetstone, in his chapter on 'the calamitie and servile bondage' of
Portugal to Spain, tells the story of Sebastian's defeat without
mentioning the part played by his English follower; [2] and

---

1 Thomas Heywood, *If You Know Not Me You Know Nobody*, Part II; *Dramatic
Works*, ed. Pearson, i,293.—It is noteworthy that what arouses Montaigne's interest
in 'cette journée fameuse par la mort de trois Roys' is the death not of Sebastian
but of the heroic Molei Molluc, King of Fez. Montaigne drew his long narrative
(*Essais*, ii,21) from Ieronimo de Franchi, *Dell' unione del regno di Portogallo alla
corona di Castiglia*, Genoa, 1585, folio 40.
2 *The English Myrror*, Book i, chapter xiii, pp.84f.

Thomas Nashe's indignation against Philip II was aroused by his treachery to the Portuguese king, not by his supposed responsibility for Stukeley's death.[1]

In 1579, about five months after the battle, a ballad, now lost, was licensed entitled *A briefe Rehersall of the bloodie Battell fought in Barbary*,[2] and in the same year there was registered a piece entitled *The Barbarie newes of the battell there* [3] which is probably represented by the extant prose tract *A Dolorous Discourse of a most terrible Battel fought in Barbarie*. The information in this pamphlet is so meagre that one is led to suppose that George Peele had other narratives at hand as sources for his tragedy *The Battle of Alcazar*.[4] This play can be dated quite definitely towards the close of 1588 or the beginning of 1589. Peele was alert not only to exploit the popular prejudice against Spain but also to take advantage of a fresh topical interest in the old story which, as we shall see, arose at that time. The piece is a bombastic melodrama, full of sound and fury, the personages so feebly characterized that their motives are not always intelligible. The text is in a state of almost hopeless confusion and its construction is so clumsy that not even dumb-shows and a 'presenter' or expositor clarify the situations. Yet it held the stage and was revived so late as 1601; and that it was popular is proved by various allusions to it. The tyrannical Moorish king is a typical stage-villain, 'black in his look and bloody in his deeds.' With this tragedy is associated an anonymous biographical play, of uncertain date but probably the mid-nineties, entitled *The Famous Historye of the Life and Death of Captaine Thomas Stukeley*.[5] Beginning not unpromisingly with

1 *Have with You to Saffron-Walden, Works*, iii,32.
2 *Stationers' Register*, 19 February 1579 (Arber, ii,347).
3 Ibid., 24 March 1579 (Arber, ii,349); Richard Simpson, *The School of Shakespeare*, i,144.
4 The original quarto, 1594, has been reproduced by Greg in the Malone Society publications; see also Peele's *Works*, ed. Bullen, i,218f. Peele may have known the *Historia de Bello Africano, in quo Sebastianus, Serenissimus Portugaliae Rex, periit . . . Ex Lusitano sermone primo in Gallicum: inde in Latinum translate per Ioannum Thomas Freigium*, Nuremberg, 1580, or the original Portuguese or the French version of this work. A brief account of Stukeley's 'voyage into Barbary,' extracted from Freigius, is in Hakluyt, vi,293f.
5 First published in 1605; reprinted in Simpson, *The School of Shakespeare*, i, with a long memoir of Stukeley. On the theory that the extant play is a patchwork of two older plays see E.H.C.Oliphant, *Notes and Queries*, Tenth Series, iii,301 and 342. Oliphant finds traces of Fletcher's hand. On *Stewtley* (doubtless Henslowe's misspell-

episodes of the adventurer's early life, it degenerates into chaotic incoherence in the last two acts where the author, wearying of his task, has clumsily cobbled together what seem to be fragments of some otherwise lost play on Alcazar.[1]

In consequence of the battle of Alcazar Portugal was presently absorbed by Spain and the long period began which is known to Portuguese historians as the Spanish Intrusion. Before long, however, rumours began to float about Europe that Dom Sebastian had not been slain in the battle but had been led away captive by the Moors. Towards the end of the sixteenth century a number of claimants to the throne of Portugal appeared who pretended to be the lost Sebastian and told more or less circumstantial stories of their escape from captivity in the desert. It would take us too far from our subject to inquire into the authenticity of any of the claims advanced;[2] nor can we give so much as a glance at the immense literature of 'Sebastianism' or at the beliefs, formerly widespread in Portugal and Brazil and perhaps even today not quite vanished, that Sebastian, like King Arthur or the Emperor Frederick II, will one day return to renew the ancient glories of his people. But we cannot neglect the contemporary interest in this matter in England. The first three claimants seem to

ing of Stukeley, *Diary*, i,44,5of.), a play performed in 1596–7 and perhaps an earlier version of the extant piece, see Sibley, op.cit., pp.153f. A play entitled *Muly Mollocco* performed by Lord Strange's men in 1592 and 1593 (*Henslowe's Diary*, i,13f.; ii,149) was, if not an independent piece now lost, either a version of *Stukeley* or else Peele's *Battle of Alcazar*. Dekker wrote a play on Stukeley which is now lost; his hand is not discernible in the extant drama. See Chambers, op.cit., iv,47, and compare p.529, note 5, below. There is also evidence of a lost play on the Moors by Dekker or at any rate a lost play on the Moors which Dekker, revising it, cut into two parts. This seems to be the point of an allusion in Dekker's *Satiromastix*, l.980, where Horace (that is, Jonson) says of Demetrius (Dekker) that he 'cut an innocent Moore' in the middle, to serve him in twice; and 'when he had done, made Poules-worke of it' (that is, the two parts were acted by the Children of Paul's).

1 Two allusions not mentioned in Simpson's memoir may be here noted. John Taylor the Water-Poet, a true-blue Protestant, says that 'bragging Stukely' promised to win Ireland for the Pope's bastard son;

> But Stukely was in Mauritania slaine,
> In that great battel at Alcazar fought.

(*Works*, Spenser Society, p.627.) There is an account of Stukeley's part in the battle in *The Arrivall and Intertainments of the Embassador*, 1637, p.27. In the Bodleian Library there is a copy, apparently unique, of *The Famous History of Stout Stukeley*, a prose narrative to which is added the ballad on the same subject. This chapbook is undated but was entered on the *Stationers' Register*, 11 May 1638.

2 See Miguel d'Antas, *Les Faux Don Sebastien*, Paris, 1866; and Montague Summers's introduction to Dryden's *Don Sebastian* (*Dramatic Works*, vi,3f.).

have made little impression there, but the fourth, Marco Tulio
Catizone, of whom reports spread from Venice, at once aroused
interest. Thomas Nashe derides the credulity of those who accept these reports. 'Greedy seagull ignorance,' he says, 'is apt
to devour any thing . . . It is currant that Don Sebastian,
king of Portugall, (slayne twenty yeares since wyth Stukeley at
the battell of Alcazar) is raysed from the dead like Lazarus, and
alive to be seene at Venice.' [1] That such gossip was still current
many years later is shown by a bit of dialogue in one of Fletcher's plays:

> *Sir Ruinous Gentry*: The first [service] that fleshed me a soldier,
> sir, was that great battle at Alcazar in Barbary, where the noble
> English Stukely fell, and where that royal Portugal Sebastian
> ended his unhappy days.
> *Wittypate*: Are you sure Sebastian died there?
> *Sir Ruinous Gentry*: Faith, sir, there was some other rumour hopped
> amongst us, that he, wounded, escaped, and touched on his
> native shore again, where finding his country at home more
> distressed by the invasion of the Spaniard than his loss abroad,
> forsook it, still supporting a miserable and unfortunate life, which
> where he ended is yet uncertain. [2]

A book or pamphlet called *Strange Newes of the Retourne of
Don Sebastian* of which no copy (if it was ever printed) is known
to survive was entered for publication in 1598. [3] Three years
later Anthony Munday issued an English version of a French
translation of a work by Fray Jose Teixeira in support of
Marco Tulio's claims. Of its immense title the essential portion
is: *The Strangest Adventure that ever Happened . . ., containing
a discourse concerning the successe of the King of Portugall Dom
Sebastian*, 1601. According to this narrative, Sebastian was
neither slain nor taken prisoner at Alcazar, but escaped sore
wounded. Ashamed of the folly and rashness which had brought
disaster to Christian arms, he would not return home but
determined to wander penitently through the world. At one

---

1 *Lenten-Stuffe, Works*, iii,212f.
2 *Wit at Several Weapons*, I,ii. Chapman seems to have accepted as true the rumour
   that Don Sebastian escaped death at Alcazar; see *The Conspiracy of Byron*, III,i,157f.
3 *Stationers' Register*, 1 February 1599 (Arber, iii,137).

time he was in military service to the Shah of Persia.[1] Later he became a hermit. When apprehended at Venice he first named himself 'the Knight of the Cross' but afterwards revealed his identity. A long list of physical peculiarities by which Dom Sebastian could be identified and which were all possessed by this claimant is given.[2] With his substantial proofs the shallow claims of other pretenders in history, such as Perkin Warbeck, are contrasted. Prophecies of the king's return—all fulfilled by the claimant—are recited. Two years later Munday published a supplement: *A Continuation of the Lamentable and Admirable Adventures of Don Sebastian*, 1603.[3] This is in part a translation from Teixeira with the addition of other documents supporting the claims of Marco Tulio who was by then a prisoner in Spain, presently to be executed. Between Munday's first and second narrative there had appeared another pamphlet, not by the same author or translator, entitled *The true History of the late and lamentable Adventures of Don Sebastian, King of Portugal, After his Imprisonment in Naples, until this present Day, being now in Spain*, 1602.[4]

Munday's earlier narrative was probably the source of the play, now lost, called *King Sebastian of Portugal* which Dekker and Chettle finished for Henslowe in May 1601.[5] It is certainly the source of the fine drama by Massinger which Sir Henry Herbert refused to license in 1630 'because it did contain dangerous matter, as the deposing of Sebastian King of Portugal.' The inherent peril lay in the possibility of giving offence to Spain. Massinger revised his play, changed its period to antiquity, turned his protagonist into Antiochus King of Lower Asia, a fugitive at Carthage, and made other alterations; and thus revamped it was licensed by Herbert in 1631 as *Believe*

---

1 Munday, *Strangest Adventure*, p.90, adds to the original text the information that Sir Anthony Sherley has written from Persia that 'a gallant gentleman, who named himselfe Le Chevalier de la Croix . . . with other gentlemen his companions' were in great reputation by reason of their valour against the Turks. Munday identifies this Chevalier with the claimant.
2 Ibid., pp.78f.
3 Reprinted in the *Harleian Miscellany*, ii (1809), 367f.
4 Reprinted ibid., ii,355f.
5 *Henslowe's Diary*, i,136f.; ii,217. This may have been a revision of the earlier play on Stukeley written by Dekker; compare pp.526–7, note 5, above. See Chambers, op. cit., iv,47; Sibley, op.cit., p.141; and M.L.Hunt, *Thomas Dekker*, p.49.

As You List, a title worthy of Massinger's bold plain-speaking on political matters, for it has a double sense: believe, if you will, that the pretender's claims are true; believe, if you will, that this is a story of ancient Carthage. With the changes in time and setting all traces of Islamic interest, if there were such (as is likely) in Massinger's original play, were removed; but in the original manuscript of the revised play scanty but unmistakable evidence remains that *Believe As You List* is at but one remove from the lost play on Sebastian for which a license had been refused.[1]

About the time when the growth of piracy was attracting to the Barbary States the anxious attention of Englishmen Thomas Heywood wrote the two parts of his *Fair Maid of the West*[2] of which several scenes are laid in North Africa. The vessel carrying Bess Bridges and her companions is 'forced for want of water' to put into Mamorrah, a Port of Barbary. Mullisheg, the King of 'Fesse' (Fez) entertains them graciously, and Part I ends with the bestowal of presents upon them and permission given for their departure. But at the opening of Part II they are in new difficulties, for Mullisheg has regretted his magnanimity because he has fallen in love with Bess. His angry Queen determines to cuckold him by giving herself to Spencer, Bess's sweetheart. By means of the familiar dramatic device of identity mistaken because of darkness, here coarsely but not unamusingly worked out, the King and Queen lie with each other, each thinking that the embraces are those

1 See C.J.Sisson's introduction to *Believe As You List* in the Malone Society edition.— Extravagant French romance vulgarized the story of the noble claimant, and it was next presented to the English public as an amorous intrigue in which Sebastian wages war in Barbary for the sake of Almeida, the sister of Mahumet of Morocco, of whom he is enamoured. After his defeat at Alcazar Sebastian and Almeida are separated but meet by chance at Venice; and the feeble tale proceeds in approximate accord with the facts and traditions to his arrest, trial, and execution (*Don Sebastian, King of Portugal, an Historical Novel, in Four Parts, Done out of French by Mr. Ferrand Spence*, 1683). In the preface to his *Don Sebastian*, 1689, Dryden acknowledges indebtedness to this French romance. Dryden retained the love-interest and complicated it by introducing the motive of incest: Sebastian, after marrying Almeyda, discovers that she is the offspring of his own father's secret love for a Moorish woman. In remorse for his unintentional crime he retires to a hermitage. The play has nothing to do with the claimant who appeared years later.

2 The date is uncertain but before 1603. Text in *Dramatic Works*, ed. Pearson, ii. Both parts were first published in 1631 when, as we have seen in Chapter VIII, there was a violent new outbreak of piracy. This doubtless lent a new topical interest to these old-fashioned plays.

of a fascinating stranger. The party of English adventurers attempt to escape but are captured and brought back; and then the Moorish monarch, who is depicted with the hearty good humour characteristic of Heywood, is moved to new magnanimity by their courage, gives over his lustful pursuit of Bess, and permits them to depart. An encounter with pirates is narrated by the Chorus at the close of Act III. The rest of their adventures take place in Italy.

In 1612, as we saw in Chapter VIII, twelve captured pirates were hanged on the same day at Wapping.[1] Contemporaneous with this wholesale execution is Robert Daborne's drama on the career of Captain John Ward, *A Christian Turn'd Turk*.[2] In his Prologue Daborne refers to former writers who in 'trivial scenes' have exhibited Ward's life as a pirate. This sounds like an allusion to some earlier play, now lost, but perhaps it points merely to the two accounts of Ward which had already appeared. In the Epistle to the Reader he calls his play 'this oppressed and much martird Tragedy,' a puzzling phrase. Perhaps the piece had suffered on the stage from the disapproval of unfriendly spectators or from such bad weather as Webster complains of in the Preface to *The White Devil*; but recalling Chapman's lament for his 'poor dismembered poems' after the censor had compelled the revision of an act of the *Tragedy of Byron*, one guesses that perhaps the censor had

1 Compare the scene of Purser and Clinton conducted by the Sheriffs to execution at Wapping in Heywood's *Fortune by Land and Sea*, V,i; *Dramatic Works*, vi,427f. This play is, however, dated about 1607 and is founded upon an account of certain English pirates of about 1586. See *Shakespeare Society Papers*, iii (1847), 7f. In various other plays (*Twelfth Night*, Fletcher and Massinger's *The Double Marriage* and *The Sea Voyage*, and James Shirley's *The Court Secret*, for example) there are pirates whose nationality is not indicated; but probably in every play where they appear or are referred to a suggestion was carried to the minds of the spectators of the roving renegades who were terrorizing shipping from their lairs on the African coast. In March 1603, a play with the curious title *The Siege of Dunkirk or Alleyn the Pirate* was purchased by the Admiral's men (*Henslowe's Diary*, i,174; ii,228). No pirate of this name appears in the records, but W.C.Hazlitt's suggestion (*Manual . . . of Old English Plays*, 1892, p.210) that Edward Alleyn took the part of the pirate and so gave his name to the play is inadmissible. In any case the play probably had nothing to do with Islam. Nothing is known of Robert Davenport's lost play *The Pirate* except that Samuel Sheppard addressed some lines to 'Mr. Davenport on his Play called The Pirate' (*Epigrams*, 1651); see Sibley, op.cit., p.123.

2 *A Christian turn'd Turke: or, the Tragicall Lives and Deaths of the two Famous Pyrates Ward and Dansiker. As it hath been publickly Acted*, 1612; ed. A.E.H.Swaen, *Anglia*, xx (1898), 174f. Nothing is known of its stage history beyond the statement on the title-page. It is not mentioned in any of the extant Henslowe-Daborne letters. Genest, op.cit., x,94f., outlines the plot.

required alterations in Daborne's play that left it 'martyred.'
Certainly the state of the text supports this theory unless we
account for the confusion on the ground that it was hastily
written to profit from the immediate interest in the subject of
pirates. Even when every allowance is made, it is a contemptible
piece of work, coarse and scabrous, bombastic and noisy, ill-
constructed and confused in style, thought, and intention. It
opens with Ward's first knavish exploit, the ship-stealing episode. Then there is a fight at sea in which the balcony of the
stage is employed to represent the poop of a vessel. A forlorn
French girl, whose lover has been slain, is taken prisoner.
Later at Tunis this girl, now disguised as a boy, attracts the
amorous attentions of a Turkish woman. The chief complication of the plot comes from Ward's attempt to cuckold a
renegade Jew. To win this Jew's Turkish wife he consents to
turn Turk. The ceremony of his renunciation of Christianity is
enacted in the dumbest of dumb-shows. A procession of Turks
bearing half-moons appears. A Mufty requires of Ward that he
kiss 'a Mahomets head.' The apostate then spurns a cup of
wine offered him by a Christian captive. (To have shown him in
the act of spurning the Cross would have probably been intolerable to the censor; in fact it may well have been at this
point that alterations were required and the tragedy consequently 'oppressed and much martird.') When it comes to
the rite of circumcision, Ward tricks the Turks by substituting
'an ape's tail' for his foreskin—the Jacobean stage never sank
lower than that. Ward's monstrous villainies occupy the remainder of the play until at last the Governor places him under
arrest and orders that he be torn piece-meal and his accursed
limbs thrown into the sea. Upon his monument (which must
have been a cenotaph) is to be inscribed: 'Ward sold his
country, turn'd Turk, and died a slave.' It is scarcely necessary to remind the reader that when this was written Ward
was still in full career with more than ten years of life before
him.

More interesting and attractive in its orientalism than any
of the plays on Moorish subjects we have passed in review,
better informed and far more realistic is Massinger's fine

romantic play *The Renegado*.[1] In order to appreciate its unusual quality we must have before us a summary of the plot.[2]
Before the opening of Act I the following events, recapitulated
in expository dialogue, have occurred. At Venice Grimaldi
the renegado had, for no clear reason, insulted the consecrated
Host and had been forced to flee oversea. He kidnapped
Paulina and, having turned pirate and Moslem, sold her to
Asambeg, the Viceroy of Tunis. Asambeg fell in love with her
but Paulina spurned his solicitations and he has treated her
with all respect and honour. Meanwhile Vitelli, Paulina's
brother, has followed her to Tunis to attempt her rescue. With
him is his spiritual adviser, the Jesuit Francisco, and his servant
Gazet, the comic character of the play. When the drama
begins Vitelli and Gazet, disguised as native merchants, are at
their stall in the market-place in Tunis. The Princess Donusa,
the niece of the Grand Seigneur Sultan Amurath, comes to the
bazaars accompanied only by a gentleman named Mustapha
who is paying court to her. At first sight she falls in love with
Vitelli; and in order to obtain a private interview with him she
resorts to the stratagem of breaking some of his wares to pieces
and bidding him bring to the palace his bill for compensation.
In the seraglio she receives him with immoderate ardour; and he,
bewildered and flattered, accepts from her all she is so ready to
bestow—not only herself but a fine suit of clothes in which he
presently struts abroad in the city. When the Jesuit Francisco
learns that he is the accepted lover of a Mohammedan princess
he admonishes Vitelli and brings him to repentance, with the
result that on his next meeting with Donusa Vitelli rudely re-
pels her advances. Their colloquy is overheard by Asambeg and
Mustapha with the consequence that they are both put under
arrest. There follows the trial-scene which readers of Massinger
learn to look for in every play from his pen. The Princess is
condemned to death, but she claims the legal alternative of an
opportunity to try to convert Vitelli to Islam; if successful, both
their lives will be spared and they may marry one another.[3]

1 Licensed 1624; published 1630.
2 For longer summaries see Genest, op.cit., vi,272f.; Schelling, op.cit., ii,220f.
3 Massinger had read somewhere that according to Mohammedan law or custom a

In the private interview which follows Vitelli passionately denounces Mahomet:

> Your juggling prophet . . .
> I will not foul my mouth to speak the sorceries
> Of your seducer, his base birth, his whoredoms,
> His strange impostures; nor deliver how
> He taught a pigeon to feed in his ear,
> Then made his credulous followers believe
> It was an angel, that instructed him
> In the framing of his Alcoran.[1]

The upshot is that Donusa, instead of converting Vitelli to Mohammedanism, is herself converted to Christianity;[2] and they are both condemned to death. But meanwhile the admirable and resourceful Jesuit Francisco has reconverted to Christianity the renegade Grimaldi. By means of a rope ladder Donusa and Vitelli escape from prison; the repentant Grimaldi receives the entire party in his ship; and they sail away leaving Asambeg and his followers discomfited.

With the Spanish sources or analogues of this lively and delightful play we are not here concerned except to say that there is a general resemblance to the Spanish pirate-romances in which the renegado is a stereotyped figure and a more particular connection with *Los Baños de Argel*, a comedy of 1615 which in turn has connections with Cervantes and his experiences as a captive in Algiers.[3] It is apparent to anyone acquainted with the literature of Levantine travel and with the chronicles of events in the Levant that Massinger had read both widely and intelligently therein. Vitelli's denunciation of Mahomet will be recognized by the reader as a theme in Christian propagandist literature whose ancestry ascends far back into the Middle Ages. There is a close resemblance between the plot of the play and the story of Ionuses Bassa

Christian, if caught with a Moslem woman, must either 'turn Turk' or else be put to death. See, for example, William Davies, *True Relation*, Sig. B₂ᵛ.

1 *The Renegado*, IV,iii.
2 There are analogous situations in *The Virgin Martyr* by Dekker and Massinger and in the anonymous play *The Two Noble Ladies or The Converted Conjuror*.
3 See Theodore Heckmann, *Massinger's The Renegado und seine Spanischen Quellen*, Halle, 1905.

and his wife Manto in Knolles's *Historie*. A parallel has been remarked between the situation of Asambeg's passion for Paulina and another story in Knolles, that of the daughter of the governor of Chalcis who refused to submit to the embraces of Mahomet II and was put to death; but the differences between these situations are greater than the resemblances, and the love of a Mohammedan ruler for a Christian captive is, as we have seen, a commonplace of Levantine romance. Details of Mohammedan customs Massinger obtained from his reading in general and perhaps, as has been pointed out,[1] particularly from Biddulph's *Travels* and Sandys's *Relation of a Journey* where he found, or could have found, information on such matters as the prerogative of the Prophet's descendants to wear green garments and the peril to non-believers who wear that forbidden colour; the jealous care with which Moslems guard their women; the dagger given the Great Turk's daughters that at need they may slay their husbands; and so forth. Somewhere Massinger read that the Sultan sends to anyone in disfavour with him the decree of death; the victim submits without a protest. Massinger does not specify the manner of execution; Biddulph says that it is by strangling and Sandys mentions the bowstring. Massinger knows that those captives in Barbary were comparatively fortunate who were not condemned to the galleys but became household servants. The bondage of the castrated slave Carazie—designed as a comic figure but repellent rather than amusing—is not severe.[2] An Englishman by birth, made prisoner by the Turks, he is now on terms of impudent leering familiarity with his mistress. In addition to this eunuch Massinger introduces a basha, an aga, and a capiaga, officials about whom he may have

---

1 W.G.Rice, 'The Sources of Massinger's *The Renegado,*' *Philological Quarterly,* xi (1932), 65f. Dr. Rice summarizes the stories in Knolles and indicates the parallels in Massinger, and notes indebtednesses to Biddulph and Sandys.—Young Malefort in Massinger's *The Unnatural Combat,* Act I, is an 'apostata' and one of 'the pirates of Argiers and Tunis.'

2 In Sir Ralph Freeman's tragedy *Imperiale,* 1639, II,ii, the sinister slave Molosso expresses his gratitude to his master for keeping him in his household and sparing him

> The restless misery of the painfull oare,
> With all the wants that ever were susteyn'd
> In a remorseless Galley.

read in Knolles. Mustapha the basha carries a scimitar and wears the mustachios characteristic of the Turks.[1] When he enters the apartment of the Princess he takes off his 'pantofles,' saying to himself:

> I am to enter
> The room where she abides, with such devotion
> As pilgrims pay at Mecca, when they visit
> The tomb of their great prophet.[2]

For all his reading Massinger was misinformed as to the place of Mahomet's burial.

The general impression made by *The Renegado* is of a romantic and picturesque yet, generally speaking, accurate and realistic orientalism unmatched elsewhere in the imaginative literature of Renaissance England. The 'juggling prophet' and the 'horned moons' of Islam; the Sultan's despotism and the jealousy of husbands; audacious lovers and amorous women; seraglios and bazaars; bashas, agas, capiagas, beglerbegs, sanzaches, chiauses, and eunuchs; the citation of the *Koran*; allusions to the Persian wars and to the siege of Rhodes—all this medley combines very successfully to create an atmosphere curiously like that of the *Arabian Nights*, a collection of stories which was not to become known in Europe for another century.[3]

VII

THE only play of the Tudor-Stuart period whose scene is laid in Arabia (other than *Revenge for Honour* where the localization is without significance) is William Lower's *The Phoenix in Her Flames*, 1639,[4] a tragedy of no great merit but written

---

1 Compare Simon Baylie, *The Wizard*, l.752: 'With Mustachoes like a Turbant Turk.'
2 *The Renegado*, I,ii.
3 Massinger's solid workmanship is brought into high relief by a comparison with the efforts—or lack of efforts—of other dramatists to achieve 'local colour.' Their orientalism generally consists of little more than oaths by Mahomet, Termagant, or Mortus Aly; allusions to concubines, eunuchs, and seraglios; and occasional vague references to the *Koran*. So finely pictorial a line as Peele's 'Silver moons . . . in banners bravely spreading o'er the plain' (*The Battle of Alcazar* I,i) is rare; a precise allusion to an article of Mohammedan costume, such as the 'high sugar-loaf hat' which the Sultan gives Erastus (*Soliman and Persida*, IV,i) even rarer.
4 *The Phoenix in Her Flames. A Tragedy. The Scene, Arabia. The Author, Master William Lower*, 1639. The play has not been reprinted. It is not included in Louis Wann's list of plays on oriental themes, *Modern Philology*, xii (1915), 164f.

with some skill and with less rant than one would expect from its date. The ingenious plot derives from the *Æthiopian History* of Heliodorus with suggestions from other sources.[1] The Prince of Damascus escapes to the Arabian desert when his city falls before the attack of the Tartars. The Princess of Egypt, who is on a journey to the court of the Prince of Persia to whom she is betrothed, is captured in the desert by a band of robbers. The same band takes prisoner the Prince of Damascus after a fight in which he kills the robber-chief. Another leader of the desert outlaws is attracted by the charms of the fair Princess and attempts to ravish her; whereupon Damascus slays him. The grateful Princess, moved by his valour, falls in love with him and woos him boldly. But Damascus is not in love with her. Meanwhile the Prince of Persia has heard that his betrothed has been taken prisoner by marauding Arabs and invades the desert to rescue her. This violation of territorial boundaries surprises and bewilders the King of the Arabs who, residing far to the South in Arabia Felix, has had no word of the violent and lawless events that have been taking place at the other limits of his domains. Damascus, who has won the confidence of the tribes of the desert, organizes them into an army, wins a battle against the Persians, and brings their Prince as a prisoner to the King of the Arabs. Forthwith, victor and vanquished, Damascus and Persia, both fall in love with Phaenicia, the daughter of the King. The two Princes, urged on by an ambitious Duke, engage in a duel. Damascus kills Persia but is himself slain by this treacherous Duke and his followers. In grief for the death of the Prince of Damascus, Phaenicia causes herself to be smothered to death in clouds of incense. The poor Princess of Egypt, having lost her betrothed who had been faithless to her and her rescuer who had rejected her advances, returns sadly home.

The courtly manners, typical of Caroline tragedy and ab-

---

1 Heliodorus's romance, better known as *Theagenes and Chariclia*, was accessible to Lower in the English translation by Thomas Underdowne, 1577. See W.B.Gates, *The Dramatic Works and Translations of Sir William Lower*, Philadelphia, 1932, pp.59f. Dr. Gates's conclusion is that 'the play was built up, probably, out of a variety of materials—situations and characters from some of the romances, other plays, and perhaps the imagination of the author.'

surdly inappropriate to the violent story, are of course hopelessly unoriental. Lower provides the usual oaths by Mahomet
and such allusions to caravans and thieves as the story requires. But in general the 'local colour' is of the crudest and
most rudimentary kind. The death of the phoenix (Phaenicia)
in the fumes of incense is certainly a novelty but not so impressive as the author evidently imagined it to be. Lower
makes some use of topographical information, as of the three
divisions of Arabia: the desert, the rocky, and the fortunate or
fertile. In the opening scene there is some slight attempt to
suggest a rough rock-strewn landscape.[1]

VIII

IF now we glance back over the way we have come in this
chapter we shall be in possession of some sort of gauge with
which to measure general knowledge of Moslem history, for
the drama is a fairly accurate reflection of the popular mind.
In the course of this summary we shall touch on a few plays
mentioned in earlier chapters or not hitherto referred to at all.
We find that the tradition of the treachery of Count Julian
by which the Moors obtained their first foothold in Spain is
the subject of a play and that the Moorish domination of
Spain forms the background of another. The Crusade led by
Godfrey de Bouillon is the principal theme of Heywood's
Four Prentices of London. The Cretan revolt against Venice
in 1361-5, into which the Turkish question intruded, is dramatized with unusual historical accuracy in The Laws of Candy
by Fletcher and Massinger.[2] The conquests of Tamburlaine

1 The history of Arabia is beyond the dramatists' range. The image which the desert
called up to Shakespeare is that of lawlessness, as in Macbeth's challenge to the
Ghost: 'Dare me to the desert with thy sword' (III,iv,104) and specifically in Corio-
lanus: 'I would my son Were in Arabia . . . His good sword in his hand' (IV,ii,24—
there is no note on the passage in the Furness Variorum). Compare Imogen's wish
that Posthumous and Cloten 'were in Afric . . . Myself by with a needle, that I
might prick The goer-back' (Cymbeline, I,i,167f.). Marston does less than justice
to Turkish criminal law when he makes one of his characters say (Parasitaster,
I,ii,254): 'May I speak out boldly, as at Aleppo?'—as though that city were beyond
the reach of the law.

2 This is the only drama of our period whose scene is set in Crete. The historical background is the discontent of the Cretans under Venetian rule. Between 1207 and 1365
there were no less than fourteen insurrections in the island; the 'war' in the play
may be any of these, perhaps that of 1361-5 which was the most memorable. The
situation is, save for one particular, quite accurately set forth at IV,ii,17f., where

form the subject of the greatest of Elizabethan dramas on oriental themes; and, probably as much because of the fame of Marlowe's play as because of the fame of his hero, the Tartar conqueror is frequently referred to elsewhere. The fall of Constantinople probably formed the historical background of Peele's lost drama on the story of Irene as it does of later dramatizations of this romantic pseudo-historical tale. The revolt of Scanderbeg was the subject of a lost play of unknown authorship. The circumstances of atrocious cruelty which marked the accession of Selim the Grim are enacted in *Selimus* and the same Sultan's conquest of Egypt in a Latin Senecan tragedy. Events immediately antecedent to the siege and fall of Rhodes, quite without warrant in history but none the less plausible to an Elizabethan audience on that account, are the subject of *Soliman and Persida*. Several allusions in the drama to the siege of Buda may point to a series of events in 1527–9 or more probably to the siege of 1602. A lost comedy on the 'taking' of Stuhlweissenburg had to do with the fortunes of a Hungarian town which changed hands several times. The siege of Vienna in 1529 is often alluded to; the reference in *Tamburlaine* to an assault on that city is unhistorical but is intended to convey to an audience a suggestion of the strength of the Ottomans. The retirement of the Knights of Rhodes to Malta is referred to more than once. In the campaign of Solyman the Magnificent against Persia, the Prince of Morocco who appears in *The Merchant of Venice* had taken part; and there are many other allusions to Turko-Persian relations. Solyman's murder of his son Mustapha at the instigation of his wife Roxolana is the subject of two or perhaps three plays. The unsuccessful Turkish attack on Malta in 1565 is a theme that enters into several plays: Marlowe's *The Jew of Malta*, Barnabe Barnes's *The Devil's Charter*, and especially Webster's *The Devil's Law-Case*; and it is a central theme of *The Knight of Malta*. The siege of Cyprus by Selim II and the capitulation of Famagusta (1571) are referred to in Mason's *The Turk* and elsewhere,

the only error lies in the statement that the Cretans were 'vex'd' by the Anatolian Turks. In reality they preferred Ottoman sovereignty to that of Venice, though Crete remained under Venetian rule till 1669.

and the audience's knowledge of these events is assumed in *Othello*. The victory of Lepanto was not put upon the stage but it forms the subject of a masque-like entertainment by George Gascoigne. Events in Barbary form the subject of several plays. The defeat and death of Dom Sebastian and Stukeley, his English follower, are twice dramatized and probably formed the subject of other plays, now lost; and Massinger's *Believe As You List* is founded upon the story of Sebastian. The career of a notorious English renegade and pirate is enacted in a sensational drama; and various incidents in the course of the long struggle with the corsairs are alluded to elsewhere.[1] The experiences of Christian captives in slave-markets are several times dramatized or described. The adventures of the Sherley brothers in Persia and elsewhere are crudely dramatized in one play and may have formed the subject of another, now lost. Finally, the blinding of Mirza by Shah Abbas and the death of the unfortunate prince afforded material for two or three tragedies of oriental palace-intrigue.

1 Into *The Knight of Malta* there is introduced a narrative of a raid upon the island of Gozo by 'Arabs' from North Africa; in Fletcher's *Rule a Wife and Have a Wife* the Turkish capture of Goletta from Don John of Austria is narrated; and in many plays there are allusions, more or less vague, to sea-fights with the Turks, by whom Moorish pirates are often intended.

CHAPTER TWELVE

EPILOGUE

COMBINED with the information derived from scores of books translated from foreign languages, the reports of the returned traveller—whether he was an ambassador or important man of affairs, factor, preacher, discharged soldier or ransomed captive, semi-professional vagabond or seeker after exotic sensations— whether he imparted his impressions by word of mouth to a small private company or through the pages of a travel-book to a larger audience—built up in the Elizabethan imagination and passed into English literature a picture of Islam as at once splendidly luxurious, admirable in its serenity, sombre in its cruelty and sensuality, and terrible in its strength. Whether or not his journey into the Levant had had a practical end in view, to serve his government or advance the trade of his country (objects generally undistinguishable from each other), such a traveller was generally uncritically receptive of impressions. There is very little in English travel-books of the period to parallel or anticipate the first-hand precision of the *Lettres edifiantes et curieuses* which from about 1570 were sent home by Jesuit missionaries and poured from the French printing-presses throughout the seventeenth century. The Jesuits were active chiefly in the far eastern field; their letters contain much precious and exact information on China (Japan remained almost unknown); they lived among the people; spoke their language; knew their lives intimately; and in their relations did much to turn sympathetic public attention to an Orient that was a reality, not a dream-world.[1] In comparison with their weighty disquisitions the narratives of the chaplains or 'preachers' to the English factors are meagre, prejudiced, impressionistic, and merely popular because these men, unlike the Catholic

1 See Pierre Martino, *L'Orient dans la littérature française*, Paris, 1906, especially p.116. Edward Pocock is the closest, and almost the only, English parallel.

missionaries, did not come into close personal contact with the native populations.

No organized topographical exploration for purely scientific purposes was undertaken by Englishmen till well after our period. The Elizabethans went into the East to discover new 'vents' for English trade. At most a trader might undertake to try to procure a chart or Arabic cosmography for such a rare inquiring spirit as Richard Hakluyt or precious documents to bring home to one of the few English Arabists; or a well-to-do and well-informed gentleman such as Fynes Moryson would make conscientious and careful observations. But even Moryson was responsible to no learned society and noted down only what attracted his own interests and tastes.

In the back of his mind the traveller carried a quantity of superstitions, fabulous lore, and old wives' tales; it was part of the baggage he took with him into the East; and when once there he was generally—though there are exceptions, such as William Lithgow—more desirous to have it all confirmed than to put it to the test of his own actual observations. What was before his own eyes he might set down accurately enough in his table-books; in earlier chapters we have had glimpses of travellers 'writing up' by night in their inns the hasty jottings made 'on the spot.' [1] Save for things for which he had 'the sensible and true avouch' of his own eyes, he was the prey to prepossessions and hearsay. The fabulous was only just beyond the horizon. His credulity was so profound that at any point he was ready to accept the most fantastic tales. Though when he journeyed through the desert he certainly heard no airy tongues syllable his name, he did not doubt that such wildernesses were demon-haunted. He did not question the likelihood that Mahomet's body was suspended in mid-air. That the palm-tree grew taller the more weight was hung upon it was not to be questioned simply because he had not put the phenomenon to the test of experiment. By the shore of the Dead Sea one could pluck fruit that was outwardly fair to view but dust and ashes within; if he had not found this fruit, that was his ill-luck, not a refutation of the old report. Somewhere in 'inaccessible'

1 See p.35, note 1, above.

Arabia [3] the phoenix was reigning in solitary beauty at the very hour when he, the traveller, might be upon the borders of that mysterious country. In far-distant Ethiopia was Prester John, the great Christian king, the potential ally of Christendom against the Moslems. Were not these and innumerable other reports confirmed by the authority of Aristotle or Pliny or Strabo or Solinus or the medieval cosmographers or the travellers of his own day? Who was he to gainsay the testimony of such learned men? The few sturdy individuals who pit their own observations against inherited traditions stand out as early representatives of the modern mind. 'Many build upon false reports,' says Lithgow, 'but experience teacheth men the truth.' The difficulty was, however, that even in the case of those who relied upon their own senses, their experiences were personal, unchecked, of small range, made generally during short sojourns in the Levant by men who brought occidental preconceptions and prejudices with them and who, in the manner of travellers, exaggerated their adventures and distorted their observations in the recounting of them. There are some notable exceptions to this rule; but in general it may be said that not until the later seventeenth century did narratives of travel become precise and reliable. The unreliability of earlier books was increased by the unconscionable habit of transferring to their own books, without acknowledgment, matter from earlier narratives, often matter quite unchecked by the borrower's own observations.

As the typical traveller was uncritical so was he undiscriminating. Everything was grist that came to his mill. 'He lesse offends,' says Fynes Moryson, 'that writes many toyes than he that omits one serious thing.' The consequence of this naïve receptivity is that when one attempts, as the attempt has been made in this book, to fashion into a single picture the observations of travellers who ventured into the Levant and the fantasies of poets and other writers who stayed at home in England, that picture must be composed of multitudinous fragments: it is a mosaic, not a painting. To neglect hundreds of bits of evidence because they are false, trifling, or absurd would

1 Milton, *Paradise Regained*, iii,274: 'Inaccessible, the Arabian drouth.'

be to omit part of the pattern; the effect is cumulative. The detail we might choose to ignore as merely frivolous may have been one of the impressions which fixed most firmly in the traveller's mind the greatness of the Ottoman Empire. Imagine an Englishman passing from the huge, dimly lighted, and almost terrifying bazaars of Constantinople—in their many nationalities of chaffering merchants a microcosm speaking eloquently of the Sultan's far-flung dominions—to the menagerie near by. It puts to shame Queen Elizabeth's collection of wild beasts at the Tower of London. What is a lion or a brown bear compared with that fairest of animals, the giraffe, which feeds so gently from his hand? Will our traveller's friends believe him when he attempts to describe it? Or if they believe him, why should he in turn refuse credence to the Hajji who tells him of the unicorn kept captive in that city of Arabia—was it Mecca or Yathrib?—that city where the false prophet is buried?

False prophet? A shadow of uncertainty flits across the thoughts of the returned traveller. Is everything that Christians tell of Mahomet and his followers true? Can it be that God suffered a disreputable impostor, such as he is described in the pulpits of Christendom and in a hundred diatribes against the Turks, to mislead so great a concourse of mankind? It is indeed difficult (thinks our traveller) to reconcile the opinions of Christian theologians with one's own impressions of the Mohammedan East. With what dignity and reserve and serenity the Moslems comport themselves; how affable they are when not aroused to controversy; how hospitable to the wayworn stranger; how tolerant even of those whose religion they hold false and abominable; how courageous in war; how evenhanded in the administration of justice. And then, their devoutness, their earnest adherence to the rules of conduct and ceremonial laid down by their religion, their admirable unity of belief and lack of divisions into sects, a unity with which the discords of Christendom contrast so shamefully.[1] This apprecia-

---

1 Hence the sense of surprise and relief implied in Christian accounts of the Turco-Persian wars, that quarrel between Sunni and Shi'a being the exception to the otherwise universal unity of Islam. Palace-intrigues and the quarrels of rival claimants to the Ottoman throne, though providing themes for the Elizabethan playwrights, are seldom thought by publicists to constitute an exception to this unity.

tion of the genial and admirable qualities of the Moslems was difficult to cultivate in an age when Christian prejudice rendered any defence of Mohammedanism suspect. The virtues practised in Islam might with weighty reservations be praised, because courtesy and courage and hospitality, when evident, did not admit of contradiction; but any sympathetic exposition of their creed was almost unthinkable when their doctrines were held to be the devil's promptings to a base-born Arabian impostor. Hence our traveller (though some thoughtful men, Bacon or Moryson for example, know better) will instinctively ascribe harmless differences of religious custom to deliberately offensive eccentricity, and fundamental contrasts to calculated insolence, defiance, and blasphemy. Englishmen of the Elizabethan age—and the traveller whose mentality we are attempting to display is representative of his time—did have some faint realization of the effect of climatic differences upon different races of men; and, perhaps directed to the thought by the theory of the cardinal humours in the human body, they remarked in some of their travel-books upon the influence which hot, dry countries exercised upon their inhabitants. But a completely tolerant outlook was beyond the Elizabethan's comprehension, a cosmopolitan point of view which embraces the idea that differences in manners and opinions are to a large degree conditioned by differences of environment and inherited traditions. That concept was not to be generally grasped for another century or more.

But the traveller did bring home confirmation of another and very different concept. All that he had to tell of the ancient countries through which he had passed would serve to strengthen in the mind of the philosophic historian the Platonic conception of a law governing the rise, florescence, and decline of civilizations. The empires of Egypt, Babylonia, Persia, Greece, Rome, Byzantium, and now Islam moved as in a vast panorama before his imagination; round the decay of the colossal wrecks of the more ancient empires the lone and level sands stretched far away; the lion and the lizard kept the courts of the kings of old. Along with a quantity of archaeological information, hastily assembled and not very well digested—'crudities gobbled up,' in Tom Coryat's phrase—this impression of the triumphs of time over all human institutions, howsoever firmly builded, passed from the traveller to such a philosophic historian as Richard Knolles and such a philosophic poet as Fulke Greville.

To the men responsible for the conduct of public affairs the traveller will have other information and impressions to impart. If he has followed the counsel given him on his departure he will have been diligent not only to observe but to note down his observations. Conferences with men who had sojourned in the East helped to shape the public policy of statesmen when, confronting Islam, the states of Christendom in times of critical decisions had a dim realization of a community of interests transcending political boundaries, uniting them in a common peril, and making them all members of a great society. The evidence brought home by actual observers doubtless strengthened this realization though it did little to produce any practical results in concerted action against the common enemy. From the traveller statesmen will wish to have the latest information upon the discipline of the Sultan's military forces and upon the organization of his civil government; upon the characteristic Ottoman methods of training selected portions of their slave populations for public service; upon the presence of Christian officials in posts of high responsibility at the Porte; upon the celebrated 'school of pages'; upon the Janissaries; upon the most recent rumours as to the likelihood of an outbreak of war and the most probable direction of the next Turkish thrust; or (if war is already in progress) as to the most efficacious means of thwarting Turkish strategy. Statesmen will also expect to be informed as to the palace-conspiracies involving some great Turkish minister of state or perhaps the heir presumptive to the throne, for such intrigues, since they are signs of interior weakness, may be interpreted as omens of Ottoman decline. The care with which English agents are guarding English interests against the intrigues and rivalry of foreigners will provoke searching questions. Estimates may perhaps be submitted of the number of Englishmen held in captivity in various parts of the Ottoman Empire and of the chances that those of wealth and rank may be admitted to ransom. Merchants trading into the Levant will seek anxiously for the latest information regarding new markets for English woollens, metals, and manufactured commodities and will probably be less interested in reports upon oriental luxuries such as silks, spices, perfumes, and the like, with which their warehouses are perhaps already overflowing. Our traveller may submit samples of some plant hitherto unknown in England which may profitably be cultivated here, or he may tell about some novel process of weaving and dyeing, or reveal some technical secret of Damascene metal-work. There was, in sum, much more dependence then than there is today on the observations and impressions of private travellers.

But statesmen and wealthy merchant-adventurers were not the only audience such a traveller might assemble round him. We can picture him at home undoing his bales and boxes while each object that comes to light reminds him of some strange or perilous experience. The bottle of water from the Jordan will be given to his parish-minister for use in christen-ings; and if that minister is not a puritan who despises holy relics he will gladly accept for his church a girdle the length of the Lord's Sepulchre. One of these parcels has in it dust from the Virgin's Grotto at Bethlehem, an excellent tonic for nursing mothers; another contains tawny sand from the desert behind Aleppo. This package may contain samples of pepper and spices, and that some bits of pitch from the oil-wells of Baku. In that long slender bundle are two rods: one is his pilgrim's staff (it must be handed down to his children's children); the other is a switch of terebinth cut on the road to Jericho (a rare curiosity worth giving to some influential courtier or perhaps to the Queen herself). That other bottle, cloudy and ill-smelling, is filled with water from the Dead Sea; and this small package has in it some powdered mummy; it, too, smells none too agreeably; it shall to the apothecary.

Having unpacked his souvenirs, our traveller, measurelessly content to be at home, sinks into a reverie, half memory, half dream, of men whom he met in far places: consuls anxious for the safety of their fellow-countrymen among the fanatic Moslems; factors responsible for precious goods stored in warehouses till opportunity presents itself to ship them to England; preachers to small colonies of Englishmen whose morals have suffered a decline in the enervating East; wretched European captives in Moslem households, perhaps eunuchs, perhaps renegades; tanned galley-slaves 'acquainted with sad misery'; [1] stately Turks wearing elaborate tulipants, disdainfully guarding their long immaculate robes from contact with the hardly tolerated infidel; other more genial Mohammedans of lower rank sitting cross-legged in coffee-houses or exercising the rites of hospitality in caravan or khan; importunate trunchmen whose enormous lies satisfy the Christian's curiosity; wild and whirling dervishes, and less extravagant devotees sedately engaged in their ceremonial ablutions in the courts of mosques; the bustle and confusion of the departing *Haj*; the display and chaffering of the bazaars; the shrill falsetto of the muezzin's call to prayer from his minaret at dawn. The confused impressions which race through his mind are not so much of garish colours and costly materials (for the Elizabethan costume is as gay in hue and of as expensive stuff as any to be seen in the East) as of fantastic patterns, their brilliance and grotesqueness exaggerated by the hard bright sunlight of the Levant.

Friends and acquaintances will not permit him to remain long in reverie, for theirs is an insatiable eagerness to hear about strange places and they wish to listen to this man who has trodden the *Via Dolorosa* at Jerusalem and seen the mummy-strewn desert beyond Cairo and watched the process of incubation and seen carrier-pigeons in flight, who has penetrated into mosques and peeped surreptitiously through guarded lattices. Perhaps in his audience in tavern or at home there is a poet or playwright whose already teeming imagination is enriched by what he now hears. There is a ready demand for coarsely piquant anecdotes of exotic sexual customs: the plurality of wives, the lawfulness of concubinage, the universal prevalence (if Christian prejudice is to be believed) of homosexuality, the

---

1 Webster, *The Duchess of Malfi*, IV,ii,29f.:
> I am acquainted with sad misery
> As the tanned galley slave is with his oar.

rite of circumcision, and the barbarous custom of castrating the guards and servants of the seraglio. The audience listens eagerly to tales of the violent cruelties and dark sensualities of the harem; and not to these scandals only but to horrid tales of cruelty to prisoners of war, of hair-breadth escapes of galley-slaves, of compulsory conversions to Mohammedanism, of the pitiable remorse of renegades, of horrible punishments such as impalement or burial alive. There are also anecdotes and impressions of another sort: of valiant fights with pirates or with banditti of the desert; of caravans almost smothered by the storms of dust and sand; of dangers at sea from water-spouts or from the cry of a mermaid. In the poet's mind rise images of surpassing splendour: the reception of ambassadors at costly banquets where the Great Turk is surrounded by crowds of guards and mutes and dwarfs and buffoons and musicians, where jugglers and acrobats and dancing-girls entertain his imperial idleness. And there are images of a more voluptuous loveliness: of gold and jewels and brocades, of haughty men and fair women who find their pleasure in fragrant gardens where fountains play by night.

SYNOPSIS OF OTTOMAN HISTORY

The following outline makes no pretence to completeness. Von Hammer-Purgstall, Creasy, S.Lane Poole, and the other historians of Turkey should be consulted for details. Names in parentheses are those by which the Ottoman Sultans were known to the Elizabethans.

The Ottoman Turks, driven from Central Asia by Mongol pressure, settle about the middle of the thirteenth century in Asia Minor, near Angora, under the overlordship of the Seljukian Empire.

1288–1326. Sultan Osman I (Ottoman). On the disintegration of the Seljukian Empire Osman declares his independence (1300). The foundation of the Ottoman Empire dates from this event. Victories over the Greeks; the Empire spreads westward towards the Sea of Marmora (1300–1326).

1326–1359. Sultan Orkhan (Orcan). Continued aggression against the Greeks. The Byzantine Empire retains no more than a foothold in Asia Minor. In Constantinople intriguers against the Emperor John Palaeologus invite Orkhan to assist in his overthrow. Hence first penetration of the Turks into Europe. They despoil the Balkans. Orkhan organizes the Janissaries.

1359–1389. Sultan Murad I (Amurat or Amurates). The Balkans as far as Adrianople controlled by the Turks, leaving the shrunken Byzantine Empire almost invested. Europe is alarmed. An allied army of Serbs, Hungarians, and so forth, assembled at the instigation of the Pope, is crushed. Murad makes Adrianople his capital (1367). Ottoman territory in Asia Minor expands and opposition there is suppressed.

1389–1403. Sultan Bayezid I (Bajazet). Execution of the new Sultan's brother. First siege of Constantinople (1395). Diversion created by the Pope and the King of Hungary; an army of Crusaders defeated by Bayezid; but the siege of the capital abandoned after heavy bribes are paid and a Moslem quarter in the city established. The last years of the fourteenth century marked by the rise of Timur the Tartar (Tamburlaine). His hosts spread westward from Samarkand, invading Syria and capturing Baghdad. Bayezid's refusal to reinstate certain dispossessed princes of Asia Minor at the request of Tamburlaine leads to the latter's invasion of Ottoman territory. Rout of the Turks near Angora; Bayezid taken prisoner and dies in captivity (1403).

1403–1413. The sons of Bayezid quarrel over their inheritance. Tamburlaine returns to Samarkand (1405). After his death his empire disintegrates amid the rivalries of his heirs.

1413–1421. Sultan Mohammed I (Mahomet). Taking advantage of this disintegration Mohammed regains all the territory lost by his father. He is memorable for his regeneration of the Ottoman power. He founded the navy and was the first Sultan to send an embassy to a Christian state (Venice).

1421–1451. Sultan Murad II (Amurat II). The second siege of Constantinople. Revolts in the eastern provinces of the Ottoman Empire and the rebellion of a pretender to the Ottoman throne cause a temporary withdrawal of the Turkish forces. The Byzantine Emperor agrees to pay a heavy annual tribute as the price of possession of the remnants of his domain. Salonica captured by the Turks (1428). A union of peoples in Transylvania and the Danube Country under Janos Hunyadi effects the expulsion of the Turks from the western confines of their empire (1442). Truce, followed by renewed war. Defeat of the Hungarians under Hunyadi at Kossovo (1448), the worst humiliation yet suffered by Europe at Turkish hands. The successful and heroic revolt against the Turks in Albania, led by George Castriota (Scanderbeg), begins in 1442 and continues till his death in 1467.

1451–1481. Sultan Mohammed II, the Conqueror (The 'Turkish Mahomet' *par excellence*). Third siege of Constantinople; fall of the city (29 May 1453). Siege of Belgrade, relieved by Hunyadi (1456). War with Venice. Turks overrun the Morea. First Turkish attempt to capture Rhodes fails (1479). Turks effect a foothold in southern Italy, at Otranto. Mohammed II the organizer of Ottoman administration; patron of learning; the greatest soldier-statesman of his age. Legends of his cruelty spread gradually into western Europe.

1481–1512. Sultan Bayezid II (Bajazet II). Turkish invasions of Austria and Poland; ruthless retaliations. New war with Venice, the Pope and the Emperor urging Bayezid to crush the Republic. A new threat to the Ottomans appears in the East with the emergence of the Shi'a heresy and the rise of the Safavi dynasty in Persia. Shah Ismail I violates Turkish territory. Bayezid abdicates in favour of his youngest son Selim and dies soon afterwards, probably poisoned.

1512–1520. Sultan Selim I, the Grim (Selimus). The struggle for the throne of Bayezid ends swiftly with the death of his two elder sons and the accession of Selim. The Persians defeated (1515) but the Turks withdraw westward. The Mameluke rulers of Egypt defeated and Egypt added to the Ottoman domains. Selim assumes the title of Caliph from the last Fatimid Caliph resident at Cairo. Syria and the Hedjaz added to the Empire, which during this reign doubles in extent. In the midst of preparations for a new attack upon Rhodes Selim dies.

1520–1566. Sultan Suleyman I (Solyman or Soliman), known to his subjects as the Lawgiver and to Europe as the Magnificent. In his reign the Ottoman Empire reaches its height of glory. Belgrade taken (1521). Siege and fall of Rhodes (1522). Budapest falls, is regained by Ferdinand of Austria, and is recaptured by the Turks (1527–9). Francis I of France asks aid of Suleyman against the Emperor Charles V as a means of preserving the balance of power in Europe. The siege of Vienna by the Turks fails (1529). The Knights of St. John, driven from Rhodes, establish themselves after years of indecision at Malta (1530). Suleyman's campaigns in Persia (1534–6); Shah Tahmasp retreats; the Turks reach Baghdad. Naval victories of the Turks in the Mediterranean under Barbarossa. War with Venice. The capture of Algiers. Growth of piracy in the western Mediterranean. The naval expedition of Charles V against Algiers fails (1541). During the fifteen-forties periods of warfare alternate with periods of truce in south-east Europe. The war in Persia drags on. The murder of Prince Mustapha (1553). The Turks besiege Malta and are driven off (1565). In the later years of Suleyman's reign the first signs of internal decay are apparent in the Ottoman Empire; the Janissaries show restiveness. Nevertheless at his death the Empire is still at its height, extending from the frontiers of Germany to the frontiers of Persia. The Balkans and the Peloponnesus are in Turkish hands. North Africa acknowledges the supremacy of the Sultan. Crete and Malta are the only outposts of Christendom in the Mediterranean.

1566–1574. Sultan Selim II. The loss of Cyprus to the Turks (1571) rouses Christendom; an alliance of the Pope, Venice, Genoa, and Spain leads to the naval victory of Lepanto over the Turks (7 October 1571). A new Turkish fleet swiftly built. A repetition of the Christian victory impossible because of dissensions among the allies. Spain captures Tunis (1572) but it is retaken by the Turks (1574).

1574–1595. Sultan Murad III (Amurat III). A weak voluptuary. Harem conspiracies result in the deposition of able ministers. On the death of Shah Tahmasp renewed war with Persia; indecisive; peace made when Shah Abbas the Great establishes his power (1590). Mutinies of the Janissaries. Yet external prestige of Turkey is still enormous; tributes paid by Venice and other states. During this reign a trade agreement is arranged between England and the Porte (1580) and the first English ambassador goes to Constantinople (1581).

1595–1603. Sultan Mohammed III (Mahomet III). War in south-east Europe. The Turks withstand a siege of Buda and capture Stuhlweissenburg (1602). The 'year of insurrections' in Constantinople and various parts of the Ottoman Empire (1603). Shah Abbas takes advantage of these dissensions to declare war on Turkey. This war continues till 1611 fitfully and breaks out again shortly thereafter. Diplomatic discussions in Europe of practicability of alliance with Persia.

1603–1617. Sultan Ahmed I (Achmet). A boy in the hands of his ministers. The period of Turkish conquests closes. Austria no longer pays tribute. Treaties are no longer imposed upon the conquered but negotiated between equal states. These are manifest signs of Turkish decadence. The first official Turkish representative visits England (1607). Barbary piracy increases.

INDEX

All references are inclusive. Anonymous works are entered under the chief word in the title. In many cases a traveller is indicated by the letter 't' following his name.

A

Abbas the Great, Shah, 50,250,278,323, 488; relations with Sir A.Sherley, 255–63,273,279,282,288; with Sir R. Sherley, 298–303,321,333–5; tolerance of Christianity, 300,302; temporary abdication, 255,516–7; cruelty to his sons, 261,333,509–14,540; in English drama, 504–14.

Abbot, George, Archbishop, 295,307, 338; *A Briefe Description of the Whole World*, 250,417.

Abel slain near Damascus, 82.

'Abn-Ul-Ahan and W.H.T.Gairdner, *The Gospel of Barnabas*, 227.

Aborisci, an Arabian 'king,' 247.

Abu Bakr, Caliph, 230,403,426.

Achmet I, Sultan, 139.

Achmet, Newes from Turkie, or the Death of, 139.

Achmeth, Visions apparus à, 437.

Acosta, Joseph de, *see* Grimestone.

Adair, E.R., *Extraterritoriality of Ambassadors*, 312.

Adams, Sir Thomas, 436.

Addison, Joseph, 'The Vision of Mirza,' 444.

Aden, 374.

Adrichomius, Christianus, *A briefe description of Hierusalem* (trans.by Thomas Tymme), 97.

Ælian, *Varia historia*, 20.

Africa, Personification of, 458.

'Agnus Dei,' The, 92,465.

Agra, 38,51.

Ahmed, *see* Achmet.

Alan de l'Isle, 14.

Alaraca (El-Arisch, Morocco), 348.

Albertus, John, Greek refugee, 137.

Alcaron, supposed god of Moslems, 389.

Alcazar, Battle of (El-Kasrel Kabir or 'Battle of the Three Kings '), 524–8.

Alcock, Thomas, t.,213.

Alcoran of Mahomet, The, see Koran.

Aldersey, Lawrence, t., Narrative in Hakluyt, 58,71–2,93.

Aldredge, Jonas, consul, 170.

Aldworth, Thomas, t.,320.

Aleppo, 44,52,83,157,220,245–6,538.

Alessio (Aibania), 475.

Alexander the Great, 7.

Alexander, Sir William, *see* Stirling.

Alexandretta, *see* Scanderoon.

Alexandria, 88–9,380.

Algiers, 343,348, Chapter VIII *passim*.

'Ali, 107,230–3,303,307,397.

Alleyn, Edward, 531.

Alphandéry,P.,'Mahomet-Antichrist,' 101.

Ambassadors, English, to the Porte, 155–62, and Chapter IV *passim*.

Amboyna (East Indies), 326,332–3.

Amboyna, Newes . . . of the cruell usage of our English merchants at, 332–3.

Ambrose, St., 14.

Amico, Bernadino, *Tratto . . . di Terra Santa*, 97.

Amurath II, Sultan, 25,474.

Amurath III, Sultan, 131,152,255, 494–5.

Andreas, Samuel, *De Sepulcro Muhammedis*, 422.

Andrew, St., Tomb of, 72.

Andromena, or the Merchant's Wife, 511–2.

Angels and the *Haj*, 425; and the Immediate Judgment, 444.

Angiolello, G.M., *Memorie*, 478–9.

Anglerius, Peter Martyr, *see* Eden, Richard.

Anne, Queen, 458,462.

Antas, Miguel d', *Les Faux Don Sebastian*, 527.

Anthropophagi, 12.

Antichrist, 101,396–7.

Antioch, 245.

Apollin, supposed god of Moslems, 389.

Apples of Sodom, *see* Dead Sea Fruit.

557